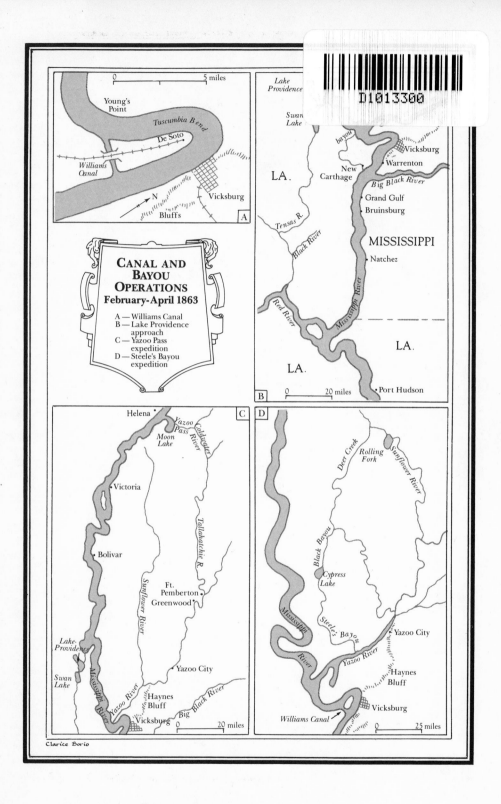

CANAL AND
BAYOU
OPERATIONS
February–April 1863

A — Williams Canal
B — Lake Providence
approach
C — Yazoo Pass
expedition
D — Steele's Bayou
expedition

Clarice Borio

The
Final Fortress:
THE CAMPAIGN FOR VICKSBURG 1862-1863

Books by Samuel Carter III

❧ The ❧
Final Fortress:
THE CAMPAIGN
FOR VICKSBURG
1862-1863
Samuel Carter III

❧

ST. MARTIN'S PRESS NEW YORK

9/6/13   *34 95*

Library of Congress Cataloging in Publication Data

Carter, Samuel, 1904–
  The final fortress, Vicksburg.

  1. Vicksburg, Miss.—History—Civil War,
1861–1865. 2. Vicksburg, Miss—Siege, 1863.
I. Title.
F349.V6C37   973.7'344   80–14928
ISBN 0–312–83926–X

FOR
MARGARET and ERWIN
. . . valiant under siege

Contents

Foreword and Acknowledgments

O F all military operations in the Civil War none was more important than the campaign for the Mississippi Valley which culminated in the siege of Vicksburg in the spring and summer of 1863.

For the South it marked, with Gettysburg, the beginning of the end. Vicksburg's fall was of more immediate significance than Robert E. Lee's retreat from Pennsylvania. Gettysburg lost the initiative, Vicksburg lost the West. The South had been mortally divided. The Trans-Mississippi, representing almost half the Confederate territory, would never be a factor in the war again.

This is the Vicksburg story, starting from the beginning of that months-long struggle. And just as Lincoln declared, at the start of the war, that Vicksburg was the key to the conquest of the Mississippi Valley, and, because it locked the two halves of the South together, the key to Union triumph in the Civil War, so Vicksburg today holds the key to much of what we know or seek to learn about the struggle.

The city itself, high on its protective bluffs and surrounded by hills that roll toward the east, is eloquent in its fortress-like location. And if one approaches Vicksburg by water—on one of the colorful stern-wheelers that travel the Mississippi from New Orleans to Memphis and beyond—one is instantly aware of what Farragut, Grant, and Sherman confronted, in that mighty stream that could not be controlled, and the treacherous, marshy banks that defied an invading army.

The *New York Times* for February 20, 1977, referred to Vicksburg as a city "obsessed with its past." Obsessed is not the right word. The city cherishes and guards the past as a foundation for the present and the future, an alloy that holds America together. There may be other sieges, other Vicksburgs, in the years and centuries ahead. Here is how we weathered one of them.

Abundant material for the narrative was found in Vicksburg's Old Court House Museum, and the author owes many thanks to Director Gordon A. Cotton for his critical reading of those sections of the manuscript pertaining to the city's history. Also my thanks to Mrs. Blanche Terry, Assistant Director, for her help and guidance in my research work at the Museum.

Further local material was obtained, with the cooperation of Charles H. Haemker, from the Vicksburg-Warren County Library, including wartime issues of the Vicksburg *Daily Citizen* and *Weekly Citizen,* and help in obtaining a microfilm record of wartime copies of the *Daily Whig.* Thanks also are due to Mrs. Mary V. Kerst for a personally conducted tour of the battlefield, and for additional papers and reminiscences collected through her longtime residence in Vicksburg.

Moving to the nearby capital city of Jackson, the Mississippi State Department of Archives and History provided a wealth of family biographies, letters, and diaries of the Civil War period, made available through the courtesy of archivists William Hanna, Dwight Harris, Mamie E. Locke, and members of their staff. Similar family histories and personal records, noted in the bibliography, were supplied by Paul Spence and Diane Wilhelm of the Illinois State Historical Society and Library, and by Richard A. Shrader of the University of North Carolina, home of the Southern Historical Collection.

My thanks are due also to Miss Donna Drew of Baton Rouge for her personal help in research conducted in that city and in New Orleans, and to M. Stone Miller, head of the Department of Archives and Manuscripts at Louisiana State University; also, to Milton Bond of Fairfield, Connecticut, for the family letters of John C. Curtis; to Librarian Elizabeth T. Edelglass of the National Archives in Washington; to Joyce Ann Tracy, Curator of Newspapers at the American Antiquarian Society; to the staffs of the Sterling Memorial Library at Yale, and of the Duke University Library at Durham; and to Professor Peter F. Walker, author of *Vicksburg: A People at War,* for checking points at which our research overlapped.

A special note of thanks is owed to Mrs. Jacqueline Wright of Springfield, Illinois, for supplying rare, personal data on the life of Major General John A. McClernand. The circumstances of the Vicksburg siege do not present the general in a favorable light, and the writer feels guilty in being a captive partner to that presentation. In point of fact, however, there were many redeeming features in McClernand's career, before and after Vicksburg—so many that Colonel Bluford Wilson, serving for three years with the general, declared that McClernand's name should be inscribed "high on the list of his Country's Great Commanders."

A large measure of gratitude also is owed to Miss Theresa Blake, Chief of Reference Services, and to the staff of the Baker Library at Dartmouth College. The lengthy, multivolume Official Records of the War of the Rebellion can generally be consulted only within the confines of a major library. The writer requested, and was graciously supplied with, photocopies of all the Official Records pertaining to the siege of Vicksburg. Being able to have these at hand, while writing of the military operations of both Union and Confederate forces, was a privilege and rare convenience.

Two precautionary notes. The following narrative is told, wherever possible, in the words of the participants, both military and civilian. Personal impressions under the stress of crisis, though humanly fascinating, are not often completely accurate. Among eye-witness accounts, it is rare that any two agree. One can only select those versions which seem to fit the situation best, aware that others may not agree with the selection or interpretation.

Then there is the matter of geographical routes and distances, important to the following of a campaign, and not always clear on the maps or in the records of that time. Mississippi was not a "tidy" area for campaigning, intersected by innumerable bayous, creeks, and marshes born of a capricious river. Naval officers generally thought of distances in terms of winding water routes: four hundred miles from Vicksburg to New Orleans, for example. General Butler's infantry, on the other hand, marching up to Vicksburg from the Crescent City, would have found the distance two hundred and forty miles by land. Particularly in quoting from personal accounts, one runs into seeming inconsistencies devolving from this factor.

It is impossible for any writer, in a work of this scope, to express full and comprehensive gratitude to all who helped or contributed to the final manuscript. But warm thanks are due to Thomas O'Connor Sloane III for his early suggestions and encouragement; to Ashton Applewhite of St. Martin's Press for patience in guiding this book to its completion; to Virginia Canfield for her expert and diligent typing of the manuscript; and to Alison Carter for her knowledgeable reading of the proofs.

Finally, immeasurable thanks to Albert Scheller, historian long connected with the Vicksburg National Military Park, for his thorough review and correction of the manuscript before its publication. If errors remain, the author alone is responsible. And if inevitable omissions prompt the reader to turn to other sources, so much the better. For Vicksburg deserves more study and appreciation than has been its lot. Volumes have been written about Gettysburg, perhaps distracting attention from a simultaneous event of even more significance. Lincoln used many memorable phrases when he spoke of Gettysburg. Vicksburg he summed up in a single pregnant sentence: "The Father of Waters again flows unvexed to the sea."

✖1✖

The Imperial River

H E was older than the Capitol itself, with its unfinished dome and half-developed mall. Older, in fact, than the Constitution. Yet in 1860 Brevet Lieutenant General Winfield Scott was still General-in-Chief of the army. Seventy-five years of age, afflicted with vertigo and dropsy, he was no longer able to ride a horse, was scarcely able to rise from the table of assorted wines and terrapin that were his sole remaining pleasures.

Yet he had been a giant in his time, a hero of the War of 1812, a victorious commander in the war with Mexico. He was still a giant, though in physical proportions only. The rest of him had largely gone the way of legend. His faltering sentences now began, "If only . . . " And his mind dwelt more on physical comforts than the exigencies of battle. His first reaction to the secession movement in the South was, "Let the wayward sisters go in peace."[1]

But, when Abraham Lincoln crept (some said "snuck") into Washington for his inauguration, Winfield Scott was the only military figure he could lean on. Lean he did, asking Scott for daily reports on the developing situation in the South and what was being done to cope with the impending crisis. Nothing much was being done. Nobody was prepared. The regular army still numbered only 16,000—as large a force as Scott had ever commanded.

Then came the fall of Sumter and the call for troops, and Lincoln summoned Scott to present a plan for the conduct of the war. The President had his own ideas, and so did George McClellan, destined, among others, to command all Union armies in Virginia. But Lincoln wanted to hear first from the aging warrior with so much past experience.

Scott's plan, on paper, was superbly simple. The United States Navy, though largely antiquated, was still intact. Few naval officers or ships had gone over to the South, as had so many West Point generals. So Scott conceived a two-point program.

First, throw a saltwater blockade around the South, from Chesapeake Bay to the tip of Florida and west along the Gulf Coast to the Rio Grande, sealing off Confederate ports from foreign commerce and supplies. This was to be coordinated with a mammoth ship-building program that the South, without the necessary shipyards, could not match.

1

Second, seize and control the Mississippi River, with coordinated forces moving upstream from New Orleans and down from Cairo, Illinois—the object, being, in his words, "to clear out and keep open this great line of communication," to stifle the Confederate states "and bring them to terms with less bloodshed than by any other means." It would also split the Confederacy in two, deny the Southeast access to the West, to supplies from Texas and the neutral corridor of Mexico.[2]

Both North and South ridiculed what was dubbed the Anaconda Plan, cartoonists depicting a comical serpent trying to squeeze the Southern states to death. And there were practical considerations. The great river and the widespread Mississippi Valley formed a massive geographic unit. As Senator James Henry Hammond of South Carolina told his dissident colleagues, "Can you hem in such a territory as that? How absurd!"

Scott himself recognized a greater obstacle, "the impatience of our patriotic and loyal Union friends," who responded fervently to Horace Greeley's cry of "Forward to Richmond!" Richmond had little military value, but it was a close symbolic target, easier to comprehend than a frontier river many miles away. And the Confederate capital appeared to be within easy striking distance. The itchy Major General George B. McClellan proposed by the Richmond route to "crush the rebels in one campaign."

Lincoln, however, liked much of Scott's plan. A Westerner himself, he had rarely in his early days been far from the tributaries of the Mississippi. He was referred to as "rail-splitter"; better to call him boatman, stevedore, and pilot. As a youth he had worked his way downstream from the Ohio, past the mouths of the Yazoo and the Big Black, to as far as New Orleans. As much as anyone, perhaps *better* than anyone, he recognized this Father of Waters, with its irrigated valley and its many tributaries, as the true heart of America. Truly, a river of destiny.[3]

The Mississippi—bringing to mind the parable of the blind men and the elephant. It could only be described as a moving object of immense vitality whose character depended on the point of contact.

To Hernando de Soto, stumbling westward to search for gold in 1541, the muddy Mississippi was a barrier. And then a tomb. His malaria-stricken body was buried in its murky depths, somewhere south of Memphis.

To the Spaniards who followed, the occasional forbidding bluffs that rose on the east side of the river were natural Gibraltars of defense. And so they constructed Fort Nogales—the name deriving from the walnut grove that topped the heights north of the later site of Vicksburg.

To Newet Vick, self-appointed Methodist minister emigrating westward from North Carolina, those same bluffs, and the fertile alluvial land below, were the logical site for a city that would prosper from the soil and the potential commerce of the river.

And so it went, each seeing the river as a complex, living thing of useful or contrary purpose. To British correspondent William Howard Russell, the Mississippi was the dreariest waterway on earth with "not a particle of romance!" To Samuel Clemens, or Mark Twain, it was "the crookedest river in the world," twisting and turning through its million-plus square miles of valley. But "as a dwelling place," wrote Twain, "it is by far the first upon our globe." Albert Bushnell Hart, historian and educator writing somewhat later, agreed with this assessment:

> The Mississippi Valley yields to no region in the world in interest, in romance, in promise for the future. Here, if anywhere, is the real America—the field, the theater, and the basis of the civilization of the Western World. The history of the Mississippi Valley is the history of the United States; its future is the future of one of the most powerful of nations.[4]

This promise reached for its fulfillment when Thomas Jefferson purchased the Louisiana Territory from Napoleon in 1803, the greatest real estate bargain in history. Jefferson wanted not so much the unmapped area reaching to the Rockies as he wanted New Orleans, the gateway to the Mississippi. In an age before railways and surfaced roads, rivers were the highways of commerce and communication; and the 15,000 miles of the great river and its tributaries formed one of the largest systems of waterways in the world.

The Mississippi alone stretched 2,348 miles from its headwaters in northern Minnesota to the Gulf. With its major tributaries, the Missouri and the Ohio, it drained a basin of 1,244,000 square miles—a third of the ultimate United States, an area larger than all of western Europe, excluding Scandinavia. The river bordered ten states: Louisiana, Arkansas, Missouri, Iowa, and Minnesota on the west; Wisconsin, Illinois, Kentucky, Tennessee, and Mississippi on its eastern bank. And its tributaries fingered virtually every state and territory between the Appalachians and the Rockies.

Twelve years after the Louisiana Purchase, when Andrew Jackson and his tatterdemalion army repulsed the British on the plains of Chalmette, the river took on a new dimension. For this was the dawning of the age of steam. Even before the Battle of New Orleans, the paddle-wheel steamer *New Orleans* successfully made the run from Pittsburgh to the Crescent City. Thereafter the slow-moving barges, rafts, and keelboats which depended on current or sail gave way to the twin-stacked floating palaces, the paddlewheel freighters, and hardworking tugboats.

In the first full decade following the War of 1812, the number of steamers pulling in and out of New Orleans increased from fewer than 200 to more than 1,200. By 1840 the city rivaled New York in harbor traffic and was the fourth busiest port in the world. In six more years, its imports and exports together were valued at $107,000,000, while the steamboat tonnage carried by the Mississippi River system exceeded that of all Atlantic ports combined.[5]

With the Louisiana Purchase, too, came the great migration westward. High prices for cotton and low prices for land, combined with unrestricted transportation on the rivers, lured people from all sections of the East and particularly from the south Atlantic states. Planters and sons of planters emigrated from Virginia and the Carolinas to the Mississippi Valley. Especially around the cotton capital of Natchez they planted their white-column, Greek Revival mansions with corridors of live oaks leading to the river and hundreds of acres of cotton, worked by scores of slaves. When there was no more room in the vicinity of Natchez, the planters moved on up to Vicksburg and beyond, to the elliptical Delta, where the black, loamy soil was richer than it was in the valley of the Nile.

Near mid-century the population of the Mississippi Valley had increased, and was increasing, faster than any other part of the United States; and, as a consequence, a measure of the political power in Washington began to shift from New England and the Atlantic seaboard to the Mississippi basin. The Cotton Kingdom—"so important to the economic life of the nation and so pregnant with the issue of slavery," wrote Frederick Jackson Turner—tilted westward.

Which meant that the Mississippi was, by all apparent rights, a national river, a "bond of Union made by nature itself," said Senator Hammond. If war or division ever came—which God forbid!—it must remain a neutral corridor, "a free and unobstructed channel of commerce for the North as well as the South." In fact, the Louisiana Convention of January 1861 put forth such a resolution; Governor John C. Pettus of Mississippi endorsed it; and the Confederate Congress, anxious to woo the Northwestern states, later voted for the measure.[6]

William Tecumseh Sherman, a Westerner with Southern credentials, would have agreed with this sentiment. Visiting the Mississippi River city of Saint Louis in the fall of 1843, he admired the sight of "the placid majestic flow that carried the life-supporting fluid of the nation." At the time he had thought of the river as, in his words, "The spinal column of America, the seat of coming empire." And later, according to his biographer, "No matter where his nomadic feet had carried him, they had kept turning back to the Mississippi."[7]

They carried him, once too often and in tragic circumstances, back to Vicksburg. For a "national" river cannot retain that role in a divided nation. The Mississippi could not be shared; and cities like New Orleans, Vicksburg, and Memphis controlled the river (in the borrowed words of one American general) "as the key [controls] the lock, or the citadel the outworks."[8]

They were thinking along those lines in Washington in early 1861.

The guns of Fort Sumter and Charleston sounded the call to war and put Scott's Anaconda Plan into motion. On April 19, a week after the bombardment of Sumter, Lincoln ordered a step-by-step naval blockade of the seceded states. While the Atlantic Blockading Squadron covered the southeastern ports, four of the fifteen ships of the Gulf Blockading Squadron were assigned to patrol the mouth of the Mississippi below New Orleans.

At the same time Illinois troops were ordered to occupy Cairo at the junction of the Mississippi and Ohio rivers, a strategic point for control and invasion of the lower Mississippi. Almost immediately, Commander John Rodgers, on orders from the War Department, purchased three river steamers and converted them to gunboats: the *Tyler,* the *Lexington,* and the *Conestoga.*

These were first steps, and from that point on, preparations to seize the Mississippi moved more rapidly at Cairo than around Union bases in the Gulf of Mexico.

During July the War Department solicited bids for the construction of seven gunboats to augment the flotilla Rodgers had assembled as a nucleus. The contract was awarded in August to Captain James Buchanan Eads of Indiana, one of those referred to by Southerners as a "pasty-faced mechanic." A forty-year-old inventor and engineer, Eads had already made his fortune on a patented diving bell for salvaging sunken vessels on the Mississippi.

Say this for Eads: he was not one easily daunted. The specifications called for light-draft vessels, drawing no more than six feet of water, yet with hulls protected by two-and-a-half-inch iron plate. Each would carry thirteen guns and have a speed of roughly nine miles an hour. All seven were to be delivered at Cairo, ready for service, on October 10—giving Eads just sixty-five days to complete the job![9]

In August, too, Andrew Hull Foote, fifty-five, with the bearded mien of a Jehovah, was summoned from the Brooklyn Navy Yard and on September 6 took command of inland naval operations at Cairo.

A United States Navy midshipman and officer for almost forty years, Foote had fought on many seas for God and country, tilting his allegiance toward God. With the zeal of a Connecticut evangelist, he preached to his crews every Sunday morning, forbade the use of liquor on his ships, believed the Bible to be superior to naval manuals, and was so addicted to prayer that (for this and other reasons) he was later called "the Stonewall Jackson of the Navy."

It was hard to say which of the two, Eads or Foote, had the more difficult assignment. Though the gunboat flotilla, when finally assembled, would be officered by naval personnel, the operation at first was under army control. This required from Foote the patience of Job; he complained that he was subject to orders "from every brigadier." He later considered his conquest of army red tape and bureaucracy a greater accomplishment than the hard-fought victories to come.

Eads, in turn, found army payments slow in coming and had to finance much of the early work himself. And there was no precedent for such a fleet. There had never been ironclads of any sort in the United States Navy (though in the East a Swede named John Ericsson was designing a curious monster called the *Monitor*). So Eads, as one contemporary writer noted, had to start from scratch:

> The engines that were to drive our first iron-clad fleet were yet to be built. The timber to form their hulls was uncut in the forest, and the huge rollers and machinery that were to form their iron armor were not yet constructed . . . telegraph lines between St. Louis and Pittsburgh transmitted instructions for the twenty-one steam engines and the five-and-thirty steam-boilers that were to propel the fleet.[10]

Even with 4,000 workmen working day and night throughout the week, it was impossible to meet the sixty-five-day deadline. By January 16, 1862, all seven ironclads were completed and commissioned, and referred to as "ninety-day wonders," and, at Foote's request, Eads converted the snag-boat *Benton* into a larger and still more powerful gunboat. He later added another converted steamer, the *Essex*. Totaling nine ironclads, the Western Flotilla, Flag Officer Foote in command, was ready for action.[11]

How ready was the South to meet this challenge on the Mississippi? On assuming Confederate command in the West on September 15, 1861, Albert Sidney Johnston was aware that the river and its valley were prime targets of the Union high command. He was informed, too, of Foote's gunboat flotilla at Cairo and believed it "strong enough to warrant the theory that a direct descent would be attempted." In that belief, fortifications and batteries had been erected at Columbus, Kentucky, Island No. 10 off northwestern Tennessee, and New Madrid, Missouri.

It was inconceivable that, short of a miracle, any ships could run that gauntlet.

Meanwhile, the blockade of the lower Mississippi (roughly the stretch from the river's mouth to Cairo) had been sketchy, but still more effective than Confederate leaders were willing to admit. Ships from England and France, traditionally trading with New Orleans, were reluctant to court trouble. On the other hand, privateers and blockade runners came and went almost at will. On June 30 the Confederate steamer *Sumter*, commanded by Raphael Semmes, slipped past the blockading vessels at the mouth of the Mississippi and, "with three lusty cheers from the crew," went on to a career of commerce raiding that raised havoc with Union shipping.[12]

To prevent such escapades, three sloops-of-war of the blockading squadron, led by the U.S.S. *Richmond*, moved up the river to the Head of the Passes, the better to seal off the Mississippi's four mouths. It was a disastrous move. In the darkness preceding the dawn of October 12, a converted Confederate ram, defiantly named *Manassas* for the South's first victory, slipped down on the group and punched a hole in the *Richmond*, which was later grounded. The ram was followed by a row of "fire-boats," barges carrying flaming tinder, which sent the rest of the Federal squadron flying—in what Commander David Dixon Porter called "the most ridiculous affair that ever took place in the American Navy."[13]

The ineffective blockade of the river's mouth continued. But the Mississippi remained free for internal traffic, from New Orleans to Columbus. So long as Columbus and New Orleans stood, the vital river was secure for the South.

It was David Dixon Porter—son of Commodore David Porter, who had commanded the famed *Essex* in the War of 1812—who first came up with a definite plan for the capture of New Orleans. According to Sylvanus Cadwallader, representing the Chicago *Times*, "Porter was vain, arrogant, and egotistical to an extent that can neither be described or evaluated."[14] Recently raised to the rank of commander, the forty-eight-year-old Porter seemed about to prove it.

Aboard the *Powhatan*, with the ships blockading the Southwest Pass of the Mississippi, Porter had contemplated capturing New Orleans single-handedly. Before the war he had made thirty trips up the river and was familiar with the channel. Reports had filtered to him to the effect that the city was ill-defended, but there was a sandbar at the entrance to the pass. "Had I been able to cross the bar with my ship," he wrote, "I would have felt justified in going up to the city and calling on the authorities to surrender. But the *Powhatan* drew three feet too much water, and there was no use thinking about such an adventure."

He did, however, return in November to Washington to report to Secretary of the Navy Gideon Welles. When Welles had listened to Porter's proposal for seizing New Orleans, he took him to the executive mansion to talk with Lincoln.

My plan [wrote Porter], which I then stated, was as follows: To fit out a fleet of vessels-of-war with which to attack the city, fast steamers drawing not more than 18 feet of water, and carrying about 250 heavy guns; also a flotilla of mortar-vessels, to be used in case it should be necessary to bombard Forts Jackson and St. Philip before the fleet should attempt to pass them. I also proposed that a body of troops should be sent along in transports to take possession of the city after it had been surrendered.[15]

Lincoln replied, according to Porter, "This should have been done sooner. The Mississippi is the backbone of the Rebellion; it is the key to the whole situation. While the Confederates hold it, they can obtain supplies of all kinds, and it is a barrier against our forces." The President then arranged for both General McClellan and State Secretary Seward to join the conference, at which Lincoln stressed the principal target of the project: Vicksburg.

"This is a most important expedition," the President told McClellan, as a prelude to asking how many soldiers the general could provide. "It is not only necessary to have troops enough to hold New Orleans, but we must be able to proceed at once toward Vicksburg, which is the key to all that country watered by the Mississippi and its tributaries. If the Confederates once fortify the neighboring hills, they will be able to hold that point for an indefinite time, and it will require a large force to dislodge them."

And Porter remembered the President stressing repetitively the importance of that mission, pointing to a map of the Mississippi Valley, saying, "See what a lot of land those fellows hold, of which Vicksburg is the key. . . . The war can never be brought to a close until that key is in our pocket."[16]

And, Lincoln insisted, "I am acquainted with that region and know what I am talking about. We may take all the northern ports of the Confederacy and they can still defy us from Vicksburg."

McClellan agreed to furnish 20,000 troops, under the command of Major General Benjamin F. Butler. The navy would provide the necessary warships. Porter himself would purchase and equip the mortar flotilla, to consist of twenty converted schooners. Then came the question of who should command the amphibious expedition. For once, Porter subjugated his vanity to the importance of the mission. He recommended Captain David Glasgow Farragut, a naval veteran of fifty years' experience, and his advice was heeded.

Porter and Farragut had been friends for nearly forty years—more than friends. They had been virtually foster brothers. Beginning at the age of nine, Farragut had served aboard the *Essex* under David's father, so capably that the senior Porter had informally adopted him. He was currently awaiting orders in a cottage on the Hudson. Porter was sent to Hastings, New York, to sound him out.

The sixty-year-old Farragut, still vigorous and active, was accustomed to doing handsprings to belie his age. Whether or not he did a few on hearing of the proffered command, he accepted with alacrity and "exclamations of delight." He knew New Orleans well from years of living in that city. Did he think it could be taken? "Yes, emphatically," he said.[17]

From then on plans moved forward swiftly and with utmost secrecy. In early December an advance contingent of Butler's troops occupied Ship Island in Mississippi Sound, sixty-five crowflight miles east of New Orleans, proverbial base of Spanish, French, and British armies seeking to invade Louisiana.

In New Orleans young George Washington Cable, then a lad of fourteen, found that "The blockade had closed in like a city gate." No other town was quite so dependent on the river, which had spawned it and which nourished it with the commercial produce of the richest valley on the continent.

Once, three-quarters of the cotton production of the South passed through the Crescent City. Now the cotton bales rotted on the wharves or in the storage depots. Business was virtually at a standstill. Towboats and river steamers, which had brought so much prosperity to the city, huddled in rows along the levee, draped in tarpaulins, their boilers cold, machinery rusting. "How quiet and lonely the harbor grew!" lamented Cable.[18]

There was activity at the foundries and dry docks across the river, where the more adaptable vessels were being converted to rams with iron-plated prows; and at the Jefferson shipyard workers were rushing to complete the great ram *Mississippi*, "a majestically terrible structure" that "would sweep the river clean!" Otherwise, "the queen of Southern commerce, the city that once believed it was to be the greatest in all the world, was absolutely out of employment."

Gold and silver had disappeared, and the town was flooded with "shinplasters," or loosely underwritten paper money, with which to bargain for the shrinking supply of goods and food. "Pah! What a mess it was!" wrote Cable. "The current joke was that you could pass the label of an olive-oil bottle, because it was greasy, smelt bad, and bore an autograph—Plagnion Frères, if I remember rightly."

The only excitement was of a military nature; there was scarcely a man to be seen out of uniform. Though most of New Orleans' native sons had already gone to war—some to fight in far-off Virginia—the "Confederate Guards," comprised of elderly merchants, bankers, lawyers, clerks, were doing their best to fill the void. Cable found this charade of old men—"gray heads, hoar heads, high heads, bald heads"—somewhat pathetic, but there was one exhibition that he thrilled to:

> Down on the steamboat landing, our famous Levee, a superb body of Creoles drilled and paraded in dark-blue uniform. The orders were given in French; the manual was French; the movements were quick, short, nervy. Their "about march" was four sharp stamps of their neatly shod feet—*un, deux, trois, quatre* —that brought them face about and sent them back, tramp, tramp, tramp, over the smooth white pavement of powdered oyster-shells.[19]

Besides the Creoles, there was the "Foreign Legion," composed of British, French, and Spanish subjects in the city. Though a pleasant diversion, this was not their war, and they were questionable material for combat service. But serving as gendarmerie, they were useful in policing the streets and enforcing martial law, and relieved Confederate soldiers of this duty.

The defense of the city was in the hands of Major General Mansfield Lovell, thirty-nine, a Maryland-born West Pointer whom President Davis had assigned to defend New Orleans. On taking over in October 1861, Lovell found the city had been "greatly drained of arms, ammunition, clothing, and supplies," which had been sent to other war zones. His land forces, moreover, consisted of only 3,000 short-term volunteers, a "heterogeneous militia, armed mostly with shotguns."[20]

Naval preparations were in equally poor shape. Commander John K. Mitchell possessed a few heavy ships, but the strongest of these, the *Mississippi,* was still on the ways, while the *Louisiana* was not yet in service. A separately commanded River Defense Fleet, under a riverboat captain, J. E. Montgomery, boasted fourteen converted gunboats that would have come in handy. But there were reports of a Federal buildup of armed ships at Cairo, aimed at descending the river. So all but six boats of the River Defense Fleet were dispatched upriver to help meet this danger.

Despite the city's unpreparedness, Lovell and the 170,000 New Orleanians put much faith in the twin forts Jackson and Saint Philip, which faced the river from opposite sides, seventy water miles below the city. Between them was stretched a floating barrier of rafts and chains; when this collapsed from the pressure of current and drifting logs, a stronger barricade was devised of dismasted schooners linked together with iron hawsers. Sandbars lay at the mouths of the Mississippi, nature itself discouraging the ascent of heavy warships.

So Lovell saw no immediate cause for worry, and the citizens also remained unruffled. The women kept busy sewing coats and blankets for the men at the front, using flannel-lined oilcloth table covers, for lack of more suitable material. The coats, pieced together with many different colored patches of this fabric, would have dazzled the Biblical Joseph. "The Federal army will fly when they see those coats!" Dora Richards observed to herself sarcastically. "Yet I helped make them."[21]

Dora had only recently returned from an extended sea voyage and a stay on her native West Indies island of Saint Croix. She had been out of touch with events and politics in America and was bewildered by this talk of divisionary war. "Surely no native-born woman loves her country better than I love America," she wrote in her journal. "The blood of one of its revolutionary patriots flows in my veins, and it is the Union for which he pledged his 'life, fortune, and sacred honor' that I love, not any divided or special section of it."

These were treasonable thoughts in New Orleans. She confined them to a personal journal, which offered a secret outlet for her Union sentiments. Otherwise she conformed to the pattern of this most Southern city, participating in bazaars to raise money for the Cause, joining sewing circles to make clothing for the troops, and even—when excitement reached fever heat with the fall of Sumter—engaging in target practice.

"We have been told," she wrote, "that it is best for women to learn how to shoot, too, so as to protect themselves when the men have all gone to battle. Every evening after dinner we adjourn to the back lot and fire at a target with pistols."

One thing Dora did not confide to her journal, as the year drew to a close, was the falling of love into her life. How or when or where she met Anderson Miller, a young Vicksburg attorney, she did not put in writing, though she later confessed that they shared pro-Union sympathies—a fact which might have attracted them to one another in this lonely life of secret exile.

It was only a few weeks before the couple's marriage in Trinity Episcopal Church in New Orleans that word reached the city of Federal troops occupying Ship Island in the gulf. There were many still alive who remembered how the British had seized that barren sandbar in December of 1814 and from it had launched their attack upon the city through Lake Borgne. General Lovell pooh-poohed the landing and informed the Richmond authorities: "I regard Butler's Ship Island expedition as a harmless menace so far as New Orleans is concerned."[22]

Not everyone shared Lovell's optimism. Probably even before their marriage, Dora and Anderson Miller had discussed their ticklish future. If there were to be a siege of New Orleans, there might well be a witch-hunt for all suspected of pro-Union sentiments. Dora had not always been discreet in idle conversations with the townsfolk. It would be well to anticipate the worst.

They could not escape downriver to the Gulf. They could only move upstream, either to Anderson's family home in Arkansas, just above the Louisiana border, or, if Arkansas were invaded, they could find sanctuary across the river at Vicksburg. For one thing was certain in this crumbling world—Vicksburg, the Queen City on the bluffs, would never fall. Vicksburg was invincible.

Vicksburg, two hundred and some land miles farther up the river, had always had a sisterly feeling for the Crescent City to the south. New Orleans was the source of many luxuries that Vicksburg's cosmopolitans enjoyed: French wines and silks and china, British woolens, Swedish glass and cutlery, and domestic sugar and molasses. Young ladies went to New Orleans for their trousseaus, which came generally from Barrier's Emporium on Canal Street, purveyors of clothing, shoes, and fabrics to Vicksburg's wealthier families.

New Orleans was also a link to the wider worlds of fashion, literature, and entertainment. Young Annie Laurie Harris, Judge Harris's daughter, whose mother was social arbiter in Vicksburg, noted that "A lady's maid among people of means was sent to New Orleans to learn hair-dressing, embroidery, and in fact everything that could perfect her in being of use to her mistress."[23] The works of Sir Walter Scott, Charles Dickens, and Lord Tennyson reached Vicksburg via the shops of Royal Street.

From the music halls of the Crescent City came the songs that Vicksburg lilted to. By a notice in the Vicksburg *Daily Whig,* New Orleans music publisher P. P. Werlein peddled his catchy, new song "Dixie," though at least one Vicksburg customer, Mahala Roach, condemned the words as "silly." A few days after the rousing Confederate anthem, "Bonnie Blue Flag," was introduced at the New Orleans Academy of Music, Vicksburg's Joe Boyer was singing it at a concert for the local military.[24]

But now, in the winter of 1862, the romance of two cities was fading to a close. After sending samples of its winter goods to Vicksburg, Barrier's announced it was suspending business, and other New Orleans merchants followed suit. Wrote Kate Stone of Brokenburn plantation across the river from Vicksburg, whose brother returned empty-handed from the Gateway City, "It may be some time before we shop in New Orleans again."[25] Even the New Orleans *Picayune* was hard to get, and Vicksburg relied on its local papers for the news.

New Orleans, to Vicksburg wives and parents, was assuming a forbidding role. It was a focal point for hotheaded sons, and not a few husbands, impatient to enter Confederate service. Kate Stone's twenty-year-old brother William rode all the way on horseback to the Crescent City. "He so fears that the fighting will be over before he gets there . . . " Volunteer units such as the Lake Providence Cadets, named for a body of water north of Vicksburg, hurried with equal impatience to New Orleans, anxious to get into action.

But few in Vicksburg believed that New Orleans itself was seriously threatened. The Federal fleet off Ship Island might try to enter the Mississippi River, but the ships would never get past Fort Jackson and Fort Saint Philip. And, if by any unlikely chance they did, New Orleans would be ready for them. Vicksburg began preparing, as all cities on the river were preparing, but only as a sensible precaution. It gave the citizens a sense of sharing in the great and holy struggle for the Cause.

Twenty miles downriver Jefferson Davis's Brierfield plantation had been left in the care of house slaves while the master was in Richmond, but the President's elder brother Joseph was looking after things from his adjoining Hurricane Plantation. Despite the impending pressure on the capital by McClellan's Union forces, Vicksburg's favorite son had time to worry deeply about affairs in his native Mississippi. Had he failed to be sufficiently concerned over the situation in the West—a virtual impossibility—publisher E. A. Pollard of the Richmond *Daily Examiner* would surely prod him.

There was no doubt in Pollard's mind, as he so declared, of "the importance of Vicksburg . . . the most important point in the Valley of the Mississippi. Thousands of men, supplies, and *matériel* were continually crossing the river —much of our provisions for the armies in the East and West being derived from Texas, parts of Louisiana, and Arkansas." The editor concluded:

> Could the Federals obtain possession of Vicksburg, all the agricultural products of the Northern and Western States would pass down unmolested to the Gulf; the enemy would gain free access to the whole river front, supply themselves abundantly with cotton, sugar, molasses, and other products, disjoin the east and west Mississippi States, and, having the Confederacy fairly on its flanks, could operate with impunity upon numberless points, divide our forces, and open a new prospect of subjugation.[26]

Which was precisely what the enemy had in mind—Lincoln had said so, clearly. Vicksburg was the key to subjugation.

❧ 2 ❧

City of a Hundred Hills

T O the worthy citizens of other states, who are seeking to build new homes in the "Sunny South" . . . Vicksburg offers fine inducements for settlement. No cloud of any kind whatsoever, now darkens its horizon, but the sunshine of a prosperous present, and the clear light of a golden future irradiates and blesses.

So wrote newspaper editor J. S. Byrne, in his preface to Vicksburg's first city directory, dated 1860–61.[1]

Byrne was a good promoter. He overlooked few of Vicksburg's attributes. Midway between Memphis and New Orleans, fronting "the greatest river in the world," with two railroads running east and west (west via ferry across the Mississippi), its commercial location was unsurpassed. There was good plantation land on all sides and across the river, and the climate was moist but temperate.

Next to fronting on the Mississippi, Vicksburg's loftiness was its chief distinction—for a city set on a hill cannot be hid. Everything seemed to be vertical, the buildings clinging to the sides of the steep hills, so that people spoke of "going up" or "going down" to visit friends, as if climbing or descending stairs. Above the waterfront the brown bluffs rose two hundred feet or more, affording a majestic view of the one-half-mile-wide Mississippi and the Louisiana shore across the way.

Unlike New Orleans, seemingly mothered solely by the river, Vicksburg was a product of both river and bluffs, the latter inspiring numerous eulogistic names. Town-booster Byrne referred to the community as the "City of a Hundred Hills." It was the "Hill City" and the "City of Terraces" to Ralph Waldo Emerson and President Millard Fillmore and, to Jefferson Davis, the "Gibraltar of the West."

Davis was closer to the target. The forbidding bluffs and rolling hills, topped by a jagged silhouette of buildings, gave the impression of a tessellated castle in the air, a medieval fortress girded for siege.

It was the bluffs, called Walnut Hills, that arrested Newet Vick's attention as, journeying west, he sighted the tree-topped heights in 1814. Fort Nogales was a ruin, abandoned a decade and a half before, and camping Indians had taken over. But the physical advantages were plain. Here was well-drained land for crops and grazing, fresh water from surrounding springs, plenty of timber from the walnut groves for building houses. Below, along the river, was flatter land on which a city could be built, and, with thirteen children of his own, and numerous relatives in his wake, he could almost populate the town himself.

With his son-in-law John Lane, Vick began platting the town, projecting a neat mathematical grid with streets named alternately after trees and presidents and presidential aspirants. Jackson Street climbed precipitously from a natural landing on the river and continued eastward as a country road to Jackson, capital of Mississippi. Levee Street paralleled the waterfront, with Washington Street two blocks above. That was enough to get things started, and about all that Vick would see of the town that would bear his name. He died of yellow fever in 1819, and his wife, a dutiful Methodist, followed him the same day to the grave.[2]

John Lane carried on, with the help of Vick's sons and nephews. Lots were sold, at first mostly to members of the clan; houses went up. Walnut, Monroe, and Cherry streets, paralleling Washington, climbed like the rungs of a ladder leaning against the heights. Hartwell Vick, serving also as postmaster, opened the first store in the little city, selling meat and groceries, building tools and agricultural equipment. Young Alexander Gallatin McNutt arrived from Virginia to set up a law office, handling deeds and claims and land disputes.

By 1825, with the population numbering 150 inhabitants, the town was chartered in the name of Vicksburg. Attracted largely by the lure of cotton, more settlers flowed in from the East, many from Virginia and the Carolinas. They were not adventurers in search of easy money. Many brought their fortunes with them, transferring their slave-dependent, gracious mode of living to fresh, promising surroundings.

Newet Vick, himself an unordained Methodist minister, bequeathed a certain moral standard to the city, and many of the early comers were ministers and men of the professions—doctors, lawyers, teachers, journalists. But, if these were the stable core of the community, the very location of Vicksburg, in the center of the Mississippi steamboat traffic, made it a target of the rougher elements that came from Natchez and New Orleans.

For skulduggery and vice, "Vicksburg under the Hill" matched "Natchez under the Hill" by the 1830s. Mollie Bunch's famous bordello was tolerated as a veiled necessity, though once the volunteer fire department was called upon to hose the action down. But there were greater offenders of public decency than Mollie, for the burgeoning city attracted what were described as "off-scourings of every river town from St. Louis and Cincinnati to New Orleans." According to Harris Dickson, Vicksburg author and historian:

> The river brought riches, and prosperity brought driftwood, scum and castaways, the river gambler, coolheaded, clear-eyed, and mannered like Chesterfield, men who carried their duelling pistols in a mahogany case and their lives in their hands.[3]

When Vicksburg citizens who patronized a gamblers' hangout called the Kangaroo began to disappear without a trace, the Reverend Hugh Bodley,

Presbyterian pastor, led an armed posse against the gaming stronghold. In a shoot-out reminiscent of far-western frontier towns, Bodley was killed as he led the attack, but five of the gamblers were captured and hanged, and a sixth, with hands bound, set adrift in a skiff on the river. A grateful town erected a still-standing monument to the martyred pastor for this bit of social surgery —specifically, the plaque read, for "Defending the Morals of Vicksburg."[4]

With lawlessness finally suppressed or kept in line (Mollie Bunch's house was given special dispensation), Vicksburg entered a period of rapid and substantial growth. The side-wheel steamers on the Mississippi, now the greatest transportation system in the nation, made the Hill City a major stop on their run between New Orleans and St. Louis. The trade in cotton and the produce of northwestern states reached such proportions that, other space lacking, "wharf boats" were used as surrogate warehouses to contain the merchandise.

In the 1830s, too, the railroads gained a foothold. William Vick, son of the city's founder, helped to promote the Clinton & Vicksburg Railway running east to Jackson, though step-by-step progress was slow, and the early cars were drawn by horses. West of the Mississippi, where DeSoto Peninsula pointed upriver, the Vicksburg, Shreveport & Texas Railroad was begun, though the name was more unfulfilled promise than reality.[5]

Expanded travel facilities brought a second wave of settlers, many of them European immigrants with special skills. Max Kuner, clock-maker, arrived from Bavaria to become a Washington Street specialist in jewelry and fine watches. Antonia Genella from Switzerland opened the first variety store in town, while his two brothers dealt in guns and pistols as a sideline. Purportedly natives of France, but more probably from New Orleans, Madame Cogniasse advertised "Corsets! Corsets! Corsets!" while Monsieur Barbiere opened a dancing academy for the elite.

A walk along Washington and Jackson Streets, with a glance around the corners, would, as time passed, reveal the signboards of commission merchants, carriage makers, men's and women's tailors and apparel shops, pharmacies, insurance agents, portrait studios, gunsmiths, wine and liquor dealers, stores selling fruits and groceries, stoves, drapes, furniture, and shoes. By mid-century there were few luxuries or conveniences that were not available to city residents.[6]

With a cosmopolitan population from many states and sections of the nation, Vicksburg hungered for news from the outside world, for reports of local and European cotton prices, for schedules of ship departures and arrivals, and for a means of announcing rewards for runaway slaves. Even in a day when all type was set by hand, numerous newspapers sprung up in the early years. Many were short-lived; others changed hands frequently. Publisher Marmaduke Shannon's *Daily Whig* and the Vicksburg *Evening Citizen,* edited by James M. Swords, were the two hardiest survivors, both publishing weekly editions for suburban readers.

Business and trade were financed through the Planters Bank, housed in a red brick building on Monroe Street. The Washington Hotel, at Washington and China Streets, reportedly somewhat like an English country tavern, took care of the visiting gentry, while the Prentiss House and the Commercial Hotel, both near the river on Levee Street, took care of the drummers and less discriminating visitors. Church spires began to punctuate the skyline, with Christ Episcopal and the Catholic St. Paul's in predominance.

The more successful professional and business men began embellishing the slopes and hilltops with mansions of varying elegance and dignity. Virginia-born merchant John A. Klein set something of a standard with his Oak Street home of Greek Revival architecture, fronted by tall white columns and double balconies that overlooked the river. Dr. William Balfour, whose shingle hung over Washington Street, maintained with his wife an impressive stucco house on Crawford Street.

On Washington Street the house originally built by Burwell Vick, son of the city's founder, became the property of William Lum, merchant and entrepreneur and part owner of the Washington Hotel. Its spacious appointments—twenty-six rooms and landscaped gardens overlooking the Mississippi—would, in another ten years, play host to extraordinary occupants, the beaten and heroic, some on the brink of death, and at least one on the brink of enduring greatness.

Near the corporation boundary on Harrison Street, John Bobb, a construction engineer and one of the early Vicksburg settlers, took over an earlier-built house of obscure design. He turned an architectural hermaphrodite into an elegant Greek Revival manor, surrounded with magnolias, boxwood, exotic Southern plants and flowers. Bobb loved those gardens almost more than life itself—as time with its penchant for tragedy would show.

Outside the corporate limits of the city, but still close enough to be a part of the community, was the plantation-type home known earlier as Wexford Lodge. It was now referred to as the Shirley House, after being purchased by James Shirley of New Hampshire and his wife Adeline Quincy. The New England Shirleys never quite seemed to belong to Vicksburg and the South. James was a man of puritan severity, his Boston-born wife a woman of stubborn reticence. The Shirley House stood in white and lonely isolation on the outskirts of the city, awaiting the role that history would assign to it.

The interior appointments of these residences were sometimes as lavish as the iron grillwork gates, the statuary, and the exotic shrubbery that graced the grounds. It was not rare to find Louis XV furnishings, Bruges carpeting, French chandeliers, marble mantelpieces brought from Italy, medallioned ceilings, and a Chickering grand piano in the corner. Young Annie Harris would remember her childhood home "as in a dream."

> It was large and spacious, a wide hall running its entire length, with rooms on either side; the front with its large fluted pillars, giving it a dignity and appearance of aristocracy that quite belonged to the times. Sixty acres of land with beautifully cultivated gardens and hot-houses surrounded it. . . . Fifteen to twenty servants were employed about the premises, for whom comfortable "quarters" had been built in the rear of the "big house."[7]

Overlooking the rooftops of all was Castle Hill with its surrounding moat, the fortresslike mansion of banker Thomas Robins, built in the early 1850s of hexagonal bricks imported from England. Robins was married to Caroline Davis, niece of Jefferson Davis, though there were no dated records of the wedding. The Castle eventually passed to Vicksburg lawyer Armistead Burwell, a Virginian by birth but in the then current secessionist debates strongly Union in his sentiments.

By the late 1850s Vicksburg was a prosperous, nearly self-sufficient city. There were schools for both boys and girls, a city hospital, and four volunteer fire-fighting companies. Planked sidewalks bordered the unpaved streets, and uphill thoroughfares were transversed with a ladderwork of stones or bricks to give horses a footing and permit the citizens to cross without sinking in the mud.

It was a precipitous city indeed, valiantly clinging to its formidable bluffs. The drugstore of Hardaway & White on the corner of Washington and Clay streets was, according to a reminiscent journalist, "the favorite meeting place of planters just in off the steamboats at the foot of the long Clay Street hill. After climbing the hill the planters and others had to sit down for a breathing spell somewhere, and Hardaway's was the handiest place and thus became the gathering point of the elite to talk crops and politics."[8]

But the very steepness of the hills was a protection to all who lived or worked above Levee Street. An editor from the Memphis *Appeal,* surveying the consequences of the 1859 flooding of the Mississippi, found Vicksburg relatively unaffected: "The fine old hills on which the city stands still raise their heads proudly beyond the 'winding wave, and mirror their image in the glossy tide.' "

The journalist complained, however, that a stranger was repelled by the steep ascent of Jackson Street, and hence "goes away with little idea of the charming beauty of the tasteful gardens, and groves, and elegant villas." He himself made the climb and waxed poetic over the "roses pouring forth their rich perfume, the birds singing in gleeful melody, the gorgeous tints of the flowers," and:

> From the hilltops the Mississippi is a grand object as its stream comes sweeping with majestic circuit round the bend on the right, and flowing, in a line wonderfully direct for that erratic stream, to the blue distance. Water always looks more beautiful when viewed from an eminence—from the heights of Vicksburg its appearance is especially charming.[9]

The water which the Memphis editor admired from the hilltops was not confined to the quirky banks of the Mississippi. Just across the river, in Louisiana's Madison Parish, it spread an arabesque pattern across the flatlands, etched by innumerable creeks and bayous. And the same was largely true of the eastward-sloping land behind the city, where the Big Black River and its tributaries watered a fruitful area of rich alluvial loam.

This was plantation country. To the north, the Mississippi, the Yazoo, and the latter's tributaries embraced a 150-mile-long elliptical area, known as the Delta, with loamy topsoil twenty feet deep. When the Yazoo Fraud, by which Georgia speculators illegally sold vast acres in the Mississippi Valley, was finally settled, the Delta was opened to settlement in 1832.

While much of the Delta remained a wilderness up to the middle of the century, the plantation belt east, south, and west of Vicksburg was under productive cultivation, contributing much to the city's prosperity. The planters shipped their cotton from Vicksburg's wharves and other nearby landings, traded with Vicksburg merchants, and often maintained dwellings in the city.

Despite geographical distance, they were an integral part of the community.

Jefferson Davis's Brierfield, at a bend in the river twenty miles south of Vicksburg, was close to the southern border of the belt. Not far away lay the Allen plantation of Nanachehaw, where James and John Allen made up for that jaw-breaking title by naming their slaves for familiar virtues, such as Patience, Chastity, and Thankful.

East of Vicksburg the Big Black River sprouted a wide border of plantations on its banks. Among them was Woodfield, seat of the socially prominent family of Egglestons. When Mahala Perkins Eggleston married wealthy Vicksburg banker John Roach, and the couple built their two-story house on Depot Street, Mahala and her children divided their time between the city and Woodfield, until John fell ill and required more of her attention.

Some miles east of the Big Black on the road to Jackson, Sid and Matilda Champion's plantation occupied the highest ground for many square miles of fertile country, peaking in what was known as Champion Hill. With access to three city markets, Vicksburg, Jackson, and the town of Raymond southwest of Jackson, Sid Champion had made a good thing of his farm and was one of the more well-to-do of Vicksburg planters.

Across the Mississippi the Louisiana bottomlands, conveniently linked by ferry to Vicksburg, drew many planters from the Deep South. Here the white-columned Greek Revival mansions, resting on comforters of cotton, boasted such proud, evocative names as Fortune's Fork, Winn Forest, Bending Willow, and Brokenburn. And when the hounds bayed on one plantation, the sound was relayed like a bugle call across the country from Bayou Macon to the Mississippi River, from Milliken's Bend to the west bank village of New Carthage.

Brokenburn, whose 1,260 acres became the property of Amanda Stone on her husband's death, was as typical of any in the region. The rambling galleried mansion, which had expanded accordionlike as the family grew, overlooked well-tended lawns, past clusters of moss-festooned oaks, to the rows of slave cabins, the stables and barns, the gins, the sawmill, and finally the cotton fields, limned by cypress marshlands.

To Amanda's elder daughter Kate, Brokenburn was the prototype of heaven. In the diary she began on reaching twenty, a portrait of her life and family unfolded page by page. "What a large household we were!" she wrote prefatorily. Besides her younger brother William, who headed the household after their father's death, were Walter and Coleman, sixteen and seventeen respectively, about to enter the University of Virginia. There were also Jimmy and Johnny, in their early teens, and the baby of the family, "Little Sister" Amanda, just eleven. Living in the house as well were Mrs. Stone's brothers, Bohana ("Uncle Bo") Ragan and Ashburn Ragan, the latter two years younger than his niece Kate.[10]

But to say that these nine comprised the family—even throwing in Aunt Lucy the cook and Webster the coachman, and other household blacks who were classed almost as relatives—would be to slight a larger tribal kinship. For, collectively, the planters comprised a clan as closely knit as each family itself; the home of one was the home of all. They thought nothing of riding twenty miles to pay a call. They came for a day and spent a week, riding and hunting in the mornings, dining with fifteen or twenty at the table, spending the evenings in music, songs, charades, and fortune-telling.

Kate, by her own description, was "tall, not quite five feet six, and thin, have an irregular face, a quantity of brown hair, a shy, quiet manner and talk but little."[11] But her daguerreotype shows regular, handsome features and direct frank eyes that seem to belie a retiring nature. In any event she was deeply involved in the world around her, and, reared as were her contemporaries on the novels of Sir Walter Scott, she believed that all men were chivalrous and brave, all women beautiful and steadfast. It was a belief that she would cling to with some difficulty in the years ahead.

By 1860 and 1861, a turning point for the state of Mississippi and the nation, Vicksburg had reached maturity as a stable, prosperous, self-contained community. From his Literary Depot, a book and print shop in the Washington Hotel, A. C. Clarke began distributing the new *City Directory* which editor Byrne had labored over. It showed that the town contained five churches, one large public school and several private academies, two hospitals, three daily papers—the *Whig,* the *Sun,* and *Evening Citizen*—and taxable property valued at $4,583,400.[12]

The town which had numbered 150 residents at the time of its incorporation now had a population of almost 5,000 within its chartered limits, second in size to Natchez in the state of Mississippi. Add those who lived and worked in the plantation belt, which surrounded the city like the rings of Saturn, and the population would be more than doubled, possibly tripled—without, however, adding greatly to the number of white citizens. Madison Parish had 11,156 residents, of which 9,863 were slaves. About the same ratio of nine blacks to every white would apply to the demography of Warren County outside of Vicksburg, the county seat.

The railway lines projected in the early 1830s had moved forward slowly but persistently. The Southern Railroad of Mississippi (formerly the Clinton & Vicksburg) had pushed east to Jackson and now extended to Meridian. Running through Jackson, the New Orleans, Jackson & Great Northern had been built as far north as Canton. There it connected with the Mississippi Central, which ran upstate to Grenada, then on into Tennessee. At Grand Junction, Tennessee, it met the Memphis & Charleston Railroad headed for South Carolina.

Thus Vicksburg had access by train and coach to cities as far east as Alabama and also to the area west of the Mississippi, via the Vicksburg, Shreveport & Texas, which still, however, had not established rails beyond Monroe, Louisiana.

Riverboat traffic clogged the landing. More long-staple cotton was shipped from Vicksburg than from any other city in the world. And the old side-wheelers faced new competition when a different sort of vessel named the *J. M. White* pulled into Vicksburg. An ingenious designer in Saint Louis had observed that wheels at the side of a vessel created, by suction, a void or depression where the paddles bit into the water. For the two side wheels he substituted a single paddle wheel positioned in the stern.[13]

The *J. M. White* launched an era of swifter stern-wheelers that took over much of the Mississippi traffic, with daily runs between New Orleans, Vicksburg, Memphis, and Saint Louis. Four times a week a steamer left the Vicksburg landing to penetrate the Yazoo River as far as Greenwood, serving the planters in the Delta. And every half hour the De Soto Ferry crossed and recrossed the Mississippi to connect with the Monroe railway, linking two halves of what was virtually one community.

Another innovation in this livelier era of shipping on the river was reported by the *Daily Whig* on November 19, 1856. MUSIC BY STEAM, read the headline, and the partial story:

> The Steamer *Amazon* had all the town agog yesterday, as she came into port from St. Louis. The *Amazon* is supplied with one of the newly invented musical steam whistles, as we believe they call the thing a "Calliope," and as she rounded in at our landing, she set up the most unearthly musical screech we ever remember to have heard. . . . She played "Oh Susannah," the "Sailors Hornpipe," and divers other pieces . . .[14]

In the city itself, the most prominent monument to progress was the new Warren County Court House, between Cherry and Monroe streets, two hundred feet above the river and considered the finest building in the state. It was a square monolithic building, with pillared verandas on all four sides, and its Irish builders had added sugar to the mortar to increase its durability. The cupola atop the structure, rivaling St. Paul's Church in skyline height, bore a four-faced clock that was the proud achievement of Max Kuner, the Bavarian watchmaker.

South of the court house on Crawford Street, the Sisters of Mercy had opened a convent and school in the former brick residence of commission merchant Manlove Cobb. Among the seventy boys and girls at first enrolled was Mahala Roach's daughter, and Mahala previewed the school before it opened on October 22. "I never saw one of these 'holy women' before," she recorded, "but I was very much pleased with them, their manners are beautiful, cheerful, intelligent, and ladylike; I am sure Nora will be pleased with them."[15]

But who can account for a child's reactions? Nora was not pleased. She had to be withdrawn, to be tutored at home by her mother. The Sisters themselves would have a long career at schooling, interrupted only by the war, and would enjoy a distinguished and heroic reputation in the history of Vicksburg.

The new *City Directory* showed other changes in the social and commercial pattern of the city. New faces appeared on Washington Street; old homes changed hands. The Planters Bank closed its doors in the 1830s, with much of its business turned over to Wirt Adams & Company, and the building became the home of Sheriff William McRae and his daughter Lucy.

An itinerant dentist named Rowland Chambers, who seemed to have plied his profession in half the towns of Mississippi and Louisiana, came to visit his son-in-law J. F. Baum, vendor of fruits and cigars on Washington Street. He began looking for a house to which he could bring his wife and family and resume his practice in the city.[16]

A young lawyer from Arkansas, Anderson Miller, had opened an office in the Masonic Building. No one knew much about Miller, except that he spent much time on business in New Orleans—the business, according to rumor, involving the courtship of a young belle from the island of Saint Croix named Dora Richards.

Dr. William Wilberforce Lord arrived from New York, to take over the pulpit of the Christ Episcopal Church. A graduate of Princeton Theological Seminary and something of a poet and literary critic, Dr. Lord brought with him his wife Margaret and two children, Lida and William, Jr., to settle in the rectory, where he installed the finest collection of books in the city.

Recreation and entertainment became more sophisticated. Such exhibits as a real Arabian camel and a personal appearance of Tom Thumb no longer drew enthusiastic crowds. P. T. Barnum rolled his circus into town, but after a few performances, it was reported, "he sold his horses and wagons and purchased a steamboat for six thousand dollars, on which he proceeded down the river."

In place of the passing carnivals and traveling displays, the Vicksburg Lyceum promoted lectures and stereopticon travelogues in Apollo Hall. Though most of the truly great music of the South came from the Negroes in the fields, the Philharmonic Society of Vicksburg was established in 1858, and Emily Shannon, the publisher's daughter, noted that "every home that could afford one had a piano, and music lessons for the daughters were considered essential."

The city had its own legitimate playhouse modeled after the Camp Street Theater in New Orleans. Professional road shows found Vicksburg a lucrative stop on the New Orleans–Cincinnati circuit. A permanent stock company settled in, presenting *She Stoops to Conquer,* but a newspaper critic soon complained of the "coarse and obscene interpretations of the actors and the whooping and yelling of the audience." The troupe thereafter stuck to Shakespeare's comedies and *Romeo and Juliet.* [17]

There were other changes to be held as marks of progress. Alone in the state, Vicksburg had its own gas company, and gaslights brightened many of the streets. And editor Byrne, in his sketch of the city for *Clarke's Directory,* noted:

> We also have two fine Volunteer Military Companies, handsomely equipped, and thoroughly drilled, the "Southrons" and "Sharpshooters," constituting the "Vicksburg Battalion"—a proud ornament in time of peace, as they would prove a bulwark of defense in danger's hour. [18]

Danger's hour seemed light years away, as the citizens shelved *Clarke's Directory* beside the works of Dickens, Byron, Dumas, and, of course, Sir Walter Scott. There would be time for reading, time for music and cotillions, time for lazy carriage rides to Sky Parlor Hill where one could picnic and watch the passing ships and the darkies working in the white-pocked fields beyond. And, as editor Byrne had assured them, there were "no dark clouds of any kind on the horizon." None visible from here, at any rate.

Visible or not, the storm was gathering, as talk of secession rumbled down the streets of Vicksburg and the daily gatherings at Hardaway & White's became choleric as the 1860 presidential candidates were weighed. The election was the immediate thing. Mississippi had already gone on record as declaring that if a Black Republican candidate (meaning Abolitionist) was chosen for the White House, "Mississippi will regard it as a declaration of hostility, and will hold herself in readiness to co-operate with her sister States of the South in whatever measures they may deem necessary for the mainte- nance of their rights . . . " It was on this platform that John J. Pettus, a strong States' Rights man, had been overwhelmingly elected governor.[19]

But Vicksburg's feelings toward secession were, at first, ambivalent, as were those of Warren County. This was cotton country, and slavery was an institu- tion on which the whole economy depended. On the other hand, war was as unthinkable as abolition. It would tear apart this blissful pattern of prosperity, and threaten the free and uninhibited use of the Mississippi and its tributaries which formed the lifeline of the cotton trade.

Young Annie Laurie Harris, the judge's daughter, wrote of these conflicting sentiments:

> The first mutterings of war were like the low, rumbling thunder that one hears on a quiet summer day, when there is hardly a cloud to be seen in the sky. The grown people used to sit and talk of the distant rumors, but not a doubt was felt that everything would be arranged to keep the Union together in a peaceful manner.[20]

Publisher Marmaduke Shannon made his presidential views known in the *Daily Whig* three weeks before election time:

> Young men! Will you see the Union of your fathers rent in twain? Will you see the Constitution torn in tatters by bands of secessional fanatics? No. NEVER, NEVER. Then buckle on your armor and go forth to do battle for the success of the Union candidates.[21]

Even after Lincoln's election, Shannon continued to fight secessionist senti- ment in the *Whig*. Though he branded the westernborn Lincoln an "obnox- ious" President, he added, "We do not mean to raise the standard of resistance. . . . Let others do what they will, for us, we will stand by the *Union, the Constitution, and the laws.*"[22]

But the showdown was coming. When the Mississippi legislature called for a choice of delegates to attend the state convention on January 7, 1861, Vicksburg elected its Union bloc of candidates over the secessionists by a vote of 561 to 175. Pro-secession editor James Swords of the *Citizen* scoffed at the results as "humble submission." Confident that "the State is certain to secede in less than two weeks," his only concern, he jokingly wrote, was what would become of Vicksburg. "Will she secede too, or will she hang on to Lincoln's Union?"[23]

Editor Swords's confidence was justified. At the state convention the ordi- nance of secession was adopted by a vote of 84 to 15, and, it was reported, "A great wave of excitement swept the audience, and grave and dignified men, swayed by a common impulse, joined in the deafening applause. In an instant the hall was a scene of wild tumult. . . . " On that note Mississippi became the first state to follow South Carolina out of the Union.

Shortly afterward, on January 26, neighboring Louisiana followed suit, and in New Orleans young Dora Richards was caught in a dilemma. Born in the Caribbean island of St. Croix, and now a resident of the most Southern of Southern states, her heart was elsewhere. As she had written in her secret diary, it was the Union, for which her American forebears had fought, that commanded her allegiance, "not any divided or special section of it." For weeks and months to come Dora would be torn between raw reality and personal emotions.[24]

With the rapid-fire secessions of Alabama, Louisiana, Texas, and Arkansas, Vicksburg found itself in the solid heart of the Southwestern Confederacy. Marmaduke Shannon, Mississippian to the core, revised his opinion as to where his duty, and that of his readers, lay: *"it is to follow the Destiny of the State and abide its fate, be it for weal or be it for woe."* He thought not in the larger terms of Union versus Confederacy, but localized the issue, writing: "It is enough for us to know that Mississippi, *our* State, *our* government has taken its position. We, too, take our position by its side."[25]

Vicksburg did not celebrate secession with marching bands and fireworks as Jackson did, but it began to make military preparations. Four more volunteer companies were organized, making six in all: the Warren County Guards, the Hill City Cadets, the Warren Dragoons, and the Vicksburg Light Artillery —to enlarge the battalion already built around the Southrons and Sharpshooters.

The latter two companies and the Warren Guards were the first to see action, when Governor Thomas O. Moore of Louisiana issued a warning that a Federal expedition was preparing to invade the Mississippi. An artillery company was sent from Jackson to Vicksburg; Captain J. F. Kerr was ordered by Governor Pettus to round up the volunteer companies and "to take such position as would enable him to prevent any hostile expedition descending the river."

Kerr led the Sharpshooters, the Southrons, and the Warren Guards up to the bluffs north of the city, once occupied by Fort Nogales, where he planted a battery of four guns. On January 11, 1861, the steamer *O. A. Tyler,* flying United States colors, rounded the bend and received a broadside from the battery that sent the vessel scurrying to safety. Vicksburg had spoken—from the cannon's mouth. Governor Pettus declared proudly that "This was the first shot fired during the war on the Mississippi River." He did not mention, perhaps did not know, that the *O. A. Tyler*'s cargo had consisted of consumer merchandise from Cincinnati.

While volunteer infantry units were organizing, Professor A. F. Cykoski, teacher of music and languages at his residence on Grove Street, appeared to see some writing on the wall. Mounted troops would, he believed, play a large part in the war to come, and, through the pages of the *Whig,* he solicited recruits for his cavalry company, insisting only that they show up promptly, bringing their own mounts. The affinity of music professors for horses is doubtless mythical, but shortly thereafter a young music master named Benjamin Grierson of Jacksonville, Illinois, was about to desert his calling for a soldier's life. He would end up terrorizing Mississippi in one of the greatest cavalry raids of Western history.

Meanwhile the city council met to allocate moneys for the purchase of munitions and the building of an arsenal outside the town. Steps were taken to provide adequate housing for volunteer units, should these reach appreciable numbers, and a resolution was proposed, and passed, urging businessmen not to stand in the way of workers or apprentices anxious to leave their employ for military service. Plans were drafted at the same time for welcoming Jefferson Davis to Vicksburg on his way to the Montgomery inaugural.[26]

The President-elect's brief visit gave the new volunteer companies a chance to show off their smart gray uniforms, to fire salutes, and parade beneath their colors, to the admiration of their townsmen. The people in turn had a chance to take stock of their new President, and found him a man of distinguished gravity and commendable modesty of dress. After the visit, Clarke's Literary Depot, like other shops, began selling framed pictures of the President along with "Jefferson Davis letterpaper" and Confederate banderoles and badges.

While a generally more martial spirit now infected Vicksburg, there was no hysteria, no war fever, no fanatical rush to arms. Life went on much as before. The volunteer companies drilled several times a week. The guns on the bluffs north of Vicksburg maintained solitary watch, facing riverward but unattended. Women wore Confederate colors, learned the words of "The Bonnie Blue Flag," and created silk flags to be carried into glorious battle by the volunteers.

Beyond the limits of Vicksburg, however, war preparations in the state of Mississippi moved more purposefully. Taking note of "the political excitement awaked by the election of a Black Republican to the Presidency," Adjutant General W. L. Sykes reported to the governor on January 18 that, for the past two months, "companies have been organizing at the rate of seven or eight per week, numbering from fifty to sixty men. The number of companies organized up to the 16th of January, 1861, amounts to 65." Earl Van Dorn, a native of Port Gibson, Mississippi, and former major of the United States Cavalry, was appointed major general in command of Mississippi volunteers.[27]

In Vicksburg itself things began to take a graver turn, as the volunteer companies were mustered into Confederate service and began departing for Florida. First to leave were the Hill City Cadets, who at dawn of March 27 were escorted to the depot by half the population of the city, many civilians bearing hampers of food and clothing for their soldier kin. There were a few tears, many cheers, to speed the company on its way to Pensacola.

In mid-April, after the bombardment of Fort Sumter, the artillery company marched to the depot, leaving their guns behind them. An uneasy feeling grew among civilians that the city was being deserted by this exodus. It was one thing to volunteer for the defense of Vicksburg or the state of Mississippi; that was a holy duty. But for the city's sons to fight in other states, perhaps to die on distant battlegrounds, was something else again.

Nevertheless, "Everywhere there were Confederate flags and bands playing martial music," wrote Vicksburg planter James Monroe Gibson, on seeing his two brothers off for Virginia. The embarking troops, he noted, were full of spirit. "The wild fox hunters whoop of the South rang out from the hills to the river—the whooping that was later called the 'Rebel Yell.' "[28]

Lucy McRae, too, felt a thrill of pride at Vicksburg's reply to the clarions of war, remembering of this time: "When the bugle sounded, and the drums called men to serve their country, the brightest and manliest of her sons responded with eagerness. Mothers, wives, and sweethearts little realized what war meant as they kissed loved ones goodby, thinking that sixty days would bring them back." No one tallied up the odds; there was no need to, with the prevailing dictum that one Southerner could lick six Yanks.

At Brokenburn across the river, Kate Stone had already seen two members of her family leave the plantation, her brother William to enlist in the Jeff Davis Guards, her Uncle "Bo" Ragan to join the Southrons. Both were at the depot bound for Richmond by the end of May—the Guards with bouquets of flowers on their bayonets, the Southrons with the "Marseillaise" on their lips.

As for Kate herself, she worked on making blankets for the troops, putting in lining with pockets "for soap, combs, brushes, handkerchiefs, etc." And with her mother selected seeds for planting crops other than cotton, so that "the North cannot starve us, try as they may. . . . " Otherwise she found the easy, familiar rhythm of plantation life a mockery of the angry passions of the South. "Oh! to see and be in it all. I hate weary days of inaction. Yet what can a woman do but wait and suffer." It was the ageless cry of women everywhere in time of war.[29]

Mahala Roach was less concerned with the national emergency. She had a crisis of her own to face. Her husband died on the first of July, leaving her, after sixteen years of marriage, with three sons and two daughters to look after. The older son Tommy, fifteen, was learning his father's banking business at Wirt Adams & Company, but the others were a handful, inspiring in her volatile nature what she called "despairing fits."

The townsfolk rallied around Mahala, as they always did when one of their number was in distress or need. In the weeks after John Roach died, the list of callers at the house on Depot Street read like a roster of the town's elite: Dr. and Mrs. William Balfour, Judge Harris and his daughter Annie, the banker Wirt Adams, Reverend William W. Lord and Margaret Lord, John Bobb, Mayor Laz Lindsay, Sheriff McRae and his daughter Lucy, and assorted Kleins, Egglestons, Barbours, and Vick descendants.

Annie Harris who, in her journal, predicted that the Union would endure despite the "mutterings of war," felt differently after April 1861. Now she recorded that "The cloud of discord grew blacker and blacker, and finally burst at the hot-headed, impulsive fight of Fort Sumter. Then it seemed as though the vengeance of heaven was upon us."[30]

There was no real reason for Annie—or Vicksburg, for that matter—to feel immediately threatened by the war. Not at this point, not directly. There would be the pain of seeing sons and husbands off to camp, the anguish of returning wounded. There would be shortages and economic ruptures. But it would be eight months after the firing on Fort Sumter before Vicksburg would hear that the Federals were converting Ship Island into a base and that Federal gunboats were assembling at Cairo.

Even so there might, in retrospect, be cause for wonder that so little was done to fortify and appreciably strengthen Vicksburg in the early months of war. Particularly in view of the massive preparations made by the state of Mississippi. Of the eighty volunteer companies raised in Mississippi, more than half were sent to Richmond, the new Confederate capital, or to Pensacola. The remainder were sent to camps in eastern portions of the state. Virtually none remained in Vicksburg.

Perhaps one explanation lay in the lingering hope that the Mississippi could remain a neutral artery of commerce, despite war—a hope shared by the northwestern states and the Confederate river cities of the South. Governor Pettus himself had urged in January that "the most prompt and efficient measures be adopted to make known to the people of the Northwestern States that peaceful commerce on the Mississippi River will neither be interrupted nor annoyed by the people of Mississippi."[31] To make a fortress out of Vicksburg would belie that good intention.

But this is idle speculation. For all eyes focused on the East in 1861. Vicksburg citizens would remember the words of Jefferson Davis on passing through the city on his way to Alabama: "I am ready, as I always have been, to redeem my pledges to you and the South by shedding every drop of my blood in your cause." They took the words "you" and "your cause" personally, as meaning Vicksburg and its preservation. As time passed, however, it began to seem that Richmond was the holy temple of that Cause. And a city as remote as Vicksburg was of no immediate concern.[32]

Except to Admiral Farragut and David Dixon Porter, who were readying their forces in the Gulf of Mexico.

❦ 3 ❦

Threat from the South

To David Dixon Porter, on that April morning of 1862, it was the opening act of a drama whose last act—if all went as planned—would equal the capture of Richmond.

In the mud-mottled waters that flowed from the Mississippi River delta, off the mouth of Southwest Pass, stood the mightiest American armada ever gathered in the Gulf of Mexico, poised to invade the river to New Orleans and from there to Vicksburg. At the latter target the fleet would be joined by the Western Flotilla of Andrew Foote, coming down from the north, to sever the Confederacy along the whole length of its spinal river.

From the deck of his flagship *Harriet Lane,* Porter could count some fifty vessels of all descriptions, from pygmy towboats to Farragut's stately ships of the line. His own flotilla, nineteen stripped-down schooners fitted with a single thirteen-inch mortar each, would spearhead the thrust, bombarding and reducing the twin forts, Jackson and Saint Philip, forty miles upriver from the mouth. With these major obstacles removed, Farragut would be free to sail on up to New Orleans and force the city to surrender.

If one believed, with Oliver Goldsmith, that "the first blow is half the battle," the subsequent assault on Vicksburg would be like picking fruit from a fallen tree. Mortally wounded, Confederate resistance in the West would crumble, and the entire might of the Union could be hurled against the isolated Eastern states.

Swarming like gnats about the two main squadrons were escort boats of multiple purposes and sizes—supply ships, gunboats, tugs, and transports. Aboard the transports were 18,000 infantry under General Benjamin Butler, to invest and occupy the conquered cities on the Mississippi's banks. To a curious degree the land and naval forces matched those of the British under Lord Pakenham and Vice Admiral Cochrane that had stormed New Orleans in 1814 and 1815—with the difference that both Farragut and Porter were familiar with these waters and this section of Louisiana, and there was no Andrew Jackson to inspire the defenders.[1]

It took twelve days, however, for the deep-draft vessels in the fleet to surmount the sandbars at the mouth of the Mississippi. Heavier ships were obliged to jettison portions of their coal and cargo, and it was not until April 16 that they reached the Scylla and Charybdis of the Mississippi: Forts Jackson and Saint Philip. Both star-shaped forts, with their tier guns and water batteries, commanded a wide sweep of the river, Jackson on the west bank, just around a bend, Saint Philip on the eastern side, a little farther up.

Below the forts stretched the crude but formidable barrier composed of half-submerged hulls of dismantled schooners linked together by iron chains and extending from shore to shore below Fort Jackson. The New Orleans *Picayune* referred to the obstruction as a "dam," and inspired among its Creole readers a war cry that would echo at Verdun a half a century and more to come: *"Ils ne passeront pas!"*

Above the floating barrier and above the forts, an improvised Confederate defense fleet stood guard. It comprised a dozen vessels of unorthodox design, most of them wooden and lightly armed, almost all converted from river steamers, tugs, and even double-ended ferries. Of the two most formidable craft—the Confederate ram *Manassas* and the sixteen-gun ironclad *Louisiana* —the former was handicapped by insufficient power for her size, and the *Louisiana* was anchored just upriver from Fort Saint Philip while work proceeded on completing her machinery.

Still farther upriver was another improvised and deadly weapon, reminiscent of the fire ships with which the Byzantine navy kept the Vikings out of Constantinople. Innumerable rafts and barges, piled twenty feet high with tinder drenched in tar and kerosene, stood moored on both sides of the river. Ignited and set adrift on the current, they would carry a wall of flame against the enemy's wooden ships as well as lighting up the targets for the gunners in the forts.[2]

The Confederates had little immediate warning of Farragut's approach. Porter kept his mortar schooners close to shore below the bend, their mastheads camouflaged with foliage that blended with the intervening treetops. Farragut held his blue-water fleet still farther back and out of sight, while he sent a small spy ship to reconnoiter the Confederate positions. Then, on the morning of April 18, the fleet commander signaled Porter to "Fire when ready!"

As the gunners scrambled to their posts, mouths open to absorb the sound, feet braced to withstand the shock, the nineteen mortars roared in unison. Tons of explosives soared up and over the river to crash with descending fury on the forts. As if by reflex the Confederate batteries snarled back. "Combine all that you have heard of thunder, add to it all you have ever seen of lightning, and you have, perhaps, a conception of the scene," recorded a Union army officer.[3]

Throughout the day some 240 shells an hour, or one every ten or fifteen seconds, plunged into and around the forts, without affecting the violence of the Confederate response. It was as savage an artillery duel as the Civil War would know. By day's end the citadels and barracks of Fort Jackson were in flames, the walls battered and the magazine inaccessible.

Though Fort Jackson withstood the attack, there had been anxious moments. Colonel Edward Higgins, the fort's commander, told Porter later: "A shell, striking the parapet over one of the magazines, the wall of which was seven feet thick, penetrated five feet and failed to burst. If that shell had exploded, your work would have ended."

By the following Tuesday, April 22, Porter concluded he had done his worst and gotten nowhere. "We had kept up a heavy fire, night and day, for nearly 5 days—about 2,800 shells every 24 hours; in all, 16,800 shells. The men were nearly worn out for want of sleep and rest. The ammunition was giving out, one of the schooners was sunk, and the rest . . . were badly shaken up by the concussion of the mortars." And the forts had shown no sign of yielding, though a Confederate deserter told Porter that their garrisons "were in a desperate and demoralized condition."[4]

From his flagship *Hartford,* Farragut had watched the bombardment with growing impatience. Porter had assured him that it would take no more than forty-eight hours to secure the forts. Five days had passed, and they were nowhere near that end.

Aboard one of the transports General Butler shared the flag officer's exasperation, referring to Porter's efforts as "that superbly useless bombardment which Farragut never believed in from the hour when it was first brought to his attention to the time when the last mortar was fired."[5]

The affair generated a degree of skepticism and distrust between the once-friendly Farragut and Porter. When Farragut called a conference of the fleet's commanders, Porter found himself too busy to attend. At the council, Farragut told his colleagues the time had come to gamble, to take great risks for the sake of greater gain. As his military secretary William Meredith recorded:

> Farragut stood facing his destiny, imperishable fame or failure. He was determined to run by the forts with his ships, and he would not cumber the fleet by towing the mortars as Porter wished him to do. Once above the defenses, and the enemy's fleet overcome, he would . . . push right on seventy-five miles up the river to New Orleans without waiting for the army.[6]

There were voices of dissent among the officers, reflecting the risks involved. Porter sent his views by courier, predicting the destruction of the fleet. His admiration for Farragut was soured by personal chagrin. Six months earlier he had seen himself capturing New Orleans single-handedly. Now he was to be left behind, to continue his battle with the forts, while Farragut sailed on to glory. To Porter's warning of disaster, Farragut replied that, if only half his fleet got through, it would be worth it.

First, however, the fleet must break the line of hulks across the river. Two plucky vessels, the *Itasca* and *Pinola,* volunteered for the hazardous mission of cutting the ties that held the floating barriers. Under cover of night they crept up to the chain, where their crews, under enemy crossfire, hacked with sledges and chisels at the cables. A link was broken. The severed ends swept back like whips with the current, carrying the *Itasca* and *Pinola* with them and leaving an off-center gap closer to the left bank of the river.

Following this maneuver, Farragut issued his "General Orders to the Fleet," one of the most momentous edicts of the Civil War: Prepare to weigh anchor at 2:00 A.M. of Thursday, April 24. It triggered feverish activity. Hulls were painted a muddy brown. Decks were sanded to prevent slipping in spilled blood. Extraneous spars were lowered from the masts. Chains were hung over the vessels' sides, adjacent to the engine rooms, like the iron mail that knights once wore to battle. All lights were extinguished, but two red lanterns were hoisted on the flagship *Hartford,* as a guidon for the fleet.

2:00 A.M., April 24: Aboard the *Governor Moore,* a converted Confederate paddle-wheel steamer waiting above Fort Saint Philip, Lieutenant Beverly Kennon heard a sound like rats gnawing the timbers in the hold. Then he recognized the grating noise as anchor cables rising through hawseholes. He went on deck. To the south, two red lights burned on the horizon, coming closer. He heard the rustle of propellers in the water. The lights were nearer now. The ghostly outline of a warship floated into view.

Kennon summoned his crew to their battle stations, where the guns had been preleveled at the fissure in the floating barrier. He gave the order: "Fire!"

Aboard the *Harriet Lane* Porter too had seen the dim procession of ships get under way, following in single file the beacons of the *Hartford.* When he heard the guns of the *Governor Moore* he knew that the movement had been detected and the Confederates had opened fire. He ordered the mortars to let loose with everything they had.

In a split second the night exploded, with the Confederate batteries and the guns of Farragut's seventeen warships adding to the din. Above the forts the fire rafts were loosed, flames rising to a hundred feet. Remembered Porter:

> From almost perfect silence—the steamers moving slowly through the water like phantom ships—one incessant roar of heavy cannon commenced, the Confederate forts and gunboats opening together on the head of our line as it came within range. The Union vessels returned the fire as they came up, and soon the guns of our fleet joined in the thunder which seemed to shake the very earth. A lurid glare was thrown over the scene by the burning rafts, and, as the bomb-shells crossed each other and exploded in the air, it seemed as if a battle was taking place in the heavens as well as on the earth.[8]

It was a small arena in which to stage so mighty a conflict—a half mile wide and not much more in length—and here more than thirty warships, spouting fire and death, battled like roiling sharks, plowing into one another, guns firing muzzle to muzzle, ships veering violently to escape imminent collision. In the center of the melee, Farragut's *Hartford* moved resolutely forward, broadside guns blazing at targets obscured by smoke and glare.

Lieutenant Kennon directed the *Governor Moore* into the heart of the free-for-all. Two converging Union vessels challenged his appearance with. "What ship are you?"

"United States Steamship *Mississippi,* " Kennon shouted, slipping between them.

Across the bow of the *Moore* passed Farragut's ship of the line, *Varuna.* Though commanding only a lightly-gunned wooden ship with an iron blade welded to her prow, Kennon rammed the *Varuna* amidships, pulled loose from the gash he had created, backed off, and rammed her again.

Listing and shuddering, the *Varuna* tried to escape upriver. Kennon pursued and headed her off, coming so close he could not depress his guns sufficiently to hit her vulnerable waterline. He depressed them anyway, blasting through the deck and bulwarks of his own ship, all but tearing out her entrails, but opening mortal wounds in the *Varuna*'s side and reducing her to a sinking wreck.

By now the *Governor Moore* was under attack by five Union vessels closing in from all sides. Their guns were raking her decks, killing the already wounded. Within minutes that seemed a lifetime, Kennon lost more than three-quarters of his crew, leaving only nineteen men undisabled. The *Moore*'s rudder was gone; her own guns had gouged holes in her forward deck and sides; the engine room was filled with searing steam from perforated boilers.

Kennon hoisted a jib sail and coaxed the dying vessel to a berth beside the wrecked *Varuna*. Then, being sure that his wounded were cleared from the vessel, he poured oil down the ladders leading to the magazine and lighted it. Leaping ashore, he watched the flames set fire to his colors on the masthead, just before the ship exploded.

Differing only in detail, the drama was reenacted up and down the roiling, contested stretch of river. Most of the Confederate ships were rams, equipped with adequate armament and able to strike a mortal blow.

Charging Farragut's three-masted *Brooklyn*, the Confederate ram *Manassas* sliced deep into her midships at full speed. A Georgia-born sailor rushed forward to inspect the damage to the *Brooklyn* and disappointedly reported it, "Not serious." A Union seaman, with the same purpose in mind, split the Georgian's skull with a well-aimed sounding lead.

Neither vessel was triumphant in this contest. It was later discovered that the *Brooklyn*'s hull had been split from waterline to keel, and only the shifting coal in the bunkers had plugged the hole and kept the craft from sinking. The *Manassas,* seeing the Union warship *Mississippi* bearing down on her, was driven into a mudbank, abandoned by her crew and set afire.

Such was the fate of three-quarters of the Southern fleet. Still below Fort Jackson, where his mortars continued pounding the twin bastions, Porter watched the smoldering hulls float by, pyres for the dead and dying on their decks. There had been no coordination in the Confederate naval action; the defending ships had fought not as a pack but as lone wolves, snapping at a passing herd.

It was not over yet. Downstream still came the fire rafts, lighting up the embattled fleet like a Wagnerian finale. Not all the fire ships, however, were successfully released, and many were carried by the current to the far bank, out of harm's way. But one was guided by a Louisiana tugboat directly toward the *Hartford*. In vain Union seamen wrestled with hawsers to veer the flagship out of its path, but the doomsday raft slid against the *Hartford* and was resolutely pinned there by the tug.

The flames swept up the flagship's hull, on up the tarred rigging and out along projecting spars. A deckhand heard the commander mutter, "My God, is it to end this way?" Then Farragut pulled himself together and ordered his crew aloft to fight the flames.

"Steady, boys, steady," Farragut shouted at them, "there's a hotter fire than this, you know, for those who flinch from duty." With bucket brigades strung out along the smoldering rigging, the sailors managed to douse the flames. Then Farragut switched his attention to the real offender. "Blast that rebel tug!" he shouted. The plucky tugboat, still pressed against the fire raft, received a pointblank shot, quivered once in agony, and sank.[9]

The battle to get past the forts, seeming to consume a lifetime, was over in an hour and ten minutes. Casualties had not been excessive for the Union fleet, less than two hundred killed and wounded. One vessel, the *Varuna,* had been lost, with two others seriously damaged, in contrast to which, only two Confederate ships survived. Farragut donned his full-dress uniform to pace the deck of his flagship, in a show of confidence and triumph.

But the fleet commander was badly shaken. "I am so agitated that I can scarcely write," he wrote to his wife the following day. He described the passage between the forts as "one of the most awful sights I ever saw or expect to witness," and expressed thanks to God that his life had been spared, "through a fire such as the world has scarcely known," later remarking, "I seemed to be breathing flame." With the Mississippi open clear to New Orleans, the dead were buried, the decks cleaned, and the fleet prepared to move upriver. Porter reluctantly remained behind with his mortar schooners to take care of the two resisting forts.

On the plains of Chalmette, made famous in the 1814–1815 Battle of New Orleans, Farragut met minor resistance from Confederate batteries below the Crescent City—then impatiently steamed on. Once New Orleans capitulated to this show of force, only Vicksburg stood between the Federal fleet and its conquest of the Mississippi Valley. And when Farragut sighted burning ships loaded with cotton, floating downstream past his fleet, he knew that the merchants of New Orleans were destroying their produce in anticipation of the city's capture.

Dora Richards and her husband, Anderson Miller, were not present to welcome Farragut's arrival at New Orleans. Promptly after their marriage, the couple had fled the city to Anderson's family home in Arkansas, just above the Louisiana border. Miller, if he had stayed, would have been subject to conscription in the Confederate army, and, though a Southerner by birth, he disapproved of the course his compatriots had taken. He would fight neither for them nor against them. So their northward trek was both a honeymoon and an escape.

For the New Orleanians they left behind, April was the cruelest month, when a city that had weathered many crises under many flags found itself endangered once again. For a year the Queen Port of the South had been throttled by the Federal blockade. Millions of dollars worth of cotton and tobacco clogged the storage houses, and the paddle-wheel steamers lay idle at the river bank. One of the busiest harbors of the world and a city of 170,000 people of mixed nationalities were moribund.

But the people up to now had felt secure. The *Picayune* had promised its readers that the chain below the forts was indestructible, that the forts were as strong as twin Gibraltars, and that "in New Orleans itself we have thirty-two thousand infantry, and as many more available in the environs."

In point of fact, most of the troops recruited in the region of the lower Mississippi were off at scattered fronts in Tennessee and Virginia. General Mansfield Lovell, garrisoning the city with 3,000 men, regarded New Orleans more as a temporary barracks than a place to be defended. Besides his own ninety-day volunteer troops, there were only the Home Guard, comprised of older men whose hair was the color of their trim gray uniforms, and the Foreign Legion composed of British, French, and Spanish volunteers, who substituted for police.[10]

New Orleans' ships, such as Captain Raphael Semmes's commerce-raiding *Sumter,* had gone to war too. The sixteen-gun ironclad *Louisiana* was down at the forts with the rest of the River Defense Fleet, and her equal in power, the *Mississippi,* was still being rushed to completion in the Jefferson boatyard. New Orleans pinned its gossamer hopes on an imaginary land and naval power, much as a later-day Paris would be lulled by a phantom Maginot Line.

When, on April 24, word arrived that Farragut had passed the forts, the city succumbed to instant panic. Merchants set fire to their cotton, to keep it from enemy hands. Warehouses went up in smoke, and the sparks ignited surrounding buildings. Fires burned throughout the night, despite a drenching rain that helped the rising Mississippi overflow its banks. The following day the Crescent City looked as if it already had been ravaged by a horde of Visigoths.

George Cable remembered how the alarm bells sounded the next morning, warning of impending danger and turning the citizens into a mob beyond control. Though the Home Guard stuck to its posts and the Foreign Legion patrolled the streets, the crowd plundered the city with a vengeance, crying "Betrayed! Betrayed!"[11] Smashing storefronts, scooping up sugar and molasses, setting fire to buildings not already burned, they paused to lynch a man whose face seemed unfamiliar.

In the rain that was coming down in sheets, young Cable walked to the flooded levee, where smoldering hulls defined the submerged banks. He wrote of asking a bystander, "Are the Yankee ships in sight?"

> He pointed out the tops of their naked masts as they showed up across the huge bend of the river. They were engaging the Chalmette batteries, on the old field of Jackson's renown. Presently that was over. Ah, me! I see them now as they come slowly around Slaughterhouse Point into full view, silent, grim, and terrible; black with men, heavy with deadly portent; the long-banished Stars and Stripes flying against the frowning sky. Oh, for the *Mississippi!* The *Mississippi!* Just then she came down upon them. But how? Drifting helplessly, a mass of flames.[12]

Farragut's *Hartford,* with its pivot gun trained on the assembled mob, anchored with the rest of the squadron off Canal Street. A captain and lieutenant came ashore and elbowed their way to the city hall, through the shouting crowd ("Shoot them!" "Kill them!" "Hang them!"), to demand the surrender of the city. General Lovell, summoned by Mayor John T. Monroe, announced blandly that he was withdrawing his troops; it was up to the civil authorities to negotiate the matter. The mayor continued to equivocate and the two Union emissaries returned empty-handed.

Farragut kept his temper. He could shell the defenseless city, but was wary of public reaction, North and South, to such a measure. He was further warned by the captain of a visiting French warship that his government and other European powers would deplore such "barbarous" extremes. Butler's troops, intended to occupy New Orleans, were still seventy-five miles to the south, and, for all Farragut knew, the two forts, Jackson and Saint Philip, were still holding out against the mortar fleet.

The forts, indeed, were holding out, declining Porter's invitation to surrender. What finally caused their capitulation on April 28 was a matter of dispute. Porter asserted that the fury of his mortars brought the bastions to their figurative knees. There were reports, too, of mutiny within the garrisons, which were composed to large degree of French and Irish immigrants seeking to evade conscription. A third view was that, with Farragut's fleet at New Orleans, the forts' commanders felt that further resistance would serve no useful purpose.

A curious incident marred the surrender ceremony aboard the *Harriet Lane,* where a flag of truce floated from the masthead. Throughout the six days of bombardment, the Confederate gunship *Louisiana* had hovered below Fort Saint Philip, immovable and apparently unsinkable, blasting with her broadside guns at any Union target within range. Now, as Porter discussed surrender terms with Brigadier General Johnson Duncan and Lieutenant Colonel Edward Higgins, the *Louisiana* made a spectacular and unforeseen appearance. Aflame from stem to stern, a drifting torch that threatened every vessel in her path, she was bearing down directly on the flagship *Harriet Lane.* [13]

In vain Porter's sailors tugged on hawsers to veer the *Harriet Lane* from the *Louisiana*'s path. But the ship came on relentlessly. It was a carefully planned and executed trick, concluded Porter. An infamous trick to send his flagship to the bottom.

Then, thirty yards away, the *Louisiana* exploded. The *Harriet Lane* tilted dangerously from the blast; the officers in the saloon were hurled indecorously from their chairs. Porter pulled himself up and, furious, charged the Confederate emissaries with violating the flag of truce. Somehow Duncan and Higgins managed to convince him that the incident had been accidental. The *Louisiana* had been burned to prevent her falling into Union hands; but the flames had also consumed her anchor ropes and set her aimlessly adrift.

The capitulation of the forts gave Farragut new psychological ammunition with which to force the surrender of New Orleans. The rest of his fleet was on the way, he told the mayor, along with troops to occupy the city. If he had to use live ammunition to convince the mayor, he would do so. Monroe replied:

We will stand your bombardment, unarmed and undefended as we are. The civilized world will consign to indelible infamy the heart that will conceive the deed and the hand that will dare to consummate it. [14]

But such defiance was mere rhetoric at this point. When Farragut landed a battalion of marines, to raise the Stars and Stripes above the custom house and lower the flag of Louisiana above the city hall, all Monroe could do was stand, breast forward, in front of the marine howitzer and challenge the Yankees to shoot.

It was a face-saving, futile gesture. The Louisiana flag came down. The city had not surrendered; it had been conquered. Or, as it was better expressed by a teenage New Orleanian, writing in her diary, "We are conquered but not subdued." Not subdued, even for a day—a citizen named William Mumford climbed the pole above the custom house and hauled down the star-spangled banner, which the mob delighted in destroying.

As General Lovell marched his evacuating troops to camps on the north and east, sending the bulk of his army under General Martin L. Smith to strengthen the garrison at Vicksburg, General Butler and his troops arrived on the first of May, to occupy New Orleans. From then on the city had a running battle on its hands, New Orleans versus "Beast Butler," as the New England general would be known.

Meanwhile Flag Officer Farragut was mindful that New Orleans was only a first step in the campaign for Vicksburg. He prepared to move upriver to the city on the bluffs, 400 river-miles away. He would not wait for Porter's mortar fleet, still guarding the conquered forts, however much Porter might object to being left behind. He did, however, plan to take with him some of Butler's troops, aware that Vicksburg could not be taken and held with naval forces only.

Butler balked at relinquishing any of his 15,000 infantry. He planned a mighty show of force, to keep New Orleans solidly beneath his heel. After publicly hanging William Mumford for tearing down the national flag, he explained, "I propose to make some further examples." But he reluctantly parted with 1,400 men under Brigadier General Thomas Williams, and Farragut loaded them aboard two transports before starting north.[15]

The flag officer sent an advance squadron upriver, led by Captain S. Phillips Lee of the *Oneida*. Lee was to sound out the Vicksburg defenses, secure the surrender of the city, and keep an eye out for a mysterious Confederate ram said to be under construction in the Yazoo River.

In the wake of Lee's advance squadron, Commander James S. Palmer aboard the gunboat *Iroquois* secured the easy surrender of undefended Baton Rouge. Catching up with Lee's flotilla, Palmer then pushed on to Natchez, where the Natchez *Courier* exhorted its citizens, "Swear! Swear! . . . never to surrender!" The exhortation fell on deaf ears. Brigadier General C. G. Dahlgren could muster only fourteen men who were willing to defend the city. Disgusted, he handed Natchez over to the civil authorities who, in turn, surrendered the city to Commander Palmer.

Lee's advance squadron was now only 115 river-miles south of Vicksburg, a three-day run. And word arrived that a second Union naval force was descending the river from the north. In the spring and early summer of 1862, the gradual Confederate withdrawal from the Tennessee River Valley had forced the evacuation of their forts along the Mississippi, driving the Southern defenders down to Memphis.

The Union pincers were closing on the major target, Jefferson Davis's Gibraltar of the West.

"Friday, April 25, 1862. Rainy, dark, and cold." Under this caption Mahala Roach recorded in her Vicksburg diary: "Soon after breakfast Tommy came in and said some Federal gunboats were at New Orleans and the City had *surrendered!* Of course we all feel dreadfully, but I think I shall stay and do the best I can—God help us all!"[16]

By the following day all Vicksburg knew New Orleans had surrendered.

There was at first bewilderment, tinged with disbelief. How could forts declared impregnable be overcome and the foremost city in the South be captured in a space of five days? "People," remembered Annie Harris, "walked the streets aimlessly, as one does when troubled, with bowed heads and saddened mien. It was like the slaying of the first born child of Egypt. Sorrow was in every house."[17]

But there was no panic, as had overtaken New Orleans. When the initial shock was over, the citizens weighed their options: stay and face whatever came, or flee to safer quarters. In the end they compromised. Older people and mothers with children began packing for a visit to friends and neighbors in the country; while businessmen closed their account books; merchants moved their cotton outside the city, to be burned if necessary; and factory owners dismantled and crated their machinery and moved it to the depot, for dispersal elsewhere.

Sunday, April 27, normally a quiet day of grace in Vicksburg, was one of feverish activity. Mahala Roach went to church, as usual, to hear "a comforting sermon from our dear Mr. Lord." But it was hard to concentrate. Outside the brick walls were the curious scrapings and mutterings of a town in motion, as if the first tremors of an earthquake had begun to undermine the streets. Wrote Mahala on returning home:

> This has been a singular Sunday, no sabbath stillness has pervaded the air, but bustle and confusion have reigned everywhere! Waggons and drays have been busy hauling up machinery from Mr. Reading's to the Cars, and carrying Cotton to the Country ready to be burned—merchants packing up their goods, and boats coming up from New Orleans to escape the Lincoln fleet. . . .[18]

Mahala was planning to move her children to her mother's plantation on the Big Black River, until the storm blew over. Other families had similar intentions. They would not leave Vicksburg for good, they told each other—just enjoy some country hospitality for a change. Thus Charles Allen found himself playing host at Nanachehaw to a Mr. and Mrs. Day who dropped in for a visit. The couple dropped the chance remark that they were "scared to death of gunboats." Allen had little choice but to invite them to stay until the gunboat threat blew over.

The city government was in a shambles. They had made no plans for this contingency. There was no real leadership, either military or political. But during the first week in May, things began to change, as troops from southern Louisiana, released by New Orleans's surrender, began pouring in.

For General Mansfield Lovell, who had left New Orleans to its fate, had no intention of forsaking Vicksburg. Before Benjamin Butler's Federal army of occupation reached the city, Lovell began moving his men and artillery up to Jackson, thence by rail to Vicksburg. Other volunteer companies from east and west Louisiana also began moving northward in advance of the Federal invasionary forces, and artilleryman Hugh Moss recorded the long trek through the bayou country in verse reminiscent of Lord Tennyson's "The Brook."

Over ridges, gullies, bridges!
By the bubbling rill, and Mill—
Highways, byways, hollow hill,
Jumping, bumping, rocking, roaring,
Like ten thousand giants snoring![19]

Reaching Vicksburg about sunset of May 5, Moss noted in his diary: "I have heard it said that a city could not be seen for its houses, but I could not see Vicksburg for the hills—it could be called a pretty place, but for the irregularity and unevenness. Next day we marched two or three miles from the city and pitched tents; soon afterwards we were given a battery of four guns —two ten-inch Columbiads and two thirty-two-pounder rifles."

Living on Depot Street near the railroad terminal, Mahala Roach witnessed the arrival of trainloads of cheering troops, most of them Louisiana regiments. She observed that many looked tired after their difficult journey and headed for the river for a drink of water. So she had water set out for them and invited the passing troops to help themselves.

"They seemed grateful," Mahala noted, but their gratitude was self-extenuating. "Soon a stream of them came pouring in, drinking and filling their canteens; two of them asked leave to stay all night and sleep on the gallery." She allowed them to stay, and began stretching pallets on the floor to accommodate more of the unexpected guests. They were soldiers, after all, and the town in turn was pleased to see them.[20]

All in Vicksburg were heartened to see the streets aswarm with gray-clad troops and the tents beginning to sprout on the surrounding slopes and in the valleys. Charles Allen, visiting the city on plantation business, was gratified to note that work on the fortifications was going on. Batteries were being planted on the river front; more guns were being hauled aloft to shelves or gashes cut into the bluffs. But with less satisfaction, he noticed another phenomenon of wartime crises: profiteering by the opportunists.

He tried to buy a sack of salt and went as high as $100 in his offer. "Duff Green & Rigsby have it, but won't sell," he wrote in his plantation book that night. "Believe [they] are partners in speculation on necessaries of life. . . . V'burg is now full of men, many of them the oldest merchants in the produce line, who are playing the game of 'Number One'; I am done with them."[21]

Marmaduke Shannon took up the cudgel against speculators in the *Daily Whig,* editorializing: "All men think all men extortioners but themselves. . . . They forget that in the Holy Book . . . extortioners are classed with murderers, adulterers, and liars, and not with common sinners. Think of this, ye church members, who are selling articles at one hundred times their value, and are thus preying upon the lifeblood of the people, and seriously jeopardizing the lifeblood of the country."[22]

On May 12 Vicksburg was given a further lift with the arrival of Brigadier General Martin Luther Smith, assigned by Lovell to take over the city's fortifications and defenses. Smith was a man who inspired confidence among both soldiers and civilians: stern as a judge, clean-shaven, taciturn, decisive.

From that point on, wrote Samuel H. Lockett, later chief engineer of the defenses, "General Smith was never absent from his post, was always equal to every emergency, and never once, while in control, failed to do the right thing at the right time."[23] Smith, for his part, was heartened by the civilian spirit, which his presence engendered, reporting,

> The citizens of the town had with great unanimity made up their minds that its possession ought to be maintained at all hazards, even though total demolition should be the result. This determination was enthusiastically concurred in by persons of all ages and both sexes, and borne to my ears from every quarter.[24]

There were qualifications, however, regarding total demolition. When the Jackson *Mississippian,* forty-two miles inland and smugly immune from bombardment by enemy warships, suggested that Vicksburg "show her earnestness in the struggle," by burning the city rather than permitting its occupation, Marmaduke Shannon took editorial exception:

> We trust that our authorities and citizens will have a little more discretion than to commit such a rash and impolitic act. Vicksburg is no Moscow, and its destruction would be of no injury whatever to the enemy, but would be a severe blow to the many families whose husbands, sons and brothers are now in the army. . . . Vicksburg has shown and will "show her earnestness in the struggle," but her people will not destroy the city. . . . If the enemy shell it, there will not be a murmur, but we will not apply the torch ourselves.[25]

At Brokenburn, Kate Stone was privately less resolved, writing in her diary that "It seems hopeless to make a stand at Vicksburg. We only hope they may burn the city. . . . How much better to burn our cities than let them fall into the enemy's hands." Her mother reflected the mood by setting fire to $20,000 worth of cotton stacked on the plantation. It was the smoke rising from that conflagration that, first sighted by Federal steamers coming up the river, misled Commander S. Phillip Lee into believing that Vicksburg would go the way of New Orleans, a city reduced to a shambles by a mob beyond control.

Under General Martin Smith's supervision, work was pushed forward rapidly on Vicksburg's defenses. On the 200-feet-high bluffs, seven batteries commanded the river, the eighteen guns manned largely by veteran artillerists sent up by Mansfield Lovell, department commander, from the conquered forts below New Orleans. "These batteries," noted Major Lockett, "were located chiefly below the city; their positions were well chosen; they had fine command of the river against a fleet coming from below." In addition, 3,600 infantry, comprising six Louisiana regiments, were camped about the city, and more Mississippi troops were on the way from Jackson and points east.

Vicksburg had become a military barracks, yet Smith refrained from putting the city under martial law, as had been done at New Orleans. A call went out, however, for militia volunteers, and on May 15 all men of military age, from eighteen to fifty, appeared before the court house to be mustered in. Charles E. Smedes, a local grocer, was awarded the rank of brigadier general of militia, and the men were required to supply their own guns, wearing whatever clothes or uniforms they chose. It was not an impressive gathering, but it exhibited a public eagerness far different from that shown at Natchez.

Sunday, May 18, was clear, sunny, and warm. At the battery below the city where, as Hugh Moss noted, "the guns were kept in readiness at all times," Moss sighted the vanguard of the Federal fleet, as it slowly steamed up from the south. The ships looked like peaceful visitors, as they anchored and rested awhile on the bosom of the swollen river. Then, from the *Oneida,* a gig was put over the side, a white flag at its bow, and it moved slowly toward the city.

A single shot across its bow called on the gig to heave to. A small steamer pulled out from the dock, made contact with the gig, and returned with a message addressed to "The Authorities at Vicksburg."

> The undersigned, with orders from Flag Officer Farragut and Major General Butler, respectively, demand the surrender of Vicksburg and its defenses to the lawful authority of the United States, under which private property and personal rights will be respected.[26]

The message was signed, "S. Phillips Lee, Commanding Advance Naval Division," and carried a footnote that the gig would return in three hours for an answer.

Lee's *Oneida* waited five hours offshore for a reply, the gig running a futile shuttle service between ship and city. At the end of that time, Lee received not one but three replies.

The first, from Mayor Laz Lindsay, spoke for the people, declaring that "neither the municipal authorities nor the citizens will ever consent to a surrender of the city."[27]

Next, Colonel James L. Autry, military governor of the post, wrote tersely, "Mississippians don't know, and refuse to learn, how to surrender. If Commodore [sic] Farragut or Brigadier General [sic] Butler can teach them, let them come and try."

General Smith, in his turn, was characteristically blunt and final: "Having been ordered to hold these defenses, it is my intention to do so. . . . "[28]

Miffed by both the content and tone of these replies, Lee led his squadron to an anchorage below the city to think things over. Baton Rouge had tumbled to a show of force. The mayor of Natchez had surrendered the city to avoid "a useless flow of blood." But the people of Vicksburg did not even seem intimidated. As he looked at the fortresslike bluffs, honeycombed with apertures that doubtless concealed hives of batteries, he saw at least one reason why.

As Commander Lee waited for orders, gunners aboard the *Oneida*—at 5:00 P.M. on May 20—fired the the first hostile shot against the Vicksburg area. The rifled projectile was directed against a column of infantry moving along the top of the bluff outside the city.

Two questions plagued the commander. His was only one advance unit of the fleet, limited in firepower. Should he wait for the rest of the divisions, coming up with Farragut—a delay that would give the Confederates more time to strengthen their defenses? Also, what of the Western Flotilla supposedly coming down from Fort Pillow to join Farragut at Vicksburg? There had been no word of its progress, no assurance that the gunboats, now commanded by Flag Officer Charles Henry Davis, had even got past Memphis. It would be risky to count on their appearance.

Lee decided to press the issue on his own. On May 21 he sent a second message, this addressed to Mayor Lindsay, expressing his intention to bombard the city. The mayor was given twenty-four hours to evacuate women and children. Lee noted that it would be "impossible to attack the defenses without injuring or destroying the town, a proceeding which all the authorities of Vicksburg seemed determined to require."[29] Lindsay replied that he would need more time to consider the proposal. Lee reiterated his determination to fire upon the defenses of Vicksburg at the earliest moment.

The very presence of the Federal fleet had seemed to stiffen Vicksburg's backbone. As Charles Allen observed, the people, rather than appearing cowed, seemed "determined to show fight." The earlier exodus, prompted by the fall of New Orleans, had removed the faint of heart and reduced the population to a hard core of unyielding citizenry. As General Smith reported,

> The inhabitants had been advised to leave the city when the smoke of the ascending gunboats was first seen, under the impression that the enemy would open fire immediately upon arrival. Hence the demand for surrender found the city sparsely populated and somewhat prepared for an attack.[30]

At dawn of the following day—Thursday, May 22—artillerist Hugh Moss saw the Federal ships weigh anchor and move slowly to a position opposite the city. There they stood, gun barrels gathering light from the rising sun.

It seemed to Moss as if the whole world waited. . . .

❦ 4 ❦

Menace from the North

"**H**EYDAY!**" cried Martin excitedly, staring at the model city with its miniature streets and public buildings, its avenues and arches. "Heyday! What's that?"

"That's Eden" said Scadder, the land agent, picking his teeth with the blade of a penknife. "But"—apologetic cough—"it ain't all built yet."

Few of Charles Dickens' readers, when his latest novel, *Martin Chuzzlewit,* reached America, would have recognized "Eden" as Cairo, Illinois (which was the author's satirised model), or the "Walley of Eden" as the Mississippi Valley. For Cairo, at the confluence of the Ohio River and the Mississippi, had become, by the middle of 1861, the northern guardian of both these crucial waterways. Once an idle stopping point for the prewar river traffic, it was Eden-like only in its lethargy, a place in which there was little more to do than watch the grass grow. A newspaper correspondent of the time described it as "preeminently lugubrious . . . you may find amusement in the contemplation of the high water mark upon the trees and houses, the stilted plank sidewalks, the half-submerged swamps, and other diluvian features of this nondescript, saucerlike, tarraqueous town."[1]

But, by the beginning of 1862, all that had changed. Cairo had become a teeming military and naval depot, its buzzing activity directed toward the conquest of the Mississippi valley.

Flag Officer Andrew H. Foote was now head of the Western Flotilla—the three timberclads *Conestoga, Lexington,* and *Tyler,* and the nine remarkable ironclads built by James B. Eads. Though difficult to keep in mind, their names would earn a place in history. Seven of these curious craft displaced 900 tons apiece—fully loaded: *Cairo, Carondelet, Cincinnati, Louisville, Mound City, Pittsburgh,* and *St. Louis.* Two later additions, the converted *Essex* and *Benton,* were of variously larger tonnage.

Going back a bit, to September 4, 1861, Colonel Richard J. Oglesby had been army commander of the post when a stubby, stoop-shouldered man in rumpled civilian clothes shuffled up to the desk, looking like a refugee from shantytown. Oglesby didn't catch the name and seemed bewildered. The stranger handed him a crumpled paper for identification. Brigadier General Ulysses

S. Grant was taking over command of the regiments at Cairo.[2]

Since his troop-drilling days at Galena, and later as colonel of the Twenty-first Illinois Infantry, Grant had moved up fast. How Congress happened to make him a brigadier general was a mystery to him; he was still waiting for his uniform to come from New York. But he took his orders from Major General John C. Frémont, commanding the department of the West, and asked no questions.

Nor was he reluctant to seek action, authorized or not. The day after his arrival, word came from Frémont that Confederate forces under General Leonidas Polk were advancing on Paducah, forty-five miles east of Cairo at the mouth of the Tennessee River. Confederate occupation of Paducah would endanger Cairo and block not only the Ohio River but access to the Cumberland and the Tennessee as well.

Grant loaded two regiments of infantry aboard some idle steamers on the river and beat the former Louisiana bishop to possession of the town. Leaving Brigadier General Charles F. Smith to hold and fortify Paducah, he returned to Cairo to receive the first of many reprimands—this from the state of Kentucky, for invading its still-neutral soil.

Later, on September 5, Captain Andrew Hull Foote arrived from St. Louis to take over from Commander John Rodgers command of the inland navy, which was under the control of the army. No two men were less alike, ostensibly, than Grant at thirty-nine and the fifty-five-year-old Foote. Yet strangely the religious-minded naval veteran and the whiskey-loving Grant got on like brothers. Both believed implicitly in the cooperation of land and naval forces. Grant, far from regarding the gunboat as a passing freak, as did the average foot soldier, saw it as a unique new ally of the infantry.

When it came to Captain Foote, his brother John recorded: "As to the comparative value of the two arms of the service—the Army and the Navy—in clearing the Western rivers of the Confederates, my brother said they were like blades of shears—united, invincible; separated, almost useless."[3] For a while Foote's gunboats and Grant's expeditionary forces seemed invincible, though the aging captain, soon promoted to flag officer, would not live to see that combination tested to the full at Vicksburg.

On the general's staff at Cairo was a young Galena lawyer named John A. Rawlins, whom Grant had heard, before the war, addressing his fellow townsmen on the sacred importance of the Union. Rawlins, Grant thought at the time, was the kind of man he would like to have beside him in a time of trial, and he wrote to Galena inviting the lawyer to become his assistant adjutant general with the rank of captain. After some delay, Rawlins arrived at Cairo and, from that moment on, was never far from Grant's side, attending to annoying details, serving as the general's conscience when it came to drinking, keeping track of the important papers—orders, records, and reports—that Grant carelessly scattered around his quarters like confetti. "I became very much attached to him," Grant later recollected.[4]

Among Grant's officers at Cairo was John Alexander McClernand, a former congressman from Illinois, whom Lincoln regarded as potentially useful to the war effort. Because of his political influence, McClernand could do much to promote recruitment in his native state of 1,800,000 population, and he had come out strongly for the Union in prewar debates between secessionists and abolitionists. In appreciation, the President had appointed him brigadier general and sent him to Cairo to serve in Grant's command.[5]

The two had never met, but, as colonel of infantry in Illinois, Grant had been present when McClernand and John A. Logan, also a politically important figure, addressed the troops. He admired "Black Jack" Logan's blunt and lusty eloquence and, almost by reflex, distrusted McClernand. He was not alone in this reaction. Described as "a swarthy, black-bearded man of slight figure and transparent egotism," McClernand was seen by Frank Wilkie of the New York *Times* as "fussy, irritable, and nervous—something fidgety about him . . . "[6]

The two generals got along well enough at first, maintaining a cool, polite relationship. But it was the beginning of a personality clash that would ripen and bear bitter fruit at Vicksburg in the months to come.

How much Grant had Vicksburg on his mind at this point is impossible to say. It was common knowledge that the campaign in the West would center on possession of the Mississippi River. That Vicksburg was the key to that objective had become a cliché. But Grant was in no position to dictate strategy; he was simply taking orders. These directed that he set his sights on Columbus, Kentucky, northernmost river stronghold of the South and western hinge of the Confederate defense line. Possession of Columbus was essential to the step-by-step descent on Vicksburg, 300 crowflight miles below.

In early November 1861, with the endorsement of General Frémont— serving the last of his controversial days as commander in the West—Grant loaded 3,000 men aboard six transports and started downriver, escorted by the *Lexington* and *Tyler*. His orders were to conduct a demonstration to assist Federal movements in southeastern Missouri. En route, Grant decided to stage a diversionary attack, and on November 7 the infantry debarked above Belmont, Missouri, where a Confederate camp lay directly opposite Columbus.

The Belmont camp was captured—with disastrous results for Grant. As the routed Confederates summoned help from across the river, the green Federal troops got out of hand, dropped their arms, and took to pillaging the enemy tents for loot and souvenirs. Only by setting fire to the camp could Grant persuade his troops to abandon their plunder and take to the transports before the reinforced Confederates had them in a trap. Grant himself, riding his horse up a narrow plank extended from a transport, barely escaped with his life.[7]

This engagement, which cost Grant 500 casualties and drew from the Northern press the first of many blasts against the general, called for some redeeming venture. If the expedition had been "a disaster," as the papers said, it had demonstrated at least that Columbus would be difficult to take. Yet so long as Columbus stood, it barred the route to the South.

Was there an alternate strategy? It was something for Grant to ponder during idle December 1861 and January 1862.

"Ye believe in God; believe also in me."

The troops attending church in Cairo would never be sure whether Flag Officer Foote was speaking for himself or for the Apostle John. Either way the words were fitting, just as it was fitting that the jut-jawed naval veteran should fill in for the missing minister. His piety often seemed a mark of greater distinction than the gold stripes on his sleeve.

His young niece, however, took exception to the text.

"Uncle Henry didn't say it right," she told her father.

"How should he have said it?" Judge John Foote asked.

"Ye believe in God; believe also in *the gunboats*."[8]

For impressive indeed were James Eads's wonderful creations, now lined up on the river like a row of snapping turtles. The seven "cities series" ironclads ordered by the War Department, which still had not been paid for, looked like something out of Jules Verne's latest fantasy. As time would tell, they would give the North the same sort of advantage in the Mississippi Valley that the Confederate cavalry, sprung full-blown from an equestrian tradition, gave to the South in the Virginia Tidewater.

The vessels were hard to describe in terms of naval architecture—not so much boats as iron sheds turned upside down and floated on almost water-level rafts. Each was roughly 175 feet long, 51 feet abeam, drawing only six feet of water or, in naval parlance, "able to navigate on heavy dew." The sides and ends of the oblong sheds were slanted inwards to deflect enemy missiles. Eight broadside guns divided between port and starboard, and three others at bow and two astern, protruded from their casemates.

Disdainful infantry would call them "turtlebacks" or "turtles," but, to the inland navy, they were still "ninety-day wonders" and things of beauty. Their maximum speed was six knots, and, although Foote complained that this was "almost too slow," Captain William ("Dirty Bill") Porter of the *Essex* interjected, "Plenty fast enough to fight with."[9]

The readying of the gunboats seemed to give direction to Grant's plans for an early spring offensive. He had reason to wonder if a straight line was indeed the shortest distance between two points, such as Cairo and Columbus, or Cairo and any other city on the river, such as Vicksburg.

Roughly paralleling the Mississippi on the east, at an average distance of a hundred miles, flowed the Tennessee, and east of that the Cumberland. A strike up the Cumberland would imperil Confederate-held Nashville, and a similar drive up the Tennessee would flank Columbus.

And much more than that. This river offensive, if effective, would deeply penetrate the Confederate defense line, running from Columbus to the Cumberland Gap in the Appalachians, and might well force Albert Sidney Johnston's army back to the northern borders of Mississippi. Then, if Grant chose to move west to Vicksburg and the Mississippi, he would have a greatly weakened enemy to contend with on his rear and flank.

With headquarters at Saint Louis, Major General Henry W. Halleck commanded this district of the Mississippi valley, replacing the discredited John Frémont and hoping to take over the entire Federal command in the West. The first week in January 1862 Grant went to Saint Louis to propose to Halleck his invasionary expedition up the rivers. Halleck gave short shrift to both the general and the project, and Grant returned "very much crestfallen" to his base.

Back in Cairo, however, he got renewed support from Flag Officer Foote, who "agreed with me perfectly as to the feasibility of the proposal." Foote's gunboat flotilla would escort the transports, adding firepower to the expedition. Jointly they appealed again to Halleck, Grant writing, "If permitted, I could take and hold Fort Henry on the Tennessee." On February 1 Halleck withdrew his previous objections. Go ahead.

Albert Sidney Johnston, commanding Confederate forces in the West, was alert to the probable targets of an enemy offensive. It was vital to hold Fort Henry and Fort Donelson, guarding the Tennessee and Cumberland—rivers that were "like a double-barreled shotgun levelled at his heart." He telegraphed Lloyd Tilghman, commanding both forts, "Occupy and intrench the heights opposite Fort Henry. Do not lose a minute. Work all night."

Whatever could be done would be too little and too late.

On February 3 Grant loaded 15,000 troops aboard nine transports and started up the Tennessee with seven of Foote's gunboats. Fort Henry had ample warning of their coming. "As far as eye could see," wrote Confederate Captain Jesse Taylor, "the course of the river could be traced by the dense volumes of smoke issuing from the flotilla—indicating that the long-threatened attempt to break our lines was to be made in earnest."[10]

Tilghman did not lack courage, but his meager garrison of 3,400 raw recruits was poorly armed, and some of his guns and most of his powder were of inferior quality. The fort itself was cursed with poor location and construction. He could put up only a token resistance. For a while he did, his batteries exchanging fire with Foote's flotilla. But meanwhile the commander ordered most of his men to get out while they could and march to Fort Donelson, twelve miles overland. He and a sacrifice garrison held the fort until they were safely on their way.

After several hours of action, on February 6, Tilghman lowered the flag and the fort surrendered. Grant had scarcely disembarked his infantry. "Fort Henry is ours," he wired Halleck. "I shall take and destroy Fort Donelson on the 8th. . . . " It was an extravagant boast, but such is the stimulus of easy victory. As Foote took his fleet back down the Tennessee to the Ohio, to advance up the Cumberland against Fort Donelson, Grant started his infantry overland to assault the fortress from the rear.[11]

During this operation Grant had a sympathetic ally in absentia—"Cump" Sherman, whom he had admired as a plebe at West Point, where Sherman had regarded Grant as a brash cadet with a mania for horses. They had seen each other only once since then, meeting accidentally in Saint Louis before the war. Both were down on their luck, Sherman out of a job and Grant peddling firewood to make a living. As a result, the encounter was awkward and uncommunicative. On parting, Sherman concluded that West Point and the army were not meant for either of them.

Now Halleck had placed Sherman in charge of the District of Cairo, with instructions to keep Grant supplied. Grant later noted:

At the time he was my senior in rank and there was no authority of law to assign a junior to command a senior of the same grade. But every boat that came up with supplies or reinforcements brought a note of encouragement from Sherman, asking me to call upon him for any assistance he could render and saying that if he could be of service at the front I might send for him and he would waive rank.[12]

The renewed contact was the start of a relationship or team of command unique in Civil War annals, in which neither rank nor personal differences would interfere. Though neither could foresee it then, it would come to full flower on the Mississippi flats and bluffs and bayous around Vicksburg.

Though Sherman sent Grant reinforcements, Fort Donelson proved a tougher nut to crack. On high bluffs overlooking the Cumberland River, its landward flank was protected by artillery and rifle pits. And its defenders, with Fort Henry's salvaged garrison, numbered approximately 17,000, including Nathan Bedford Forrest's cavalry. When Forrest saw Foote's gunboat flotilla approaching up the Cumberland, he turned to a former preacher in his regiment, Captain D. C. Kelley, with the cry, "Parson, for God's sake pray! Nothing but God Almighty can save us now!"

Without the Almighty's intervention, the gunboats were placed at a disadvantage. Their slanting sides, intended to deflect enemy shells, presented their surfaces head-on to the fire from the high bluffs. Instead of glancing blows, the heavy shot struck the vessels at right angles, shattering their armor plate and, as one officer recorded, tearing sheets of iron from their sides "as lightning tears the bark from trees."

The gunboats approached the fort with guns blazing. Virginia-born Commander Henry Walke of the *Carondelet* was the first to open fire and the last to give up. He later reported grimly of shots that crashed through his armor plate, shattered his guns, turned the decks slippery with blood. "Two shots entered our bow-ports, killed four men and wounded several others. They were borne past me, three with their heads off. The sight almost sickened me, and I turned my head away."[13]

Foote's flagship received a direct hit on its pilot house, killing the pilot and seriously wounding Foote himself. That afternoon the crews buried their dead ashore where, to Captain Walke, the sound of Grant's artillery, "like the rumbling of distant thunder, was the only requiem for our departed shipmates."

With the failure of the gunboats, Grant wired Halleck that he anticipated "a protracted siege," in contrast to the easy conquest of Fort Henry. He was wrong. The three top officers of Fort Donelson, often at odds with one another, agreed that their position was untenable. They sought to fight their way out, failed, and by messenger requested Grant's conditions for an armistice.

Grant replied: No terms but unconditional surrender. Protesting this "ungenerous and unchivalrous" ultimatum, General Simon P. Buckner surrendered the garrison after his two superiors had fled. But not Nathan Bedford Forrest. "I did not bring my men here to surrender," he told his superiors, and he found a gap in the investing line, through which to lead his cavalry in flight to Nashville.[14]

The fall of Fort Donelson not only opened a path of invasion deep into the South, it created an overnight hero for the Union. "Unconditional Surrender" Grant, the initials U.S. labeled him throughout the nation. Northern newspapers hailed his success as the first important Union victory of the war. Congress voted him the country's gratitude, and Lincoln awarded him the two stars of a major general.

Only Halleck withheld praise, seeing Grant's victory eclipsing his own military status. "Give me command of the West," he telegraphed McClellan. "I ask this in return for Forts Henry and Donelson." Shortly thereafter Halleck's request bore fruit.

Without waiting for orders, Grant started for Nashville, next logical target for the army and already in a state of panic over the fall of Donelson. His independent actions in the next few days gave Halleck all the fuel he needed to downgrade the general to his own advantage. "Why do you not obey my orders?" he wired Grant, sending him back to Fort Henry. At the same time he telegraphed McClellan, regarding Grant, "It is hard to censure a successful general immediately after victory, but I think he richly deserves it."[15]

Few heroes in history have been so quickly toppled from their pedestals. Two weeks after his conquest of the forts, Halleck was authorized to arrest the general, "If the good of the service requires it." He put General Charles F. Smith in charge of Grant's army with orders to march into southern Tennessee, placing Grant on standby orders. Grant in turn asked to be relieved of further duty under Halleck.[16]

The matter was resolved in part when Halleck got his wish and was appointed Federal commander in the West. His authority assured and free of any threat of competition, he felt differently about the major general. Countermanding previous orders, he asked Grant to resume command of the army "and lead it on to new victories."

It was not the end of the friction between Grant and Halleck. At a later date, after the battle of Shiloh, Grant would again resolve to quit the service, embittered, among other things, by newspaper rumors of his drunkenness on duty. It was Sherman who would talk him out of it, reminding Grant of the criticism he himself had suffered from the press. "Grant stood by me when I was crazy," he later wrote, "and I stood by him when he was drunk." The half-jocular comment said a lot.

The two would never be far apart, except for distance, after that. In fact it was Sherman who fortuitously picked the site of Grant's next engagement: Pittsburgh Landing near Shiloh Church.

After the rout of the gunboats below Fort Donelson, Flag Officer Foote, still suffering from leg and arm wounds, withdrew the flotilla to Cairo for repairs, leaving the timberclads *Lexington* and *Tyler* to accompany Grant's transports up the Tennessee. Ill but not discouraged, Foote still believed that control of the West meant control of the Mississippi. And this meant fighting on the river, with Vicksburg the ultimate target and his Western Flotilla the key to conquest. *Ye believe in God; believe also in the gunboats.*

A naval reconnaissance in force, by Foote's gunboats on March 4, revealed that Columbus had been evacuated. This time the gunboats were accompanied by mortar scows. The fall of forts Henry and Donelson had rendered the Confederate grip on Columbus untenable. Guns and garrison had been transferred to New Madrid and Island No. 10, sixty miles downriver, where the Confederates prepared to make another stand.

While Foote proceeded down the river, General John Pope marched 20,000 troops down the west side of the river to New Madrid. With a force outnumbering the Confederate defenders three to one, he easily took possession of the post on March 13 and waited for Foote's flotilla to catch up.

But between Foote and New Madrid lay a formidable Southern stronghold, Island No. 10, named for being the tenth of such midstream sandbars coming down from Cairo. Bristling with batteries, the narrow strip effectively sealed off the river for descending vessels. In Confederate eyes it was impassable. Its loss, believed General P. G. T. Beauregard, second in command to Albert Sidney Johnston, would "be followed by the loss of the whole Mississippi Valley," even the loss of the war. Its battery commanders were instructed to hold Island No. 10 "at all costs."[17]

Pope and his infantry, of course, were no longer impeded by Island No. 10; they had simply walked around it on their way to New Madrid. And Foote, on his part, was reluctant to risk his fleet by running the gauntlet of the island's guns.

He did, however, attempt to subdue the fort with his gunboats and mortars, bombarding the island for three weeks without apparent results. When urged repeatedly by Pope to try running the batteries with one of his ironclads, the flag officer told the general that, if he did so, he would lose the boat and its officers and men, "which sacrifice I would not be justified in making."

It was not unreasoning timidity. He faced a disadvantage not encountered on the Tennessee. At Fort Donelson he had been fighting upstream, which meant that a disabled gunboat drifted back to safety. This time the current would be working against him.

It was Commander Henry Walke of the *Carondelet,* a man and ship determined to make history, who volunteered to make a test run past the batteries. Reluctantly Foote consented. He would not order any of his commanders on such a hazardous mission, but if one volunteered, his conscience was at least appeased.

Walke swaddled the *Carondelet* with protective cargo, chains and lumber piled around the vulnerable sections of the ship until she resembled, in the captain's eyes, "a farmer's wagon prepared for market." Then, anticipating the possibility of close-quarter fighting, he armed his men like a pirate's crew, with pistols, cutlasses, and hand grenades. If this were not enough to repel potential boarders, a hose was connected with the boilers to scald the attackers with steam. Finally, Walke made provisions to sink the ship if threatened with capture, rather than risk the uncertain results of setting it afire.[18]

On the night of April 4, the *Carondelet* slipped downstream with a protective hay barge laden with coal strapped like a tumor to her side. Cloaked in darkness the freakish collage was soundless and invisible. Then the unexpected happened, both endangering and salvaging the mission. A sudden thunderstorm exploded, threatening to silhouette the *Carondelet* and make a perfect target for the batteries. But, at the same time, the gunners in the fort were quick to depress their muzzles, to keep the rain out, and were caught unprepared as the *Carondelet* slid past. This curious conflict of circumstances, Walke believed, "was the cause of our escape."

Unscathed, the *Carondelet* reached New Madrid a little after midnight. She was given a tumultuous welcome by the army, and Walke gave the order to "splice the mainbrace"—whiskey rations for the crew.[19]

If one gunboat could make it, another could. Two nights later the *Pittsburgh* ran the Confederate batteries to help cover Pope's army as it crossed the river. There was no battle. Seeing itself cut off and isolated, with Pope below and Foote above, Island No. 10 and the Tennessee land batteries surrendered, yielding the garrison and quantities of guns, ammunition, and supplies.

The date was April 7, 1862, the day that the battered Confederates withdrew from Shiloh, after the bloodiest fighting of the war to that date. It was hard to claim that Grant had won that battle; the cost had been too great for either side to win. But he retained the field; Corinth was threatened; and the Confederates had lost one of their outstanding leaders in Albert Sidney Johnston. As George Cable of New Orleans remarked, "The South never smiled after Shiloh."

Meanwhile, a unique flotilla was being readied by Colonel Charles Ellet, Jr., who was a civil engineer before receiving his army commission. For some time Ellet had been alerting the War Department and the navy to the urgent need of rams in inland waters. His advocacy of sharp-pointed vessels that could slice a wooden ship in two gained credence in March at Hampton Roads, when the iron-plated *Virginia*—formerly the U.S.S. *Merrimack*—clashed to a draw with the Federal ironclad *Monitor*. Metal ships had come to stay.[20]

War Secretary Edwin M. Stanton sent for Ellet, quickly approved his formula for rams ($F = MV^2$, or force equals mass times the square of the velocity), made him a colonel, and gave him a contract for as many vessels as he thought were needed for successful operations on the Mississippi.

Ellet scoured the adjacent rivers for nine mothballed steamers and brought them to Cairo for refitting. He strengthened their bulkheads, fashioned their bows into iron-plated beaks, and rebuilt their engines to deliver a speed of fifteen knots, making them the fastest river craft afloat.[21]

All this took time, and, while Ellet worked on his shipsplitting inventions, Flag Officer Foote moved against Fort Pillow with his gunboats and mortars. On April 14, the mortar boats were towed into position by tugs and began pounding Fort Pillow, two miles distant, with thirteen-inch, 200-pound shells. This operation was to continue for the next several weeks.[22]

The bombardment was tedious work for the mortar crew and mildly entertaining to Fort Pillow's garrison, who amused themselves by tracking the shells. One Confederate noted how "one of these little pills would climb a mile or two into the air, look around a bit at the scenery, and finally descend and disintegrate around the fort, to the great interest and excitement of the occupants."

At this time the wounds suffered by Flag Officer Foote at Fort Donelson required medical attention. At his own request, command of the Western Flotilla was turned over to Charles Henry Davis, a veteran saltwater captain of about the same age. Davis, of an aristocratic Boston family, was described by one of his officers as "a charming and lovable man," but whether he had Foote's drive and decisiveness only time would tell.

Foote said farewell to the fleet, as it continued operations against Fort Pillow, Tennessee, on the left bank of the Mississippi. He was, he wrote later, "glad to be done with guns and war." He could be satisfied with his accomplishments. He had molded the Western Flotilla into a first-class naval unit. He had cleared the Mississippi between Cairo and Fort Pillow, a distance of two hundred miles by water. Below Fort Pillow stood only Memphis, and after Memphis was clear sailing down to Vicksburg.

General Pope and his army were also separated from the expedition, being summoned by Halleck to aid in the drive against Confederate-held Corinth, where General Beauregard had succeeded Johnston in command. It would seem that, henceforth, the gunboats and mortars under Flag Officer Davis and the rams under Colonel Ellet would have to carry the burden of the fighting on this portion of the river.

Some genuine excitement came directly after Foote left, when Confederate Captain James Montgomery brought his River Defense Fleet up from Memphis to drive the Federals away. Six of Montgomery's fleet had been lost in the fighting below New Orleans; the remaining eight carried a single gun apiece, but their prows were plated with railroad iron for their use as rams. All were commanded by riverboat captains—a breed of men, complained General Lovell, that "will never agree on anything once they get underway."

But, if they lacked agreement, they made up for it with enterprise. Three of Montgomery's rams smashed into the Federal ironclad *Cincinnati*, inflicting severe damage, which sent her to the bottom in eleven feet of water. Coming to the *Cincinnati*'s rescue, the *Mound City* was ripped open by another Confederate ram and sank on a shoal.[23]

Impending disaster cued the descent of Captain Walke and his irrepressible *Carondelet*, with the rest of the Union gunboats following. Walke plowed into the center of Montgomery's wolfpack, until he had three Confederate rams in front of him and two behind. Then he let go with bow and stern guns simultaneously, like a scorpion shooting venom from both tongue and tail. None of the other gunboats joined in the uneven fray—"I never could understand why," Walke later wrote—but he hardly needed them. Able to duck the Confederate rams and fire at the same time, the *Carondelet* succeeded in wounding four of Montgomery's vessels before all eight withdrew to safety beneath Fort Pillow's batteries.

In its first real test since New Orleans, the River Defense Fleet had not done too badly. Montgomery returned to Memphis and a hero's welcome; he had, it was felt, stopped the Federals cold. "They will never penetrate farther down the Mississippi," he assured General Beauregard at Corinth. And at this point even Flag Officer Davis could believe it. With only the gunboats and the clumsy mortars, his chances of breaking through to Vicksburg appeared slim indeed.

Living beside a river, there was a tendency to look upstream for whatever might arrive, be it friendly or hostile, driven by sail or steam, or simply carried by the current. Vicksburg, however, did not know which way to look. The fall of forts Henry and Donelson had torn apart the Confederate curtain protecting the valley on the northeast, and Grant's invasion of Tennessee had stretched that rent to the Mississippi border.

Just south of the city stood Farragut's deepwater fleet, with the gunboats aligned on both sides of the river. And now came the word that New Madrid and Island No. 10 had fallen, and another Yankee naval force was threatening Fort Pillow. If Fort Pillow yielded, there was only Memphis and the battered River Defense Fleet to block the enemy's descent on Vicksburg. It was generally believed, wrote Kate Stone in her diary, that Memphis was "doomed, and the Yankee gunboats will then descend the Mississippi and get all the cotton they can steal."

Wherever one turned, gray clouds of smoke lay over the land, like a pall of doom, as planters responded to Beauregard's order to destroy their cotton. The bales burned slowly and had to be prodded and turned over, day by day, to stay ignited. The air was heavy with the odor of scorched fiber, reminding the planters that their fortunes were being reduced to ashes. Many were ruined and knew it; yet none held back. All grimly waited for the arrival of the gunboats, prepared, in Kate's words, "to welcome them with bloody hands to hospitable graves."[24]

Dora Richards and her bridegroom, Anderson Miller, had ended their flight from New Orleans at Miller's hometown in Arkansas, a hundred miles above Vicksburg, on the west bank of the river. They had not been there long before Dora was obliged to write in her diary, "The serpent has entered our Eden." The serpent was the combined rancor and suspicion she had sought to leave behind in New Orleans, where an incautious word suggesting Union sympathies branded one a traitor. Here, even in his family's native village, Miller was suspect for being out of uniform, and Dora herself was constantly tripping over those "incautious" words.

When local merchants refused to sell them food and supplies, maintaining that their stocks were rationed for "the poor," Miller decided it was time to move. The river was swollen by spring flooding, forcing those in the Valley to live like Venetians, with boats or rafts at every door. Using their boat, the Millers crossed the Mississippi, planning to avoid the gunboats at Vicksburg by marching overland to the Yazoo River and thence downstream to the Terraced City where Miller's uncle had a home.[25]

In Vicksburg the railway depot teemed with the wounded from Shiloh, and Mahala Roach was one of those who did what she could to make them comfortable and find beds in the City Hospital and private homes. "It was a sad sight," she wrote, "and makes us realize that the war is near us indeed." Annie Harris, the judge's daughter, also wrote of the large number of wounded soldiers in the city and noted that "each household received as many as could be accommodated, the ladies sleeping on mattresses in order that the sick might be comfortable."

Along with the incoming wounded, trains brought fresh troops almost daily from other parts of Mississippi and Louisiana. For many of these, there were not sufficient tents and quarters. Annie Harris wrote of soldiers sprawling at night on her father's lawn and eventually, as space gave out, on the front veranda:

> ... as a result it was not safe to go out of doors after night-fall for fear of stepping on an arm or leg of some poor fellow, who, with only his blanket around him, would lie under our bright-curtained windows listening to the sounds of the voices within, sounds . . . of home. We had not the heart to drive them away, though we found it anything but agreeable to be in the midst of so many men.[26]

At Brokenburn, Kate Stone and her mother were cut off from Vicksburg, unable to cross the Mississippi in the face of Yankee gunboats. Kate's brother William and her Uncle Bo were still with their regiments in Virginia, and her younger brother Coleman ("Coley"), now eighteen, had joined a cavalry company formed by their neighbor, Beverly Buckner of Winn Forest. The company was in camp near Jackson, and Kate had been able to visit Coley once before the gunboats came.

Kate wrote in her diary of the "stirring events of the last sixty days . . . the two-day battle and victory at Shiloh . . . the long bombardment, heroic defense, and final surrender of Island No. 10; the attack on and successful defense of Fort Pillow." She could not know, at that time and from that distance, that Shiloh had been a disaster and the successful defense of Fort Pillow only temporary.

At Cairo, Charles Ellet was putting the finishing touches on his rams when word came that Montgomery's River Defense Fleet had attacked Flag Officer Davis's flotilla above Fort Pillow and knocked out two of its gunboats. Ellet received a wire from Secretary Stanton, urging him to speed up construction of the Union rams and get them down to Davis in a hurry.

Ellet finished all nine in record time and, perhaps for expediency, appointed captains from members of his family. He gave himself command of *Queen of the West,* his younger brother Alfred captaincy of the *Monarch,* and so on down the line of relatives to his teenage son and namesake with the appropriate middle name of Rivers, whom he placed in command of the *Lancaster.*[27]

On May 25 the strange-looking vessels dropped down the Mississippi to augment Flag Officer Davis's fleet. Some days later, on June 5, a joint army–navy operation was launched against Fort Pillow, meeting with no sign of resistance. Personnel of the ram *Monarch* were first to enter the fort and to find it as deserted as a tomb. Upon the evacuation of Corinth, General P. G. T. Beauregard had ordered the fort to be abandoned, together with Fort Randolph farther down. The river was open clear to Memphis.

Approaching Memphis early on the sixth, the gunboats and rams found Montgomery's River Defense Fleet drawn up in a line across the river. Crowds of civilians thronged the bluffs in the early dawn to witness the impending battle. The morning was clear and still, remembered Alfred Ellet aboard the *Monarch,* when a single shot broke out:

> It was the first gun from the River Defense Fleet moving to attack us. Colonel Ellet was standing on the hurricane-deck of the *Queen of the West.* He immediately sprang forward, and, waving his hat to attract my attention, called out: "It's a gun from the enemy! Round out and follow me! Now's our chance!" Without a moment's delay the *Queen* moved out gracefully, and the *Monarch* followed. By this time our gunboats had opened their batteries, and the reports of guns on both sides were heavy and rapid.[28]

As dense smoke rose from the river, all the spectators saw were pairs of smokestacks piercing the clouds and flashes of fire from the gunboats. Beneath the pall the *Queen of the West* plunged forward to see the Confederate *General Lovell* coming at her head-on. Neither wavered; then the *Lovell* veered off suicidally, and the *Queen* plowed into her amidships. "The vessel," wrote Ellet, "was cut almost in two and disappeared under the dark waters in less time than it takes to tell the story."[29]

The *Monarch* in turn struck the Confederate *General Price* a glancing blow that sheared off one of her paddle wheels and knocked her out of the fight. Then Alfred Ellet's ram drove into the *Beauregard,* crushed her side, and finally made for the *Little Rebel,* which was seeking to escape. The *Monarch* headed her off and pushed her like helpless flotsam up against the shore.

Ellet had not misconceived the violence of his formula $F = MV^2$. In little more than ninety minutes, the entire River Defense Fleet had been virtually eliminated. Seven of the eight Confederate vessels had been destroyed or run ashore, to be abandoned by their crews. Only the *Van Dorn* escaped. To sum up, Alfred Ellet wrote:

> The battle of Memphis was, in many respects, one of the most remarkable naval victories on record. For *two* unarmed, frail, wooden river steamboats, with barely enough men on board to handle the machinery and keep the furnace-fires burning, to rush to the front, between two hostile fleets, and *into* the enemy's advancing line of eight iron-clad, heavily armed, and fully manned steamrams, sinking one, disabling and capturing three, and carrying consternation to the others, was a sight never before witnessed.[30]

Many Memphis ladies on the bluffs, it was reported, wept as they watched the Confederate Defense Fleet torn to shreds. "A deep sympathizing wail which followed each disaster went up like a funeral dirge from the assembled multitude, and had an overwhelming pathos."

It was a dirge that could be heard in Richmond, where Mary Chesnut wrote in her ever-perceptive diary, "In my heart I feel: all is gone now." And it could be heard, one almost believed, in distant Vicksburg, where the fall of this Southern stronghold, two hundred miles to the north, opened for the enemy a clear path to the Terraced City.

And Vicksburg already had almost more than it could cope with.

❧ 5 ❧

Firm as the Eternal Hills

T HOUGH she was across the river and many cotton fields west of Vicksburg, Kate Stone seemed to feel the waves of apprehension radiating from that threatened city. Her brother Coley's company had reportedly returned to Vicksburg, to stand with the defenders on the bluffs, but Kate and her mother had had no word from him. Feeling the need of companionship, they both left Brokenburn to spend the night with Elizabeth Savage at Salem Plantation. The next morning, May 19, 1862, Kate noted in her diary:

> We listen hourly for the cannonading to begin at Vicksburg. Surely the gallant Mississippians will not give up their chief city without a struggle.
>
> > *Better the fire above the roll,*
> > *Better the shot, the blade, the bowl,*
> > *Than crucifixion of the Soul.*
>
> Better one desperate battle and the city in flames than tame submission.[1]

In Vicksburg itself, from the porch of his house overlooking the Mississippi, Dr. Rowland Chambers kept anxious vigil over the gunboats on the river. The itinerant dentist had arrived in Vicksburg with his wife and children just a few weeks earlier. He had anticipated a long and settled practice in this peaceful place, near his married daughter. The Federal gunboats on the river seemed to cloud that outlook, but it was too late now to move on. He was trapped in this unfamiliar city and would make the best of it.

The number of Confederate troops in and around the town was multiplying rapidly, as more of General Lovell's troops arrived by forced marches from New Orleans. Lieutenant Jared Young Sanders of the Twenty-sixth Louisiana Infantry, Colonel Winchester Hall commanding, had already encamped on the eastern slopes behind the city. Exasperated at what he considered a bungled operation at New Orleans, Sanders wrote to his father, "I am determined to *fight* now and *forever,*" and he expected "some sharp, quick & effective blow to be struck in a very short time." From which side the blow would come, he did not specify.[2]

Private Granville L. Alspaugh of the Twenty-seventh Louisiana Infantry had also just arrived, but shared none of Sanders's resolution. He had joined the army only two months earlier at the age of sixteen, and already he was sick of it—homesick, as much as anything. With youthful sarcasm he wrote to his mother in early May, suggesting she "send some of the boys up here to help us work on the fortifications. It is nice fun rolling dirt. . . . For my part I am willing to quit."[3]

At his battery on the bluffs, Confederate gunner Hugh Moss kept a sleepless eye on the black-hulled vessels on the river. "Detachments were kept at the guns all the time in readiness," he noted. South of the city on the river eleven more masts had come into view as the body of Farragut's fleet caught up with the advance flotilla under Phillips Lee. Leaving the troop-bearing transports out of sight, the vice-admiral's flagship had drawn nearest to the city, with the powerful warships *Brooklyn* and *Richmond* close by. Hugh Moss watched the exchange of semaphore signals between the *Hartford* and Commander S. P. Lee's *Oneida* and wondered what was coming.

According to all reports attending Lee's ultimatum, the city expected the attack to start at eight or nine o'clock on Thursday evening, May 22. But the time passed; nothing happened. Above the layer of excitement and anxiety that gripped the population rose a cloud of quandary. What was the enemy waiting for? Was Commander Lee restrained by his conscience from the shelling of civilians? Was this a war of nerves, perhaps? Thursday passed, Friday the 23rd was uneventful. Saturday was warm and sunny, and the city went about its business.

That Sunday, May 25, Dr. William Lord, the Episcopal minister, held services as usual in the church on Main and Locust Streets. This duty fulfilled, he helped his wife Margaret and their son and daughter pack and prepare to leave the city for the Big Black River plantation of Mr. Uriah Flowers, "a patriarchal bachelor of the old school." They would take with them the family treasures including the rector's books; what silver they had would be buried in the churchyard. Dr. Lord himself would remain in Vicksburg to attend to his duties at the church and to serve in his new role of chaplain to a Mississippi brigade.[4]

The preparations were timely, the intentions wise, but subsequent events made the family's immediate escape impossible.

Monday, May 26, 1862. "Clear, bright, and fine," was the local report. Mahala Roach learned from visitors that it was "very dull in town," and after some sewing and mending spent the rest of the day engrossed in the romantic novel H. C. Clarke's was peddling, *Love Me Little, Love Me Long*. At precisely five o'clock came the delayed and scarcely audible report. A dot of white smoke on the river, a thin streak arcing across the sky, marked the first shell of the war to fall on Vicksburg.

After the long waiting and the tension, this first aimless shot was something of an anticlimax. As were those that followed. Rowland Chambers noted in his diary that "the enemy . . . fired about 20 shots and shells; and after sundown retired down the river to their old positions; and everything was quiet until Tuesday 27 when the enemy came up and commenced shelling the town about 3 PM."

In this bombardment the Federal gunners were closer to the range. Chambers got his wife and children into what he referred to as "our fort," presumably a homemade shelter, "and kept them there until dark when the firing ceased for a short time. We then got out & ate supper and had just done when the firing commenced and continued at intervals until 3 o'clock in the morning, shell and shot striking a number of houses [and] the Methodist church."[5]

That day, though she knew the city was under bombardment, Mahala Roach returned from Woodfield to Vicksburg to check on her ailing mother. She no sooner reached town than she found a crowd had gathered near her house where "one man had a glass through which we took a look, watched the boats throw shells for a short time, then all rode up to the hill . . . to have a good view of the boats." She observed:

> After several shots towards the batteries, they suddenly aimed a shell, apparently at our group! I felt awfully when I heard the shell whizzing above my head— of course we all ran from the dangerous spot.[6]

After safely getting back to the plantation, Mahala learned that:

> . . . the shell which went over our heads while we were on the hill, struck the Methodist Church and knocked a hole in it. Duff Green's new house was injured, also Mr. Klein's kitchen. I never had such feelings in my life, more of *horror* than fear; the great excitement kept me from mere *fear* . . .[7]

In the basement of the Episcopal rectory, where Dr. Lord had installed his family for safety, young Willie Lord, the pastor's son, got his first taste of wartime siege. He later recalled his childhood impressions of that brief scene in their underground retreat, where the family spent the night on piles of coal overspread with rugs and blankets. He remembered:

> . . . my mother and sisters huddling around me upon the coal-heap, my father, in clerical coat, and a red smoking-cap on his head, seated on an empty cask and looking delightfully like a pirate (for I knew nothing of cardinals in those days), our negro servant crouching terror-stricken, moaning and praying in subdued tones in a neighboring coal-bin, and all lighted by the fitful glow of two or three tallow candles, the war became to me for the first time a reality, and not the fairy-tale it had hitherto seemed.[8]

Throughout both days the Vicksburg batteries, those on the bluffs and those on the river, scarcely bothered to return the enemy's fire, "for the double purpose," wrote an officer, "of saving the limited ammunition and keeping the men fresh for any assault that might be made." But the enemy's transports still stayed out of range, and there was no threat of an assault.

Though there was little actual damage done to the city, Colonel Winchester Hall observed, when the firing ceased, that "Vicksburg looked as if the simoon of war already had swept over it . . . city deserted by all who could leave, business houses that were not closed were barren of goods. . . . " Rowland Chambers likewise noted in his diary for May 27 that "the women became much alarmed and determined to leave town in the morning." The following day he moved his family and servants to an unspecified refuge in the country, then returned to his home and practice in the city.

Max Kuner, the Washington Street jeweler, was hard-pressed to find means of flight, since all horses and mules had been requisitioned by the army. He finally found a rickety wagon and broken-down nag he was able to hire and moved his family to an abandoned plantation manor ten miles out of town. He discovered that four other families had had the same idea, and all settled down as squatters in the neglected mansion "with pigs in the basement."[9]

The exodus, however, was not one of panic or despair. Brigadier General Martin Smith, in charge of defense, made periodic inspections of the city and found that the morale of the civilians remained high. This factor, he believed, "unquestionably had its influence on the ultimate result. Our cause probably needed an example of this kind, and assuredly a brighter one has never been given."[10]

Marmaduke Shannon continued to publish the *Daily Whig,* anxious only that his supply of paper might be cut off by the Federal blockade. In his editorial column he noted with pride that the citizens were unperturbed by the sporadic fire of the enemy; they calculated the periods when the streets were relatively safe and went about their business with commendable composure.

After May 28 the Federal fleet remained largely inactive for more than a week, during which General Smith's command at Vicksburg was substantially increased. Four more regiments of Louisiana volunteers arrived, along with five companies of cavalry, another battery of field artillery, and four companies of Mississippi troops. These he distributed along the riverfront, from Walnut Hills to Warrenton, to guard against a land attack. All things considered, Smith's defenses were in good shape.

There was a secret weapon in the offing that Smith had not counted on— secret as of then, at any rate. It was presaged by the appearance, during the bombardment, of a stranger in the city, staying at the Prentiss House. He was Lieutenant Isaac Newton Brown, a forty-five-year-old navy veteran and native of Kentucky. But what was a naval officer doing in Vicksburg where no Confederate naval force existed?

Brown was, as it turned out, awaiting reassignment from Secretary Mallory's office in Richmond. On May 28 his orders came. They were "to proceed to Greenwood, Miss., and assume command of the Confederate gunboat *Arkansas,* and finish and equip that vessel without regard to expenditure of men and money."

Brown doubtless knew something about the *Arkansas;* a vessel by that name had been under construction in Memphis before that city was attacked. But few knew that the *Arkansas* had been towed away to safety before the destruction of most of the defending fleet. Brown started at once for Greenwood at the head of the Yazoo River, more than two hundred miles by water north of Vicksburg.

There he got his first surprise. "It being the season of overflow," he wrote, "I found my new command four miles from dry land."[11]

He studied his charge from a distance—and then closer to. What looked like no more than a hunk of flotsam was indeed the *Arkansas,* as much as could be seen of her. Brown's first comment was a masterpiece of understatement: "Her condition was not encouraging." And he added:

The vessel was a mere hull, without armor; the engines were apart; guns without carriages were lying about the deck; a portion of the railroad iron intended as armor was at the bottom of the river, and the other and far greater part was to be sought for in the interior of the country.[12]

Brown, however, appeared to have some of the ingenuity of his namesake, Isaac Newton. Also some of the persistence. In the following weeks, while Vicksburg faced the first real crisis in its forty years of existence, Brown worked with herculean energy to make a first-class fighting vessel out of virtually nothing. To what extent he might succeed was something for the future to decide.

Just below Vicksburg on the flagship *Hartford,* Flag Officer Farragut weighed what seemed to be the first real setback since he left the Gulf. Up to now he had been riding high. He had successfully run the forts below New Orleans and captured the Queen City of the South, and this triumph had been followed by the easy conquests of Baton Rouge and Natchez.

But here at Vicksburg the intimidating presence of his fleet and the shelling of the city had accomplished nothing. The Confederates thought so little of it that they had not bothered seriously to return the fire. Commander Phillips Lee, having reported the city's refusal to surrender, shared the admiral's frustration, writing, "I had hoped that the same spirit which induced the military authorities to retire from the city of New Orleans rather than wantonly sacrifice the lives and property of its inhabitants would have been followed here."

It hadn't been.

Surveying the batteries on the bluffs, many too high for his naval guns to reach, Farragut summoned General Thomas Williams for a conference. The fleet alone, Farragut admitted, could not reduce the city. If Williams's troops were put ashore, could they storm the defenses with help from the naval guns? Williams thought not—not with only 1,400 men, when the Vicksburg garrison numbered, by his estimate, around eight thousand.

Meanwhile Farragut's position was precarious; it was fortunate, though a bit humiliating, that Vicksburg's batteries had chosen to ignore him. He had hoped to meet up with Charles Davis and his Western Flotilla, but Davis was still far up the river above Fort Pillow. He sent a message down to Butler at New Orleans, which contained a thinly-veiled rebuke:

As they have so large a force of soldiers here, several thousand in and about the town, and the facility of bringing in 20,000 in an hour by railroad from Jackson, I think it would be useless to bombard it as we could not hold it if we took it.[13]

Plainly he was exaggerating (20,000 men by railroad in an hour!) and suggesting that it was Butler's niggardliness in not supplying sufficient troops that was responsible for his predicament. He would have to call this expedition "a reconnaissance in force," and return with most of the vessels to New Orleans. If he remained, there was the risk of running out of provisions, and the even greater risk of his fleet being grounded as the level of the Mississippi dropped. So, five warships departed down the river, accompanied by all the transports. Six gunboats remained to keep watch on Vicksburg.

News of Farragut's withdrawal and of Butler's indifferent support of the expedition raised a small storm in Washington. Navy Secretary Gideon Welles was outraged that the thrust at Vicksburg had been abandoned, while Assistant Secretary Gustavus Fox protested, "Impossible! Sending the fleet up to meet Commodore Davis was the most important part of the whole expedition. The instructions were positive."[14]

Fox promptly sent a dispatch to Farragut at New Orleans: "It is of paramount importance that you go up and clear the river with utmost expedition." All other naval operations, he insisted, "sink into insignificance compared with this." Fox followed this with a second message, reflecting Lincoln's concern over Farragut's retreat from Vicksburg:

> The President requires you to use your utmost exertions (without a moment's delay, and before any other naval operations are permitted to interfere) to open the Mississippi and effect a junction with Flag Officer Davis.[15]

Reluctantly the admiral prepared to start back up the river. This time Porter would accompany him with most of his mortar fleet, since the mortars with their high trajectory could reach and even clear the Vicksburg bluffs. And he persuaded Butler to part with enough of his infantry to raise General Williams's forces to 3,200 men. These, along with some light artillery, were loaded on transports at Baton Rouge.

Sergeant John C. Curtis—"Cool Curtis" to the troops—was with the Ninth Connecticut Infantry that boarded the transport *Diane* at Baton Rouge. With three other infantry regiments and several batteries of artillery, they started for Vicksburg on June 20, putting to shore from time to time to diversify the voyage. After a week on the river Curtis wrote to his father in Bridgeport, Connecticut, of an event not recorded in John Allen's journal:

> On our way up we stopped at Col. Allen's plantation. He is Col. of the 4th Louisiana Volunteers, and he is now in Vicksburg. We confiscated everything in eating line such as chickens, geese, sheep, eggs, milk and sugar. Capt. Coats and I took possession of the Overseers House. We made him cook every thing we wanted and when it came about time to bunk in, Cap. and his Lieut. took possession of one of the beds and the overseer had the other so I was left out. I was bound I would not sleep on the floor so I made the overseer roll over backside and got in with him. He did not like to sleep with a Yankee much but I made him Grin & Bear It.[16]

Farragut's earlier trip up the Mississippi had alerted the riverside communities to this second coming. Confederate guerrillas lurked along the banks. Snipers peppered the fleet and transports as they passed. Williams was warned that Confederate guns at Grand Gulf, sixty miles by water below Vicksburg, would be apt to give them trouble. The Connecticut and Wisconsin regiments, along with some light artillery, were put ashore to wipe them out.

Intense heat took a greater toll than enemy fire in this operation. Horses as well as men fell by the roadside; one man died of sunstroke. But the Confederates were easily frightened off by their appearance at Grand Gulf, and Sergeant Curtis reported that "Every house that night was reduced to ashes. The

Western boys done most of it. They can beat our Regt. all to nothing steal-
ing."

Steaming against an adverse current, the Union armada did not reach
Vicksburg until June 25, less than four weeks after it had left. In the interval
the city had had a chance to strengthen its defenses. The gunboats, which
Farragut had left behind to harass the defenders, had done little damage. "One
or two would come up and engage our battery every day," wrote Hugh Moss,
"but at too long a range to do execution on either side."

The citizens began preparing bomb-proof shelters in their yards or cellars,
and a few moved into natural caves and crevices on the sloping east side of
the hills. But civilian life was not greatly disrupted. Marmaduke Shannon of
the *Daily Whig* kept his readers posted on the gunboats' operations. A notice
of June 5 advised: "As a matter of course, we may expect another bombardment this evening. They generally commence at five o'clock. Admission free,
but stand from under."[17]

News items in the Vicksburg *Citizen.*

Friday, June 20, 1862: Major-General Earl Van Dorn has assumed command of the Confederate Department of Southern Mississippi and East Louisiana, with the special responsibility of the defense of Vicksburg.

A Federal naval expedition under Flag Officer Farragut has left Baton
Rouge with 3,000 troops under Brigadier-General Thomas Williams, report-
edly on its way to Vicksburg, with the intention of establishing a base on the
De Soto Peninsula ("Swampy Toe") opposite the city.

Colonel S. H. Lockett of the Army of Tennessee has been ordered to report
to General Smith as the latter's Chief Engineer in charge of fortifying Vicksburg.[18]

On assuming his post as engineer, Colonel Lockett was pleased to find that
"vigorous preparations" were going on in Vicksburg, noting:

> The garrison was engaged in strengthening the batteries already constructed, in
> making bomb-proof magazines, and in mounting new guns recently arrived.
> Several new batteries were laid out by myself on the most commanding points
> above the city; these were afterward known as the "Upper Batteries." The work
> of making an accurate map of Vicksburg was also begun.[19]

General Smith's garrison was also further strengthened. In addition to the
regiments already present, more troops from the state of Mississippi swelled
the number of defenders. "They were already veterans," Lockett noted, "and
many of them were skilled artillerists." And they had come to stay. There was
no more talk of "terms of enlistment" or "ninety-day volunteers." Those
belonged to the days of complacency, before the war grew hot. And it was hot
in Vicksburg.

Even sixteen-year-old Private Granville Alspaugh began to change his attitude toward the service. "Dear Ma," his letter of June 14 began. "You wrote
me to come home but I could not even if I wanted to; my age dont let me out
of the army. I dont want to come home if I could. . . . I dont like to back
out. . . ."[20]

Wednesday, June 25. "Clear, hot and dusty—cloudy P.M.," was the prediction. Through the morning haze artillerist John Moss, at his river battery, got his first glimpse of the returning fleet, the tall masts pricking the skyline as they rounded Davis's Bend.

Seen closer, it was a far more impressive armada than that with which Commander Phillips Lee had earlier tried to intimidate the city. The rest of the gunboats, Farragut's capital ships, and, new to the scene, the mortar schooners. Nine of the latter took up positions along the eastern shoreline, out of range of the batteries. The other eight kept close to the Louisiana shore, their masts camouflaged with foliage to make them nearly invisible against the banks of willows.

Here was the clear and present danger. But there was another threat, as yet invisible from Vicksburg.

At Salem Plantation not far from Brokenburn, Kate Stone was among those assembled to stand watch against the coming of a second hostile fleet, comprised, wrote Kate, of "what we have been looking for for weeks—the Yankee gunboats descending the river. We hope they will be the first to be sunk at Vicksburg. . . . They are polluting the waters of the grand old Mississippi."[21]

The "gunboats," however, were only the vanguard of Charles Henry Davis's Western Flotilla, coming down from Memphis in the hope of linking up with Farragut. They were really the new Federal rams commanded by Colonel Alfred W. Ellet aboard the *Monarch*. To Kate Stone, the rams looked "dark, silent, and sinister." She hated them with all her heart and wished them at the bottom of the river.

When one of the Federal ships seemed to be edging toward the shore, Kate and the other guests at Salem Plantation gathered up the family silver and jewelry and carried them out into the fields for hiding. But the alarm proved false. The enemy vessel appeared only to be anchoring in sheltered water.

South of Vicksburg, by means of land communication across De Soto Peninsula, Farragut got word that advance units of Davis's flotilla were only twenty miles above him. Remembering Lincoln's insistence, and that of the Navy Department, that he "effect a junction with Flag Officer Davis," Farragut was left with no alternative. He must run the Vicksburg batteries and get upriver from the city.

It was always risky business for saltwater ships, built for ocean fighting and maneuvering, to run the gauntlet of river batteries. And what, precisely, would be gained was hard to say. But one thing would be accomplished. Farragut would have fulfilled instructions and also demonstrated that his fleet could move up and down at will, unintimidated by the guns of Vicksburg. He would make the run on Saturday, June 28. Meanwhile the gunboats and mortars would soften up the enemy's defenses with a night-and-day bombardment.

The mortars opened the barrage on the afternoon of June 26, resuming the following morning when Rowland Chambers was aroused from his bed "by the report of a big gun." During the day, several of General Williams's rifled cannon joined the barrage from positions on De Soto Point where earlier Williams had established camps and set up artillery for shelling the city from across the river. Volunteers crept up to the Mississippi shoreline after dark, planting stakes to mark triangulations for the gunners; lanterns, with one side blacked out, were hung on the stakes to make them visible at night.

The following day, June 27, the mortars were again brought into action, and the barrage increased in fury. Hugh Moss changed his sneering opinion of earlier Federal bombardments, confessing that now "their mortars annoyed us considerably, night and day." Rowland Chambers sat on his gallery after supper and watched the bombshells patterning the sky. "It was the most grand display of fireworks, the shells ascending and descending in every direction, many bursting high up in the air, others near the ground. But the greatest number burst on the ground."[22]

Vicksburg citizens, accustomed to seeking shelter on slopes east of the city, could not escape the elliptical path—high up, and down—followed by the mortar shells. But it was random firing; the gunners could not see over the hills; no civilians were killed, few soldiers wounded. As Colonel Lockett noted:

Vertical fire is never very destructive of life. Yet the howling and bursting shells had a very demoralizing effect on those not accustomed to them. One of my engineer officers, a Frenchman, a gallant officer who had distinguished himself in several severe engagements, was almost unmanned whenever one passed near him. When joked about it, he was not ashamed to confess: "I no like ze bomb; I cannot fight him back!"[23]

Lockett measured one of the craters made by a shell and found it seventeen feet deep. It would be impossible, he thought, for civilians or soldiers to find bombproof shelters from such engines of destruction. Yet find them or build them they would. Though not yet convinced of the necessity, the people began going underground. Tentative molelike probes were made into the brown loess soil of the hillsides, an effort that would in time define a way of life.

Though, after forty-eight hours, the Federal bombardment revealed little damage to the Confederate batteries on the bluffs, Farragut prepared to make his move. As in the run past forts Jackson and Saint Philip, protective iron mail was hung about the vulnerable sections of the vessels. Extraneous spars were lowered; the magazines cushioned in bales of cotton; all lights extinguished. At 2:00 A.M. two red lights were raised on the mizzenmast of the *Hartford,* as a signal to get under way. One hour later the flagship began moving upstream, the fleet filing in its wake. It was still dark at four o'clock, when their coming was detected. The Marine Hospital Battery opened fire; Farragut turned loose his naval guns; and the mortar schooners belched a hail of iron on the city. Hugh Moss remembered that "the shells fell so fast that they looked like stars falling from the heavens—it was a sublime but dangerous scene—the very earth trembled beneath us." Sergeant John Curtis of the Federal infantry aboard the waiting transports was equally awed: "I never saw such a magnificent spectacle in my life."

It was by far the heaviest bombardment Vicksburg had as yet sustained. The guns and mortars of thirty-six warships competed with ten land batteries for one short strip of Mississippi water a half mile wide. "The roar of the cannon was now continuous and deafening," wrote General Martin Smith; "loud explosions shook the city to its foundations; shot and shell went hissing through the trees and walls, scattering fragments far and wide in their terrific flight; men, women, and children rushed into the streets, and amid the crash of falling houses, commenced their hasty flight to the country for safety."[24]

One never made it. Mrs. Alice Gamble, reported the *Whig,* was running for shelter when she was struck "by a bloody messenger of tyranny, and after a short but painful agony, she yielded to her God a spirit too pure for this sinful world . . . in our country's history, *her* name is certainly worthy of a bright page and an everlasting mausoleum." She was Vicksburg's first civilian casualty; she would not be the last.[25]

To Marmaduke Shannon, "the scene in the city beggared all description. . . . Men, women and children, both black and white, went screaming through the streets, seeking a place of safety—some dressed and others almost nude. Mothers were running with little babes in their arms, crying 'Where will I go,' and some would stop and crouch under the first hill, while the shell was bursting above them. We noticed one man with his wife in his arms, she having fainted with fright at the explosion of a shell within a few feet of her. . . . "

Within minutes, Marmaduke Shannon noted, the hills to the east were covered with people seeking safety. "Even the stock, and almost every living thing in the city, was panic stricken and fled. Horses, mules, cows, dogs, etc., could be seen speeding through the town, out of reach of the missiles. Such a scene we have never before witnessed, and we hope we never shall again."[26]

As in the passage of forts Henry and Saint Philip, the battle was sudden, violent, and explosive; but it lasted barely three hours. By 6:50 A.M., as the sun broke through the smoke clouds, the *Hartford* and all but three of Farragut's ships had passed the batteries. None was sunk, and only one of the trio, still downstream, was slightly damaged.

One new arrival watched the engagement. Major General Earl Van Dorn had reached the city, with a brigade predominately of Mississippi infantry and assurance from President Davis that "The people will sustain you in your heroic determination, and may God bless you with success." Van Dorn, in turn, was able to make his first report to Davis one of reassurance: "Bombardment heavy yesterday and this morning. No flinching. Houses perforated; none burned yet . . . all sound and fury and to brave men contemptible."[27]

It had been considerably more than sound and fury. Though the Confederate defenders had lost only two men killed and three men wounded, Farragut had suffered 45 casualties. But he had passed the batteries, and had made contact with Davis's advance flotilla as instructed. He capsuled his success in a report to Washington:

> The forts have been passed, and we have done it, and can do it again as often as may be required of us. It will not, however, be an easy matter for us to do more than silence the batteries for a time, as long as the enemy has a large force behind the hills to prevent our landing and holding the place.[28]

When Flag Officer Charles Davis joined the fleet on July 1 with four ironclads and six mortar scows, it was time to assess the situation. Farragut had run the batteries. The two fleets from north and south had joined forces. But what now? The transports with General Williams's infantry were still below the city. They were too slow, too vulnerable, to try to pass the batteries. And anyway, Farragut believed, there were not enough of them to attempt a land assault on Vicksburg.

Previously Williams and Farragut had agreed on a plan to dig a canal across the base of the peninsula for the purpose of bypassing the river batteries at Vicksburg. This accomplished, Federal ships could pass up and down at will, out of range of the batteries. And, if the river performed as it should and followed the new channel, Vicksburg would be isolated and left high and dry.

Williams launched the task on June 27, utilizing his troops and impressing slave gangs from the neighboring plantations in Louisiana. Wrote Kate Stone of Brokenburn, "The excitement is very great. The Yankees have taken the Negroes off all the places below Omega [two miles from Brokenburn], the Negroes generally going most willingly, being promised their freedom by the vandals." Many planters hustled their slaves to back-country hideaways, and, observed Kate, "We hope to have ours in a place of greater safety by tomorrow."[29]

Though the operation was an army one, supposedly involving labor by the troops, most of the heavy work was left to blacks. Sergeant "Cool" Curtis found himself simply an observer, along with the rest of his regiment. "Gen. Williams is now to work changing the course of the Mississippi and that makes Vicksburg no account," he wrote to his Bridgeport family. "We have a thousand niggers to work on the proposed cut-off. I think it will be completed in a very short time."[30]

Curtis enclosed his own drawing of the project, inaccurate as to detail, but none the less illustrative of the purpose and general location and direction of the project relative to Vicksburg. The actual plan called for a canal that would stretch from the right bank of the Mississippi, six miles upriver from Vicksburg, to an exit on the river three and a half miles below the city. It would be a mile and a half long and fifty feet wide.

The last of these specifications gave trouble from the start. With the spring floods subsiding, the level was falling day by day. This meant that, once the channel's upper end was opened to the river, there might not be sufficient flow to fill it, much less scour out the channel and enlarge it.

Meanwhile, as this work went on, the Federal mortars below De Soto Point continued to lob shells into Vicksburg day by day. But as so often happens in warfare, the bombardment simply stiffened the backbone of the defenders. According to Colonel Charles E. Hooker:

> Even the citizens who remained became accustomed to the steady dropping of the shells, and went about their daily business. Women and children who remained sheltered in caves would come out and divert themselves by watching the fiery instruments of destruction, taking refuge again when the shots would concentrate on their neighborhood.[31]

Above the bend, Farragut's fleet was safe from retaliatory fire from the Vicksburg batteries. But the flag officer was haunted by rumors of a Confederate warship under construction somewhere on the Yazoo River. On June 26 two of the new Ellet rams, the *Monarch* and *Lancaster,* commanded by Lieutenant Colonel Alfred W. Ellet and his teenage nephew, set out on a search-and-destroy mission up the river.

Fifty miles from its mouth they approached two Confederate gunboats and a ram, which had escaped from Memphis. Alarmed at the sight of the Union rams, the Southern officer in charge ordered all three burned to avoid capture, and the Ellets returned.

One Union officer who could not tolerate reverses and delay was David Dixon Porter. He still smarted from having been left behind during Farragut's first thrust at Vicksburg. Now, though the fleet was reunited, he found himself and his mortar boats in an exasperating situation. They could expend countless tons of ammunition shelling the Confederate defenses but, he found, "the soldiers in the hill forts refused to stay shelled out."

From his vantage point below the city, he studied again the baffling fortifications of Vicksburg, "scattered over the hills in groups, the guns fifty yards apart, concealed from view." Every so often Confederate shells would whistle over his ships, some throwing up water spouts around them, all too many crashing through the vessels' timbers—a constant reminder of how well the city was defended. Porter concluded:

> The whole power of the Confederacy had been set to work to save this Gibraltar of the Mississippi, the railroads poured in troops and guns without stint, enabling it to bid defiance to Farragut's ships and the mortar flotilla. . . .
> Our combined fleet lay there and gazed in wonder at the new forts that were constantly springing up on the hill tops . . . while water batteries seemed to grow on every salient point. It was evident enough that Vicksburg could only be taken after a long siege by the combined operations of a large military and naval force.[32]

Experts would later say that Vicksburg could have been taken any time that summer, had Halleck committed sufficient troops to the endeavor. Even at this moment, the large naval force which Porter advocated was at hand. But to pit Williams's 3,200 infantry (which Porter considered "perfectly useless") against Van Dorn's 15,000 Confederates in fortified positions would, in the commodore's mind, be suicidal folly.

Moreover, in the hot and humid weather, there was increasing sickness among the naval crews and Williams's infantry, attributed to poor food and water and the "vapors" or "miasmas" of the Mississippi. Many Confederates were suffering, but to a less degree. Hugh Moss came down with what he described simply as "a sickness." Vicksburg hospitals being full, he was taken to a private home in the adjacent country, there to remain for several months "completely prostrated."

The work on the canal had proved especially exhausting, despite the help of 1,200 to 1,500 blacks. Wrote Lieutenant Colonel Richard B. Irwin of Williams's staff, "By the 11th of July, the cut . . . had been excavated through the clay (with much felling of trees and grubbing of roots) to a depth of thirteen feet, and a width of eighteen feet. . . . " But the deeper the workers dug, the further the water level fell. Irwin noted:

> The grade was now about 18 inches below the river level, and in a few hours the water was to have been let in. Suddenly the banks began to cave, and before anything could be done to remedy this, the river, falling rapidly, was once more below the bottom of the cut. Williams at once set about collecting more hands and tools with the purpose of carrying the cut below the lowest stage of water, forty feet if necessary; this he calculated would take three months.[33]

For the first time food was becoming scarce, in a city not fully prepared for military occupation. Grateful as Vicksburg was for the presence of Van Dorn's thousands of troops, they also occasioned some resentment. They took whatever they needed from whatever source, good-naturedly but freely. Rowland Chambers found his orchard depleted of ripening peaches and noticed that one of his pigs was missing.

It seemed hardly appropriate to celebrate July Fourth, of which the long-suffering Chambers noted in his diary: "This is a lovely morning, perfectly cloudless with a gentle breeze, and not too hot to be pleasant; everything quiet, and a person could hardly realize that he was in the center between two large armies intent on nothing but death and destruction of everything within reach."

Chambers's morning euphoria did not last. As the sun rose higher, Farragut celebrated Independence Day with a twenty-one-gun salute from all his vessels but one, accompanied by sporadic bombing by Davis's mortars. But the date would be better remembered for Van Dorn's General Order Number 9, imposing martial law on the beleaguered town. The measure was as unpopular here as at New Orleans, arousing such indignation that the order was later countermanded by the Richmond War Department.

Marmaduke Shannon gave slight notice to Van Dorn's edict in the *Whig,* but the following week he published an appraisal of the situation, under the simple heading of OUR CITY:

> The "terraced hill city," which for more than two months has withstood the demands, the threats, and the shells of the enemy, presents today a desolate, yet withal a sublime appearance. Our streets which of old teemed with the tide of business, now echo the tread of the sentinel as he paces his weary rounds, while our residences, around which cluster all the endearing and holy sentiments inseparable from associations of home, are dismantled, defaced, and in many instances destroyed.[34]

As Winchester Hall had done, he likened the devastation to that caused by a passing simoon, and itemized the destruction caused by its "poisonous blast." The horror was "rendered cumulative by the sporadic showers of shot and shell which are hurled upon us at morning, noon, and night." Yet Shannon closed with a moving tribute:

> In the midst of all this, Vicksburg, proud, gallant little Vicksburg, firm as the eternal hills on which she reposes, gazes boldly and defiantly upon her enemy, and, with a feeling of inexpressible but justifiable pride she beholds two immense fleets . . . unable to cope with her, compelled not only to keep a respectful distance, but, astounding as it may seem, actually forced to dig a new channel for the Mississippi! How humiliating to the United States, how more than glorious to her.[35]

Farragut meanwhile chafed at his fleet's inactivity and seeming impotence. The ocean-going vessels, although they had performed well so far, were not ideal for operations in a tricky river. And another worry: the subsiding waters of the Mississippi—which had made ludicrous General Williams's ditch-digging efforts on the peninsula—also threatened to leave Farragut's vessels stranded above Vicksburg. On July 10 he inquired by wire of the War Department: "In ten days the river will be too low for the ships to go down. Shall they go down, or remain up the rest of the year?"[36]

Two days earlier a wire had come from Secretary Welles directing the flag officer to send David Dixon Porter and twelve of the mortar schooners to Norfolk, Virginia, for service on the James. Porter left the fleet on July 10, taking with him more than half the mortar flotilla along with a number of gunboats to tow the schooners. Farragut was not perturbed by the loss; the mortars had done little to reduce the Vicksburg batteries; and on an optimistic note he informed the department that he expected "soon to have the pleasure of recording the combined attack of army and navy, for which we all so ardently long."

Of more concern than Porter's absence were the persistent rumors of a Confederate warship being built in the upper reaches of the Yazoo River. Even if the reports were true, "I do not think she will ever come forth," he stated. But Flag Officer Davis proposed an expedition to investigate. On July 15, three of the vessels, the Ellet ram *Queen of the West* under Lieutenant James Hunter, the *Carondelet* under Commander Henry Walke, and the wooden gunboat *Tyler* under Lieutenant Commander William Gwin, started up the Yazoo.

They would never get far beyond the river's mouth. Downstream came a legendary ship with the sting of a scorpion, to change the whole complexion of this, the first prolonged assault on Vicksburg.

❧ 6 ❧
"The *Arkansas* Is Coming!"

THERE are bronze generals on horseback, marble Confederate riflemen on pedestals, staunch granite gunners at the breech. But there are few Civil War monuments to ships in inland cities. Vicksburg, however, would have been justified in erecting an enduring memorial to one extraordinary craft deserving of its gratitude. Should the city ever do so, it would be the weirdest looking monument in history.

The vessel's own dramatic history gained momentum in the summer months of 1862, at a place called Greenwood in the upper Yazoo River. Here Lieutenant Isaac Newton Brown strove to reverse the parable of mountains bringing forth a mouse; his assignment was to turn a drowned mouse into a man-eating shark. Brown compared his work to that of Oliver Hazard Perry who, in ninety days on the wooded shores of Lake Erie, had built a navy with which to devour the British Great Lakes Fleet in 1813.[1]

Brown was building only one ship, the *Arkansas.* But he faced the same problem of starting from scratch, creating something out of virtually nothing. He had no work force, no materials, no machinery. The half-sunken hulk, four miles from dry land, was all but inaccessible, and the iron intended for her armor plate was at the bottom of the river.

One of Brown's officers, George Gift, found this "fearfully discouraging, but Brown was undismayed." The lieutenant proceeded methodically, step by step. He commandeered the nearby river steamer *Capitol* and used her derricks to fish up the sunken railroad iron. Then he had the *Arkansas*'s hull towed down to Yazoo City, a hundred and ten miles below, where the *Capitol* was lashed alongside to serve as a working platform. Here the real job of turning a derelict wreck into a first-class fighting ship began.

Two hundred men were conscripted from a nearby army detachment to work on strengthening the deck and hull.

Additional railroad iron was rounded up from all points of the compass and brought to the nearest depot to be hauled by wagon to the site. Fourteen blacksmith forges were drawn from the neighboring plantations to forge and

67

shape the iron plate. Extemporized drilling machines powered by the engines of the *Capitol* were used to bolt the armor plate to the hull.

Local lumberjacks were hired to cut the wood to make gun carriages. Since no such apparatus had ever been made in Mississippi, Brown scoured the neighborhood and found "two gentlemen from Jackson" who agreed to build five carriages apiece.[2]

All this went on in 100-degree heat, unsheltered from the sun, within sound of the guns of the Federal fleet at Vicksburg, only six cruising hours distant. Moreover, the water level of the Yazoo, responding to that of the Mississippi, was dropping fast, putting added pressure on the work force. To speed things up, ordinary boiler plate was substituted on ticklish sections of the hull—it would look like railway iron to the enemy—and the ship was camouflaged with the only paint available, a dull brown.

At the end of five weeks, wrote George Gift, "we had a man-of-war (such as she was) from almost nothing." While, in the words of Lieutenant Brown, "The *Arkansas* now appeared as if a small seagoing vessel had been cut down to the water's edge at both ends, leaving a box for guns amidships." Two guns protruded from both ends of the shed, the ends of which slanted upward to deflect shells fired at close range, with three guns in each broadside, making ten in all. A small pilot house jutted from the roof, and a single smokestack rose from the furnace room below, where two reconstructed engines would supposedly provide a speed of eight knots under full steam, half that figure if obliged to run against the current.[3]

On July 12 the *Arkansas* was as finished as she would ever be, a vessel built largely of improvisation and ingenuity. George Gift was baffled by her appearance: "What she was designed for no man probably knows. I imagine that she was intended for a powerful iron-clad gun boat, with an iron beak for poking, and several heavy guns for shooting." Gift settled for calling the ship "an hermaphrodite-iron-clad."[4]

Brown could not wait longer to add improvements or refinements. At Yazoo City the lieutenant began rounding up his officers and crew. He obtained a hundred seamen from the three vessels destroyed to escape capture during Colonel Ellet's search-and-destroy mission up the Yazoo and got sixty more from the swashbuckling Missouri guerrillas of Brigadier General Jeff Thompson, finally rounding out his crew with volunteers from Louisiana units. None of the Missourians had ever served aboard a naval vessel, but, Brown believed, would have "the cool courage natural to them on land." Some of his officers had served in the "old" navy. "The only trouble they gave me," the lieutenant wrote, "was to keep them from running the *Arkansas* into the Union fleet before we were ready for battle."

Much remained to be done, but Brown could not afford the time if he was to have enough water left to navigate. On July 12 the *Arkansas* cast off and headed downriver to Satartia, fifty river miles above Vicksburg, where his crew was organized and drilled.

A day or so later, on the run downriver from Satartia, the jerry-built engines failed to operate in unison and cut out unpredictably. With one engine lagging or stalled, the *Arkansas* spun around in dizzy circles that no rudder could control. Escaping steam from a leaky boiler so drenched the magazine that they had to stop at a bank of the river and spread out the powder on tarpaulins, shaking and turning them to hasten the drying process.

They were as ready as they would ever be when, on the morning of July 14, the *Arkansas* resumed its way down the river to reach Haynes Bluff at midnight. Brown planned a surprise attack on the combined Union fleets at dawn. Van Dorn had sent word that thirty-seven Federal men-of-war were visible from Vicksburg, with possibly more upriver. Odds of one to thirty-seven were an acceptable challenge, given the advantage of surprise.

On the way downstream, Brown stopped the *Arkansas* near a riverside plantation and sent Lieutenant Charles Read ashore to get any fresh information he might obtain. Read found only an aged negress, who professed to know nothing about Union ships or Union pickets. "And, if I did, I wouldn't tell."

"Do you take me for a Yankee?" Read protested. "Don't you see I wear a gray coat?"

"Sartin you's a Yankee," said the woman. "Our folks ain't got none dem gumboats."[5]

Brown was forced to move on without any local intelligence, to find that the factor of surprise that he was counting on had vanished. By the first glow of dawn he saw three Federal vessels approaching at full steam—later identified as the ironclad *Carondelet,* the ram *Queen of the West,* and the timberclad *Tyler.*

A newspaper correspondent, possibly drawing on his imagination, reported later that three Confederate deserters had revealed the presence of the *Arkansas* to Commander Davis, that Davis had posted lookouts on the Yazoo's banks to watch for the mystery ship, and that early on the morning of July 15 these sentinels "came down like a streak of lightning, screaming, "The *Arkansas* is coming! The *Arkansas* is coming!' " True or not, it hardly mattered. The *Arkansas* was here.

In full-dress uniform, his tawny beard parted by the wind, Brown stood at the head of the cannon shed, ordering those at the bow guns to hold their fire. The rearward thrust would delay their speed; he was going for the swift kill and might not have another chance. He recognized the *Carondelet* and recalled that he had known her captain well; he and Henry Walke had been messmates in old navy days. Perhaps from a sense of traditional service rivalry, he ordered the pilot to steer directly for the ironclad.

The *Carondelet* fired with all of her batteries facing the *Arkansas,* then swung around and fled, followed by the *Queen* and *Tyler.* The *Tyler* and *Carondelet* pointed their stern guns at the pursuing *Arkansas.* Brown steered the *Arkansas* on a zig-zag course, to mask the boiler plate on her armor. But he kept blazing away at the *Carondelet* and observed with satisfaction that, while his own shots were peeling the metal skin off his opponent, the enemy's missiles "were deflected over my head and lost in air."

Not all, however, were deflected. "I received a severe contusion on the head," the lieutenant was forced to admit, "but this gave me no concern after I had failed to find any brains mixed with the handful of clotted blood which I drew from the wound and examined." Another Federal shell, seconds later, crashed into the pilot house, killing the pilot and injuring his standby. James Brady, one of Jeff Thompson's Missourians, took over the wheel and Brown hazily remembered: "I was near the hatchway at the moment when a minié-ball, striking over my left temple, tumbled me down among the guns. I awoke as if from sleep, to find kind hands helping me to a place among the killed and wounded."[6] Regaining consciousness, Brown saw the *Carondelet* listing among the willows in shallow water, helpless, with her steering mechanism shot away. Brady had swung the *Arkansas* around and his broadside guns were pumping shells into the stricken vessel, causing her to reel and thrash like a mortally wounded animal. "Our last view of the *Carondelet,*" wrote a United States seaman aboard the *Tyler,* "was through a cloud of enveloping smoke with steam escaping from her ports, and of her men jumping overboard," while Brown laconically observed, "We neither saw nor felt the *Carondelet* again."[7] After the *Arkansas* passed, the *Carondelet* grounded.

The *Tyler* and *Queen of the West* were fleeing downstream to the mouth of the Yazoo, and to the protection of the combined Federal fleets on the Mississippi. They had the advantage of greater speed. An unlucky shot on the *Arkansas'* vitals had carried away the flue connecting furnace and smokestack. Raw flame was pouring into the engine room, raising the temperature to 130 degrees. Men could work only in relays. An unwary crewman peered through a porthole and was instantly decapitated. When ordered to throw the headless body overboard, a sailor cried, "But I can't do that, sir! It's my brother!"[8]

Aided by the current the *Arkansas* chugged into sight of the Federal fleet above Vicksburg. Brown saw "a forest of masts and smokestacks . . . in every direction, except astern, our eyes rested on enemies. . . . It seemed at a glance as if a whole navy had come to keep me away from the heroic city."

As at Memphis, the sound of cannon on the river brought swarms of civilians to the bluffs, to the rooftops, to the levee, to watch the battle. One among them, Edward Butler, noted the "pandemonium" that heralded the appearance of the *Arkansas.* "People cheered, sang, danced, and hugged one another." A newspaper editor believed that "Probably no vessels in history had the hopes of so many people riding with her"; while an artillerist with a battery on the bluffs observed, "We knew that the odds against the solitary vessel were overwhelming and of course our excitement was almost unendurable."[9]

Aboard the *Arkansas* Lieutenant Brown was forced into an instant battle plan. His was one vessel against ships of two Union fleets: seven rams, five ironclads, and Farragut's squadron of saltwater ships. But he had taken that fleet—if not the three gunboats in the Yazoo—by surprise, and many Federal vessels had not got up enough steam to maneuver.

His chances were best in the very center of his antagonists, hugging the enemy vessels like a boxer in a clinch—so close that their rams would not have room enough to strike him, and their guns, if they missed, risked disabling their own ships. The *Arkansas* would be able to fire willy-nilly, certain of hitting an enemy target in any and all directions.

Plunging into the center of the Union fleet, Brown trained his sights on the flagship *Hartford,* and in minutes "every gun on the *Arkansas* was at its work." With vast clouds of smoke obscuring everything, the men could only direct their aim at the flashes of enemy guns—flashes that seemed to form a circle that was slowly closing in on them.

Brown found it like being in the crater of a volcano—"The *Arkansas* from its center firing rapidly to every point in the circumference, without the fear of hitting a friend or missing an enemy." Through rents in the smoke he saw his guns tearing gaping wounds in the superstructures of surrounding vessels.

The *Hartford* and the *Iroquois* were blasted by direct hits, the *Benton* less seriously damaged. One of Porter's mortar schooners, the *Sidney Jones,* lying south of Vicksburg and outside the naval action, was mistakenly fired on by Federal attackers.

A Union ram, the *Lancaster,* suddenly bore down on the *Arkansas*'s port beam. "Go right through her, Brady," ordered Brown. A shot from the *Arkansas* penetrated the *Lancaster*'s steam drum. Clouds of steam enveloped the ram, scalding a number of the crew, who jumped overboard. Wrote Brown, "We passed through the brave fellows struggling in the water under a shower of missiles intended for us."[10]

Faltering engines, aided by the current, took the *Arkansas* downstream, away from the wolf pack. But steam pressure had dropped to twenty pounds. "With our firemen exhausted, our smoke-stack cut to pieces, and a section of plating torn from the side," Brown concluded that "humanity required the landing of our wounded—terribly torn by cannon-shot—and of our dead." He ordered the pilot to head for the landing at Vicksburg and the protection of the city's batteries.

At the wharf below Jackson Street, Vicksburgians rushed to greet the heroic ship with its flag still flying from a pole temporarily erected for that purpose. "As she landed," wrote one observer, "our pent-up enthusiasm burst into uncontrollable manifestations in a variety of ways. Some jumped up and shouted, others rolled over and over upon the ground, while not a few burst into tears of gratitude over the merciful deliverance."

But as people peered over the rail or through the portholes their jubilation vanished. Lieutenant George Gift, with one arm smashed, and surrounded by his dead or dying crew, knew what repelled them. He remembered later:

> A great heap of mangled and ghastly slain lay on the gun deck, with rivulets of blood running away from them. There was a poor fellow torn asunder, another mashed flat, whilst in the "slaughter-house" [gun shed] brains, hair and blood were all about. Down below fifty or sixty wounded were groaning or complaining, or courageously bearing their ills without a murmur.[11]

"It was a little hot this morning all around," Lieutenant Brown wrote, in summarizing the day's engagement. He had lost a number of his crew in the second encounter with Farragut's fleet, more through the expiration of their one-trip enlistment, and the *Arkansas* had been severely mauled. Sheets of armor plate dangled like loose skin from her sides. The smokestack resembled a sieve, and gaping holes punctured her gun shed.

On top of everything, the ship was out of fuel. Brown directed the vessel downriver to the coalyard below Depot Street, to refill the bins and effect whatever repairs were possible at this stage. After two battles in a single morning, the *Arkansas* was "not in fighting condition," Brown laconically recorded. But he was convinced that she would fight again.

Brown was proved right sooner than he thought.

Aboard the wounded flagship *Hartford,* Flag Officer Farragut struggled to control his temper. Surveying the wreckage around him, he saw evidence of "Damnable neglect, or worse." Most galling of all was the fact that a hybrid Confederate craft, which looked as if it had been pieced together from a junk pile, had made a joke of two Union fleets of more than twenty first-class fighting ships. And now that offending vessel was mocking him beneath the guns of Vicksburg.

The flag officer had to redeem himself, and quickly. He could only do that by taking his deep-water fleet past the Vicksburg batteries again and, with combined and massive firepower, sink the *Arkansas* before the sun went down. Flag Officer Charles Davis was opposed to the move, but he agreed that his gunboats would keep the water battery, north of Vicksburg, occupied, while Farragut led his fleet down for the kill.

Aboard the *Arkansas,* but disabled by his shattered arm, Lieutenant George Gift could only serve as an observer. But he early sensed that "the enemy intended mischief." When he heard the Vicksburg batteries explode and the Union naval guns reply, he surmised the enemy's intent: "The sea-going fleet of Farragut was to pass down, drag out and literally mob us; whilst the iron-clad squadron of Davis was to keep the batteries engaged."[12]

Down they came, gun barrels gleaming in the last rays of the setting sun. But the timing was unfortunate for Farragut. While light from the west made silhouetted targets of his line of ships, it did little to identify the rust-colored *Arkansas* against the dark bank. It was Brown who gave his position away. Perhaps it was the sight of his prime antagonist, the *Hartford,* or simply the sound and smell of gunpowder he could not resist. But in any event, "Unfit as we were for the offensive," he confessed, he ordered the captain to get under way and head for the center of the oncoming fleet.

The order was never executed. A shot from the *Oneida* crashed through the side of the *Arkansas,* made havoc of her engine room, killed or wounded some of the crew, and lodged in the opposite bulkhead. Inert, her engines shattered, the *Arkansas* stayed where she was, her broadside guns pumping shells into the passing Union vessels, at such close range that Brown could hear the groans of their wounded—and was dismayed that "these sounds were heard with a fierce delight by the *Arkansas*' people."

"To be a spectator of such a scene was intensely exciting," wrote George Gift, continuing:

> The great ships with their towering spars came sweeping by, pouring out broad-side after broadside, whilst the batteries from the hills, the mortars from above and below, and the iron-clads, kept the air alive with hurtling missiles and the darkness lighted up by burning fuses and bursting shells. On our gun-deck every man and officer worked as though the fate of the nation hung on his individual efforts.[13]

"Why no attempt was made to ram our vessel, I do not know," wrote Lieutenant Brown. But the *Arkansas,* helpless and immobile as she was, was not struck or boarded by any of the line of ships which seemed content to discharge their guns in her direction, then pass on down the river. Darkness had come before the ordeal was over, the last of Farragut's vessels was below the city. Aboard the *Arkansas* there were more dead to be buried, more wounded to be cared for, still more repairs required. But the ugly duckling with the falcon's claws still snugly nested beneath the guns of Vicksburg as if she had been hatched there.

"It was a day long to be remembered by the people of Vicksburg," Rowland Chambers wrote in his diary for July 15. He himself remembered best the tremendous volume of smoke that smothered the Mississippi, and the muffled sound of bursting shells coming from beneath that pall. But Vicksburg would never forget the sight of that gallant Confederate vessel, seeming to bleed from every deep gash in her side, as she limped victoriously into port with the flag still flying from a makeshift pole. The city needed such a triumph, to resuscitate its pride and confidence after weeks of punishing bombardment.

At her mother's Woodfield plantation on the Big Black, Mahala Roach had listened all day to the distant cacophony of guns, "the heaviest I ever heard," and concluded that "my poor, devoted house is gone at last . . . well, God's will be done." That evening came news that the *Arkansas* had scored "a brilliant victory . . . this is some good thing for us." She longed to go to the city and see if her home had been spared, but was feeling "quite unwell" from no other discernible cause than apprehension.[14]

Not far below Mahala's home on Depot Street, the *Arkansas* was recovering from her wounds, as surviving members of the crew worked fiercely to repair the damage. But during these days of convalescence, neither Davis's squadron above the city, nor Farragut's fleet below, gave the lone Confederate vessel any rest. The mortars and naval guns splattered near-misses around the hull, dowsing the crew with refreshing spray, destroying quantities of perch and bass.

"Just look at that, will you!" shouted one Confederate crewman to his neighbors. "The upper fleet is killing fish for the lower fleet's dinner."[15]

Despite all he had been through, Brown was not ready to settle for just three victories. He itched to get back on the offensive. While the engines were being repaired, he kept up steam in the boilers, sending up plumes of smoke to warn the Federals that he might come forth at any moment—"thus compelling the enemy's entire force, in the terrible July heat, to keep up steam day and night."

Meanwhile the lieutenant sought to replenish his decimated crew. In addition to the dead and wounded, the surviving Missourians had returned to Jeff Thompson's guerrilla brigade. He asked Van Dorn for replacements from the troops in Vicksburg. Van Dorn was willing, provided the men volunteered. A good many did, but, on seeing the battered condition of the *Arkansas,* they reneged; the ship was a death trap. Brown was left with only enough men to handle two guns and keep the engines running.

Frustration had taken its toll of Farragut. Nothing had gone well in front of Vicksburg, since he had wired Secretary Welles that he was certain of success. The canal across the peninsula had been a dismal failure and was abandoned. Large numbers of his sailors were on the sick list, as were many of General Williams's troops. On top of all, the Mississippi was still falling. Unless they moved quickly, they might never move at all.

But there was unfinished business to attend to. Secretary Welles had wired him, and Farragut agreed, that the squadron must redeem itself by "the destruction of the *Arkansas.*" Davis, at first, wanted no part of another attack. "I have watched eight rams for a month," he said, "and I have difficulty watching one." But he finally agreed to send two vessels, the ram *Queen of the West* and the powerful *Essex* with "Dirty Bill" Porter in command, to destroy the Confederate warship in her berth.

Their planned strategy, put into effect at dawn of July 22, seemed foolproof. The *Essex* and the *Queen of the West* would both drive their iron beaks into the enemy's exposed side.

Brown was ready for them; in fact, he even proposed to go out and meet them. As he saw the *Essex* steaming at him "like a mad bull," he ordered the forward lines slackened. The current swung the ship's bow out into the river so that she presented her sharp prow, and not her vulnerable side, to the attackers. The guns of the *Essex* and *Arkansas* blasted at one another, muzzle to muzzle up to the moment of impact, which was no more than a glancing blow.

While Brown's ship was damaged in the exchange and fourteen men were killed or wounded, the *Essex* returned to midstream, then, under heavy fire from the river battery, headed downriver. The *Queen,* meanwhile, coming in for the kill, was able to deliver only a sidewise blow, inflicting little damage, grounded briefly on the shallow bank, then headed upriver to safety.

When the crew of the *Arkansas* cleared up their decks after the affray, they were surprised to find that, in addition to other missiles, the *Essex* fired "marbles that boys used for playing. We picked up a hundred unbroken ones on our forecastle. There were 'white-allies,' 'chinas,' and some glass marbles."[16]

"Thus," Lieutenant Brown wrote, "closed the fourth and final battle of the *Arkansas,* leaving the daring Confederate vessel, though reduced to twenty men all told for duty, still defiant in the presence of a hostile force perhaps exceeding in real strength that which fought under Nelson at Trafalgar."[17]

Five days of standoff elapsed before Farragut finally gave up on the *Arkansas* and Vicksburg. Vast quantities of coal had been consumed in keeping steam up on the ships, and the water beneath their keels was still diminishing. He had received a belated reply to his wire of July 10, as to whether he should "go down or remain up the rest of the year." Welles's instructions had been: "Go down river at discretion."

On July 24 Farragut's fleet weighed anchor and steamed south with the transports, leaving one ironclad and one ram behind, to patrol the river below Vicksburg and blockade the *Arkansas.* On July 28 Flag Officer Davis headed upstream for Helena, Arkansas, three hundred miles above. Though they were acting under Welles's authority, the Secretary of the Navy expressed his disgust with the whole Vicksburg operation:

> The most disreputable naval affair of the war was the descent of the steam ram *Arkansas* through both squadrons, until she hauled into the batteries of Vicksburg, and there the two Flag Officers abandoned the place and the iron-clad ram, Farragut and his force going down to New Orleans, and Davis proceeding with his flotilla up the river.[18]

General Van Dorn, commanding the troops in his native Mississippi, gave credit to more than the *Arkansas* for the ultimate Federal retreat, recognizing what would become more and more apparent—that the defense of Vicksburg was becoming a national not a local issue:

The power which baffled the enemy resided in the breasts of the soldiers of seven States, marshaled behind the ramparts at Vicksburg. Mississippians were there, but there were also the men of Kentucky, of Tennessee, of Alabama, of Arkansas, of Louisiana and of Missouri, as ready to defend the emporium of Mississippi as to strike down the foe at their own hearthstones.[19]

To Vicksburg, after weeks of tension and excitement, the slipping away of the enemy fleet seemed anticlimactic. It was like a sharp change in barometric pressure—not enough energy left for celebration, simply a great weight lifted from the shoulders of the city.

It would take some getting used to. Rowland Chambers's ears still rang from the final day's bombardment, during which he took to the bomb-proof cave he still referred to as a "fort." Here, as he wrote in his diary, the shells landed so close "that we could feel the shocks very sensibly. This is the first time I have felt alarmed. My nerves are completely unstrung; I can hardly write."

The next day, however, he was back tending his vegetable garden, where he found the enemy had planted a fifteen-pound shell "2 feet 10 inches deep." Presumably it was unexploded, and presumably, too, he gave it a wide berth. Of destruction in the city around him, Chambers observed, "The principal part of the town has been much damaged; scarcely a house has escaped."[20]

With Vicksburg free of enemy harassment, the refugees began returning. Mahala Roach, though most of the time at her mother's plantation with the children, had never truly been away. At Woodfield, she had "fretted and yearned for home," and her heart dwelt always in "that sweet starlight dream, on my own familiar gallery."

Once or twice Mahala allowed her young son Tommy to visit the city and check on the property. When he returned with a piece of shell that had struck the house, she insisted on going herself and found "two *holes* made by Yankee balls," and her desk and bookcase damaged. Otherwise the place was intact, except that the soldiers had picked her strawberries and flowers.[21]

Dora Richards and her bridegroom, Anderson Miller, had begun the last lap of their flight from New Orleans two days after the *Arkansas*'s triumphant descent down the Yazoo River. They had heard the guns, but had not realized that the Confederate ram was clearing their projected path to Vicksburg. That morning, July 18, they started by boat down the Yazoo, following backwater bayous wherever possible, but saw no enemy and met with no interference beyond fallen trees and floating branches.[22]

As they emerged from the mouth of the river, Dora would never forget her first glimpse of that section of the Mississippi. "It was the vision of a drowned world, an illimitable waste of dead waters, stretching into great, silent, desolate forest." They passed the night at the plantation home of a "Colonel K"—Dora was still reluctant to spell out the names of her benefactors, for fear her Union sympathies might get them into trouble—and arrived in Vicksburg the following day, having traveled a total of 125 miles in nine generally-rainy days in an open boat. The couple put up at the Washington Hotel, from which point Miller undertook a dual endeavor: searching for legal work and trying to avoid the conscript officers.

From her hotel window Dora had her first view of the city, foreign and peculiar to her Leeward Island eyes. She noted in her diary: "Looking at it from a slight elevation suggests the idea that the fragments left from world-building had tumbled into a confused mass of hills, hollows, hillocks, ditches, and ravines, and that the houses had rained down afterwards. Over all there was dust impossible to conceive."

There would always be dust kicked up by intermittent shelling from the vessels on the river. But Vicksburg was returning, bit by bit, to normalcy, with most of the stores reopened, though with drastically diminished stocks. Supplies from the Trans-Mississippi arrived in limited amounts via the Red River, which flowed into the Mississippi between Natchez and Port Hudson. But there was one problem Vicksburg faced, common to embattled cities everywhere. That was the presence of Confederate troops, already numbering between 15,000 and 20,000, and destined to reach 30,000 in the months to come.

Mahala Roach felt gratitude and pity for the soldiers. Many were young, far from home, and lonely; and her house and heart were open to them. She invited them in, to fill their canteens and help themselves to her abundant crop of figs. And because of them, she was not afraid to be alone at night, nor did she lock her doors. "The pickets, with the guns, at the street corners, seemed protection for me."

Annie Harris saw the military presence in the city through romantic, youthful eyes:

> Among the soldiers were many elegant, refined gentlemen, and the young girls enjoyed gay times. Suppers, dances, and card parties, were frequently given; and often in the midst of fun and frolic, the roll of the drum would be heard, and the gallant knights would vanish to the call of duty. Flirtation and lovemaking were everywhere. Rings were exchanged, and promises given to be fulfilled in peaceful times. It was not difficult to be a belle with so many admirers of the opposite sex, waiting for active service.[23]

To many, however, the Confederate army seemed something like the invasion force they were here to repel. Welcome at first in the presence of the Union fleet, they now resembled a barbarian horde—only a portion of whom were Mississippians—who had taken over the community. There was the customary pilfering by soldiers on the loose; fruits, vegetables, chickens and livestock disappeared. But more than that, by tripling and then quadrupling the city's population, the troops helped drain the city of supplies, created shortages, sent prices soaring.

Food was becoming scarce. Butter sold for $1.50 a pound, and flour was virtually unavailable. A substance that passed for coffee was brewed from sun-dried pieces of sweet potato. Annie Harris's mother found it necessary to forage for provisions in the manner of a military commissary, using her coachman as guide and protector. By driving miles through the country, she was able to buy salt for $45 a bag and turkeys at $50 a head. Otherwise, noted Annie, "We lived on bacon and cornmeal, and a salted mackerel was considered a delicacy."

On the plantations around the city and across the river, things were relatively better, though described by Kate Stone of Brokenburn as "on a war footing—cornbread and home-raised meal, milk and butter, tea once a day and coffee never." But she noted with some relish:

Common cornbread admits of many variations in the hands of a good cook—eggbread (we have lots of eggs), muffins, cakes, and so on . . . and there are chickens, occasional partridges, and other birds, and often vegetables of all kinds minus potatoes; and last but not least knowing there is no help for it makes one content.[24]

Shortages also applied to clothing. Dresses of homespun fabric, linen or calico, were worn like badges of distinction. Hats were woven of palmetto, "and with trimmings of flowers, were light and pretty." Among the men, broadcloth was worn, Kate Stone observed, "only by the drones and fireside braves." Dyed linsey was the fashionable material for coats and pants. "Fashion is an obsolete word," wrote Kate in her diary, "and just to be decently clad is all we expect."

Appearances no longer marked the gentleman, and no one cared. One impressive figure whom Kate encountered on the street, "a splendid-looking fellow he was, had a piece of fish in one hand, a cavalry saddle on his back, bridle, blankets, newspapers, and a small parcel in the other hand; and over his shoulder swung an immense pair of cavalry boots. And nobody thought he looked odd."

With Vicksburg virtually free of threatening enemies, communication with all parts of the Confederacy was reestablished. Lieutenant Jared Sanders of the Twenty-sixth Louisiana Infantry was at long last able to write to his mother of conditions in the city:

The inhabitants have returned to the far-famed city since the departure of the investing fleets, & the ferryboat has come out the Yazoo River, to which river she had fled, & resumed her accustomed trips across from Vicksburg to the Louisiana shore.[25]

After two months of being shuttled from camp to camp throughout central Mississippi, Sanders's regiment had settled in at Camp Hall, eighteen miles east of Vicksburg, ready to move into the city's peripheral defenses at a moment's notice. "All is monotony & laziness here," he wrote, "as is the case in all the camps." Of Vicksburg itself he added:

I frequently visited that place during the bombardment which lasted *two months,* & on the roads that led into town were to be found *tents*—filled with women & little children. Many & many a family were thus driven from that luxury and comfort of a home to buffet the winds and weather beneath the unsubstantial roofs of cloth tents. Many found friends & vacant houses, but, of course a whole city population could not find accommodations of that kind & hence many bought tents & literally *camped* out as soldiers do.[26]

Sanders ended his letter by reporting the "easy capture" of Baton Rouge by General John C. Breckinridge. It was a misleading statement. The Confederate attempt to retake the Louisiana capital was only temporarily successful. But Baton Rouge in early August did become the setting for a grand finale—the last act of a drama that began just three weeks earlier, when the *Arkansas* came down the Yazoo River like a lone wolf on the prowl.

"Vicksburg was now without the suspicion of an immediate enemy," wrote Isaac Brown. And since repairs on the *Arkansas* were "fairly under way," the lieutenant obtained from the Navy Department a four-day furlough to visit friends in Grenada, Mississippi, a hundred and thirty miles north of Jackson. He turned command of the *Arkansas* over to First Lieutenant Henry Stevens "to sustain without me the lassitude of inaction."[27]

Brown himself was suffering from more than lassitude. After sixty strenuous days of preparing his ship for action, fighting four battles with her and sustaining troublesome wounds, he was close to collapse. On reaching Grenada, he wrote, he was "taken violently ill" and found himself confined to bed.

Earl Van Dorn, meanwhile, with his Vicksburg troops relieved of enemy threat, assigned 4,000 men to Breckinridge, with instructions to go downriver and try to recapture Baton Rouge. Easier said than done. En route to the Louisiana capital, Breckinridge wired Van Dorn that the city's garrison numbered at least 5,000 defenders. He asked that the *Arkansas* be sent down, "to clear the river and divert the fire of the gunboats," in support of his attack. Van Dorn ordered Stevens to comply.

Stevens promptly telegraphed Brown at Grenada asking for advice. Brown replied "with a positive order to remain at Vicksburg" until he could rejoin the ship.

Still feverish and scarcely able to stand, Brown stumbled to the railroad depot, climbed aboard the first train, and rode back to Jackson couched on a pile of mail sacks. At Jackson he ordered a special train to Vicksburg, and there received the news that the *Arkansas* had left four hours earlier. "I was completely cured by this intelligence," the lieutenant wrote, "and immediately hurried to Pontchatoula, the nearest approach by rail to Baton Rouge. . . . "

Stevens had had no choice but to leave without his commander, Van Dorn insisting, "beyond all reason," that the *Arkansas* reach Breckinridge by August 5. Under full steam, the substitute commander made the 260-mile run on schedule, only to have his engines crack from the strain within sight of Baton Rouge. Capriciously, the *Arkansas* veered right and ran aground.

"There lay the enemy in plain view," wrote George Gift, "and we as helpless as a shear-hulk." Stevens hastened repairs on the balky engines, meanwhile throwing excess iron overboard to get the ship afloat. By dawn of August 6 the ship was under way again. "Like a war horse she seemed to scent the battle from afar," wrote Gift, "and in point of speed outdid anything we had before witnessed."[28]

The enforced speed was her undoing. This time the port engine broke down under pressure, and the *Arkansas* was once again aground.

Of all the ironies in this situation, the most mortifying was the sight of the approaching *Essex,* which had discovered her predicament. She had withstood the *Essex* at Vicksburg. She could do it again, under normal circumstances, but . . .

Unable to move or bring his guns to bear upon the enemy, Stevens faced up to his only option. Tears streaming down his face, he ordered his men to swim to shore. Then he set fire to the vessel, leaping to safety himself before the flames took over.

As one by one the *Arkansas's* guns exploded when the fire reached them, the *Essex* was forced to back off. Even on the brink of death, the Confederate ironclad kept her enemy at bay.

It was just as well that Isaac Brown did not see his ship go down. He had transferred from train to horseback at Pontchatoula, to catch up to his errant vessel. He would catch up and get aboard her somehow. But all he saw from the bluffs above Baton Rouge, when he arrived there, was his arch enemy the *Essex,* circling around the eddy where the *Arkansas* had sunk.

There were only ripples and detritus to mark her grave. But the *Arkansas* needed no monument to be remembered. In twenty-three days she had created an undying legend in the history of naval warfare. No other ship on record had accomplished so much, so bravely, with so little. Brown consoled himself with the knowledge that her deck "had never been trod by the foot of an enemy." And because of her, the "proud and beautiful city," as Van Dorn referred to Vicksburg, remained still proud and beautiful.[29]

❧ 7 ❧

A Galaxy of Generals

I T was "the most anxious period of the war to me," wrote Ulysses Grant of the spring of 1862.[1]

It had been growing more difficult for him week by week since, after Fort Donelson, he had gone to Nashville without authority and incurred the wrath of his superior. Thereafter Halleck had either censured or ignored him. Then came Shiloh, with Sherman's rise to favor—"that single battle had given me new life," wrote Sherman—while Grant was made the scapegoat for the frightful Union casualties.

Time and again Grant asked to be relieved from serving under Halleck. When he finally made up his mind to quit the army, only Sherman, friendly to both men, could have talked him out of it. And did. "I begged him to stay," wrote Sherman, "illustrating his case by my own." The Northern press had called Sherman "crazy" only six months earlier, when he'd been furloughed from active service. Now they were calling Grant incompetent and a drunkard. Sherman had been since restored to favor, as Grant would be, if he waited out his critics.[2]

With Halleck's promotion to general in chief of the Union armies and his departure for Washington on July 17, 1862, Grant was free of his *bête noire*. Arriving at Corinth near the northern Mississippi border, he took over command of the District of West Tennessee. In a practical sense he was really a departmental commander, but no announcement of this was forthcoming until mid-October. "This place [Corinth] will be your headquarters," Halleck wrote to him. As for instructions, "You can judge for yourself." Grant was in something of a quandary.

More important, the magnificent army of 120,000 with which Halleck had captured Corinth had been broken up into several pieces. An army under the command of Major General Don Carlos Buell was slowly working its way along the Memphis and Charleston Railroad toward Chattanooga. Grant was left with less than 50,000 men, and these were widely dispersed, with various units at Corinth, at Bolivar and Jackson, Tennessee, and at Memphis under General Sherman. He moved his headquarters to Jackson, to facilitate communications with his scattered commanders.

As to the Federal objective in the West, that much was clear: the conquest of Vicksburg and possession of the Mississippi. With Union forces extending up to Baton Rouge, and down the river as far as Memphis, the target was a relatively narrow corridor. Only the single railway line that ran east from Vicksburg connected the Western half of the Confederacy with the Atlantic seaboard. "To dispossess them of this," wrote Grant, "became a matter of the first importance."[3]

Had Halleck kept the army intact, a massive attack on Vicksburg in late summer might have brought that city to its knees. Now the opportunity was gone. Grant commanded only scattered and "immobile garrisons," no one of which was sufficient for offensive action. Moreover, the general wrote, "We were in a country where nearly all the people, except the Negroes, were hostile to us and friendly to the cause we were trying to suppress." He had hundreds of miles of railroad to guard; his every move was watched and reported; Southern guerrillas threatened his communication lines. "I was put entirely on the defensive," he recorded.

Confederate General Joseph Eggleston Johnston, shortly to appear on the western horizon, was aware of Grant's dilemma. Of the scattered Federal troops he later wrote, "Their wide dispersion put them at the mercy of any superior or equal force, such as the Confederacy could have brought against them readily. . . ."[4] General Earl Van Dorn, commanding the department that included Vicksburg, had 22,000 men at his disposal (Union estimates ran as high as 40,000), a match for any one of Grant's detachments.

Then the balance tilted toward the Union side, as Van Dorn sought to take advantage of the situation. The Confederate commander felt he no longer had to worry about Vicksburg. His "beautiful and devoted city" was secure. Port Hudson guarded the river approaches on the south. The Federal fleets were no longer in the area.

Accordingly, Van Dorn set his sights on forcing Grant out of Western Tennessee. He could do this, he thought, by retaking Corinth. The loss of that key Union stronghold would threaten Sherman at Memphis and Grant at Jackson, and conceivably extend the Confederate Western front clear up to the Ohio River. It was a gamble, but the odds were not unfavorable. Van Dorn's forces almost equaled those of Union General William Rosecrans at Corinth.

There followed two days of bloody fighting, October 3 and 4, 1862, during which the Confederates lost 4,200 men—almost a quarter of Van Dorn's army and almost double the casualties of the defenders. Van Dorn was forced to withdraw, and Corinth remained secure in Union hands.

To Grant, who had not been present and had left the fighting up to Rosecrans, the victory was like an open sesame. "The battle relieved me from any further anxiety for the safety of the territory within my jurisdiction." He was free to consolidate his forces for a drive on Vicksburg and wrote to General Halleck of this project. Halleck offered no reply, but Grant's position was strengthened when, on October 16, he was given official command of the new Department of the Tennessee, placing the likely approaches to Vicksburg in his field of operations.

If Van Dorn's defeat had helped consolidate Grant's plans for moving against Vicksburg, it also affected Jefferson Davis's plans for the defense of his Gibraltar of the West. In early October the President replaced Van Dorn with

Lieutenant General John C. Pemberton, former commander at Charleston, South Carolina. Van Dorn's services, however, would not be lost to the Confederate defenders. Pemberton made his predecessor chief of all Southern cavalry in Mississippi and East Louisiana.

"Men born Yankees are an unlucky selection as commanders for the Confederacy," wrote Mary Boykin Chesnut in her indefatigable Richmond diary.

To substantiate this statement, she cited, among other examples, Vice-President Alexander Stephens, Mansfield Lovell at New Orleans, and John Clifford Pemberton, then major general commanding the Department of South Carolina, Georgia, and Florida.

Mrs. Chesnut's entry was dated April 29, 1862, and seemed based more on bias than place of birth. Stephens was a dyed-in-the-wool Georgian who had once opposed secession, as had many Southerners. Lovell was Maryland-born with unquestioned Southern sympathies. Only Pemberton of Pennsylvania could qualify as a native Northerner, though siding with the South since the beginning of the war.

To her curious comment Mrs. Chesnut added an equally curious quotation: "Whom the Gods would destroy, they first make mad."[5]

Pemberton would not be driven mad, though he would be exposed to the pressures of perhaps the weightiest command in the Confederacy, barring only that of General Robert E. Lee in Virginia. In addition to the exacting job itself, he would always be suspect, a victim of his Northern birth. Overlying that onus was a brusqueness of manner that dispensed with all amenities, a Yankee practicality and drive that in themselves were alien to the magnolia-conditioned natives of his first command at Charleston.

Born in Philadelphia, which his ancestors had helped to settle as early as 1682, Pemberton had made a career of the army since his graduation from West Point in 1837. He had fought in Florida, in Mexico, and on the Plains against the Indians. Stationed later at Fort Monroe, Virginia, he met, wooed, and married petite Martha Thompson of Norfolk—she twenty-two, he thirty-four—forsaking the precept that Philadelphians should marry only Philadelphians.

It was not only his marriage to Martha that turned his sympathies toward the South. It was also a matter of principle. According to his grandson and namesake, he had always been a strong States' Rights man and "never wavered in his view that the South was right." If and when secession came, he would "follow the right as he saw it."

Resigning from the United States Army in April of 1861, Pemberton served first on Joseph Johnston's staff in northern Virginia, then as second in command to General Lee at Charleston. When Lee was summoned back to Richmond, Pemberton, by then major general, commanded a large portion of the Confederate east-coast defenses.

His Northern birth was discounted by official Richmond. None, least of all Jefferson Davis, doubted his loyalty. But, to the residents of Charleston, who had found Robert E. Lee just barely tolerable, this stern-visaged, stern-willed Yankee was anathema. When Pemberton cracked down on the illegal sale of cotton to the enemy, one of the few pursuits by which some Southerners could make a living, the cry went up for his removal. Charlestonians demanded the return of Pierre Gustave Toutant de Beauregard, the flamboyant commander who had fired on Fort Sumter.

So Davis gave them Beauregard and sent Pemberton west with the rank of lieutenant general commanding the new Department of Mississippi and East Louisiana, with the particular responsibility of defending Vicksburg.

Arriving at Jackson, Mississippi, on October 14, 1862, Pemberton paused only long enough to set up headquarters in the capital, then pushed on to Vicksburg. Though appreciative of what had been done to fortify the city, he was appalled at what remained to be accomplished.

Realistically, Vicksburg's line of defenses stretched from Snyder's Bluff on the Yazoo, some ten miles above the city, to Port Hudson north of Baton Rouge—a distance of 250 river-miles. Farragut's fleet and Butler's army at New Orleans threatened one end of that line. Sherman at Memphis and David Dixon Porter—the latter having returned from the East to take over command of Charles Davis's Mississippi fleet—jeopardized the other end. Grant's forces in Western Tennessee were poised to threaten the Southern Railroad of Mississippi, Vicksburg's lifeline, connecting with the whole Confederate West. With the loss of the western end of the Memphis & Charleston Railroad, the Confederate West was more than ever dependent on the Southern line.

Of the 24,000 men of Van Dorn's original army, Pemberton concluded that "A very considerable part of these troops may be properly characterized as irregular, having little organization and less discipline." He noted that "the deficiency of guns for water defense was extreme both as to number and to character." Further, "there was scarcely an earthwork worthy of the name of defense." Making a personal inspection of Port Hudson the day after he arrived, he concluded that "if we intend to hold it, no time should be lost in greatly strengthening the defenses and increasing the garrison."[6]

There followed four weeks of frenetic activity that Vicksburg would not easily forget. None was unhappy to see Van Dorn replaced, but this dynamo of Yankee energy, manipulating troops, guns, and geography like props and puppets on a string, was new to even this war-hardened city. Mahala Roach was told one morning that a battery was to be placed on her trim front lawn that overlooked the river: ". . . and soon after breakfast the work began—tearing down fences, digging, etc., etc. I felt very badly about it, but found it was no use to do so—I must bear my part of annoyance and trouble, as much as anyone else."[7]

More upheaval was to come as the troops, along with slaves impressed from the plantations, were put to work erecting additional hill and river batteries, felling trees and dismantling houses that were either in the way or might obstruct the line of fire. North of Vicksburg, Snyder's Bluff overlooking the Yazoo was strongly fortified, while farther down, the area about the racetrack was strewn with abatis. A line of earthworks, redoubts, and rifle pits extended over the hills and hollows to the rear of the city to block a drive from the east. Guns and earthworks crowned the bluffs at Warrenton six miles below—so that Vicksburg was ringed with forts like a medieval city.

No more did Lieutenant Jared Sanders of the Twenty-sixth Louisiana complain of monotony and laziness in camp. It was a time for every man to "rush to the field," and "we will soon close a war otherwise doomed to be long & bloody." In general, army morale rose in response to more decisive leadership, though Louisiana Private Granville Alspaugh complained of excessive drilling and being up all night as corporal of the guard. He wrote to his mother that "there is no chance to get home till this war is over but I think I will run away Christmas and come home any how. I dont think they will do worst than kill me. . . . "[8]

The citizens, too, were enlisted in these preparations. In addition to volunteer hospital work for disabled soldiers, women were urged to make and repair clothing and blankets for the troops. At Brokenburn, Kate Stone devoted herself to knitting gloves. She omitted the fingers, to give the soldiers greater freedom in aiming and triggering their guns. Informed that a rifleman usually removed his gloves in battle, she knitted the fingers and sewed them on.

Dora Miller, still hiding her Union sympathies, was concerned with her own immediate problems. She and her husband had been forced to leave the Washington Hotel and were looking desperately for a place to live. They found that "Boarding-houses have all been broken up, and the army has occupied the few houses that were for rent." Frustrated in trying to find quarters, the couple agreed to part for a time, and Anderson lodged his wife on a farm some twenty miles east of town until conditions eased.

Though some of the citizens were reported as showing "a good deal of temper and irritation" at the martial restrictions imposed upon them, the commander had established a provost marshal guard of a hundred men to police the city, which at least kept rambunctious troops in hand.

In general, Pemberton had got a good reception from the local press. Both Marmaduke Shannon of the *Whig* and J. M. Swords of the *Citizen,* though wary at first, soon gave the general their approval. A few weeks after his arrival the *Whig* hailed Pemberton as "a man worthy of trust and confidence," and added: "Brief as has been his command he has brought order out of chaos, and if after the well-nigh fatal blunders of his predecessor [Earl Van Dorn] it is possible to defend ourselves against the Yankees we believe he will do it."

Equally warmly the *Daily Citizen* praised the new commander for his efficiency in completing and perfecting the defenses planned for Vicksburg by Chief Engineer Lockett, noting:

> With the practised eye of a master—the science of an engineer—he surveyed the ground at Vicksburg—at Port Hudson and at other points, and determined at a glance what was necessary, what was practicable, what was possible—the problem being to render our position impregnable and set the assailants at defiance.[9]

One outsider concerned with Pemberton's arrival to take over the Confederate command was "Sam" Grant. The two had met in 1845, when both were serving under General Zachary Taylor in the war with Mexico. Grant later said of his future opponent, "a more conscientious, honorable man never lived," and added:

> I remember when an order was issued that none of the junior officers should be allowed horses during the marches. Mexico is not an easy country to march in. Young officers not accustomed to it soon got foot-sore. This was quickly discovered, as they were found lagging behind. But the order was not revoked, yet a

verbal permit was accepted, and nearly all of them remounted.

Pemberton alone said, No, he would walk, as the order was still extant not to ride, and he did walk, though suffering intensely the while. This I thought of all the time he was in Vicksburg and I outside of it; and I knew he would hold on to the last.

Yes, he was scrupulously particular in matters of honor and integrity.[10]

It was the kind of integrity, Grant realized, that would never yield—a quality that he himself would have to reckon with.

That September, Abraham Lincoln had an unexpected visitor, one of the galaxy of generals now assembling, by chance or order, to decide the fate of Vicksburg.

John Alexander McClernand, age fifty, was a hard man to pigeonhole in this category. He had been a lawyer, a newspaper editor, a Mississippi trader, a successful and ambitious politician in the state of Illinois. During five terms in Congress he had been a Democrat, an anti-Abolitionist, yet a staunch supporter of the Union. Except for a brief stint as volunteer militiaman in the Black Hawk War, he had had no military training or experience.

But he had drive, and, as a man of influence from Lincoln's home state, he had pull. When, after First Manassas, McClernand applied for a commission in the army, Lincoln appointed him brigadier general under Grant at Cairo. Grant, who had not overcome his initial distrust of the Scotch-Irish McClernand, had later found fault with his subordinate's performance at Fort Donelson and Shiloh—with more prejudice than justice. McClernand, commanding a division, had fought well at Shiloh.

The following summer McClernand left for Washington on leave, announcing peevishly that he was "tired of furnishing the brains for the Army of the Tennessee." He had no trouble getting in to see the President, who brought Secretary Stanton into the discussion. The visitor had a proposition for seizing Vicksburg, an objective dear to Lincoln's heart.

McClernand's proposition was this: give him permission and he would raise an army of his own in the midwest—recruits, not drawing on existing Union forces—and would personally lead that army in a crushing blow on Vicksburg, ending with the capture of that city and possession of the Mississippi River.

Lincoln bought it; so did Stanton. On October 20 the President handed McClernand his sealed orders, drawn up by the Secretary. They authorized the major general to proceed to the states of Illinois, Indiana, and Iowa and recruit troops in that area.

In conclusion, the instructions read: "When a sufficient force, not required by the operations of General Grant's command, shall be raised, an expedition may be organized under General McClernand's command against Vicksburg and to clear the Mississippi River and open navigation to New Orleans."

To these secret papers, marked *Private* and *Confidential,* Lincoln added a postscript, urging that the project "be pushed forward with all possible dispatch, consistently with the other parts of the military service."[11]

The whole transaction was extraordinary, a masterpiece of ambiguities and contradictions. McClernand was basically a politician with no proven military talent. Yet he was selected by Lincoln for one of the most formidable operations of the war, even though the President knew that Vicksburg was in Grant's department and that Grant himself was preparing to move against the Mississippi stronghold. Moreover, not only was Grant not told of this decision, but General in Chief Henry W. Halleck was kept in the dark about the matter.

One other person knew of the deal, inadvertently, according to his own account. David Dixon Porter had just been given command of the Mississippi Squadron with the rank of acting rear admiral, replacing Flag Officer Davis. Before leaving for Cairo, he called on Lincoln, found him "in excellent humor," and later recorded his conversation with the President:

> "I promised you," he said to me, "that you should see Vicksburg fall, and now you shall do it. I want to ask you something about your plans, for, knowing all about the place, I suppose your measures for capturing it must be matured by this time."
>
> I assured the President that my plans were very simple. A large naval force, a strong body of troops, and patience, were the only means of capturing Vicksburg. . . .
>
> "Well," said the President, "whom do you think is the general for such an occasion?"
>
> "General Grant, sir. Vicksburg is within his department, but I presume he will send Sherman there, who is equal to any occasion."
>
> "Well, Admiral," said the President, "I have in mind a better general than either of them; that is McClernand, an old and intimate friend of mine."[12]

Porter didn't know McClernand and said as much. The President expressed surprise, saying, "He saved the battle of Shiloh when the case seemed hopeless." When Porter courteously disagreed, giving Grant the responsibility for Shiloh, the President corrected him. The credit belonged to McClernand, "a natural-born general."

"Well, Mr. President," said Porter, "with all due deference to you, I don't believe in natural-born generals except where they have had proper military training, and it seems to me the siege of Vicksburg is too important a matter to trust to anybody except a scientific military man. . . . "

Lincoln, however, requested Porter's full cooperation in the project, gave him a letter of introduction to McClernand, and asked him to call on the Illinois general before leaving Washington. Porter did so. He found the President's protégé at his hotel, "and he [McClernand] talked in the most sanguine manner of taking Vicksburg in a week!"

Porter did not report to Lincoln on the interview. He told Assistant Navy Secretary Gustavus Fox that he hadn't the time; he was leaving for Cairo in two hours to see Grant. He informed Fox of McClernand's plan to raise troops in the northwestern states and added: "He is shortly to be married, and if he proposes to recruit an army in that way, I think it will be hardly worth while to wait for him."[13]

Despite Porter's often faulty observations, he was right on one point. McClernand had more than dreams of military glory on his mind. He was engaged to Minerva Dunlap of Jacksonville, Illinois, twenty-four years his junior, and sister of his first wife, long deceased. What better way to celebrate a marriage than a honeymoon on the Mississippi River, with a ringside view of the bridegroom's army storming the Queen City on the Bluffs? And after glorious victory, what next? Andrew Jackson had risen to President as hero of the Battle of New Orleans.

While McClernand hurried back to Springfield and Porter traveled on to Cairo, Lincoln wrestled with another problem in command. Who should replace Butler at New Orleans? General Butler, with his intransigent, sometimes outrageous policies, had not only aroused unnecessary hatred in Louisiana but had embarrassed his own government. Above all, he had balked at cooperating properly with Farragut in the amphibious campaign for Vicksburg during the preceding summer.

Lincoln's choice of General Nathaniel P. Banks as successor to Butler was as strange as his selection of McClernand to command the Vicksburg expedition. Banks, like Butler, was a Massachusetts politician, one whose indifferent performance in the East had won him the nickname, based on his initials, of "Nothing Positive" Banks.

The President made it plain what he expected of his new commander in the Department of the Gulf. The opening of the Mississippi was listed as Banks's top priority. The Confederate river stronghold of Port Hudson represented the most serious obstacle to Banks's projected drive up the Father of Waters. It must be taken. In these instructions no mention was made of McClernand's covert role.

"It is generally regarded as an axiom of war," wrote Grant of his first attempt to capture Vicksburg, "that all great armies moving in an enemy's country should start from a base of supplies, which should be fortified and guarded, and to which the army is to fall back in case of disaster."[14]

Though he established his base at Columbus, Kentucky, on the Mississippi, he started his movement south in early November, by concentrating his army about the railway at Grand Junction, Tennessee. From here he wired Halleck: "I will go on to Holly Springs and maybe Grenada, completing railroad and telegraph as I go." He planned to reach these places by following the tracks of the Mississippi Central, depending on the railroad for communications and provisions.

There was a weakness he recognized in this procedure. In previous campaigns, notably his move against Fort Donelson and up the Tennessee, he had relied on the rivers for supplies. With Union gunboats on the waterways, he'd felt secure. Railroads were a different proposition. With Confederate cavalry on the loose, under such men as Earl Van Dorn and Nathan Bedford Forrest, tracks could be torn up, bridges burned, and depots wrecked, faster than they could be repaired. The deeper he pushed into Mississippi, the more precarious his lifeline to Columbus would become.

Sherman had advocated going down the Mississippi. "I am daily more convinced," he wrote to Grant, "that we should hold the river absolutely and leave the interior alone . . . with the Mississippi safe we could land troops at any point. . . . "[15] But this had been tried by Foote and Davis and, from the south, by Farragut and Butler. The bluffs of Vicksburg had proved too forbidding. Better to approach the city from the rear. Grant would rely on Sherman at Memphis to protect his right flank, as he marched his army south toward Jackson, Mississippi, east of Vicksburg.

Accompanying the expedition was war correspondent Sylvanus Cadwal-

lader, representing the Chicago *Times.* Cadwallader's credentials were a subterfuge. Newspaper reporters were in bad odor with the Union army, especially
with Grant and Sherman, who had suffered from their invective. Cadwallader's predecessor had been jailed for releasing confidential information. It
was the newcomer's secret mission to secure the prisoner's release, with argu-
ments and documents supplied to him by his employers on the *Times.*

Despite this initial deception, which Grant quickly penetrated, Cadwallader
remained in the general's good graces as a trustworthy reporter and a person
of good judgment. He won the approval, too, of Grant's adjutant, John Rawlins. In time both Rawlins and Cadwallader became among Grant's more
trusted personal allies, remaining close throughout his campaigns in the
West.

As Grant marched his 30,000 troops toward Holly Springs, Pemberton
shifted his forces from Vicksburg and Jackson up to the Tallahatchie River to
block their further progress south. Then, his flank threatened by Federal
troops, which had crossed the Mississippi from Arkansas, Pemberton pulled
back to Grenada on the Yalobusha River, sixty miles below the Tallahatchie.
The retreat might be a trap, thought Grant, designed to lure his army deeper
into hostile Mississippi, exposing his rear to Confederate attack.

Already his line of supplies was dangerously long, almost two hundred miles
back to Columbus. He began stockpiling provisions and ammunition at Holly
Springs, deciding to make this his new base of operations. But more than
military considerations made him hesitate to push across the Tallahatchie and
force a showdown with Pemberton at Grenada.

"At this stage of the campaign," he wrote, "I was very much disturbed by
newspaper reports that General McClernand was to have a separate and
independent command within mine, to operate against Vicksburg by way of
the Mississippi River." He recorded his reactions with restraint:

> Two commanders on the same field are always one too many, and in this case
> I did not think the general selected had either the experience or the qualifications
> to fit him for so important a position. I feared for the safety of the troops intrusted
> to him, especially as he was to raise new levies, raw troops, to execute so
> important a trust.[16]

Indignantly Grant telegraphed Halleck, demanding to know what was going
on behind his back: "Am I to understand that I lie still here while an expedition
is fitted out from Memphis, or do you want me to push south as far as
possible."

Halleck was equally indignant at not being told about McClernand's ma-
chinations. In fact, the mishandled affair seemed to heal the rift between
himself and Grant and establish a bond of sympathy between them. He wired
back: "You have command of all troops sent to your department, and have
permission to fight the enemy where you please."[17]

That was all the reassurance that Grant needed. He sent word to Sherman,
asking him to bring his two divisions down to Oxford, leaving only enough
men to garrison Memphis. Together they would smash through Pemberton's
forces by sheer weight of numbers, then proceed on to Jackson and from there
to Vicksburg.

In Richmond, Jefferson Davis was keenly disturbed by the war reports from his adopted state of Mississippi and the growing threat to Vicksburg, telling Robert E. Lee that, "In Tennessee and Mississippi the disparity between our armies and those of the enemy is so great as to fill me with apprehension." From Pemberton were coming pleas for reinforcements, either from Braxton Bragg's Army of Tennessee or from over the river in Arkansas, where Theophilus Holmes commanded the Trans-Mississippi Department with a questionably estimated 50,000 troops.

It was difficult to give advice, much less official orders, over such an intervening distance. He needed someone on the spot, to serve as mediator or coordinator and bring "greater cooperation among the armies." James A. Seddon, his new secretary of war, convinced him of the right man for the job, and on November 24 Davis appointed Joseph Eggleston Johnston, fifty-five, commander of all Confederate troops between the Alleghenies and the Mississippi.

It is reasonable to suppose that Johnston was as reluctant to accept the post as Davis was to offer it. There had never been any love between them. Some said their hostility dated from West Point days and a feud over the daughter of a tavernkeeper in the town. Whatever the cause, it took their wives to maintain peace between them, and Varina Davis personally called on General Johnston to wish him well in his assignment.

Johnston himself was eager to get back in service, though not fully recovered from the wounds he suffered when commanding the Confederate army at Seven Pines. Yet he balked at this particular appointment, telling Davis he considered himself "unfit for duty."[18] Presumably he meant for duty in the field, yet he ended up with "full power to direct the entire Western campaign." It was considered by some a graver responsibility than that incurred by Johnston's successor in Virginia, General Lee. Lee had one army to command; Johnston had two—that of Braxton Bragg in Tennessee and of Pemberton at Vicksburg.

Even before he left Richmond for his assigned headquarters in Chattanooga, Johnston urged the transfer of Holmes's idle troops in Arkansas to Mississippi. Jefferson Davis supported him in this appeal, though not going as far as making it an order. Holmes refused, maintaining that political necessity demanded that he keep his troops in Arkansas. It was a border state, and needed to be guarded in full force.

Becoming more alarmed, Davis decided to visit the troubled area himself. Governor Pettus had urged him to do so. "You have often visited the army of Virginia," he wired the President. "At this critical juncture could you not visit the army of the West? Something must be done to inspire confidence." Senator James Phelan added his plea: "If ever your presence was needed . . . this is the hour . . . you can save us or help us save ourselves from the dread evils now so imminently pending."

Davis responded to these pleas and to the dictates of his conscience. "I propose to go out there immediately," he told Lee, "with the hope that something may be done to bring out men not heretofore in service, and to arouse all classes to united and desperate resistance."[19]

He left Richmond in secret, to avoid arousing alarm and speculation, and stopped off at Chattanooga to pick up Johnston before going on to confer with

Braxton Bragg at Murfreesboro. He persuaded Johnston and Bragg to send 9,000 of the latter's troops to support Pemberton in Mississippi, and then, with Johnston still in tow, proceeded on to Vicksburg by way of Jackson, arriving at the Terraced City on December 19, 1862.

By rights, Vicksburg should have welcomed its adopted son with some measure of enthusiasm. But the city was too preoccupied with its peril to do more than observe the minimum courtesies. General Martin Smith lined up his troops for a formal review by their commander in chief. But, according to William Chambers, by the time the President's party arrived, "the men had been in line six or seven hours without food, and did not feel as enthusiastic as they did in the early morning." As a member of the provost marshal's guard, Chambers himself was able to get a good view of the President:

> He is a spare made man, and I should say a rather ugly one. His complexion is sallow and his face is on the "hatchet" order. He was attired in plain citizen's dress, and I should think there was little in his appearance to mark what he really is—one of the most noted men now living—and, as I think, posterity will regard as one of the greatest.[20]

Of General Johnston who stood beside the President, Chambers noted: " 'Old Joe' looked the most perfect specimen of a soldier I ever saw. 'Rough and ready' in exterior he impresses one at a glance that he is no ordinary man." Which seemed to be the reaction to "Little Joe" or "Uncle Joe" wherever the Virginian went. He lacked the dash of Sherman or the common touch of Grant, but he inspired a curious devotion among the troops he headed, even in defeat.

For two days the President's party inspected the Vicksburg defenses, from Snyder's Bluff on the Yazoo to Warrenton sixteen miles below. Then they traveled by rail through Jackson, to visit Pemberton's army and entrenchments at Grenada. Here Johnston discovered, and later confessed to, a basic difference between him and Pemberton. At both Vicksburg and Grenada, Johnston was critical of the Confederate fortifications and preparations, writing that "in discussing the defense of his department, Lieutenant General Pemberton and myself differed widely as to the mode of warfare best adapted to our circumstances."[21]

Simply stated (though not by Johnston), Pemberton preferred to fight from fixed positions, strongly fortified; Johnston tended to favor movement and mobility that might keep the enemy off balance. Little Joe would gladly relinquish any amount of real estate if it led to ultimate victory; Pemberton considered each position under his command a sacred trust, to be defended at whatever cost. It was a difference that would affect not only their future relations but also the fate of Vicksburg.

Meanwhile Grant, having maneuvered Pemberton's Confederates back from the Tallahatchie to Grenada, paused to reconsider his position. From Admiral Porter in Cairo had come news confirming McClernand's plan to launch a private expedition against Vicksburg. New recruits, reported Porter, were daily pouring through Cairo on their way to Memphis, which would be the base of this new, independent operation.

Grant forthwith revised his strategy. "I was authorized to do as I thought best for the accomplishment of the great object in view," he later wrote. What was best in this case was to prevent McClernand from taking over the expedition—more important than trying to battle through Pemberton's defense line in an effort to reach Jackson.

He talked it over with Sherman, recalling Halleck's telegraphed assurance that "You have command of all the troops in your department." Surely this gave him authority over McClernand's new recruits assembling at Memphis. What if Sherman should go back to Memphis, team up with Porter's fleet, and snatch the expedition out from under McClernand's foxy nose?

It was what Sherman had advocated all along: an expedition down the Mississippi. With the aid of Porter's gunboats, Sherman could effect a landing below Snyder's Bluff on the Yazoo River and storm the city from the north. Grant's important role would be to keep Pemberton's forces pinned down at Grenada, leaving Vicksburg defended by only the 6,000 troops of General Martin Luther Smith's command.

Sherman promptly left with one division for Memphis, where his command would be reinforced by two more divisions, and on that day Grant wired Halleck: "General Sherman will command the expedition down the Mississippi. . . . I will cooperate from here." That, he thought, would settle the McClernand matter.

Grant made no secret of his motives, later admitting:

> My action in sending Sherman back was expedited by a desire to get him in command of the forces separated from my direct supervision. I feared that delay might bring McClernand, who was his senior and who had authority from the President and Secretary of War to exercise that particular command—and independently.[22]

Admiral Porter was motivated by the same desire. He had taken command of the Mississippi Squadron at Cairo, eager to share in the Vicksburg expedition. "I thought myself lucky to have two such generals as Grant and Sherman to cooperate with." His fleet was constituted much as it had been under Flag Officer Davis, with the recent addition of a number of "tinclads," or shallow-draft, lightly armored gunboats.

Even before Sherman arrived back at Memphis, Porter had assembled a flotilla at the mouth of the Yazoo River for the purpose of destroying Confederate batteries and mines, and setting up landing areas for Sherman's troops. He was in for an ugly surprise. A Confederate naval officer in New Orleans, named Beverly Kennon, had for some time been experimenting with an electrically activated torpedo, or mine. He had come to Vicksburg in the fall of 1862 to impart his knowledge to a couple of other inventive naval officers, Zedekiah McDaniel and Francis M. Ewing.

Guided by Kennon's experiments, McDaniel and Ewing gathered several glass demijohns and filled them with powder obtained from the artillery. Copper wires with primers attached were inserted in the necks of the flagons, and the demijohns were affixed to floats that would suspend them just below the surface of the water. Strategically anchored in the channel of the Yazoo, the copper wires were extended to camouflaged "torpedo pits" on shore, where volunteers stood by secretively to detonate the mines.[23]

On December 12, as the Federal squadron of five vessels steamed up the Yazoo, the ironclad *Cairo,* one of James Eads's proudest creations, struck first one of these demijohns, then another. Twelve minutes later it was at the bottom of the river, beneath thirty-six feet of water. The *Cairo* had at least made history. This was the first recorded incident in naval annals in which a warship had been sunk on contact with a mine.[24]

On the day of this disaster Sherman reached Memphis and moved full speed ahead with preparations for the Vicksburg expedition. Two infantry divisions detached from the Department of the Ohio arrived at Memphis and were added to his own expeditionary force, giving him roughly 32,000 troops, including another division waiting to join him at Helena.

Meanwhile, he wrote, "Admiral Porter dropped down to Memphis with his whole gunboat fleet, ready to cooperate in the movement. The preparations were necessarily hasty in the extreme, but this was the essence of the whole plan, viz., to reach Vicksburg as it were by surprise. . . . "[25]

Vicksburg would not be surprised—the *Cairo*'s foray up the Yazoo had provided ample warning—but McClernand surely would be. On December 12 he had telegraphed Washington from Springfield, to report that he had sent forward 40,000 men for his assault on Vicksburg, was ready to move, and was awaiting only his official orders. After waiting almost a week for a reply, he began to suspect that there was monkey business going on and sent identical messages to the President and Secretary Stanton: "I believe I am to be superseded. Please advise me."[26]

Stanton referred the message to Halleck, who apparently intended to ignore it. McClernand forced his hand. On December 16, he wrote directly to Halleck: "I beg to be sent forward, in accordance with the order of the Secretary of War on the 21st of October, giving me command of the Mississippi expedition."

That at least got some results, though not what McClernand had expected. In a last-minute effort to straighten out the mess, Halleck telegraphed Grant, "The troops in your department . . . will be divided into four corps. It is the wish of the President that General McClernand's corps shall constitute a part of the river expedition, and that he shall have immediate command under your direction." He asked Grant to forward these instructions to McClernand.[27]

To the general in Springfield, there was a galling difference between leading his own army and serving as merely a corps commander under Grant. His instinct was to rush down to Memphis and confront his superior with a *fait accompli.* But he was committed to the calendar date of December 23, when his marriage to Minerva Dunlap was scheduled to take place. He put aside all other considerations and headed for Jacksonville on a special train bearing the governor and other selected guests invited to the ceremony.

Of the reception that followed the wedding, the Springfield *Journal* reported:

> The Dunlap House was crowded with the youth, beauty, and intelligence of Jacksonville. . . . First came the bride and groom, the former dressed in beautiful white satin with a magnificent veil falling over her shoulders nearly to the floor, and the usual orange flowers in her hair; the latter in the full uniform of a major

general. . . . The bridegroom, although much older than his lovely partner for life, looked very well indeed, and bore himself admirably upon the occasion. . . . Promenading, dancing, and conversation concluded the entertainment of the evening.[28]

Immediately after these festivities the bride and groom, along with the ushers and bridesmaids and Governor Richard Yates, embarked on a special train for Cairo. There the entourage would transfer to a Mississippi steamer bound for Memphis where the general would assume command of his awaiting army. The wedding party and the governor would accompany the expedition down to Vicksburg, to enjoy a grandstand seat at the conquest of that city.

On the afternoon that McClernand led his young bride to the altar, General Sherman was on the Mississippi River, some miles below Helena and 400 crowflight miles from Jacksonville. Aboard the steamer *Forest Queen,* he distributed maps and final instructions to his four division commanders: Generals Frederick Steele, George W. Morgan, A. J. Smith, and Morgan L. Smith. In the projected capture of Vicksburg, he told them, "We are to act our part —an important one of the great *whole.* "[29]

Theirs was not a single, unsupported operation. General Grant was determined to hold Pemberton's army in northern Mississippi; Admiral Porter's gunboats were already taking their positions above Vicksburg—"each in perfect harmony with the whole."

That was the key: perfect harmony with the whole. If their mission was successful, Sherman told his commanders, it would be "probably the most decisive act of the war."

❊ 8 ❊

Assault on the Bluffs

Eearl VAN DORN, so thoroughly a Mississippian that he had river water in his veins, knew Holly Springs like the back of his hand. He knew every dip in the surrounding landscape, every possible access leading to the little railroad town.

Only two months earlier, in October 1862, before Pemberton had taken over the command of troops in Mississippi, Van Dorn had headquartered in Holly Springs. And good-naturedly, "Cump" Sherman, in command of Federal-held Memphis, arranged for his former fellow cadet at West Point to enjoy a few of the amenities of life. He saw to it that Van Dorn was regularly supplied with cigars, liquor, boots, and gloves—simply by looking the other way as these were smuggled out of Memphis.

But fraternity between antagonists, however common in this war, could be carried only so far. It reached its limit when Sherman's patrols overtook a sedately decorated hearse lumbering innocently out of Memphis. A hearse and coffin without mourners in attendance seemed to call for an investigation. The casket was pried open and found to contain medical supplies for Van Dorn's army at Holly Springs. Thereafter Sherman cracked down on the traffic, feeling his courtesy had been abused.

Since then Van Dorn had been demoted, if demoted is the proper word, from command of the army to head of Pemberton's cavalry, a role he would have performed better to begin with. Now, in the still dark hours of December 20, he was visiting Holly Springs again, instructed by his new commander to destroy the abundance of arms, ammunition, and supplies that Grant had assembled there for his invasionary expedition. The post was only scantily garrisoned by some 1,500 Illinois and Wisconsin troops commanded by Colonel R. C. Murphy of the Eighth Wisconsin Infantry.

In the woods surrounding Holly Springs, Van Dorn's 3,500 gray-clad horsemen waited for the crack of dawn. Then, with the spine-tingling Rebel yell, first heard in chorus at Manassas Junction, the gray riders swept into town from multiple directions. Surprise was complete. Most of the garrison was rounded up and captured before having time to fall in line, after which the raiders put the torch to ammunition dumps, provision depots, trains and storage sheds, sending up in smoke, according to Van Dorn's estimate, some $1,500,000 worth of supplies essential to Grant's continuance of his campaign.[1]

If Van Dorn did little more in the Civil War—and little more, he did—he had with this single blow pulled the rug out from under Grant in Mississippi and thwarted the first land assault on Vicksburg. Sherman did not know it yet and would not know it, until he, too, was crippled indirectly by this strike at Grant's supplies.

Grant would never forgive Colonel Murphy for this capture of his garrison. Murphy, he insisted, "was warned of Van Dorn's approach, but made no preparation to meet him. He did not even notify his command." He considered Murphy's role in the affair "disgraceful."[2] But there was more bad news to come.

In conjunction with Van Dorn's thrust at Holly Springs, Nathan Bedford Forrest, at Pemberton's request, led his Confederate cavalry in an auxiliary raid on Grant's supply lines. Of all Confederate cavalry leaders in the West, observed Cadwallader, Forrest was the only one whom Grant sincerely dreaded, largely because he "was amenable to no known rules of procedure, was a law to himself for all military acts, and was constantly doing the unexpected, at all times and places."[3]

This was one of those times and places. Detached from Bragg's army below Nashville, Forrest led his force of some 2,500 peerless horsemen across the lower Tennessee in mid-December. Routing opposing Federal troops near Lexington, the hard-riding column struck the railroad lines between Jackson, Tennessee, and Columbus, Kentucky, burning bridges, trestles, depots, tearing up sixty miles of track and tearing down all telegraph wires on the route.

Grant sought to inform Sherman that this twin catastrophe "cut me off from supplies, so that further advance by this route is perfectly impracticable." But Grant had been isolated from all contact, and Sherman never got the message (only some hearsay he would not believe), and never learned that one half of their plan had gone awry. He would continue his downriver drive, confident that, when he reached Vicksburg, Grant would have taken care of Pemberton and would be waiting with his army to aid Sherman in the final, critical assault.

What Grant feared most, had happened. His supplies destroyed by Van Dorn, and his means of replacing them destroyed by Forrest, he had no choice but to pull back to Grand Junction, leaving Pemberton free to return with his army to Vicksburg. And leaving Sherman to stumble blindly, and alone, toward disaster.

Grant's immediate problem was getting his troops back safely to Grand Junction, where they'd started from. Mississippians were openly exultant over Van Dorn's raid and the Yankee general's obvious embarrassment. Civilians taunted the general by asking how he planned to feed his army, with his supplies at Holly Springs destroyed. Grant told them bluntly that he expected the Mississippians to feed his soldiers, since it was their troops who had destroyed his depot.

Accordingly, as Cadwallader reported, "Trains of wagons, heavily guarded, were sent out by scores, for twenty-five miles on both sides of the road from

Yocknapatafa to Holly Springs, and stripped the country of all food for men and animals. Mills were erected, grain ground, fat stock driven in and slaughtered by thousands, and abundant supplies obtained. To people's inquiries as to what the inhabitants should live upon, Gen. Grant advised them to move further south. His army would not be allowed to starve while there was anything to live upon within reach."[4]

"I was amazed," Grant later wrote, "at the quantity of supplies the country afforded. It showed that we could have subsisted off the country for two months . . . without going beyond the limits designated. This taught me a lesson which was taken advantage of later in the campaign. . . . "[5]

But this happy discovery did little to ease his immediate concern for Sherman's plight. There was still no way of informing that general that half of their joint endeavor had collapsed. Already, Grant knew, elements of Pemberton's 22,000-man army were on the way back to Vicksburg. There, with General Smith's garrison of 5,500 troops, the combined Confederate forces would be more than a match for Sherman's expeditionary force.

In Vicksburg, elation over the exploits of Van Dorn and Forrest was tempered by news that Porter's fleet was in the Yazoo River, and Sherman was on his way from Memphis. Until Pemberton's army had time to return from the Yalobusha, the city was defended only by the small garrison under General Smith. The women of the community drafted a petition for a day of prayer, and the council, meeting on December 20, passed a resolution calling for twenty-four hours of "Humiliation, Fasting, and Prayer to Almighty God, that Vicksburg may be spared from the Hand of the Destroyer. . . . "

General Smith tightened up restrictions on the civilian population. All new arrivals must register with the military authorities, while all who could leave the city were advised to do so. Rowland Chambers needed no urging. "After a family consultation we thought prudence the better part of valor." He put his wife and children on the train for Clinton, some miles short of Jackson, while "I remained at home to try and take care of the place as best I could under the circumstances."[6]

On December 26 General Pemberton, back at Vicksburg, issued a more commanding proclamation:

> It is earnestly recommended that all the noncombatants, especially the women and children should forthwith leave the city . . . the places of supposed protection with which I am informed many have provided themselves during the progress of a battle here, may prove wholly insufficient for their safety. When the city becomes crowded with the soldiery, it will be impossible to afford the helpless those aids and facilities which humanity might seem to demand.[7]

The *Daily Whig* published notices of country homes accepting refugees, one advertisement reading: "A few nice persons, who come well recommended, can get board at my house one mile from Bovina. . . . Boarders must furnish themselves with lights and bedding. Board can be had only while the enemy threatens Vicksburg."

William Chambers had been detached from picket duty on the Yazoo and brought back to Vicksburg to serve in the newly-formed provost marshal's guard, created to keep order during the emergency. The 100-man detachment, he discovered, included 75 French Creoles from Louisiana, "but few of whom could speak or understand a word of English." Chambers was posted with two of them at the court house, "utterly in the dark as to my duty." There was no conversation to relieve the tedium. He found himself looking forward for diversion to the ear-splitting clamor of the court house bells that sounded out the hours.[8]

With Christmas approaching, Mahala Roach decided to leave the city for Woodfield till the storm blew over. She had learned to live with the guns that General Smith had planted on her lawn, even felt a sense of propriety over the battery and the gray-clad artillerists. But now two companies of Louisiana Artillery had settled on the field below. They had no tents, and when it rained Mahala invited them to use her gallery for shelter. Then she offered them Tommy's room to put their baggage in. By nightfall, ten of them were sleeping on the floor.

Finally the wagons arrived from the plantation to pick up her trunks and baggage, and Mahala took leave of her beloved home. First, however, she turned over her keys to the captain commanding the battery, inviting him and his troops to make use of the house. That night she was safe at Woodfield, nursing a sore throat and reading a "kind message" from a distant cousin, President Jefferson Davis, who had just arrived in Mississippi.[9]

Davis and Johnston, after their tour of inspection of Confederate defenses in the region, had returned to Jackson where the President was scheduled to address the Mississippi legislature and attending visitors on December 26. In the opinion of Governor Pettus and Senator Phelan, who were with him on the platform, this was the real purpose of his visit: to inspire confidence among the people of Mississippi by his words and presence.

Davis could speak with conviction of a natural and warm attachment to his adopted state. Though as President he could favor no one section of the South above another, "Yet my heart has always beat more warmly for Mississippi, and I have looked on Mississippi soldiers with a pride and emotion such as no others inspired."

He excoriated the Northern aggressors who had singled out Vicksburg as the target of their barbarous invasion. " 'But vengeance is the Lord's,' and beneath His banner you will meet and hurl back these worse than vandal hordes." He had "every confidence in the skill and energy of the officers in command" and the valor of the troops defending Mississippi, and adjured them, "Vicksburg must not fall!"[10]

He had barely sat down to polite applause when the cry went up for "Johnston! Johnston!" All but raising the rooftops with their clamor, the audience would not be denied. "Little Joe" finally took the stand, and his words were as brief as Davis's were long:

Fellow citizens: My only regret is that I have done so little to merit such a greeting. I promise you, however, that hereafter I shall be watchful, energetic, and indefatigable in your defense.[11]

Johnston remained at the capital, to set up temporary headquarters in the city, while Davis went to visit his brother Joseph at a new plantation he had bought near Bolton. The Yankees coming up from New Orleans had burned

Hurricane, the old plantation on Davis Bend, and the President's Brierfield was later pillaged, though the slaves had escaped and the manor itself remained.

In fact, Yankee troops appeared to be on the rampage all up and down the Mississippi valley. At Brokenburn, Amanda Stone purchased a secluded farm on a nearby bayou, to which she sent her slaves for safety. For the whole neighborhood, all of Madison Parish, in fact, was suddenly alive with bluecoats. From Milliken's Bend on Christmas Day, General Sherman dispatched Burbridge's infantry brigade and a detachment of the Sixth Missouri Cavalry —to wreck the Vicksburg, Shreveport & Texas Railroad and generally disrupt communications between the city and the Trans-Mississippi states.

Brokenburn's slaves escaped the roving eyes of the marauders, but a matter of much greater import struck the household. That morning Kate's younger brother Johnny had set out on foot for Milliken's Bend to catch a glimpse of the reported gunboats and had not returned by nightfall. It would be four anxiety-ridden days before the family would learn what happened to him.

As it turned out, Johnny had been picked up by a Federal patrol and taken aboard a gunboat to be questioned on the disposition of Confederate "troops, guns, government stores, etc." With the insouciant smile of a fourteen-year-old, Johnny acted the role of a deaf mute and enjoyed himself immensely. His refusal to be intimidated aroused the admiration of the crew. "Hang on, bub," they whispered to him on the side—and Johnny did.

After three days of interrogation, Colonel Clark Wright came aboard to wring the truth from this recalcitrant. The men, said the colonel, were anxious to see Johnny hanged—as others had been—for withholding information. He wanted to spare him such a fate, if Johnny would only tell him what he knew, in confidence. Johnny smiled sunnily and kept his lips sealed, and in final exasperation they released him. "Clark was just kidding," he told Kate on arriving home. "I knew they'd never hang me."[12]

Christmas at Woodfield was also made anxious by reports that Yankee troops were attempting to land at Blake's Plantation on the Yazoo River, "prepared for their grand attack on us." In her diary Mahala Roach invoked God's help in this, "the hour of our great need," and she closed her journal on a somber note: "Now I am an exile and may soon be homeless—the tide of war has rolled to our very doors, and a battle is raging a few miles from our home."[13]

"You may calculate on our being at Vicksburg by Christmas," Sherman had written to Grant on leaving Memphis. "River has risen some feet, and all is now good navigation. Gunboats are at mouth of Yazoo now, and there will be no difficulty in effecting a landing up Yazoo within twelve miles of Vicksburg."

He was close to schedule, as the expedition reached Helena two days later to pick up Frederick Steele's division of 12,000 troops. But there had been no reply from Grant, and at Helena disturbing rumors reached him of Confederate raids on Grant's supply line. Sherman refused to be alarmed. If the rumors were true, the raids might "disconcert" his colleague, but he still expected and assured his commanders that "General Grant . . . will meet us on the Yazoo."[14]

Leaving Milliken's Bend later on Christmas Day, the armada proceeded down the Mississippi to Young's Point and tied up. The procession of transports and warships made "a magnificent sight," recorded Sherman. "Admiral Porter's gunboats took the lead; others were distributed throughout the column, and some brought up the rear. . . . Some few guerilla parties infested the banks, but did not dare molest so strong a force as I then commanded."[15]

A detachment of Porter's gunboats went ahead to secure the Yazoo for a distance of twenty miles. The naval task force had more to worry about than mines. Lieutenant Jared Sanders with the Twenty-sixth Louisiana Infantry had been sent to the banks of the Yazoo to "annoy the gunboats." While a man with a rifle might seem hardly a match for an ironclad vessel with eight-inch naval guns, the odds were in favor of the hidden snipers. Sanders discovered he could pick his targets at will among the men and officers on deck and generally score a kill. The gunboats could only reply by shelling the surrounding woods where no enemy was visible.[16]

The day after Christmas, while Davis was addressing the Mississippi legislature, Pemberton returned to Vicksburg with some troops from Grenada. A Christmas Eve ball at the Crawford Street home of Dr. and Mrs. William T. Balfour, attended by a number of officers, was terminated by news that, in addition to the gunboats, enemy transports had been sighted on the river. At dawn of Christmas Day, General Smith ordered the Vicksburg garrison under arms, and regiments holding the Walnut Hills line were alerted.

Sherman's sixty transports and supply vessels steamed up the Yazoo from the Mississippi, and the following morning more than 30,000 troops representing four divisions were disembarked at the Johnson Plantation near the mouth of Chickasaw Bayou.

The maps which Sherman had distributed to his commanders—the two Smiths, Steele, and Morgan—showed Chickasaw Bayou originating at McNutt Lake and meandering northeasterly for about one mile in front of Walnut Hills, then turning north and flowing to the Yazoo River. A triangular belt of lowland, five miles across at the base, its apex at Snyder's Bluff, lay between the Yazoo and the bluffs. The entire area, alternately wooded and cleared, was cut up by bayous and sloughs.

What the maps did not show was the forbidding nature of that stretch of bottom land, traversed by Chickasaw Bayou, which could not be easily forded in the face of enemy resistance. It was a terrain as difficult, Sherman observed, as man and nature could possibly make it. Rifle pits, artillery, and abatis covered every feasible approach over this area to the bluffs.

"Sherman at every point encountered obstacles of which he had never dreamed," wrote Admiral Porter, comfortably aboard his flagship. "Forests had been cut down in the line of Chickasaw Bayou, and through the *chevaux-de-frise* the soldiers, standing up to their waists in water, had to cut their way with axes across the dismal swamps." And that was not all:

To add to Sherman's difficulties, the rain came on—and such a rain! The heavens seemed to be trying to drown our army; the naval vessels and transports were the only arks of safety. The level lands were inundated, and there were three feet of water in the swamps where our army was operating.[17]

Battling his way inland from the Yazoo toward the bluffs, Sherman divided his forces, sending the two divisions under Morgan Smith and A. J. Smith to the right toward Vicksburg, partly to find an opening nearer the city, partly as a feint to draw off Confederate defenders in the center of the line. It was in the center, opposite the triangular fork of Chickasaw Bayou, that he planned to launch his main attack, with General Morgan supported by Frederick Steele's division.

On December 28, as Morgan's troops reached the fork in Chickasaw Bayou, Confederate resistance stiffened. In dead center of the Devil's Triangle, between fork and bluffs, were nests of rifle pits manned by the Twenty-sixth Louisiana under Colonel Winchester Hall. "General S. D. Lee rode to our regiment," wrote Lieutenant Sanders with the regiment, "and told us we had the post of honor." But they would pay dearly for that honor.

The Federals hammered at the rifle pits for seven hours. "It was almost impossible to look over the works so fast flew the enemy's shot," wrote Jared Sanders. "We lost eight killed and four wounded that evening. It was so sad to hear the groans of the dying around us. The brave boy who was killed in our company had his brains blown partly out and he lay there picking out the remainder with his fingers, & uttering most piteous moans."[18]

Monday, December 29, dawned cool and cloudy, with a sense of impending battle in the air. The Twenty-sixth Louisiana crawled out of their blankets, instantly restless and reaching for their rifles. To keep them occupied, Colonel Hall ordered them out on reconnaissance. With strict orders: just look around; avoid any contact with the enemy. But the mist was lifting from the flats, and minutes later the Louisianians were face to face with a regiment of Morgan's bluecoats.

"The temptation was too much for the naughty boys," wrote Colonel Hall like a scolding father. They eagerly opened fire and kept on peppering the "bluebellies" until all had fled. As the Louisianians started in pursuit, Hall drew his revolver and ran to block their path, threatening to shoot the first man who should try to pass him.[19]

After which the withdrawn Federals were treated to a baffling sight. Either to punish his insubordinate troops or keep them out of further mischief, Hall lined them up and put them through the manual of arms, followed by close-order drill. War was full of surprises, but this exhibition of military calisthenics, staged in full sight of the enemy before a major battle, was in a category by itself.

Sherman that morning stood beside General Morgan at the front. Facing them was the amphitheater of Walnut Hills, with gun emplacements and rifle pits at its base, paralleling the Valley Road, and batteries guarding Snyder's Bluff five miles to the left.

The general explained his battle plan to Morgan, who would command his own division, supported by that of Frederick Steele. The two Smiths would keep the graybacks occupied on the left end of the Confederate line near Vicksburg, while Porter's gunboats would keep the defenders occupied at the right end of the line near Snyder's Bluff. Morgan, supported by Steele, would cross the three hundred yards of flats separated by the bayou, for the main assault against the center of the enemy line at the base of the bluffs. As

Sherman recorded in his *Memoirs*: "General," said Morgan, "in ten minutes after you give the signal I'll be on those hills."[20]

Morgan did not remember, even denied, making such a boast. He did recall, however, that, after Sherman had left, his Assistant Adjutant General, John H. Hammond, returned to give Morgan "his exact words": "Tell Morgan to give the signal for the assault; that we will lose 5,000 men before we take Vicksburg, and we may as well lose them here as anywhere else."

According to Morgan, "I told him to say to General Sherman that I would order the assault; that we might lose 5,000 men, but that his entire army could not carry the enemy's position in my front; that the larger the force sent to the assault, the greater would be the number slaughtered."[21]

Despite these contradictory views, General Morgan called his brigades into line for the attack. He noted that others shared his fatalistic view of the result:

> Colonel [John F.] De Courcy, who was an officer of skill and experience, approached and said; "General, do I understand that you are about to order an assault?"
>
> I replied, "Yes; form your brigade!"
>
> With an air of respectful protest he said: "My poor brigade! Your orders will be obeyed, General."[22]

At ten o'clock Federal artillery began its opening bombardment, and the Confederate batteries replied. To Kate Stone at Brokenburn, the gunfire sounded as if coming from the next plantation, while at Woodfield Mahala Roach found the cannonading "Fearful." In Vicksburg itself the tremors seemed to carry through the earth as if on conduits, and to Rowland Chambers it was as if the hills themselves began to shake.

Finally, toward noon, the shelling ceased. Sherman had given the signal to attack.

Jared Sanders, whose company had suffered so heavily the day before, found the Louisiana troops again the center of attack, and recorded with literary relish the advance of the Federal ranks "in daring style, with banners flying." At first they seemed unaffected by the hail of shells from the batteries on the heights, but:

> Very soon our infantry opened fire upon them & our cannon belched forth a perfect stream of lead and iron. Then could be seen the grandest and most magnificent aspect of war, an angry collision of hostile forces. . . . It was magnificent to look upon, and I enjoyed it greatly. . . .
>
> When they came closer to our lines I could see men falling by crowds—officers tumbling from their horses & horses dashing over the field; and then our brave men began to fire in such volleys upon them that they could advance no further but turned about & made off "at a run." Shout after shout rose from our lines that told—"Victory was ours."[23]

On the right of Sanders's regiment, Private William Chambers saw the action only obliquely, through a fringe of intervening willows, but "How the nerves quivered and the heart wildly beat to join the fray!" He waited for an order to advance, which never came. He only heard, above the booming

artillery, "the din of small arms, piercing the sky with its clear, shrill alto."
Then "the shouts of victory along our lines swelled louder and louder."

From behind the Federal lines, General Morgan at first saw only the backs
of his advancing troops as they "came under a withering and destructive fire.
A passage was forced over the abatis and through the mucky bayou and
tangled marsh to dry ground."

So far so good, but at this point, wrote Morgan, "All formations were
broken; the assaulting forces were jammed together, and, with a yell of desperate determination, they rushed to the assault and were mowed down by a storm
of shells, grape and canister, and minié-balls which swept our front like a
hurricane of fire." They were terribly repulsed, the general admitted, but there
was no rout or panic, and the troops retreated "slowly and angrily. . . . "

DeCourcy's brigade and Blair's brigade, each mustering an attacking force
of four regiments, on opposite sides of Chickasaw Bayou, pushed toward the
Confederate line, seized advanced rifle pits, only to be driven back by a hail
of bullets and artillery projectiles. To the right of DeCourcy the Fourth Iowa
of Thayer's brigade gained the far bank of the bayou, where it was pinned down
by murderous fire. Other regiments of the brigade wandered off in the wrong
direction and failed to cross the bayou.

A half-mile to DeCourcy's right, the Sixth Missouri crossed Chickasaw
Bayou at the Indian Mound. On the opposite side the infantrymen were halted
by intense fire. Efforts by pioneers to mine the abrupt bank were unsuccessful.
Sherman observed of their predicament:

> The men of the Sixth Missouri actually scooped out with their hands caves in
> the bank, which sheltered them against the fire of the enemy, who, right over
> their heads, held their muskets outside the parapet vertically, and fired down.
> So critical was the position, that we could not recall the men till after dark, and
> then one at a time.[24]

Fierce enemy resistance foiled efforts to throw a bridge over Chickasaw
Bayou between Indian Mound and the line of DeCourcy's advance.

It was Sherman's first independent command in the field, and it had ended
in disaster. He would in time blame no one but himself, "rather than throw
it off on any generous and brave men or set of men." But, anticipating diatribes
from the Northern press, which followed in abundance, he insisted that "There
was no bungling on my part, for I never worked harder or with more intensity
of purpose in my life. . . . "[25]

And of Morgan's hapless brigades and those who had failed to come to their
support, the general was sharply critical, especially so in the light of Morgan's
promise to be "on those hills" within minutes. In reply, besides denying that
he had ever made such an extravagant boast, Morgan claimed that his troops
had fought valiantly and well and had been defeated only by terrain.

There was justice in the latter claim, and according to Morgan he had called
Sherman's attention to the problem when the point of attack was selected:

> Our troops had not only to advance from the narrow apex of a triangle, whose
> . . . sharp sides bristled with the enemy's artillery and small-arms, but had to
> wade the bayou and tug through the mucky and tangled swamp, under a wither-

ing fire of grape, canister, shells, and minié balls. Such was the point chosen for the assault by General Sherman. What more could be desired by an enemy about to be assailed in his trenches![26]

In any event the Federal repulse had been complete. Sherman's casualties totaled 1,779. The Confederates had lost 187. Morgan asked that a flag of truce be sent to the enemy, with permission to bury the dead and rescue the wounded. At first, Sherman rejected the proposal as an admission of defeat, but later changed his mind. It was a moot point. He himself had declared of the expedition: "Our loss had been pretty heavy, and we had accomplished nothing, and had inflicted little loss on our enemy."[27]

Nevertheless, he thought of renewing the assault, but not against Walnut Hills or anywhere opposite Chickasaw Bayou, where Morgan had been proved right. His whole army was not strong enough to take that line. Further up, however, around Snyder's Bluff, he would have the support of Porter's gunboats. He borrowed a horse and rode upriver in search of Porter.

"That night," wrote Porter, "General Sherman came aboard my flagship drenched to the skin. He looked as if he had been grappling with the mud and got the worst of it." Despite the general's cavalier message to Morgan that he was ready to sacrifice 5,000 men if necessary, Porter found him depressed by the losses which he had suffered, and by the knowledge that the Northern press would crucify him with "their ridiculous stories about Sherman being whipped, etc." Porter tried to cheer him up by saying: "Only seventeen hundred men! Pshaw! That is nothing; simply an episode in the war. You'll lose seventeen thousand before the war is over, and will think nothing of it. We'll have Vicksburg yet. . . . "[28]

The two decided on a plan to storm Snyder's Bluff. Porter's gunboats would cover the landing and provide artillery support for the attack. The position at Chickasaw Bayou would be retained for a simultaneous assault on the Walnut Hills line. Steele's division and Giles Smith's brigade, comprising 10,000 troops, were embarked aboard the transports for the trip upriver.

With the fate of the *Cairo* in mind, the admiral sent one of Ellett's rams in advance, to explode any mines that might be in their path. "If we lose her, it does not much matter," the admiral decided. Colonel Charles R. Ellett indignantly concluded otherwise. He attached a wooden framework to the bow of the ram, to snare the torpedoes forty-five feet ahead before they made contact with the ship.[29]

The attack on Snyder's Bluff, set for dawn of New Year's Day, never got off the ground. It rained heavily throughout the preceding night, and the current was so strong that the vessels had to be fastened to the trees. "The wind," wrote Porter, "howled like a legion of devils, though which side it was howling for I have no idea."

The next morning Porter sent word that his fleet was fogged in; the gunners could not even see the bluffs. Sherman in turn noted that the Yazoo River was approaching flood conditions, and concluded that it was the better part of wisdom to abandon the campaign.

He had had no word from Grant, who had not come to his support. And, while waiting for the fleet to return for the troops, Sherman could hear, from the direction of Vicksburg, the whistles of arriving trains, apparently bringing up Confederate reinforcements. He could also see "battalions of men marching up . . . and taking posts at all points on our front." He concluded later that, had he renewed the attack, "we might have found ourselves in a worse trap, when General Pemberton was at liberty to turn his whole force against us."

His official report of this first land assault on Vicksburg was the shortest he ever submitted:

> I reached Vicksburg at the time appointed, landed, assaulted and failed, re-embarked my command unopposed and turned it over to my successor.[30]

The successor, of course, was John McClernand who, Sherman wrote laconically, "it was rumored had come down to supersede me."

Steaming down from Cairo with his bride of seven days, McClernand had reached Memphis on December 30 and looked around for the army he'd recruited. There was no army. It had left, he was told, with General Sherman on December 20.

McClernand found this "strange." First he had been reduced from leader of the expedition to commander of an army corps; now the whole army had gone on without him. He continued downriver aboard the *Tigress,* like a frantic father in pursuit of an abducted offspring and, near the mouth of the Yazoo, caught up with Porter and the gunboat fleet. The admiral sent word at once to Sherman: "McClernand is at the mouth of the Yazoo, waiting to take command of your army!"[31]

Coming on top of the disaster at Chickasaw Bayou, it was a bitter pill to swallow. Sherman wrote to his wife Ellen that he would "submit gracefully. . . . The President has a perfect right to choose his agents." But, to his brother John, he confessed his true emotions. "Mr. Lincoln intended to insult me and the military profession by putting McClernand over me. . . . I never dreamed of so severe a test of my patriotism as being superseded by McClernand."[32]

Nevertheless he hurried downriver ahead of the army transports, to confer with the Illinois general aboard the *Tigress.* The black-bearded, foxy-eyed McClernand was no harbinger of sweetness and light. With what seemed like secret satisfaction, he told his visitor of Grant's misfortune at the hands of Forrest and Van Dorn. Sherman no longer could count upon his friend and ally for support. He, McClernand, was taking over what would now be known as the "Army of the Mississippi." It would be divided into two corps, one under Sherman, the other under General Morgan, whom Sherman blamed in large degree for the failure at Chickasaw Bayou.

Beyond the patronizing remark that Sherman had "done as well as could be expected under the circumstances," the new commander had little to offer. "At that time I don't think General McClernand had any definite views or plans of action," Sherman wrote. "If so, he did not impart them to me. He spoke in general terms of opening the navigation of the Mississippi, 'cutting his way to the sea,' etc., etc., but the *modus operandi* was not so clear."[33]

Sherman, however, itching to redeem his repulse at Vicksburg, did have a plan for the army now returning to Milliken's Bend. Twenty miles up the Arkansas River lay Fort Hindman, better known as the Post of Arkansas, held by some 5,000 Confederates under Brigadier General Thomas Churchill. So long as the post remained, the enemy had a base from which to interfere with

Federal use of the Mississippi River. Sherman proposed, with 10,000 troops and the aid of Porter's gunboats, to take possession of the fort.

McClernand liked the idea—liked it so well that he took it over for himself. He would personally lead the army up the Arkansas, and conquer that state for the Union. He had no instructions from Grant to do so, but the move, in Grant's absence, would establish his authority as *de facto* head of the Army of the Mississippi.

Waiting until the last minute, when no countermanding order could be received, he telegraphed Grant announcing this new expedition into Arkansas, whose results would be "the counteraction of the moral effect of the failure of the attack near Vicksburg and the reinspiration of the forces repulsed by making them the champions of a new, important, and successful enterprise."[34]

Since Porter's gunboats were essential for support, the two generals called on the admiral aboard his flagship to discuss the plan. They found Porter surprisingly brusque and uncooperative. He had known of Sherman's project and had previously approved it. Why this sudden change?

Sherman took Porter aside and wormed the reason out of him. Porter admitted he couldn't stand McClernand, resented every inch of the man. If Sherman were leading the expedition, he would go along, but not with McClernand in command. It took a good deal of tact, but Sherman persuaded him to put personal feelings aside, for the sake of the common goal. Porter finally acquiesced, but he would go along himself, not simply assign the gunboats to McClernand.

On January 5 the expedition got under way. Disembarking from transports on the morning of January 10, the troops approached the Post of Arkansas. That evening Porter's gunboats shelled the fort until after dark. That night, in bright moonlight, army scouts reconnoitered the post and reported most of the outlying rifle pits abandoned.

But Sherman, after the slaughter at Chickasaw Bayou, was taking no chances. He did his own reconnoitering:

> Personally I crept up to a stump so close that I could hear the enemy hard at work, pulling down houses, cutting with axes, and building intrenchments. I could almost hear their words, and I was thus listening when, about 4 A.M. the bugler in the rebel camp sounded as pretty a reveille as I ever listened to.[35]

Daylight of January 11 revealed a line of rifle pits supported by artillery extending westerly from the fort to a bayou. The intervening ground totaled 700 yards in width with little natural protection for attacking troops. At 1:00 P.M. the gunboats renewed bombardment from the river, and Sherman's corps on the right and Morgan's on the left slowly advanced under heavy fire, "once or twice falling to the ground for a sort of rest or pause."

As the fight grew steadily hotter, Sherman noted that "the rebel troops fired wild," but the field guns "kept things pretty lively." When he realized that the gunners were aiming at himself and his staff, he "made his staff scatter." As the gunboats drew closer, Sherman saw their flags over the parapet of the Post of Arkansas.

They saw something else, as well—a Confederate soldier on the ramparts, waving a large white flag, while smaller flags sprouted all along the battlements. Sherman gave the order to cease fire and rode forward to accept the fort's surrender. "I saw that our muskets and guns had done good execution; for there was a horse-battery, and every horse lay dead in the traces . . . and dead men lay around very thick."[36]

It had been a costly conquest. Against less thann 150 Confederates killed and wounded, the attacking force suffered more than 1,060 casualties. Though twenty-year-old Private Isaac Jackson of the Eighty-third Ohio Infantry was shocked at the heavy losses in his regiment, he took comfort in the aftermaths of victory, writing to his brother back in Harrison, Ohio,

> I lost my blanket in the engagement and got a large white bed quilt in the fort to serve in its place. I have small trophies I wish to send home . . . could have picked up almost *anything* after the surrender. I nearly forgot to tell you that we captured 4,793 prisoners, 4 or 500 mules, several pieces of artillery and plenty of other kinds of property and ammunition.[37]

It had been Sherman's and Porter's victory all the way. McClernand had had "a man up a tree" to keep him informed of the progress of the battle. When Sherman called to report in person:

> . . . I found General McClernand on the *Tigress,* in high spirits. He said repeatedly: "Glorious! glorious! my star is ever in the ascendant!" He spoke complimentarily of the troops, but was extremely jealous of the navy. He said, "I'll make a splendid report. . . . "[38]

The "splendid report," designed to reflect glory on McClernand, was the seed of his undoing. In it, according to Sherman, he "almost ignored the action of Porter's fleet altogether." Porter was outraged, and Sherman shared his indignation. Together they wrote to Grant, with whom communications were restored, urging him, according to Grant, "to come and take command in person, and expressing distrust of McClernand's ability and fitness" for so important a position.

Accordingly, as McClernand withdrew his army to the mouth of the Arkansas River, Grant came down from Memphis to investigate. On first hearing of the attack on the Post of Arkansas, he regarded it as a wasteful deviation from the main campaign for Vicksburg. On learning of the capture of 5,000 Confederate troops who might otherwise have interfered with the campaign, he changed his mind and considered the conquest of Fort Hindman "very important."

What bothered him now, however, was the uncertain status of McClernand. "It was evident to me that both the army and the navy was so distrustful of McClernand's fitness to command that, while they would do all they could to insure success, this distrust was an element of weakness. It would have been criminal to send troops under these circumstances into such danger."[39]

He would have been glad to put Sherman in McClernand's place, "to give him an opportunity to accomplish what he had failed in the December before." But Sherman was McClernand's junior, and, though Halleck had given him authority to relieve or replace the Illinois general, there was a certain code of justice to be followed.

"Nothing was left, therefore," wrote Grant, "but to assume the command myself."[40]

A week elapsed, while Grant returned to Memphis to make certain that "all the territory behind me was secure," and while McClernand brought his expeditionary force almost 200 miles downriver to Young's Point, on the west bank of the Mississippi, south of Milliken's Bend. Here Grant rejoined the army and took over command from McClernand on January 30.

If he expected an uproar from the dispossessed commander, he was anything but disappointed. The general, he wrote, "took exception in a most characteristic way—for him." As so often with a man whose wrath is boundless, McClernand did himself more harm than those he castigated. With vituperative letters, he attacked on all fronts—accusing Grant of "creating confusion," Stanton of betrayal, and Halleck of "wilful contempt . . . and utter incompetency." He crazily demanded of Lincoln that he, the President, take over Halleck's duties as general in chief, suggesting that he at least could do no worse.

With extraordinary patience, Lincoln replied that he was already beset by "too many *family* controversies (so to speak)," and he begged the Illinois general, for his own sake and the nation's sake, to confine his attention to the common goal of Union harmony and victory. It was enough to hold McClernand in check—for the present, at any rate.

It had been nine months, roughly, since Farragut had started up the Mississippi in the first thrust toward Vicksburg, only slightly more than that since Foote had started down from Cairo. In that time the campaign for the city and the Mississippi Valley had been one of shifting fortunes and directions, fluctuations in authority, changes in command. No central figure had emerged to bring cohesion to the operation.

Now there was a single general whose control extended over both banks of the river, including a piece of Arkansas and Louisiana, who had the unqualified support of President Lincoln and General Halleck, the approval of Admiral Porter, and the undivided loyalty of General Sherman. And as Ulysses Grant saw it at the end of January 1863, "The real work of the campaign and siege of Vicksburg now began. . . . "[41]

❧ 9 ❧

Of Time and the River

I F, as Grant stated, the real work of the campaign for Vicksburg was beginning, part of the job was determining how and where to start. Despite the crushing blow dealt to him at Holly Springs the previous December, he still believed that the strategic point of attack was from the rear or east of Vicksburg, following—as he had intended—the line of the Mississippi Central Railroad down to the vicinity of Jackson and then swinging west.

He had failed in this approach before. But he was wiser from that failure. If he tried again, he would establish his depot at Memphis rather than Columbus, giving him a shorter supply line to defend and a base that could not be easily destroyed. And he had learned from losing his supplies at Holly Springs that it was highly possible to live off the land in fertile Mississippi.

There was one grave drawback, more political than military, to persisting in this plan. Northern morale was at an all-time low. The November elections had gone against the Washington administration. Volunteer enlistments had declined; army desertions had increased. After the December setbacks at Fredericksburg and Chickasaw Bayou, many Northerners saw no satisfactory ending to the war.

Rumors of a growing Copperhead conspiracy in some northwestern states, aimed at a Western Confederacy independent of the Union, were coupled with "Howls from New England," where Boston arch abolitionist Wendell Phillips predicted that, if the war continued in its present vein, "the West will desert the East and join her natural ally who holds the mouth of the Mississippi."[1]

The influential journal *New Mercury* replied: "Just so, Mr. Phillips." And went on to say, "We believe the North has already put forth the greatest strength she will ever exert in this struggle. She is capable of more, but *she has lost heart in the cause.*" She had lost heart, the editor believed, because of the "gross mismanagement" of the Washington administration and its generals.[2]

In early January 1863 the New York *Herald,* which a year before had boasted of "crushing the rebellion in ninety days," confessed to see "no speedy termination of our troubles," while the New York *Times,* three weeks late in giving the details of Sherman's rebuff at Chickasaw Bayou—and blaming the delay on deliberate government concealment of the facts—called that "shame" to the nation "one of the greatest and most disgraceful defeats of the war."[3]

If, in the face of all this fatalistic criticism, Grant pulled his troops back from in front of Vicksburg and took them with the fleet upriver to Memphis, it would popularly be regarded as a "backward movement" or retreat—and a lengthy 350 river-mile retreat at that.

"There was nothing left to be done," he wrote in recollection, "but to *go forward to a decisive victory.* This was in my mind from the moment I took command in person at Young's Point."[4]

So far as manpower went, his reunited forces were more numerous than any he had hitherto commanded. McClernand's visionary "Army of the Mississippi" was no more. Grant reorganized the troops and their commanders into four corps: the Fifteenth under Sherman, the Thirteenth under McClernand, the Seventeenth under James Birdseye McPherson, with General Stephen Hurlbut's Sixteenth Corps retained on standby in Tennessee.

Excluding the Sixteenth Corps, Grant's Army of the Tennessee totaled some 62,000 men. The editor of *Harper's Weekly* appraised it more extravagantly:

> No monarch of Europe ever gathered together so many men, so many vessels of war, so many guns for any single purpose. In comparison with the forces commanded by McClernand, Grant, Banks, Porter, and Farragut, the allied expedition to the Crimea was an insignificant affair . . .
>
> Should the war be finally settled by a pitched battle in the heart of Mississippi, as Jeff Davis predicts, the forces engaged will probably be twice as numerous as those that fought at Waterloo, and our army ought to exceed that of the rebels by a large percentage.[5]

The reference to Banks and Farragut in this encomium was, by then, an irrelevant tribute. Neither, at that time, was waging a campaign to conquer Vicksburg or Port Hudson. Despite the instructions given Banks, that "The President regards the opening of the Mississippi River as the first and most important of our military and naval operations," he was moving slowly. His 30,000 troops were more than double the number of Confederates holding Port Hudson, above Baton Rouge, but "Nothing Positive" Banks remained cowed. He called on Washington for heavy artillery. "The enemy's works at Port Hudson . . . are formidable. Our light field guns would make no impression on them."[6]

So, while Lincoln saw the campaign for the Mississippi as a two-pronged drive from both north and south, it appeared that Grant would be obliged to act alone—for now, at least. Both the President and Halleck seemed to some extent aware of this.

"You must not rely too confidently upon any direct cooperation of General Banks and the lower flotilla," Halleck cautioned Grant, "as it is possible that they may not be able to pass or reduce Port Hudson." The most to be hoped for was that Banks's operations, whatever they turned out to be, might "occupy a portion of the enemy's forces and prevent them from reinforcing Vicksburg."[7]

Meanwhile Grant's southern flank at Vicksburg remained unprotected, nor could he move in that direction. Porter's vessels could not pass the batteries to get below the city. Which was part of Grant's dilemma, as he saw it: "The problem was to secure a footing upon dry ground on the east side of the river from which the troops could operate against Vicksburg."[8]

Sherman's defeat at Chickasaw Bayou had demonstrated that Grant could not effect a tenable landing above the city—without going so far north that an overland approach would be impractical. South of the city the terrain provided more suitable ground for offensive operations. But how were ships to get below the batteries, to escort the troops across?

In effect, Grant's immediate war was with the river, with time and the river. The January rains had been among the worst on record. The Vicksburg *Whig* for January 9, 1863, reported that the Mississippi was rising at the rate of two and one-half inches a day, had climbed two feet in the previous week. It was a question of moving fast before all flat land on the west bank of the river became a sheet of water or waiting interminably for the river to subside—and delay was as bad as retreat in the eyes of a disheartened nation.

Weighing both the objective and the problems, Grant launched a series of what he chose to call "experiments" and what history might call the battles of the bayous. They were moves suggested not so much by him or his associates as by the nature of the river and by previous attempts to tame it. One of these early, aborted efforts lay under his nose, the vestiges of the trans-peninsula canal begun by General Thomas Williams during Farragut's blockade of Vicksburg the preceding summer.

Williams's intentions then were the same as Grant's intentions now—to provide a channel for the fleet to pass below the city without having to run beneath the batteries. Lincoln had had a personal interest in the scheme since he first heard about it, and now Halleck urged Grant by telegraph to "Direct your attention particularly to the canal proposed across the point. The President attaches much importance to this."[9]

Even before he returned from Memphis, Grant ordered work renewed on the canal. Marmaduke Shannon of the *Whig* reminded his readers that he had repeatedly urged the Vicksburg authorities to fill in the abandoned ditch before the Federal fleet returned and made some use of it. Now, in January, the *Whig* reported:

> The enemy have at last got a boat into the canal, destroying the prognostications of the "wiseacres" who last summer declared the canal could never be made navigable, and that it was useless to fill it up. A steamer supposed to be a dredge boat was seen yesterday plying up and down the canal, and we suppose that a few more days will suffice to make it navigable for the enemy's gunboats.[10]

Shannon's alarm was premature. What he or his reporters evidently saw was a small light-draft steamer, the *Catahoula,* commandeered by Lieutenant Wilson for an exploratory tour of the abandoned waterway. Aboard with Wilson was Chicago correspondent Sylvanus Cadwallader, who was not impressed with what he saw. Swollen as the Mississippi was, it was not high enough to fill the shallow ditch, of which the reporter noted:

It was standing full of still water, without any current whatever and quite as much inclined to empty itself into the river above Vicksburg as below it. My first feeling was one of great disappointment. The canal was shallow and narrow, and not one-tenth part of the work had been expended on it which I foresaw would be necessary for heavy transports, to say nothing of Porter's ironclads.[11]

Cadwallader believed that Wilson "fully agreed with my estimate." But when Grant returned from Memphis he made his own inspection of the channel. He instructed Wilson to make some changes in its course, especially in the angles of its junctions with the Mississippi, and "to widen and deepen it throughout," to accommodate ships of greater draft and wider beam than had been presaged for its predecessor.

Even with these proposed enlargements Cadwallader remained pessimistic, writing later that "As a matter of historical interest it may be stated that very little water ever ran through it, and the theory that a small stream once diverted into it would soon widen and deepen it, until it became the main channel of the river, was completely exploded."

Yet the work went on, of therapeutic value to the troops if nothing else. All but one army corps was involved. From Tennessee, McPherson's corps proceeded to Lake Providence, seventy miles upriver from Vicksburg on the west bank of the Mississippi. Thus they escaped the canal digging operations on De Soto Peninsula. Meanwhile they were enjoying other benefits as well. McPherson discovered, as Grant had learned on returning from Holly Springs, that one could live high off the land in the Mississippi Valley. McPherson's industrious foragers treated their chief and themselves to a daily menu of "roast turkey, chicken, meat pies, corn bread, wheaten cakes, and stewed fruit."

Sherman and McClernand's troops were assembled at Young's Point, ten miles upriver from Vicksburg and opposite the mouth of the Yazoo. Together they contributed 1,000 men a day to work on the canal with picks and shovels, aided, as in General Williams's earlier effort, by gangs of blacks impressed or hired from the neighboring plantations. It was a battle on two fronts. At one and the same time, Sherman noted, "We were digging the canal while fighting off the water of the Mississippi which continued to rise and threatened to drown us."[12]

Along with this unequal struggle, living conditions for the troops were dreadful. With the winter rains and rising river, dry ground was at a premium. The men camped on the levees or lived aboard the transports. Grant maintained headquarters in the ladies' cabin of the riverboat *Magnolia,* on which the Chicago correspondent Sylvanus Cadwallader managed to wangle quarters of his own. Sherman was forced to room in the house of a Mrs. Groves, "which had water all around it, and could only be reached by a plank-walk from the levee built on posts."

And there was the everlasting mud, extending horizontally and perpendicularly to infinity. Isaac Jackson, customarily complaining to his sister Sarah of the bitter January cold, now wrote with satisfaction, "Last night it was so cold it froze the mud so that we could walk over it without breaking in." He was able to tramp to the levee for a glimpse of Vicksburg, four or five miles distant. "I could see their fine buildings with their nice shade trees. . . . We can only see that part of the city which lays next to the river. They say the largest part of the city lays the other side from the river."[13]

When the mud thawed with the rising sun, the quagmire gave rise to a grim, mephitic crop. Many of the dead from Sherman's assault at Chickasaw Bayou had been loosely buried in a strip of bottom land between the river bank and levee. Now, observed Cadwallader, "Teams that were still contriving to drag through to the transports for supplies would often strike the end of the box or coffin and heave it clear out of the ground."[14]

The exhausted workers now had another imperative: reburying the uprooted dead. There was no high ground for miles around, where a spadeful of earth was not replaced by water. But the banks of the levee proved reasonably firm and these, according to Cadwallader, were soon "literally honeycombed with excavations."

One coffin, accidentally emptied, was appropriated by a member of the burial party. He smuggled it aboard the *Magnolia* to be used as a bedstead, unaware that its original occupant had died of smallpox. Whether or not this caused the subsequent outbreak of illness in camp—"There are but few who have not had a sick spell," Isaac Jackson wrote—it forced Rawlins to have the *Magnolia* fumigated and kept the regimental surgeons overworked and apprehensive.

In early February Grant wired Halleck, "Work on canal proceeding as rapidly as possible." A response came not from Halleck but from Lincoln: "Cannot dredge boats be used with advantage on the canal? There are four lying idle at Louisville. . . . " Dredge boats appeared, and the work went faster.

Comfortable aboard the *Black Hawk,* Porter and his naval crew observed the infantry's bedevilment with wry amusement. Porter saw Sherman sloshing and swearing through the mud, "half sailor, half soldier, with a touch of the snapping turtle," and invited the general aboard for a glass of hot rum.

"If this rain keeps up," the admiral assured his guest cheerfully, "we won't need a canal. The whole peninsula will disappear, troops and all, in which case the gunboats will have the field to themselves."[15]

Sherman was not amused. With growing impatience, he concluded that "trying to turn the Mississippi by a ditch" was "a pure waste of human labor." To Grant he wrote: "The river is about full and threatens to drown us out. The ground is wet, almost water, and it is impossible for wagons to haul stores from river to camp, or even for horses to wallow through."

Scathing criticism came from other sources, predictably the Northern press, which had made Grant and Sherman particular targets for abuse. Grant's "Big Ditch" was another sign of that general's "imbecility." Despite this anti-Grant campaign and Sherman's discouragement over the canal, Cadwallader recorded:

> This work was pressed forward with all the force that could work at it, until the rise of the river, which came soon after, did actually overflow about all of Young's Point and rendered its further prosecution impossible. It had been so nearly completed that one or two light draft vessels had traversed nearly its entire length. Our delay in completing the work had been so great that the Confederates had planted batteries on the opposite shore exactly opposite its mouth by which an enfilading fire could destroy vessels in the lower two-thirds of its length.[16]

In point of fact, Grant himself was becoming disillusioned in the project. It was simple logic that the Confederates would shift some of their guns to face the mouth of the canal, as soon as it neared completion and became a threat. But, as others despaired, Grant maintained a show of optimism. Even if the work should fail, it was keeping the troops occupied, and idleness was fatal to morale.

Moreover, the Big Ditch was only one ace up his sleeve in the winter's campaign for Vicksburg. He wired Halleck, "What may be necessary to reduce the place, I do not know, but, since the late rains, think our troops must get below the city to be used effectively." And he had a possible way of getting the troops below the city, which was shaping up before the work on the canal was winding up.

"Vicksburg is daily growing stronger," Pemberton telegraphed Jefferson Davis the first week in January, adding simply: "We intend to hold it."[17]

He had every reason to feel confident and buoyant. Not only was his own star in the ascendancy, outshining the cloudy suspicions born unfairly of his Yankee heritage, but Vicksburg itself had valiantly withstood—with only insignificant losses and a massive sense of pride—the first furious assault of Federal land forces. Echoing many calamity howlers in the North, the Southern press coupled Sherman's repulse at Vicksburg with Lee's fierce stand at Fredericksburg, as marking a turning of the tide toward Southern victory.

In an editorial headed WIDE AWAKE, Marmaduke Shannon wrote in the *Daily Whig:*

> One of the last signs of evidence of the sagacity of our government, is to be found in the fact that it has determined to spare no cost or labor in defending Vicksburg —or in other words, the key to the navigation of the Mississippi River. Great as is the importance of holding the capital of the Confederacy, or our seaboard cities, the great Valley of the Mississippi is infinitely of greater moment.[18]

Shannon followed this up with a later comment dated January 10:

> All the information we receive from the North, through the abolition journals, indicates that the backbone of invasion has been broken, and that the South is fast getting into position from which it can descry the dawn of independence in the horizon. Common sense is beginning to teach the Northern people the utter hopelessness of the task they have undertaken, and from the present signs in the abolition sky, the great "anaconda" will soon lie prostrate at our feet.[19]

The Jackson *Mississippian,* which had always taken a somewhat patronizing attitude toward its neighboring city on the river, pulled out all stops in its assessment of the present struggle:

> Too much importance cannot be attached to the engagement already commenced at Vicksburg. The contest there is yet undecided. . . . But if we prove ourselves equal to the emergency that is now upon us, and baffle the enemy at Vicksburg and Port Hudson . . . the war will be virtually closed.
> The banks of the Mississippi, either at Port Hudson or Vicksburg, will be the theater of the last grand battle waged by an intolerant fanaticism against the dear

bought rights of a free people. . . . The curtain is now rising upon the last act of the drama. If we play our part well, as we will do, our cause is safe.[20]

Port Hudson, too, glad to regard itself an ally of its sister city on the north, hailed "the heroic example of the gallant little city of Vicksburg, in beating back the vandal foe." Observed the editor of the Port Hudson *News*, "The very hills resound with praises of her determined, brave and self-sacrificing people, and will stand as living monuments . . . to the heroic, daring and gallant defense of their own uncontaminated soil." Lest his readers fail to heed the inherent message, the editor added:

> Port Hudson, a modest little village, . . . is now destined to take its place, side by side, and hereafter will ever be associated with the Hill City in the defence of the Mississippi valley and the discomfiture of the Yankee invaders. What Vicksburg has done Port Hudson will do.[21]

"With unconcealed emotion and frank gratitude," according to his grandson, General Pemberton expressed to his troops "his high appreciation of their recent gallant defense of this important position," continuing:

> All praise is due them, not alone for so bravely repulsing the renewed assaults of an enemy vastly superior in numbers, but equally for the cheerful and patient endurance with which they have submitted to the hardships and exposure incident to ten successive days and nights of watchfulness in the trenches, rendered imperatively necessary by the close proximity of the opposed armies.[22]

Vicksburg, as the general had said, was indeed growing stronger, with the arrival of reinforcements from Braxton Bragg in Tennessee and additional units from the state of Georgia, where the Augusta *Chronicle* declared that "Whatever may be the fate of Vicksburg, she has done enough to deserve a place in history beside those cities whose defense has been the most heroic, and whose names have become illustrious." The *Chronicle* expressed pride that Georgia battle flags should stand with those of other states on that "rock which stands immovable against the raging flood of invasion. . . . "

Yet, although Pemberton's forces had increased by 13,000 between Christmas and the second week in January, there had been one serious depletion. As newly-appointed commander in the West, Joe Johnston had transferred most of Pemberton's cavalry under Earl Van Dorn—as many as 6,000 mounted troops—to Braxton Bragg's department, leaving Pemberton only a small detachment of Mississippi horsemen.

Though it sowed the seeds of dissension between them, Pemberton made no immediate complaint. Johnston assured his subordinate that one reason for the move was to help keep Federal forces out of Mississippi and Middle Tennessee, which would mean, in effect, protecting Vicksburg's vulnerable eastern flank. But it left Pemberton "sightless," without the cavalry necessary for reconnaissance. Had Grant been anywhere near his rear, in Mississippi, he would have worried more. But now Grant's army was in plain sight, muddied down across the river, and the terrain north of Vicksburg was so badly flooded that Pemberton had little fear of an attack by land.

And army morale among the troops at Vicksburg, as generally follows victory, was reassuringly high. A correspondent for the *Daily Whig* reported, shortly after Sherman's withdrawal from Chickasaw Bayou:

> We passed along our line on Sunday forenoon and were much gratified by the spirit manifested by the troops. Their courage seems to rise with the emergency, and there appears a determination in every eye to make our flag their pillar of fire by day and by night, and to allow nothing upon its folds but the record of its glories.[23]

Private William Chambers and his comrades of the Forty-sixth Mississippi were in a jocular mood as they returned to camp from the front-line trenches —as he recorded in his journal: "It was raining again and the road was desperately muddy. The whole way was lined with newly arrived soldiers, who amused themselves near the *real* slippery places, by calling to some imaginary person *up a tree* and seeing some fellow lose his footing, as he looked upward while walking along." Chambers himself "slid down a steep hill in a sitting posture, with my haversack of cooked food, and several shovels full of slush boiling over between my thighs."[24]

Sergeant William H. Tunnard of the Third Louisiana Infantry was among those newly arrived troops replacing those withdrawing from the trenches. They wasted no time in getting settled. "In the absence of tents," he wrote, "the men excavated houses in the abrupt hill-sides, forming the roofs of rough shingles, firmly supported by posts—erecting, in fact, those rude shelters with a celerity truly astonishing, for which soldiers are proverbially famed."

Defending, as they henceforth would, the northern approaches to Vicksburg, "they were nerved to a determination never before witnessed, and, notwithstanding . . . were full of life and fun." Tunnard, however, was conscious of the grave responsibility involved. "The stake now being played for was a tremendous one, being the possession of the Mississippi River, the destiny of the whole valley, and the vital life and safety of the country."[25]

Lieutenant Jared Sanders, after the Federal withdrawal, wrote in a letter addressed to "dear friend" on January 4: "I think the war is beginning to close; and that *six months* will find us 'home again.' " He had talked to many Yankee prisoners who insisted that "They don't want to fight us any more. They say the army . . . does not expect to take Vicksburg." The troops of Sanders's Twenty-sixth Louisiana Infantry reaped unexpected benefits from the battle of Chickasaw Bayou:

> Our men have many large overcoats & other Yankee equipments. Some of them got over 100$ in "green-backs." For 10$ in Yankee green-backs one can get 15$ in Confederate notes in Vicksburg. Smugglers buy them to trade off to the enemy for contraband goods. There is a great deal inspiring excitement on the battlefield. . . .[26]

The plundering of enemy dead and wounded on the field, even though rightfully the spoils of victory, were frowned upon by both sides in the war. But the Twenty-sixth Louisiana, which had allegedly been first to open fire in the battle and had borne the brunt of the subsequent fighting, returned as heroes to the city. Colonel Hall received so many gifts for his men from grateful citizens that he published "A Card of Thanks" in the *Daily Whig:*

> With the enemy at our homes, and our property in their possession, the present, to the regiment, is timely and priceless. God bless our peerless Southern women! May history and tradition accord to them the proud niche won by their faith and works in the great cause; and may that live on in the memory of our volunteer army until every eye is too dim to recognize the beautiful, and every heart too feeble to give one throb for affection.
>
> WINCHESTER HALL, Colonel Com'g.[27]

The colonel evidenced his own faith in his troops and those defending Vicksburg by deciding that the city was now a safe enough place to bring his family. His wife and four children arrived by horse and carriage, and Hall boarded them at Mrs. Down's home on the edge of town, while he himself lived with a number of fellow officers at the Masonic Hall.

Marmaduke Shannon, alternating caution with enthusiasm, told the readers of the *Daily Whig* on January 6, "our heart beats lighter and freer. Everywhere our cause is propitious and everywhere we find men in command who have given assurance of their ability. Forward is the flight of our young eagle! Onward presses the gallant army of the young Confederacy, and backward sullenly retire the beaten legions of the abolitionists."

Temporarily, at least, the citizens reflected this euphoria. Rowland Chambers, after the Yankees had withdrawn from Chickasaw Bayou ("minus about 1500 who stay to enrich the soil") wrote with uncustomary fervor in his diary: "The clouds disappeared last night and the sun rose in all its splendor as tho the God of the universe was smiling on us with approval of our endeavor to maintain our independence and bless us in a righteous cause, and may it be so for Christ sake."

By the end of January, "Grant's Big Ditch," which Marmaduke Shannon had warned would be completed in two weeks, was no longer a matter for concern. From Sky Parlor Hill at the top of the bluffs, from which the citizens got a good view of the river and the Federal camps on the peninsula, the army of workers looked like bewildered ants, mired in mud and going nowhere. Of more interest were the antics of the Yankees not affixed to picks and shovels, chasing hogs around the ruined depot.

A *Whig* reporter noted on January 29 that the first pursuit was not successful. The next day the band returned, one with a sword, the rest with guns. By mid-afternoon they succeeded in cornering a sow between the river and the levee. At this point Confederate batteries on the east bank sided with the hog. "Two shots were sent over causing them [the Yankees] to fall back in double-quick time; a third shot . . . forced them to give up the pursuit of hogs and retire to their camps."

Dora Richards Miller remained discreetly reticent in her diary during January. She and her husband, secretly sharing Union sympathies, kept to themselves. Of Sherman's repulse at Chickasaw Bayou, Dora noted indifferently that "the only paper here shouts victory as much as its gradually diminishing size will allow." Not only newsprint but stationery was in short supply. Anderson Miller was lucky to find some sheets of colored paper, "and we have whiled away some long evenings cutting envelopes and making them up."

Books, too, were scarce. A. C. Clarke, more pessimistic than most as to the future, had moved his Literary Depot from Washington Street to Georgia but still solicited business through advertisements in the *Daily Whig*. From this source Dora was able to obtain a copy of Harriet Beecher Stowe's *Sunny Memories of Foreign Lands*—which constituted her only reading, aside from letters "from friends here and there in the Confederacy." True to her code of reticence, she did not name the friends, but noted:

> One of these letters tells of a Federal raid to their place, and says, "But the worst thing was, they would take every toothbrush in the house because we can't buy any more; and one cavalryman put my sister's new bonnet on his horse, and said 'Get up, Jack,' and her bonnet was gone."[28]

The plundering by Federal raiders on the loose throughout the countryside, though often exaggerated in the telling, added fuel to Vicksburg's hatred of the enemy. Marmaduke Shannon reported that Union soldiers, unable to achieve a military victory, were venting their wrath on the helpless and neighboring plantations. Giving names and locations, Shannon cited instances of buildings burned, livestock stolen or killed, women robbed of their jewels, "and other outrages so sickening that we refrain from reciting them. There is scarcely an inhabited plantation along the river that has not suffered as severely as those we have alluded to above."

Jefferson Davis, however, had had generally encouraging news from his faithful black overseer, Ben Montgomery, presiding over what had been left of Hurricane and Brierfield Plantations on Davis's Bend. Enough crops had been planted, mostly corn, to keep the community going through the winter; adequate wood had been cut and laid aside; and much of the scattered livestock had been recovered. Ben seemed to have things well in hand:

> I find that the present number of people here [at Hurricane] and Brierfield will require about 15 bushels meal weekly for bread, besides some will be necessary for some of the stock & some little for the hogs that are here to prevent them from straying off. So I think of getting more while it is to be had. . . .
>
> To avoid exhausting my little means I am devoting some time to shoemaking for some of the neighbors that desire. The tanning will be continued. I am having bark gathered for the purpose, having lost all by the preparation made sometime since to move. . . .[29]

The community would all move to the land near Bolton purchased by Joe Davis for their refuge—though there seemed little place left to hide in Mississippi. Mahala Roach was, nonetheless, saying goodbye to Vicksburg—for good, for all she could see of the future—and taking her brood to the Eggleston plantation far to the east. "With thanksgiving to God for having spared my dear children and Mother to me," she wrote:

> My life this year, forms a great contrast to last year; then I was in my home, surrounded by all that could make life desirable; the dreadful war had not then

affected *me,* and I led a gay rather careless life—Now I am exile, and may soon
be homeless—the tide of war has rolled to our very doors, and a battle is raging
only a few miles from our home. Still, amid all this apparent trouble, I am more
contented, and *happy,* and thank God that I am.

May I lead a better, truer life, and become more fitted to receive those blessings
another year.[30]

With this last entry she put aside her diary as a legacy for the future—a sort
of last testament to which, whatever happened, she would find little more of
significance to be included.

At Brokenburn, uncomfortably close to the Federal concentration at
Young's Point, Kate Stone was overjoyed at having her older brother William
home on furlough. He had been slightly wounded in the foot at Fredericksburg. His presence seemed to assure Kate that "Altogether we are getting the
better of our foes." But the convalescent captain, less optimistic, insisted on
finding a more remote place to hide the plantation's slaves, for, as Kate
observed:

He is sure we will all be forced to leave this place as the enemy intends going
into camp at the [Milliken's] Bend, and in the event of their defeat at Vicksburg
which is certain, will lay this whole country waste, sending out bands of Negroes
and soldiers to burn and destroy.[31]

Marmaduke Shannon shared the captain's apprehension, writing in the
Whig: "We are surprised to hear people advance the opinion that the enemy
have given up the idea of taking Vicksburg. The opening of the Mississippi is
too important to be given up without at least a struggle. They are only preparing a more gigantic plan and a larger force to precipitate against us." With
some qualifications, he was right.

As Mark Twain had noted and as Grant discovered, charts of the Mississippi, in whatever rare form they existed, were as unreliable as the Father of
Waters himself. For the Mississippi was a river with imagination, and a mind
of its own. It would change direction on a whim and slice through a jutting
bank to leave behind an island. Or it would climb banks to seek a different
channel, and leave behind a lake.

Such a body of water was Lake Providence, some seventy river-miles north
of Vicksburg. Crescent-shaped and six miles long, it had once been a bed of
the Mississippi, until the river shifted capriciously a mile or more to the east.
Now the landlocked lake drained south, through a torturous chain of bayous
and streams that eventually reached the Red River and rejoined the Mississippi.

Who or what focused Grant's attention on this network of waterways is hard
to say. He writes only that, at the end of January, while work was in progress
on the trans-peninsula canal, "We were busy in other directions, trying to find
an available landing on the east bank of the river, or to make water-ways to
get below the city, avoiding the batteries."

The Lake Providence route not only got below the city, it bypassed, by some
forty miles, the Confederate batteries at Warrenton and Grand Gulf, to emerge
on the main river just above Port Hudson. An amphibious expedition could
here unite with the forces of Banks and Farragut to squeeze the Confederates

out of Port Hudson, then jointly move up the Mississippi for a naval and land attack on Vicksburg.

On first arriving at Young's Point, Grant sent one of his engineers up to Lake Providence to look the situation over, and on January 30 he wrote to Admiral Porter:

> By inquiry I learn that Lake Providence, which connects with Red river through Tensas Bayou, Washita [Ouachita] and Black rivers is a wide and navigable way through. As some advantage may be gained by opening this, I have ordered a brigade of troops to be detailed for this purpose, and to be embarked as soon as possible. I would respectfully request that one of your light-draught gunboats accompany this expedition, if it can be spared.[32]

On the same day he sent a message to McPherson, who was commanding the Seventeenth Corps near Lake Providence, to put his troops to work on the project, writing, "This bids fair to be the most practicable route for turning Vicksburg." He was sanguine about the clogged streams, marshes, and twisting bayous to be cleared. "All these are now navigable to within a few miles of this place, and by a little digging, less than one-quarter that has been done across the point before Vicksburg, will connect the Mississippi and Lake, and in all probability will wash a channel in a short time."

Hitherto skeptical of all these backwater expeditions, Sherman agreed with Grant that this route offered possibilities, greater at least than the peninsula canal. "It is admirable," he wrote to Grant, "and most worthy of a determined prosecution. Cover up the design all you can, and it will fulfill all the conditions of the great problem. This little affair of ours here on Vicksburg point is lost."[33]

Both generals agreed that James Birdseye McPherson was the man to oversee the job. First in his class at West Point and a former instructor in engineering, the Ohio-born major general, thirty-five, had served as Grant's chief engineer earlier in the war. He was perhaps the most popular general in the army, somehow combining high moral principles with an easygoing camaraderie. Sherman considered him "a noble, gallant gentleman," and prophesied, "If he lives he'll outdistance Grant and myself." Though destined to die at Atlanta in the summer of 1864, McPherson came close to fulfilling that prediction.

With one of his two divisions, McPherson pitched into the job at once. To cut through from the Mississippi to Lake Providence, a distance of one half mile, was easy. He would leave that to the last. The lake at that time was eight feet below the level of the river; when completed, the cut would not only even up the difference but the inrushing water would help to scour out the subsequent channels he proposed to dredge.

These were the real problem, the bayous leading southward from Lake Providence. As Grant himself observed, when he later reviewed the operation:

> Bayous Baxter and Macon are narrow and torturous, and the banks are covered with dense forests overhanging the channel. They were also filled with fallen timber, the accumulation of years. . . . Bayou Baxter, as it reaches lower land, begins to spread out and disappears entirely in a cypress swamp before it reaches the Macon. There was about two feet of water in this swamp at this time. To get through it, even with vessels of the lightest draft, it was necessary to clear off a belt of heavy timber wide enough to make a passage way. As the trees would

have to be cut close to the bottom—under water—it was an undertaking of great magnitude.[34]

McPherson's ingenuity was up to the task. He and his engineers devised a circular saw on a shaft that extended perpendicularly downward from a floating platform. The sharp-toothed disk could be rotated by two men using their arms as pistons on a camshaft, and could be raised or lowered to the proper level on the underwater stump. When the severed trunks floated to the surface, two boats hauled them clear of the channel in a second operation—a long, time-consuming business.

When early in February, Grant visited McPherson at Lake Providence, he found that men and horses had hauled a small thirty-ton steamer overland from the Mississippi to the lake, for purposes of reconnaissance. "The work had not progressed so far as to admit the water from the river into the lake," he observed. But he was given a tour of the site aboard the little steamer on which "we were able to explore the lake and bayou as far as cleared."

The trip, as he recorded, gave rise to serious misgivings. "I saw then that there was scarcely a chance of this ever becoming a practicable route for moving troops through the enemy's country." He recalculated the distance as being 475 miles from the lake to the lower Mississippi and doubted that Porter's ironclads could get through if the water level dropped.

And he would need the gunboats to protect his troops. The Confederates still held most of the Mississippi between Vicksburg and Port Hudson, and a good part of the Red River valley. On almost any navigable section of the route, he noted, "The enemy could throw small bodies of men to obstruct our passage and pick off our troops with their sharpshooters." Nevertheless, the general wrote, "I let the work go on, believing employment was better than idleness for the men."[35]

The work went on through February into March, but at a slower pace. It was not without moments of satisfaction, even pleasure. No longer needed for reconnaissance, the little steamer became an excursion boat for McPherson and his staff and guests. On moonlit nights it puffed across the placid lake, with the regimental band on deck to serenade the passengers. At the foot of the lake a cotton plantation offered an inviting stop, with a well-stocked cellar for refreshment. It would often be after midnight before the steamer returned to the base, the passengers flushed with vintage wines, the band impartially rendering "Dixie" and "Yankee Doodle" for the benefit of the aroused camp.

The soldiers, too, who worked in relays, had time off for relaxation. Lake Providence was stocked by nature with abundant bass and bream, and the men fished, or went off with their rifles to hunt for game. There was occasional excitement in encounters with Confederate patrols, marked by one memorable incident reported by a New Orleans war correspondent. It concerned a runaway slave named Jim Williams, twenty-six years old, who, impatient with the slowness of Union plans to enlist colored troops for combat, left his master and stole up to Lake Providence to work as cook for McPherson's corps. According to the reporter, he was not long in getting into action:

Learning that a Union scouting party was going out Tuesday [February 10] to hunt Confederate guerillas around Lake Providence, Jim borrowed a mule and musket and quickly found himself on the firing line, with Union men dropping dead around him.

In a running fight, Jim managed to flush out three guerillas, demanding their surrender. Two threw down their guns, but when the third fired at the Negro, Jim shot him through the head. He brought in the other two as prisoners.[36]

In writing of the incident for *Harper's Weekly,* Theodore R. Davis noted "constantly recurring" additions to the army, comprising what the soldiers called "recruits of color." While the blacks who flocked to the Union armies —men, women, and children on the way down Freedom Road—were regarded as contraband of war and treated somewhat as wayward children, Grant tended to pút the able-bodied men to work on military projects with an eye to their becoming soldiers.

When the crucial time came for opening the cut between the Mississippi and Lake Providence, the results surpassed the most imaginative expectations. The deluge all but blotted out the lake and Bayou Baxter, sweeping over the landscape in a copper-colored sheet of water. Theodore Davis noted that "The flood . . . inundated a large district of country in Louisiana, some portion of which was a fine cotton-growing region." The flood waters reached as far as Madison Parish, and Marmaduke Shannon speculated in the columns of the *Whig* that, happily, this might drive the Yankees from their base at Young's Point.

For now at least the Lake Providence route was as open as it ever would be, a little too open, perhaps, but Grant had long since set his sights on yet another scheme for reaching Vicksburg. In permitting the work at Lake Providence to continue, as a means of keeping the troops employed, Grant wrote that the operation served, too, "as a cover for other efforts which gave a better prospect for success."

But there was still the recalcitrant river to contend with and the unpredictable surprises it produced. Two seemingly unrelated incidents were reported in the *Whig.* On January 24 the steamer *City of Vicksburg* came up the river with supplies and docked at the city wharf. She had been struck three times by Union artillery on the right bank but had suffered no serious damage or personal injuries.

Three days later Marmaduke Shannon informed his readers:

There is a steamer lying at a little town on one of the tributaries of the Mississippi, which might be used to patrol the river below here. It is the towboat *Webb,* formerly of New Orleans, and one of the fastest steamers that ever turned a wheel. She is well adapted to the business, having undergone improvements at New Orleans before that city fell. She has rifled guns already mounted.[37]

As ships go, the vessels seemed to offer little promise of impending action. But as provocative bait for an enemy on the prowl, they could be lethal. And, in fact, they were.

❧ 10 ❧

The Queen and the Dummy

No matter what happened on its banks or any of its two hundred-odd tributaries, Ol' Man River just kept rolling along. And in its bosom the Mississippi held the fate of both the armies flanking it at Vicksburg. Grant needed it desperately, to get below the city. Vicksburg and Pemberton needed the river even more, for food and supplies essential to survival.

Though generally the Mississippi was impartial, making its own decisions as to course and boundaries, it was now on the side of the Confederates who held 240 precious miles of coffee-colored water, from Vicksburg to Port Hudson. This stretch included, of course, the mouth of the Red River, twisting southward from the west. Down the Red and up the Mississippi to the hungry wharfs of Vicksburg came pork, beef, flour, cotton, salt and sugar, from Texas and Louisiana.

This free flow of traffic was a mockery to Rear Admiral Porter and his ironclads, unable to pass the Vicksburg batteries to put a stop to it. In addition to this frustration, the fleet had played only a minor role in Grant's efforts to reach or get around the city, aside from tossing occasional shells into the hilly reaches for their nuisance value.

Under the circumstances, Porter could hardly be blamed for this constraint. Cadwallader of the Chicago *Times* would castigate him nonetheless, calling him "by all odds the greatest humbug of the war. He absolutely never accomplished anything unaided. He bombarded Vicksburg for months; threw hundreds of tons of metal into the city; never hit but one house and never killed a man. The Confederates laughed at him."[1]

Whether or not he sensed this criticism, the rear admiral was in receipt of a telegram from Gustavus Fox, assistant secretary of the navy, responding to one of his own routine reports. "If you open the Father of Waters, you will at once be made an admiral; besides we will try for a ribboned star. . . . Do your work up clean, and the public will never be in doubt who did it."[2]

Even the secretary seemed to sense that Porter's public image was diminishing, but he offered a heady anecdote in the promise of an admiral's stripes—

122

if Porter could earn them, which meant reconquering the Mississippi below Vicksburg. Thus goaded, Porter decided to get at least one ram below the city, to harass Confederate shipping on the river, and on February 2 the *Queen of the West,* its sides protected with cotton bales, prepared to run the batteries under its teenage commander, Colonel Charles R. Ellet, whom Porter considered a "gallant young fellow, full of dash and enterprise."[3]

Aboard the *Queen* were two newspaper correspondents, toward whom neither Porter nor Grant shared Sherman's intractable antipathy. They were Albert Bodman, who signed himself "Bod," of the New York *Tribune,* and Finley Anderson of the New York *Herald,* the latter replacing a previous *Herald* reporter whom Sherman had had arrested and recalled. Anderson, noted Sylvanus Cadwallader, "seemed completely infatuated by the promise of excitement and adventure, and no persuasions could induce him to forego this trip."[4]

Ellet's orders were to slip past the batteries under cover of darkness, showing no lights, and at minimum speed to keep excessive smoke from giving him away. Sneaking up on Water Street, he was to ram and disable the Confederate steamer *City of Vicksburg,* which lay against the bank. "If you can fire turpentine balls from your bow field pieces into the light upperworks, it will make a fine finish to the sinking part," suggested Porter. This accomplished, the *Queen* would continue down to the Red River to intercept supply ships destined for Vicksburg, destroying or capturing everything in sight.[5]

The scenario was promising, but allowed for no departure from the script. Expecting to get under way at 4:00 A.M., Ellet found a malfunctioning in one of the paddle wheels, which delayed the start till daybreak. The Vicksburg batteries thus had a well-lit target, but even so, recorded Ellet, "we were only struck three times before reaching the steamer."

The *City of Vicksburg,* however, was lying at such an angle that the *Queen* could strike only a glancing blow with her armored prow. Ellet reported that "at the very moment of collision the current, very strong and rapid at this point, caught the stern of my boat, and, acting on her bow as a pivot, swung her around so rapidly that all her momentum was lost."

The colonel remembered Porter's instructions to let loose his turpentine balls, and just as the *Vicksburg* rewardingly burst into flames, the first of a swarm of Confederate shells began raining on the *Queen.* The cotton bales banked against the vessel's sides caught fire, and as Ellet reported:

> The flames spread rapidly, and the dense smoke, rolling into the engine room, suffocated the engineers. I saw that if I attempted to run into the *City of Vicksburg* again, my boat would certainly be burned. I ordered her to be headed downstream, and turned every man to extinguishing the flames. After much exertion, we finally put out the fire by cutting the bales loose. . . . We were struck twelve times, but, though the cabin was knocked to pieces, no material injury to the boat or to any of those on her was inflicted.[6]

The *Queen* proceeded downriver to a point below the mouth of the Red River, turned about, and headed back toward Vicksburg after completing a short run up the Red River. En route, three steamers were seized and destroyed. On February 5 the *Queen* completed her successful foray and tied up at a landing near the downriver end of Grant's Canal.

Encouraged by this exploit Admiral Porter ordered the *Queen*, accompanied by the captured *De Soto*, converted into a cottonclad, to set forth on another raid against Confederate shipping below Vicksburg. Ellet requested and received a barge-load of coal which Porter floated down to him from Milliken's Bend. "This gives the ram nearly enough coal to last her a month," Porter reported to Washington, "in which time she can create great havoc, if nothing happens to her."

Proceeding downriver on February 10, Ellet was able to create considerable havoc, destroying flatboats loaded with supplies, confiscating hundreds of bales of cotton. According to Shelby Foote, he burned at least three plantation manors on the Atchafalaya, "apparently undismayed even when one planter's daughter sang 'The Bonny Blue Flag' full in his face as the flames crackled." As the raid on Confederate shipping continued, Grant was able to wire Halleck: "This is of vast importance, cutting off the enemy's communications with the west bank of the river."[7]

With the *De Soto* following behind, Ellet steamed up the Red River on February 12 and landed the greatest prize so far, halting the Confederate steamer *Era No. 5* with a shot through the vessel's stern. Officers aboard the *Era* swarmed on to her deck, "hoisted white sheets and waved white handkerchiefs in token of surrender." The captured vessel yielded 4,500 bushels of corn, a paymaster's roll of $32,000, and military personnel from Texas and Louisiana bound for Vicksburg.

Flushed with initial success, the youthful commander Ellet thirsted after more. Word came of another Confederate supply ship farther up the river, at a place called Gordon's Landing. The *Era* was left behind under guard while the *Queen* and the *De Soto* ran upriver. Approaching Gordon's Landing from around a bend, the *Queen* came under fire from a hidden four-gun battery. Ellet fired his bow gun at steamers fleeing upriver, when the pilot either misjudged the channel or deliberately ran the *Queen* aground.

Stuck solidly in a mudbank, only four hundred yards below the battery, the ram was a sitting duck for Confederate gunners. "Bod" Bodman of the New York *Tribune* tried to recreate that nightmare for his readers. "Shots were flying, shells were bursting, and worse than all we could not reply. . . . Your correspondent sought the pilothouse, and thus became an unwilling witness of the terrible affair. Three huge thirty-two pounder shells exploded upon the deck and between the smokestacks, not twenty feet from our heads."[8]

Shells also exploded below deck, shattering the machinery, puncturing boiler and pipes and filling the engine room with scalding steam. Firemen, engineers, and crewmen scrambled on deck, some throwing cotton bales into the river to be used as life preservers, others simply diving overboard in panic. As the ship began listing, Bodman expected any minute to be "launched into eternity." Worst of all, there seemed to be no one in command. Colonel Ellet had mysteriously disappeared. Recorded Bodman:

> I was in the pilothouse when the explosion occurred, and took the precaution to close the trapdoor, thus keeping out a quantity of steam. There was still enough to make breathing almost impossible, that came through the window in

front of us. I had sufficient presence of mind to cram the tail of my coat into my mouth and thus preventing scalding.

Shortly we discovered that to remain would induce suffocation, and we opened the trapdoor and, blinded by steam, sought the stern of the vessel. Groping about the cabin, stumbling over chairs and Negroes, I sought my berth, seized an overcoat, leaving an entire suit of clothes, my haversack, and some valuable papers behind, and emerged upon the hurricane deck.[9]

With shells still exploding overhead, Bodman lowered himself by a rope to a waiting lifeboat which carried survivors back to the *De Soto*. Others reached the cottonclad by riding the current on cotton bales, last among them Colonel Ellet who had stayed with his ship until she settled in ten feet of water. Finley Anderson of the New York *Herald,* who had boarded the *Queen* in a starry-eyed search for adventure, did not make it; he later found his dénouement in a Texas prison camp.

The *De Soto* was hardly adequate for a mass evacuation, and her rudders were lost after the vessel grounded. To prevent her capture, live coals from the furnace were strewn about her hold and she was left to burn, while her crew and the survivers of the *Queen* transferred to the *Era.* As they headed downstream for the Mississippi, Bodman wrote for his paper:

The night was a terrible one—thunder, lightning, rain, and fog. . . . All hands were set to work to throw overboard the corn to lighten her, and we were slowly crawling down the river. We know to a certainty that we shall be pursued. The [Confederate] gunboat *Webb* is lying at Alexandria, and we know that she will start in pursuit of us whenever she learns of the destruction of the *Queen* and of the escape of a portion of her crew.[10]

Like so many Confederate fighting vessels, the *William H. Webb* was a converted side-wheeler, fitted with an iron prow for ramming, under the command of Captain Pierce. She had been hidden in Alexandria on the Red River since the fall of New Orleans. Now she came forward, accompanied by two "cottonclads" or steamers protected by cotton bales, to raise, repair, and take over the *Queen of the West.*

It would take several days to salvage the *Queen,* and Albert Bodman's fears were largely imaginary when he wrote, aboard the *Era* steaming for the mouth of the Red River, "Our only hope lies in reaching the Mississippi quickly, whence we shall make the best of our way to Vicksburg. The *Webb* is a model of speed, and can make fourteen miles an hour against the current. If we do not get aground, and if our machinery does not break, we hope to outrun her. If I am captured, a visit to Vicksburg will be my portion. We shall see."[11]

It was not the *Webb* that Bodman and his fellow fugitives had most to fear, but the man at the wheel of the *Era,* the same pilot who—"designedly or otherwise," in Bodman's estimation—had run the *Queen* aground below the battery. After the escape ship reached the Mississippi, the pilot edged toward the western bank and ran aground again.

To Bodman, his chances of visiting Vicksburg as a prisoner seemed all but certain. The vessel, he wrote, "laid for four mortal hours within ten feet of shore," subject to capture at any moment by Confederate guerrillas or the supposedly-pursuing *Webb.* While Colonel Ellet weighed the possibilities of building dugouts with which to slip past Port Hudson to Union territory, the crew cut trees to be used as levers to dislodge the *Era.*

All breathed a sigh of relief when, after a night of pushing and heaving, the ship finally eased out of the mud and was afloat again. All day she crawled up the Mississippi, with no fuel other than water-soaked cypress to provide a speed of only a knot against the current. Precious time had been lost, time enough for the *Webb* to have passed them in the night; she might be waiting for them farther up the river. Bodman had just retired to his cabin, to catch up on stolen sleep, when he heard the lookout's cry: "Gunboat ahead!"

"Bod" joined the others in a rush to the hurricane deck. Bearing down upon the *Era,* through the dusk and mist, was a stygian vessel with tall, dark smokestacks, prophesying doom.

Grant, of course, had been blissfully unaware of the fate of the *Queen of the West* when he wired Halleck of her successful raid on Confederate commerce on the river. In fact, he had been so impressed with the results accomplished that he urged Admiral Porter to send another Federal ship downriver to help the *Queen* add other trophies to her string of scalps.

Porter agreed. He chose for the mission the ironclad *Indianola,* largest and proudest of his Union fleet, with powerful guns enclosed in casemates forward and astern. These guns were capable of wide-angle fire. Driven by four engines powering twin screws and paddle wheels, the *Indianola* was flanked by two coal barges lashed to her sides, to provide fuel for herself and the *Queen.* The supply was sufficient to cover operations for several weeks in hostile waters.

Captained by Lieutenant Commander George Brown, the *Indianola* successfully passed the batteries at Vicksburg and Warrenton the night of February 13. It was her smokestacks that the apprehensive crew of the *Era* saw approaching through the morning twilight. Their spirits were "raised to heights of exaltation," Bodman wrote, when they recognized the vessel as a Union ironclad:

> We were, some of us, hatless, bootless, and coatless. All of us were hungry. We had eaten nothing for the last forty-eight hours but a little stale and sour corn-meal, found in the bottom of a barrel aboard the *Era* at the time of her capture. The good people of the *Indianola* acted the part of the good Samaritans; they clothed and fed us, and made us comfortable. Captain Brown invited Colonel Ellet and the two Bohemians [newspaper correspondents] into his cabin and regaled us with a delicious cup of coffee.[12]

From his coffee-klatch guests, Brown learned of the fate of the *Queen of the West* and the likely presence of the *Webb,* possibly accompanied by other enemy vessels, in the vicinity. Proceeding downriver, the *Indianola* and the *Era* encountered the *Webb,* which turned about and outdistanced her pursuers.

Leaving the *Indianola* near the Red River, the *Era* steamed for Vicksburg. Colonel Ellet had switched pilots, and she made a profitable voyage, stopping at several plantations to confiscate sufficient cotton bales to pad the vessel's sides against enemy shells. She successfully passed the batteries at Grand Gulf and Warrenton, but was peppered by sharpshooters from the eastern bank. "One hundred shots for an unarmed steamer within thirty-five miles is no trifle," Bodman wrote laconically.

From February 17 to 21, the *Indianola* blockaded the mouth of the Red River, watching for the *Webb*. During four days of waiting, Brown received surprising news from up the river. The Confederates had raised and repaired the *Queen of the West*. Captained by James McCloskey and carrying, in addition to her deck guns, a body of skilled Confederate sharpshooters, the captured Union ram was now part of a mini-fleet that included the *Webb* and the two converted cottonclads.

Still impeded by the barges clinging to the *Indianola's* sides, Brown on the 21st headed back up the Mississippi. He would deny that he was running from a fight, writing that his purpose was "to communicate with the squadron as soon as possible, thinking that Colonel Ellet had not reached the squadron, or that Admiral Porter would expect me to return when I found that no other boat was sent below."[13]

It was a long haul, with the two coal barges strapped to either side. Brown was reluctant to let the barges go; he still hoped to meet the gunboat Colonel Ellet had requested, and if he did the extra coal might be essential. Just above the head of Palmyra Island on the night of February 24, the commander became aware of shadowy outlines in the dark behind him. When he recognized the *Queen* and *Webb*, he swung the *Indianola* around to interpose one of the barges between him and the pursuers. As Brown later reported:

> The *Queen of the West* was the first to strike us, which she did after passing through the coal barge lashed to our port side, doing us no serious damage.
> Next came the *Webb*. I stood for her at full speed; both vessels came together bows on, with a tremendous crash, which knocked nearly everyone down aboard both vessels, doing no damage to us, while the *Webb's* bow was cut-in at least eight feet, extending from about two feet above the water line to the keelson.[14]

While this clash of giants was going on, the Confederate cottonclads poured a tormenting fire on the *Indianola*, which Brown ignored. He saved his own ammunition for his principal enemies, the *Webb* and *Queen*. The injured *Webb* rammed him again, this time on the starboard side, splitting apart the protective barge and leaving its wreckage dangling like seaweed. In the pitch-black darkness, Brown's gunners could only fire wildly, but the listing hulk of the *Indianola* was hard for the enemy to miss.

For an hour or more the Union ironclad held out against the wolf pack that surrounded her. Several times the *Webb* ploughed into her flanks, while the *Queen of the West* sheered off her starboard rudder and crushed her starboard wheel. With each blow the *Indianola* shuddered and settled lower in the water. Brown found his ship "in an almost powerless condition," as the *Webb* bore down again:

> She struck us fair in the stern and started the timbers and starboard rudder-box so that the water poured in in large volumes. At this time I knew that the

Indianola could be of no more service to us, and my desire was to render her
useless to the enemy. . . .[15]

It was a form of naval suicide. The more punishment the *Indianola* took,
the less valuable she would become to her antagonists. Brown made no effort
to evade the *Webb* when he saw her coming at him for the final time. He could
feel the shock of contact and could hear the water plunging through the new
gash in her side. But he kept the vessel in deep water and let her bleed to death,
until he was certain her wounds were mortal. Then:

Knowing that if either of the rams struck us again in the stern, which they then
had excellent opportunities of doing on account of our disabled condition, we
would sink so suddenly that few if any lives would be saved, I succeeded in
running her bows on shore by starting the screw engines.[16]

Somewhere near the point where, two years earlier, Jefferson Davis had
boarded the Mississippi steamer that would carry him to Vicksburg for the trip
to his inauguration, the dying Union vessel came to rest. Perhaps there was
symbolism in this circumstance. The second of two of the finest ships in the
Federal inland navy, which had threatened Confederate custody of the Mississippi for almost a year, was now a humiliating corpse on Davis Bend. If there
were ghosts in the ruins of Hurricane Plantation, they were having the last
laugh.

Brown surrendered the stranded *Indianola* to McCloskey of the *Queen*, who
put troops from the cottonclads aboard the Union vessel to raise and repair
it for Confederate use. Commander Brown and the crew of the ironclad were
sent to Texas as prisoners of war, along with Finley Anderson of the *Herald*.
Albert Bodman managed to elude the Southern captors, and raced overland
to Young's Point to carry the news of the disaster to the Union fleet.

At New Orleans the still frustrated Farragut, unable himself to pass Port
Hudson, excused his own predicament in part on Porter's failure, complaining
that "Porter has allowed his boats to come down one at a time & they have
been captured by the enemy, which compels me to go up & recapture the whole
or be sunk in the attempt. The whole country will be in arms if we do not do
something."[17]

Once again the 240 precious miles of river between Vicksburg and Port
Hudson were solidly in Southern hands. Vicksburg had reason for rejoicing.
The defenders had driven back Sherman at Chickasaw Bayou; now they had
got the better of Porter on the Mississippi. Marmaduke Shannon reported that
"Piping and dancing have been the order of the night for every night this
week."

But, ever the guardian of the city's conscience, the publisher also warned
that on the very night the *Indianola* had run the Confederate batteries, "some
of the high officers were tripping the light fantastic toe with the ladies of the
town." Such frivolity and dalliance were not in keeping with the times and
might well bode ill for the future. And another thing:

"Whiskey is to be master of the Confederacy, not the Yankees," the publisher warned in a front page editorial in the *Whig.* Victory celebrations and
relief from tension could be carried too far, by both citizens and soldiers.

Vicksburg, "Gibralter of the West," as seen from the Mississippi River in this contemporary lithograph. *(St. Louis Mercantile Library)*

Panoramic view of Vicksburg and the Mississippi from the hills behind the city. From a contemporary engraving. *(Harper's Weekly)*

Commodore Andrew Hull Foote, U.S. naval veteran and original commander of the Federal gunboat squadron on the upper Mississippi. Photo by Mathew Brady. *(National Archives)*

Rear-Admiral David Glascow Farragut, whose Gulf fleet captured New Orleans and the lower Mississippi, but failed to force the surrender of Vicksburg. *(Harper's Weekly)*

Commodore Porter camouflaged the masts and rigging of his mortar schooners with foliage designed to blend with the forested banks of the Mississippi. *(Harper's Weekly)*

Farragut's flagship *Hartford* is set ablaze by a Confederate fire raft during the battle with the forts below New Orleans, April 24, 1862. *(Harper's Weekly)*

The makeshift Confederate ram *Arkansas* (right) battles the formidable Union gunboat *Carondelet* at the mouth of the Yazoo, July 15, 1862. *(Leslie's Illustrated Newspaper)*

Confederate President Jefferson Davis, near neighbor of Vicksburg at his Brierfield Plantation, urged Pemberton to hold the city at all costs. *(Library of Congress)*

Rear-Admiral David Dixon Porter commanded Farragut's mortar fleet and later the Mississippi gunboat squadron above Vicksburg. Photo by Mathew Brady. *(National Archives)*

Porter's fake monitor, without guns, crew, or engine, spouting fabricated smoke, terrorized Confederates as it floated down the Mississippi. *(Harper's Weekly)*

Major-General Martin Luther Smith, commanding the defenses of Vicksburg, refused to surrender the city to the Union fleet, May 18, 1862. *(Library of Congress)*

Porter's Mississippi Squadron runs the Vicksburg batteries by night, April 15, 1863, to aid Grant's crossing of the river below the city. *(Naval History of the Civil War)*

Gangs of blacks impressed from surrounding plantations helped to clear "Grant's canal" across De Soto Peninsula. The canal proved useless. *(Harper's Weekly)*

Lieutenant-General John Clifford Pemberton, Pennsylvania-born commander of Confederate forces defending Vicksburg. *(National Archives)*

Shannon suggested that the hospitals be moved outside of town. The medicinal whisky was disappearing at a mysteriously rapid rate, and more than one officer was seen to enter the convalescent ward and later emerge reeling back into the streets.[18]

At Young's Point on February 24, Porter had heard the sound of the battle off Davis Bend and correctly diagnosed another setback to his fleet. But, despite Ellet's request that a third ship be sent to the rescue, Porter had nothing strong enough to run the batteries. The next morning, February 25, he got news of the *Indianola*'s fate and reported the same by wire to Halleck. It was proof of the need for an expanded Union navy on the Mississippi.

Meanwhile, though unable to send ships down to retrieve the captured *Indianola,* Porter debated other means of preventing the Confederates from salvaging the vessel. The plan he conceived was a masterpiece of guile, which the admiral with uncommon modesty referred to as "a cheap expedient, which worked very well."

Starting with an abandoned flatboat, Porter put the men of his squadron to work adding log rafts, tapered to a point, to both ends of the hollow craft. A formidable-looking shed of canvas and planks was erected in the center, with portholes from which protruded charcoal-blackened logs resembling guns. Two huge housings for imaginary paddle wheels flanked either side, each bearing the crudely-lettered legend DELUDED PEOPLE, CAVE IN.[19]

For further realism two unusable lifeboats hung from inoperable davits, and between them rose twin dummy smokestacks made of pork barrels rising one upon another. Mud-insulated iron pots were placed beneath each funnel, in which tar and oakum could be burned to send clouds of black smoke up the chimneys. At the bow of the makeshift monitor there rose the Jolly Roger flag of skull and crossbones; over the stern hung the Stars and Stripes.

The behemoth, 300 feet in length, had taken twelve hours to build, at a cost of $8.63 for materials. Porter proudly compared his creation with the U.S.S. *Monitor* which had balked the *Merrimack/Virginia* at Hampton Roads the year before, writing that "Ericsson had saved the country with an iron one, why could I not save it with a wooden one?" It was a tongue-in-cheek question, but the answer exceeded his expectations—the expectations being that his fearsome dummy would at least draw Confederate fire and cause the useless expenditure of ammunition.

At midnight of February 25/26 the craft was towed closer to Vicksburg, the tar-and-oakum furnace was lit, and, with no one aboard, the craft was set adrift. The smoking behemoth was quickly spotted by Confederate lookouts, and one of Porter's expectations was fulfilled. "Never," wrote the admiral, "did the batteries of Vicksburg open with such a din; the earth fairly trembled, and the shot flew thick and fast around the devoted monitor."

The shot not only flew thick around the sham monitor; it went right through it and out the other side. Yet, to the amazement of the Vicksburg gunners, the fearsome ship proceeded on, as fast as the current could carry it. Here indeed was an unsinkable vessel, immune to shells, whose officers appeared so confident of her invulnerability that they did not even fire back at their attackers.

No sooner had she passed the batteries than the current began to play tricks with the drifting imposter. She was saved by a fortuitous audience that had come to the Louisiana shore to cheer her on. As Porter noted, "Some of our soldiers had gone down to the point below Vicksburg to see the fun, and just before reaching Warrenton the mock monitor caught the eddy and turned toward the bank where these men were gathered."[20]

The soldiers spent several hours trying to push the vessel back into the mainstream—and by daylight had succeeded. The Jolly Roger streaming from her bow, the faithful stacks ejecting columns of black smoke, the stygian ship drifted on and on. Upstream came the *Queen of the West* in quest of supplies at Vicksburg.

McCloskey caught sight of the monster in his path, "with her guns run out and her deck apparently clear for action." He swung the *Queen* around and headed downstream, with the monitor riding the five-knot current in pursuit.

At Davis Bend some miles below, another scene in this peripatetic river drama was unfolding with unseemly haste and little preparation or rehearsal. Passing by on the *Queen* in his flight from the anonymous, pursuing monster, McCloskey warned the salvage crew aboard the *Indianola* of the "great ironclad" that was descending on them. Orders were sent from Vicksburg to destroy the *Indianola,* to prevent her recapture by the Federals. Then, joined by the *Webb* in flight, McCloskey headed the *Queen* for the Red River.

Aboard the stranded *Indianola,* the lieutenant directing the salvage operations was at first reluctant to destroy the vessel. He waited to test the validity of McCloskey's warning. Finally convinced that Union gunboats were around the bend, he threw the light guns overboard, exploded the heavier guns, and set fire to his charge. "With the exception of the wine and liquor stores of *Indianola,* nothing was saved," it was officially reported.

Possibly the wine and liquor helped to ease the hardship of that night ashore, as the frustrated detail watched their captured prize burn and smolder to her waterline. But the next morning brought an astonishing sight. The mysterious enemy ship was precisely where it had been the night before, twelve crowflight miles upstream, no smoke emerging from its funnels and no crew or officers apparent on its deck.

A venturesome group rowed up to inspect the vessel. They found it rooted solidly in a mudbank, its wooden guns and canvas superstructure looking clownish in the morning sun. They read the legend on its paddle-wheel housing —DELUDED PEOPLE, CAVE IN—and realized they had destroyed the *Indianola* in the face of a gigantic hoax.

In Vicksburg, Marmaduke Shannon refused to concede that either he or readers of the *Whig* had been deluded. Instead, he reprinted a derisive article from the Richmond *Examiner*—headlined THE INDIANOLA AND TURRETED MONSTER—in which the writer somehow managed to pin the blame on Navy Secretary Mallory for the gullibility of Confederate military personnel. First, the *Examiner* noted, had come Grant's use of "the modern horror—the iron gunboat" on the Tennessee.[21]

"After that," wrote the editor, "the gunboat panic seized the whole country, and it became a serious question at the Navy Department whether liberty and the Southern Confederacy could exist in the presence of a cannon floating on a piece of wood in the water." It took the Union failures at Drewry's Bluff in

Virginia and at Chickasaw Bayou above Vicksburg to cure the Confederate fear of gunboats.

"But of late a new terror has turned up," wrote the editor, continuing:

The telegram brings us tidings of something which is tremblingly described as a "Turreted Monster." Gunboats are deemed not more dangerous than dug-outs, but when the case is altered to an interview with a "Turreted Monster" then the brave defenders of the Father of Waters can do nothing better than make towards the Mountains.[22]

The reported fate of the prize ship *Indianola* the writer found "more disgraceful than farcical. Here was perhaps the finest ironclad on the Western waters, captured after a heroic struggle, rapidly repaired, and destined to join the *Queen of the West* in a series of victories. Next we hear that she was of necessity blown up, in the true Merrimac Mallory style, and why?

"Laugh and hold your sides lest you die of a surfeit of derision, O Yankeedom! Blown up because forsooth a flat-boat or mudscow, with a small house taken from the back-garden of a plantation put on top of it, is floated down before the frightened eyes of the Partisan Rangers. A Turreted Monster!" The *Examiner* continued:

"A most unfortunate and unnecessary affair," says the dispatch. Rather so! "The Turreted Monster proves to be a flat-boat, with sundry features to create deception." Think of that! "She passed Vicksburg on Tuesday night, and the officers (what officers?) believing her to be a Turreted Monster, blew up the *Indianola,* but her guns fell into the enemy's hands." That is passing odd. Her guns fell into "the enemy's hands after she was blown up." Incredible![23]

The *Examiner* concluded that if Admiral Porter would only build a few more monitors of logs and canvas, the Federal navy could do without its ironclads and win the war with dummies, "a powerful and almost invincible fleet."

With Grant's army strung out for miles along the west bank of the Mississippi, from Delta Point to Lake Providence, the Louisiana planters lived in constant apprehension. Kate Stone's brother William had left Brokenburn to return to his regiment in Virginia. Brother Coley was with Pemberton across the river, and young Johnny was often out scouting to see if any marauding Yankees, who seemed everywhere, were getting close to the plantation.

"We are in a helpless situation," wrote diarist Kate, "three ladies and two little girls and not a white man or even a gun on the place, not even a boy till Johnny gets back." Appraising the situation on March 12 she wrote:

The enemy have now been three months before Vicksburg doing nothing against the city, but scourging this part of the country. The opinion now is that they will not attack this place at all. The deserters say they will not fight at Vicksburg. They say that the place is impregnable, that they will not fight to meet certain defeat, and that there is great dissatisfaction among officers and men. They will not pay off the men for fear they will desert.[24]

"I must think," Kate resolved, "there will be no attempt to storm the city." But a gnawing doubt remained. "I cannot think they will make all this preparation and gather this great army without at least making an attempt to capture it."

Across the river Dora Miller, who could see the Federal fleet from a hilltop near her home, recorded that "The slow shelling of Vicksburg goes on all the time, and we have grown indifferent." It had become a popular diversion to climb to Sky Parlor Hill for a good view of enemy activities. In fact, Sky Parlor Hill became something of an amusement park, with a band to entertain spectators, a telescope with which to view the operations of the Union fleet, and smartly uniformed Confederate officers to entertain the guests. Dora overheard one woman ask an officer, apropos of the Federals across the river:

"How can they ever take a town that has such advantages for defense and protection as this? We'll just burrow into these hills and let them batter away as hard as they please."

"You are right, madam," said the officer, "and besides, when our women are willing to brave death and endure discomfort, how can we ever be conquered?"

The talkative lady glanced at Dora's husband, Anderson Miller, in civilian clothes, and raised her voice:

"The only drawback," she said, "are the contemptible men who are staying home in comfort, when they ought to be in the army if they had a spark of honor."[25]

There were plenty of grandstand critics on Sky Parlor Hill—it was a forum for opinions on the conduct of the war—and Dora, with her Union sympathies, had learned to keep her mouth shut. Not so, twenty-seven-year-old Mary Webster Loughborough. Mary had recently arrived from Alabama with her two-year-old daughter, to be with her husband, Major James M. Loughborough, attached to General Moore's staff. New to the scene, but eager to get acquainted with her surroundings, one of the early entries in her diary recounted her first visit to Sky Parlor Hill:

> I was most provoked by the criticism of a couple of beardless youths (who are not old enough to be conscripts and who have not the gallantry to volunteer); they were talking to some young ladies of the wretched manner in which Vicksburg was defended and the evident inability of our artillerists. Poor [Major F. N.] Ogden, who has always done so well, received a very severe castigation.[26]

For the moment the whole defense of Vicksburg lay with the artillerists atop the bluffs and on the river front, with the infantry generally encamped behind the hills. Now back with Major Ogden's Eighth Louisiana Artillery Battalion, after six months of convalescence in the Soldiers' Home in Jackson, Hugh Moss found himself "in, I thought, good health and ready to encounter the hardships which soon followed." His Third Battery required the attendance of "nine men per diem. All that were well had to go on from four to six hours a day, according to the number of men for duty."

Private Granville Alspaugh of the Twenty-seventh Louisiana Infantry no longer complained of being homesick. On permanent duty patrolling the city he had met, and was wearing the ring of, a local lass named Mollie Pierce, "not pretty but she will do." By letter he reassured his mother that "you need not be afraid of my marrying her; I have no such idea." Perhaps he found the name Mollie irresistible. He inferred in his letter that his heart remained with the girl next door in Clinton—Mollie Gurney.[27]

Despite the intermittent shelling Rowland Chambers found the city relatively quiet, "as if war had never been known." But his peace was rudely interrupted when in early March his home was appropriated for an army hospital. "The soldiers are all the time annoying us in every way," he wrote uncharitably in his diary. Sick soldiers could become the worst of all.

Chambers protested to General Smith and gained a small concession. He would be allowed to stay in the house, though in the servants' quarters, provided he turned his limited medical experience to caring for the ill and wounded.[28]

Though there was plenty of illness in Vicksburg among soldiers and civilians both—in the span of two weeks Marmaduke Shannon lost three children to diptheria—it was far worse among Grant's waterlogged troops across the river. "There are but few that have not had a sick spell," Private Isaac Jackson of the Eighty-third Ohio wrote his sister Sarah. Grant himself confessed that, at Young's Point, "troops could scarcely find dry ground on which to pitch their tents. Malarial fevers broke out among the men. Measles and small-pox also attacked them."

The Cleveland *Plain Dealer* reported of the Union army at the end of February: "The moist, warm weather, the close steamboat quarters, hard fare and bad water have caused a melancholy amount of sickness and death. One-sixth of the army is said to be on the sick list, and the admissions to hospitals about 300 per day. Some 30 to 50 a day died during the month of February." To this a Missouri newspaper amended: "The cruelty of our hospitals—so called—transcends any torture ever devised for criminals."[29]

Newspaper correspondents, on a dull day, fed upon these miseries, one writing: "Fifteen or thirty men of the [Grant's] command die every day and getting necessary rations for the sick seems to be more trouble than anyone wants to go to." The reporter quoted another general as saying that "it is easier to dig two graves than sign one set of requisitions for rations." A regimental surgeon visiting a hospital ship reportedly found twenty-two dead men on the deck, and certified: "I believe before God that some of them died for want of proper nourishment."[30]

Private Isaac Jackson seemed less concerned with health than the morale and conduct of the army. "There is not a day passes but gambling, card-playing, swearing and every other kind of vice is in full progress," he wrote to his brother Ethan Jackson, adding that the troops had become "very low-spirited":

When we first landed at Young's Point the army was in a very bad fix indeed. They were very badly demoralized. The infernal traitors had been sending their corrupt communications to their friends in the army, and they circulate it as much as possible. We had every kind . . . [of] rumors intended to discourage the army which they succeeded in, in great degree.[31]

Who the infernal traitors were, Isaac did not specify, but suggested that Northern Copperheads were behind the stories circulated to demoralize the army. General Sherman was more specific. It was the newspaper correspondents who reveled in the army's difficulties and defeats. A reporter, in Sherman's eyes, was at best a rumor monger and at worst a spy.

The press fought back, goaded by the censorship that Sherman had attempted, ineffectually, to impose. A correspondent for Murat Halstead's Cincinnati *Gazette* wrote viciously: "There never was a more thoroughly disgusted, disobedient, demoralized army than this one, and all because it is under such men as Grant and Sherman."

The *Gazette* concluded that "We want a general who can perfect the organization of forces, improve their discipline, strengthen their confidence in themselves," while the Louisville *Journal* raised the question, "If Gen. Halleck is unable to find any generals who can take Vicksburg, why doesn't he go and try it himself?"[32]

Already there were calls for Grant's removal, one coming expectedly from John McClernand, who urged President Lincoln to take over the command himself. Lincoln, however, never seemed to waver in his confidence in the Ohio general. "I think we'll try him a little longer," he concluded.[33]

If Grant was troubled by these personal attacks, he appeared to take them in stride and keep his silence. Which he could do. Permitted an interview with the Union commander, one correspondent found Grant "a man who could be silent in several languages." Perhaps the criticism that disturbed the general most appeared in the soft-spoken New York *Times,* which reported Grant as "stuck in the mud of northern Mississippi, his army of no use to him or anybody else."

This hit close to the mark and to his own appraisal of the situation. His army was stuck in the mud, but due to circumstance and not mismanagement. Not until spring, when the river subsided and the land dried out, could any major military operation be considered. Meanwhile, in mid-February, he sent McClernand's corps up to Milliken's Bend, where the flooding was less serious and firm ground could be found, keeping Sherman with him at Young's Point.

Work on the trans-peninsula canal and at Lake Providence continued. But, as Grant had written earlier, he allowed these projects to go on as a cover for "other efforts which gave a greater promise of success." Earlier, too, he had conferred with his chief topographical engineer, Lieutenant Colonel James Harrison Wilson. Admittedly he was getting nowhere on the west side of the Mississippi; he could not, he complained, "just sit in front of Vicksburg and look at it." He would have to get across the river, and somehow approach the city from the north and rear.[34]

Did Colonel Wilson have any ideas? He did.

❧ 11 ❧

Battling the Bayous

"EUREKA!"

It was what James Harrison Wilson reportedly cried, as he looked across the flatlands of the Delta stretching eastward from the levee. For here, he believed, was the solution Grant had been groping for.[1]

Six years before, the dike that he was standing on had not existed. The waters of the Mississippi had flowed freely through what was known as Yazoo Pass, six miles below Helena on the east bank of the river. Steamers could follow the fourteen-mile pass through Moon Lake to the Coldwater River, on down to the Tallahatchie, which turned into the Yazoo above Greenwood, Mississippi. It was the shortest and easiest route from Memphis to Yazoo City, which for many years had serviced the plantations in the Delta.

But the main river had flooded too often through the pass, destroying crops and property, and shortly before the war the state had sealed off the pass, with a levee a hundred feet thick and eighteen feet high. It was possible to use the streams and rivers of the Delta—the Sunflower, Deer Creek, Steele's Bayou, and other tributaries of the Yazoo—but no longer was there a direct connection with the Mississippi below Helena.

It would be a simple matter, as Grant had suggested and Wilson now discovered, to open the levee and let the Mississippi through again. In this project, the river would be on their side. Already high and rising, its waters would scour out the neglected channel and provide a passage for gunboats and troop-bearing transports to the Coldwater River—down the Coldwater, Tallahatchie, and Yazoo rivers to the flank and rear of Vicksburg, without having to pass the batteries at Snyder's Bluff.

Wilson's enthusiasm for the new route was contagious. This passageway through Yazoo Pass was destined, Grant wrote, "to prove a perfect success." Sylvanus Cadwallader regarded it as the "most celebrated" of all the bayou expeditions, while contemporary chronicler John Fiske referred to it as "perhaps the most gigantic flanking movement ever attempted in military history."[2]

Gigantic in length it was, some seven hundred miles or more from Young's Point—up the Mississippi, through the pass, and down to Vicksburg. But it seemed like a surefire back door to the city on the hills. And it was naively assumed that it would take the Confederates by surprise.

By the first week of February the expedition had been organized. Admiral Porter would not personally go along, but he placed Lieutenant Commander Watson Smith in charge of a ten-boat flotilla, including the powerful gunboats *De Kalb* and *Chillicothe,* to escort the fourteen transports bearing 4,500 troops under Brigadier General Leonard Ross. General McPherson was told to stand by at Lake Providence and be prepared to send additional troops as needed.

On February 2 Wilson began to cut the levee. According to Porter—who tended to minimize others' efforts and exaggerate his own—"a few men dug a trench with spades, and in an hour the water was rushing in. . . . " It would take more than a few men working with spades for an hour to penetrate an eighteen-foot-high earthen wall one hundred feet thick at the base. The next day Wilson planted explosives in the levee and blew it up, creating a chasm eighty feet wide and sending the "water pouring through like nothing else I ever saw except Niagara."³ By next morning the gap was seventy-five yards wide.

The Mississippi being eight to nine feet higher than the pass, it required four days for the turbulent water to even up these levels and enable vessels to pass through. Even so, the velocity of the current tossed the boats around like toys, in competition with the logs and dead trees carried on its surface. Past Moon Lake, five miles beyond the Mississippi, the expedition was slowed by additional problems. The channel narrowed; overhanging branches of cypress and cottonwood knocked over smokestacks, ripped off cabins and pilothouses, shattered the paddle wheel of one ship, and stove in the planks of another.

"Most of the lighter vessels," Porter wrote, "were perfect wrecks in their upper works. Their machinery and boilers held out, and that was all that was required of them. It was a painful and ever-to-be-remembered expedition to those who took part in it."

Wild grapevines threw a canopy over the channel, forcing the pilots to pick their way through twilight. At times the boats were stopped short by what were called "Red River rafts," or mounds of fallen trees and branches "held securely by running vines or wedged in so strongly with a key-log that it would require hours of labor before they could get the raft loose and let it go drifting down with the current."⁴

The Confederates, far from being taken by surprise by this invasion, had arrived on the scene well ahead of them. Gangs of blacks had been impressed from the plantations to fell trees across the stream, as many as eighty to a mile, "so that," wrote Wilson, "for miles there was an entanglement so thick the troops could cross it from bank to bank."⁵

Some of the trees were four feet thick and weighed as much as forty tons. When block and tackle proved insufficient to remove them, labor parties of five hundred each snared the trunks with hawsers and hauled them out with muscle power. Even Wilson was surprised at the speed and success of the operation, writing: "Seeing such an exhibition of strength it is easy enough to understand how the Egyptians moved the great stones, columns, and slabs from their quarries to their temples and pyramids."⁶

It took two weeks to clear the pass and wait for the transports to catch up, and not until February 28 did Watson Smith's flotilla emerge on the Coldwater

River to hear the cry, "On to Vicksburg, boys, and no more trees to saw!" From here on, down the Coldwater and Tallahatchie, it seemed clear sailing, and Wilson wrote to Rawlins, "I am confirmed in the opinions expressed in my previous reports concerning the practicability of this route. . . . "[7]

Wilson's optimism was premature. He had been given a sample of Confederate foresight in the blockage of Yazoo Pass. Farther down the Coldwater River, near the mouth of the Tallahatchie, yet another surprise awaited him.

At Vicksburg, Pemberton had been alerted to the breakthrough at the pass. He warned President Davis that this might enable a Federal expedition to come down the chain of rivers, so that, "either from above or below there is a possibility that troops may be landed and Vicksburg be invested by land or water." Even if Union forces never reached the city, Federal warships on the Yazoo River might cut off his supply of food from the plantations in the Delta.

Under Major General William Wing Loring, Pemberton rushed 2,000 troops up the Yazoo to block the Tallahatchie River, a few miles above Greenwood. Here, using cotton bales and sandbags, they hastily constructed breastworks, which they named Fort Pemberton, and mounted thirteen guns, the largest of which was a thirty-two-pounder rifled cannon.[8]

The fort's location was its greatest strength. Built on a narrow neck of land between the Tallahatchie and Yazoo Rivers, it rested virtually on an island, unapproachable by land. Alongside, blocking the channel in the Tallahatchie River, lay the sunken hulk of the *Star of the West,* the ship that had attempted to carry provisions to Fort Sumter just before the war. Since captured by the Confederates and hidden in the Yazoo River, the sunken Union steamer now blocked the stream to her former owners, more effectively than had she been afloat and fully armed.

Lieutenant Commander Watson Smith was brought up short at the sight of the low-lying fort in his path. Ever since the ordeal of hacking through Yazoo Pass, Wilson noticed that Smith had acted strangely or, as Porter put it, "showed symptoms of aberration of mind." He was in a blue funk now, hesitating several days before risking an attack. Then, on March 11, he sent the gunboats *Chillicothe* and *De Kalb* to open fire on the fort.[9]

The attack resulted in "inglorious failure." One shell from the thirty-two-pounder rifle plunged into *Chillicothe*'s port side and hit an eleven-inch gun being loaded. Both shells exploded, tearing nuts off the bolts securing the armor and flinging metal about like bullets, killing or wounding thirteen of her crew. The gunboats retreated to repair the damage.

Wilson, becoming increasingly exasperated, looked for other means of advancing the attack. He located a hummock seven hundred yards upriver from the fort. Here he established a three-gun battery with which to shell Fort Pemberton, hoping, he wrote, to "add backbone" to the expedition—and adding only to his own frustration.

Two days later the gunboats attacked again, discreetly maintaining a distance of eight hundred yards. Their fire did only minor damage to the fort, where General Loring paced the parapet shouting, "Give 'em blizzards, boys!" Confederate artillery scored a number of hits on the Union gunboats; and once again the Federal boats withdrew—bequeathing to Loring the enduring sobriquet, "Old Blizzards."[10]

For three more days the ill-starred venture rested at a standstill. There was no dry ground on which to put the troops ashore; no way to storm the works by land. Wilson complained that if the gunboats had only moved faster through the pass and down the river, they might have reached Fort Pemberton before the breastworks were completed. If Ross had only disembarked his troops in the marsh, they might have assaulted the parapets somehow, but under the mushy circumstances Ross was unwilling to take the risk.

And as for Lieutenant Commander Watson Smith who, according to Wilson, "let one 6 1/2-inch rifle stop our navy. Bah! They ought to go up to 200 yards and 'make a spoon or spoil a horn.' . . . I have no hope of anything great, considering the course followed by our naval forces under the direction of Acting Rear Admiral, Commodore, Captain, Lieutenant Commander Smith."[11]

The gunboats launched one final attack on March 16, fulfilling Wilson's dark predictions. The navy was powerless against the strategically positioned fort. There was no room to maneuver; no way to get past it or behind it. The only approach was by the straight and open line of river which gave the Confederates an unobstructed target.

Lieutenant Commander Smith broke down completely, shouting at his men in gibberish. Replaced by Lieutenant Commander James P. Foster of the *Chillicothe,* he was shipped for convalescence to the North. (A year later, though he participated in the Red River campaign, his "symptoms of mental aberration" proved fatal.)

Wilson himself, deeply concerned about "my reputation at headquarters," was at something of a breaking point. He was convinced, he wrote to Rawlins, that "the rebels are making great calculations to bag us entire." So, "as things stand now . . . the game is blocked on us here as well as below." He might, however, have taken note of one thing. As the gunboats and transports stood passive on the river, there was no fire from the fort or from its garrison.

Wilson tried one more strategem. In response to his suggestion, Federal forces on the Mississippi made a second cut in the levee above the Yazoo, to increase the flow of water into the Coldwater and down the Tallahatchie. If this should cause the river to rise even as much as two feet, the Confederates might be flooded out or drowned like rats. Nothing happened.[12]

Thoroughly discouraged, Ross and Foster agreed to abandon the expedition. But withdrawing up the Tallahatchie and Coldwater Rivers, they encountered a brigade of reinforcements sent by McPherson under Brigadier General Isaac Quinby. Taking new heart, the combined land and naval forces returned to Fort Pemberton where, on March 23, Quinby prepared to renew operations.

Before an attack could be launched, however, Colonel Wilson arrived on the scene with an order from Grant directing an immediate withdrawal. Quinby complied with the directive and "returned with but little delay."[13] On April 4 the Federals began heading upriver and arrived at Helena six days later.

So ended the third struggle with the waterways, including Grant's efforts with the trans-peninsula canal, and the fifth attempt to capture Vicksburg, including Farragut's siege of the previous summer and Sherman's repulse at Chickasaw Bayou. Wilson compared the compounded futility with that of a young lad trying to capture a sapsucker high in a tree. As the boy climbed upwards branch by branch, and the bird kept ahead of him hop by hop, bystanders jeered that he would never reach his prey. "Well, if I don't catch it," said the youngster, "you can bet your life I'll worry it like hell."

Wilson believed that at least they had worried the enemy like hell. But he did not know the principal, ironic cause of the Confederates' concern. By the end of the last attack upon the fort, as the Federals pulled back for good, Loring's troops and Loring's gunners were virtually out of ammunition.

To Vicksburg, Grant's battle with the bayous was a distant but intriguing sideshow, one they were well aware of but unable to attend. Because of the secrecy of the Federal expeditions, Marmaduke Shannon could get no news from loyal correspondents, but relied extensively on the Memphis papers to provide his patrons with some interesting reading. He took impish delight in reproducing the headlines on the front page of the Memphis *Bulletin* for March 7:

LATEST FROM THE FLEET

SUCCESS OF THE CANALS

VICKSBURG FLANKED

PROBABLE EVACUATION[14]

To these nuggets, Shannon appended: "The *Bulletin* reports three canals nearly completed—one at Vicksburg, one into Lake Providence, and one to connect the Mississippi with the Yazoo." In the last reference, Shannon must have been referring to the blown dike which had opened Yazoo Pass. The Yazoo was a tributary of the Mississippi; no canal was needed to connect them.

More amusement than apprehension was aroused by these reports, as Shannon had anticipated. From Sky Parlor Hill the people could see for themselves the diminishing operations on the trans-peninsula canal across the river. The upriver end, that nearest Young's Point, had caved in altogether from the pressure of the rising Mississippi, and the result had been to fill the ditch with about as much debris and silt as water. More dredges were brought in and the work went on, but Confederate artillerists on the east bank, with their guns aimed at the south end of the passageway, kept the dredges away from the downriver end of the canal.

As for the Lake Providence bugaboo, an unknown number of Confederate partisan rangers, reported as "two or three companies," had raided the Federal camps engaged in the digging and dredging operations, killing a few and leaving a few of their own behind as prisoners. They had then moved north to cut a levee on the Mississippi several miles above the site. The result of this was to flood the area around Lake Providence to a degree that made further work impossible for several days and required the bringing of heavier dredges down from Memphis. Indignantly, the Memphis *Bulletin* pointed to the wanton destruction of crops and buildings in the area: "Thus the responsibility for flooding the country and destroying millions of property will rest, not upon the Federal Army, but upon the rebels themselves."[15]

News of Watson Smith's repulse at Fort Pemberton had come direct from the wounded troops that General Loring sent back to Vicksburg. Though not expecting further trouble from this quarter, Loring maintained a garrison at the outpost in the event of any further attempt by Federal vessels to descend the Yazoo.

The consequence of these three expeditions, which from Vicksburg's immediate standpoint might be termed extracurricular, was a lessening of pressure on the city itself, though Dora Miller wrote in mid-March that "The slow shelling of Vicksburg goes on all the time, and we have grown indifferent. It does not at present interrupt or interfere with daily avocations. . . . " Marmaduke Shannon's militant pen was directed at a paean to the season: "Beautiful and glorious rose blossom spring has come again, sending upon us its balmy breezes, and filling everything with a new life."

The columns of the *Whig* were filled with letters advising on the timing and methods of spring planting, the importance of raising edible crops in preference to cotton, an edict from General Pemberton requiring that all corn grown in excess of a planter's immediate needs would be requisitioned by the army, and an anonymous letter from a dowager protesting that, for a city in such dire danger, there was too much festivity and entertaining going on in Vicksburg. To which Marmaduke Shannon replied editorially, and somewhat out of key for him:

> We believe in being joyful even in the midst of war. A little mirth mixes well and profitably with both business and philanthropy. Life would be stupid, both in labor and leisure, without that gaiety within us which responds to the cheerfulness and beauty around us.[16]

Though supplies in the city were adequate but limited, prices continued to soar. The peripatetic editor James B. de Bow found real estate selling at "enormous prices." Room and board had doubled to eight dollars a day since the first of January, with other costs proportionately higher. To wit: "Flour was $125 per barrel, meat 75¢ a pound, broadcloth $50 per yard, shoes $30 a pair, boots $75, sugar $1 per pound, coffee $5 per pound."[17]

Yet despite these burdens, de Bow found that the citizens maintained a cheerful, even prosperous façade. It was indeed a period of relative euphoria in Vicksburg, brought in part by tidings from the rest of the South that the Hill City had become a symbol of Confederate pride and uncompromised resistance. It hardly seemed possible now that it could ever have been otherwise.

Of the affair that had ended at Fort Pemberton, Admiral Porter wrote: "It was just one of the episodes of the war (my consolation when I met with failure), and I never wanted to hear of the Yazoo expedition again."[18]

But, in contrast to that nightmare, Porter had just turned up an admiral's dream. Exploring by tugboat the country north of Vicksburg, so flooded that almost any gap through the forest was navigable, Porter realized that, in what he called "this topsyturvy world," there were no land barriers. One could go anywhere, sailing through the tops of trees that floated like sargasso weed on the surface of this wilderness sea. As he noted: "Great forests had become channels admitting the passage of large steamers between the trees, and now and then wide lanes were met with where a frigate might have passed."[19]

This being so, with the water measuring as much as seventeen feet in depth, Porter could sneak his gunboats, drawing only six feet, through the torturous passages running north and eastward to the deeper water of the Sunflower River, a major artery of the Delta region, which reached the Yazoo above the batteries at Snyder's Bluff and far below Fort Pemberton. By this route, he thought, "I was sure of getting in the rear of Vicksburg, and could send some more shells into the hills that would keep them fastened down to eternity."

He took Grant a little way up Steele's Bayou, so that the general might look the situation over for himself. Grant was still concerned with the fate of the Yazoo Pass venture, having heard only that the gunboats had been thwarted at Fort Pemberton. He was pondering ways of sending reinforcements up to General Ross. But the vista Porter opened to him had a dual potential. It could be a way of getting troops to Ross, bypassing the batteries at Snyder's Bluff; or it could be a way of landing troops behind the bluff and approaching Vicksburg from the rear.

The more the general thought about it, the more the rescue mission turned into an expedition against Vicksburg, using Sherman's troops and vessels from Porter's fleet. Given his orders, the admiral assembled five gunboats, four tugs, and four mortar scows, and on March 14 the flotilla entered Steele's Bayou, first link in the network of waterways. It was a long circuitous chain, 200 miles or more, connecting two points only thirty-five miles apart: the Mississippi at Steele's Bayou and the mouth of the Sunflower River above Haynes Bluff. Yet, even with three amphibious failures behind him, it appeared to Grant as the most promising of all.

On March 16, Grant gave Sherman his official instructions:

GENERAL: You will proceed as early as practicable up Steele's Bayou, and through Black Bayou to Deer Creek, and thence with the gunboats now there by any route they may take to get into the Yazoo River, for the purpose of getting an army through that route to the east bank of the river, at a point from which they can act advantageously against Vicksburg.[20]

Sherman chose his troops from Brigadier General David Stuart's division. He selected the Eighth Missouri as a "pioneer regiment, being many of them boatmen," that would precede the expedition.

Loaded aboard a steamer named appropriately *Diligence,* the Missourians were supplied with "axes, saws, and all the tools necessary" to clear a passage for the transports, which would follow them.

Sherman went ahead in a tug on a personal reconnaissance and met Porter at the confluence of Black Bayou and Deer Creek. Porter assured him at that point that he had passed the most difficult section of the waterway, "and that he would be able to reach the Rolling Fork and Sunflower." Sherman was dubious.

It was the last time on this expedition that the two would meet under tolerable conditions. Sherman dropped back to be close to the slower-moving transports, battling against overhead obstructions.

Porter's certainty that he would reach the Sunflower did not, at the time, appear unwarranted. Deer Creek north of Black Bayou provided relatively clear sailing. Still it was a curious sight to see a naval flotilla winding through the woods where "sometimes a rude tree would throw Briarean arms around the smoke-stack of the tin-clad and knock its superstructure sidewise."

"This," the admiral wrote in retrospect, "was one of the most remarkable military and naval expeditions that ever set out in any country, and will be so ranked by those who read of it in future times." Of its diluvial setting, reflecting the book of Genesis, Porter wrote:

> Here was a dense forest, deeply inundated, so that large steamers could ply about among the trees with perfect impunity. They were as much at home there as the wild denizens of the forest would be in dry times.
> The animals of all kinds had taken to the trees as the only arks of safety. Coons, rats, mice, and wild cats were in the branches, and if they were not a happy family, it was because when they lay down together the smaller ones reposed within the larger ones.[21]

This Peaceable Kingdom tableaux held a hidden menace. From time to time, one of the ironclads struck a tree and shook loose from its branches a deluge of vermin, "among them rats, mice, snakes, and lizards," and sometimes a stunned raccoon. Sailors with brooms stood ready to brush them off, but the raccoons were coaxed to leave of their own volition while the insects chose to cling close to the invaders.

The vision of wildcats lurking in the trees caused Porter to wonder if Confederates, as well, were somewhere poised to spring upon him, either by land or water. He recalled the nightmare of the *Arkansas,* and knew that the Southerners were building rams at Yazoo City. But he learned of their condition through a "truthful contraband," who told him, "Dey has no bottom in, no sides to 'em, an' no top on to 'em, sah, an' deir injines is in Richmon'."

There were other threatening possibilities. The Mississippi water level could subside and leave them stranded. Or the enemy could block the head of the creek with cotton bales, cutting off the inflow of water and leaving his flotilla mired in a bed of mud. For Porter was certain that Vicksburg and Pemberton by now had heard of the invasion; and in his mind he composed an imaginary telegram, such as the Confederate general might now be sending to Jefferson Davis in Richmond:

> SHERMAN AND PORTER PIROUETTING THROUGH THE WOODS IN STEAMERS AND IRONCLADS. ARE KEEPING A LOOKOUT ON THEM. HOPE TO BAG THEM ALL BEFORE TOMORROW.[22]

But during that first day Porter kept his composure, and, when they came to a point "where the forest was close and composed of very large trees," he relapsed into poetic reverie:

> In the distance, between the trees, would spring into sight gray sunless glens in which the dim, soft ripple of day seemed to glimmer for a second so fancifully, indeed, that it required but a slight stretch of imagination to see wood-nymphs disporting in their baths.

And farther upstream:

> Every turn of the wheels sent an echo through the woods that would frighten the birds of prey from their perches, whence they were looking down upon the waste of waters, wondering (no doubt) what it all might mean, and whom these mighty buzzards, skimming over the waters and carrying everything before them, could possibly be.[23]

He began to conjecture, in this sylvan setting, what would happen when the trees became too dense. He found out, when a mighty monarch of the woods loomed in their path. "Ram that large tree there," he told the captain of the *Cincinnati*. Eight hundred tons of ironclad, at a speed of three knots, slammed into the trunk, lifted it from its water-softened roots, and "sent it out of all propriety." Porter ordered the crew of the following vessel to shove it clear of the channel, and went on to knock down six or eight more giant oaks in the same manner.

As the squadron proceeded up Deer Creek, the route became narrower, the banks steeper, the depth shallower. The boats inched through, with only a foot of clearance on each side, and barely two feet of water beneath their keels. Porter recorded:

> We had not entered the bayou more than half a mile before we saw the greatest excitement prevailing. Men on horseback were flying in all directions. Cattle, instead of being driven in, were driven off to parts unknown. Pigs were driven by droves to the far woods, and five hundred negroes were engaged in driving into the fields all the chickens, turkeys, ducks, and geese, and what were a few moments before smiling barn-yards, were now as bare of poultry as your hand.[24]

The natives need not have feared for the safety of their livestock. What Porter was interested in was cotton; he would confiscate any that he found. And now he was surprised to see bale after bale of the white stuff being piled in mountains on both sides of the channel—six thousand bales, Porter estimated, straddling the waterway like Scylla and Charybdis. Two men were seen applying torches to each of the two piles, and soon the rising columns of smoke obscured everything around them.

"How long will it take that cotton to burn up?" Porter shouted to an onlooking black.

"Two days, Massa," the slave assured him cheerfully, "maybe t'ree."

The admiral turned to the *Cincinnati*'s captain. "Ring the bell to go ahead fast," he ordered, "and tell those astern to follow after me."

All ports were shut, and all crews stood ready with buckets of water. The men wet themselves thoroughly, and drenched the decks and hulls, and, as the *Cincinnati* led the flotilla through the arch of flame and smoke, Porter recalled that "the heat was so intense that I had to jump inside a small house on deck covered with iron, the captain following me. The helmsman covered himself up with an old flag that lay in the wheelhouse. The hose was pointed up the hatch to the upper deck and everything drenched with water, but it did not render the heat less intolerable."[25]

Passing through the inferno, the men were scorched and the boats were blistered, but neither suffered greatly. The smoke proved of greater danger.

While still smothered in it, "there was a dreadful crash which some thought was an earthquake." The *Cincinnati* had struck an overhanging bridge, split it in two, and hurled its wreckage to the banks.

Once clear of the smoke, they saw that another bridge awaited farther down. There a burly plantation overseer regarded the boats contemptuously, a bare-breasted woman by his side. Porter was as much concerned at the loss of valuable cotton as with the act of defiance in burning it.

"Why did those fools set fire to that cotton?" Porter asked the man.

"Because they didn't want you fools to have it," was the reasonable answer.

After further repartee, the admiral told the overseer angrily, "I want nothing more with you, but I am going to steam into that bridge of yours across the stream and knock it down."

"You may knock it down and be damned," the other told him. "You'll find it a hard nut to crack. . . . "

The *Cincinnati* cracked it with a single blow, then met another bridge upstream and "down it went like nine-pins." The flotilla passed on through a stand of tenacious willows rising from the bottom of the bayou. "The small sprouts, no larger than my little finger, caught in the rough plates of the overhang and held us as the threads of the Lilliputians held Gulliver." It took an hour to cut the willow branches loose.[26]

The course of Deer Creek became more and more convoluted, to the point where the gunboats, following each other at a respectful distance, were all pointed in different directions at any given moment. "One would be standing north, another south, another east, and yet another west. . . . One minute an ironclad would apparently be leading ahead, and the next minute would as apparently be steering the other way."

With no room to maneuver or move at full speed in the narrow channel, trees in their path could not be knocked down. And if an ironclad became wedged between two of them, they could only be freed with saws and axes. As a result of this hacking and jarring, "the branches would come crashing on deck, smashing the boats and skylights and all the frame-work that they reached."

The gunboats tied up to the trees for the night, after a day of frustration and little progress. There had been no sign of Confederate activity. Yet Porter was certain that Pemberton had been well informed. Too many people had seen them pass, especially curious blacks who tracked along the banks beside them, entranced with the convolutions of "Mas' Linkum's gunboats."

But, according to Porter, if Pemberton knew of their progress, "he didn't know (or I thought he didn't) that I had two [actually four] mortarboats with which I expected to bombard Vicksburg in the rear!"

Or possibly Pemberton did know, or at least suspected. Early next morning the sailors heard the sound of chopping in the distance. Confederates up to mischief? Porter loaded a twelve-inch howitzer on one of the tugboats and sent it ahead to investigate. In twenty minutes he heard three blasts from the howitzer, then the whistle of the tug returning. Recorded Porter:

> The officer in charge reported that he had suddenly come upon a large body of negroes under the charge of some white men carrying lanterns, cutting trees on the banks of the stream we were in; that they had felled a tree three feet in

diameter, and this had fallen right across the bayou, closing the stream completely against our advance.[27]

Proceeding ahead on the tug, the sailors had no great trouble removing the tree with block and tackle, but immediately heard the sound of axes further up the stream. Again the tugboat with howitzer was sent ahead; the howitzer barked; the chopping stopped; and the tug returned with two captured blacks, who reported that they and three hundred other negroes had been impressed by officers from Vicksburg and forced to fell trees across the waterway with pistols at their heads.

The third day was a repetition of the second. More battles with obstructing trees where "snakes of every kind and description had followed the rats and mice to these old arks of safety." But the advance party aboard the tug made one encouraging discovery near the junction of Deer Creek and Rolling Fork —an Indian mound that could serve as a fort. A lieutenant commander asked Porter to let him fortify it. "It would be," he said, "a *point d'appui* for Sherman's troops in case they were attacked!" Porter supplied two howitzers, and the lieutenant planted a battery on the mound with enough men to attend the guns.

The flotilla was now only six hundred yards from the Rolling Fork, but Porter noticed "at the head of the pass a large green patch extending all the way across. It looked like the green scum on ponds." He asked one of the ubiquitous negroes what it was.

"It's nuffin but willers, sah," the black assured him. "When de water's out ob de bayou—which it mos' allers is—den we cuts de willers to make baskits wid. You kin go troo dat like a eel."[28]

The tug went ahead to test the willows, and promptly got stuck. The *Carondelet* came up from behind to push it out, and did not even reach the tug. The vinelike tentacles wrapped themselves around the hull "and held us as if in a vise." The *Carondelet* tried to back out, but couldn't move. They tried to dislodge the withes with boathooks, got up a full head of steam, and tried again. The vessel did not move an inch. Then:

> We got saws, knives, cutlasses, and chisels over the side, with the men handling them sitting on planks, and cut them off, steamed ahead, and only moved three feet. Other withes sprung up from under the water and took a fresher grip on us, so we were worse off than ever.

It was like some horror tale from Edgar Allan Poe—chained to the bottom of a forest, with imaginary pendulums descending from above. What made it worse were reports of a steamer coming up the Rolling Fork and landing two miles below. Then, breaking the tension, two shells screamed above their heads and exploded over the Indian mound.

The battery on the mound returned the shots, but by then the enemy's fire had reached sixteen shells a minute. Porter saw the sides of the fortified mound alive with his officers and men. "They were tumbling down as best they could; the guns were tumbled down ahead of them; there was a regular stampede." So much for the strong point around which Sherman's men could rally—when they came.

Porter's naval guns could not be elevated above the banks but, estimating the enemy's distance by the sound, the mortars opened fire. The gunners must have been born beneath a lucky star. Miraculously the enemy artillery fell silent.

But the respite, Porter knew, would be a brief one. A second steamer was reported having joined the first. Both were some two miles away, but the admiral could see them through his glass: loaded with troops in Confederate gray![29]

Pemberton's movements to check the Steele's Bayou expedition had been well-informed, well-timed, and almost in perfect step with the invaders. Reports from local inhabitants, and even the columns of smoke from burning cotton on Deer Creek plantations, revealed the progress of the Union amphibious column headed toward the Rolling Fork.

The night following Porter's entry into Deer Creek, Colonel Samuel W. Ferguson moved his reinforced combat team south to the Rolling Fork. During the afternoon of March 20, elements of Featherston's brigade reached the Rolling Fork from Snyder's Bluff and strengthened Ferguson's command. Ferguson routed Porter's sailors from the Indian mound and began to close in on the fleet.

To the south of the endangered gunboats, another force under the command of Stephen D. Lee had moved north from Snyder's Bluff and began obstructing Deer Creek, six miles above its outlet on the Yazoo River, to forestall a possible Federal withdrawal in that direction.

Someone, however, possibly Pemberton himself, had suggested a short cut as a means of saving time—Deer Creek, which left the Yazoo above Haynes Bluff and ran west of the Sunflower River directly to the Rolling Fork. By this unhappy choice, the steamers encountered the same obstacles that Porter's gunboats had experienced. In fact, William Chambers's account of the voyage up Deer Creek sounds like a repetition of Porter's recollections of his own experiences.

"Its channel was crooked and narrow, and we frequently collided with overhanging trees," recorded Chambers. There was "a great deal of bumping and thumping to the imminent danger of our smoke stacks, scape pipes, and Jack-staff of the steamer as well as the hats of those of us who were on the hurricane deck. . . . "[30]

After six miles of battling through this "cheerless waste of waters," the steamer could go no further, and the party was lucky to find an abandoned scow against the bank. It would hold no more than half a regiment; the other three and a half regiments would have to wait until the way ahead was cleared. It seemed for a while that their turn would never come, for the first boatload, in which William Chambers found himself, became stranded on a sunken cypress. It took several hours, with all the troops at work, to free the scow. Chambers would never make it to Rolling Fork.

Porter was by that time in an all-out battle with Ferguson's sharpshooters. He knew now that Confederate reinforcements were arriving on his rear. Nothing could make his predicament worse—but something did. Down from the Rolling Fork, riding a sudden cataract of water, came an avalanche of fallen trees, thrashing and thrusting end over end.

Another fiendish Confederate device to bury them beneath a logjam! Only weeks later would Porter discover that this new threat was not created by Confederates but by Federal troops on the Mississippi River, as they made a second cut in the levee above Yazoo Pass, in an effort to flood Fort Pemberton. "What was good for those fellows," Porter wrote in retrospect, "was bad for us."

As they fended off the descending logs, Porter heard from an itinerant black that the steamers in Rolling Fork had landed two thousand men "who were marching to get into our rear." Laconically the admiral noted, "Pleasant, that!"

He stepped ashore to query the Negro who had brought the news. How did he know these things? "I'm de county telegraph, sah," the black man told him. Could he carry a message to General Sherman, down the banks of the bayou? He could. "I kin take a note to Kingdom Kum if yer pay me half a dollar." Porter wrote the message on a piece of tissue paper:

> Dear Sherman:
> Hurry up, for Heaven's sake. I never knew how helpless an ironclad could be steaming around through the woods without an army to back her.[31]

He rolled the paper in a piece of tobacco leaf and gave it to the Negro, who concealed it in his hair.

"Go along the road," he told the black, "and you can't miss him."

"I don't go de road," the telegrapher said. "I takes de ditches."

During the night the gunboats backed several miles downstream. At the confluence of Deer Creek and Black Bayou, Sherman had been waiting for two days for the transports. The 800 pioneer troops under Giles A. Smith had been clearing out the bayous up to this point, but these were all the troops that had arrived. On Thursday, March 19, he heard the sound of heavy guns "booming more frequently than seemed consistent with mere guerilla operations." He guessed that Porter was in trouble.

Then came Porter's message, containing more than the admiral had quoted in his recollections. According to Sherman, "The admiral stated that he had met a force of infantry and artillery which gave him great trouble by killing the men who exposed themselves outside the iron armor to shove off the bows of the boats, which had so little headway that they would not steer. He begged me to come to his rescue."

Sherman ordered Giles Smith and his men to move as fast as possible to the stalled flotilla, and to tell the admiral that he and the rest of the troops were on their way. Then, alone in a canoe, he paddled downstream to hurry up the transports. One boatload had already landed, and he met the steamer *Silver Wave* arriving with another contingent, two regiments and a brigade in all. Those on shore were loaded into a coal barge towed by a tug which preceded the *Silver Wave*, "crashing through the trees, carrying away pilot-house, smoke-stacks, and every thing above deck."[32]

By nightfall they had covered only two and a half miles. Sherman debarked the troops on the spongy soil. Even through this impossible terrain of marsh and canebrake, they could walk a lot faster than the boats could move. The night was dark as pitch and the men put pine-cone torches in the barrels of their guns to light the way.

If Porter's voyage among the treetops was a legendary one, surely this was one of the fabled marches of the war. The troops groped through the wilderness in single file, each following the lights ahead of him, often waist-deep in water. The plucky drummer boys kept up a low staccato beat to animate the marchers; the flickering torches were reflected in a thousand pools; the chatter and whisper of frightened wildlife rose and fell in rhythm to their progress.

At midnight they rested for some hours in an open cotton field, to resume the march by daylight. The next morning, wrote Sherman, "We could hear Porter's guns, and knew that moments were precious. Being on foot myself, no man could complain, and we generally went at the double-quick. . . . " Now they could see the footmarks of Giles Smith's regiments which had preceded them, and the sound of the naval guns grew closer.[33]

Smith, meanwhile, had reached the stranded navy in the proverbial nick of time. The regiment met with a party of 400 Confederates armed with axes, which had got around and below the fleet, and were felling trees to block Porter's only possible escape route. Driving these off before their job was finished, Smith reached the flotilla on the afternoon of the twenty-first, to find it already snared between fallen trees in front and a sunken coal barge in the rear.

In trying to back out of the willows, the barge, which had been last in the original column, had automatically become first, and had been sent to the bottom by the other boats descending on it. Sailors now trying to raise the obstruction were harassed by Confederate marksmen closing in. The snipers, wrote Smith, were "out of range of the admiral's guns. Every tree and stump covered a sharp-shooter, ready to pick off any luckless marine who showed his head. . . . "[34]

As directed by Sherman, Smith reported to Porter for instructions. He found that Porter had all but given up. Expecting to be boarded, Porter had his crew poised at battle stations. Emphasizing his concern Porter had placed his men on half-rations. Smith's troops lost no time in spreading out and dispersing the Confederate sharpshooters. Free from enemy fire, operations began to raise the coal barge and remove obstructions. Once the way was clear, the fleet resumed backing down Deer Creek.

The next day, cheer after cheer rose from the boats. Porter looked up and saw "Old Tecumseh" a hundred yards down the bank, riding bareback on a borrowed nag. Behind him, marching across an open cotton field, came column after column of men in muddied blue. In a theatrical role belonging normally to the marines, the army had arrived!

It was all an anticlimax after that. Sherman's troops were spread along the banks, for several miles on both sides, to keep the Confederates at a distance. The gunboats, with their rudders removed, drifted backward downstream in a series of ungainly bumps and grinds, while the infantry hooted with good-natured glee at the discomfited bluejackets.

Back at the mouth of the Yazoo, Porter defined the expedition once again as "One of the episodes of war," but insisted to Sherman, "We will take Vicksburg yet. . . . " He later wrote of the Steele Bayou venture that, "It didn't amount to much in effecting changes in the condition of Vicksburg, but we gained a lot of experience which would serve us in the future."[35]

Being only human, the admiral confessed chagrin at having his navy rescued by the army. As others did. Secretary of the Navy Gideon Welles wrote of the affair, "The accounts from Porter are not satisfactory. He is fertile in expedients, some of which are costly without adequate results."

Grant, however, was more charitable. "The expedition failed," he wrote, "probably more for want of knowledge as to what would be required to open this route than from any impracticability in the navigation of the streams through which it was supposed to pass." It sounded as if he had not given up on the bayous, and an account of the affair in *Harper's Weekly* seemed to bear this out.

The *Harper*'s story told of a Federal officer captured at Steele's Bayou by Confederates who asked him:

"What in the devil is Grant here for? What does he expect to do?"

"To take Vicksburg," was the answer.

"Well, hasn't the old fool tried this ditching and flanking five times already?"

"Yes," said the officer, "but he has thirty-seven more plans in his pocket.[36]

Not thirty-seven, as it turned out. Only one. But it was one on which he would stake his reputation, that of the army, and the whole campaign for Vicksburg. It was the last roll of the dice.

❧ 12 ❧

Last Desperate Gamble

Friday, March 27, 1863.

Already it was early summer in the Mississippi Valley. The trees were in full leaf, the dogwood and azalea were in bloom, the fragrant air was rich with promise. And if Grant had had a crystal ball, he might have seen another March 27 shaping in the future, two years hence, when he, Sherman, Admiral Porter, and President Lincoln would meet aboard the *River Queen* at City Point, Virginia, and plot the road to final victory at Appomattox.

Right now, victory seemed as elusive as the floating seeds of cottonwood. He was willing to concede that his battles with the bayous had, in every instance, ended in abysmal failure. After the repulses at Fort Pemberton and on Deer Creek, the Lake Providence scheme was abandoned, as was the canal across De Soto Peninsula. Both projects, Grant confessed, had been "no more successful than the other experiments with which the winter was whiled away."

His mind was further burdened by a telegram from Halleck, dated one week earlier:

> The great objective on your line is the opening of the Mississippi River, and everything else must tend to that purpose. In my opinion the opening of the Mississippi will be to us of more advantage than the capture of forty Richmonds.[1]

Yet after more than two months he was still no closer to Vicksburg than he had been in late January, when he took over command of the army from McClernand. And public feeling in the North, observed Sylvanus Cadwallader, was becoming "troublesome. The cry of 'On to Vicksburg' was as common as 'On to Richmond.' "

The Northern press, reflecting the temper of a war-weary nation, needed a scapegoat for the stalemate in the Mississippi Valley. Grant remained the obvious target. His campaign for Vicksburg had, apparently, no other objective than "digging ditches." The acrimonious correspondent for the Cincinnati *Gazette,* whose reports were forwarded to Washington, charged that "Our noble army . . . is being wasted by the foolish, drunken, stupid Grant. He can't organize or control or fight an army. I have no personal feelings about it, but I know he is an ass."[2]

Through such insidious reports the image of Grant, to many back home, was that of a self-indulgent malingerer, lounging aboard the *Magnolia* with a bottle in his hand. Major General Charles Hamilton, holding a command in the Sixteenth Corps, wrote to Senator Doolittle of Wisconsin: "*Grant is a drunkard.* His wife has been with him for months only to use her influence in keeping him sober. He tries to leave liquor alone but he cannot resist the temptation always."

"I believe I am the only friend Grant has," said President Lincoln, as the protests reached the White House. He and the general had never met. But Lincoln, with his X-ray vision, had never lost faith in what he saw as the basic Grant—a steadfast, responsible, determined man whom one could count on. Though he still was being badgered to replace the general with, among others, George McClellan, he dismissed all such suggestions. "I cannot spare the man; he fights."[3]

Secretary Edwin Stanton of the War Department rarely agreed with the President on anything—and didn't now. Dictatorial, suspicious, fearful, Stanton distrusted Grant. For one thing, the general was tardy with reports, which showed a disrespect for top authority and left Stanton unsure of what was going on in Mississippi. Was it true, as he had been told, that Grant was "idle, incompetent and unfit to command men in an emergency?"

He needed an informer out in Mississippi, a sort of superspy who could win Grant's confidence and then report to the secretary regularly on the general's conduct and his handling of the Vicksburg operation. Stanton had such a man on call—a man named Dana.

New Hampshire-born Charles Anderson Dana, forty-four, had, after his Harvard graduation, spent some years at the communal utopia of Brook Farm in Massachusetts, lecturing, meditating, and refurbishing his mind.[4] From there he made a mighty leap to an editorship on Horace Greeley's New York *Tribune,* a post which he held until a disagreement between him and Greeley ended the association.

Having thereafter performed some confidential missions for the War Department, he was not surprised to be summoned to Washington in March of 1863, for an interview with Secretary Stanton. Wrote Dana:

> He wanted some one to go to Grant's army, he said, to report daily to him the military proceedings, and to give such information as would enable Mr. Lincoln and himself to settle their minds as to Grant, about whom at that time there were many doubts, and against whom there was some complaint.[5]

Dana's "cover," Stanton explained, would be that of special commissioner of the War Department, investigating payroll distribution in the Western armies. The code word for the Vicksburg operation would be "Cupid," and all messages would be transcribed in cipher.

This cloak-and-dagger secrecy turned out to be superfluous. When Dana arrived at Milliken's Bend on April 6, Grant and his staff knew precisely who had sent him and the purpose of his mission. Some of the staff grumbled sotto voce about "a spy in our midst," but Grant had nothing to hide and warmly welcomed the ex-journalist.

"Indeed, I think Grant was always glad to have me with his army," Dana later wrote. "He did not like letter writing, and my daily dispatches to Stanton relieved him of the necessity of describing every day what was going on in the army."[6]

Grant, often secretive, opened up to Dana on his hopes and plans and the reasoning behind them. While Sherman continued to urge that the army return to Memphis and move against Vicksburg from the rear, through the interior of Mississippi, Grant still rejected this proposal. To press and public it would appear as a step backward, a repetition of the strategy that had led to disaster in December.

An alternative was a frontal assault on Snyder's Bluff, using all his troops and the guns of Porter's fleet. "This will necessarily be attended with much loss," he wrote to Banks at New Orleans with a hint of rebuke for that general's absence, "but I think it can be done." Considering further the cost, he changed his mind in favor of a plan that he'd been brooding on since January.[7]

His goal was to get his army below the Confederate batteries, cross the river south of Vicksburg with the aid of Porter's fleet, and come on the city from the rear. He thought he had found a way to do it.

Between Milliken's Bend and Young's Point a chain of bayous and creeks twisted west and south through the Louisiana town of Richmond and approached the main river again at the village of New Carthage, almost equidistant in crowflight miles between the Confederate batteries at Warrenton and the fortifications at Grand Gulf.

A short canal beginning at Duckport Landing, connecting the Mississippi with the first of these bayous, would open a forty-mile inland waterway sufficient to accommodate tugs, barges, and small steamers without exposing them to Vicksburg's guns. If there were not enough vessels to carry the whole army to New Carthage, the infantry could make the overland trek on foot, while supplies followed them by boat.

The general outlined his plan, and the chain of waterways involved, to Porter in a letter dated April 2:

> I am satisfied that an attack on Haynes (Snyder's) Bluff would be attended with immense sacrifice of life, if not with defeat. This, then, closes out the last hope of turning the enemy by the right. I have sent troops through from Milliken's Bend to New Carthage, to garrison and hold the whole route and make the wagon road good. . . . With this done, there will be good water communication from here to Carthage for barges and tugs . . . [these] to be fitted up for the transportation of troops and artillery. With these appliances I intend to move 20,000 men at one time.[8]

And he added, "I would, admiral, therefore renew my request for running the blockade at as early a day as possible." By blockade, he meant the river batteries at Vicksburg.

Grand Gulf, roughly sixty river-miles below the city, on the east bank of the river, was the leading obstacle. It would have to be reduced before he could operate with safety against Vicksburg. He hoped with diminishing confidence for help from Banks and Farragut at New Orleans, who were facing a similar problem with Port Hudson. On March 14 Farragut tried to pass Port Hudson's fifty-odd guns with seven of his vessels, but only his flagship *Hartford* and an escort made it. Banks's army, under that general's timid leadership, never got within a few miles of the place.

It would be principally up to Porter, then, to get his gunboats below Vicksburg, escort the transports Grant would need to cross the Mississippi, and protect the landing. Porter was game, but he warned the general that the move was irreversible. Once past the batteries, his gunboats would have reached the point of no return. They could make it downriver; they could never make it up again. Moving slowly against the current, under fire, they would be shattered like so many eggshells.

In short, this was an all-or-nothing gamble. If it failed, the outcome would be final. Grant would still be on the wrong side of the river. Porter and he would be separated. There would be nothing left to try. And the nation's faith in Grant and in the army—in the whole war effort in the West—would be severely shaken. These were heavy stakes that Grant was playing for.

Many of Grant's staff thought the whole plan risky if not reckless. Sherman considered it a "desperate and hazardous" move. "Grant trembles at the approaching thunder of popular criticism and must risk anything," he wrote to his wife, but "it is my duty to back him."[9] Perhaps the only hot-blooded enthusiasm for the venture was that of Grant's twelve-year-old son Fred, who had left school to be with his father at Young's Point and had since befriended Admiral Porter aboard the latter's flagship *Black Hawk*.

There were objections, too, to Grant's choice of McClernand and his Thirteenth Corps to lead the military expedition down the inland waterway. But the choice was logical. McClernand was not only the senior corps commander, he was already at Milliken's Bend and in a position to start at once. On March 31 an advance contingent of a thousand men including infantry and cavalry, equipped with two mounted howitzers, and engineers with a pontoon train left Milliken's Bend for Richmond. They would reconnoiter the road and open communications to New Carthage.

Army morale improved dramatically. After a winter of discontent, things were moving; something was happening at last. "A great change has taken place," wrote Isaac Jackson of McClernand's corps. "A *very* dark hour has passed, and a clear sky again appears. . . . The men are in excellent spirits. . . . "

Perhaps the summerlike spring of southern Mississippi was a factor. From Walnut Bayou, Private Jackson wrote to his brother Ethan:

We have a fine time while out here. We don't have to work very hard . . . 6 or 8 hours a day. And we have a very pleasant place to come while out here, alongside the bayou on the gently sloping bank which is nice and grassy. We have plenty of rafts which we ride on and, then, the bayou is one of the prettiest places to swim in the world. It is also an excellent place to fish . . . [10]

But it was hard work, too. McClernand himself was impressed by the ingenuity and diligence of his men. Houses were torn down and the lumber used to build bridges over streams. Felled trees and fence rails were used to lay corduroy roads across the marshes. And, at the Louisiana town of Richmond, the troops had some trouble dispersing Confederate resisters. But the advance contingent was near New Carthage on April 6, where the foragers treated their general to a dinner of "sweet potatoes, stewed chicken, and coffee laced with real cream."

By the second week of April McClernand was able to report to Grant that the route from Milliken's Bend was open to a point near New Carthage. But then the Mississippi started playing tricks. The water level, rising since January, had begun to fall, changing the channels into empty ditches, turning the creeks into sunken, muddy roads. All right for troops; no longer possible for transports or for barges carrying supplies.

Admiral Porter's job took on a new dimension. It was no longer a matter of getting the gunboats past the Vicksburg batteries. Transports and supply ships must be somehow brought down with them. Again Porter warned Grant of the risks involved. Gunboats were one thing, but the thin-skinned transports and powerless barges would be at the mercy of Vicksburg batteries. However, if there were no other choice . . .

Dana alone remained brimming with confidence. In a letter to a friend discussing the Vicksburg problem, "toughest of tough jobs," he wrote, "Like all who really know the facts, I feel no sort of doubt that we shall before long get the nut cracked." Dana ventured to prophesy:

> Probably before this letter reaches you . . . the telegraph will get ahead of it with the news that Grant . . . has carried the bulk of his army down the river through a cut-off which he has opened without the enemy believing it could be done; has occupied Grand Gulf, taken Port Hudson, and, effecting a junction with the forces of Banks, has returned up the river to threaten Jackson and compel the enemy to come out of Vicksburg and fight him on ground of his own choosing.[11]

It was pure conjecture, but closer to ultimate truth than Dana realized. Even so, he qualified this prediction, adding: "Of course this scheme may miscarry in whole or in part, but as yet the chances all favor its execution, which is now just ready to begin."

It began on April 16, as Porter prepared his flotilla to run the gauntlet past the batteries. Eight warships and three transports. A coal barge was lashed for protection to the port side of each gunboat, leaving, however, the port guns free to fire. Each transport had a barge on each side. Heavy logs and bales of hay and cotton padded the vulnerable portions of the vessels. They would start downriver after nine that evening, in single file; no lights, no noise, using minimum power and letting the current do the work.

Though the night, when it came, was clear and cloudless, and Vicksburg stood silhouetted like a starlit Camelot, the bank-shadowed river was in almost total darkness.

On the morning of April 16 the Vicksburg *Whig* reported the concentration of Federal warships up the river, around the bend, but assured its readers that "There is no immediate danger here. We do not regard the fleet's coming down as at all pointing to an attack here."

As further sign of diminishing enemy pressure on the city, the editor noted "unusual quietness among the Yankees across the river"—so many Federal troops having, in fact, mysteriously disappeared—and concluded that the threat to Vicksburg "is virtually ended."

Even General Pemberton felt the worst was over, informing Joe Johnston by letter dated April 11 that "most of Grant's forces are being withdrawn to Memphis."

A new optimism bordering on euphoria crept over the city. The people came out of their homes to stroll in the early summer sun, to exchange experiences with their neighbors, shop for whatever goods remained after two years of blockade. Despite shortages and soaring prices, observed the peripatetic newspaper correspondent James de Bow, it was remarkable how well everybody managed to dress. Women sported silks and laces, ribbons and flounces, like April flowers. The men, noted de Bow, favored army clothes and colors and "the everlasting gray suit."

Mary Loughborough, shopping Washington Street for accessories to wear that evening at Major Watts's ball, found it hard to credit the tranquillity and beauty of the city. "Was it a dream?" she asked herself. "Could I believe that over this smiling scene, in the bright April morning, the blight of civil war lay like a pall?"[12]

In the commodious hillside home of Major William Watts (Ret.), servants were putting up decorations for the evening's cotillion, polishing silver, laying out tableware, and arranging chairs for the musicians. Elsewhere in the city, during that afternoon of April 16, officers gave their boots and uniforms to orderlies for cleaning; women studied themselves in mirrors, looking for ways to make the same old dress seem brighter, with a bit of lace here, a ribbon there.

As afternoon faded into evening, the warships at the fleet anchorage at the mouth of the Yazoo fell quietly into formation, a mile-long line of them. They were not all the Union fleet by any means, for Porter was saving a substantial portion of his naval power to maintain his position above the city. But, if these got past the guns of Vicksburg, it would be enough to reduce the batteries at Grand Gulf, and to get Grant's troops across the river. And when Banks and Farragut took possession of Port Hudson—which they surely must in time— the Confederacy would be split in two.

The evening was still young at Major Watts's house as Mary Loughborough and her officer husband stepped outside for a view of the river in the starlight:

> We sat on the long veranda in the pleasant air, with the soft melody and rich swell of music from the band floating round us, while ever and anon my eyes sought the bend of the river, two miles beyond, where the Federal transports, brought out in bold relief by the waning, crimson light of the evening, lay in seeming quiet.[13]

Above the bend and beyond the range of Mary's eyes, a more subdued social gathering was taking place. General Grant was entertaining members of his family and staff aboard the steamer *Von Phul,* anchored just to the side of the assembled gunboats. His wife, his son Fred, and the younger children were among the guests, along with McClernand and his bride. Sherman had gone downriver with one of several yawls, to be at the finish line below the city, when and if the fleet got through, but Rawlins and Dana were on the *Von Phul,* and James Wilson had one of the Grant children on his lap.

Young Fred Grant remembered of his father, "He was quietly smoking, but an intense light shone in his eyes." The cigar, the tension, were only natural. For Grant, at least, this was the moment of truth, an evening that could make or break him. For the others, there was tingling curiosity, as they watched the twinkling lights of Vicksburg and listened to the distant music from the bright house on the hill.

Ten o'clock passed. Aboard the *Von Phul* Dana saw the dark shapes in the river start to move, keeping a distance between them of two hundred yards. Squinting, he tried to identify them by their outlines. "First," he noted, "came seven ironclad turtles and one heavy armed ram; following these were two side-wheel steamers and one stern-wheel, having twelve barges in tow." The barges, Dana believed, bore supplies for McClernand's forces at New Carthage, while one far astern carried ammunition.[14]

Beneath the bright chandeliers reflected on the polished floor, Mary Loughborough twirled in the arms of her major to the strains of *Listen to the Mocking Bird*. Around the crystal punch bowl officers lounged and helped themselves with growing liberality and laughter. As the tune came to an end and the white-gloved dancers clapped for more, Mary wondered about the haunting words with which the waltz had ended: "After many a summer dies the swan. . . . "

On the high bluffs north of Vicksburg, Hugh Moss stood by his battery and watched the moving shadows on the river. He knew what they were—Porter's ships trying to pass the city and get below, to ferry Grant's troops across the river for a march on Vicksburg from the rear. He heard a musket shot. Some idiot firing at the column before it even got in range.

The ships had reached the bend, showing no lights, drifting soundless with the current. There were more musket shots, and Moss realized they were signals. From the wharf below the city, volunteers in gray pushed off in skiffs and headed for the farther shore.[15]

From the deck of the *Von Phul* Dana saw a sudden flash from atop the bluffs, followed by an ear-splitting boom. Then the whole line of sky two hundred feet above the river spouted sheets of flame. From the gunboats came an answering blast; and along the Louisiana shorelines, set afire by the skiff-born volunteers, abandoned wooden buildings glowed like torches, silhouetting the armada for the gunners on the heights.

Young Fred Grant remembered that "fires were burning along the whole front of the city" as well as on the Louisiana bank across the way, "and the river was lighted up as if by sunlight." James Wilson recalled that "the whole scene was grand and awe-inspiring. One of the Grant children sat on my knees with its arms around my neck, and as each crash came, it nervously clasped me closer. . . . "[16]

In the ballroom of the Watts house, a young girl in bombazine heard the explosions above the music and looked in fright to the brigadier general who was dancing with her. "What do we do?" she cried.

"Flee to the country for safety," he mockingly advised, and took her in his arms again.

The terrified girl took him literally, fleeing out into the night.[17]

Beside his battery, with his ears plugged against the noise, Hugh Moss saw one of his shells strike a transport, the *Henry Clay* as it turned out, and set the vessel afire. Just then he heard that one of his gunners, creeping down through the trees for a closer look, had been accidentally shot. "The sentinel called out to him to halt; being rather deaf, he did not hear the warning and a bullet pierced his heart."

William Chambers was also on the bluffs, as spectator rather than combatant, which he regretted. "It was a sight never to be forgotten," he recorded, "and while a sensation of awe came over me to behold such a display of man's destructive energy, it awoke the savage in the heart and filled it with an enthusiastic desire to be in the thick of the work of death."[18]

From the upper gallery of their midtown house, Dora Miller and her husband held box seats from which to view the drama. "The burning houses made the river clear as day," remembered Dora. Their first reaction was that the city was being bombarded in preparation for assault, and that the enemy would soon be landing just below them. In their excitement, they leaned so far over the balcony that a passing friend informed them later, "It's a wonder you didn't get your heads shot off, with grapeshot whizzing all around you."[19]

At the head of the moving armada, aboard the lead ship *Benton,* Admiral Porter, half-blinded by the terrific glare from both sides of the river, thought for a moment that the city was on fire. He had seen one of the transports aflame and had given up on several of the barges. But the gunboats were getting through, thank God for that!

As the firing subsided after midnight, Dana estimated that 525 shells had been hurled at the fleet during that hour and a half, or one every ten seconds, but none except the transport *Henry Clay* had been damaged beyond repair.

From the yawl below the city, Sherman considered the spectacle "truly sublime." But the sight of the *Henry Clay* drifting downriver helplessly, a flaming torch, was "more terrible than anything I have ever seen." It was fortunate that he had picked this spot to await the fleet. The men aboard the yawl were able to rescue the pilot who was clinging to a floating plank; the captain and crew of the *Henry Clay* managed to make shore unaided.[20]

By daybreak of April 17 the flotilla, minus one transport and three barges, reached New Carthage, and Grant, unable to contain himself, had his horse saddled and rode forty roundabout miles down to congratulate the victors.

Those in Vicksburg might not yet be fully aware of it, but the passing of half the Union fleet to a point below the city marked a milestone on the road to their destruction. Similarly, the inland movement of troops on the west bank of the river, cutting a wide swath through Madison Parish to New Carthage, marked the end of an era for Louisiana planters.

Kate Stone would never see lilacs again, she wrote, without remembering the tragic incidents of that fateful April, 1863. First had come the Yankees marching south from Milliken's Bend, a couple of whom had sighted her favorite horse in the Brokenburn corral. She had run to open the gate, to let the animal escape, but one of the Federals had held a pistol to her head, while his companion rounded up the horse. "I cried the rest of the day and half the night," Kate recorded in her diary.[21]

Then came word of her brother Walter's death in Mississippi. "He was but a boy and could not stand the hardships of a soldier's life." Tragedy piled upon tragedy. The plantation livestock, and what cotton had not been burned, had been confiscated by the Yankees. "Our house is stripped of furniture, carpets, books, piano and everything else, the carriage, buggy, harness, and everything of that kind."

As Porter's gunboats passed the Vicksburg batteries, and McClernand led the Union army toward New Carthage, Kate Stone and her mother decided to leave Brokenburn, possibly forever. They would flee to Texas, as so many of their neighbors planned to do. For life had become intolerable for the planters west of Vicksburg. The deliberate opening of dikes along the Mississippi tributaries—by the Federals to form assorted waterways to Vicksburg, by the Confederates to flood the enemy out of their west bank camps—had half-submerged that section of Louisiana.

The Stones obtained a dugout to carry them over the flooded terrain to Delhi, nearest stop on the railroad to Monroe. The clumsy craft bore an overwhelming load: "All seven of us, Mamma, Aunt Laura, Sister, Beverly, I and the two boys, with an assorted cargo of corn, bacon, hams, Negroes, their baggage, dogs and cats, two or three men, and our scant baggage." It took six hours in the scorching sun to paddle the dugout to Delhi, a bottleneck for refugees from the neighboring plantations.[22]

For most of the plantation slaves, it was a new day dawning. Seeing the Federal soldiers ranging over the plantations, helping themselves to mules and horses, plundering smokehouses and granaries, upset all behavior patterns for the blacks. The field hands, especially, threw in their lot with the passing soldiers, for a sample of "this hyah freedom business." And when the army marched on, hundreds of blacks—men, women, and children—went with them, arms laden with hams and chickens, jugs of molasses, sacks of flour.

By depriving the surviving planters of essential labor and thus damaging the South's economy, the contrabands, or liberated blacks, were considered of service to the Union. Officers were required to accept them and to show consideration for their welfare, which was often a burden, sometimes a tragedy, for those who so impetuously clutched at freedom.

Frank B. Wilkie, New York *Times* reporter, was aboard the steamer *Silver Wave* when she stopped on the river to pick up a raftload of escaping slaves. When the raft was made fast to the stern of the vessel and the *Silver Wave* resumed speed, Wilkie was horrified to see the bow of the escape craft dip further and further beneath the water, frightened blacks scrambling sternward, until the whole contraption slipped below the surface, leaving no trace of its human cargo.[23]

In Vicksburg, Rowland Chambers noted that many were fleeing the city after the passage of the Union fleet. On the other hand, Lavinia Shannon informed her daughter, "A good many families still remain in town and some have moved back." The two observations were not contradictory. Those of little faith were leaving, while the stout of heart remained. Marmaduke Shannon, of course, was committed to the *Whig,* though he moved the typesetting racks and forms to Mrs. Shannon's bedroom. It was quieter and safer there.

The gunboats of the upper fleet, continued their intermittent shelling, as did the thirty-pounder rifled guns, which Grant had mounted on De Soto Point. "They have inflicted little damage as yet," reported the *Whig* on April 21, "but their shells are a considerable annoyance, as the iron visitors burst into fragments frequently in the heart of the city, causing pedestrians to 'skedaddle' in fine style."

From time to time, but careful of ammunition, the Confederate cannon growled in reply. Wrote Dora Miller who claimed to have grown accustomed to the rattling of windows in the house:

> One of the batteries has a remarkable gun they call "Whistling Dick," because of the screeching, whistling sound it gives, and certainly it does sound like a tortured thing. Added to all this is the indescribable Confederate yell, which is a soul-harrowing sound. I have gained respect for the human ear, which stands it all without injury.[24]

Some Confederate guns that had been sent to Fort Pemberton on the Yazoo were recalled and some transferred to Grand Gulf just below New Carthage, where Grant's army appeared headed. With a lengthened defense line, Confederate strength was being thinly spread, and Pemberton wrote to Jefferson Davis that "The passage of batteries at Vicksburg by a large number of enemy vessels . . . shows conclusively that we have an insufficient number of guns. . . . Vicksburg and Port Hudson, and if possible Grand Gulf, ought to be greatly strengthened in guns. . . . "[25]

He wrote essentially the same to General Johnston, adding: "Enemy has now nine boats between Vicksburg and Port Hudson. He has land-forces at New Carthage from Grant's army, and can reinforce them to any extent. He can use his nine boats to cross his troops to this side."

The whole Union move had Pemberton in something of a dither. He sorely missed his cavalry, most of which Johnston had transferred to Braxton Bragg in Tennessee. Three weeks before, he had telegraphed Johnston in Tullahoma: "Have you separated the Cavalry with Gen'l Van Dorn from my command entirely? If so, it very much diminishes my ability to defend the Northern portion of the state as the planting season comes on." Among other uses, the protection of mounted troops was essential "to enable planters to sow crops."[26]

With not enough horsemen for reconnaissance, Pemberton was "a blinded leader, dangerously in the dark." As his grandson wrote: "Without cavalry, he had no way of knowing what disaster might result from movement in any direction; or what opportunity he might lose completely at any time by failure to concentrate or disperse his forces."

"What news have you? What from Vicksburg?" President Lincoln anxiously telegraphed General Stephen Hurlbut at Memphis on April 20.

Hurlbut had no ready answers. But Grant, back at Milliken's Bend, was at that moment deciding Vicksburg's fate with the posting of his "Special Orders No. 110 to the Army in the Field." There was a tone of finality in the fourteen crisp provisions, as if it were the last chance he might have to issue such a manifesto. As indeed it could be.[27]

Defining the army's goal—"to obtain a foothold on the east bank of the Mississippi, from which Vicksburg can be approached by practicable roads" —the orders confirmed the sequence of the march. McClernand's corps, already at New Carthage, would spearhead the amphibious invasion; McPherson would follow from Lake Providence, and Sherman, still north of Vicksburg, would make up the rear.

Only the minimum of camp equipment would be taken on the march, no tents except those needed to protect provisions. Each man would carry his own rations. Commanders were authorized to forage for "beef cattle, corn, and other necessary supplies," provided the troops took only those of military value. Major supplies, including food, forage, and heavy equipment, along with an ample supply of coal, would arrive by boat.

But the latter provision of the order offered problems. The inland waterway so laboriously cleared from Duckport, through Walnut and Roundaway Bayous and Bayou Vidal to New Carthage, no longer contained enough water in the canal to handle even the smallest craft. Wagon trains—even were there enough of them—would be hard-pressed to carry such quantities with sufficient speed, over the circuitous inland route. Only transports, coming directly down the Mississippi, could do the job.

As Grant knew, the steamers would have to pass the Confederate batteries without the protection of Porter's remaining gunboats stationed above Vicksburg. The admiral had made it plain that, once below the fortified bluffs, the gunboats could not return, whatever the emergency. The transports would be on their own.

There was a sense of *déjà vu* as the six transport steamers were assembled at the bend, each loaded with a hundred thousand rations. When civilian crews balked at the hazardous assignment, the vessels were quickly manned by army volunteers who vied with one another for the privilege of serving. "If ten thousand men had been wanted instead of one hundred and fifty," Dana wrote, "they would have engaged with zeal in the adventure."[28]

On April 22 the ships were readied for the run. Bulwarks of hay and cotton shielded vulnerable sections of the steamers, and barges were lashed to their sides for protection. Grant's instructions were "to drop noiselessly down with the current from the mouth of the Yazoo, and not show steam until the enemy's batteries begin firing, when the boats were to use all their legs."

Private Jake Wilkin of the 130th Illinois was not among the volunteer crewmen. He was standing on shore close to Grant's headquarters steamer, the *Von Phul,* which was stationed behind De Soto Peninsula with the general back on board. Wilkin saw the lead transport *Tigress* glide past, followed by her five companions, and in that tense moment his gaze wandered to the upper deck of the *Von Phul* where Grant stood like "a man of iron, his wife by his side. He seemed to me then the most immovable figure I ever saw. . . . No word escaped his lips, no muscle of his earnest face moved."

All others aboard the *Von Phul,* Wilkin noted, seemed consumed with anxiety and apprehension for the fate of the flotilla. Yet, he added:

Grant alone appeared oblivious to what was going on. . . . If those boats failed
to reach the army below, it would be without provisions, without forage, and,
still worse, without adequate means of crossing the river and gaining the necessary footing on the east side. If the boats were sent to the bottom, as the Rebels
confidently hoped, thirty thousand men or more would be helpless on the west
bank of the river.[29]

Thirty projectiles struck the *Tigress*. One shot tore a gigantic hole in her
stern causing her to sink below Vicksburg, the crew escaping on floating bits
of wreckage. The other five steamers got through and shortly reached McClernand's forces above New Carthage, to be greeted with the strains of "Three
Cheers for the Red, White, and Blue."

After midnight, the guns of Vicksburg had cooled, the river was silent once
again. And Jake Wilkin remembered that Grant had still not said a word.

With both the gunboats and the transports below Vicksburg, the stage was
set for the cross-river invasion of Mississippi. By that time McClernand's
corps, 16,000 strong, moving in a snakelike column, had covered most of the
distance from Milliken's Bend toward Hard Times Landing, nearly opposite
Grand Gulf. To Grant's disgust, the political general had taken his bride along,
with her servants and baggage, and had invited Governor Yates of Illinois to
be present at the fateful crossing of the Mississippi, in which he, McClernand,
would be first man over.

Sergeant Charles E. Wilcox of the Thirty-third Illinois Infantry was with the
vanguard of McClernand's troops. He had formerly been working on the
ill-starred peninsula canal and had welcomed the rumor, recorded in his diary,
that "this huge army is going to move to [New] Carthage on the Mississippi,
below Vicksburg, in this state." Though he thought the prospect "larky," his
joy was soon refined. Once on the way, and past Richmond, Louisiana, Wilcox
found the roads cumbersomely muddy, the weather torturously hot.[30]

On April 16 the Illinois troops heard the sound of heavy artillery fire from
Vicksburg. They surmised that Porter's gunboats had run the batteries and
would be there to greet them at New Carthage, now only four miles distant
on their line of march. Some days later the advance regiments bivouacked at
Perkins Plantation, just opposite Davis Bend and the Confederate President's
estate, and seventeen miles upriver from Hard Times Landing.

In the wake of McClernand's troops, McPherson's corps was hurrying down
from Milliken's Bend, the men suffering intensely from the April heat and
discarding the jackets and extra clothing they would later need in the chilly
Mississippi nights. Sherman was still at Young's Point with his Fifteenth
Corps, awaiting Grant's order to move south with the rest, and still nursing
a dim view of the whole planned operation.

At New Carthage, on April 17, Porter's gunboats were assembled and
awaiting the supreme test. At first the admiral was confident that he could
reduce the batteries at Grand Gulf, while admitting that his gunboats might
be "knocked about a bit." But the thin-skinned transports were more vulnerable. And what resistance would the troops meet from the entrenched Confederates when they stepped ashore? And as they later marched through the interior
of Mississippi? He recommended that Grant consider a crossing farther down
the river.

Even Grant confessed to seeing "great difficulties" in the venture. He had had no word as yet from Banks. But Grant had two aces up his sleeve. Both were premised on an "if."

If he could keep Pemberton's forces pinned down at Vicksburg, unable to reinforce Grand Gulf, and *if* he could distract Confederate forces in Mississippi, keep them diverted elsewhere, he would have an easier time in crossing the river and in establishing a beachhead on the other side.

With these two goals in mind, he suggested that Sherman remain at Young's Point and, when the crucial day arrived, feint an assault against Drumgould Bluffs above Chickasaw Bayou. It would be purely a demonstration, a threatening maneuver to keep Pemberton occupied and make him reluctant to send more troops to Grand Gulf. Grant did not make this an order, since the fake assault would obviously lead to nothing, and the press and public might unjustly accuse Sherman of another failure.

Sherman scoffed at this reservation. "Does General Grant think I care what these newspapers say?" he demanded. "We will make as strong a demonstration as possible." And to Grant he wrote, "You are engaged in a hazardous enterprise, and for good reason wish to divert attention; that is sufficient for me and it shall be done." He assured Grant that the troops would understand the purpose of the move and would not be put off by scurrilous news reports.[31]

This settled, Grant turned to his other planned diversion. The Southern cavalry, led by Earl Van Dorn and Bedford Forrest, had throttled his first attempt to get at Vicksburg from the rear, by cutting his supply line and disrupting his communications. Why couldn't he turn the tables on the enemy and do the same?

So far there had been little use made of mounted troops in the operations around Vicksburg. For one thing, the tricky terrain, with its creeks and gullies, hills and marshes, was unsuitable for cavalry maneuvers. And up to this point in the war, the Union cavalry had yet to find itself, or have an opportunity to prove itself.

In the South, where riding was a way of life, volunteer companies had sprung full-blown into existence, led by such talented commanders as Jeb Stuart in the East and Bedford Forrest in the West. In the North, which had no similar equestrian tradition, horses were generally regarded as draft animals for farming or transportation. It took two years of training to turn the average Yankee into a cavalryman on a par with his Southern counterpart.

Moreover, Northern generals tended to look upon mounted troops as secondary to the infantry, useful in courier or picket work but not much else. Grant was one of the exceptions. Since the age of eleven, he had lived and worked with horses and at West Point had been the finest rider in his class, astonishing his fellow cadets with his extraordinary feats of horsemanship.

After graduation he applied for a commission in the cavalry. "I had the vanity to think that as a cavalry officer I might succeed very well in the command of a brigade," he wrote.[32] Though he was turned down for want of a vacancy in that arm, he still dreamed of serving as an officer of mounted troops. Right now, however, he turned his mind to a more practical consideration.

A cavalry raid through Mississippi, similar to Forrest's recent raids in Tennessee, would siphon off enemy cavalry in pursuit, disrupt Pemberton's communications and supplies, and divert attention from his crossing of the river and the operation at Grand Gulf. Possibly another, simultaneous, raid through northern Alabama would draw Bedford Forrest far from the neighborhood of Vicksburg and keep that "Wizard of the Saddle" off his back.

Grant already had his eye on a likely leader for the raid through Mississippi: Colonel Benjamin Henry Grierson, attached to Hurlbut's Sixteenth Army Corps in Memphis. Sherman had called his attention to Grierson almost a year earlier, writing from Memphis that "Colonel Grierson has been with me all summer and . . . is the best officer I have had yet." And back in February Grant had suggested to Hurlbut:

> It seems to me that Grierson, with about five hundred picked men, might succeed in making his way south, and cut the railroad east of Jackson, Miss. The undertaking would be a hazardous one, but it would pay well if carried out. I do not direct that this shall be done, but leave it for a volunteer enterprise.[33]

Nor did he direct who should lead the expedition, though he stated that he considered Grierson "better qualified" than others in the cavalry.

Now, with few restrictions or directions, he was about to turn "Grierson's Hooting Hellions" loose on Mississippi soil—in what would become one of the most spectacular and fruitful forays of the Civil War. As Pemberton's grandson later wrote, "Vicksburg and Pemberton's army from this time on were to be subjected to warfare of a different pattern: encirclement, preceded by widely scattered cavalry infiltrations. Unopposed, the cavalry kept going—even to the sea."[34]

❧ 13 ❧

Raid of the Hellions

HORSES! My God, how he hated horses! His aversion dated from the age of eight, when Benjamin Henry Grierson had been kicked in the face by a rambunctious pony—a blow that temporarily blinded him and gashed his cheek from chin to ear, leaving a facial scar he bore for life.

Raised in Youngstown, Ohio, young Grierson had rejected a commission to West Point in favor of a life in music. He had organized and led his own band, composing musical skits and symphonic numbers for regional performances. When marriage forced him to make a living, he tried teaching music in Youngstown and Jacksonville, Illinois, then turned to a general merchandising business, which brought him close to bankruptcy by 1861.

At that time few people, including Grierson himself, would have visualized this gangling thirty-five-year-old Scotch-Irishman—who hated horses and distrusted those who rode them—as a commander of mounted troops. He had had no military training, aside from a brief stint with the Ohio State Militia, during which, he wrote, "the men worked systematically to get the officers drunk"—after which they roguishly pushed them into the canal.

Yet, responding to Lincoln's call for volunteers in the spring of 1861, he was startled to find himself enrolled in the one branch of service that he most abhorred: the cavalry. And a major, at that! He appealed to Henry Halleck for a transfer to the infantry but, he noted, "General Halleck jocularly remarked that I looked active and wiry enough to make a good cavalryman."[1]

He made a good cavalryman, a conscientious officer, and an accomplished rider and rose rapidly to colonel of the Sixth Illinois Cavalry. His only link to his musical past was the jew's harp he played while jogging in the saddle, a pertinent occupation, since music, whether represented by Philip Sheridan's marching band or Jeb Stuart's banjo-playing escort, was an integral part of Civil War cavalry operations.

Grant's instructions for Grierson's now-projected raid—which the general hoped would siphon off troops from the defense of Vicksburg—were deceptively simple: strike due south through Mississippi, wrecking Confederate depots and supply routes; cut the Southern Railroad of Mississippi, the Mobile & Ohio, and the Mississippi Central, all directly or indirectly servicing Vicks-

164

burg; meanwhile "destroying all telegraph wires, burning provisions and doing all mischief possible"; and, finally, return home by way of Alabama.[2]

Actually the route of return was optional; Grierson was "to use his own best judgment as to the course it would be safest and best to take."

Three regiments, aggregating 1,700 troops in all, made up the expedition: Grierson's own Sixth Illinois, the Second Iowa under Colonel Edward Hatch, and the Seventh Illinois commanded by Colonel Edward Prince. Six two-pound guns manned by a detachment of the First Illinois Light Artillery accompanied the troopers, towed by teams of horses fleet enough to keep pace with the cavalry.[3]

The column left its base camp at La Grange in southwest Tennessee on April 17. The first three days, moving south into Mississippi, were uneventful. To Sergeant Richard Surby of the Seventh Illinois, they were downright beatific:

> The morning . . . was a beautiful one, with a gentle breeze from the south. The fruit trees were all in full bloom, the gardens were fragrant with the perfume of spring flowers, the birds sang gaily, all of which infused a feeling of admiration and gladness into the hearts of all true lovers of nature.[4]

Sergeant Stephen Forbes, a regimental buddy, had thoughts that ran in counterpoint to this. "Perhaps it seems a little strange that we should think anything about pleasant weather, we, who have come down here to kill our fellows and carry distress to families, to dislocate the country and destroy life by wholesale."

Besides a compass and a rough map, Grierson carried with him a secret report from a loyal Mississippian (name undivulged) that "described routes by which a cavalry column might move through Mississippi, locations of well-stocked plantations, Confederate warehouses, the varying loyalties of the people in different sections of the state, the probable presence of guerillas, the geography of the country, and the distance between towns."

With this as an aid, the colonel started a series of diversionary raids by small detachments of his troopers, a tactic he would use throughout the entire expedition. The purpose was partly to gather provisions as needed and destroy Confederate property and military stores, and partly to mislead Confederate pursuers as to the location and intention of the raiders.

One detachment feinted toward the Mobile & Ohio Railroad on the east; another feinted toward the Mississippi Central on the west; still others ranged in all directions, foraging for supplies and horses and anything the land could offer.

Though Grierson tried to discourage indiscriminate pillaging, the column began to leave a sorry trail of plundered plantations in its wake. Reports of the villainy of "Grierson's thieves" *(They took every single thing I had . . . There was not even a grain of corn on the place to make hominey after they were gone)* spread across the state, alerting local communities in the raiders' path and trickling back in the form of rumors to Pemberton in Jackson.

The fourth day out from La Grange, learning that Colonel Clark Barteau's brigade of Confederate cavalry was on his trail, Grierson took protective action. Weeding out "all men and horses in any ways disabled or unfit for hard marching," he grouped them with prisoners so far taken on the raid, and started them in columns of four directly back to La Grange. These jettisoned hundred (known as the "Quinine Brigade") would leave tracks, and doubtless those who saw them pass would report to the authorities that Grierson's cavalry was marching back to Tennessee.

The following day he resorted to a more elaborate maneuver, detaching one whole regiment—Colonel Hatch's Second Iowa—for a diversionary strike at the Mobile & Ohio Railroad. With 600 troopers and one gun from the horse artillery, Hatch was to cut the railroad and then head back for the base camp at La Grange, presumably luring Barteau's cavalry to follow in pursuit.

Below Houston, Mississippi, where all Confederate government property was destroyed, Hatch's regiment reversed direction, spreading out to obliterate Grierson's hoofprints pointing south. The single gun was turned four times around, to suggest that the entire battery was going with them and that, in fact, all of Grierson's cavalry was returning to La Grange.

"These detachments," Grierson wrote, "were intended as diversions, and should the commanders not have been able to carry out their instructions, yet, by attracting the attention of the enemy in other directions, they assisted us much in the accomplishment of the main object of the expedition."[7]

The main objective was the severing of the Southern Railroad—Vicksburg to Jackson and points east—supplying essential war materials for Pemberton's survival in the hard-pressed city. Grierson would not know till all was over how well his diversionary tactics worked. Colonel Barteau had been hot on his trail until the Confederates reached the point where Hatch's brigade had reversed direction. Barteau assumed from the hoofprints and gun tracks that the whole Union cavalry was heading back to Tennessee. He took off in pursuit, leaving Grierson's main column free to move unmolested toward the target.

"A cavalry raid at its best," wrote Sergeant Stephen A. Forbes of the Seventh Illinois, "is essentially a game of strategy and speed, with personal violence as an incidental complication. It is played according to more or less definite rules, not inconsistent, indeed, with the players killing each other if the game cannot be won any other way; but it is commonly a strenuous game, rather than a bloody one, intensely exciting, but not necessarily very dangerous."[8]

So it might seem at this point. But the two remaining regiments of the brigade, now reduced to less than a thousand men, were pushing ever deeper into hostile territory. Grierson needed scouts to patrol his front and flanks and keep an eye out for the enemy.

Lieutenant Colonel William Blackburn, a swashbuckling officer, was asked to organize the scouts. He selected eight men from his regiment, the Seventh Illinois, appointing Richard Surby the sergeant in command. The men adopted makeshift uniforms pieced together from captured or stolen clothing—gray slouch hats, gray shirts, and butternut-dyed trousers. Since they could pass for either friend or foe, the brigade agreed on countersigns to distinguish them from the enemy.[9]

Thereafter, complained the rest of the brigade, it was the Butternut Guerrillas who had all the fun. Back-country people, having had no news of the Union raiders, mistook them for Confederates and cheered them on. Passing one plantation manor, Surby was flagged down by hands waving from a window. He ordered the squad to halt.

"No sooner done," he wrote, "than the front door flew open and three lovely looking females dressed in white appeared at the opening, their faces beaming with smiles, and in a voice soft and sweet invited us to dismount. . . . "

On learning that the scouts were hungry, the women ran back into the house "and soon returned with two black servants following, loaded down with eatables . . . half a ham, biscuits, sweet cakes, fried sausage, and peach pie, all in abundance were pressed upon us, while one of the young ladies plucked some roses and presenting one to each as they bade us adieu, with many blessings and much success in our 'holy cause.' "

And the ironic reason for this hospitality? All the menfolk on the plantation, husbands, sons, and brothers, were off with the troops defending Vicksburg. The women were trying to do their bit to help that "Holy Cause."[10]

As Grierson's main cavalry pushed farther south, the land seemed to sink beneath them, seemingly weighted by the moisture-laden atmosphere. This was Mississippi bottomland, flooded by the overflowing streams. Grierson recorded that the column rode for miles on end, "horses belly-deep in water, so that no road was discernible." Meanwhile the distant New York *Times* reported, apparently by crystal ball, that, "The water everywhere was three to four feet deep, with every few hundred yards a mire hole in which frequently man and horse were lost to view."

South of Louisville on April 23, the raiders were less than forty miles from the Southern Railroad, with only the upper Pearl River intervening. The Butternut Guerillas reconnoitered the approaches to the only bridge across the river and had a stroke of luck. Sergeant Surby found a white-haired native by the roadside and, in courteous Southern tones, inquired if any Confederates were patrolling this vicinity. Yes, the old man said, his son was part of an armed squad guarding yonder bridge, with orders to burn the structure the minute that Federal cavalry was sighted in the neighborhood.

Surby drew his revolver. "It lies in your power," he told the patriarch, "to save your buildings from the torch, to save your own life, and probably that of your son, by saving the bridge." He ordered the old man to carry that ultimatum to the guards and insist that they withdraw.[11]

It was a tense moment at the crossing, as the Confederate guards were presented with this bitter choice. Surby's heart was in his mouth. Were the bridge destroyed, the whole mission might be thwarted. With infinite relief he saw the Confederates finally mount their horses and withdraw. An hour later Grierson's cavalry crossed the river, and the following day they were approaching Newton Station on the Southern Railroad. Once in possession of Newton Station, they could stifle supplies to the Hill City on the Mississippi —the Gibraltar that all the might of Federal navies and armies in the West had not been able to reduce.

Following customary procedure, Colonel Blackburn rode ahead with a battalion of two hundred men to seize and hold the town until the others could arrive. The battalion struck Newton just in time to capture two arriving trains, loaded with commissary stores, provisions, arms and ammunition, half of which was destined for Pemberton's troops in Vicksburg. The trains were shunted to a siding and set afire, the exploding ammunition sounding like an artillery barrage.

Hearing the din and presuming that Blackburn had run into trouble, Grierson spurred his cavalry to the rescue. "On they came," wrote Sergeant Surby, "expecting battle but instead, found the men had charged a barrel of whisky, which they were confiscating. I did not see a man that had more or less than a canteen full."

Grierson weaned the men away from the whisky and put the whole brigade to work on what was the main purpose of the expedition. The two regiments separated, ranging east and west on both sides of the depot, tearing up tracks, toppling telegraph poles and cutting wires, burning trestles and bridges. All military stores at Newton Station were destroyed; all rolling stock was blown up and the wreckage scattered on the roadbed.

It would take the Confederates days or even weeks to repair the damage— while Vicksburg went without supplies that were essential to its life.[12]

At his headquarters in Jackson, Pemberton teetered on the horns of a dilemma. Three days after Grierson's cavalry had left La Grange, the Confederate commander began hearing rumors, unspecific, of heavy troop movements across the Tennessee border. "The enemy," he memorialized, "are endeavoring to compel a diversion of my troops to Northern Mississippi." Were he to yield to that compulsion, he would weaken his defenses on the eastern flank of Vicksburg.[13]

Now more than ever he regretted and resented the transfer of his cavalry, Van Dorn's 6,000 mounted troops, to Braxton Bragg in Tennessee. Without cavalry to give him eyes, he was kept in dangerous ignorance of what Grant was up to across the river and of what this new threat of invasion from the north amounted to.

On April 22 he telegraphed General Johnston in Tullahoma: "Heavy raids are making from Tennessee deep into the State. . . . Cavalry indispensable to meet these raids. . . . Could you not make a demonstration with a cavalry force in their rear?"[14]

The following day, having had no reply from Johnston, he wired Jefferson Davis: "I have so little cavalry in this department that I am compelled to divert a portion of my infantry to meet raids in Northern Mississippi. If any troops can possibly be spared from other departments I think they should be sent here."[15]

He got no satisfaction from his two superiors. Both seemed to feel that Bragg's Army of Tennessee was in greater need of cavalry and troop support than Pemberton. Then came the news of Grierson's raid on Newton Station, followed by reports that Grant was shifting his army to Hard Times Landing, across the river south of Vicksburg. The real and present danger to the city was increasing by the hour.

Though Pemberton released all available troops for the pursuit of Grierson, they seemed unable to get their clutches on the man. "These raids endanger my vital position," he wrote to Johnston in a last appeal for help. "However necessary cavalry may be to the Army of Tennessee, it is indispensable to keep my communications. The enemy are today at Hazlehurst, on the New Orleans and Jackson Railroad. *I cannot defend every station on the road with infantry.*

Am compelled to bring down cavalry from Northern Mississippi here, and whole of that section is consequently left open."[16]

"And so," noted Dee Brown in his definitive account of Grierson's raid, "began the rapid draining away to the east of Pemberton's reserve strength, in pursuit of less than a thousand elusive cavalrymen, while Grant across the Mississippi was preparing to strike him hard on the west with a force of thirty thousand."[17]

In Vicksburg during the receding weeks of April, the sense of impending danger from across the river mounted. Mary Loughborough had found that "resting in Vicksburg seemed like resting near a volcano," while Dora Miller noted in her diary for April 28, "For many nights we have had but little sleep, because the Federal gunboats have been running past the batteries. The uproar when this is happening is phenomenal." Dora could not resist leaving her bed and climbing the stairs to watch the fireworks:

> From the upper gallery we have a fine view of the river. The Confederates had set fire to a house near the bank, and soon a red glare lit up the scene and showed a small boat towing two large barges, gliding by. Another night, eight boats ran by, throwing a shower of shot, and two burning houses made the river clear as day.[18]

Dora could only surmise that these intrepid Union vessels were carrying still more supplies to Grant's army somewhere farther down the river.

Across the river Kate Stone and her family, after leaving Brokenburn en route for Texas, found themselves trapped at Delhi in a bottleneck of traffic fleeing the plantations:

> The scene beggared description: such crowds of Negroes of all ages and sizes, wagons, mules, horses, dogs, baggage, and furniture of every description. It was just thrown in promiscuous heaps—pianos, chairs, rosewood sofas, wardrobes, parlor sets, with pots, kettles, stoves, beds and bedding, bowls and pitchers, and everything of the kind just thrown pell-mell here and there, with soldiers, drunk and sober, combing over it all, shouting and laughing. While thronging every-where were refugees—men, women, and children—everybody and everything trying to get on the cars, all fleeing from the Yankees or worse still, the Negroes.[19]

She was aware of no enemy action across the river in Mississippi. Nor, at first, were the residents of Vicksburg. Then, the last week in April, came chilling rumors that the city was imperiled from a new direction by a new kind of offensive weapon, cavalry. All knew or had read of spectacular Southern cavalry achievements in both the East and the West. And what current rumors referred to as Grierson's "Hooting Hellions" sounded suspiciously like John Hunt Morgan's "Terrible Men" and the fearsome destruction they had wrought.

Had this type of scourge been adopted by the enemy, to be used for the first time, or one of the first times, against Vicksburg?

Though his mail and telegraph communications had been disrupted by Grierson's raiders, Marmaduke Shannon was finally able to apprise his public of the situation. In the April 29 *Whig* he gave an account of the departure from

La Grange, the attack on Newton Station, and the general composition of the expeditionary force, but no positive information on their numbers.

Their destination was thought to be Baton Rouge, but, wrote the publisher, "We believe they will strike higher up—somewhere between Natchez and Grand Gulf, where they will receive the protection of the gunboats, and if necessary be crossed over to the Louisiana shore." With Vicksburgians doubtless more concerned with Grant's descent of the Mississippi and probably seeing no connection between this and Grierson's cavalry invasion, Shannon saw fit to publish an admonitory editorial:

> There is but little hope of the Yankee expedition, which is marauding through our State, being apprehended. So little did we dream of such a raid that there was very little in readiness to meet it, and hence Grierson is able to go from one end of our State to the other, pillaging and destroying property as he goes along. We hope that this expedition will teach us a lesson. Bitter experience has always been our tutor in this war.[20]

Shannon closed with the premonition: "This raid is evidently a prelude to some gigantic move for which we should keep on the *qui vive.*" He urged immediate steps be taken to prevent its repetition and forestall whatever further move it indicated.

Pemberton was taking all immediate steps he could. Wirt Adams's cavalry was on its way in pursuit of the marauders, and Lieutenant Colonel Clark Barteau, in northeast Mississippi, was sent orders to ride with his troops to Hazlehurst. General Franklin Gardner at Port Hudson and commanders at other Confederate bases within striking distance had been urged to contribute units, mounted or otherwise, to the chase.

But the people, especially noncombatant males, must become involved. In cooperation with Governor Pettus, Pemberton sent out a call on April 27 for the mobilization of "Mounted Gunmen." The stated object was "to organize citizens, within a radius of ten or more miles of each important depot and railroad concentration, that they may be prepared to meet raids of the enemy. . . . So soon as forty men enroll themselves, they will be organized and authorized to elect their officers." Places and dates for enrollment were given for each locality (in Vicksburg, Hardaway & White's, for one) and there were few qualifications required.

One important effect of this announcement was to direct the public attention, now so concerned with Grant's descent of the Mississippi, to this new threat to the Mississippians' villages, homes, and families. In its strong support of the Mounted Gunmen, the *Whig* focused its columns on Grierson's expedition. This was no isolated raid but an integral part of Grant's maneuvers across the river. "It is the new plan for reducing Vicksburg."

In case there were citizens unaware of this, Marmaduke Shannon spelled it out in the *Whig* for April 30:

> The Yankee scheme for the reduction of Vicksburg is beginning to develop itself. Demonstrations, simultaneously, are to be made down the Mobile and Ohio railroad, the Mississippi Central, and the Mississippi and Tennessee railroads. At the same time, Banks is to move on Port Hudson in conjunction with Far-

ragut; Grant and McClernand are to move against our city from below; while Porter is to make as much as possible out of the gunboat fleet.

By thus striking simultaneously at so many points, they hope to be successful, believing we have not the men to cope with them over so vast an amount of territory. It is in anticipation of these moves that "gunmen" are called out for local defence. They can do excellent service and enable old veterans, now doing guard duty, &c., to swell the army and enable us to hold the Mississippi. The severe struggle is yet to come—let us hold ourselves in readiness for it.[21]

Though his information and predictions were not wholly accurate, Shannon saw the comprehensive picture more clearly than most. This, he believed, and stated on April 30, was "THE DARKEST HOUR that the Southern people will be called upon to endure during the remainder of the terrible crisis which threatens our national existence. No greater effort can be put forth by the infuriated and implacable enemy that is now testing the . . . ability of the Confederate States to maintain their independence."[22]

Throughout it all—while "Grierson and his Yankee followers are still enjoying themselves by roving about through our State"—Shannon could not withhold reluctant respect for this leader of the mounted hellions. "This fellow Grierson is certainly a gallant chap, and his ride will compare favorably with anything yet recorded, even in the South, where so many deeds of noble daring have been related. . . . " He continued:

Where they will turn up next or what damage they will do, Heaven only knows. We have for several days heard a good deal about expeditions that will "gobble" them up, but thus far the expeditions have accomplished nothing. . . . Mississippi's brow has remained untarnished until now. Her escutcheon was without a blemish. . . . But a stigma, a stain of reproach, has at last been placed upon her. . . . How long will they [Grierson's troopers] be permitted to go? How long before they are apprehended?[23]

As he asked the question, other questions were raised concerning a new breed of Union cavalry—further distant from Vicksburg but equally concerned with its destruction.

Across the Mississippi in Louisiana, and now south of Vicksburg, the bulk of the Federal army was still on the march, McPherson's corps following McClernand's to New Carthage. From Holmes Plantation not far from New Carthage, Isaac Jackson wrote to his brother of their new location. Holmes, the Southern plantation owner, was "downriver somewhere," and the corps had moved in in his absence.

The planter would not know the place when he returned. His fences had been torn down for firewood. His livestock had been confiscated by the army. His Negroes had all left. His sawmill, pride of the plantation, was being operated by the Union soldiers, making lumber for constructing river craft. As to the future:

Where we are going I cannot say but before this reaches you perhaps I shall know. Some think that when all things are ready there will be one grand crossing of the Mississippi and then on to Vicksburg. Others think that we will keep on this side of the river and go down and aid in the reduction of Port Hudson and then back to Vicksburg. We have news of several gunboats running the blockade. I expect it is so, for we heard firing in that direction the other night.[24]

Shortly after Isaac's letter was on its way, General Grant was boarding one of Porter's ships for a run downriver to Hard Times Landing, opposite the left-bank fortress of Grand Gulf. It was from this point, even in the face of Confederate batteries at Grand Gulf, that Grant hoped to take his troops across the river. Yet Porter, as he regarded the high bluffs of Grand Gulf, honeycombed with gun embrasures, thought the action too risky. He had learned (and given credit to a false report) that the fort was garrisoned by 12,000 Confederate troops, enough to repel any landing force, despite the fire cover of the gunboats. He urged Grant to consider some point farther down the river.

But Grant had had enough of mud and swamps and battling through everlasting water. Over at Grand Gulf was solid land. If he could get a toehold on it, he could keep it. He would rely on Porter's gunboats to neutralize the Confederate batteries, on Sherman to keep Pemberton pinned down at Vicksburg, and on Grierson's raiders to keep Confederate reinforcements from converging on his path.

He had not heard from Grierson since the colonel had left La Grange, but General Hurlbut had reported that the raiders had "destroyed the railroad below and near Tupelo, and in the confusion may get fairly started across Alabama before they are known." It was pure conjecture, and wrong at that, but Grant was ready to believe it, and believe that his projected crossing of the Mississippi would be less impeded as a consequence.

Far to the north and east another diversionary thrust in Grant's behalf was going on—one that deserved more credit than the average accounts of Vicksburg would accord it. Colonel Abel Streight, a stocky broad-shouldered Yankee of forty, was leading a cavalry column on a raid through northern Alabama, designed to wreck Confederate communications and to keep "that Devil Forrest" occupied, while Grant prepared to cross the river below Vicksburg.

Streight's "Independent Provisional Brigade Designed for Temporary Purposes," which left Eastport, Mississippi, two days after Grierson left La Grange, numbered roughly 1,700 troopers or the same as Grierson's initial band. But there was one unique difference. Streight had mounted his cavalry on mules, believing that these hybrid animals were more durable, required less care and sustenance, and were better adapted than horses to the rough terrain of northern Alabama.

Many would be the derisive smiles directed at this motley mule-borne expedition. But, just as Grierson siphoned off troops from the defense of Vicksburg, Streight lured Bedford Forrest, most dreaded of Confederate cavalry commanders, out of range of the Federal thrust into Mississippi.

After an exhausting three-day running fight through rugged Alabama terrain, Forrest caught up with his quarry on May 3, just short of the Georgia border, and Streight surrendered. But the mule-mounted cavalry had served its purpose. Forrest had been diverted from the defense of Vicksburg. And

Streight's plucky band would be remembered by a popular Tennysonian ballad that circulated through both North and South:

> *When can their glory fade?*
> *Honor the charge they made!*
> *Honor the Mule Brigade,*
> *Long-eared six hundred!*[25]

Having left Newton Station in charred ruins on April 24, Grierson knew that his destruction of the Southern Railroad would arouse a hornet's nest of virulent avengers. To return to La Grange the way he had come was out of the question. Confederate cavalry would be swarming to the north and south of him and from such Southern military bases as Columbus, Mississippi. But he guessed that Grant was preparing to cross the river for the ultimate assault on Vicksburg. What better objective than to join Grant in that epoch-making venture?

Also, by moving west instead of south, he could destroy another vital railway line, the New Orleans & Jackson & Great Northern, feeding Vicksburg from the Gulf. Only one obstacle intervened, halfway between Newton and the Mississippi River: the lower Pearl River, more formidable here than farther north. There was no bridge, only a single ferry by which to cross. To secure that ferry, Grierson wrote, was "a matter of life and death," and he sent Colonel Prince ahead, with two battalions of the Seventh Illinois, to take possession of the landing.

Prince arrived at the Pearl after dark, to find no guard at the wharf and the ferry tied up on the farther shore. A volunteer tried to swim the river and secure the ferry single-handed, but horse and rider were tumbled downstream by the galloping current. His shouts, however, aroused attention on the distant bank. A soft voice with a Mississippi drawl called through the darkness:

"You-all want across?"

"First Regiment, Alabama Cavalry from Mobile!" Prince shouted back. "Get over here—and hurry up about it!"[26]

The ferry was small and could carry no more than two dozen men and horses at a time. With the rest of Grierson's cavalry catching up, it took the rest of the night and part of the next day to get the whole brigade across. During this tedious operation, Grierson "accepted an invitation to breakfast with my officers at a fine home near the ferry. The breakfast was well served, the ladies were all smiles," believing, apparently, that they were entertaining Alabama cavalry hastening to the defense of Vicksburg.

At Hazlehurst on the New Orleans & Jackson Railroad, the raiders unleashed the same destructive energy that devastated Newton Station. Freight cars loaded with ammunition were exploded, buildings and stores were set afire, tracks were ripped up on both sides of the depot. But before tearing down the telegraph wires Grierson resorted to a prank he may have learned by hearsay from John Morgan. He sent a message to General Pemberton:

> The Yankees have advanced to Pearl River, but finding the ferry destroyed they could not cross, and have left, taking a northeasterly direction.[27]

The harassed Confederate general concluded that Grierson was heading back for the Vicksburg railroad to further disrupt the city's lifeline. Frantically he tried to summon Colonel Barteau and his weary cavalry back from northern Mississippi.

Hatch's diversionary raid—which had led Barteau and his troopers on a wild goose chase—had been a staggering success. Always managing to keep a lap ahead of their pursuers, the Iowans had wrecked portions of the Mobile & Ohio Railroad, had taken scores of prisoners, had captured 200 horses and mules with as many able-bodied blacks to handle them, and, racing toward the Tennessee border, had burned their bridges behind them.

Colonel Barteau overtook and almost stopped them forty miles below the Tennessee border, near a place called Camp Creek. Here the Iowa horsemen turned to face their Confederate pursuers in what was to be a showdown fight. And here, after several futile charges, the Confederates were forced to end the fight when the Iowans crossed Camp Creek and burned the bridge. Barteau's exhausted troopers had run out of ammunition.

With Barteau out of the picture, Pemberton called on other cavalry and infantry detachments to take up the pursuit of Grierson. In Jackson he enlisted the support of a notorious partisan chieftan named Colonel Robert Richardson —not as contemptuous of the rules of war as William Quantrill, but guilty of many military misdemeanors. Forgiving him for past offenses, Pemberton named him commander of a regiment of Mississippi mounted infantry and sent Richardson to block the approaches to Jackson and the Vicksburg railroad.

Though acutely aware that Vicksburg was threatened by Grant's troops across the river from Grand Gulf, Pemberton saw more immediate danger in the raiders on his flank and rear. He strove to wall them in. Richardson would hold all highways leading north. General Loring at Meridian was instructed to watch out for Grierson if he moved east. And General Franklin Gardner at Port Hudson sent Colonel W. R. Miles and his Louisiana Legion to block possible escape routes to the south.

Finally, and closer at hand, Pemberton instructed General Bowen at Grand Gulf—who was bracing himself for Grant's assault from over the river—to send Colonel Wirt Adams's cavalry to help to intercept the raiders if they moved west. "Follow them up without delay. Annoy and ambush them if possible. Move rapidly."

Thus Grierson's tiring horsemen had already achieved an important objective of the raid: the diversion of troops from the defense of Vicksburg. Forty-eight hours later Grant crossed the Mississippi virtually unopposed.

For Grierson, however, the trap was closing. Confederate forces were zeroing in from all points of the compass. Enemy scouts were everywhere, wrote Sergeant Surby, reporting on their movements. "Rebel forces were concentrating and sent to intercept us, hem us in, and annihilate us. . . . Retreat was impossible, even if such an idea had occurred to us, we having destroyed our only hope in that quarter—bridges and ferries."[28]

Strangely, they were conceded a begrudging admiration from their foes. The Jackson *Appeal* acknowledged that "the penetration of an enemy's country, so extensively, will be regarded as one of the gallant feats of the war, no matter whether the actors escape or are captured." A Southern planter whose fields they camped on told them wistfully, "You fellows are doing the boldest thing

I ever heard of. But I'm afraid that you'll be captured. Yes, sir," (sadly) "you'll be trapped."

Grierson himself later wrote of a Southern lady who came to her plantation gate to watch them pass and asked to speak with the commander. When this was arranged, she told the colonel that her husband was serving with the Confederate forces and she herself was loyal to the Cause, but that this raid "beat anything she ever heard of, or had ever read of in history; and if the North *should* win in the end and Grierson should run for President, her husband would vote for him or she'd get a divorce."

The Federal raiders' first clash with Wirt Adams's cavalry—in fact, the first serious resistance they met—occurred near Union Church on April 28. The horsemen in blue had bivouacked two miles outside the town to rest and graze their horses when, Grierson reported, "our pickets were fired upon by a considerable force." Stephen Forbes observed:

> In a short time the camp was all in confusion, men running as fast as they could in every direction, carrying saddles, leading horses on the gallop, gathering up carbines and sabers and buckling on belts, while the air was filled with cries and oaths and quick impulsive exclamations and sharp stern orders and shouts of "Fall in here, men, quick!" "Dry up that noise and load your guns!" "Gallop—march!"[29]

As the rebel yell was raised and the gray line of horsemen swept toward them, "galloping and shooting in a cloud of dust and smoke," the Union cavalry let loose a volley that wounded several and unsaddled many more. The Confederates quickly withdrew, but Grierson learned from captured prisoners that these had been only the vanguard of Adams's cavalry. The rest were preparing an ambush.

From Union Church, Grierson's troopers returned to the New Orleans & Jackson line at Brookhaven, burned the railroad station and freight cars, and damaged the railway.

At Summit on April 30, it was the moment of truth for the Federal commander. Much as he would have liked to join Grant and share in the march on Vicksburg, he had no assurance that Grant had crossed the Mississippi. He estimated that at least 20,000 Confederate troops—cavalry, infantry, and artillery—were on his trail, "sent out to destroy us." Weighing all factors, Grierson made his choice. "Hearing nothing more of our forces at Grand Gulf and not being able to ascertain anything definite as to General Grant's movements or whereabouts, I concluded to make for Baton Rouge."[30]

At daybreak, he turned his column to the southwest—"a straight line for Baton Rouge, and let speed be our safety." That night they camped on the plantation of a Dr. Spurlark, where Grierson decided to treat his staff to a chicken dinner to make up for weeks of spartan eating. He trudged to the hen coop, only to find that the soldiers were ahead of him and had all but cleaned out the supply of chickens. Only one remained, and that was being carried off by a hungry and possessive private. Recalling the incident later, Grierson wrote:

Saber in hand, I went for that private. Over the hen coop, around the pig-sty, through the stable, behind the smokehouse, between the horses, and under the horses, dodging the trees, and jumping the briers, down the steps, and smashing the trellis—the hen squawking, I vociferating, the laughing officers cheering the novel chase, till over a picket fence went the soldier, dropping the fowl under my saber. It did not require much plucking by this time, but I had earned my fricasee.[31]

When they awoke the following morning, May 1, to start the last hazardous dash for safety, they were a hundred miles from Baton Rouge, all but a few miles lying in enemy-held territory, where General Gardner's Port Hudson infantry and cavalry were looking for them. The troopers had been in the saddle for two solid weeks, with only snatches of food and rest. They were hungry, weary, and forever wet. The byroads through the Mississippi bottom-lands were deep in omniverous mud from the excessive April rains. "We lost several animals drowned," wrote Grierson, "and the men narrowly escaped the same fate."

But their luck so far had been phenomenal. Of the 900 men in the two regiments only one had been killed—a Butternut Guerilla hit in a shoot-out near Philadelphia, Mississippi. Four had been wounded; three left behind by reason of illness; six were missing and presumably captured. Nowhere had they met with serious reversal or defeat. Sergeant Surby remained in a lyrical mood, writing of that May Day morning as they started out for Baton Rouge:

A gentle breeze floated through the trees, causing a rustling among the green leaves of the oaks. Perched among the branches was the mocking bird, singing a variety of notes, the whole impressing the beholder with a sense of the Creator of all this beauty. . . . We little dreamed what a change would be produced in a few hours.[32]

The change was produced at Wall's Bridge over the Tickfaw River, three miles north of the Louisiana border. Here Blackburn's scouts in their tatter-demalion uniforms encountered three Confederate pickets.

"We're reinforcements for Adams's cavalry," Surby told them.

With surprising cordiality the Confederates greeted them, at which point the scouts raised their pistols and took the three men prisoner. Blackburn rode up, followed by the advance platoon. His intervention brought disaster that might have been avoided if, as Grierson later wrote, Blackburn had been "as discreet and wary as he was brave"—which is to say:

The passage of the Tickfaw might have been a complete surprise and accomplished without loss but for the incident of firing the alarm. Unfortunately, Lieutenant Colonel Blackburn, calling on the scouts to follow him, dashed forward to the bridge without waiting for the column to come into supporting distance.

Seemingly the sight of the open bridge persuaded Blackburn to throw caution to the winds. He galloped over the planks with Surby at his heels. They were half way across when a rifle snapped. Blackburn's horse reared, screamed, and tumbled, pinning its rider, bleeding profusely, beneath its body.

Surby reined up to aid his commander. "Go on! Go on!" yelled Blackburn. The sergeant wheeled his horse around to ride off the bridge, felt a burning pain in his leg as the saddle seemed to slip beneath him—and remembered nothing more.

Now the whole platoon was thundering over the bridge, sabers drawn and firing as they came. On the far side, concealed in woods, the Ninth Louisiana Partisan Rangers from Port Hudson held their fire until the Federals had crossed the river—then let loose a shattering volley. Seven bluecoats pitched from their saddles, of whom three were hit and four others captured. The survivors veered back across the bridge in panic.

Grierson's main column, alerted by the fusillade, came up at full gallop. Informed of the ambush, the colonel ordered up the horse artillery and shelled the woods with a blanketing barrage. Then, splitting his brigade three ways, he led his troops in a hell-for-leather charge—one column across the bridge and over the fallen Blackburn, who was still yelling, "On! On!", and the other two columns fording the river for a flank attack from both sides. Remembered one Confederate on the far side of the river:

> We could hear the sound of galloping horses, a chorus of yells, and then with a quick sharp rattle a little cloud of smoke arose, whiz, skip, cling, the bullets came howling past our heads, spattering the trees unmercifully. Then suddenly came a quick flush in the face, a feeling at the small of the back as if a charge of electricity was passing through it, then a desperate attempt to keep cool, and whang went the carbines one after another all along the line. "Stand firm! . . . Hold your ground, men!"[33]

But, instead of standing firm, the Louisianians broke and scattered, leaving their dead and wounded for the Federals to tend to. Blackburn and Surby were too severely hurt for further service in the saddle. Grierson had Surby dressed in a regulation uniform to prevent his being shot as a spy and left the wounded at a neighboring farmhouse with the regimental physician. Then, without further pause, the column galloped southwest.

Wall's Bridge was the first calamitous setback of the raid and a warning of the hazards that still lay ahead. Recorded Grierson:

> The enemy were now on our tracks in earnest. We were in the vicinity of their stronghold [Port Hudson] and, from couriers and dispatches which we captured, it was evident that they were sending forces in all directions to intercept us. The Amite River, a wide and rapid stream, was to be crossed, and was in exceedingly close proximity to Port Hudson. This I determined upon securing before halting.[34]

Captain Henry Forbes had vivid recollections of that all-night, sleepless ride to the Williams Bridge over the Amite River, with the men dozing off in the saddle, heads nodding to the monotonous rhythm of the horses' hooves. This time a single scout, who looked "as honest and harmless as a Presbyterean deacon," was sent ahead to check the bridge guards. From a distance he saw two soldiers on duty at the river and brought this information back to Grierson. The Butternut Guerillas rode forward and captured the couple.

"The best of the story is yet to be told," wrote Captain Forbes. It was an understatement, referring to one of those strange events, reported later, that change the course of battles and of history. A Tennessee unit dispatched by General Gardner from Port Hudson had already reached Clinton and was prepared to intercept and crush the Federal invaders.

Having arrived with time to spare, the unit postponed its march to the Amite when "the good citizens rejoiced at the foreseen capture of Grierson and his raiders [and] tendered a complimentary dance to the officers of the command."

So the music played and the Tennesseans danced. And, as in Brussels fifty years before, on the eve of the Battle of Waterloo, "there was a sound of revelry . . . and bright the lamps shone o'er fair women and brave men." Just as, during that most famous ball in history, Napoleon stole the night's march from Wellington, Grierson's raiders slipped quietly over the Amite under the enemy's collective nose.

"While . . . we were stretching our legs for the bridge," wrote Captain Forbes, "the Confederate gentlemen were stretching theirs in the cotillion. After they had danced they marched. After we had marched we danced— when we learned they arrived at the bridge just two hours after we crossed it."[35]

Ten weeks later General Gardner admitted with chagrin that the elusive raiders had caused his surrender of Port Hudson, "by cutting off communications and supplies." He afterwards met Colonel Grierson and showed him a sheath of telegrams that had compounded his confusion. "Grierson was here; no, he was *there,* sixty miles away. He marched north, no, south, or again west." Confessed the general: "The trouble was, my men ambushed you where you did not go; they waited for you till morning while you passed by night."[36]

Saturday, May 2. The raiders were now only thirty miles from Baton Rouge, less than that from the Union lines and safety. They had hoodwinked Gardner's units for the moment but were still in hostile territory, and, as Captain Forbes observed, fatigue became another enemy:

> Men by the score were riding sound asleep in the saddles. The horses, excessively tired and hungry, would stray out of the road and thrust their noses to the earth in hopes of finding something to eat. The men, when addressed, would remain silent and motionless until a blow across the thigh or shoulders should awaken them, when it would be found that each supposed himself still riding with his company, which might be miles ahead.[37]

As they passed the rich plantations of Louisiana, slaves by the score poured out to join "the Yankees come to free the black folks." On overloaded mules, and with wagons piled with household furnishings and children, they fell in behind the column in ungovernable numbers, forming the sort of ragtail procession that would later follow Sherman on his march through Georgia.

At one plantation within sight of Baton Rouge, where the column stopped for food and rest, the men sprawled on the lawn, too tired to eat, and fell into obliviating sleep. Grierson, however, accepted the hospitality of the manor where "I astonished the occupants by sitting down and playing upon a piano which I found in the parlor and in that manner I managed to keep awake."

He did not reveal what music he played, possibly one of his own compositions from his youth, but he did recall his thoughts during that recital:

Only six miles then to Baton Rouge and four miles would bring us inside the lines guarded by the soldiers of the Union. Think of the great relief to the overtaxed mind and nerves. I felt that we had nobly accomplished the work assigned to us and no wonder that I felt musical; who would not under like circumstances?[38]

He was still playing when a scout rushed in with news that a large force had been sighted in the west. This close to the Union lines, Grierson was dumbfounded. He had thought that Gardner's troops were twenty miles behind him. Mounting his horse he rode out alone to investigate. True! Both sides of the road to Baton Rouge were flanked by two companies of cavalry, dismounted and deployed, with carbines at the ready.

Grierson also dismounted and, waving a white handkerchief, walked toward their captain, J. Franklin Godfrey, who wore the distinctive insignia of the Union cavalry on his jacket. It took a good deal of fast talking to convince that Federal officer that Grierson was indeed a bona fide commander of the Sixth and Seventh Illinois Cavalry that had crossed through all of Confederate Mississippi from La Grange in Tennessee.

Godfrey in turn explained the reason for his skepticism and show of force. One of Grierson's orderlies who had dozed off in the saddle had been carried by his horse into the Union lines. He was taken for a spy and grilled by General Christopher Augur at Baton Rouge. Augur refused to believe that he was a wayward member of a Federal cavalry unit from distant Tennessee. It was a trick, designed to lure his troops into a trap. He sent Captain Godfrey to "ascertain the truth."

Once the matter was resolved, Grierson's cavalry rode in behind this welcoming committee, and all of Baton Rouge turned out to greet the heroes. A triumphant parade was the last thing that the weary troopers wanted, but the residents demanded it. Bravely the brigade responded, forming a two-mile-long procession of mud-stained men and horses followed by a tatterdemalion horde of blacks with their mules and wagons and boisterous children—surely one of the most raffish marches in Louisiana history.

A hundred and ten miles to the north, the last of Grant's troops had already crossed the Mississippi and were ready for the march on Vicksburg. Grateful to Grierson for having diverted Confederate forces from his landing site, the general was lavish in his praise. He reported to Halleck that "Colonel Grierson's raid from La Grange through Mississippi has been the most successful thing of the kind since the breaking out of the rebellion." He believed, from information received, that, "Grierson has knocked the heart out of the State [of Mississippi]."[39]

Grant's colleague and the arch critic of cavalry, Sherman, was, for him, effusive, calling Grierson's raid "The most brilliant expedition of the war."[40]

In his own account, Grierson confined himself to the barest facts, noting that his troopers had ridden over 600 miles in less than sixteen days and had lost approximately 26 men. "During the expedition we killed and wounded about 100 of the enemy, captured and paroled over 500 prisoners, many of them officers, destroyed between 50 and 60 miles of railroad and telegraph, captured and destroyed over 3,000 stand of arms, and other army stores and Government property to an immense amount; we also captured 1,000 horses and mules."[41]

Had he possessed all the facts, he might have added that he had diverted Confederate cavalry from Grant's landing on the east bank of the Mississippi and lured away General Pemberton's reserve force at the Big Black River bridge. If Vicksburg should ever fall, the name of Ben Grierson, music teacher, would be stamped upon the ruins.

❦ 14 ❦

"The Road to Vicksburg
Is Open"

WEDNESDAY, April 29, 1863. Sergeant Charles E. Wilcox, of the Thirty-third Illinois Infantry at Hard Times Landing, noted in his diary:

> The sun rose throwing an impressive splendor upon the exciting scenes of the early morn. Every boat—transport and barge—lies at the landing, about five miles above Grand Gulf, covered till they are black with troops. Every heart here is full of anxiety and emotion; wondering eyes and eyes not altogether tearless, gaze ever and anon upon the *Father of Waters* where lie the formidable fleet of gunboats and rams, transports and barges, the latter heavily loaded with troops whose courage and valor are sufficient, when combined with that of the rest of this mighty army to redeem this lovely valley of the Mississippi from fiends and traitors who are desecrating it.[1]

The embarkation of the troops had been delayed. At Somerset Plantation, despite repeated proddings from Grant to get things moving, General McClernand had held up the operation for twenty-four hours, while Illinois Governor Richard Yates addressed the troops. "The Governor," wrote Sergeant Wilcox, "received from our battery and colors the usual salute—fifteen guns, colors drooping, small arms and swords presented. . . . 'Twas a very pleasant affair, the whole thing."

After this pleasant affair, General McClernand retired to the nuptial chamber to spend the evening with his bride.

The next morning, April 29, as the troops waited aboard the transports and barges safely out of range, Porter's gunboats tackled the Grand Gulf batteries and, as the admiral had predicted, got "knocked about a bit." More than a bit. None of the gunboats escaped damage. Eighty-one shells struck the supposedly "shot-proof" *Tuscumbia*, killing or wounding thirty of her crew. More than forty-seven shells struck Porter's flagship *Benton*, smashing her steering wheel, gouging great holes in her armor plate. The others fared only slightly better.

After that five-hour duel, it became apparent that Grand Gulf, with its

181

fortified bluffs, was as impregnable as Vicksburg from the river. Grant looked for a point downstream where he could cross to high ground out of reach of the defenders' guns. A "colored man" approached Grant and told him that a good landing was available at Bruinsburg and from there a good road led to Port Gibson.

An Illinois soldier, present at the interview, recorded the answer in words he thought a black man ought to use:

> Dar is only one way, General, and dat is by Bruinsburg, eight miles furder down. Dar you can leave de boats and the men can walk on high ground all the way. De best houses and plantations in all de country are dar, sah, all along dat road.[2]

That night the disembarked troops marched overland to De Shroon's plantation opposite Bruinsburg. Charles Dana rode beside Grant through the mud and darkness and made a moral estimation of the general's character. When Grant's horse stumbled and nearly pitched its rider to the ground, Dana thought expectantly, "*Now* he will swear." But, "Pulling up his horse, he rode on, and, to my utter amazement, without a word or sign of impatience." Dana still had not heard the overburdened general use an oath throughout the campaign.[3]

That night, too, Porter slipped his vessels past the Grand Gulf batteries. The enemy's guns he had futilely tried to silence earlier that day remained miraculously quiet of their own accord. The next morning, April 30, the river-crossing began without incident. By the next day 23,000 soldiers of McPherson's and McClernand's corps were on Mississippi soil at Bruinsburg.

For that unopposed landing, Grant would later thank Ben Grierson and his mounted hellions for keeping the Confederates elsewhere occupied. And he also owed a lot to Sherman. . . .

Sherman's April 30 and May 1 demonstration against Haynes Bluff had been a masterpiece of showmanship—or "a jolly lark," as his chief engineer, Captain William Jenney, saw it from one of the troop-bearing vessels on the river above Vicksburg. "Sherman spread his command over the decks of the transports with orders that every man should . . . look as numerous as possible." The gunboats fulminated smoke and steam; "the transports whistled and puffed and made all the noise they could."[4]

Having thus aroused the attention of the garrisons at Snyder's and Drumgould's Bluffs, Sherman's men landed beyond range of the batteries, circled back through the woods to reboard the transports out of sight, and came downriver "to go through the same farce again."

Surveying the action from Haynes Bluff, Confederate Major General Carter Stevenson saw ten regiments landing, then another ten, and then another. He telegraphed Pemberton at Jackson to ignore Grant's threat to Grand Gulf. It was just a bluff. The real attack was here. "The enemy are in front of me in force such as has never been seen before at Vicksburg. Send me reinforcements."[5]

Pemberton promptly ordered 3,000 troops on their way to Grand Gulf to return immediately. They had already traveled thirty miles, but raced the same distance back without a rest. On reaching Vicksburg, the men were reported as "perfectly exhausted, and lay along the road in groups, completely fagged out." Vicksburg citizens brought carriages to carry the spent troops to the bluffs—arriving in time to see Sherman's armada, mission accomplished, blandly sailing down the Yazoo.

"This diversion," wrote Sherman later, "made with so much pomp and display, therefore completely fulfilled its purpose, by leaving General Grant to contend with a minor force, on landing at Bruinsburg, and afterward at Port Gibson and Grand Gulf."[6] Grant's message to Sherman was brief but appreciative. "All right," he commended. Then, almost as an afterthought, "Join me below Vicksburg."

On May 1, with two-thirds of his army on the east bank of the Mississippi, Grant was able to write later, "I felt a degree of relief scarcely ever equalled since. . . ."

> I was now in the enemy's country with a vast river and the stronghold of Vicksburg between me and my base of supplies. But I was on dry ground on the same side of the river as the enemy. All the campaigns, labors, hardships and exposures from the month of December previous to this time that had been made and endured were for the accomplishment of this one object.[7]

Grant's first move was to push his army toward Port Gibson, ten miles northeast, whose capture would outflank Grand Gulf and lay open the invasion route to Vicksburg. Confederate General John Bowen raced from Grand Gulf to block the Federal drive to Port Gibson. Though heavily outnumbered —with only two brigades from his own division and two brigades sent from Vicksburg—Bowen hoped for reinforcements he'd been told were on the way. That afternoon he positioned his available troops at a fork in the road three miles below Port Gibson.

Bowen had only one thing in his favor.

As Grant noted: "The country in this part of Mississippi stands on edge, as it were, the roads running along the ridges except when they occasionally pass from one ridge to another." The terrain was "the most broken and difficult to operate in I ever saw." The Union attackers were forced to approach the Confederate line over erratic ridges, unable to support each other, separately vulnerable. Four miles below Port Gibson, Grant ran into Confederate pickets about 12:30 A.M., May 1. After some exchange of fire, the Federals pushed forward a short distance, before suspending operations until daylight.

William Chambers of the Forty-sixth Mississippi Infantry was among the reinforcements hurried down from Vicksburg in support of Bowen, and Chambers got his first taste of an enemy invasion of his native state. He found Port Gibson a beautiful city, the streets broad and regular, the houses handsome, comparing favorably to his own home town in Covington County. "But," he noted, "I had no time to observe anything." Actually he observed a great deal, as he later wrote:

> In the streets all was confusion. Men with pale faces were running hither and thither, some with arms and seeking a command, women sobbing on every side, children in open-eyed wonder clinging to their weeping mothers not understanding the meaning of it all, and negroes with eyes protruding like open cotton bolls

were jostling each other and every body else and continuously asking about "dem Yankees."

The ladies cheered us through their tears, and besought us to drive the invaders from their homes. One lady while she prayed Heaven to protect us, said we felt as near to her as though we were her own sons going forth to battle. The wounded, too, were meeting us, some in vehicles and some on litters, and many a poor fellow with a shattered limb or a gaping wound would wildly hurrah for the "brave Mississippians."[8]

The reinforcements arrived in time to check the Federal onslaught until late afternoon. Bowen's limited strength, recorded *Harper's Weekly,* "made victory for him impossible, for Grant almost inevitable." Though they fought stubbornly, gave ground reluctantly, the day-long battle left 787 Southerners dead or wounded and missing on the field, with the rest in near collapse. Chambers saw one of his fellow Mississippians, unscathed in the battle, sink exhausted against a tree trunk, carelessly discharging his musket and blowing his arm off at the elbow.

A successful Federal flank attack near the Bruinsburg Road forced Bowen to break off the action, abandon Port Gibson, and retreat toward Grand Gulf. Charles Dana had not yet seen Grant in action and arrived too late to witness the fight. But he stopped at a small field hospital behind the battlefield, "and the first thing my eyes fell upon as I went into the yard was a heap of arms and legs which had been amputated and thrown into a pile outside. I had seen men shot and dead men plenty, but this pile of legs and arms gave me a vivid sense of war such as I had not before experienced."[9]

Grant was breakfasting in Port Gibson when he looked up to see, approaching on the road outside, two horsemen who oddly resembled Don Quixote and Sancho Panza. They were Charles Dana and Grant's son Freddy.

Aboard a steamer, Freddy had wakened to find his father gone and the army in transit to Bruinsburg. Determined not to be left behind, he hitchhiked across the river on a transport and set out on foot to find the general. Along the way he met Charles Dana, also following the army. The two teamed up and wangled a pair of captured horses from the infantry. When Grant first saw the couple, they were mounted on two enormous animals, swaybacked and languid with age, with dilapidated saddles and bridles made of clothesline.

With more pride than annoyance, Grant decided to keep Freddy with him for the balance of the campaign. The lad was old enough "to take in all he saw and retain a recollection of it that would not be possible in more mature years." Besides, his ebullient youth and cheerful disposition were a tonic for the troops. Fred himself remembered that "the sight of a small boy on the big white horse made some sport on the road for the soldiers as I passed—or those who passed me."[10]

With McClernand's troops in possession of Port Gibson, Grant rode to Grand Gulf, since evacuated and held in fee by Porter's gunboats. Aboard an ironclad he had his first bath in a week, borrowed clean underwear, and sat down for a meal. From Grand Gulf, Porter took vessels from his fleet downriver, to blockade the Red River.

For the time being Grant planned to make Grand Gulf his base for the projected campaign against Vicksburg. Here wagon trains or vessels coming down from Milliken's Bend with food, forage, and ammunition could be landed in accordance with the progress of his army. But a message from "Nothing Positive" Banks changed his mind. Written three weeks earlier, it informed Grant that Banks had not as yet reduced Port Hudson but instead had gone off campaigning in Louisiana, was now a hundred miles away, and would not be able to begin operations against Port Hudson until May 10, a week from then.

Grant decided to ignore for the present any major cooperation with Banks. To wait a week, he realized, would give Pemberton time to reinforce Vicksburg and its outposts, enable the forces in Mississippi to rally to the state's defense, and seriously jeopardize the campaign. Moreover, Banks's forces when they arrived would add no more than 10,000 to 13,000 men to his army, which hardly outweighed the disadvantages of delay.

"I therefore determined to move independently of Banks," Grant wrote, "cut loose from my base, destroy the rebel force in rear of Vicksburg, and invest or capture the city."[11]

The affair at Holly Springs the previous December, when his depot and supplies had been destroyed by Earl Van Dorn, had taught him one important lesson. Mississippi was a fruitful state; one could live off the land, getting ample food and fodder from the still luxuriant plantations. So long as he had ammunition, and that should be certain before he started, the troops could forage for themselves.

It was a move that violated all military precedent—and one in direct defiance of Halleck's instructions, which had been to send one corps to cooperate with Banks against Port Hudson. Yet to get approval from Washington would take more precious time. Better to make his point by means of a fait accompli.

Even Sherman—who would later make the same decision at Atlanta and march to the sea without a fixed base to rely on—urged Grant not to abandon Grand Gulf but to "stop all troops till your army is partially supplied with wagons." Grant assured his colleague that, when all his army was united, "we could be in Vicksburg in seven days." Every day lost was "worth two thousand men to the enemy." He could not afford to wait. "A delay would give the enemy time to re-enforce and fortify."[12]

Which was what Pemberton was doing, to the best of his ability.

Though, with little cavalry for reconnaissance and with many key defense points to keep track of, Pemberton was reduced to speculation as to the enemy's movements and intentions. As more rumors and reports arrived, he concluded that the goal was Vicksburg.

Headquartered at Jackson until May 1, he was more immediately concerned with Grierson's raid, which was drawing off his forces in pursuit. It was not until April 28 that he first learned of Grant's intended crossing of the Mississippi, when General Bowen telegraphed from Grand Gulf that "transports and barges loaded down with troops are landing at Hard Times on the west bank."

From that moment on, Pemberton would never know a moment's peace. Earlier, Vicksburg was a fortress to be held, and one which had been held successfully against attacks by land and river. Now it was a sacred trust to be defended, one on which the future of the Southern Cause depended. If he allowed its defenses to be weakened for whatever reason, "I should have been in heart a traitor to that cause. . . . "[13]

He immediately telegraphed Bowen at Grand Gulf: "Have you now force enough to hold your position? If not, give me the smallest additional number with which you can." At the same time, he ordered Major General Carter Stevenson, in command at Vicksburg, to ready 5,000 troops for quick transfer to Grand Gulf when the call came.

At the same time, too, he wired both Johnston at Tullahoma and President Davis in Richmond, informing them that much of Grant's army was at Hard Times, "indicating an attack at Grand Gulf with a view to Vicksburg." Of Johnston he asked that the Army of Tennessee protect the approaches to Vicksburg in central Mississippi, and to Davis he reemphasized his need for cavalry support.

For years to come, questions would be debated as to what steps Pemberton took to prevent Grant's landing and subsequent march through Mississippi. And, from another angle, what steps Johnston took to help his subordinate in this emergency. The fact is that both did what they could in the confusing circumstances. Without the "eyes" of cavalry, Pemberton had no precise information on Grant's operations and designs. Without such information, Johnston was reluctant to weaken Bragg's army in Tennessee by detaching troops for Mississippi that might not, in fact, be needed.

Finally, on May 1, when Grant's crossing was confirmed, Pemberton sent identical messages to Johnston and the President:

> Enemy can cross all his army from Hard Times to Bruinsburg below Bayou Pierre. Large reinforcements should be sent me from other departments. Enemy's movement threatens Jackson, and, if successful, cuts off Vicksburg and Port Hudson from the east. Am hurrying all reinforcements I possibly can to Bowen.[14]

The reinforcements, which included William Chambers's Mississippians, reached Bowen but were not sufficient to hold Port Gibson. Nor would Pemberton get any help from Lieutenant General Kirby Smith, commanding Confederate forces west of the Mississippi. He had tried to tap that source before, urging Smith at least to disrupt Federal communications on the right bank of the river. From Smith, as from Braxton Bragg and Joseph Johnston, came the answer: No men could be spared for Vicksburg. In Johnston's May 2 reply to Pemberton's plea for help, there was no mention of reinforcements or the return of Van Dorn's cavalry. The telegram read simply: "If Grant's army lands on this side of the river, the safety of Mississippi depends on beating it. For that object you should unite all your forces."

The instructions left Pemberton more baffled than before. With his army widely distributed at Vicksburg, Jackson, and Port Hudson, how was he to unite his forces to "beat" Grant without exposing one or more of those key points to danger?

He would not abandon Vicksburg or leave it insufficiently attended. "With Vicksburg for his base," the Confederate general wrote, "he [Grant] would at once have had the game in his own hands." And "was not Sherman's large force—two thirds of my entire strength—still at Haynes Bluff on the city's very rim, prepared to march in if I marched out?"[15]

A lot of the questions answered themselves, when Grierson ended his raid at Baton Rouge, when Grand Gulf and Port Gibson fell, when Sherman left the area north of Vicksburg to rejoin Grant, and when the united Federal army began its march northeastward into central Mississippi. There was only one thing Pemberton could do: leave a sufficient force to garrison Vicksburg, and place himself between the advancing Federals and the imperiled city.

Grant's army, after leaving Port Gibson and moving north and east, had a choice of either Vicksburg or Jackson as its destination. Waiting for Sherman's corps to catch up, McPherson's corps hugged the south bank of the Big Black River, keeping watch over Hankinson's Ferry by which the Confederates might approach Grant's army. When Sherman arrived, McPherson bore to the right, toward Raymond, while Sherman's corps, after crossing the river, rejoined the army on May 8 and followed behind McClernand.

As Grant had foreseen, the countryside provided abundant food and fodder for troops, now numbering 43,000 or thereabouts. With equipment commandeered from the plantations, a wagon train was improvised, perhaps the strangest caravan of any war. Elegant state carriages, upholstered phaetons and barouches, surreys with the fringe on top—all drawn by horses, mules, oxen, and anything with four legs—were loaded down with hams and chickens, bags of sweet potatoes, sacks of corn, buckets of honey, and baskets of fruit and vegetables. If the South purported to be starving from the Federal blockade, there was no evidence of it in this part of Mississippi.

While a New York *Times* correspondent, assigned to the army, found the Mississippi maidens "plump, rosy, engaging and delicious," he also found plantation food delicious, dining on "roast turkey and duck, wheat bread, biscuits, and an abundance of vegetables." In the ranks, Isaac Jackson of the Eighty-third Ohio Infantry found the area "great mutton country. We live fat. Plenty of the best mutton and beef."[16]

Charles Dana, with the mind of a scholar and the heart of a poet, saw the march in somewhat different terms, writing to a young acquaintance, unidentified:

> The plums and peaches here are pretty nearly ripe. The strawberries have been ripe these few days, but the soldiers eat them up before we get a sight of them. The figs are as big as the end of your thumb, and the green pears are big enough to eat. But you don't know what beautiful flower gardens there are here. I never saw such roses; and the other day I found a lily as big as a tiger lily, only it was a magnificent red.[17]

Osborn Oldroyd of McPherson's corps was getting his first taste of real campaigning, having missed the fighting at Port Gibson. He found foraging a cornucopia of mixed delights. Osborn watched while two of his companions chased a chicken to its refuge beneath an outhouse raised on stilts. The more agile of the two men caught the chicken; but the other discovered a coffee pot brimful of silver dollars, apparently concealed there by the owner. The lucky finder, Tom McVey, distributed most of the coins among his comrades, finding the load too heavy for his pockets.

The nineteen-year-old Oldroyd found the march through southern Mississippi a source of inspiration:

> O, what a grand army this is, and what a sight to fire the heart of a spectator with a speck of patriotism in his bosom. I shall never forget the scene of today, while looking back upon a mile of solid columns, marching with their old tattered flags streaming in the summer breeze, and hearkening to the firm tramp of their broad brogans keeping step to the pealing fife and drum, or the regimental bands discoursing "Yankee Doodle" or "The Girl I Left Behind Me."[18]

In contrast, the Confederate concentration below Vicksburg, and along the railroad east of Vicksburg, seemed to lack both heart and hope. "This was one march in which the command 'close up' was wholly unnecessary," William Chambers noted. The men had scarcely had an hour's rest since moving south to intercept the enemy. "My feet had blood blisters on the soles," wrote Chambers, "and the others were no better off. We had marched about 150 miles in less than four days, besides the fighting, and this was no timid performance for troops unused to long marches."

Then Chambers sounded a still more somber note. "But what distressed me more than anything else, was the conduct of our officers." Out of discretion, perhaps, he did not elaborate; but added and underscored: "*And some men had already begun to suspect the motives as well as doubt the judgment of Gen. Pemberton.*"[19]

By contrast, Joe Johnston, a native of Virginia and one who made retreat a hallmark of his strategy, never lost the confidence of those he led. Yet a Pennsylvania Yankee leading Confederates in retreat would in months to come be judged more harshly—and unfairly.

Never before, since he took command of the army at Young's Point in January, had Grant radiated so much optimism.

"The road to Vicksburg is open," he assured his colleague, General Sherman; and to Halleck in Washington—unaware of quite different instructions Halleck was sending him by way of Banks—he wrote: "This army is in the finest health and spirits. Since leaving Milliken's Bend they have marched as much by night as by day, through mud and rain, without tents or much other baggage, and on irregular rations, without a complaint, and with less straggling than I have ever before witnessed." They would keep marching, he assured the general in chief, and "not stop until Vicksburg is in our possession."

He even took time on May 10 to write to General Banks in Baton Rouge:

> Many days cannot elapse before the battle will begin which is to decide the fate of Vicksburg, but it is impossible to predict how long it may last. I would urgently request, therefore, that you join me or send all the force you can spare to cooperate in the great struggle for opening the Mississippi River.[20]

Banks would neither join him nor send troops to join him. Halleck might forgive Grant for deciding at Grand Gulf to leave "Nothing Positive" Banks behind. Banks, however, would not forgive him, and Grant would never really care.

Charles Dana, dividing his time between young Freddy and the general, continued to take Grant's measure in accordance with Stanton's instructions. But he no longer anticipated weaknesses in the general's character or conduct. The man was sober, tough as rawhide, and dependable. Only young Freddy had a complaint; he preferred to eat with the troops instead of with his father, since the foraging soldiers set a better table. Grant's meals, in Freddy's estimation, "were the worst I ever saw or partook of."

As a sergeant, Osborn Oldroyd's opinion of the general would have probably meant more to Grant than Dana's. While the Twentieth Ohio guarded Hankinson's Ferry across the Big Black River, Oldroyd overheard his comrades speculating on their destination. Some thought that they would march direct to Vicksburg, others that Grant was feeling for a weak spot in the enemy's defenses. And, wrote Oldroyd,

> . . . one cool head remarked that it was all right wherever we went while Grant was leading, for he had never known defeat. Confidence in a good general stiffens a soldier—a rule that ought to work both ways. Surely no leader ever had more of the confidence of those he led than General Grant. . . . The enemy are doing all they can to hinder us, but let Grant say *forward,* and we obey.[21]

Lieutenant General Pemberton would have been envious of that encomium. As Oldroyd wisely stated, confidence should work both ways, stiffening the spirit of both soldiers and their leader. It was a factor that was fading, if not missing, in the Mississippi army.

Late in the morning of May 12 the van of McPherson's corps neared Fourteen Mile Creek, two miles south of Raymond. Brigadier General John Gregg prepared to resist the Federal advance with the 3,000 troops of his brigade. Gregg's instructions from Pemberton were, "If the enemy advance on you too strong, fall back on Jackson." The enemy did advance too strong, a whole division confronting Gregg's brigade outside the town.

The major burden of driving the Confederates from Raymond fell fortuitously to the Third Division troops of Major General John A. Logan, a man in whom Grant placed increasing trust and toward whom Sylvester Cadwallader felt both admiration and suspicion. While Logan was known as a "political general," the reporter admitted he evinced a certain military brilliance. But he also swore, he drank, and he had other traits unsuitable to the two stars of his rank.

Cadwallader chose a curious example to "give some insight into the habits and character of Gen. John A. Logan" during the campaign:

> I saw him on one occasion . . . with nothing on him in the way of clothing but his hat, shirt and boots, sitting at a table on which stood a bottle of whiskey and a tin cup, and playing on the violin for a lot of darky roustabouts to dance. When the exercise began to flag, which it generally did at short intervals in the face of such temptations, potations were indulged in by players and dancers.[22]

Yet Logan kept his mind on business as he led his troops in the attack on Raymond. Sergeant Oldroyd, who had seen little fighting since the army crossed the Mississippi, found himself in the forefront of the battle as "Black Jack" Logan threw his second brigade down an embankment and across a creek to fall on the heads of the Confederates.

"They fought us desperately," Oldroyd wrote, "and no doubt they fully expected to whip us early in the fight, before we could get reinforcements." The regiment next to the Twentieth Ohio wavered, but "Logan dashed up, and with the shriek of an eagle turned them back to their places. . . . " It was the sight of Logan riding up and down the line, "firing the men with his own enthusiasm" that kept the troops firmly in position.

"For two hours the contest raged furiously," Oldroyd wrote, and "the creek was running red with precious blood spilt for our country. . . . Into another part of the line the enemy charged, fighting hand to hand, being too close to fire, and using the butts of their guns."[23]

At the end, when the surviving Confederates had fled, Oldroyd found half of his company killed or wounded. He saw Colonel Manning F. Force, regimental commander, seated against a tree and openly weeping at the loss, his face and uniform streaked with the powder of exploding shells.

The army camped that night at Raymond where the citizens had prepared a dinner for the Confederate defenders, who had not stopped to eat it. One of the residents, Marmaduke Shannon's married daughter, Anne Martin, was among those expecting to welcome Gregg's victorious troops on their return. Now she retreated to her home and locked the doors, and after the Federal invaders had departed, Anne wrote to her sister in Vicksburg:

> For a week that immense army continued to pass through . . . pouring into town, flaunting their star-spangled banner, playing Yankee Doodle, and, oh the desecration! the Bonnie Blue Flag. . . . All night the fife and drum was heard as fresh regiments passed. . . . I prayed most earnestly for protection during the night for we could hear them tearing down fences, shooting cattle, shouting and going on and we expected every minute to be broken in on.[24]

Finally the doors to Anne's home were broken down, and the rampaging Yankees "took everything but one sidesaddle, and even pulled the curtains down and tore them in strings." She saw the men gathering up their household plunder, "showing around jewelry and silverware that they had stolen." And she warned her sister never to hide anything underground for safety. Their neighbors' baby had been buried in their yard, "and would you believe it: that child's remains were dug up no less than three different times in search of treasure."

By nightfall of May 12, Gregg's forces were bivouacked between Raymond and Jackson, with no Southern troops between them and the Mississippi capital. Confederate casualties on the field at Raymond were reported as 515 in killed, wounded, and missing.

It was just as well that neither Dana, Secretary Stanton's confidant, nor Rawlins, Grant's self-appointed guardian, was with the general on the night following the battle of Raymond. Sylvanus Cadwallader was sitting in Colonel Duff's tent when, around midnight, "General Grant came into the tent alone, in the dark, and requested a drink of whiskey. Col. Duff drew a canteen from under his pillow and handed it to him. The general poured a generous potation into an army tin cup and swallowed it with great appreciation."

Cadwallader was surprised to see the general take a second cupful, then a third, before retiring. He was also surprised when Duff pledged the reporter to "discreet silence" on the incident. Later, Cadwallader learned that Governor Richard Yates had entrusted a barrel of whisky to Duff's care, and that "Grant knew about it. I also subsequently learned that Duff had catered to Grant's inordinate desire for stimulants long before this, and continued to do so till his 'muster out' at City Point [in 1865]."[25]

The next day, however, Grant's mind was crystal clear. The fall of Raymond brought his campaign into sharper focus, which he detailed later. "As I hoped in the end to besiege Vicksburg I must first destroy all possibilities of aid. I therefore determined to move swiftly towards Jackson, capture that place without delay, destroy or drive any force in that direction and then turn upon Pemberton."[26]

He ordered McPherson to cut the Vicksburg to Jackson railway line at Clinton and then move east on Jackson. Sherman's corps would advance on the capital from Raymond, while McClernand would be positioned within supporting distance. The Federal advance had brought Pemberton out of his Vicksburg headquarters on May 12 to join his forces strewn along the railroad line near Edward's Station, east of the Big Black River.

It was becoming an intricate game of chess, involving careful moves and countermoves. And the worst of it was that neither player knew precisely which of his opponent's pieces occupied what squares on the chessboard.

Joe Johnston, at long last, was on his way to take command of the defense of Vicksburg. The dapper, diminutive Virginian, with the trim Van Dyke and halo of silvering hair, had been at Tullahoma on May 9 when the telegram arrived from Secretary Seddon:

> Proceed at once to Mississippi and take chief command of the forces there, giving those in the field, as far as practicable, the encouragement and benefit of your personal direction . . .[27]

He took with him 3,000 troops from Bragg's magnificent Army of Tennessee and was told he could expect more men from Beauregard at Charleston. Johnston wired back, "I shall go immediately, although unfit for field service."

"Old Joe" (the "old" was largely a term of affection; he was only fifty-six) still suffered from the wounds received at Seven Pines twelve months before. He was dispirited by the death of Stonewall Jackson, who had been mortally wounded by his own men at Chancellorsville, deeply troubled, too, by the assassination of Earl Van Dorn at Spring Hill, Tennessee.

The gallant cavalier, Van Dorn, had been shot in the head by a local doctor, George B. Peters, for allegedly paying excessive attention to Peters's wife. (In Richmond, diarist Mary Chesnut was diverted by the gossiping ladies trying to rhyme "maids and women all forlorn" with Earl Van Dorn.) Van Dorn's death seemed to mark a milestone in the Confederate West, where cavalry leadership had been so great a factor.

Johnston arrived at Jackson on May 13 to find only Gregg's 6,000 soldiers in the city and Grant's three-corps army within striking distance of the capital. He telegraphed Seddon that he found himself cut off from communication with General Pemberton. *"I am too late,"* he lamented. Too late to hold Jackson, at any rate; with his limited force, he could fight only a delaying action, meanwhile trying somehow to link up with Pemberton.

He promptly sent a message to Pemberton at Edward's Station. Written in triplicate and dispatched by three separate couriers for safety, it read:

> I have lately arrived, and learn that Major General Sherman is between us with four divisions at Clinton. It is important to re-establish communication, that you may be re-enforced. If practicable, come up in his rear at once. To beat such a detachment would be of immense value. The troops here could cooperate. All the strength you can quickly assemble should be brought; time is all-important.[28]

Time was running out so far as Jackson was concerned. During the morning of May 14, Sherman and McPherson's troops sloshed through pouring rain and mud to storm the city from the south and west. The Confederates were driven back into the city, after brief but bitter fighting, and Johnston—abandoning seventeen pieces of artillery—promptly withdrew his forces six miles northward up the Canton road.

To Osborn Oldroyd's disgust, Sherman's corps was first into the city, leaving his own regiment "covered with mud instead of glory." But he recorded one memorable moment when he came upon a Confederate soldier lying mortally wounded by the roadside. He bent over to give the man a drink from his canteen. "His piteous glance at me at that time I shall never forget. It is on the battlefield and among the dead and dying we get to know each other—nay, even our own selves."[29]

As soon as the road was cleared, Sylvanus Cadwallader rode with young Freddy Grant into the city and, wrote Cadwallader, "started for the Capitol at full speed to secure the large Confederate flag which waves from a staff on the roof." Reaching the building they ran up the stairs leading to the garret, only to meet "a ragged, muddy, begrimed cavalryman descending with the coveted prize under his arm. To say that our disappointment was extreme but mildly expresses the state of our feelings."

Freddy, however, continued his search for the spoils of war. Wandering through the Capitol he entered Governor Pettus's office, to find what he believed was the governor's pipe abandoned on a desk. "I confiscated it," he wrote, "ostensibly for the national service, but actually for my own private use. It had the advantage of being still loaded and lighted."[30]

"If there ever was a jubilant army," recorded one Yankee soldier, "Grant's army in Jackson was that night." Grant himself stopped at the city's finest hostelry, the Bowman House, occupying the bed that Johnston had slept in the night before, and the next morning, May 15, he and Sherman visited a factory still working at full blast, producing equipment for the Southern armies. No one, Grant wrote later, seemed to notice them:

> We looked on for a while to see the tent cloth which they were making roll out of the looms, with "C.S.A." woven in each bolt. There was an immense amount

of cotton, in bales, stacked outside. The operatives were told they could leave and take with them what cloth they could carry. In a few minutes cotton and factory were in a blaze.[31]

The sparks were only the first of a mighty conflagration that, for Sherman, was something of a rehearsal for the burning of Atlanta. "He did the work most effectually," Grant acclaimed, while a correspondent for the Northern press reported: "Foundries, machine-shops, warehouses, factories, arsenals and public stores were fired as fast as flames could be kindled." Sherman later declared that "Jackson, as a railroad center or Government depot of stores and military factories, can be of little use to the enemy for six months."

Similarly, a resident of Jackson found the city "a wreck of its former self. . . . Look where you will, ruin meets the eye." Landmarks such as the two railroad depots, the Catholic Church, and many public buildings were destroyed, while in the residential district some solitary chimneys rose above the rubble. These lone-standing columns of stone, that later in the war were known as "Sherman's sentinels," gave the capital the temporary name of "Chimneyville."[32]

Lieutenant Colonel Arthur James Fremantle, a young English officer on a busman's holiday, visited Jackson while many of the buildings were still smoking. It was one of his first impressions of the Civil War that he had come to America to write about, and he added the charge of wholesale looting to the list of Union depredations. He extravagantly claimed, perhaps on hearsay, that "during the short space of thirty-six hours, in which General Grant occupied the city, his troops had wantonly pillaged nearly all the private houses. They had gutted all the stores, and destroyed what they could not carry away."[33]

By noon of May 15, while Sherman remained with two divisions in Jackson to complete the work of destruction, McClernand's and McPherson's corps were marching for Edward's and Bolton. Johnston was still encamped on the road to Canton, and Pemberton's forces stood astride the Southern Railroad, almost midway between Vicksburg and the burning capital. Chief engineer Lockett was summoned to Edward's Station to construct fieldworks "at favorable points." As Lockett wrote:

> The position was naturally a strong one, on high ground, with the cultivated valley of Baker's Creek in its front. Here General Pemberton wished to wait to be attacked by Grant. There can be no doubt that if he had been allowed to do so a desperate and bloody battle would have been fought on that ground, the issue of which might have been different from that of the two unfortunate engagements which did actually occur.[34]

In Vicksburg, before leaving for Edward's Station and the Big Black River, Pemberton once again published an order for all noncombatants to leave the city. "Heretofore, I have merely requested that it be done; now I demand it." But Mary Loughborough joined the determined band of citizens who refused to leave. Where could they go? In any direction they might encounter Federal troops, reportedly ranging through Hinds County around Jackson. Who would protect them then? Mary and others pleaded with officers sent to enforce the order:

"We declared that we would almost starve—that we would meet any evil cheerfully in Vicksburg where our friends were—where we were housed, quiet, and contented. So, laughingly, they said they were completely overcome by our distress and would arrange it so that we could stay if we wish.

"But remember," the officers said, "if trouble comes, you must meet it with your eyes open."

"Yes," the ladies said tactfully, "we can meet trouble where you are cheerfully."

Added to the population that insisted on remaining were the incoming refugees from Jackson and the threatened country and plantations to the east. Vicksburg, which had earlier been a place from which many sought to flee, had now become a haven, secure behind its fortifications as no other place in Mississippi was secure. Mary Loughborough expressed the sentiments of many, both residents and refugees, in writing:

Ah! Vicksburg, our city of refuge, the last to yield thou wilt be; and within thy homes we will not fear the footstep of the victorious army, but rest in safety amid thy hills! And those whom we love so dearly will comfort and sustain us in our frightened and panic-stricken condition—will laugh away our woman's fears, and lighten our heart from the dread and suffering we have experienced.[35]

✣ 15 ✣

Hill of Death

I T was a whooping, singing, cheering Union corps that marched out of
Jackson with McPherson on the morning of May 15, leaving behind a city still
in flames.

"The last few days have been full of excitement," wrote Osborn Oldroyd,
"and although we have marched and fought hard, and lost some of our best
men, besides getting tired and hungry ourselves, we are more resolved than
ever to keep the ball rolling." Their battle cry, "On to Vicksburg," rang with
new conviction. They had marched from the Mississippi to the captured
capital in fourteen days, won three significant victories, and the Fortress City,
only forty miles away, no longer loomed as the invincible Gibraltar of the
West.

That the troops were leaving the conquered capital so quickly, with such
sure direction, was due to an extraordinary piece of luck. Not only luck, but
the chance result of a ruse that had been planted several months before. In
war-torn Memphis, General Stephen Hurlbut had openly castigated and ex-
pelled a citizen on charges of disloyalty. The professed traitor was drummed
out with exaggerated fanfare and publicity.

In point of fact, the exiled citizen was a loyal Union man, with instructions
to enter Mississippi as a Union deserter and to infiltrate the Confederate high
command.[1]

The mission was highly successful. Reaching Jackson, he was accepted as
a Southern sympathizer, inducted into the army, and later appointed to Joseph
Johnston's staff, when that general reached the capital. And it was he who was
chosen as one of three couriers to deliver Johnston's first dispatch to Pemberton, instructing the Vicksburg general to advance from Edward's Station,
come up on Grant's rear, and join forces with Johnston's troops as they moved
west from Canton.

Now Grant knew precisely what the enemy was planning and how best to
thwart it. Giving Sherman another day for the destruction of the capital, he
ordered McPherson's corps to start immediately for Bolton, twenty miles west
of Jackson on the Southern Railroad—"the nearest point where Johnston
could reach the road."

195

At the same time he informed McClernand, still near Raymond: "It is evidently the design of the enemy to get north of us and cross the Big Black River and beat us into Vicksburg. We must not allow them to do this. Turn all your forces toward Bolton Station and make all dispatch in getting there. . . . "[2]

Grant himself left Jackson only shortly behind McPherson's column, to arrive at Clinton later that day. Everything had been breaking in his favor. The interception of Johnston's orders to Pemberton would enable him to keep the Confederates divided—an essential requirement should Johnston receive expected reinforcements. And though he had ignored Halleck's instructions to cooperate with Banks before marching into Mississippi, it would be hard to censure the success already gained.

Moreover, Charles Dana—who had stopped regarding himself as a watchdog over Grant but, rather, as one sympathetic to the general's operations—showed him a telegram received from Secretary Stanton:

> General Grant has full and absolute authority to enforce his own command, and to remove any person who, by ignorance, inaction, or any other cause, interferes with or delays his operations. He has the full confidence of the Government, is expected to enforce his authority, and will be firmly and heartily supported; . . . You may communicate this to him.[3]

That settled, in Grant's mind at least, not only any clash with Halleck on the question of insubordination, but also the troublesome matter of McClernand. But he would take no action regarding the Illinois general at this point. Things were going too well as it was.

Grant waited with his staff at Clinton till the morning of May 16, when he learned from a train crew of the Southern Railroad that Pemberton was indeed obeying Johnston's orders and marching east with "eighty regiments of infantry and ten batteries." If so, the trap Grant was planning should be well prepared.

That morning, too, elements of McPherson's and McClernand's corps began marching toward Edwards from their bivouac. Sylvanus Cadwallader rode with Logan's division in the vanguard of McPherson's corps and witnessed a strange clash between the allied columns. General Alvin P. Hovey's division of McClernand's corps was first to reach the crossing of the Clinton and Raymond roads, obtaining the right of way over Logan. Reported Cadwallader:

> Logan was compelled to halt till Hovey had passed this intersection, and then start on squarely in Hovey's rear. I rarely ever witnessed such an exhibition of rage, profanity, and disappointment as Logan then gave. The air was just blue with oaths, till speech was exhausted. McPherson's arrival a few minutes after was the signal for another outburst. But there was no apparent remedy. Hovey had the road by right of prior occupation . . .[4]

Logan would have his moment of glory when he met the enemy, and McPherson even now felt confident enough to inform Grant by courier that "Pemberton was soon to be caught!"

Neither McClernand nor McPherson knew precisely where they might encounter Pemberton's forces. They found out quickly when McClernand's advance was engaged, some miles southeast of Edward's Station, by Wirt Adams's cavalry, guarding the Raymond Road.

For Pemberton, who two days earlier had been in position at Edward's Station in fieldworks prepared by Lockett, the place and time of the encounter was unfortunate and unexpected. But much had happened in the intervening hours. On the morning of May 14, he had received Johnston's first dispatch (that had also fallen into Grant's hands) ordering him to move his army eastward, toward Grant's rear, and join forces with Johnston who was still awaiting reinforcements.

It was perhaps the hardest dilemma Pemberton would have to face. He had received instructions from Jefferson Davis that Vicksburg and Port Hudson must be held "at all costs." And the President had also advised him that: "In your situation . . . it is necessary to add conciliation to the discharge of duty. Patience in listening to suggestions . . . is sometimes rewarded."[5]

Yet to follow Johnston's order to leave his fieldwork at Edward's Station, to confront a Union force of unknown size, meant moving still further from endangered Vicksburg, exposing his flanks to attack from north and south, and jeopardizing his communications and supply line with the fortress city.

His quandary sprang from a basic difference in the attitudes and tactics of the two commanders. Pemberton was dedicated above all to the defense of Vicksburg. The city's survival as a Confederate Gibraltar was to him a sacred trust. Johnston, who never regarded any point in geography as indispensable or worthy of great sacrifice, put Vicksburg secondary to the conquest or dispersal of the Union forces under Grant. He had come to Mississippi to beat Grant, not to hold a city—and had shown as much when he readily abandoned Jackson to avoid a battle that might jeopardize his meager forces.

Basically a lonely man, conscious of being suspect because of his Northern birth, Pemberton eased his dubiety by doing something he had never done before in his thirty years of military service. He summoned his generals to a council of war. In this difficult situation he needed their total agreement and cooperation. Should they advance east to meet the enemy on relatively open ground, as Johnston had instructed? Or was there an alternative?

According to one of the conferees, Inspector General Jacob Thompson, *"there was not a voice in favor of moving on Clinton."* But though this statement was made only two months later, Thompson's memory was faulty. There was marked division of opinion in the group. Some agreed to the move on Clinton; General Loring, among others, favored marching southeast toward Dillon's Plantation, thereby cutting Grant's supply line with the Mississippi—unaware that Grant had determined to abandon that supply line some days earlier.[6]

Disliking both alternatives, Pemberton reluctantly agreed to Loring's plan, sending a missive to Johnston informing him of this decision and the reasons for the move. Forced to wait for supplies from Vicksburg and further delayed on the march by flooded streams, the Confederate column made scant progress toward Dillon's on May 15.

The rumble of artillery fire caught the attention of Confederate officers at an early morning briefing. Shortly thereafter, Colonel Wirt Adams rode up to bring news of a Federal column advancing on the Raymond Road. A short time later a courier arrived with a second dispatch from Johnston, stating that "our being compelled to leave Jackson makes your plan impractical." The commanding general reiterated his instructions that Pemberton should advance toward Clinton and attempt a junction with Johnston's troops.[7] This time Pemberton moved to comply with his superior's orders. Reversing direction, the wagon train headed for Edward's Station and the Brownsville Road without any marked difficulty.

As the sound of battle drew nearer, Pemberton realized it was time to make a stand. It was not what he had wanted, not as he had planned, but the position forced upon him was fortuitously favorable. He deployed his army on a prominent ridge running from the southwest to the northeast. Champion Hill, an elevation seventy feet high, dominated not only Sid and Matilda Champion's plantation but much of the surrounding country. The lower slopes were covered with dense woods and undergrowth; the approaches were serried by gullies and ravines. Even Grant later admitted that the Confederates, whether by chance or design, had chosen well.

On this ridge Pemberton placed his three divisions in position: Loring on the right astride the Raymond Road, Bowen in the center, and Stevenson on the left. Extending three miles in length, the line was manned by 23,000 troops. In midmorning, around 10:30, the battle was joined.

Grant rode up just as Brigadier General Alvin Hovey prepared to launch the first full-scale attack on the Confederate left, where troops of Major General Carter Stevenson defended the slopes of Champion Hill and the ridges to each side. His arrival was timely, bolstering Federal confidence up and down the line. Sergeant Charles Longley of the Twenty-fourth Iowa Infantry—who had "sensed the silent prayers" of his companions, as they waited for the order to attack—noted the rise in their spirits "once the imperturbable face of the great commander appears."

Minutes later, the initial charge, led by Brigadier General George F. McGinnis, surged 600 yards up Champion Hill with bayonets fixed. Reported McGinnis:

> The whole line moved forward as one man, and so suddenly and apparently so unexpected to the rebels was the movement that, after a desperate conflict of five minutes in which bayonets and butts of muskets were freely used, the battery of four guns was in our possession, and a whole brigade in support was fleeing before us, and a large number of them taken prisoner.[8]

Off to McGinnis's left, another of Hovey's brigades struggled through thickets left of the Jackson Road and across a clearing to disperse the Confederates holding the crossroads, capturing the battery at that point.

"On and upward you go; thicker and faster falls the hissing hail," wrote Sergeant Longley. "Suddenly the added elevation brings into view a battery, and the same instant the horrid howling of grape and canister is about us."

There was a halt in the ranks as the attacking Union infantry sought to find gray-clad targets in the labyrinth of trees. Longley sighted his man, pressed the trigger, saw him fall backwards, the gun spinning from his hands.

At this moment, while every human instinct is carried away by a torrent of passion, while kill, *kill,* KILL, seems to fill your heart and be written over the face of all nature—at this instant you hear a command (it may have come from the clouds above, you know not) to "Fix bayonets, forward, charge!" and away you go with a wild yell in which all mouths join.[9]

To McGinnis's right, "Black Jack" Logan's division had surged on to smash the remainder of Stevenson's division. Stevenson's battered regiments fell back to a new line a half mile to the rear. Meanwhile, Grant had ordered McClernand to press forward on the enemy's center and right. "I sent him repeated orders by staff officers competent to explain to him the situation." It was several hours before McClernand received the order and put his divisions in motion.

It was now an hour after high noon. The struggle was still unresolved. The steep slopes were littered with the dead and wounded of both sides. On the Confederate line, Pemberton instructed Bowen to shift to the left in support of Stevenson, who had so far borne the brunt of the attack. At the same time he ordered Loring to come to Stevenson's assistance. With several enemy divisions in his front, Loring stalled and waited to see how things developed.

A Confederate counterattack launched at 2:30 P.M. promised to change the complexion of the battle. From his vantage point atop Champion Hill, McGinnis, who regarded the battle as "one of the most obstinate and murderous conflicts of the war," saw the gray tide rising ominously. Sweeping forward, Bowen's veterans drove Hovey's division from the ground gained earlier in the fight. The grayclads swarmed up Champion Hill, then headed down the far slope with irresistible force. Within an hour of vicious fighting, the Confederates had pushed the bluecoats back three-quarters of a mile. To General Hovey, his division "seemed to be melting under the intense Mississippi sun."

Faced with impending disaster, Grant threw in Brigadier General Marcellus M. Crocker's Division, which had just arrived. General Hovey quickly assembled sixteen guns with which to rake the Confederate ranks, and once again McClernand was ordered to advance.

Throughout the battle, observed Adjutant S.H.M. Byers of the Fifth Iowa Infantry, General Grant "stood leaning complacently against his favorite steed, smoking—as seemed habitual with him—the stump of a cigar. . . . I was close enough to see his features . . . clear, calm, and immovable."

Byers had little time to study the general's features. Almost at once, without time to fix bayonets, his regiment was ordered into the battle for the hill, and a moment later "we were charging the enemy's position with bare muskets . . . for half an hour we poured the hot lead into each other's faces." Then Byers saw his regiment outflanked and "heard a hundred Rebel voices yelling: 'Stop! Halt! Surrender!' " The captain followed the reaction of his regiment:

We ran, and ran manfully. . . . The grass, the stones, the bushes seemed melting under the shower of bullets. . . . We tried to halt, and tried to form. It was no use. Again we ran, and harder, and farther, and faster. We passed over the very spot where, half an hour before, we left Grant leaning on his bay mare, and smoking a cigar. Thank God! he was gone.[10]

Six hundred yards short of the Champion plantation manor, the Southern advance ground to a halt. Facing a heavy fire to the front and increased pressure on the flank, Bowen's Missourians and Arkansans grudgingly fell back. Bowen's withdrawal coupled with Loring's failure to come up prompted Pemberton to order a retreat. Some regiments retired in disorder.

Officers did their best to check the Confederate stampede. Colonel Edward Goodwin of the Thirty-fifth Alabama Infantry ordered his troops to fix bayonets and prepare to charge their fleeing comrades, "but even this could not stop them," he confessed. "The colors of three regiments passed through. . . . We collared them, begged them, and abused them in vain."[11]

Concerned about the proximity of Union troops on his flank and rear, Loring decided to avoid the direct road to Edward's Station and seek a route farther south. After a night of aimless thrashing about in bottomlands, Loring became convinced that he could not catch up with Pemberton. Thereupon, he marched his division eastward to Crystal Springs. Several days were to elapse before he joined forces with Johnston at Jackson.

The question uppermost in Pemberton's mind during the last critical hour of the battle—"Where is Loring?"—was now resolved, though Pemberton would not know the exact answer for a while longer. Loring and his troops were lost to him for good.[12]

The sanguinary battle of Champion Hill (or "Battle of Baker's Creek," as the Confederates would name it) was the decisive engagement in the campaign for Vicksburg and was costly to both sides. Grant lost 2,441 men killed, wounded, or missing. Pemberton suffered greater casualties: 3,840 men killed, wounded, or missing, along with twenty-seven guns and all of Loring's wandering division.

Among the Confederate dead was the courtly Brigadier General Lloyd Tilghman, who had gallantly defended Fort Henry against Grant's forces in 1862. Upon the spot where he fell, the Vicksburg *Herald* later noted—where "his noble life ebbed away and the sad earth drank his blood with greedy thirstiness"—a young peach tree grew to maturity and put forth leaves of blood red, and the fruit it bore was also scarlet—a phenomenon observed throughout the tree's life.[13]

Hovey, who lost a third of his troops on the blood-stained turf of Sid Champion's plantation, wrote later, "I cannot think of this bloody hill without sadness and pride. It was, after the conflict, literally the hill of death."

Wilbur Crummer of the Forty-fifth Illinois Infantry also would never forget the post-battle scene on that hill of Golgotha:

All around us lay the dead and dying, amid the groans and cries of the wounded. Our surgeons came up quickly, and, taking possession of a farmhouse, converted it into a hospital, and we began carrying ours and the enemy's wounded to the surgeons. There they lay, the blue and the gray intermingled; the same rich, young American blood flowing out in little rivulets of crimson; each thinking he was in the right. . . . With no anesthetic to soothe agony, but, gritting their teeth, they bore the pain of the knife and saw, while arms and legs were being severed from their bodies.[14]

Charles Dana rode over the battlefield with Colonel Rawlins, shortly after the smoke had cleared, and wrote of one memorable moment:

> On the hill where the thickest of the fight had taken place we stopped, and were looking around at the dead and dying men lying all about us, when suddenly a man, perhaps forty-five or fifty years old, who had a Confederate uniform on, lifted himself up on his elbow and said:
> "For God's sake, gentlemen, is there a Mason among you?"
> "Yes," said Rawlins, "I am a Mason." He [Rawlins] got off his horse and kneeled by the dying man, who gave him some letters out of his pocket. When he came back Rawlins had tears on his cheeks. The man, he told us, wanted him to convey some souvenir—a miniature or a ring, I do not remember what—to his wife, who was in Alabama.[15]

Sylvanus Cadwallader reported the engagement not to the press but in a letter to his wife, captioned, "Champion's Hill, 18 miles east of Vicksburg, May 16th."

> . . . We have had another terrible battle . . . as hotly contested as any could be. The rattle of musketry was incessant for hours. Cannons thundered till the heavens seemed bursting. Dead men, and wounded, lay strewed everywhere. . . . I find it impossible to get a list of the killed, for "dead men tell no tales," and in these cases no one tells for them. Missing, means dead in this army. My heart sickens at the suspense many families must suffer.[16]

And after noting that Grant had defeated Pemberton "quite badly," Cadwallader added a postscript: "Vicksburg must fall now. I think a week may find us in possession—it may take longer, but the end will be the same. . . . "

Grant felt that he might have settled Vicksburg's fate that very day, had McClernand attacked the defenders' right and then cut off the enemy's retreat, as McPherson was driving back the Confederate left. "Had McClernand come up with reasonable promptness," Grant later wrote, "I cannot see how Pemberton could have escaped with any organized force."[17]

Pemberton had, justifiably, a similar complaint. Had Loring come up to support the Confederate hard-pressed left, Stevenson's troops might have held out against Hovey's division and McPherson's corps—long enough at least to prevent many men and guns from being captured. But Loring had disappeared, he knew not where.

At another plantation, six miles away, General Sherman, hurrying his two divisions forward to the sound of battle, stopped for a drink of water. Beside the well he saw a soiled book lying on the turf and, having it handed to him, noticed the title, *The Constitution of the United States*. On the flyleaf, in bold slanting script, appeared the name of the owner, *Jefferson Davis*.

He learned from a Negro on the premises that the abandoned plantation did indeed belong to the Confederate President. Apparently it had been purchased as a place of safety, for the slaves and possessions removed from Brierfield on Davis Bend. Sherman discovered further:

His brother Joe Davis's plantation was not far off; one of my staff officers went
there, with a few soldiers, and took a pair of carriage horses, without my
knowledge at the time. He found Joe Davis at home, an old man, attended by
a young and affectionate niece; but they were overwhelmed with grief to see their
country overrun and swarming with Federal troops.[18]

Private William Chambers of the Forty-sixth Mississippi Infantry, whose
regiment had been patrolling the west bank of the Big Black River, heard the
roar of artillery from Champion's plantation, as his company hurried eastward
to join Pemberton's main army. By late afternoon they got as far as the railroad
bridge across the Big Black, to find the Confederate forces routed from Champion Hill and preparing to make a last stand at the bridge.

Most of Pemberton's two divisions had already crossed the bridge with the
remaining field guns and were posted on high ground along the right bank,
facing eastward. Here the river made a shallow horseshoe turn, and, on the
opposite bank, along the line of a meandering bayou, other Confederate troops
had prepared a forward defense line of rifle pits and cotton-bale parapets,
running from one end of the horseshoe to the other.

One glance at these preparations convinced Chambers that Pemberton's
precarious stand was doomed. "While I make no pretensions to military
science, it seems to me that a blunder was made, *if these works were intended
to guard the approaches to Vicksburg.*" East of the bridge the ground was flat
and level, offering little protection, and the river would cut off their retreat if
the troops on the forward defense line were overrun by superior numbers.

What Chambers would not know was that Pemberton hoped to keep the
bridge open only long enough to allow Loring's missing division, whereabouts
unknown, a chance to cross over and rejoin the army. There was a purpose
behind this risk of sacrifice. Nevertheless, wrote Chambers, "I dreaded the
battle as never before. It seemed to be impressed on me that I should be killed
in the fight, and the thought of meeting my God unprepared never seemed half
so appalling before."[19]

But the battle that Chambers dreaded lasted for only a brief span. When the
pursuing Federal army closed in on the Big Black at noon, the forward
defenders a half mile beyond the east bank scarcely put up a fight—perhaps,
as one officer observed, because they were more conditioned now to flee than
stand. This time four of McClernand's regiments spearheaded the Federal
assault, led by a fighting Irishman, Brigadier General Michael Lawler, whose
maxim was, "If you see a head, hit it!"

Lawler's brigade slugged through the bayou, swarmed over the trenches and
took hundreds of prisoners, while the rest of the defenders stampeded for the
bridge. Ubiquitous young Freddy Grant, seeing the Southerners routed from
their earthworks, could not contain his enthusiasm. He leaped his horse over
the abandoned breastworks and followed the fleeing Confederates to the banks
of the Big Black, writing later:

I was watching some of them swim the river, when a sharpshooter on the
opposite bank fired at me and hit me in the leg. The wound was slight, but very
painful; Colonel [C.B.] Lagow came dashing up and asked what was the matter.
I promptly said, "I am killed." The Colonel presumed to doubt my word, and

said, "Move your toes"—which I did with success. He then recommended our hasty retreat.[20]

Freddy's father also met with a curious surprise during that engagement. An officer from General Banks at Baton Rouge handed Grant a letter. It was Halleck's dispatch of May 11, instructing Grant to delay his advance into Mississippi and join with Banks's forces before attacking Vicksburg. It had been sent to Banks rather than Grant himself, since Halleck was uncertain as to where Grant was.

The officer bearing the missive insisted that Grant return at once to the Mississippi River. Grant brushed the courier aside. If General in Chief Henry Halleck could know the present situation, he would never insist that those orders be obeyed. Confirming this view, Grant heard the sound of "great cheering" from the Federal units pressing the attack. "I immediately mounted my horse and rode in the direction of the charge, and saw no more of the officer who delivered the dispatch."[21]

By that time Pemberton's army was in full retreat toward Vicksburg, leaving the Black River bridge behind in flames. Of that panicky flight, William Chambers wrote: "Our brigade brought up the rear, and so far as I could see was the only one that preserved any semblance of discipline. Had the enemy closely followed us that day, he could probably have entered the city without serious opposition."

Major Samuel H. Lockett, who perhaps had staked too much on the hasty defenses he had built at Edward's Station, now abandoned, rode back with Pemberton toward Bovina. Lockett remembered:

> I was the only staff officer with him. He was very much depressed by events of the last two days, and for some time after mounting his horse rode in silence. He finally said: "Just thirty years ago I began my military career . . . and today —the same date—that career is ended in disaster and disgrace."[22]

Lockett tried to revive his spirits, but, the general's grandson believed, "Pemberton had lost confidence in himself and his men." It was a situation not of his own making. He had been caught in a vise between Jefferson Davis, demanding that Vicksburg be defended at all cost, and his immediate superior, General Johnston, demanding that he evacuate Vicksburg and unite with Johnston's army.

He had been forced to make his own lonely decisions, take his own risks, and abide by the consequences; he could expect no understanding or compassion.

In Vicksburg, Emma Balfour noted, "No news from any quarter—not a word. . . . " The *Daily Whig* had become a casualty of war. On the previous Saturday, May 9, the newspaper's plant on China Street near Washington had been burned to the ground, perhaps set afire by a shell from the river, perhaps by an arsonist among the Federal spies suspected of being in the city.

There had been previous announcements that the *Whig* would suspend publication, from lack of paper and the protests of its staff that they were working under constant danger. But this time Marmaduke Shannon seemed

to mean it. He had lost four of his children in Raymond to war-related
afflictions, and now his life's work was gone as well.

The *Citizen,* under editor James M. Swords, struggled to carry on intermit-
tently, but the editions were smaller. Communications with the outside world
were shrinking.

The news blackout added to the general feeling of anxiety and panic in the
city. Not to know anything was to suspect the worst. On Saturday, May 16,
Emma Balfour wrote in her diary of "a dispatch from General Pemberton
ordering a train out to Edward's depot to bring in our supplies which are in
danger. This looks ominous, but I still have hope."

By Sunday morning, however, hope seemed to vanish, as word came of the
battle at Champion Hill and the disaster at the Big Black River. Her pen
trembled as she scratched the words: "We are deserted—our army in confusion and the carnage, awful! Whole batteries and brigades taken prisoners—
awful! awful!" Lieutenant Underhill, a friend of the family, broke down and
wept as he told of the Confederate calamity at the Big Black.

"Oh will God forsake us now?" wrote Emma. "I cannot believe it. He may
chasten us, and [words undecipherable] I will not be disheartened or discouraged!"[23]

Mary Loughborough, alone with her two-year-old daughter on that pleasant, sunny Sunday, was on her way to the Methodist Church, when she heard
the sound of cannon from the east and, querying a passing officer, was told that
Pemberton was on the run, and many ministers and physicians had gone out
to attend the wounded and the dying on the battlefield.

Though concerned for the safety of her daughter and herself, Mary continued on to church where a traveling minister occupied the pulpit, and after
"simple, fervent words and prayers," urged the ladies of the congregation to
"make arrangements for supplying lint and bandages for the wounded." She
remembered:

> As we returned home, we passed groups of men at the corners, with troubled
> faces; very few soldiers were seen; some battery men and officers needed for the
> river defenses, were passing hastily up the street. Yet, in all the pleasant air and
> sunshine of the day, an anxious gloom seemed to hang over the faces of men:
> a sorrowful waiting for tidings, that all knew now, would tell of disaster.[24]

By noon the vanguard of the soldiers of retreat began to reach the outskirts
of the city. In front of a Southern mansion on the road into Vicksburg, William
Chambers saw a group of young ladies waiting for them. "With tears and
smiles they greeted us and spoke words of cheer; and as our regiment filed by
one sweet young voice said: 'Remember, Mississippians never surrender!' "
They would see no more smiling faces as they neared the city.

Dora Miller, unlike her neighbors, felt a sense of relief at this turn in events.
She and her husband had been having Sunday breakfast when an employee of
Miller's hammered at their door to report that "Pemberton had been whipped
at Baker's Creek and Big Black, and his army are running back here as fast
as they can come and the Yanks after them in such numbers nothing can stop
them."

The report that the Yankees would be there by evening did not greatly disturb her. "A city besieged is a city taken," she quoted in her diary, "so if we live through it we shall be out of the Confederacy." It was what she and her husband, Anderson, had secretly longed for—to be back among Union friends and sympathizers. Yet she was moved to compassion when a group of weary, dust-covered Confederates rested for a moment on her doorstep. From their speech, she gathered that they were Acadians from Louisiana, and she asked them gently what the news was.

"Ritreat! Ritreat!" they said in broken, almost-sobbing English.[25]

As the formerly quiet city came to life, wrote Mary Loughborough, "the stir of horsemen and wheels began, and wagons came rattling down the street— going rapidly one way, and then returning, seemingly, without aim or purpose; now and then a worn and dusty soldier would be seen passing with his blanket and canteen; soon straggler after straggler came by, then groups of soldiers worn and dusty with the long march."

Mary went down to the roadside where a group of neighboring housewives were demanding of the soldiers: "What is the matter! Where are you going!"

"We are whipped," was the grim reply, "and the Federals are after us. . . . "

"Oh! Shame on you!" cried the ladies, "and you running!"

"It's all Pem's fault," said one.

"It's all your own fault," said the Greek chorus. "Why don't you stand your ground? Shame on you all!"

Mary could not help but feel sorry for "the poor worn fellows, who did indeed seem heartily ashamed of themselves; some without arms, having probably lost them in the first break of the companies." Despite their own state of shock, most of the householders invited the crestfallen troops into their yards for water and food, and listened to their story. It was General Pemberton's fault, they said. They had never run before, but when they saw the rest of the army crumble at the Big Black, "We could not bear up alone." One old soldier was blunter than the rest, insisting:

> Oh, we would ha' fit well; but General Pemberton came up and said: 'Stand your ground, boys. Your General Pemberton is with you'; and then, bless you, lady! the next we see'd of him, he was sitting on a horse behind a house—close, too, at that; and when we see'd that, we thought 'tain't no use, if he's going to sit there.'[26]

Afterwards, Mary learned, as did the others, that Pemberton had done his best to rally the troops by his presence and personal intervention. But now, "Where these weary and wornout men were going, we could not tell. I think they did not know themselves."

Later that afternoon, Emma Balfour recorded the shifting panorama in the troubled city:

> I hope never to witness again such a scene as the return of our routed army. . . .
> Nothing like order prevailed, of course, as divisions, brigades and regiments were broken and separated. As the poor fellows passed, every house poured forth all it had to refresh them. I had every one on the lot and there were some visitors carrying buckets of water to the corner for the men. Then in the back gallery I had everything that was eatable put out—and fed as many as I could.
> Poor fellows, it made my heart ache to see them, for I knew from all I saw

and heard that it was want of confidence in the general commanding that was the cause of our disaster. I cannot write more—but oh! there will be a fearful reckoning somewhere.[27]

Within forty-eight hours General Pemberton—who, for a while, had overcome his Yankee background to become a symbol of confidence in the city—had become the scapegoat for a situation that was nearly unavoidable. Dr. Joseph Alison, Confederate army physician in Vicksburg, who reportedly had "never seen troops more dispirited or more demoralized," observed, "A rumor is circulated that Gen. Pemberton has sold Vicksburg and many believe it."[28]

Even the *Daily Whig,* which had done so much to rally support for the commanding general, now posthumously blamed Pemberton for the disaster. Alexander Abrams of the defunct newspaper's staff wrote of "the gallant men who had left Vicksburg three short weeks before, in all the pride and confidence of a just cause, and returning to it a demoralized mob and a defeated army, all caused through one man's incompetence."

Rowland Chambers, the erstwhile dentist now living in the servant's quarters of his home-turned-hospital, had worried all during the week about his family in refuge in the country east of Vicksburg. Now he, too, became convinced that "Pemberton is not the rite man in the rite place." He felt his judgment verified as he recorded that "our army has fell back from the Bigblack to Vicksburg. The hills are covered with men in every direction, and the day of our doom appears close at hand. Only the God of heaven can save us and in him I trust; . . . "[29]

As the trickle of returning soldiers turned, by late afternoon, into a flood, even Dora Miller with her secret Union sympathies was moved to sympathy and pity:

I shall never forget the woeful sight of a beaten, demoralized army that came rushing back,—humanity in the last throes of endurance. Wan, hollow-eyed, ragged, footsore, bloody, the men limped along unarmed, but followed by siege-guns, ambulances, gun carriages, and wagons in aimless confusion. At twilight two or three bands on the court-house hill and other points began playing Dixie, Bonnie Blue Flag, and so on, and drums began to beat all about; I suppose they were rallying the scattered army.[30]

Lieutenant Jared Sanders of Martin Smith's division, with other troops garrisoning Vicksburg, began to move to new positions in the rifle pits surrounding Vicksburg, where some would remain for weeks to come. Wrote Sanders in his diary for May 17: "Great excitement in town. The 26th [Louisiana] regiment ordered to pits on the lines of fortifications below the city. Heard of the battle of the Big Black which is disastrous to us. Slept in trenches." They would be sleeping in trenches for days and weeks to come.

That evening saw fresh troops marching into Vicksburg from the guns at Warrenton and from the batteries on Walnut Hills. These were undefeated, hitherto inactive companies, in marked contrast to the battered remnants of the army from the east. Their arrival, noted Mary Loughborough, did much to lift the spirits of the women in the city.

"You'll stand by us, and protect us?" the women cried. "You won't *retreat* and bring the Federals behind you."[31]

Yet in a sense, retreat or withdrawal was what they were doing. For the defenses at Warrenton below the city, as well as the batteries on the bluffs above, were being abandoned to bring all men and movable armament within the fortifications surrounding Vicksburg, in preparation for impending siege.

Throughout the night the influx from the east took on a grimmer aspect, as Mary Loughborough saw "the ambulances passing with wounded and dead; and one came by, with officers riding near it, bearing the dead body of General [Lloyd] Tilghman, with blood dripping slowly from it." Rowland Chambers, putting his limited skills in dentistry to use in caring for the injured, dressing wounds, and even assisting in amputations, wrote later, "It was more human suffering than I ever saw at one site before; . . . "

Former *Whig* reporter Abrams observed another tragic column mingled with the returning companies from the east—hordes of civilian refugees. "Many planters living near the city, with their families, abandoned their homes and entered our lines with the Confederate forces. . . . There were many gentle women and tender children torn from their homes by the advance of a ruthless foe, and compelled to fly to our lines for protection; . . . "[32]

The number of civilian refugees would swell the population of a city already overcrowded by the presence of the military, amplifying the serious problem of supplies. But Abrams's attention was captured for the moment by "the Sabbath-night uproar, in which the blasphemous oath of the soldier and the cry of the child mingled, and formed a sight [sic] which the pen cannot depict."

Though the streets became quieter as night wore on, Mary Loughborough remained deeply troubled, wondering, "What will the morrow bring forth?" None could be certain of the answer. But Lieutenant Jared Sanders of General Smith's garrisoning troops—who saw the last Confederate survivors reaching Vicksburg, "everybody looking *blue*"—noted in his diary:

> It is now a foregone conclusion that we are to be besieged by the approaching enemy. Rumors place the Yankees within a few miles of our works. Now will we be tested by the *state* of preparations in which the defenders of Vicksburg have placed the city—how much provisions—how much ordance stores they have . . .[33]

Dr. Alison saw the city's situation in a different but no brighter light, writing that evening:

> The enemy have a line entirely around us, leaving us no outlets. Our only hope now is that we can hold out until Johnston arrives with reinforcements and attacks Yankees in rear. Gen. Pemberton says he can hold out as long as provisions last, and our commissaries say they can feed the army six weeks. If so, we may yet be rescued.[34]

McClernand's pursuit of the Confederates to Vicksburg was held up for a day by the destruction of the railroad bridge across the Big Black River. By that time, Sherman with his two divisions, hurrying up from Jackson, had joined General Grant near Bridgeport. Both had hoped somehow to get around Pemberton's left flank and beat him into Vicksburg.

The Federals worked frantically to span the river. A pontoon bridge was thrown across at Bridgeport, and farther downstream three bridges over the Big Black were built of rafts, felled trees overlaid with timber, and bales of cotton serving as pontoons. By midnight the troops started crossing over, regiment by regiment in single file, guided by torches staked on the banks or carried by the men.

Sherman remembered that "the whole scene was lit up by fires of pitch-pine. General Grant joined me, and we sat on a log, looking at the passage of the troops by the light of those fires; the bridge swayed to and fro under the passing feet, and made a fine war picture."[35]

The next morning, Monday, May 18, the rest of the army finished crossing, to the drumbeats of the marching bands and the strains of "The Girl I Left Behind Me." Osborn Oldroyd felt a thrill of pride as they approached the abandoned enemy fortifications, convinced now that "the combined Confederate army could not keep us out of Vicksburg."

> It was a grand sight, the long lines of infantry moving over the pontoons, and winding their way up the bluffs, with flags flying in the breeze, and the morning sun glancing upon the guns as they lay across the shoulders of the boys. Cheer after cheer went up in welcome and triumph from the thousands who had already crossed and stood in waiting lines upon the bluff above. This is supposed to be the last halting place before we knock for admittance at our goal—the boasted Gibraltar of the West.[36]

Once assembled in formation the army marched in three columns, westward, toward the city. McClernand's corps followed the line of the railroad. McPherson and Sherman, accompanied by Grant, followed the Bridgeport Road toward Vicksburg. A company of Union cavalry swooped up on Snyder's Bluff and found the stronghold abandoned, the guns spiked, and only a handful of men remaining. The latter were quickly gobbled up.

For Sherman it was a memorable moment. It was a few miles away from here, in December, that he had launched the first, supposedly decisive, land attack on Vicksburg. And there it was that he had suffered the most humiliating defeat of his career. During a winter of repeated failures on the river and the bayous, he and Grant had often disagreed—without ever losing confidence in one another. This occasion seemed to seal the bond between them. Sherman turned to his commanding general.

"Until this moment," he said emotionally, "I never thought your expedition a success; I never could see the end clearly till now. But this is a campaign; this is a complete and successful campaign whether or not we take the town."[37]

For Vicksburg, too, the date of May 18 was a momentous one. It was precisely a year ago that Commander Phillips Lee had appeared with units of Farragut's fleet below the city and demanded its surrender. It was a time to remember the Confederate reply: *Mississippians don't know the meaning of the word "surrender!"*

✣ 16 ✣

Cordon of Steel

ONCE back within the walls of Vicksburg, on May 18, Pemberton's mood of despair transformed to one of resolution. As Lockett reminded him, "Things were not so bad as they seemed to be." He still had two strong divisions in the city, those of Generals John Forney and Martin Smith, fresh troops whose morale was high. Discounting his losses at Champion Hill and the Big Black, his army of defense would number roughly 31,000, smaller than Grant's estimated 45,000, but having the advantage of fighting behind fortified positions.

Moreover, in Davis's telegram instructing Pemberton "to hold Vicksburg at all hazards," the President had added that, "if besieged he would be relieved." And Lockett further assured the general that "Vicksburg was strong and could not be carried by assault." In fact, Lockett had hurried back to the city ahead of Pemberton, to see to the repair and strengthening of the defenses.

As originally laid out by Lockett in September 1862 after a month of study, the land fortifications consisted of an eight-mile arc, extending from Fort Hill on the bluffs a half-mile above Vicksburg and following an irregular course of hills and ridges to South Fort, overlooking the Mississippi three miles below the city. The front of the city was still, of course, protected by the river batteries, which had been on alert all year against the threat of Porter's gunboats on the river.

Strong forts covered six roads that entered Vicksburg, as well as the railway line from Jackson, and smaller forts, redoubts, lunettes, and batteries were placed at strategic intervals along the line. All were connected by rifle pits and trenches to form an unbroken chain, with ramparts topped by parapets to protect the garrisoning troops. Outside a fort ran a ditch as much as eight feet deep and fourteen feet in width. In front of the fortifications trees had been felled, to clear the line of fire—their tangled branches, interlaced with telegraph wires and sharpened stakes, creating a formidable abatis.[1]

Unoccupied for many months, many of these defenses had deteriorated, with earthworks damaged by the heavy rains of winter. Lockett, in charge of preparations, put Smith's and Forney's troops to work repairing and strengthening the line. Handicapped by lack of shovels (only 500 were available), the soldiers made improvised spades of wood and, where necessary, used their bayonets as picks.

The lighter artillery had been brought in from Warrenton and Walnut Hills when these positions were evacuated to consolidate the city's defenses, and 102 guns were positioned strategically along the eight-mile line. To these were added "Quaker Guns," a common ruse throughout the war: round logs painted black to resemble the muzzles of cannon, and mounted at embrasures in the ramparts. As Lucy McRae of Vicksburg later wrote, "when General Grant made his reconnaissance he could not tell a log from a cannon."[2]

For the moment there were ample provisions and supplies. Boatloads of corn had been brought down from the Delta, or Yazoo Basin, before the evacuation of the outlying bluffs, and the troops retreating from the Big Black had been ordered to gather up everything usable or edible from homes, farms, and plantations on the way.

Nothing would be left for the approaching enemy. Wagons were filled with trussed-up chickens and turkeys, peas, corn, rice, and sugar. Cattle, cows, sheep, hogs, and mules were rounded up and driven ahead of the retreating army. As Emma Balfour observed from her window overlooking Crawford Street, "From twelve o'clock until late in the night the streets and roads were *jammed* with wagons, cannons, horses, men, mules, stock, sheep, everything that you can imagine that appertains to an army—being brought hurriedly within the intrenchment."

With what had already been stockpiled in the city, Pemberton had sufficient provisions to feed his army and the noncombatant population for an estimated six weeks, maybe more. Ammunition might become a problem; the infantry and artillery were cautioned against wasting shells and bullets. Pemberton could not hold out forever, but Johnston was not more than fifty miles away and had indicated he expected reinforcements.

Then, at noon of May 18, came the blow. Pemberton was handed a message from Johnston, dated the day before and marked as being sent from camp near Brownsville. At least that meant that Little Joe was moving westward toward the Big Black River, in a position to attack Grant's flank, but the contents of the message caught the Vicksburg general by surprise:

> If Haynes Bluff is untenable, Vicksburg is of no value and cannot be held. If, therefore, you are invested in Vicksburg, you must ultimately surrender. Under such circumstances, instead of losing both troops and place, we must, if possible, save the troops. If it is not too late, evacuate Vicksburg and its dependencies, and march to the northeast.[3]

Evacuate Vicksburg! To Pemberton, it was almost unthinkable. As he later wrote in his official report, it would have meant "the surrender of the Mississippi and the severance of the Confederacy." Moreover, "I believed it to be in my power to hold Vicksburg. . . . I knew, perhaps better than any other individual . . . its capacity for defense. . . . I had ample supplies of ammunition as well as of subsistence to stand a siege."

Moreover, "I knew and appreciated the earnest desire of the government and of the people that it should be held."[4]

Nevertheless, and for the second time in his life, Pemberton summoned a council of war. Confronting his general officers with Johnston's message, he made no comment of his own, but asked if they considered it practicable or advisable to carry out the orders. In his reply to Johnston he reported: "The opinion was unanimously expressed that it was impossible to withdraw the army from this position with such *morale* and material as to be of further service to the Confederacy." And he concluded:

I have decided to hold Vicksburg as long as is possible, with the firm hope that the Government may yet be able to assist me in keeping this obstruction to the enemy's free navigation of the Mississippi. I still conceive it to be the most important point in the Confederacy.[5]

Then, with Lockett's advice, the Confederate commander set about preparing to meet Grant's approaching army, already covering the eastward valleys with a quilting of blue beneath ascending clouds of dust. Judging from the direction of these marching columns and from reports from Confederate skirmishers outside the city, two likely points of attack appeared: the Graveyard Road into Vicksburg from the east and the Jackson Road, also approaching from the east.

In the fortifications commanding these two arteries, Pemberton placed his two fresh divisions, Martin Smith holding the line from Fort Hill to the stockade on the Graveyard Road, Forney's troops covering the interval from that point to the Railroad Redoubt. Stevenson's battered division was spread out from the railway to the Warrenton Road at South Fort, overlooking the river and facing roughly south, where, for the moment, no enemy threat was evident.

Altogether some 31,000 troops were available to man the ramparts with Bowen's division being held in reserve behind the center of the line, for use as needed. Contingents posted in advanced rifle pits to delay the enemy's advance were withdrawn as the Federal army began closing in on May 18.

That night, with the lights of a hundred campfires pinpointing the hills and valleys around Vicksburg, the city waited.

Approaching Vicksburg on the Jackson Road, an officer on McPherson's staff observed,

A long line of high, rugged irregular bluffs, clearly cut against the sky, crowned with cannon which peered ominously from embrasures to the right and left as far as the eye could see. Lines of heavy rifle-pits, surmounted with head logs, ran along the bluffs, connecting fort with fort, and filled with veteran infantry. . . . The approaches to this position were frightful—enough to appall the stoutest heart.[6]

Grant's engineers also took an apprehensive view of the defense of the city, noting the "intricate network of ravines and ridges" with sides so steep that no troops could get a foothold, and "in many places entanglements which under fire were absolutely impassable." In short, Vicksburg, it was observed, "owed much of its strength to the difficult ground, obstructed by fallen trees in its front, which rendered rapidity of movement and *ensemble* in an assault impossible."

Lieutenant Colonel James Wilson noted another factor to be considered. Grant's troops had been marching and fighting for twenty days, living off the land as best they could. True, they had won five strenuous battles in the interval and were flushed with the spirit of success. Still, Wilson believed, it would have been better to give them time to simmer down, rest up, and, with the guidance of their officers, prepare more carefully for the assault.

But the blue-coated troops themselves, now rimming the city's walls, were keyed up to the point of cockiness. "This day beholds a cordon of steel, with rivets of brave hearts, surrounding Vicksburg," Osborn Oldroyd wrote on May 19, and he added: "We have come here to compel [the Confederates] to surrender . . . and they cannot say us nay."[7]

Echoing this sentiment, Sergeant Charles Wilcox of the Thirty-third Illinois Infantry observed on that same morning, "We have now completely invested this place and believe we'll take it with the whole garrison in a day or two."[8]

Grant himself was in no mood for delay. "The enemy had been much demoralized at Champion's Hill and the Big Black, and I believed would not make much effort to hold Vicksburg," he recorded. The quicker he struck, the less time for Pemberton's army to regain its equilibrium and prepare for an attack. Grant's order for the day, May 19, declared:

> Corps commanders will push forward carefully, and gain as close position as possible to the enemy's works, until 2 P.M.; [at that hour] they will fire three volleys of artillery from all the pieces in position. This will be the signal for a general charge of all the army corps along the whole line.[9]

That Grant felt certain of victory was indicated by a closing line: "When the works are carried, guards will be placed by all division commanders to prevent their men from straggling from their companies." Sherman, normally less sanguine than his colleague, was equally confident of quick success. He ordered his officers to charge on foot, and to let their servants bring their horses to them after Vicksburg fell. Further, his troops were instructed to "keep close at the heels of the enemy when they fled, and not permit them to rally inside the works."[10]

There was only one dissenting voice in all this optimism. The day before the attack, Admiral Porter, having challenged the guns of Fortress Vicksburg for well nigh a year, wrote to General Hurlbut in Memphis: "I am not authorized to say so, but my opinion is that General Grant should be reinforced with all dispatch; he will have the hardest fight ever seen during the war."[11]

It turned out to be a hard fight, principally for the Federals. On the Grave-yard Road, Sherman was closest to the city, only 500 yards from the left of Pemberton's line, where Grant hoped for a quick decision. At the boom of the signal guns, all three brigades of Blair's division plunged forward into chasms filled with fallen timber, across fields of canebrake, scythed by Confederate fire as sharply concentrated as a knife blade.

It seemed incredible that any should survive that storm of lead. But men of the 113th Illinois, seeing "the very sticks and chips, scattered over the ground, jumping under the hot shower of Rebel bullets," pushed close to the ditch below the ramparts.

Colonel Thomas Kilby Smith saw his Second Brigade halt and regroup three times before reaching within 400 yards of the parapets, by which time they were "thoroughly exhausted." Eventually, however, they gained the base of the rampart where they were pinned down by the fire from above. Smith refused to order them to further effort, reporting later: "A few men could have been got over by the aid of a ladder of bayonets or digging holes in the embankment, but these would have gone to destruction." Besides, Confederate sharpshooters "were picking off our officers with devilish skill."[12]

It was the same all down the line of attack, where Union troops were surprised and stunned by the Confederate resistance. With McPherson's forces on Sherman's left, Brigadier General Thomas Ransom reported, "After advancing two hundred yards, with severe losses, to the first line, I found the ravine in my front, which I had not had time to reconnoiter, impassable for troops."[13]

Captain Charles Ewing of the hardened Thirteenth United States Regulars saw three of his color bearers shot down, seized the flag himself and carried it up to the edge of the ramparts before a bullet took his finger off. Every officer in Ewing's company was wounded, and almost a third of his troops were lost. As with the other assailants, those who survived slipped down into the ditches for protection and there, out of range of enemy fire, remained until nightfall permitted them to creep back to their lines.

In the midst of their predicament Sherman's troops ran out of cartridges. A fourteen-year-old drummer boy, Orion P. Howe, serving with the Fifty-fifth Illinois Infantry, volunteered to garner ammunition from other nearby commands, and his regimental commander sent him off to do so. A few yards away the runner stopped. "What caliber?" he shouted. "Fifty-four!" cried the colonel, and the boy raced off.

As he approached the rear, General Sherman noticed the lad, observed that he was wounded and bleeding, and stopped him.

"What is the matter, my boy?" the general asked.

"They shot me in the leg, sir," Orion said but rejected suggestions that he go to the field hospital. He had volunteered to get that ammunition, and he was going to get it.

Nevertheless, wrote Sherman, "Even where we stood the shot and shell fell thick and fast and I told him to go to the rear at once. I would attend to the cartridges, and off he limped."[14]

Orion was not seen again on the field of battle, and it was not until thirty-three years later, in 1896, that he was awarded the Medal of Honor for his bravely assumed but uncompleted mission. Ironically, if one report can be believed, it was just as well that the mission remained uncompleted. For the colonel's instruction had been faulty; the cartridges, had Orion delivered them, would have been of the wrong caliber.

At the end of the day, for what it was worth, Union battle flags stood planted on the outside of the Southern ramparts—but not a single Federal soldier had pierced the parapets.

Sherman was frank in admitting defeat. "My troops reached the top of the parapet, but could not cross over. The rebel parapets were strongly manned, and the enemy fought hard and well. My loss was pretty heavy; . . . " In a letter to his wife he expressed himself more graphically: "The heads of columns have been swept away as chaff thrown from the hand on a windy day."

Grant had lost nearly a thousand men in the attack, the Confederates less than a hundred. He dismissed the failure by recording that the assault had "resulted in securing more advanced positions for all our troops, where they were fully covered from the fire of the enemy." From these advanced positions, once they were thoroughly consolidated, he would try again.

Sylvanus Cadwallader, too, seemed to regard the battle of May 19 as simply a temporary setback. His opinion of Grant—as a man of destiny who would not be denied the capture of the city—had risen considerably in the past two weeks. In a letter headed, "In front of Vicksburg, May 21st 1863," Cadwallader wrote:

> . . . Nothing like this campaign has occurred during this war. It stamps Gen. Grant as a man of uncommon military ability—proves him the foremost one in the west; if not in the nation. The plan [of campaign], although suggested by Rawlins and Wilson, was his own. . . . I think it brilliant. All his plans have worked to a charm. . . . Officers in high command, including some of the general's staff, believe firmly that we shall be in Vicksburg within a week at farthest. Their means of judging are superior to mine of course, and cause me to doubt my own judgment—which is that the place will hold out for at least another month.[15]

In Vicksburg, the people had been braced for the battle that they knew was coming.

"Last night," wrote Emma Balfour on that fateful Tuesday, "we saw a grand and awful spectacle. The darkness was lit up by burning houses all along our lines. They were burnt that our firing would not be obstructed. It was sad to see. Many of them we knew to be handsome residences put up in the last few years as country residences—two of them very large and handsome houses, but the stern necessity of war has caused their destruction." She continued, in her diary:

> We have provided ourselves with a cave as Gen. [Stephen D.] Lee says there will be no safety elsewhere. Our entrenchments are a mile and a half to three miles from town, varying with the nature of the country. Of course shells and balls [from the enemy] will reach any part of the town and the gunboats from the other side can throw to beyond our entrenchments. When the Gen. asked if we were provided with a rat-hole, I told him it seemed to me that we were all caught in a rat-hole.[16]

Emma may have been heartened somewhat by having a new and reassuring neighbor; General Pemberton had established his Vicksburg headquarters in the house next door, on Crawford Street.

Mary Loughborough, however, believed that since the entrenchments were so far from the center of the city, "We would be out of danger, so we thought." She was glad she had resisted the temptation to leave town, "for we felt that now, indeed, the whole country was unsafe, and that our only hope of safety lay in Vicksburg."

When she heard the boom of cannon and rattle of musketry, sounding "like the quick successive dropping of balls on sheet iron," Mary stood on the back veranda where,

> . . . we could plainly see the smoke before the report of the guns reached us.
> . . . Groups of people stood on every available position where a view could be obtained of the distant hills, where the jets of white smoke constantly passed out from among the trees.
> Some of our friends proposed going for a better view up on the balcony around the cupola of the court house. The view from there was most extensive and beautiful. . . . The hills around near the city, and indeed every place that seemed commanding and secure, was covered with anxious spectators—many of them ladies—fearing the result of the afternoon's conflict.[17]

A few spectators turned their eyes toward the river where several transports had got up steam as if for an amphibious attack—which never came. Four ironclads held positions below Vicksburg, firing at the city and the Confederate batteries; but the upriver gunboats were differently disposed, preparing for an attack on Yazoo City.

It was hard for the civilians on the hills to follow the course of the battle, nothing to observe but noise and smoke. Emma Balfour accordingly remained in her sewing room, "praying in my heart, oh so earnestly for our cause," but all too conscious of the battle sounds a few miles east of her house on Crawford Street. She was interrupted when her black maid Nancy rushed in, "actually pale," exclaiming:

"Oh, Mistress, the Yankees are pouring over the hill and our men are running. Just come to the gallery and you can see!"

Emma ran to the back gallery with her glass and did observe Confederates running past the house, seemingly a whole brigade. But she guessed correctly. They were not retreating, but were being rushed as reinforcements to another threatened point in the defenses. Emma told Nancy things were "not so bad as she had thought and quieted her a little."

Toward sundown, Mary Loughborough wrote an epitaph to that momentous day: "So twilight began falling over the scene—hushing to an occasional report the noise and uproar of the battle field—falling softly and silently upon the river—separating us more and more from the raging passions surging around us. . . . "[18] But twilight also bore the rumble of wagon wheels and the tread of stretcher-bearers bringing in the wounded.

To the Hansford house on Farmer Street, Colonel Winchester Hall arrived by ambulance. He had been shot in the leg during the assault on Martin Smith's line, had been given a swallow of whisky and then was left lying in a wagon rut, where another Federal bullet struck him. At the sight of his anxiously awaiting wife, however, he was raised to the best of humor. "Hurrah for Vicksburg!" he shouted at her. "Hurrah for the Confederacy!"[19]

Hall had entered the day's conflict in a spirit of defiance, and would end it in that manner. His Louisiana regiment had been posted north of the Stockade Redan from where, as dawn broke, the colonel could see the Union officers deploying their troops on the opposite hills. Hall summoned the regimental band to serenade the enemy with "Dixie" and other patriotic Southern airs. This bit of bravado, however, was shortly silenced by Brigadier General Francis Shoup who considered the overture "untimely."

But Hall's spirit on returning home expressed the intense relief that all in Vicksburg felt, both citizens and soldiers. Pemberton himself had reason to be briefly satisfied. His troops had performed even better than he hoped they would, although Rowland Chambers reported the "skulking of some cowardly men," who hid in the hollows and behind trees and in caves and "lay there all day just like so many scared dogs." But the Confederate general recognized that the day's engagement did not qualify as an assault in force. The real test was yet to come. He sent a dispatch that night, smuggled through enemy lines, to President Davis, which reflected his concern:

> We are occupying the trenches around Vicksburg. The enemy is investing it, and will probably attempt an assault. Our men have considerably recovered their *morale*, but unless a large force is sent to relieve it, Vicksburg before long must fall. I have used every effort to prevent all this, but in vain.[20]

He did not mention Johnston in the dispatch, perhaps because their views were so disparate that he actually entertained small hope of help from that direction. Yet Johnston was still commander in the West and the only general with any force, however small, capable of coming to his aid.

Johnston's magic name, in fact, was on everybody's mind and lips, soldiers and civilians both. Faith in Little Joe for their salvation grew almost proportionately to their loss of confidence in Pemberton. Emma Balfour prayed, "If we can only hold this place 'til Johnston can come to our aid from outside!" Mrs. Lord, the rector's wife, had believed that Johnston's evacuation of Jackson combined with Pemberton's retreat to Vicksburg were "parts of a great plan of these two Gens. to surround Grant's army—but . . . I was sadly undeceived."

Even after the successful resistance of May 19, the anxiety remained. "Not," wrote Mrs. Lord, "the fear that Gen. Pemberton was a traitor but, although loyal to the South and personally brave, he was yet wholly incapable to act as Gen. of an army . . . that is still our almost only fear: That when the time comes, as we hope it will in a few days, when it will become necessary for him to sally out and attack them [the Federals] in front, while Johnston fights on their rear, his inefficiency will again lose us the victory."[21]

During the day the Lord house had been out of range of Federal shells and musketry. Mrs. Lord's young daughter, Lida, later remembered:

> All day the cannonading was terrific and the air was full of conflicting rumors, but toward evening the news was brought that in three tremendous charges the enemy had been repulsed with great slaughter. Then began the moral reconstruction of our army. Men who had been gloomy, depressed, and distrustful now cheerfully and bravely looked the future in the face. After that day's victory but one spirit seemed to animate the whole army, the determination never to give up.[22]

Colonel Hall presented good evidence of that determination. The following morning he talked a regimental surgeon out of amputating his wounded leg, settled for having a piece of bone removed, and, after being sewed up, looked to the safety of his family. Grant was still shelling the city from the east, but the greater danger came from mortars placed on scows across the river, which found the area of the Hansford home a convenient target.

Hall moved his wife and children behind a hill to the rear of the house. Here two tents were pitched and a portion of the hillside cut away as an emergency refuge for the children.

"During the afternoon," wrote Hall, "a shell was heard. A soldier passing at the same moment, seeing this scooped hole in the upright bank, sought shelter in it from the coming shell. It exploded directly over him, the concussion killing him instantly, in the very spot where my children had sought shelter frequently during the day. Fortunately, they were at that time occupied with their dinner. . . . The tent I occupied was thrown down by the concussion. I was covered with earth, and it gave me a considerable shock."

Hall would move his family twice again in forty-eight hours—first behind Sky Parlor Hill, then, with the aid of an artillery officer who, "noting the forlorn condition of my family, and my own helplessness," guided them to rooms on the second floor of a dwelling on the river front "just below the built up portion of the city."[23]

Elsewhere Vicksburg residents began digging in the hillsides, prepared to join the legion of cave dwellers in this Gibraltar of the West. The mortar scows, in position two miles to the west, were under orders to shell the city night and day. Noted Mrs. William Lord, "the terrible mortars began to desolate our homes." Dr. Lord, though he still spent much of the time at the rectory, insisted that his wife and son and daughter take refuge in the cave of Gerard Stiles and his family, formerly of Locust Street.

"Imagine," wrote Mrs. Lord later, "one of these Vicksburg hills in the very heart of the town—caves dry . . . and intersecting each other, reaching again to the front, forming in that way several passages and fire openings." Her son Willy described the underground shelter in more detail:

It was shaped like the prongs of a garden rake, the five excavations from the street or road all terminating in a long central gallery, so that in case any one of them should collapse escape could be made through the inner cave and its other branches. The entrance galleries at either end were reserved for servants and cooking purposes, and the intervening galleries and inner central gallery were occupied as family dormitories, separated from each other by such flimsy partition of boards, screens, and hanging as could be devised.[24]

Eight families, besides a number of single people and "innumerable servants," shared quarters in the cave, among them Mrs. William McRae and her three younger children, Sheriff McRae "having such aversion for a cave that he would not enter one." Young Lucy McRae remembered that:

Mother took pillows, comforts, provisions, and clothing into the cave with her. There were about two hundred people in this cave, mostly women and children (some men, of course, too). The mortars, which were planted just opposite the city on the Louisiana side, kept up a continual fire upon us. All along on the ground in this cave planks were laid, that our beds might be made as comfortable as possible under the circumstances.[25]

Surveying the Mississippi from her back veranda, Mary Loughborough took note of a puzzling procedure. Ordinarily, with Porter's gunboats lurking on the river, there was little traffic between the east and west banks. But now she saw two large yawls shuttling back and forth, leaving the city wharf loaded with men, and returning empty. She learned that the men were Union prisoners who, instead of being held in town, were being paroled and sent across to the Federal encampment to avoid the necessity of feeding them.

Somehow this gave Mary an uneasy feeling. The city, initially victorious, was nonetheless trapped within an impenetrable circle; nothing could be brought in by land or river. She concluded, with considerable prescience, "We might look forward truly now to perhaps real suffering."

The reality of war and the inevitable suffering of civilians had already overtaken the James Shirley family, longtime residents of the Vicksburg area. The Shirley House, one of the county's older mansions, stood 400 yards outside the fortifications, east of the third Louisiana Redan. Adeline Shirley's husband, a former Vicksburg attorney, was from New Hampshire, and she herself was a Boston-born Yankee—considerations that had not yet caused them any trouble.[26]

But on May 17 and 18, with the Confederates retreating and the Federals advancing from the Big Black River, Adeline realized her predicament. Her husband was at Clinton, seeing to the safety of their daughter attending college in that village. Except for her fifteen-year-old son, she was alone in the house with two black servants, caught in a sudden no-man's-land between two hostile armies.

Yet she stubbornly refused to leave, even when retreating Confederates threatened to burn down the house to clear their line of fire. As her daughter Alice later heard the story from her mother, when the order came to set fire to all surrounding buildings, and a Confederate soldier approached the house with a torch of flaming cotton, he was shot by one of McPherson's pickets in the vanguard of the Union army.

"The poor fellow," wrote Alice, "crept away under the shelter of some planks, where he died alone, his body being found next day and buried under the corner of the house."

Saved from the Confederates, Mrs. Shirley now had to face the advancing Union soldiers who, as a precaution, fired through the door and windows of the house. "My mother thought rapidly," wrote Alice. "The thing to be done was to hang out a flag of truce, and quickly she secured a sheet to a broom handle, and sending it by our carriage driver to the upper front porch . . . it was soon waving a truce to the bullets."

Suspicious Federal troops still stormed the house, however, and Alice recorded, "Household treasures were soon destroyed under the ruthless hands of the soldiers," until a kindly Union officer intervened. That afternoon the first clash between Union attackers and Vicksburg's defenders began, and "The dead and the dying were brought into the old house. Here in the midst of terrible war my mother and brother remained for two days."

Meanwhile the two blacks fashioned a cave of sorts in a hill behind the house, with a blanket strung across the opening. Here Adeline, with her son, a trunk, and a rocking chair, was found some days later by her returning husband. Under the direction of General Grant himself, the family was moved to a plantation three miles away, where abandoned slave cabins offered temporary shelter.

But the Shirleys, James and Adeline, would return someday—to be buried beside their home which, despite what happened to it in the coming weeks, was one of the few antebellum manors to survive the siege of Vicksburg.[27]

The free-lance British observer, Lieutenant Colonel James A. L. Fremantle, was still in Jackson when he heard the "great bombardment going on at Vicksburg." Like a cub reporter he had scrambled around the mutilated capital, seeking information from every man or officer that he could buttonhole, getting arrested as a spy (partly because his Saville Row shooting suit was suspect in a population clothed in homespun), and being rescued by a staff officer of Brigadier General "States' Rights" Gist who had just arrived from Charleston with his brigade, to reinforce Joe Johnston.

Fremantle wangled permission to visit Johnston's camp near Livingston. From his four days' traveling through Mississippi, he had concluded that "The great object of the Confederates must, of course, be to unite their forces under so able a general as Johnston, and then relieve Vicksburg." He wanted to meet the Western commander and find out what he proposed to do about the situation.

Reaching Livingston he found the Confederate camp in a state of gloomy pessimism. "I now heard everyone speaking of the fall of Vicksburg as very possible, and its jeopardy was laid at the door of General Pemberton, for whom no language could be too strong. He was freely called a coward and a traitor. He has the misfortune to be a Northerner by birth, which was against him in the opinion of all here."

The British colonel was officially welcomed at Livingston with Virginia courtesy, and he noted of Johnston: "To me he was extremely affable, but he certainly possesses the power of keeping people at a distance when he chooses, and his officers evidently stand in great awe of him." Yet the Southern general obviously commanded great respect. "Many of the officers told me they did not consider him inferior as a general to Lee or anyone else." When the two men, Fremantle and Johnston, got down to discussing the immediate military situation, the visiting Englishman recorded:

> He told me that Vicksburg was certainly in a critical situation, and was now closely invested by Grant. He said that he (Johnston) had 11,000 men with him (which includes Gist's), hardly any cavalry, and only sixteen pieces of cannon; but if he could get adequate reinforcements, he stated his intention of endeavoring to relieve Vicksburg.[28]

Before leaving the area Fremantle noted the arrival of considerable reinforcements. Loring's division, separated from Pemberton after the Battle of Champion Hill, reached Jackson with 5,000 of his men; another brigade, 2,000 strong, arrived from Charleston; and Brigadier Generals Albert C. Rust and Samuel B. Maxey's forces from Port Hudson were reported nearing Jackson. Fremantle estimated Johnston's strength by then as almost 25,000, present or within marching distance. This prompted the colonel to make further inquiry:

In the evening I asked General Johnston what prospect he thought there was of early operations, and he told me that at present he was too weak to do any good, and he was unable to give me any definite ideas as to when he might be strong enough to attack Grant.[29]

In Vicksburg, Pemberton, too, was unable to get any definite commitment from his superior. On May 19 and 21 he sent two dispatches to the general, the first reporting the successful repulse of the initial Federal assault, and estimating Grant's investing forces at "not less than 60,000"—an exaggerated figure.

The enemy, Pemberton wrote, was continuing to cannonade the city with his long-range guns. "That we may save ammunition his fire is rarely returned. At present our main necessity is musket-caps. Can you send them to me by couriers or citizens? An army will be necessary to relieve Vicksburg, and that quickly. Will it not be sent? Please let me hear from you if possible."

In his second dispatch from Vicksburg Pemberton reported the appearance on the river of "two large [Federal] transports loaded down with troops. They are evidently reinforcing their present large force." And he asked again:

Am I to expect reinforcements? From what direction and how soon? Can you send me musket-caps by courier? . . . The men credit and are encouraged by a report that you are near with a large force. They are fighting in good spirits, and the reorganization is complete.[30]

By this time communication between the two commands was difficult, if not impossible. Messages had to be smuggled through enemy lines by couriers risking death or capture. Probably no one was to blame that Pemberton did not get his musket-caps, much less any reinforcements, in time for the next offensive that he knew was coming.

Meanwhile, he ordered that "ammunition should be hoarded with the most zealous care." General Stevenson was instructed to organize a civilian guard to protect the powder magazines. Skirmishing on the front, "without special object," was forbidden "as being a useless waste of ammunition." And when, on May 20, Admiral Porter's mortar scows were shelling the city, the Confederate batteries were told to hold their fire.

With steadily strengthened defenses, with rising confidence among the troops, Vicksburg waited through two days of tension. Only a few faint-hearted civilians believed with Rowland Chambers that "the day of our doom appears close at hand." Trial and hardship might await them, yes, but for most Vicksburg still stood as firm as her eternal hills.

In a postmortem conference on May 20, Grant and his three corps commanders, Sherman, McPherson, and McClernand, analyzed the unsuccessful battle of the day before. They compared notes, according to Sherman, and agreed that the assault had failed for two principal reasons: the natural strength of the Confederate position, and "because we were forced by the nature of the ground to limit our attack to the strongest parts of the enemy's line"—namely, where the three main roads approached the city.

These were difficult conditions to surmount, but a more careful reconnaissance of the terrain, and a better deployment of troops resulting from that
study, might diminish their significance. In any event Grant decided, with
Sherman's concurrence, on another all-out assault on Vicksburg, later giving
as his reasons:

> Johnston was in my rear, only fifty miles away, with an army not much inferior
> in numbers to the one I had with me, and I knew he was being reinforced. There
> was danger of his coming to the assistance of Pemberton, and, after all, he might
> defeat my anticipation of capturing the garrison if, indeed, he did not prevent
> the capture of the city.
> The immediate capture of Vicksburg would save sending me the reinforce-
> ments which were so much wanted elsewhere, and would set free the army under
> me to drive Johnston from the State. But the first consideration of all was—the
> troops believed they could carry the works in their front, and would not have
> worked so patiently in the trenches if they had not been allowed to try.[31]

The assault was set for the morning of Friday, May 22, by which time
Grant's commissary line, from the Yazoo River and other sources of supply,
would be perfected and in operation. Moving as they had without a wagon
train or base, the troops had had their fill of beef, pork, chicken, and yams,
easily appropriated from plantations that they passed. For a change, if nothing
else, they wanted bread, in any and all forms.

Grant was made aware of this as he passed down the line on an inspection
tour and heard one of the soldiers say, in a soft but well-directed voice, "Hard
tack!" All down the line the troops took up the cry of "Hard tack! Hard tack."
The general paused to tell them gently that roads were already being built from
the Yazoo River to their camps behind the lines, and they would soon have
a more varied diet. Whereupon, Grant observed, the cry of hard tack "instantly changed to cheers."[32]

Possession of Walnut Hills and the neighboring bluffs not only cleared the
way for adequate supplies for the besieging army but also put Grant in easy
communication with Porter and his upper squadron near the mouth of the
Yazoo. Porter agreed to cooperate in the next assault. The mortar fleet would
keep the city under heavy fire from the river, while Porter's lower fleet would
come up and join in the bombardment.

During the next two days, both sides strengthened and consolidated their
positions, the Federals pushing their trenches ever nearer to the ramparts.
Lieutenant Sanders complained that "Enemy seems to be fond of flaunting
their miserable old flag close to our works." One arrogant Yankee, protested
Sanders, dug himself a rifle pit within 100 yards of the Confederate defenses,
the better to fire at the loopholes in the parapets. This particular Yankee would
be heard from later.

But, while there was almost constant artillery fire from the Union batteries
on the east, as well as from the river, the closeness of the two lines bred a
curious camaraderie—which existed so often in the war, during even the most
critical of campaigns. Noted Captain J. H. Jones of the Thirty-eighth Mississippi Infantry:

On the night of May 21st preceding the assault, the fratricidal feature of the war was called to our attention in a most pathetic manner. Just on our left was [Brigadier General Martin E.] Green's Missouri brigade, and, by the irony of fate, a brigade of Missourians on the Federal side was directly opposed to them. They discovered this in some way, and until late at night we could hear the Confederates calling to their old neighbors and asking of the loved ones in their far-away homes.[33]

Similarly, in his journal for that day, Sergeant Tunnard of the Third Louisiana noted that conversation with the enemy was common, due to their proximity. A Missourian in his regiment found "some acquaintances" among the opposing Federals and was invited into their lines where he was treated to food and beverages unavailable to the Confederates. After "a sociable chat and several drinks," he returned to his company, "very favorably impressed with the generosity of the Yankees." Tunnard continued:

The evening chats, after the day's deadly sharpshooting, revealed the fact that there were members of both armies who were personally acquainted, and, in one instance, two members of the Third Regiment found a brother in the regiment opposed to them.[34]

General Sherman, during this two-day period, reconnoitered the terrain in front of his position and decided to direct his attack on both sides of the Stockade Redan and strike at the defense works to the north. But this time he must solve the problem of the ditch below the Confederate parapets, which had baffled so many of his soldiers in the first assault.

A party of 150 volunteers, calling themselves the Forlorn Hope, vowed to overcome the barrier. They first planned filling the ditch with stalks of cane, but Sherman advised that a wooden bridge be thrown across just prior to the main assault. The only nearby source of planks was the house where Grant was sleeping. The commanding general was aroused from his bed to stand by, while his temporary quarters were dismantled, board by board, and left in the form of tidy piles of lumber.

Similarly engineers of McPherson's corps, on Sherman's left, were put to work fashioning forty ladders, fifteen or twenty feet long, to be dragged by ropes to the foot of the ramparts with the first wave of advancing Union troops. These would be used to scale the walls of the Great Redoubt, the largest fort on the line.

McClernand's troops prepared to attack the right of Vicksburg defenses, the line held by Stevenson's division from the railroad to the river, and a belt on the other side of the railroad held by Forney's division. Relatively inactive in the May 19 engagement—and still seeking glory that he felt had been denied him when Grant took over the army—McClernand was determined that his Thirteenth Corps should win distinction in this battle. He pushed his troops as close as possible to the Confederate defenses to be first in the assault.

Not far from the Third Louisiana Redan, Osborn Oldroyd of the Twentieth Ohio noted, "We can see the court house of the city with a Confederate flag flying over it. What fun it will be to take that down, and hoist in its stead the old stars and stripes." One thought marred this bright anticipation: "We are ragged and dirty, for we have had no change of clothes for over a month.

. . . If we were to enter Vicksburg tomorrow, some of our nice young fellows would feel ashamed to march before the young ladies there."[35]

Within the city's defenses Dr. Joseph Alison was not too worried about tomorrow. "We certainly are in a critical situation," he wrote in his diary for May 21, but he added: "We men are in fine spirits and satisfied that we can hold out a month. Johnston must relieve us soon. [President] Davis can't intend to sacrifice us, and will send reinforcements before long."[36]

Hope seemed to be divided equally between the blue and gray.

That night the men of both armies slept on their weapons in the trenches. It was uncomfortably hot, but the stars were out. Beyond the spires of Vicksburg, Oldroyd could visualize the sleepy Mississippi flowing by, an imperturbable nepenthe. His last thought was, "We want to jump into that once more and have a good bath."

❦ 17 ❦

Rivets of Brave Hearts

Friday, May 22, 1863.

It was a bright, clear morning in Mississippi and destined to turn warmer as the day advanced.

South of Vicksburg, General Nathaniel Banks was approaching Port Hudson, southernmost anchor of Confederate defenses on the river. As he began his campaign, pitting his 14,000 men against Franklin Gardner's garrison of half that number, he appealed to Grant for reinforcements. Grant turned him down. He could spare no men, for "Vicksburg is the vital point."

In Richmond, Virginia, an anxious and ailing President Davis, distraught from having no adequate information from Joe Johnston, went over the Western commander's head to telegraph Braxton Bragg in Tennessee:

> The vital issue of holding the Mississippi at Vicksburg is dependent on the success of General Johnston in an attack on the investing force. The intelligence from there is discouraging. Can you aid him?[1]

Similarly, Davis consulted Robert E. Lee on the wisdom of sending detachments from the Army of Northern Virginia to help in the defense of Vicksburg. Lee had what he thought was a better idea to aid Pemberton and ease the Federal pressure on Vicksburg: create a diversion in the east with a thrust into Pennsylvania.

So, no immediate help for now from any source. Except for the phantom presence of Joseph Johnston, elusive Confederate commander in Mississippi, the City of a Hundred Hills was on its own.

All but surrounding Vicksburg, Grant's troops were poised for the attack. Since five o'clock Porter's gunboats and mortars on the river, and Grant's artillery on the north and east, had been softening up the city with a fierce bombardment. Captain J. H. Jones of Brigadier General Louis Hébert's Confederate brigade recorded: "It was the grandest and most awe-inspiring scene I ever witnessed. The air was ablaze with the burning and bursting shells, darting like fiery serpents across the sky, and the earth shook with the thunderous roar."[2]

Osborn Oldroyd remembered how, waiting for the order to advance, the men of his regiment "were busy divesting themselves of watches, rings, pictures and their keepsakes, which were being placed in the custody of the cooks, who were not expected to go into action." They left addresses of parents, wives, or sweethearts to whom the articles should go "in case I never return." After this, the corps moved up to the rifle pits within 400 yards of the Confederate ramparts, where the air was so thick with smoke from the bombardment that they could not see the enemy parapets.[3]

With Logan's division of McPherson's corps, Wilbur Crummer of the Forty-fifth Illinois remembered that, as the bombardment began, "sharpshooters at the same time began their part," and over the thunder of artillery was heard "the sharp whiz of the minié ball."

Sylvanus Cadwallader observed the bombardment from what he had thought would be a safe position, between McPherson's and McClernand's corps, and reported that:

> The cannonading from both sides was terrific. The air was filled with hollow shot, percussion shells, and about every kind of missile ever thrown from heavy guns. At this time we were using many Hotchkiss shells having wooden bases fastened to metal points with wires and strips of tin. They were so imperfectly manufactured that the wooden base was blown off a large proportion of the time before they reached the enemy. . . . It was a common remark that they killed more of our own men by flying to pieces prematurely than the killed and wounded of the enemy combined.[4]

At precisely 10:00 A.M. by the officers' synchronized watches, the Federal assault was launched: Sherman's corps striking down the Graveyard Road at the Stockade Redan; McPherson advancing against Forney's division on the Jackson Road to Sherman's left; and McClernand attacking the center of Pemberton's line on both sides of the railroad tracks.

Sherman's assault was led by the Forlorn Hope, carrying their planks and ladders. Under murderous fire some of the volunteers advanced to the ditch. Several hardy men struggled part of the way up the slippery exterior slope, then slid back into the ditch for safety, to be joined shortly by troops charging behind them. The Confederates held their fire until the main line of the infantry was in close range, then, noted Sherman, "rose behind their parapet and poured a furious fire upon our lines; and, for about two hours, we had a severe and bloody battle, but at every point we were repulsed."[5]

Those who were pinned to the bottom of the ditch were isolated; they could not move forward or back. From their parapets the Southerners rolled shells with lighted fuses down into the ditch, there to explode with devastating fragmentations. Some Federals used their bayonets to try to parry the shells before they exploded and to hurl them back into the Confederate entrenchments.

To the left of Sherman, McPherson's corps was meeting stiff resistance in the Jackson Road area. With the troops defending this section of the Confederate defenses, J. H. Jones of Forney's division watched as "the Federals formed three lines of battle . . . and began a steady advance upon our works."

Their lines were about one hundred yards apart. They came on as rapidly as the fallen timber would permit, and in perfect order. We waited in silence until the first line had advanced within easy rifle range, when a murderous fire was opened from the breastworks. We had a few pieces of artillery which ploughed their ranks with murderous effect. Still they came bravely on.[6]

Jones was moved to admiration, considering the charge "a gallant sight, though an awful one. . . . Surely no more desperate courage than this could be displayed by mortal men." The Confederates' clear field of fire worked strikingly to their advantage. As the bluecoats came plunging up the slope, "they invariably fell backwards, as the death shot greeted them. . . . Some of them fell within a few yards of our works. If any of the first line escaped, I did not see them."

The following Union troops, "when they recognized the impossible, sought refuge among the fallen timber." There they remained until nightfall. Jones noted, however, that some suicide-minded Missouri troops had succeeded inplanting a battle flag upon the exterior slopes of the Great Redoubt, where "it waved defiantly all day until it was carried off by its owners, who had found shelter in the ditch."

On the left, facing the center of Pemberton's line, McClernand brimmed with confidence that morning. This, he resolved, was to be his day, but he wouldn't turn down any help that he could get. Brigadier General John McArthur was on his way from Warrenton to attack South Fort, southern anchor of the Confederate line. To divert McArthur's troops to his own command, he sent a message to the general: "Hope circumstance will justify you in Immediately joining me with your whole division. . . . With your assistance I have no doubt I will be able to force the enemy center and reach Vicksburg tomorrow."[7]

He wouldn't wait for McArthur's reply, which was just as well; McArthur ignored the request and proceeded toward South Fort. Before he could organize an attack, however, he received a message he could not ignore—an order from Grant for McArthur to march to McClernand's front. Starting at dawn and continuing till 10:00 A.M., McClernand's siege and field artillery shelled the center of Pemberton's defenses. Then to the sound of bugles his whole battle line moved forward.

There was a dramatic success when the troops of one brigade, according to McClernand's report, "carried the ditch, slope, and bastion of a fort." A dozen men of the Twenty-second Iowa Infantry, led by Sergeants Joseph Griffith and Nicholas Messenger, entered the Railroad Redoubt through an opening—chewed out by artillery fire—at the salient angle. In a terrific hand-to-hand struggle, the Iowans drove the Confederates from the fort. Some hours later Griffith and his band repelled an enemy sortie and then captured thirteen grayclads. With no reserves on hand, the Federals were unable to exploit this tenuous penetration.

Other regiments in that first wave of the assault were cited in the Illinois general's report. "The colors of the 22nd Iowa were planted upon the counterscarp of the ditch, while those of the 48th Ohio and the 77th waved over the bastion."

On the other side of the tracks two other brigades had "rushed forward and carried the ditch and slope of a heavy earthwork and planted their colors on the latter." The fighting increased in ferocity as Federal units mounted repeated attacks against the Second Texas Lunette, which guarded the Baldwin's Ferry Road. The Confederates were hard-pressed to maintain this key position.

Placing battle flags on the outer rim of any of the enemy's defenses indicated gallantry on the part of certain individuals, but little more—though McClernand would make the most of it. Other regiments of McClernand's corps suffered severely. Sergeant Charles Wilcox, with the Thirty-third Illinois Infantry, was forced to mount a ridge in close proximity to the enemy's line, then, to reach the objective, had to run along the top of the ridge in the line of enemy fire. "Here is where our poor boys suffered terribly, the ridge being covered with the dead and wounded."

Some of the brigade plunged into a depression on the ridge for shelter, and Wilcox remembered:

> We lay there for about eight minutes and yet it seemed an age to me, for showers of bullet and grape were passing over me and not a foot above me, and on my right and left were my comrades dying and dead as well as living. What an awful eight minutes that was. . . . Twice I exclaimed aloud, that my comrades might hear, *"My God, why don't they order us to charge,"* and then I thought perhaps all of our officers were killed and there was no one to order us forward.[8]

"Some who were wounded groaned and shrieked, others were calm and resigned," wrote Sergeant Wilcox. "Generally those that were the slightest wounded, shrieked the loudest, thinking they were wounded the worst." But one of the injured resorted to a tactic that forced a smile from Wilcox. He simply lay down and started rolling down the opposite slope of the ridge and kept on rolling until safely out of enemy range. The rest of the regiment sought positions from which they could safely return the Confederate fire without undue exposure. They had already lost a good half of those engaged.

Sylvanus Cadwallader, from his point of observation, wrote of this engagement:

> As McClernand's advance neared the rebel works, it came into plain view from my place of shelter. It had been so mercilessly torn to pieces by Confederate shot and shell that it had lost nearly all resemblance to a line of battle, or the formation of a storming column. Officers and men were rushing ahead pell-mell without much attention to alignment. The small number in sight could no longer be mown down by artillery, as the guns of the forts could not be depressed sufficiently.
>
> When they crossed the deep ditch in front of the earthworks and began to ascend the glacis, they were out of musketry range for the same reason. . . . A straggling line, continually growing thinner and weaker, finally reached the summit, when all who were not instantly shot down were literally pulled over the rebel breastworks as prisoners. One stand of our colors was planted half way up the embankment and remained there until a daring Confederate ventured over, and carried it back inside.[9]

Cadwallader had seen enough and returned to Grant's headquarters, where he learned more. McClernand reported he had found his forces vigorously counterattacked by the Confederates, who had brought up reinforcements—until, wrote the Illinois general, "failure and loss of my hard-won advantages became imminent." He again requested reinforcements from McArthur, and promptly at noon sent a message to Grant by courier:

> General: We are hotly engaged with the enemy. We have part possession of two forts, and the Stars and Stripes are floating over them. A vigorous push ought to be made all along the line.[10]

Sherman was with Grant at the time, having reported his failure to make a dent in the Confederate defenses, and being assured by the general that McPherson's corps had done no better. Grant handed him the message from McClernand, with the comment:

"I don't believe a word of it."[11]

Undoubtedly Sherman was skeptical as well, but, he wrote later, "I reasoned with him [Grant] that this note was official, and must be credited, and I offered to renew the assault at once." Grant then directed Sherman and McPherson to make the diversion requested by McClernand.

McPherson sent Isaac F. Quinby's division to support McClernand's effort. McClernand was elated by this "welcome intelligence," writing that "the works in which I made my lodgment were commanded by strong defenses in their rear, but that with a division I doubted not that I should force my way through the hostile lines."[12]

What happened next is a matter of conflicting views. According to McClernand, Quinby's three brigades, "coming up late in the evening and much exhausted," never saw action. As a matter of fact one of these brigades engaged three regiments of Brigadier General Martin E. Green's Confederates in a bitter thirty-minute fight just north of the Second Texas Lunette.

Cadwallader wrote, however, that "instead of using Quinby as a support to his own troops, McClernand ordered them to the front in the forlorn hope of retrieving the fortunes of the day, and attempted to make a second assault, with his own demoralized troops, on Quinby's flank. One of his colonels flatly refused to obey this order and declared that he would take the consequences of his disobedience rather than lead his men to certain death."[13]

Finally, the colonel—declaring "Good God! no man can return from this charge alive!"—led his men gallantly forward and, according to Cadwallader, "fell dead at the first fire."

"The whole affair," wrote Cadwallader, "was miserable and inexcusable to a point past endurance."

On the right end of the line, Sherman and McPherson had attacked as ordered, to take the pressure off McClernand—and been similarly thwarted. Wrote Sherman of the three separate assaults made by his men that afternoon:

> It was a repetition of the first, equally unsuccessful and bloody. It also transpired that the same thing had occurred with General McPherson, who lost in this second assault some most valuable officers and men, without adequate result; and that General McClernand, instead of having taken any single point of the rebel

main parapet, had only taken one or two small lunettes open to the rear, where his men were at the mercy of the rebels behind their main parapet, and most of them were actually thus captured.[14]

Viewing Sherman's morning assault from the Confederate defenses held by Martin Smith's division, William Chambers recorded that to the right "column after column was hurled against our works, only to be driven back in confusion, leaving the ground in front of our lines literally blue with the dead and wounded Federals." He continued:

Never before had the idea I once entertained of what a battle was like, been so nearly realized as now. The spectacle of perhaps sixty or seventy thousand men *all fighting at once;* with upward of three hundred cannon belching forth their thunder, is a scene I cannot attempt to describe. In these charges the enemy reached our trenches in many places, and desperate hand-to-hand conflicts occurred. A few prisoners were taken, it was those whose trepidity carried them into our works, where they were made captive.[15]

Despite counterattacks, the Federals maintained a tenuous grip on the Railroad Redoubt for several hours, until a contingent of Colonel Thomas N. Waul's Texas Legion volunteered to dig them out. "With promptness and alacrity," reported Colonel Waul, "they moved to the assault, retook the fort, drove the enemy through the breach they entered, and tore down the stand of colors still floating over the parapet . . . "

Waul sent the colors, with a note of the action, to General Stephen D. Lee who declared, "A more daring feat has not been performed during the war."

For the first time Cadwallader was severely critical of Grant. The commanding general, he believed, had failed to make a proper reconnaissance of McClernand's section of the battlefield. "Had he been near enough to obtain a clear view of it, his guilt would have exceeded McClernand's, and instead of reinforcing him he should have peremptorily withdrawn him from the field." Later the reporter wrote:

I remember distinctly that I gave Grant and Rawlins the first complete account of its failure—stated that I was in plain view of the rebel earthworks—that McClernand never gained a footing inside of them—and that the small number of his men who actually reached the crest, or scrambled over it, were there yet as prisoners. I was questioned closely concerning it; and shall never forget the fearful burst of indignation from Rawlins, and the grim glowering look of disappointment and disgust which settled down on Grant's usually placid countenance, when he was convinced of McClernand's duplicity, and realized its cost in dead and wounded.[16]

The cost had indeed been terrible: for the Federals, 3,200 dead, wounded, and missing; Confederate losses were less than 500. And, after thinking it over, Grant two days later knew wherein the blame lay:

General McClernand's dispatches misled me as to the real state of the facts, and caused much of this loss. He is entirely unfit for the position of corps commander, both on the march and on the battlefield. Looking after his corps gives me more labor and infinitely more uneasiness than all the remainder of my department.[17]

Assigning the blame was of little comfort now. Two onslaughts on the city had failed dismally. As Grant acknowledged: "This last attack only served to increase our casualties without giving us any benefit whatever. As soon as it was dark our troops that had reached the enemy's line and been obliged to remain there for security all day, were withdrawn; and thus ended the last assault upon Vicksburg."[18]

In Vicksburg none could know that this would be the last all-out attack against the city. It hardly mattered; they were under siege from two sides, land and river, and none was so sanguine as to think that Grant would simply go away. Things could get worse before they got better; and they would only get better when Johnston arrived to deliver them from Grant's iron grasp.

At his river battery below the town, Hugh Moss kept his sights set on the Union gunboats on the river, which were giving his fellow artillerists "hotter work than we expected . . . the mortars also played on us rapidly." They had been warned of the stepped-up bombardment by an intercepted dispatch from Grant to a commander in the Union fleet, advising that the army would continue to press on Vicksburg from the east, while the gunboats and mortars should pummel the city from the river.

Forced underground for shelter, Emma Balfour had suspended writing in her diary during the battle of Friday, May 22, when "The shells exploded around us all day." She took up her pen again on Saturday, to report that the day before:

> . . . the gunboats towed some mortars into range, and there was a rushing into caves . . . we went into a cave for the first time. . . . Just as we got in, several machines exploded, it seemed just over our heads, and at the same time two riders were killed in the valley below us by a twenty-four pound shell from the east side, so you see we were between two fires.[19]

In the cave Emma felt "a sense of suffocation from being underground . . . there was no way of escape . . . we were hemmed in, caged." She preferred the risk of living in her house to being packed in with so many others, although writing, "we are having a cave of our own built, but I certainly shall stay out as long as I can."

In their crowded underground shelter near the center of the city, Margaret Lord and her two children found they were not secure from danger. The bombardment during the Friday battle was so severe that Mrs. Lord could feel the whole earth shake. A bombshell, striking the top of the hill, detached a mass of earth from the ceiling of the cave, its initial fall throwing young Lucy McRae to the floor. A visiting soldier flung himself over the girl's small body to break the force of the avalanche—which, Mrs. Lord believed, surely would have killed her—and soon both were dug free, Lucy unscathed and the soldier badly bruised.

It was only the beginning of their trial by terror. "The worst sufferers during a battle are the non-combatants," Mrs. Lord's daughter Lida wrote, remembering from her cave life that: "Candles were forbidden, and we could only see one another's faces by the lurid lightning-like flashes of the bursting bombs. Sometimes a nearer roar, a more startling beam, would cause us all to huddle closer together and shut our eyes, feeling that our last hour had come. Frightened women sobbed, babies cried, tired and hungry children fretted," and the badly shaken Lucy McRae "moaned incessantly and piteously."

Later during the bombardment, Lida remembered, another bombshell struck the side of the hill, collapsing one of the entrances. A voice shouting, "Good God! Out of the cave! Out of the cave!" provoked a panic among the crowded refugees, until young Willie Lord heard his father's powerful voice calling, "All right! Nobody hurt!" The panic was checked in the nick of time when, wrote Lida Lord, "many were rushing for the openings, while others, blinded and terrified, were plunging farther back into the hill. For, truly, though there were horrors enough within, where else could the poor souls go?"[20]

Mary Loughborough, however, stayed in her house, though remaining dressed throughout the night. She was not too frightened by the gunboats; their presence had become familiar. But, when shells from the battlefield began exploding near her home, she was severely shaken. Then toward evening came the "loud rush and screams of the mortar shells," and she ran to a small cave near the house and remained there during the night, "by this time wearied and almost stupefied by loss of sleep."

The caves, wrote Mary, "were plainly becoming a necessity." She was more convinced of that when a shell crashed into her house and through the room where lately she had been sleeping. She noted, too, that "some persons had been killed on the street by fragments of shells." Still, she would never get over the sense of fear and utter hopelessness of a night spent beneath the ground:

> Terror stricken, we remained crouched in the cave, while shell after shell followed each other in quick succession. I endeavored by constant prayer to prepare myself for the sudden death I was almost certain awaited me. My heart stood still as we would hear the reports from the guns, and the rushing and fearful sound of the shell as it came toward us.
>
> As it neared, the noise became more deafening; the air was full of the rushing sound; pains darted through my temples; my ears were full of the confusing noise; and, as it exploded, the report flashed through my head like an electric shock, leaving me in a quiet state of terror the most painful that I can imagine— cowering in a corner, holding my child to my breast—the only feeling of my life being the choking throbs of my heart, that rendered me almost breathless.[21]

Morning found the subterranean refugees "more dead than alive, with blanched faces and trembling lips." One of Pemberton's staff officers warned the emerging cave dwellers that "Vicksburg would not in all probability hold out for more than a week or two," and while the ladies protested, "Oh, never surrender!" Mary Loughborough, after the night's experience, did not know whether she really cared or not. One thing was certain, life in Vicksburg would be greatly altered in the days ahead, for "so constantly dropped the shells around the city, that the inhabitants all made preparations to live under the ground during the siege."

Dora Richards Miller, despite her secret hopes for a Federal "liberation" of the city, found little comfort in the present situation. "We are utterly cut off from the world, surrounded by a circle of fire. Would it be wise like the scorpion to sting ourselves to death?"

The cellar in which Dora and her husband stayed for safety was so damp that the bedding had to be carried out for airing every day, with the knowledge that it might be destroyed by the constant shelling. Except for this chore, she and her husband spent much of their time rereading Dickens's novels by the dim light in the cellar. But, "the confinement is dreadful," wrote Dora. "To sit and listen as if waiting for death in a horrible manner would drive me insane. I don't know what others do, but we read when I am not scribbling in this [journal]."[22]

The dentist-turned-doctor Rowland Chambers, whose diary was badly in need of spelling corrections ("terable" for "terrible"), felt that "we have now experienced all the horrors of war except being in the thickest of the battle . . . shot, shell, and minié balls are passing over and around us in all directions. The whir of the parrot shell is frightful; the whiz of the minié ball has an indescribable effect. When you hear one, you know it has passed you, but [it] leaves a dread of the next one; . . . "

Chambers found himself tending wounded Yankees brought to his home, now converted to a hospital. He wrote in his diary that night that "one of them had a hole shot in the side of his head and his brains were running out of it." Another told Chambers that death was the common lot of all of them, and he, for one, much preferred dying to living in this nest of rebels.[23]

Though Winchester Hall was being cared for by his wife in their boarding house, his lieutenant in the Twenty-sixth Louisiana, Jared Sanders, remained with the rest of the regiment in the fortifications ringing Vicksburg, with little to eat, little to quench their thirsts, and with seemingly one thought in mind, which echoed the hopes of Hugh Moss at the river battery: "We are looking anxiously for *Joe Johnston.*" The underscoring was his own.

A light rain fell during the night. Some of the Confederates crept out on the battlefield in search of trophies—Federal kepis with the company insignia above the brim, buckles stamped with the initials "U.S.," officers' swords and pistols. And above all the Enfield rifles and the Union cartridge boxes. For Pemberton, early on, had exhorted the men to gather up enemy arms and ammunition every chance they got. Back in the breastworks they exchanged souvenirs as children exchanged picture cards and marbles.

But for the majority of weary defenders, wrote Sergeant Willie Tunnard of the Third Louisiana, the post-battle evening offered no repose:

> Heavy details were made to rebuild and repair those portions of the works ploughed up and torn down by the heavy firing of the enemy's batteries during the day. It was no light task, after fighting all day beneath the rays of the summer's sun, thus, amid the shadows of night, to use pick-axe, spade, and shovel, carry heavy sandbags, strengthen the torn-down breastworks with heavy timbers and cotton-bales, in order to be protected during the approaching day's combat.[24]

For all expected that the fight would be renewed—and, though of different character, it was. During May 23 the gunboats and mortar barges on the river, and the Federal artillery to the east, continued to shell the city unremittingly.

Musketry fire was constant; no combatant, on either side, dared to raise his head.

But there was no further Federal assault upon the earthworks, although the dawn-to-dusk bombardment continued throughout Sunday. Emma Balfour came out of the cave where she had spent the night to survey the damage to her neighborhood. She discovered that four of her neighbors' homes had been struck by shells and one "literally torn to pieces." Miraculously, no one in the houses had been injured, but Emma learned that two Vicksburg civilians had been killed, as well as a small child, crushed to death by falling debris.

Already, in this brief tour of inspection, Emma was learning the secrets of survival in a city under fire:

> You must understand that it was not in the usual way we walked down the street, but had to take the middle of the street when we heard a shell, and watch for it. You may imagine our progress was not very fast. As soon as a shell gets over your head you are safe for, even if it approaches near, the pieces fall forward and do not touch you; but the danger is that sometimes while watching one, another comes and may explode or fall near you 'ere you are aware.[25]

Many Federal shells failed to explode, and, after stumbling on five of them, Emma brazenly started picking them up and taking them home as keepsakes, writing two days later: "I have quite a collection of shells which have fallen around us and if this goes on much longer I can build a pyramid." Unknowingly, Emma was presaging a new hobby in the city, collecting shell casings, broken glass of different colors, pieces of shrapnel and Federal bullets—especially the soft-lead minié balls (named for their French inventor), which could be molded into miniature figures, animals, elves, and dollhouse furniture.

In addition to the rain of shells, the rattle of musketry, the choking stench of smoke and powder, a dreadful odor permeated Vicksburg, reaching even to the center of the city. Though two miles within the breastworks, Rowland Chambers complained, "The smell of the dead bodies is horrible." Despite a deep-seated humanitarianism, Grant perversely would not request a truce in which to gather up the wounded and the dead, even though the vast majority were his own soldiers. It would be an admission of weakness or defeat; and he would not confess to either.

In fact, his official report to Halleck in Washington carried a note of optimism and achievement: "Vicksburg is now completely invested. . . . Today an attempt was made to carry the city by assault, but was not entirely successful. . . . The nature of the ground about Vicksburg is such that it can only be taken by a siege." He estimated that the siege would take no longer than a week, provided General Johnston did not "send a large army upon my rear."[26]

A siege was the last thing that Grant wanted and was what he had tried to avoid by his hasty May 19 assault upon the city. But in his *Memoirs* he described it as simply a tactic of "out-camping" the enemy without incurring further losses. Besides:

> The experience of the 22d convinced officers and men that this was best, and they went to work on the defenses and approaches with a will. . . . As long as we could

hold our position the enemy was limited in supplies of food, men and munitions of war to what they had on hand. These could not last always.[27]

However, with Johnston somewhere to the east and reportedly receiving reinforcements, Grant would have to prepare for fighting on two fronts. Detachments of troops began extending the siege line which ultimately would stretch for twelve miles, paralleling the Confederate defenses. Subsequently, reinforcements would construct a second system of breastworks, facing the other way, in anticipation of attack from Johnston.

And meanwhile the bloated corpses still lay on the battlefield, intermingled with the wounded, beneath a scorching Mississippi sun. Some of the wounded, noted William Chambers, had been there for two days "without a drop of water or a particle of shade."

Even for the Confederate soldiers, Pemberton reported, it was a harrowing ordeal to see the enemy "lying in every attitude of agony, on the open fields, in the trenches and the ditches, and among the slashed trees. . . . " Wrote Captain J. H. Jones of Forney's division facing McPherson's front: "The stench was unbearable. The sight was horrible. The reeking bodies lay all blackened and swollen, and some with arms extended as if pleading to Heaven for the burial that was denied them by man."

Finally Pemberton could stand it no longer. On May 25 he sent a flag of truce across the lines with a letter addressed to General Grant:

> Sir: Two days having elapsed since your dead and wounded have been lying in our front, and as yet no disposition on your part of a desire to remove them being exhibited, in the name of humanity I have the honor to propose a cessation of hostilities for two hours and a half, that you may be enabled to remove your dead and dying men. . . .[28]

If Grant was not inclined to take care of the matter, Pemberton added, all the Union general had to do was withhold his fire while Confederate troops undertook to bury the Yankee dead and round up the Yankee wounded to be cared for. Grant agreed to the truce proposal, but he replied that it would take time to circulate the cease-fire order to his scattered commanders. He suggested 6:00 P.M. for the truce to take effect. Hostilities would halt for Pemberton's prescribed two hours and a half.

"Now commenced a strange spectacle in this thrilling drama of the war," wrote Sergeant Willie Tunnard of the Third Louisiana:

> Flags were displayed along both lines, and the troops thronged the breastworks, gaily chatting with each other, discussing the issues of the war, disputing over differences of opinion, losses in the fight, etc. Numbers of the Confederates accepted invitations to visit the enemy's lines, where they were hospitably entertained and warmly welcomed. They were abundantly supplied with provisions, supplies of various kinds, and liquors. Of course, there were numerous laughable and interesting incidents resulting from these visits.[29]

Union infantryman Osborn Oldroyd noted that both armies "mingled together in various sports, apparently with much enjoyment. Here a group of four played cards—two Yanks and two Rebs. There, others were jumping, while everywhere blue and gray mingled in conversation over the scenes which had transpired since our visit to the neighborhood. . . . From the remarks of some of the rebels, I judged that their supply of provisions was getting low. . . . We gave them from our own rations some fat meat, crackers, coffee and so forth, in order to make them as happy as we could."

Oldroyd talked with one "very sensible rebel who said he was satisfied we should not only take Vicksburg, but drive the forces of the South all over their territory, at last compelling them to surrender." Isaac Jackson, also of the Union infantry, wrote of the Confederates he saw or chatted with: "A great many never went back. They say that they will have to give it [Vicksburg] up."[30]

On the other side of the coin, Confederate private William Chambers noted of this mixed assembly that "Old acquaintances were hunted up, and the broken ties of friendship . . . were reunited." But Chambers added with emphatic underscoring: "Although our foes were elated over their recent victories . . . yet *I found not a man but what was willing to go home and leave the South alone!*"

The brief truce, to bury the dead and gather up the wounded, served another purpose. Officers of both sides seized the opportunity to inspect the enemy's positions, single out points of weakness, and plan their future strategies accordingly. Sherman, particularly, was so inclined, writing later of the Union failures of May 19 and 22: "I have since seen the position at Sevastopol, and without hesitation I declare that at Vicksburg to have been the more difficult of the two."

On the excuse of delivering a message from behind the lines to Pemberton's engineer, Sam Lockett, Sherman suggested they share a fallen log where they could sit and talk awhile. After some polite conversation, during which both surreptitiously examined the terrain, Sherman remarked, "You have an admirable position for defense here, and you have taken excellent advantage of it."[31]

The Confederate engineer was flattered; he himself had been in charge of fortifying the position. As the conversation grew more pleasant and diverting, Lockett lost all track of his mission. "Intentionally or not," wrote the colonel of his chat with Sherman, "his civility certainly prevented me from seeing many other points which I as chief engineer was very anxious to examine."

As the bugles signaled the end of the truce, Chambers saw two brothers, one in blue, the other gray, "clasp hands in farewell and go in opposite directions," reconciled to resume the firing on one another. Willie Tunnard recorded another parting, as a Confederate captain who had been drinking with a Yankee officer and sharing the latter's viands, shook hands with his host. Said the latter:

"Good day, Captain; I trust we shall meet soon again in the Union of old."

Said the captain, smiling wryly: "I cannot return your sentiment. The only union which you and I will enjoy, I hope, will be in kingdom come. Good-bye, sir."[32]

Only Jared Sanders had ugly memories of those few hours of respite on the battlefield. He stood on the parapet watching the intermingling of friend and foe below him, unwittingly silhouetted to provide a perfect target. The temptation was too much for a Federal sharpshooter who, complained Sanders, "took a *deliberate fire* at me—the ball passing harmlessly by. It was an infamous act." Sanders's comrades agreed with him, and shouted an angry warning to the Federals not to try that sort of thing again.[33]

The brief and eerie silence following the truce gave no assurance to the city or its garrison. As long as the Federal troops were there, attack at any time must be anticipated. Yet the only move suggesting another attack came from Porter's gunboats on the river. Prompted by the ever-restless Sherman, the admiral sent one of his mightiest ironclads, the *Cincinnati*, to destroy the Confederate batteries on the north edge of the city and clear the area for an assault by land.

When the ironclad appeared on the morning of Wednesday, May 27, Hugh Moss recorded, "There was great commotion in the city—women and children and even men ran for their rat holes thinking that there would be a general attack in front and indeed this was the opinion of officers and men." Troops rushed to the rifle pits; Moss and his fellow artillerists manned their batteries.

Aboard the *Cincinnati*, Richard D. Hall, naval surgeon, was writing a letter to his wife, explaining the action. If the *Cincinnati* took the main battery and expunged the rifle pits, "Sherman and his men will go into Vicksburg." Hall never finished the letter. A shell crashed into the hull of the *Cincinnati*, and the fight was on.

It was a day to remember for Hugh Moss. The ironclad, intrepidly coming ever closer, firing blast after blast, finally came into the range of Moss's battery, "and we gave her all we had. Cheer after cheer from the men above told us that some good had been done for the monster had become companion to the fishes under the waters of the great Mississippi."[34]

The *Cincinnati* was ingloriously driven to the far bank of the river, where just as ingloriously she sank. Sergeant Willie Tunnard recorded in his diary: "This combat was witnessed by hundreds of ladies, who ascended on the summits of the most prominent hills in Vicksburg. There were loud cheers, the waving of handkerchiefs, amid general exultation, as the vessel went down." He concluded:

A large number of articles from the sunken boat were picked up in the river, including hay, clothing, whiskey, a medical chest, letters, photographs, etc. We often wonder if the surgeon on the *Cincinnati*, who so comfortably penned a letter to his affectionate wife as the boat neared our batteries, escaped unhurt.[35]

There would be no more attempts to assault the city from the river. From this point on the danger would lie east of Vicksburg, where both armies, within and outside the fortifications, waited apprehensively for Johnston.

William Chambers remembered that on the day that Pemberton's forces returned to Vicksburg and turned to face the enemy approaching from the Big Black, "we were exhorted to hold the place for only twelve hours longer, being assured that General Johnston would join us, by that time, at the head of a heavy force." Nine days had passed, and during that interval, wrote Chambers:

We were repeatedly informed that he was coming!—that dispatches had been received from him stating that he had gained important victories, and that the siege would surely be raised in two or three days at farthest. This was repeated so often and the men were so often disappointed that they naturally became skeptical and despondent.[36]

Chambers added, however: "Without boasting, I can say that I did not entirely despond during all those dreary days."

Nor did Pemberton despair. Though it was hard to reach Johnston by courier—through enemy lines and only by night—he gathered that the general had by now approached the Big Black River. No answer had come to his May 20 request for reinforcements, but on May 29 he received a message from Johnston dated May 19 and reading: "I am trying to gather a force which may relieve you. Hold out."

This was followed by a still more encouraging dispatch from the Confederate commander: "Bragg is sending a division. When it comes, I will move to you. Which do you think is the best route? How and where is the enemy encamped? What is your force?"[37]

Replying to these questions to the best of his ability, Pemberton added: "My men are in good spirits awaiting your arrival. You may depend on my holding this place as long as possible." Receiving no answer for several days he followed this up with a more urgent message:

"When may I expect you to move, and in what direction?"

Again, no answer. Grant dug in; the Federal batteries and the gunboats on the river shelled the city. The days passed. Pemberton waited; all Vicksburg waited. Though the city was still locked within a cordon of steel, as Osborn Oldroyd had observed, his reference to "rivets of brave hearts" might equally have been applied to the Confederates.

❊ 18 ❊

The Noose Draws Tighter

"**V**ICKSBURG was so important to the enemy," wrote General Grant, "that I believed he would make strenuous efforts to raise the siege."[1]

So he must tighten his grip upon the city. His twelve-mile-long line enclosing the Confederate defense perimeter, running from the river a mile and a half above Vicksburg and back to the river three miles below the city, was roughly 600 yards from the Confederate defenses. He would move it closer, step by step, digging approach trenches toward the main Confederate strong points, then extending parallels like fishbones radiating from a spine. As each advanced trench was occupied, parapets of logs and earth were raised along its forward rim to protect the troops from enemy musketry.

There was a shortage of trained engineers, essential to siege operations. But Grant and his chief engineer Frederick Prime discovered that with Yankee ingenuity they could do without them. The enterprising infantry could do the job. As one of the latter noted:

> Every man in the investing line became an army engineer day and night. The soldiers worked at digging zigzag approaches to the rebel works. Entrenchments, rifle pits, and dirt caves were made in every conceivable direction. When entrenchments were safe and finished, still others, yet farther in advance were made, as if by magic, in a single night.
>
> Other zigzag underground saps and mines were made for explosion under forts. Every day the regiments foot by foot, yard by yard, approached nearer the strongly armed rebel works. The soldiers got so they bored like gophers and beavers, with a spade in one hand and a gun in the other.[2]

Wrote Isaac Jackson of the Eighty-third Ohio to his brother John in early June, "Now we have good rifle pits all around, and Battery after Battery planted on the hills all around their works. . . . We will soon be as strongly fortified as they." But he noted that Confederate sharpshooters kept "popping away" at the soldier-engineers. "It sounds like shingling a house. First one pops and then another." But Grant was bringing up heavy siege guns; they should make the Confederates pull in their heads.

To protect the diggers, sap rollers, or "bullet-stoppers," were fabricated, to be pushed ahead of the advancing engineers and troops. As explained by Wilbur Crummer of the Forty-fifth Illinois Infantry: "Suppose we take two empty barrels, and lash them together, one on top of the other, then wrap them round and round with willow saplings, fill them with earth, put a cover on, lay them down, and you have a sap-roller."[3]

The construction might vary to include any movable mass that protected the Federal diggers as they pushed toward the Vicksburg earthworks. Seeing others thus engaged, Grant's chief of commissary, Robert Macfeeley, regretted that he was too fat to be of use in this endeavor—unless they could use his barrel-shaped frame for a roller. "He was a large man, weighing two hundred and twenty pounds," Grant observed, "but as we were sure to lose him if we used him as a sap-roller, I let him off."[4]

To augment his supply of siege guns, Grant coaxed from Porter a number of naval cannon. These were placed at strategic elevated points along his line. As the line pushed forward, parallel by parallel, so did the batteries, shelling the Confederate works from ever closer range.

But mortars were needed to lob their projectiles above and over the intervening hills. So, Grant recorded, "wooden ones were made by taking logs of the toughest wood that could be found, boring them out for six or twelve pounder shells, and binding them with strong iron bands. These answered as coehorns, and shells were successfully thrown from them into the trenches of the enemy."

With so long a siege line around the city, the Union general worried at first about sufficient troops to man the trenches. He did not have to worry long; for as Sherman wrote, Grant was now the hero in the War Department's eyes. He may have ignored instructions, as he did in not cooperating with Banks, but he had reached the gates of Vicksburg and was not to be denied.

Concerned by reports of a Confederate concentration in the Jackson-Canton-Yazoo City area, Grant, late in May, ordered two divisions on occupation duty in Tennessee to the Vicksburg front. In addition, he applied to General Halleck for reinforcements. Halleck responded by transferring to Grant's command two divisions from Kentucky and one division from Missouri. His army which had numbered 50,000 at the end of May would reach 77,000 by mid-June—more than double the number of Pemberton's defending troops.

On June 22 Grant organized an army of 34,000 under Sherman to bar an approach by Johnston and to strengthen and expand defenses from the Yazoo to the railroad bridge across the Big Black River, for, he wrote, "we were now looking west, besieging Pemberton, while we were also looking east, to defend ourselves against an expected siege by Johnston." The reinforcements from Missouri were placed on the far left, to strengthen the siege line south of Vicksburg.

Since the previous summer, colored recruits had, in certain cases, been accepted in the Union Army—"colored" being the term applied to freed blacks, many of them former slaves. In the early months of 1863 Grant had been encouraged by the War Department actively to recruit black troops. Now, elements of an African Brigade, recruited in Louisiana, were posted at Milliken's Bend—twenty miles upriver from Vicksburg—to defend the Union communications and depots on the western bank.

The city was now so closely invested that, as one Confederate remarked, "a cat could not have crept out of Vicksburg without being discovered." And Grant himself felt sufficiently confident to wire Halleck that, "The fall of Vicksburg and the capture of most of the garrison can only be a question of time." When one of his staff suggested that Johnston might fight his way into the city and greatly strengthen Pemberton's defense force, Grant replied:

> No, we are the only fellows who want to get in there. The Rebels who are now in want to get out, and those who are out want to stay out. If Johnston tries to cut his way in, we will let him do it, and then see that he don't get out. You say he has thirty thousand men with him? That will give us thirty thousand more prisoners than we now have.[5]

In Richmond, Jefferson Davis, already deeply troubled by affairs in his native Mississippi, grieved over the desecration of Brierfield, his plantation home, enshrining thirty years of pleasant memories. Rogue troops were blamed for the atrocity.

The main house was left standing by the vandals, but the interior was ravaged—furniture destroyed, rugs and paintings ripped with bayonets, almost everything of value stolen, including the gold-headed cane he had carried as United States Secretary of War under Franklin Pierce. Over the entrance in crude letters at one time had been painted, "This is the house that Jeff built," and to humiliate him further a band of liberated blacks had been installed as "guests" of the Confederacy's President.

His brother Joseph's adjoining plantation, Hurricane, had suffered more severely, even though Joe had not been active in the war. All of the owner's fondly-collected books, china, glassware, paintings and sculptures had been smashed or burned. Most of the slaves had earlier been removed to Fleetwood, Joseph's plantation refuge near Bolton, where he lived with his granddaughter Lise and where Sherman had stopped to pay his respects on his march from Jackson toward Vicksburg.

Fleetwood, too, was threatened by troops on the way to Vicksburg, with orders "to leave no board unburned." According to Lise, writing in her journal, "The ladies watched them [Federal soldiers] break open trunks and rob them of silver, jewels, and other valuables." The vandals were about to apply the torch when a wily servant shouted that rescuers were coming, and the soldiers fled without setting fire to the house.[6]

Since then, despite the President's urging that he come to Richmond, Joseph had remained at Bolton "to be among my people," and had frequently called on Johnston at his camp near Jackson. In his brother's behalf he had tried, in vain, to get information from the general as to his plans for aiding Pemberton. President Davis likewise could get no satisfactory answer to his pleas that Johnston move to the relief of Vicksburg.

"I hope you will soon be able to break the investment, make a junction [with Pemberton] and carry in munitions," he telegraphed Johnston. "If my strength permitted I would go to you."

Many felt that Davis himself should take over the command in Mississippi, believing that his mere presence would inspire Pemberton's defending army and prompt Johnston to get moving. But with Robert E. Lee preparing his invasion of Maryland and Pennsylvania, the President thought it best that he remain in Richmond. Braxton Bragg had been obligingly transferring troops to Johnston and, as the President told Lee, "All accounts we have of Pemberton's conduct fully sustain the good opinion heretofore entertained of him."

But confidence in Pemberton was greater in Richmond than in Vicksburg. Even his practical order that the troops and artillerists conserve their ammunition roused resentment and dejection. "In our regiment," wrote William Chambers of the Forty-sixth Mississippi Infantry, "a willingness to capitulate soon became evident. They realized they were starving; they saw themselves surrounded by a force five times greater than their own; they beheld the enemy entrench himself and build stronger and better forts than ours; and they saw their comrades being shot down every day, *while they were not permitted to fire a gun!*"[7]

Vicksburg citizens, however, had recovered from the shock of the early enemy assaults and had steeled themselves to an acceptance of their situation. Emma Balfour believed the constant enemy bombardment was intended to "wear out the women and children and sick, and General Pemberton would be obliged to surrender the place on that account." If so, she thought, the Union high command was unaware of the mettle of Southern womenhood.[8]

True, a few timid souls petitioned Pemberton to request a truce and permit the women and children to leave the city safely, but Emma told the general that "I hoped he would never grant anything of that kind. . . . " And since only five signatures could be obtained for the petition—hardly worth Pemberton's attention—it was plain that the women and youth of Vicksburg chose to stay and see things through.

In fact, wrote Alexander Abrams, formerly of the *Whig* staff,

> Not the slightest fear was expressed of the city ever falling into the hands of the enemy; not a man, woman, or child believed such an event at all likely to occur, but all anticipating the defeat and destruction of Grant's army as soon as Johnston arrived with the fifty thousand men he was reported to have under his command.[9]

Fifty thousand men! *Such stuff as dreams are made on.* But already the hopes of the city had shifted focus, from Pemberton to the magic name of Johnston. The *Daily Citizen* fanned this new allegiance. In an early June edition, shrunk by paper shortages to a size of six by eighteen inches, the editor told his readers: "The utmost confidence is felt that we can maintain our position until succor comes from outside. The undaunted Johnston is at hand."

Though life under siege could never return to normal, the citizens clung to habitual routine as to a life raft. Dr. William Lord, continuing as chaplain in the army, still held Sunday services in the partially damaged Episcopal Church. One devout member of the congregation noted that "organs and church music mixed up with a bombardment is a powerful combination. . . . "

Dr. Lord's fellow chaplain William L. Foster, serving with the Mississippi troops, observed "there is no Sabbath quiet here. War knows no Sabbath." Yet, contrarily, one Vicksburg man and wife told Samuel Clemens some years later, "It got to be Sunday all the time. Seven Sundays a week—to us anyway." The couple remembered:

We hadn't anything to do, and time hung heavy. Seven Sundays, and all of them broken up at one time or another, in the day or in the night, by a few hours of awful storm of fire and thunder and iron. At first we used to shin for the holes a good deal faster than we did afterwards.[10]

Emma Balfour didn't know which to fear the most, the mortars from the river or the shells from the Union Parrott guns. The Parrott shells confined their impact to a limited target; one could be lucky, or safe by taking due precautions. The mortars, in turn, could be followed in flight by their lighted fuses, but when they plunged earthward, "Then look out," wrote Emma, "for if they explode before reaching the ground, which they generally do, the pieces fly in all directions, the very least of which will kill one, and most of them of sufficient weight to tear through a house from top to bottom."[11]

Houses nearest the levee were most subject to enemy fire from across the river. Dora and Anderson Miller were enjoying a candlelit evening in the upstairs of their home, when Anderson suddenly shouted from the window:

"Run!"

"Where?"

"*Back!*"

They had scarcely reached the door when a Parrott shell plunged through the roof, throwing both to the floor. "Then we found the entire side of the room was torn out." Soldiers rushing to the rescue helped them board up the wall to keep out prowlers, and the Millers moved back to their accustomed cellar.[12]

Nearby, on June 1 another shell set fire to a house, and the conflagration burned an entire block of homes and businesses on Washington Street. So complete was the destruction that many believed an arsonist had been at work again, possibly the same enemy agents that burned the *Whig* plant.

Diminishing food supplies were becoming critical in Vicksburg. "On this day," wrote Sergeant Tunnard on June 4, "all surplus provisions in the city were seized, and rations issued to citizens and soldiers alike. To the perils of the siege began now to be added the prospect of famine." Only native peas were plentiful and became a universal staple. The peas could be ground into flour and used for baking bread—which Ephraim Anderson found "the hardest of hard tack . . . one might have knocked down a full grown steer with a chunk of it."

While civilians, cooking outside the entrances to their caves when enemy shelling was light, improvised with pastry concoctions of rice and milk, and coffee brewed from sweet potatoes, the army was put on short rations: fourteen ounces of food per soldier daily, which included four ounces each of bacon, flour, or meal, the rest comprising peas, rice, and sugar. It was less than half the amount of rations normally issued and led, some believed, to sharply increased sickness among the debilitated troops.

Fresh water was a problem, for which the polluted Mississippi offered no solution. Supplies from the underground springs in the hills were rationed, and the Lords were forced to buy their water from a farmer's wife who lived within the Confederate defenses. When the woman's soldier-husband returned from the trenches on furlough and found his wife was charging for each bucketful, he "walloped her good for meanness," and thereafter the water was issued to first comers free.

Dora Miller considered herself lucky. "We hear of others digging up the water from ditches and mudholes," she wrote, but:

> This place has two underground cisterns of good cool water and every night in my subterranean dressing room a tub of cold water is the nerve-calmer that sends me to sleep in spite of the roar. One cistern I had to give up to the soldiers, who swarm about like hungry animals seeking something to devour. Poor fellows! My heart bleeds for them. They have nothing but spoiled, greasy bacon, and bread made of musty pea-flour, and but little of that.[13]

Dora was used to sick or wounded men, not sufficiently disabled to be cared for in the hospitals, seeking refuge on her gallery. She believed she had saved the lives of some, especially one young soldier in gray who arrested her attention. "He looked as if shells had lost their terrors for his dumb and famished misery." She mixed him a saucerful of cornmeal gruel, added some milk and sugar and nutmeg, and placed the dish before him as before a starving cat. He gulped it down with tears in his eyes and thanked her brokenly. "I shall get better," he promised.

Washington Street merchants—those who survived the earlier conflagration in their district—were not above making exorbitant profits on their limited supplies of hoarded food: $200 for a barrel of flour, $30 for the same amount of sugar, corn $100 a bushel, and bacon $5 a pound. And the people resented equally the Southern planters on the Big Black River who were selling their hoarded produce to the Yankees. Actually, the planters had no choice; the markets of Vicksburg had been sealed off from them; and what the commissaries did not buy, the Yankees simply took.

In fact, Vicksburg citizens caught outside the Confederate defenses suffered as greatly as those within. Ida Barlow's house, north of the city limits, was now behind Sherman's line of siege, and Ida wrote: "Our home was surrounded by Yankees both day and night, and the headquarters of Gen. Grant were only about a mile from our home. We were utterly in their power and in a constant state of uneasiness for fear we should be killed."[14]

One morning a company of Sherman's troops stopped at the house, to ask if any Confederate guerrillas had been seen in the vicinity. Mr. Barlow assured them none had been around. The officer led his men away, only to encounter a volley of rifle fire from a hillside ambush. The captain was killed, and a number of the troops were wounded. The wounded were carried back to the house to await an ambulance.

Meanwhile, wrote Ida, "The Yankees were so enraged with my father, saying he had known the rebs were hiding under the hill, which he did not, that they at once put the torch to our home and told my father that if he was on the premises at sundown they would hang him."

With their house "a mass of smouldering ashes," the Barlow family fled to their grandfather's home some miles away. They were still behind enemy lines, but, despite the charges made against them, they were allowed to draw Federal army rations.[15]

This feeding of the enemy *by* the enemy gave Private Francis Tupper of the Fifteenth Illinois Cavalry some food for thought—that under the surface all men and women are akin:

When we came here we had nothing to eat and the soldiers ate up everything the folks had for ten miles around. They are now of necessity compelled to come here and ask for something to live upon, and they have also discovered that they have the best success when the youngest and best-looking one in the family comes to plead their case and they have some very handsome women here. They are well educated and were rich before their niggers ran away. If I was to meet them in Illinois I should think they were born and brought up there.[16]

Though the food provided to the Union army was supposedly superior to that which Pemberton's men survived on, the Barlows found it humiliating to apply to Grant's commissary for subsistence. Not only humiliating, Ida wrote, but the food itself was "awful—fat pickled pork, hard tack so old it had bugs in it, a little flour and coffee. My grandmother soaked the hard tack in water overnight to soften it, then fried it in the grease that came out of the meat, and drank the coffee without sugar."

Ida was wryly consoled by reports from the city, where "the inhabitants who were packed away in caves like rats in a hole," that indicated many were living on the edge of famine. It was bantered about among the garrisoning troops that Vicksburg had a new commander, more invincible by far than Pemberton. "General Starvation" was his name.

"The siege is still progressing favorably," wrote Osborn Oldroyd of McPherson's corps on June 5. The Federals had advanced their approaches and parallels closer to Vicksburg's defenses, concentrating especially on approaches to Confederate forts guarding the routes leading to the city: the Stockade Redan on the Graveyard Road; the Third Louisiana Redan flanking the Jackson Road; and the Railroad Redoubt overlooking the railway leading to the city. Eventually thirteen of these approaches would extend toward the Confederate perimeter.

It had not been easy. Sharpshooters on both sides rarely refrained from testing their marksmanship. Confederate riflemen, moving from one slot in their breastworks to another, looked to Isaac Jackson like gray mice scampering from hole to hole. A man could amuse himself raising his hat on the tip of his bayonet, above the breastworks, then counting the number of bullet holes he would have suffered with his head inside the cap.

As the Union sap-rollers pushed inexorably forward, Grant accused the enemy of using "explosive musket-balls"—a "barbarous" and cruel device. The source of this false impression was probably a new Confederate expedient for stopping the persistent rollers. The troops fired musket balls, the bases of which had been stuffed with cotton fiber soaked in turpentine, making an effective incendiary.

During delays, Grant's impatience grew. Though he kept busy supervising operations on the Vicksburg front, organizing expeditions to reconnoiter the surrounding countryside, and organizing a strike force to cope with the threat posed by Johnston's army, there were times when it seemed that there was nothing he could do but watch and wait. He paced the lines like a stalking tiger, often hoisting himself above the parapet for a better view of operations. A Minnesota soldier, seeing a stocky man in a sloppy uniform exposing his head to enemy fire, shouted, "You god-damn idiot, you'd better get down or you'll get shot!"

Another irate private, yelling to the general to "get off that mule," remarked, when cautioned that he was speaking to his chief commander, "I don't care who he is, what's he fooling around here for anyway? We're shot at enough without taking chances with him."[17]

Colonel Rawlins, the general's self-appointed conscience, was aware of the strain that Grant was under. But the colonel was also aware, and apprehensive, of another threat to Grant's hold upon the army and upon himself.

Passing the general's headquarters on June 5, the third week of the siege, Rawlins noticed an open case of wine outside the tent. He ordered it removed, over Grant's protest that he was saving it to celebrate the fall of Vicksburg. Judging from the empty bottles, the celebration had begun a little early.

That night Rawlins composed a letter reaffirming a concern that he had earlier expressed to Grant in person:

> The great solicitude I feel for the safety of this army leads me to mention, what I had hoped never again to do, the subject of your drinking. . . . Tonight when you should, because of the condition of your health if nothing else, have been in bed, I find you where the wine bottle has just been emptied, in company with those who drink and urge you to do likewise, and the lack of your promptness and decision, and clearness in expressing yourself in writing conduces to confirm my decision.[18]

Rawlins's decision was to retire from Grant's staff, unless the general swore off alcohol forever.

Grant would not receive this admonition for another three days, during which he jeopardized his whole career. That night he left with Charles Dana and a small escort of cavalry for, ostensibly, a voyage of inspection up the Yazoo River. Commandeering the steamboat *Diligence,* on its way downriver, Grant ordered the vessel to turn around and head back for Satartia. He wanted, he said, to reconnoiter the route down which Joe Johnston might attack, though nothing suggested that Johnston, still east of the Big Black River, was about to do so.

It so happened that Sylvanus Cadwallader, the newspaper correspondent, was aboard the *Diligence* when Grant took over, and, though Charles Dana tactfully reported that "Grant was ill and went to bed soon after we started," Cadwallader had a different impression:

> I was not long in perceiving that Grant had been drinking heavily, and that he was still keeping up. He made several trips to the bar room of the boat in a short time, and became stupid in speech and staggering in gait. This was the first time he had shown symptoms of intoxication in my presence, and I was greatly alarmed by his condition which was fast becoming worse.[19]

The correspondent had no authority to act in such a situation. He appealed to Grant's aide-de-camp, Lieutenant H. N. Towner, to get the general to his cabin and keep him there. When Towner demurred, Cadwallader demanded of Captain Harry McDougall of the *Diligence* that he lock up the bar and "lose the key." Then Sylvanus himself guided the wobbly general to his cabin, bolted the door, and threw the remaining whisky bottles out the window. He wrote later:

> On finding himself locked in he [Grant] became quite angry and ordered me peremptorily to open the door and get out instantly. This order I firmly, but good-naturedly declined to obey. I said to him that I was the best friend he had in the Army of the Tennessee; that I was doing for him what I hoped some one would do for me, should I ever be in his condition; that he was not capable in this case of judging for himself; and that he must, for the present, act upon my better judgment, and be guided by my advice.[20]

The Chicago correspondent then persuaded the general to lie down, and fanned him to sleep—an unhappy mariner saving his Ulysses from the sirens.

When, however, the *Diligence* grated against the wharf at Satartia, Grant woozily climbed off the bunk and insisted on taking his cavalry escort ashore and riding back to Vicksburg. Though Captain E. D. Osband of the escort had no choice but to obey, Cadwallader threatened to shoot or hamstring the horses if he complied. Satartia was deep in hostile territory and the countryside infested with Confederate guerrillas. For Grant to try to ride through it with only a handful of horsemen would be suicidal. In the end, the general was persuaded to remain on board while the *Diligence* started back downriver.

The next morning, as the ship arrived at Haynes Bluff, Dana observed that "Grant came out to breakfast fresh as a rose, clean shirt and all, and quite himself." Finding that they were more than halfway back to Vicksburg, the general sent some of his escort down to headquarters to pick up any news. During the wait for their return, Cadwallader was "thunderstruck" to find that Grant had somehow obtained a new supply of whisky and was soon as intoxicated as the afternoon before.

When the escort got back, Grant ordered the captain of the *Diligence* to proceed downriver for debarkation at Chickasaw Bayou, now a main landing for Federal supplies. Again Cadwallader intervened. The ship would arrive close to midday, when the wharf would be swarming with Union officers and men. For Grant to be seen in his present condition, Cadwallader believed, "would lead to utter disgrace and ruin." He conspired with Captain McDougall to "accidentally" ground the vessel on a handy mudbank on the way, and keep it stranded until after dark.

Reaching the Chickasaw landing that night, Cadwallader helped to disembark the horses, and then looked around for Grant. The general had disappeared. Docked nearby was the sutler vessel of "Wash" Graham, dispenser of red-eye spirits and cigars. Suspecting the worst, Cadwallader searched the ship till he came upon Grant surrounded by bottles, a glass of whisky in his hand.

Cadwallader was not above losing his temper. He told the general the horses were waiting, that at best they would not reach headquarters until after midnight, there was no time to waste. Grant responded in surprising fashion. Marching determinedly down the gangplank, he leaped on his horse, named Kangaroo, gave it the spur, and "darted away at full speed before anyone was ready to follow."

Then began a wild, dark steeplechase. Cadwallader took off after the general, ahead of the rest of the cavalry. Unable to overtake his quarry, he could only dimly trace Grant's mad ride down the murky and torturous roadways, over rickety bridges spanning sloughs and bayous. He recorded later:

Each bridge had one or more guards stationed at it, to prevent fast riding or driving over it; but Grant paid no attention to roads or sentries. He went at about full speed through camps and corrals, heading only for the bridges, and literally tore through and over everything on his way. The air was full of dust, ashes, and embers from camp-fires; and shouts and curses from those he rode down in his race.[21]

But in his condition Grant could not keep up the pace. Cadwallader finally overtook him, scuffled briefly for possession of his horse's reins, then led Kangaroo into a thicket and forced Grant to dismount. In minutes the general was sound asleep. Cadwallader stood by, ready to cut the insignia from the commander's uniform should a Confederate patrol discover them. When the cavalry escort finally arrived, after a frustrating search for their general, Cadwallader sent one of them to camp to report to Rawlins, "and no one else," asking that an ambulance be sent to pick up Grant.

During the ride back in the ambulance, Cadwallader was rewarded with some satisfaction. "On the way he [Grant] confessed that I had been right, and that he had been wrong throughout, and told me to consider myself a staff officer, and to give any orders that were necessary in his name." When they reached camp where the anxious Rawlins waited, Grant "shook himself together," bade his two would-be guardians a polite and sober goodnight, "and started toward his tent as steadily as he ever walked in his life."[22]

It was Grant's last lapse of the campaign. And it was the source of a curious fraternity, even of conspiracy, between the three men, Grant, Cadwallader, and Rawlins. Despite his previous admonition, Rawlins would take no action on the bacchanal; the general had hit bottom, and the only way was up. Cadwallader, who had greatly exceeded his authority, gained Grant's confidence and gratitude instead of his resentment. And, as for Grant himself, Cadwallader wrote of the incident, "To my surprise he never made the most distant allusion to it then, or ever afterward." Nor would Cadwallader or Rawlins ever mention it until the war was over.

"I am still without information from you, later than your dispatch of the 25th," wrote Pemberton to Johnston on June 7. "I have sent out couriers to you almost daily. . . . The enemy is so vigilant that it is impossible to obtain reliable information. When may I expect you to move, and in what direction?"[23]

Normal communication between the two commanders appeared all but severed by the Federal investment. Couriers could sneak between Vicksburg and Johnston's army only by night, over difficult trails often picketed by Union soldiers, at the constant risk of death or capture. Yet many volunteered for the assignment, using devious methods and devices. "Dispatches from Pemberton to Johnston," wrote a Federal captain, "were discovered in a rebel woman's hair."

Some volunteers traveled by secret waterways between the Big Black and the Yazoo, then tried to slip past Porter's gunboats on the Mississippi. One of these, well known to Emma Balfour among others, was Major Lamar Fontaine who two years earlier had composed the lyrics of one of the war's more popular ballads, "All Quiet Along the Potomac Tonight." A stanza of Fontaine's verse seemed to reflect the experience of snaking through the woods by dark, watching for the glint of a picket's rifle:

> Hark! Was it the night wind that rustles the leaves?
> Was it the moonlight so wondrously flashing?
> It look'd like a rifle! "Ah, Mary, Goodbye!"
> And his lifeblood is ebbing and plashing; . . .[24]

One of the more successful and persistent couriers was Absalom Grimes who, despite imperative secrecy, appeared to operate out of Saint Louis with an accomplice identified as "Bob." His personal account of his adventures may be somewhat spurious. However: On May 25, a few days after Grant's investment of Vicksburg, Grimes states that he and his colleague made their way to Yazoo City, where they procured a double-ended skiff, a pair of oars, and such assorted items as two saucepans, wire, staples, and a hammer. They also engaged a local tinsmith to fashion and sodder four large watertight boxes to contain dispatches and mail for Vicksburg. These were fastened to the bottom of the skiff by wire.

Once on their way downriver after sundown, the oars were secured to the floor of the boat, the saucepans were used as more quiet paddles. Above its mouth, the Yazoo had been blocked by the Federals by a chain of rafts. Absalom and Bob tilted their boat until it was filled with water almost to the gunwales, then slipped overboard and used their saucepans to propel the nearly submerged craft beneath and past the chain.

Below the mouth of the Yazoo lay the ever-watchful Union fleet. Climbing back into the skiff, still riding barely above water level, the couriers pushed on. Three naval spotlights continuously swept the Mississippi, and the boatmen used their saucepans sparingly for fear the metal might reflect the passing flashes. The skiff they did not worry about. All but submerged, Grimes observed, "It presented little to arrest the eye of a lookout."

At midnight they reached the Vicksburg landing, vowing never to expose themselves again to such a harrowing ordeal. But the enthusiastic gratitude of civilians and soldiers committed them to carry on the service. They were supplied with Federal uniforms from enemy prisoners and, thereafter, with the four tin boxes strapped to the keel and the boat apparently empty, they excursioned freely up and down the Mississippi. Sailors on Porter's gunboats regarded these blueclad infantry, rowing for pleasure on the river, as an "exhibition of lunacy" unworthy of their notice.[25]

There was more involved in this courier service than the exchange of vital information. While Pemberton at times appeared unduly cautious in hoarding ammunition—time would show that he had an ample reserve of shells for his batteries—there was no doubt that his troops were short of musket caps. Vicksburg women became adept at making paper cartridges, and there was sufficient powder, but percussion caps were needed to explode the powder when the musket's hammer fell. Pemberton noted early in the siege of "having one million more of cartridges than caps, without which latter, of course, the former could be of no possible value." Recorded Pemberton's grandson:

> Every way was tried to convey caps into the beleaguered city; even hollow logs were filled with them and floated to the shore near the city. Men packed caps round their persons and then tried to get in the town. A few succeeded; the most failed.[26]

Lamar Fontaine was credited with getting 18,000 caps through the Union fleet to Pemberton. "His skiff was so small," wrote Osborn Oldroyd, "and moved so silently over the water that it was difficult to distinguish from a floating log." But the largest shipment, 200,000 caps, carried by eight Confederates from Johnston's camp east of the Big Black, was captured in its entirety, leaving the Vicksburg troops still woefully undersupplied.

But, if Johnston found it hard to keep in touch with Pemberton, and vice versa, he was in ready communication with Jefferson Davis, who kept goading him to action, and with Kirby Smith, who was commanding Confederate forces west of the Mississippi. Since early May Pemberton had been urging Smith to break Grant's threat to Vicksburg by attacking Federal forces on the west bank of the river, then to cross over, bringing reinforcements to the city.

Now Johnston also urged that Smith do something to take the pressure off Pemberton. And in June, Smith finally responded; the safety of his own department depended on Pemberton's survival. Though necessarily concerned with the fate of Port Hudson, he told General Richard Taylor, son of Zachary Taylor, "the stake contended for near Vicksburg is the Valley of the Mississippi and the Trans-Mississippi Department; the defeat of General Grant is the *terminus ad quem* of all operations in the West this summer. . . . "[27]

On June 7, the day that Grant returned from his two-day frolic to Satartia, Taylor led an army of 3,000 men from the Tensas River against Federal bases on the west side of the Mississippi above Vicksburg. Dividing his army, he sent one brigade against the Federals at Young's Point, another against the base at Milliken's Bend, whose defending garrison was made up principally of Colored troops.

Taylor's report of the action does him little credit:

> Both attacks were made at dawn, and, with the loss of some scores of prisoners, the negroes were driven over the levee to the protection of gunboats in the river. . . . As foreseen, our movement resulted, and could result in nothing . . . the time wasted on these absurd movements cost us the garrison of Port Hudson, nearly eight thousand men; but the pressure on General Kirby Smith to *do something* for Vicksburg was too strong to be resisted.[28]

Except for some earlier skirmishing around Port Hudson, it was the first real action that any colored troops had seen. Though they had had scant training, they fought well, despite inferior weapons.

Charles Dana considered Taylor's thrust "the most serious attack from the west during the siege," which indeed it was, and noted also:

> This engagement at Milliken's Bend became famous from the conduct of the colored troops. General E. S. Dennis, who saw the battle, told me that it was

the hardest fought engagement he had ever seen. It was fought mainly hand to hand. After it was over many men were found dead from bayonet stabs, and others with their skulls broken open by butts of muskets. "It is impossible," said General Dennis, "for men to show greater gallantry than the negro troops in that fight."[29]

And Dana noted: "The bravery of the blacks in the battle of Milliken's Bend completely revolutionized the sentiment of the army with regard to the employment of negro troops. I heard prominent officers, who formerly in private had sneered at the idea of the negroes fighting, express themselves after that as heartily in favor of it. Among the Confederates, however, the feeling was different. All the reports that came to us showed that both citizens and soldiers on the Confederate side manifested great dismay at the idea of our arming negroes. They said that such a policy was certain to be followed by insurrection with all its horrors."

Though Union casualties at Milliken's Bend had been heavy—almost four times those of the Confederates—Grant wrote favorably of the operation. "In this battle most of the troops engaged were Africans, who had little experience in the use of firearms. Their conduct is said, however, to have been most gallant, and I doubt not but with good officers they will make good troops."[30]

A more unique reaction to the battle was that of Sergeant Charles Wilcox, who was moved to an unusual commitment. Someday he would like to command a company of colored troops. He discussed his chances, two days later, with a major in his brigade in the hope that he could do *"something* for me" —but Wilcox would not achieve his goal till three months later. Meanwhile, on June 10, he wrote in his journal:

Talking with an intelligent negro to-day about enlisting he said, "Now, Mr. Wilcox, since this affair," (we had just been speaking of the bravery that the black troops exhibited in the late fight at Milliken's Bend, La.,) *"I feel that I'm as much of a man as any one."* The fight had made him our compeer and he felt exceedingly joyful over it. He asked for the privilege of going in my company when I get it up. Of course he shall have the chance . . . if I have the opportunity.[31]

The last word on the fight across the river was, however, delivered by General Grant who tersely observed, "We had no further trouble in that quarter during the siege."

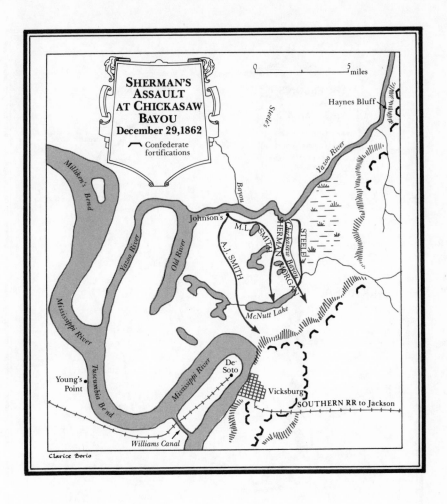

SHERMAN'S ASSAULT AT CHICKASAW BAYOU
December 29, 1862

⌒ Confederate fortifications

0 ——————— 5 miles

Haynes Bluff

Steele's

Bayou

Yazoo River

Milliken's Bend

Yazoo River

Old River

Johnson's

M.L. SMITH

A.J. SMITH

STEELE

SHERMAN

MORGAN

Chickasaw Bayou

McNutt Lake

Mississippi River

Tuscumbia Bend

Young's Point

De Soto

Mississippi River

Vicksburg

SOUTHERN RR to Jackson

Williams Canal

Clarice Borio

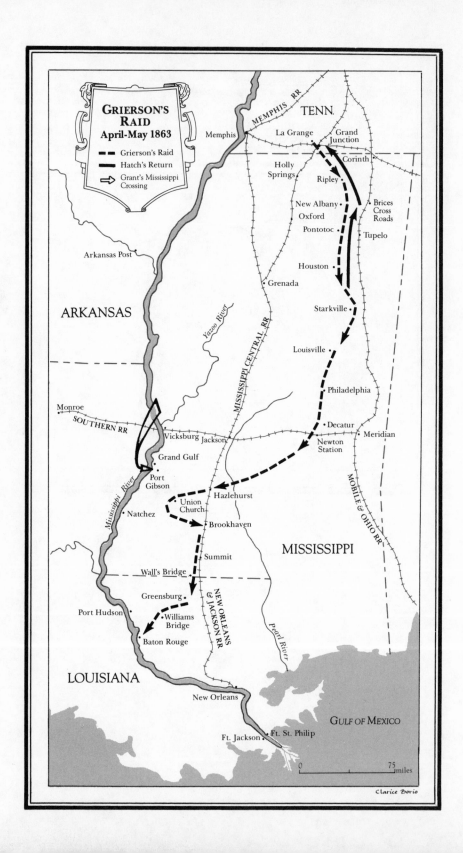

GRIERSON'S
RAID
April-May 1863

- - - Grierson's Raid
——— Hatch's Return
⇨ Grant's Mississippi
Crossing

TENN.

Memphis   La Grange • Grand
                              Junction
                         • Corinth
Holly
Springs   Ripley •

        New Albany •   • Brices
        Oxford •   Cross
        Pontotoc •   • Tupelo Roads

              Houston •

        • Grenada

              Starkville •

                    Louisville •

                         • Philadelphia

                    • Decatur   • Meridian
Monroe
    SOUTHERN RR   Newton
         Vicksburg Jackson• Station
                    • Grand Gulf

Arkansas Post

ARKANSAS

                    Port
                    Gibson
         • Natchez Union   Hazlehurst •
                    Church •
                         • Brookhaven   MISSISSIPPI

                         • Summit

         Wall's Bridge •

         Greensburg •

Port Hudson •   • Williams
                       Bridge
              • Baton Rouge

LOUISIANA

         New Orleans •

                              GULF OF MEXICO

              0   75
                           miles
         Ft. Jackson • • Ft. St. Philip

Clarice Borio

Major-General William Tecumseh Sherman, Grant's right-hand man in the Vicksburg campaign, led the first land assault against the city. *(Library of Congress)*

Major-General Ulysses S. Grant, commander of Federal forces in the Vicksburg campaign, later became general-in-chief of all U.S. armies. *(Library of Congress)*

Colonel Benjamin Grierson's first great Union cavalry raid diverted Confederate forces from opposing Grant's crossing of the Mississippi. *(Harper's Weekly)*

The Battle of Champion Hill, May 16, 1863, last and bloodiest engagement of the campaign leading to the siege of Vicksburg. *(Leslie's Illustrated Newspaper)*

Before daylight, General Blair's Union division crosses the Big Black River, last obstacle on the march to Vicksburg, May 18, 1863. *(Battles and Leaders of the Civil War)*

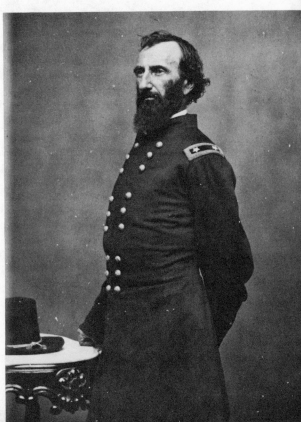

Major-General John Alexander McClernand, controversial Union corps commander, was removed by Grant during the fourth week of the siege. *(Library of Congress)*

A fused bomb threatens besieged civilians outside a Vicksburg cave during the intermittent bombardment of the city. Drawn by Howard Pyle. *(Harper's Monthly Magazine*

Union attackers shelter in dugouts behind the Shirley House, at the north end of the Federal siege line in June, 1863. *(Old Court House Museum)*

Assault on Vicksburg, May 22, 1863. Attacks at major points of Pemberton's defenses failed to break the line and forced Grant to resort to siege. *(Leslie's Illustrated Newspaper)*

Federal sharpshooters man the trenches and parapets during the siege of Vicksburg, pressing on the city from north, east, and south. *(Leslie's Illustrated Newspaper)*

The fight at the crater. After exploding a mine beneath the 3rd Louisiana Redan, June 25, 1863, Federal troops tried in vain to penetrate the gap. *(National Archives)*

General Joseph Eggleston Johnston, C.S.A., tried but failed to lead reinforcements to the aid of Pemberton at Vicksburg. Photo by Mathew Brady. *(National Archives)*

Generals Grant and Pemberton, behind the Union siege lines, discuss terms for the surrender of Vicksburg, July 3, 1863. *(Harper's Weekly)*

❧ 19 ❧

The Mounting Fury

"T HE siege continues with increasing fury," wrote Osborn Oldroyd in mid-June. "Yet," he added, "there are grumblers in the North who are complaining of our slow progress, and treasonable articles are published in some papers [asking], 'Why don't Grant move?' "[1]

It was true that the closer the lines converged—and the two armies were already within conversation distance of each other—the more the resistance between them hardened by compression. But Grant himself had rarely been more optimistic. He had long since learned to shrug off criticism, confident that the War Department, Henry Halleck, and the President were solidly behind him.

"All is going on here now just right," he wrote to acquaintance George B. Pride on June 15, and added:

> We have our trenches pushed up so close to the enemy that we can throw hand grenades over into their forts. The enemy do not dare show their heads above the parapets at any point, so close and so watchful are our sharpshooters. The town is completely invested. My position is so strong that I feel myself abundantly able to leave it so and go out twenty or thirty miles with force enough to whip two such garrisons.[2]

The reference to moving out twenty or thirty miles, and whipping the second of two garrisons, referred to the likelihood of his having to confront Joe Johnston when and if Johnston moved upon the army's rear.

His confidence was not unwarranted. Indeed, Grant's force had, by the end of the month, virtually reached full strength, with some 220 pieces of artillery, batteries of naval guns, 77,000 men hemming in the city, Porter's gunboats on the Mississippi, and more Federal batteries aimed at Vicksburg from the west. Grant's huge mortars were rarely silent, and Oldroyd "could see the balls distinctly, as they flew across the hills towards Vicksburg." The infantryman concluded that "The buildings in the city must, by this time, be pretty well riddled with shot and shell."

Oldroyd was right. Alexander St. Clair Abrams, formerly of the *Whig* and

released from military service due to wounds, remained an on-the-spot observer of the city under siege, writing:

> By the middle of June, Vicksburg was in a deplorable condition. There was
> scarcely a building but what had been struck by the enemy's shells, while many
> of them were entirely demolished. The city had the appearance of a half-ruined
> pile of buildings, and on every street unmistakable signs of the fearful bombard-
> ment it had undergone, presented themselves to the observer.[3]

Confederate army surgeon Joseph Dill Alison, long accustomed to human
misery, wrote in his diary at about this time:

> I have read of besieged cities and the suffering of the inhabitants, but always
> thought the picture too highly painted. But now I have witnessed one and can
> believe all that is written on the subject. Rations though short, are still enough,
> and we have good water most of the time, so do not as yet suffer on that source.
> But the stench from dead mules and horses (killed by shell) is intolerable.[4]

As the siege rolled on, Confederate Colonel Robert S. Bevier noted, "The
enemy's efforts to reduce the city redoubled; the thunder and roar of artillery,
both night and day, were incessant, and the rattle of musketry was unremitting," while Dr. Alison observed: "Our situation now becoming desperate. No
place of safety. If you stand still there is danger from the pieces of shell that
fill the air, and if you move the danger becomes greater. The whole town is
enfiladed."

The whole town was also going underground, with grim determination.
Cave construction became big business in the city. Unemployed blacks, noted
Mary Loughborough, "hired themselves out to dig them, at from thirty to fifty
dollars according to size."[5] Free-lance realtors did a thriving business. As more
prosperous tenants moved to what they considered safer localities, their caves
were sold to the less fortunate, or leased, at an average monthly rental of $15.
"For Rent" signs appeared on many abandoned homes, for those willing to
take their chances above ground.

Originally, most of the caves constructed had faced east, away from the
gunboat and mortar fire from across the river. But as Grant stepped up his
bombardment from the city's rear, the danger came from both directions. To
overcome this double exposure the William Lord family decided to leave the
cave that had partially collapsed from an exploding shell, nearly crushing
young Lucy McRae to death.

At the suggestion of an army major, a new site was selected behind the city
hospital, now serving military needs, in the continuing hope that the yellow
flag above the building would prove something of a safeguard. Here on a
well-drained hillside what amounted to a double cave was scooped out, with
entrances facing east and west, so that if one were obstructed the other would
offer an escape hatch.

Lida Lord considered it "the coziest cave in all Vicksburg." An open walk
with a parapet six feet high led to a side door and formed a sort of outdoor
patio, "overhung by creeping vines and shaded by papaw trees. . . . Here the

rector smoked his cocoanut pipe, and the children made mud pies and played with paper dolls cut from a few picture-papers and magazines that happened somehow to be among our belongings."

> This cave [wrote Lida] ran about twenty feet underground, and communicated at right angles with a wing which opened on the front of the hill, giving us a free circulation of air. At the door was an arbor of branches, in which, on a pine table, we dined when shelling permitted. Near it were a dug-out fireplace and an open-air kitchen, with table, pans, etc.
>
> In the wall of the cave were a small closet for provisions, and some niches for candles, books, and flowers. We always kept in tin cups bunches of wild flowers, berries, or bright leaves which the children gathered in their walks. Our cave was strongly boarded at the entrances, and we had procured some mattresses which made comfortable beds. For a time we slept in the tent, and only used the cave for a shelter.[6]

Cave life embraced the gamut of birth to death, with the dying sometimes commemorated by the newly born. The family of Wixforth Bitterman, Vicksburg carriage-makers, shared their cave with ex-newspaperman George Rogers and his mother. When Mrs. Rogers died during the siege, Jane Bitterman's sister became the proud mother of a son, whom she and her husband named Roger in memory of the deceased.

Jane described her cave as "far more pleasant than most people imagine. A hallway ran the entire length of the four bedrooms arranged on either side. Beyond the hall was a large square room used as a dining room and from this a continuation of the hall that led to another entrance." She remembered that:

> The beds were arranged upon planks that were elevated on improvised stands, planks covered the ground floor and these in turn were covered with matting and carpets. The walls around were covered with strips of carpets, eliminating some of the dampness.[7]

Still shaken by their first experience with cave life, when young Lucy had been buried beneath falling walls, the McRaes found their new cave not much safer. Mrs. McRae had a tent pitched just outside, "so that when the mortars did not have the range we could sit there and watch the shells as they came over. They were beautiful at night."

One time, however, when Mrs. McRae was brushing Lucy's hair at a washstand in the tent, "we heard the report of the mortar, heard the shell rattling over, and knew it was near."

"Get in the cave!" shouted Mrs. McRae.

Lucy didn't quite make it, remembering, "I only had time to jump into a small hole we children had dug out in the side of a hill, when a piece of shell came down into the tent, demolishing the wash-stand by which we had stood. I felt the heat as it came down. Mother's face, white with anxiety for me, peeped out from the cave door. There I sat, stunned with fear."[8]

Such narrow escapes were commonplace during these weeks of constant shelling. An aged black servant of the William Lum household was chopping wood in the yard of the family's Washington Street home and was momentarily called off the job. When he returned, he found much of his work completed, if somewhat sloppily. A shell had struck directly on his sawbuck, shattering the woodpile into manageable pieces.

In many ways the children of this semisubterranean city found cave life more of an adventure than a hardship, reacting to danger with a nimble scorn of fear. Wrote Lida Lord:

> It was curious to see how well trained the little ones were. At night, when the bombs began to fly like pigeons over our heads, they would be waked out of a sound sleep, would slip on their shoes, and run, without a word, like rabbits to their burrows. In the daytime they climbed the trees, gathered papaws, and sometimes went blackberrying up the road, but never far, for the first sound of cannonading sent them scampering home.[9]

Yet, as in any siege, the children suffered and their mothers suffered for and with them. Young Willie Lord watched one youngster chasing a butterfly outside a nearby cave—with an anxious mother in pursuit. The infant laughed and dodged ahead of the parent, but the mother was playing a deadly game. Just as the woman stretched out her hand to catch the child, a plummeting shell took her arm off at the shoulder. With her remaining arm the mother swept her offspring to her side; the loss of a limb was little to pay for the salvation of her son.

"Another mother," wrote Lida Lord, "had her baby killed on her breast. My own little brother, stooping to pick up a minié ball, barely escaped being cut in two before our eyes, a Parrott shell passing over his back so close that it scorched his jacket. There were many other narrow escapes and some frightful casualties. . . . "

Serious casualties occurred among those who, weary of cave life, sought to return to their homes, if only for the night. Twenty-year-old Savilla Schaeffer recalled a "terrible scene" in a neighboring house on Adams Street, where a woman who was ill insisted on remaining with her four-month-old son. "With terrific force an immense shell tore through the room, and in its wild journey caught the baby, dashed it against the wall and embedded it there, mashed and mangled." Savilla hoped never to return again to that "street of living death."

Through it all, some social life managed to survive in this half-world of catacombs. The Lords were close to the camp of a Missouri brigade, whose officers often spent the evenings in their cave "making its gloomy recesses echo with songs and laughter." To their repertoire of standard favorites, "Dixie," "The Bonnie Blue Flag," and "Maryland, My Maryland," they added a parody of an old-time song, "Then Let the Old Folks Scold If They Will,"

> *Then let the big guns boom if they will,*
> *We'll be gay and happy still,*
> *Gay and happy, gay and happy,*
> *We'll be gay and happy still.*[10]

Vicksburg's conversion to an underground community had something of a parallel along the Union siege lines. Whole encampments were established in the shelter of escarpments. Hillsides were hollowed out to form what Wilbur Crummer called "a sort of cave," with poles put up and covered with oil cloth to form an al fresco shelter at the entrance. "It was a queer phase of war to us all," wrote Lieutenant Cyrus Dickey who watched his comrades tunnel into the hillsides east of Vicksburg. "The timid boys who have not dug caves for themselves try to buy out others who have dug their holes."[11]

The side of the hill on which the Shirley House stood, 400 yards east of the Third Louisiana Redan, was honeycombed with caves and dugouts. And, as in Vicksburg, the rain washed landslides down on the besiegers, or a wayward Confederate shell would collapse the walls and roofs protecting them. They were perversely comforted by the thought of how much worse it must be in the cave-infested city, which they scathingly rechristened "Prairie Dog Village." At least, most of the Federal troops had sufficient food, and, even if they hadn't, one Union officer wryly asserted, "I think we would starve better than the Rebs do."

But the mid-June heat, often exceeding 100 degrees Fahrenheit in the shade, was suffocating to the Union soldiers, less accustomed to the Mississippi climate than the Southerners. "This is an awful hot country here full of bugs of all sorts," wrote Brigadier General Willard Ward Orme of Herron's division to his wife back home, adding that, along with an attack of bilious diarrhea,

> I am now suffering terribly from the effects of mosquitoes & other bugs—I am full of bites all over. There is a small insect about the size of a pin's point which bites its way into the flesh & makes a very sore place—This insect is called a "chicker" or "jigger."—We are all suffering from its depredations. They are much worse than the "wood tick"—I have to stop after every sentence I write to scratch myself & drive off the bugs. . . .[12]

And while he longed for the "cool recesses and shady trees" of his home in Illinois, "its comforts & luxuries," Orme could see no immediate relief in sight. "We are still closely investing the city," he wrote, "and digging our way nearer to the enemy's forts every night." But: "The rebels hold out well, & it may be a month before they give up, or it may be a week."

Night and day the lines grew closer, as the digging went on, and Union trenches snaked toward the Southern defenses. By miscalculation, one Federal work crew looked up from their tools to discover themselves at the feet of Confederate pickets. The Southerners informed them they were trespassing, but it would be hardly sporting to shoot them for an unintentional mistake. Officers of both sides met in consultation. It was decided to reposition the Confederate pickets, so that the Union operation could remain without corrective digging.

There was a curious, friendly sort of rivalry between the defenders of the goal and those of the Federal offensive, such as one might see between competing sports teams. "We are on speaking terms with the enemy at the [Third Louisiana] redan," reported Confederate General Shoup. "The picket parties at that point agree upon short truces, during which neither party is to fire. Notes are thrown across from one party to another. Some trading going on in coffee, etc. Have forbidden communications, but after sundown the firing ceases and there is a good deal of talk going on between the enemy and our own people. . . . Brothers, relatives and friends are constantly inquiring after each other."[13]

Of this fraternity between opposing troops, cavalryman Francis W. Tupper observed:

> Our 6th Missouri regiment is in the trenches opposite the rebel 6th Missouri, and the boys call them the "bogus six" to distinguish them from ours. At night firing ceases as a general thing . . . they post their pickets outside of the works and ours are advanced and posted near them. They have great times talking together. They know every regiment of ours that has ever been in a fight and are always asking where they are and they also know the numbers of the regiments that have fought them the hardest.[14]

Commonly shared rules of courtesy and fair play made life more tolerable for both sides. Carl Sandburg related the story of two Confederate majors who sent a bouquet of flowers to General Sherman on the north end of the siege line. An accompanying note expressed the donors' thanks to Sherman for not having bombed their section of the city, where a dance had been held the night before.

Whether or not Sherman had silenced his guns by specific request was not made clear. But the secretly sentimental general—who was writing to his wife at this time of the beauty of June foliage and the singing of the mocking birds —might well have acceded to such a request if it were made.

In Grant's camp, Sylvanus Cadwallader basked in newfound favor, since rescuing his chief from drunken disaster at Satartia, and Rawlins, too, was closer than ever to the general. McClernand, however, was still a thorny issue in Grant's side. It had been three weeks since McClernand's apparent duplicity had contributed to the fiasco of May 22. Although both Halleck and Stanton had indicated that he had the right to remove McClernand, Grant was reluctant to take action against one whom Lincoln had befriended. He simply avoided contact with the commander of the Thirteenth Corps.

McClernand, however, still brooded over his subordinate position under Grant and what he considered a lack of recognition of his talent and achievements. When James Wilson brought him an innocent request from Grant to strengthen his forces at Hall's Ferry, McClernand bridled:

"I'll be God damned if I'll do it," he shouted. "I am tired of being dictated to—I won't stand it any longer, and you can go back and tell General Grant!"

This was followed by a blasphemous denunciation of the chief commander and his staff. Wilson was stunned by this reaction. And then furious. He drew his horse abreast of McClernand's.

"It seems to me," he said, "that you are cursing me as much as you are cursing General Grant. If this is so, while you are a major general and I am only a lieutenant colonel, I'll pull you off that horse and beat the boots off you."

McClernand begrudgingly apologized. "I was simply expressing my vehemence on the subject matter, sir, and I beg your pardon." But Wilson, still smoldering with indignation, reported the interview to Grant. Grant took the matter in good humor. Opposed to blasphemy, he was amused by McClernand's excuse of "expressing himself with vehemence" and thereafter applied that definition to those swearing in his presence. He told his chief of staff:

"While I shall not notice this violent outburst, I'll get rid of McClernand the first chance I get."[15]

The chance was shortly handed to him on a silver platter. Soon after the abortive May 22 assault, McClernand, it was later learned, had delivered a congratulatory order to his troops in the form of an address. Referring to his corps as the "Army of the Mississippi," he praised his men for their valor and "successes" and disparaged the conduct of Sherman and McPherson, which, he implied, had deprived his "army" of its rightful victory.

Then, in an unprecedented move, McClernand sent copies of the order to the Northern press, a violation of War Department ethics.

Sherman first read a copy of the order in the June 13 issue of the Memphis *Evening Bulletin.* He found it "manifestly designed for publication for ulterior political purposes . . . perverts the truth to the ends of flattery and self-glorification." He stormed into Grant's tent, demanding that McClernand be relieved.

Grant gave McClernand a chance to explain, then decided to replace him. Fittingly, perhaps, it was James Wilson who carried the order of dismissal to McClernand, undoubtedly a mission which the colonel relished. After donning full dress uniform for the event, Wilson managed to arrive at McClernand's tent at 2:00 A.M., to awake that general from a sound sleep. McClernand digested the order calmly, then exclaimed:

"Well, sir! I am relieved!" Then, after thinking it over, he added, "By God, sir, we are both relieved!"—referring, Wilson thought, to Grant, though the sentiment embraced all three of them.[16]

McClernand would not retire gracefully. He protested all the way back to Illinois to Stanton, Halleck, and particularly Lincoln. Reminding the President that he, McClernand, had proposed the whole campaign for Vicksburg and raised many of the troops, his removal seemed to him outrageous and unjust. Lincoln replied with gentle, tactful wording: "General Grant and yourself have been conspicuous in our most important successes and for me to interfere and thus magnify a breach between you could not but be of evil effect."[17]

Charles Dana saw the general's dismissal as catastrophe averted. Had anything happened to Grant in the ensuing weeks, McClernand, as next in rank, would command the entire Vicksburg operation. With Sherman and McPherson detesting the Illinois general, a sentiment returned in full, there would be scant cooperation, much less harmony, in the campaign. McClernand, however, would never be assuaged. He would continue to rail at his alleged mistreatment for the duration of the war, and even afterwards.

Command of the Thirteenth Corps was assigned to Maryland-born Edward O. C. Ord (the O. C. for "Otho Cresap"), a friend of Sherman's since West Point days, and one of whom Sherman said, "a more unselfish and manly person never lived." Ord would remain as a corps, and later an army, commander under Grant until the final days at Appomattox.

"The works of the enemy are progressing rapidly and begin to assume a formidable appearance," wrote Pemberton in his record of the second week of

June. In a similar vein Henry Ginder, an engineer in Pemberton's employ, informed his Louisiana wife, "Truly we are surrounded by a wall of fire." Ginder could not understand why none came to their assistance—especially, "What makes Johnston act so slowly?"—unless the importance of relieving Vicksburg loomed so large in the Confederacy's conscience that its leaders, including President Davis, were reluctant to take risks by moving speedily.[18]

Pemberton had as yet received no reply to his second request for information on Johnston's plans, sent to that general on June 7. The Virginian began to loom in his imagination as something of a legendary Sphinx, crouching passive and silent, somewhere east of Vicksburg. He resorted to getting information from the enemy. Several swift nighttime raids on Sherman's line brought back a number of prisoners who declared that "Johnston's army was still at Canton, 25 miles north of Jackson."

With this as a possible lead, Pemberton tried again. Warning Johnston that "We are losing many officers and men," he told the general:

> I am waiting most anxiously to know your intentions. Have heard nothing of you nor from you since May 25. I shall endeavor to hold out as long as we have anything to eat. Can you not send me a verbal message by courier crossing the river above or below Vicksburg and swimming across again opposite Vicksburg?[19]

Two days later Pemberton received, not precisely an answer—none could be expected in so short a time—but a courier-borne dispatch along with some badly needed musket caps. The information in the dispatch was disheartening. Written by Johnston on May 29, and taking fifteen days to reach the city, it stated:

> I am too weak to save Vicksburg. Can do no more than attempt to save you and your garrison. It will be impossible to extricate you unless you cooperate and we make mutually supporting movements. Communicate your plans and suggestions, if possible.[20]

Not knowing how many troops Joe Johnston had, or how much artillery or cavalry, if any, it was hard for Pemberton to figure out what "mutually supporting movements" the Virginian had in mind. He had hoped from the beginning that, as commander of the West, Johnston would take the initiative and attack Grant from the rear. Pemberton did not want simply to save his garrison; he wanted to save the city, conscious as he was of President Davis's admonition: "To hold both Vicksburg and Port Hudson is necessary to our connection with Trans-Mississippi."

The support which Pemberton wanted was any action on Johnston's part that would help to ease the pressure on the city. But he wasn't even sure, from the dispatch dated two weeks earlier, where Johnston was. On June 14 he tried again to establish communications with the general, reporting that the enemy was now "within *25 yards of our works.* He will probably attempt to sink a mine. I shall try to thwart him. I am anxiously expecting to hear from you to arrange for cooperation."

Johnston meanwhile remained passively at Canton, 50 miles away. He telegraphed War Secretary Alexander Seddon that, even with reinforcements so far sent, his army numbered less than 26,000.

"My only plan is to relieve Vicksburg," he assured the secretary, but added, "My force is too small for the purpose. Tell me if you can increase it, and how much."[21]

Seddon regretted he could send no more troops from Braxton Bragg to Johnston, without seriously weakening Bragg's hold on Tennessee. Nor could any troops be sent from Virginia, where Lee was preparing his second invasion of the North. "You must rely on what you have, and the irregular forces Mississippi can afford." To which Johnston responded with an old refrain: "I have not at my disposal half the number of troops necessary."

It was not Joe Johnston's finest hour. Naturally cautious, he was taking no chances—at a time, however, when taking some risks for the sake of immeasurable gain was vital.

In Vicksburg few were fully aware of the inescapability of their predicament. There were increasing shortages of food and water, continuing danger from exploding shells, the hardships and tedium of cave life. But sooner or later help would come from Johnston—and, needless to say, Pemberton did not share his doubts on this point with civilians. Few tried to leave the city, and those who got permits to do so were forbidden by Grant to pass through the Federal lines.

J. M. Swords, militant editor of the *Daily Citizen,* fought on several fronts to strengthen morale and the spirit of resistance. He railed against the enemy within the walls, the extortionists and profiteers who capitalized on the city's plight to fatten their wallets. He called on every able-bodied civilian to march to the parapets. And he urged noncombatants to "sustain and encourage our generals in the tented field."

General Pemberton, the editor acknowledged, might not be the equal of Robert E. Lee, but the "harsh criticism and animadversion" recently leveled at the local commander could only damage the cause, create distrust among the troops.

As for the soldiers themselves, wrote Swords:

> The army at Vicksburg now stands among the veteran troops of the world, and it is but just that full credit should be given it by the Government and by every portion of the Confederacy. No other army has been placed in such a critical position in this war, and those who are compelled to endure the privations and hardships of a protracted siege against such immense odds, should be remembered by a grateful country, and their merits fully and liberally rewarded.[22]

Swords had just finished running off the issue when a thirteen-inch bombshell plummeted into the *Daily Citizen* building, boring through two floors to the basement, scattering type and dust and broken glass, but injuring none of the workers in the place.

Irate but composed, Swords belittled the incident. Plainly, the hand of the Almighty had prevented the destruction of the city's voice, the only newspaper remaining since the *Whig* suspended publication with the burning of its plant.

Swords reminded his readers that "In a few days we shall have relief and the people again be enabled . . . to give thanks to God for our deliverance from the toils of enemies."

Dora and Anderson Miller were finally forced to leave the basement of their house, the shells were falling so heavily in that quarter of the city. "The churches are a great resort for those who have no caves," wrote Dora. "People fancy they are not shelled so much, and they are substantial and the pews are good to sleep in." But she shunned close contact with the public. Instead, the couple took refuge in Anderson Miller's office, sleeping on piles of old newspapers spread out on the floor.[23]

Those rejecting churches or caves sometimes sought shelter behind or near the city hospital, hopeful that the yellow flag—antecedent of the Red Cross emblem—would protect them from the enemy artillery. It was an idle expectation. No direct effort was made by either Grant or Admiral Porter to shell the city's hospitals, but, because of their prominence they were, like the court house cupola, rangemarkers helpful to the gunners and not easy to avoid.

Editor Swords, however, saw nothing accidental in "the immense mass of destructive missiles" hurled, he believed, deliberately at the hospitals:

> Towards these buildings, now the majority in the city, the enemy directs his special attention; and wherever a yellow flag—the emblem of the sick and wounded and suffering—is visible, there the humane Yankee directs his one-sided, dastardly warfare . . . how long, how long, oh Lord! shall we witness these acts of the barbarian?[24]

Dr. Joseph Alison confirmed in his diary: "The wounded are killed in the hospitals, surgeons wounded while attending to their duties." And Alison found the hospitals so overcrowded that "Some poor fellows are compelled to lay out in the open air and get attention from any doctor who happens to pass that way."

During the second week of June a direct hit was scored by a thirteen-inch mortar shell on the city hospital, the shell exploding on the main floor where the surgeons were at work. One doctor, buried and maimed beneath the debris, managed to tie up his severed arteries to keep from bleeding to death before his colleagues were able to amputate his leg. Dr. Alison himself barely escaped death from flying fragments. Altogether, eight men were killed and fourteen wounded in the hospital explosion.

The city and military hospitals, even with their emergency cots arranged on the grounds outside, could not take care of the flow of casualties from the trenches. In an undated entry in her journal, Annie Laurie Harris wrote:

> Wounded soldiers came in large numbers, and each household received as many as could be accommodated, the ladies sleeping on mattresses in order that the sick might be comfortable. On our lawn were encamped some of the men who were ready to defend Vicksburg. Many of those disliked tent-life, and would insist on our front gallery . . .[25]

Scarcely a woman in Vicksburg was not involved in administering to the care and comfort of the wounded, emerging from their homes and caves as necessary. The Confederate troops, noted Sergeant Tunnard, "gained renewed courage from the example thus given them by the heroic women of the Hill City." The Catholic Sisters of Mercy, those who remained after their seminary work had been suspended, were seen by Ephraim Anderson hovering over the beds of sick and wounded, "like ministering angels carrying balm and healing to the poor soldiers, cheering the hope of recovery or soothing the last moments of expiring life."[26]

The Union army, too, was not without its Florence Nightingales, compelled by conscience to the front from often distant places. Jane Currie Hoge of Chicago, with a son in Grant's army, arrived with a medical delegation, inspecting Union military hospitals. She found the field hospitals clean, sanitary, and beneficial from being in the open air, and she took in her stride the grim work of the army doctors, the piles of amputated arms and legs, and the knowledge that half the victims of this surgery were doomed to die.

Though hers was supposedly only a tour of inspection, Mrs. Hoge remained to take care of Federal wounded behind the lines. She remembered many weary days and nights in a tent on the Chickasaw Bayou where "the muttering of delirium . . . grated painfully on a pained ear and aching heart. Huge insects, stinging and whirling round the single candle that flickered in the night air, greeneyed lizards, slimy serpents, hooting owls and flittering bats were companions as cheery and welcome as Macbeth's witches on the heath."[27]

While Union soldiers, for the most part without a woman's comforting attendance, admired from a distance the courage of Vicksburg ladies—hurrying to and from the hospitals under fire, or climbing to the exposed hilltops to wave encouraging handkerchiefs at their Confederate defenders on the ramparts—they need not have looked far for examples of similar feminine fortitude on their side.

Few in Grant's army took particular notice of Private Albert Cashier of the Ninety-fifth Illinois Infantry, McPherson's corps, who was in the thick of the fighting around Vicksburg. Cashier was regarded as "unusually quiet and reclusive, but withal a good soldier," one colleague recalling that 'He was the smallest man in the company.' But Private Cashier held a unique distinction. "He" was a woman, disguised in regimental blues, whose identity was not discovered until the war was over.[28]

The siege ground on into its fourth week. "How very sad this life in Vicksburg!" wrote Mary Loughborough in her journal, "how little security can we feel, with so many around us seeing the morning light that will never more see the night. . . . How blightingly the hand of warfare lay upon the town! even in the softening light of the moon—the closed and desolate houses—the gardens with the gates half open. . . . At times it seemed like a ghost town, abandoned, as the residents remained inside their caves."[29]

Some 240 river-miles to the south, as all in Vicksburg knew, Port Hudson had been under siege since May 28, shelled from both the river and the land. With only a small civilian population, the suffering of noncombatants was proportionately less, but for the troops of both sides conditions were equally insufferable. Lieutenant Colonel Richard B. Irwin, assistant adjutant to General Banks, might have been writing of Vicksburg when he noted:

The heat, especially in the trenches became almost insupportable, the stenches quite so, the creeks dried up, the creek lost itself in the pestilential swamp, the springs dried out, and the river fell, exposing to the tropical sun a wide margin of festering ooze. The illness and mortality were enormous.[30]

Yet Banks tried again on June 14 to break General Gardner's hold on the fortress, assaulting the city from both sides and again being repulsed with serious casualties. Port Hudson's resistance was a heartening example to its northern neighbor, and editor Swords reminded his readers they were not alone. If Port Hudson could hold out against such constant Federal pressure, so could Vicksburg.

Behind Grant's lines in their grandfather's house, the Barlow family, sisters, wives, and mothers, were inclined to show a dangerous contempt for the surrounding enemy. Miss Elizabeth Read, Ida Barlow's cousin, was told by her servant one night: "Miss Bettie, dem dar Yankees is a sleeping on your Piano."

Elizabeth bounced into the parlor and found several hulking men in blue stretched out on the grand piano for a comfortable nap. She ordered them "to dismount." A young soldier swung his legs toward the floor, and told her:

"We'll get down if you'll come and play for us."

"I will not play for you," she said, "but I will play for these Confederate prisoners you have here." Ida Barlow, witnessing the scene, recalled:

So while she was playing the handsome fellow came and turned the music for her. She noticed that he wore a beautiful diamond ring, and told him she knew he had stolen it from a Southern girl. He held out his finger and said, "You can have it if you can get it off my finger." She said, "Give me your knife." He did so, and she whacked it with the knife until the blood flew. He said, "Why I believe you would kill me if you could!"

Elizabeth told the soldier, No, but she would kill his captain if she could. He unbuckled his belt and handed her his pistol, saying, "Now you have the chance." At that moment, Ida Barlow's aunt entered the room, screamed when she saw the pistol, and forestalled any impending mayhem.[31]

Mary Loughborough was in her cave when a shell from the river ploughed into the hillside, for a moment threatening to bury her alive. When the dust and debris settled, however, she found only a section of wall had collapsed, and she and her daughter were shaken but safe. Only such incidents, and "this thrilling knowledge of sudden and horrible death occurring near us," wrote Mary, "breaks the daily monotony of our lives."

In chronicling the "sad news of a Vicksburg day," Mrs. Loughborough wrote in her diary for June 15:

A little negro child . . . had found a shell; in rolling and turning it, had innocently pounded the fuse; the terrible explosion followed, showing, as the white cloud of smoke floated away, the mangled remains of a life that to the mother's heart had possessed all of beauty and joy.

A young girl, becoming weary in the confinement of the cave, hastily ran to the house in the interval that elapsed between the slowly falling shells. On returning, an explosion sounded near her—one wild scream, and she ran into her mother's presence, sinking like a wounded dove, the life blood flowing over the light summer dress in crimson ripples from a death-wound in her side, caused by the shell fragment.[32]

Animals as well as humans suffered from the rising fury of the siege. Grazing cows died in torn-up pastures, horses were killed in the streets and in the camps —sometimes chopped up for meat, often hauled down to the Mississippi River to turn the water foul with floating corpses. Dogs ran in packs like wild wolves, terrified by the concussions, or simply sat down and yowled in misery. In a year to come, the city of Atlanta, too, would shiver at the eerie sound of dogs tormented by a human madness that they did not understand.

But tragic drama calls for moments of comedy relief. Lida Lord remembered that each day, without fail, her father walked over shelterless land, from their cave to the Episcopal Church, "always carrying with him his pocket communion service, apparently standing an even chance of burying the dead, comforting the dying, or being himself brought home maimed, or cold in death." Returning one evening, with a sharp eye out for the lighted fuses of falling shells, he saw a burly wagoneer "slip off his horse and get under it in a hurry." As Lida Lord relayed her father's story of the frightened drover beneath the horse:

> His head appeared, bobbing out first from one side, then from the other. Above him in the air, bobbing too, and with a quick uneasy motion, was a luminous spark. After a full minute spent in vigorous dodging, the man came out to prospect. The supposed fuse was still there, burning brilliantly.
> "Darn the thing!" he grunted. "Why don't it bust?"
> He had been playing hide-and-seek for sixty seconds with a fine specimen of our Southern lightning-bug, or firefly![33]

Running out of newsprint, Swords began printing the *Daily Citizen* on the blank side of flowery-patterned wallpaper. Joseph Schmalz, the Main Street carpenter, first read the news, then turned the *Citizen* around and covered the wall of his cave with the pink and green flower motif appearing on the reverse side of the sheet. Opportunistic delivery boys, taking advantage of the general shortage of both news and paper, raised the *Citizen*'s list price of 25 cents to 50 cents an issue, pocketing the difference.

Few outside journals reached the city, though editor Swords, among others, would have been interested to read in the neighboring Jackson *Mississippian* —which had earlier recommended that Vicksburg be burned and abandoned to the enemy—now had changed its tune. Resuming publication with the departure of Grant's occupation forces, the *Mississippian* observed:

> All eyes are now turned eagerly towards Vicksburg. . . . Let her hold out yet and her fame will be more enviable than Gibraltar's or Sevastopol's. Let her still hold out and those who have participated in her defense will deserve and receive . . . the gratitude of a nation. And she will hold out. We are confident that she is invincible. . . . Vicksburg will rise from the ordeal nobly defiant and wreathed in perennial glory.[34]

❧ 20 ❧

"Ho! For Johnston!"

THE rumors danced on the horizon like confetti, illusive, hopeful, insubstantial as the summer breeze. Joe Johnston was on his way to the relief of Vicksburg. The gallant Virginian—the one Confederate general Grant confessed to fearing most among Southern leaders, not excluding Robert E. Lee —was bringing with him, some said 30,000, others 40,000, veteran troops to break Grant's iron chain around the city.

By mid-June the unconfirmed reports had pyramided. Ephraim Anderson learned that dispatches from Johnston stated that "we had only to hold out a few days longer and we would be relieved. Glorious anticipation!" Sergeant William Tunnard heard that Johnston was already at Clinton with 25,000 troops "and positively asserted that he was approaching to succor the garrison."[1]

William Chambers observed that every time artillery fire was heard from the east, the troops conjectured that "Gen. Johnston was coming at last. *How high rose the hopes for our men!*" At the same time, James Pepper, courier serving with Forney's division, was writing in his diary of "flying reports of Johnston's being in [Grant's] rear," later recording that Johnston was at Mechanicsburg and Satartia, west of the Big Black, and "was only waiting for a *very* important train expected hourly at Canton, and he would move his force 100,000 strong on to Vicksburg."[2]

Hugh Moss was another Confederate diarist who had exaggerated hopes of Johnston's numbers and proximity. "More news from Johnston," he wrote at this time. "Two men couriers arrived last night and stated that he was 25 miles from here when they started and on his way with 75–100 thousand men, his advance guard then skirmishing with the enemy. May he arrive here in due time, for we are now living on almost nothing."[3]

Even the Federal troops and high command were plagued by this rash of hearsay. "Johnston is getting lively again, and beginning to kick up dust in the rear," wrote Osborn Oldroyd the fourth week of June, as he prepared to march east with Sherman's forces to confront the Southern general. But what manner of dust was being kicked up, Oldroyd didn't know. Charles Dana had a hard time keeping up with the unsubstantiated tales of Johnston's whereabouts and confessed, "Almost every one of my dispatches to Mr. Stanton contained rumors of the movements of the Confederates, and the information was so uncertain that often what I reported one day had to be contradicted the next."[4]

Though many Southerners were skeptical—they had hoped and waited for so long, only to be disillusioned—editor Swords of the *Daily Citizen* tried to weave the fragmentary rumors into a paragraph of reassuring type, skillfully avoiding any reference to solid fact. In the issue of June 18 appeared this front page item:

HO! FOR JOHNSTON!—The most agreeable news nowadays is to hear from Gen. Johnston. But we have nothing to record of his movements, except that we may look forward at any time to his approach. We may repose the utmost confidence in his appearance within a very few days. We have to say to our friends and the noble army here that relief is close at hand. Hold out a few days longer, and our lines will be opened, the enemy driven away, the siege raised, and Vicksburg again in communication with the balance of the Confederacy.[5]

Among the civilians, the Lords, the Loughboroughs, the McRaes, and the Yankee-surrounded Barlow family all wrote of waiting with tense expectancy for Johnston. Their confidence in Pemberton was waning, and they had seen the deteriorating condition of the troops that manned the parapets. More and more, "Little Joe" loomed as their only hope of deliverance, and wish was father to the thought that his coming was, as the *Citizen* assured them, only days away.

According to William Drennan, who shared his Vicksburg quarters with a commissary officer, the people believed what they wanted to believe. "A man knows nothing. . . . As rumor, with her thousand tongues is more busy than ever . . . I find myself unusually credulous—believing some things that I usually would not think bore a semblance of truth. So much for being enclosed in the fortifications of a city."[6]

In point of fact, Johnston was still encamped between Canton and the upper reaches of the Big Black River, with an estimated 31,000 Southern troops. And the tug of war continued between his demands for reinforcements and the dilemma of the War Department. Was it more important to hold Tennessee with undiminished support for Braxton Bragg? Or to swing the emphasis to Mississippi with its vital river bordering the state?

Johnston's June 15 telegram to Secretary Seddon tolled a message of impending doom. Without additional support and with the odds so heavily against him, "I consider saving Vicksburg hopeless."

Seddon's reply was instantaneous:

Your telegram grieves and alarms me. Vicksburg must not be lost without a desperate struggle. The interest and the honor of the Confederacy forbid it. I rely on you to avert the loss. If better resources do not offer, you must attack. It may be made in concert with the [Vicksburg] garrison, if practicable, or otherwise without—by day or night, as you think best.[7]

Strong language. Johnston took three days to think it over before replying. He advised the secretary that perhaps Seddon did not appreciate the difficulties presented by Grant's strong position, his superior numbers, his heavy artillery commanding every road to Vicksburg—and added:

> The Big Black covers him from attack, and would cut off our retreat if defeated. We cannot combine operations with General Pemberton, from uncertain and slow communications. . . . I will do all I can, without hope of doing more than aid to extricate the garrison.[8]

Seddon shortly wired that he did indeed appreciate the difficulties Johnston faced, and, while he deferred to that general's superior judgment and "military genius," he felt it was time to take risks and "follow the most desperate course the occasion may demand." Whatever course Johnston followed, the secretary wrote:

> Rely upon it, the eyes and the hopes of the whole Confederacy are upon you, with the full confidence that you will act, and with the sentiment that it is better to fail nobly daring, than, through prudence even, to be inactive. . . . I rely upon you for all possible to save Vicksburg.[9]

One who did not doubt that Johnston might be on the way was Grant. He had hoped to capture Vicksburg and its garrison before the Confederate general could threaten his siege line from the rear or cooperate with Pemberton on ways to evacuate the town and save his army. Time was no longer strictly on the Union general's side. An early arrival by Johnston could force him into a two-front war, the last thing that he wanted.

On June 22 he took immediate steps to forestall this possibility. First and most importantly he placed seven divisions under the command of Sherman to expand and strengthen the defense line from Snyder's Bluff to the railroad bridge across the Big Black River. It was not an assignment Sherman relished —he had hoped to be in on the kill at Vicksburg, when and if it came—but, as he wrote to his brother John, "With Grant I am a second self." Whatever Grant's left hand needed, Sherman's right hand would provide.

Two days earlier Grant launched an all-out artillery attack, in the hope of bringing the city to its knees or cracking its defenses. Rawlins took down the order the night before, for delivery to all divisions:

> At 4 A.M. on the 20th instant a general cannonading will be commenced from all parts of the line on the city of Vicksburg. Firing will continue until 10 A.M. . . . Troops will be held under arms from 6:30 A.M. ready to take any advantage of any signs the enemy may show of weakness, or to repel an attack should one be made.
>
> It is not designed to assault the enemy's works but to be prepared.[10]

It would be the most massive bombardment of the whole campaign. All 220 of Grant's land guns would take part in the action, along with David Porter's naval guns and mortars, and the batteries across the river. Though Vicksburg had stood up under previous barrages, the weight of this one would, Grant hoped, be overwhelming. No amount of ammunition would be spared—beyond 100 rounds for each piece of field artillery, and 20 rounds for siege guns, to be held back "for emergency."

No amount, in fact, was spared. Major Charles J. Stolbrand, Chief of Artillery in Logan's division under corps commander McPherson, estimated that his four batteries expended 13,500 rounds of ammunition during the siege of Vicksburg, a good proportion during the furious hours of June 20.[11]

Pemberton wrote of the bombardment, placing its start an hour earlier, "At 3 o'clock this morning the enemy opened a tremendous artillery fire along his whole line, which was continued for six hours without cessation. The gunboats also participated and the storm of shot and shell was terrific, greatly exceeding in severity anything yet witnessed since the commencement of the siege."[12]

Of that "terrific bellowing," Osborn Oldroyd noted, "there was every variety of tone . . . from the squeak of a little feist to the roar of a bulldog. The sound of some brass pieces was so loud as to drown out the reverberations of the larger guns. . . . " The smoke was so thick, according to Oldroyd, that the Confederates could have walked out of the city, had they wanted to, without being discovered, though the Union troops were standing by in line of battle to contain them—or to break through their defenses, should the siege guns open up a hole.[13]

In William Tunnard's company, the sergeant recorded, "all concurred in the opinion that such a tremendous cannonading had never been equalled in their experience, and the volume of sound surpassed anything yet heard. It seemed as if heaven and earth were meeting in a fearful shock, and the earth trembled under the heavy concussions. . . . The cannonading kept up steadily all day."[14]

In the city proper, Dora and Anderson Miller decided to stay in their cellar during the bombardment, though invited to share a cave with others. But Dora made the mistake of going upstairs to rest in her own bed during a lull in the firing. The subsequent experience convinced her, "mine is not an American constitution." She wrote in her diary:

> . . . a shell burst right outside the window. . . . Pieces flew in, striking all around me, tearing down masses of plaster that came tumbling over me. When [her husband] rushed in I was crawling out of the plaster, digging it out of eyes and hair. When he picked up a piece as large as a saucer beside my pillow, I realized my narrow escape. . . . It has taken all the afternoon to get the plaster out of my hair, for my hands were rather shaky.[15]

Lucy McRae's family and several others who shared their cave were informed, the night before, of an impending bombardment of the city. An officer persuaded them they would be safer "nearer the lines under cover of the hills." They hastily packed up tents and baskets of food and headed north across Glass Bayou bridge—a dangerous route by day but relatively safe at night— and pitched their tents in a ravine behind the batteries and earthworks of General Martin Smith's division.

The night passed quietly enough, with the whole family huddled together in their tents, until, wrote Lucy, "Just about daylight we were aroused by the belching cannon, and before we could think where we were a cannon-ball that had spent its force on the side of the hill came rolling into the tent."

The ladies screamed, "and in less time than it takes to tell we were all up and out of the tent. Balls were whizzing, cannon booming from the rear, mortars replying in rapid succession from the front."

The group felt they were in dead center of the falling bombs, and Mrs. McRae commandingly led the flight back to town, a Confederate officer warning them to stay off main roads and keep close to sheltering banks. Tents and provisions were cast aside as impediments to speed; the children were crying and the mothers praying, as the shells exploded around them; and young Lucy was still clinging to her mother's hand when she found herself back in the blessed safety of their cave.[16]

It was not an ideal time for swimming in the Mississippi, but Chaplain Foster was caught in the crossfire while trying to bathe before daylight at the river's edge. While he was enjoying himself in the refreshing but polluted waters, the bombardment opened, "certainly the heaviest that occurred during the siege." Shot striking the water, Foster observed, made "a peculiar sound," as if coming "in contact with a rock." He got out in a hurry, to find Vicksburg in confusion and the citizens scurrying for their caves.

To a degree, the Confederate troops on the outer fortifications suffered less than the civilian population. "No spot within the city," wrote Winchester Hall, "was safe or knowingly spared. Women, children, and the wounded were exposed more than the soldiers in the trenches." Those caught outside the caves and dugouts found themselves in sudden, unexpected peril. According to a contemporary chronicler:

> One man had his head shot off while in the act of picking up his child. One man had a shell explode close by him and lift him some distance in the air. One shell exploded between two officers riding on the street and lifted both horses and riders into the air without hurting man or beast. A little girl, the daughter of a Mrs. Jones, was sitting at the entrance of a cave, when a Parrott shell entered the portal and took her head off.[17]

"The screams of the women of Vicksburg were the saddest I ever heard," wrote Mary Loughborough. "The wailings over the dead seemed full of heartsick agony." Mary came close to sharing personally in their tragedies. Her husband, Major James Loughborough, had implored his wife to take to their cave when the firing began, and to stay there with their child and servants.

Mary had scarcely settled in that gloomy cavern, clutching her baby daughter in her arms, when,

> a Parrott shell came whirling in the entrance and fell in the center of the cave before us all, lying there smoking. Our eyes were fastened upon it, while we expected every moment the terrific explosion would ensue. I pressed my child closer to my heart and drew nearer to the wall. Our fate seemed almost certain.

All remained motionless, transfixed by this "missile of death"—until one of the servants, the black boy George, rushed forward, picked up the shell, and hurled it through the door. The explosion they waited for, second by second, never came; the fuse burned itself out harmlessly. But Mary let the shell remain where it had fallen, for all to see, as a monument to George's courage and their own miraculous escape.[18]

Two bombshells burst simultaneously near the Lords' cave. Again, miraculously no one was injured, though, wrote Lida Lord, "The air was filled with flying splinters, clods, fragments of iron and branches of trees. The earth seemed fairly to belch out smoke and sulphur, and the roar and shock were indescribable." In the adjoining Confederate camp, Lida observed:

> The tents were in ruins. One of the officers was astride a table, without any idea of how he got there, and one was flat on the ground, with his scalp slightly grazed and bleeding. The mess-cook, a white man, was on his knees, with his hands clasped to his back, frantically clutching his suspenders and howling dismally. He was with much trouble convinced that he had escaped without a scratch.

"That evening," remembered Lida, "in reaction to our fright, we had quite a merry time. We made taffy, and the 'boys' sang us many a rollicking song." Among those rollicking songs was a lyric set to the tune of "Listen to the Mocking Bird," of which one verse and chorus:

> 'Twas at the siege of Vicksburg
> Of Vicksburg, of Vicksburg,
> 'Twas at the siege of Vicksburg,
> When the Parrott shells were whistling through the air.
> Listen to the Parrott shells,
> Listen to the Parrott shells,
> The Parrott shells are whistling through the air. [19]

The cannonading began and ended so early that Saturday morning that J. M. Swords was able to publish an account of the bombardment in the June 20 edition of the *Daily Citizen*. He observed that "Fully two thirds of the enemy's shells passed over our breastworks and came hissing into the city," but at the time of going to press he had no deaths or substantial damage to report, as a result of "this demonstration of fiendish spleen."

"It remains a matter of conjecture," wrote Swords, "as to what was the purpose of the enemy—whether a feint to cover some of their movements, or the indulging of the vain hope that they can dismay our gallant defenders, we know not." But in customary hyperbole, the editor described the city as undiminished in its defiance, and assured his readers that they "will yet have the gratification of seeing their foe retreating in dismay and disorder to their northern homes. . . . "[20]

The following day was as normal as any day could be in Vicksburg under the circumstances. William Drennan was amazed at how people came out of their burrows at the risk of life and limb, writing: "You can see women gaily dressed promenading the streets, if there is a slackening of shells, and men would give any price for a drink of whiskey—so much they wish for extra excitement. I saw Mrs. Lum walking the street with a gold laced official and she appeared as thoughtless as any one could be."[21]

As always in times of trial and crisis Vicksburg could be thankful for its sense of humor. "Professor" David Porter was complimented for his "grand pyrotechnic exhibition," gratuitously given for the people's benefit. And amused attention was paid to an abandoned house that, before the bombardment, had carried the sign FOR RENT: INQUIRE OF DAVIS & PEMBER-

TON. After a shell had ripped through the building the sign was painted over to read: RENTED: BY GRANT & McPHERSON.

From a military standpoint, Vicksburg had not been badly hurt by the bombardment. The damage to the fortifications could be repaired. The troops, sheltered behind their earthworks, had not suffered serious casualties. But casualties from other causes were continuing and unremitting. Lida Lord, from her family's cave in the hills, could see the Confederate troops in their entrenchments, and observed:

"The men suffered terribly. The hot sun burned and blistered them, while the freshly dug earth poisoned them with malaria. They were half starved, shaking with ague, and many of them afflicted with low fevers and dysenteric complaints. . . . Many succumbed and had to be taken to the hospital, where kind ladies tended them as best they could." On the other hand:

> If the men suffered, the officers had compensation; they were absolute heroes in the eyes of the prettiest girls in the South, who knitted their socks and hemmed their handkerchiefs, put blossoms in their buttonholes when they started for the batteries, and welcomed them back to an evening in the caves, where home-made candies, flowers, songs, flirtations, and whist combined to wring some festivity even out of these gloomy hours. And when the officers could not leave their posts, the girls, fearless as they were fair, made up riding parties to the forts and trenches, going in the twilight so that they could see and dodge the fuses of the shells.[22]

General Pemberton saw the city's situation in more critical light. He was deeply concerned with the worsening condition of the troops. On the day of the bombardment, he summoned his most trusted courier, Captain George D. Wise, to carry a report of the enemy's artillery attack to Johnston, with, more importantly, yet another plea for help:

> I hope you will advance with the least possible delay. My men have been thirty-four days and nights in trenches without relief, and the enemy within conversation distance. We are living on very reduced rations, and, as you know, are entirely isolated. What aid am I to expect from you? The bearer, Captain Wise, can be confided in.[23]

Wise himself later wrote to Pemberton that "you gave me verbally some directions for Gen. Johnston not contained in your dispatch. . . . They were substantially as follows—that you had full & correct reports from all the departments under your command . . . [and that] you could not hold out longer than the 10th day of July. . . . You urged me to impress upon Gen. Johnston the urgent necessity for speedy action on his part. . . . "

Wise also recalled that Pemberton, unwilling to put too much on paper for fear of his courier's capture, also told the captain that his troops were too weak to fight their way out of the city, but that if Johnston could approach by the Graveyard Road which left Vicksburg on the east, Pemberton would try to sneak his army through Hall's Ferry Road as soon as he had evidence of Johnston's presence.

To complete the record of Wise's mission, one must follow the captain to

Jackson, and for the time being leave the story there. For he would not report back to Pemberton. Instead, he was captured by McPherson's forces, trying to return to Vicksburg. Before his capture, however, he did reach Johnston in the Mississippi capital where, as Wise later related to Pemberton, the Western commander

> informed me that he was in no condition to make a movement in your favor; that he had not sufficient troops, and that he had been unable to obtain the requisite number of horses for artillery purposes & at the same time to haul the necessary supplies for his army. After thus explaining his own situation & his inability to strike a blow for the relief of the garrison of Vicksburg, he added:
>
> "Tell Genl. Pemberton that the determination manifested by him, and Genl. E. Kirby Smith's expected cooperation, encourages me to hope that something may yet be done to save Vicksburg; but if it should become necessary to surrender, that he [Pemberton] should make propositions to Genl. Grant, as my making them would be an impolitic confession of weakness."[24]

Then Johnston did a strange and prescient thing. He gave Wise a letter to General McPherson, requesting that the captain be given considerate treatment if captured.

There is no reason to believe that at this time Pemberton had any thought of surrendering. He would like to have been able to lead his army out of Vicksburg, still intact—but only to team up with Johnston to drive Grant away and save the city. In the Confederate fortifications William Chambers recorded that "It was now a common topic of conversation that the garrison was to cut its way out of Vicksburg. . . . In view of the condition of the men, such an attempt would have been utter madness."

It would have been madness to engage the weakened army in a battle to cut through the Union lines. But according to Sergeant Tunnard, "A large number of skiffs were constructed and conveyed to the lower portion of the town. . . . The conviction seemed finally to settle on every mind that a desperate attempt would soon be made to cross the river with the army, and escape into the Trans-Mississippi Department. . . . "[25]

Grant also wrote in his account of the campaign that "On the 21st of June I was informed that Pemberton was preparing to escape, by crossing to the Louisiana side under cover of night; that he had employed workmen in making boats for that purpose. . . . The rebel pickets also said that houses in the city had been pulled down to get material to build these boats with. Afterward this story was verified."[26]

It is hard to doubt Grant, or ignore the reports of soldiers on the scene. But it is equally hard to visualize or credit this extraordinary project, and Pemberton makes no mention of it in his diary or reports. To try to carry an army of 30,000 men across the half-mile-wide Mississippi—in small, hastily-constructed boats, and in the face of not only batteries on the other side but Porter's gunboats standing in the river above and below the city—seems preposterous. Grant himself had not dared to cross the river in the face of Grand Gulf's batteries, even with Porter's gunboats to protect him and no Confederate warships intervening.

"We are now swiftly nearing the end of our siege life," wrote Mary Lough-borough in the latter part of June. "The rations had nearly all been given out." Lucy McRae also recorded that "our provisions were becoming scarce, and the Louisiana soldiers were eating rats as a delicacy, while mules were occasionally carved up to appease the appetite. Mother would not eat mule meat, but we children ate some, and it tasted right good, having been cooked nicely. Wheat bread was a rarity, and sweet-potato coffee was relished by the adults."[27]

Lida Lord referred to the tales of eating rats as "Canards!" And they probably were, in large degree, originating often from hearsay or the reports of gloating Northern correspondents. If the Louisianians ate rats, they were, more likely than not, muskrats—for muskrats had long been an acceptable part of diet in that section of the country.

Yet Sergeant Tunnard, himself a Louisianian, insisted "It is a difficult matter for persons surrounded with abundance to realize the feeling produced by extreme hunger. . . . It must be felt to be realized; and if once felt, the idea of eating dogs, cats, rats, or even human flesh would contain nothing repulsive or repugnant to the feelings."[28]

With the army under reduced rations and on the information that some citizens were hoarding food, Martin Smith's troops conducted a house-to-house search of the city, a procedure arousing mixed feelings in the population. Less mixed were their feelings when the City Guard raided a grocery at the corner of Levee and Clay streets and confiscated sixty-nine bottles of whisky. The liquor, they said, was for medicinal use at the hospitals—an explanation that might have held up, had not most of the Guard been drunk by nightfall.

Writing at about this time, Alexander Abrams noted:

Starvation in its worst forms now confronted the inhabitants. . . . All the beef in the city was exhausted, and mules were soon brought in requisition, and their meat sold readily at one dollar per pound, the citizens being as anxious to get it as they were, before the investment, to purchase the delicacies of the season.

It was also distributed among the soldiers, to those who desired it, although it was not given out under the name of rations. A great many of them, however, accepted it in preference to doing without any meat, and the flesh of the mules was equal to the best venison.[29]

Abrams himself tried eating mule meat for three or four days, "and found the flesh tender and nutritious, and, under the *peculiar circumstances,* a most desirable description of food."

The Chicago *Tribune,* with tongue in cheek, published a bill-of-fare allegedly purloined from the "Hôtel de Vicksburg," which listed, among its daily courses, Mule Tail Soup, Mule Foot Jelly, Mule Salad; and among its side dishes and entrées:

> *Mule head stuffed à-la-Mode.*
> *Mule ears fricaseed à-la-Gotch.*
> *Mule side stewed, new style, hair on.*
> *Mule brains à-la-omelette.*
> *Mule tongue cold à-la-Bray.* [30]

The reports of mule consumption spread so rapidly and widely that Commodore James S. Palmer—with Farragut's fleet, which was still supporting Nathaniel Banks's efforts to take Port Hudson—wrote to Admiral Porter at Vicksburg, inquiring about this new Confederate nutriment, and "if it be true, that diet assimilates them wonderfully to the animal that is said to sustain them, for to my mind they have become more stubborn and obstinate than ever."

In their hillside cave, the Lords suffered from a different animal kingdom problem. Wrote Lida Lord: "We were almost eaten up by mosquitos, and were in hourly dread of snakes. The vines and thickets were full of them, and a large rattlesnake was found one morning under a mattress on which some of us had slept all night." Along with the other cave-dwellers, the Lords had grown used to hunger and a diet of mule meat and pea-flour bread, but thirst added to their misery. Water had to be drawn by the panful from household cisterns and rationed out as if to shipwrecked drifters in a lifeboat.

To the credit of Pemberton's command, the military did not intrude on or appropriate any of a family's private source of water. Bucket brigades carried water from the Mississippi River to the soldiers in the camps and on the barricades—a factor which further contributed to their declining health.

At their refuge home behind Grant's lines, the Barlow family were adequately fed on Union rations, but were still beset by confrontations with the enemy. When a crowd of Yankees visited the home, Ida Barlow's aunt feigned sickness to discourage them. But a more accommodating houseboy was heard to say, "Come this way, I'll show you where they keep the goodies." He led the soldiers into the pantry, whereupon, wrote Ida:

> My aunt jumped from the bed and grabbed an old musket that my uncle always kept by the bedside and jerked out the bayonet that was the end of it and struck one of the Yankees in the breast. He was borne away to the surgeon and the entire family thought our time had come and we would all be slain, but an officer was outside and he came in and had a private conversation with my grandfather and that was the end of that.

On another evening, remembered Ida, "Several Yankees brought in a Confederate spy whom they had captured and sat around our fire, saying that at 9 o'clock they would take him out and shoot him. My grandfather begged for his life but to no good, so the prisoner gave up his great Army coat and blanket and was led out behind the gin house. Out of the darkness came the report of pistol shots which sent him to his death."

Civilian hopes continued to feed hungrily on rumors. "Our ears were always strained to catch the first sound of Johnston's guns," wrote Lida Lord. "Every extra-heavy cannonading was a message of hope, and every courier brought in, it was said, news of most encouraging victories."[31]

One such courier named Bob Lowder of Saint Louis arrived on Sunday, June 21, the thirty-fifth day of the siege, to send the spirits of both soldiers and civilians soaring. Reportedly, he had passed the gunboats on the Yazoo dressed as a fisherman and trolling a baited line behind his skiff. Nearing the city where the Union ships became ubiquitous, he abandoned his boat and, waiting for darkness, floated down the current on a plank.

He brought with him dispatches for General Pemberton, but when grilled as to their contents he avowed that he was sworn to secrecy. He admitted, however, that he had come from Johnston's army which "consisted of the very flower of the South Carolina, Virginia, and Kentucky troops," adding, "I can only tell you that in three or four days you will hear the biggest kind of cannonading, and will see the Yanks skedaddling up the Yazoo."[32]

Three or four days! If Bob Lowder's report could be relied on, that meant that Johnston could be expected on June 24 or 25. The day of deliverance was close at hand. Among the garrison, wrote Sergeant Tunnard, "A feverish excitement prevailed of hearing something definite from General Johnston, and, as day after day passed without any reliable information of succor, the anxiety became intense."

Meanwhile, as William Chambers realized and as Union soldiers shouted gleefully across the lines to their opponents, they were prisoners in their own proscribed world, "and a dreary world it was." Chambers consoled himself by reading the New Testament, the works of Bulwer-Lytton, and Charles Dickens's new novel, *Great Expectations,* somehow smuggled through the blockade.

At the time that James Pepper was writing in his diary that "The news of Johnston still seem to be reliable," Pemberton received by courier on June 21 another communication from the general. It was not a reply to his dispatch sent by Captain Wise, now a prisoner of war. But, though dated June 14, it helped to clarify their relative situations. Wrote Johnston in part:

> All that we can attempt is to save you and your garrison. To do this, exact cooperation is indispensable. By fighting the enemy simultaneously at the same point of his line, you may be extricated. Our joint forces cannot relieve the siege of Vicksburg. . . . Inform me as soon as possible what point will suit you best. . . . General [Richard] Taylor, with 8,000 men, will endeavor to open communication with you. . . .[33]

It was not what Pemberton had hoped to hear. There was no suggestion that Johnston planned to attack Grant's rear and raise the siege of Vicksburg. But dependent as he was on help from Johnston, Pemberton would have to take what he could get. He promptly replied:

> If it is absolutely impossible, in your opinion, to raise the siege with our combined forces, and that nothing more can be done than to extricate the garrison, I suggest that, giving me full information in time to act, you move to the north of the railroad, drive the enemy's pickets at night, and at daylight the next morning engage him heavily with skirmishers, occupying him during the entire day, and that on that night I move by the Warrenton Road by Hankinson's Ferry, to which point you should previously send a brigade of cavalry, with two field batteries, to build a bridge there and hold that ferry; also Hall's and Baldwin's, to cover my crossing at Hankinson's. . . . I await your orders.[34]

Two days later, hard on the heels of his earlier message, came another dispatch from Johnston, dated June 22, this one in reply to Pemberton's appeal for help on June 15:

General Taylor is sent by General E. Kirby Smith to cooperate with you from the west bank of the river, to throw in supplies, and to cross with his force, if expedient and practicable. I will have the means of moving toward the enemy in a day or two, and will try to make a diversion in your favor, and, if possible, communicate with you, though I fear my force is too small to effect the latter. . . . If I can do nothing to relieve you, rather than surrender the garrison, endeavor to cross the river at the last moment if you and General Taylor communicate.[35]

Considering Smith's and Taylor's past failures to do anything substantial to relieve beleaguered Vicksburg, and Taylor's defeat at Milliken's Bend, Pemberton put little faith in help from across the Mississippi. And to cross that river, as Johnston suggested, in the face of enemy batteries and gunboats, was, Pemberton wrote, "beyond all possibility of even partial accomplishment." Which left previous rumors of boat-building efforts in the city, and Grant's report of half-finished boats stacked up in Vicksburg, something of a mystery.

All that Pemberton could do for now was to wait for Johnston's confirmation of his plan to lead his army via the Warrenton Road to Hankinson's Ferry, a movement which could not be accomplished unless certain of support. He would have a long wait. In fact, he got no further word at all from Johnston. And despite that general's assurance that Pemberton could expect support from Kirby Smith, he got no word from either Smith or Richard Taylor. He was a man alone, and Vicksburg was his problem—with none prepared to share it with him.

"We were now looking west, besieging Pemberton," Grant had written "while we were also looking east to defend ourselves against an expected siege by Johnston."[36]

In point of fact, Grant's own concern now focused more on Johnston than on Pemberton. Pemberton could be contained in Vicksburg, and the city could be expected to collapse, in time, from hunger and privation. But Johnston, reportedly being reinforced by Braxton Bragg, was still a free agent—a brainy, shrewd strategist whom Grant admired—and who posed a constant threat to the rear of the Union siege line.

It would be well, Grant thought, to meet Johnston "at least fifteen miles out," and Sherman was prepared to do so. His eastern defense line spanned a twenty-mile arc, from Snyder's Bluff to the railroad bridge across the Big Black, with batteries posted on strategic heights. It was up-and-down terrain, a stretch of hills and valleys, ridges and ravines—good country for defense.

Charles Dana, still reporting faithfully to Stanton, visited Sherman several times and observed that "he had occupied the commanding points, opened rifle-pits wherever they would add to his advantage, obstructed the crossroads and most of the direct roads also, and ascertained every point where the Big Black could be forded. . . . By his rapid movements . . . Sherman produced the impression that his forces were ten times as numerous as they really were."[37]

But there was no sign of Johnston, who, to use Sherman's word, appeared to be "vibrating" between Canton and Jackson in a state of indecision. There were only wary Confederate pickets keeping watch from the east bank of the

Big Black River. This lack of challenge (Vicksburg was where Sherman wanted to be, where the action was) made the red-headed general increasingly waspish and impatient.

A captured Confederate officer was brought into his presence, a lieutenant of poetic bent, who fulsomely praised the magnolia trees outside the general's tent.

"How beautifully those leaves wave—be-ee-utiful!" he said and, getting no response, repeated soulfully, "Be-ee-utiful!"

"Well, damn it, can't you let 'em wave?" the general snapped.[38]

Dana also visited Admiral Porter on the Mississippi and found that Porter too was looking east and west, blockading Vicksburg against Pemberton's possible crossing of the river and watching out for Kirby Smith's rumored attack from the Louisiana side. But the real work at Vicksburg was the siege. "No amount of outside alarm loosened Grant's hold on the rebel stronghold," Dana wrote, "and the siege went on steadily and effectively. . . . Grant soon had seventy-seven thousand men around Vicksburg, and Pemberton's last hope was gone."

In the Union lines infantryman Isaac Jackson wrote to his sister that "I hope it will not be too much longer before we get this stronghold. We keep working and pegging away at [it] day and night. It will fall eventually." The pegging away in Jackson's section was directed principally at the Second Texas Lunette, "the best fort the rebels have," confronting Ord's corps near the center of the Vicksburg line.

The Mississippi climate was too hot for Jackson's taste, but there were compensations. "Among other things I love to sit and listen to the mocking bird sing. They are plenty here and the prettiest singers I ever heard, and they never get tired. There used to be one came where our gun was planted and sit on an old, dead tree and sing. I could lay in my tent and see him."[39]

The Federal besiegers were so close now and the trenches so contiguous to those of the defenders, that one Union officer became enraged when a Confederate digger accidentally tossed a shovelful of earth on top of him. "That fellah hit me with a clod!" he protested loudly. Not all such incidents were accidental. An enemy head, just yards away, was fair game for a rock, a dead rat, or anything handy for pitching at it.

James Wilson, an engineer by training, was one who did not believe that Vicksburg's defenses could be overcome by ordinary means. From past experience, such as that of May 22, he concluded that "no well-constructed, well-defended line of earth-works" could be successfully assaulted without making "every possible preparation, not only for the attack, but for instantly following up every preliminary success. . . . The assailants should work with all their might for a surprise or for some other advantage which would neutralize the entrenchments to be attacked."[40]

Grant's thoughts were in the same direction. His siege guns had made no irreparable dent, much less a gap, in the Confederate fortifications. He would not rely on another infantry assault across open ground, nor depend entirely on his artillery. Both had been tried and failed. He would, as he was doing now, burrow under the Vicksburg fortifications, plant mines, and blow them up, then employ infantry and artillery to exploit the gap.

❧ 21 ❧

Blow, Gabriel, Blow

THE Third Louisiana Redan would have its own history in the war, and a monumental one at that. But among Confederate troops the V-shaped fort had a unique distinction. It was the proud possessor of a glee club.

Sergeant Tunnard, who equated his Louisiana regiment with the Spartans at Thermopolae, was entranced by their musical performance. "What a strange spectacle!" he wrote, extolling the "spirit of heroism manifesting itself by the men composing and singing, with harmonious voices and enthusiastic chorus, songs regarding their situation."[1]

Captain J. H. Jones of the Thirty-eighth Mississippi, same brigade as the Third Louisiana, was equally appreciative of the glee club, noting, "It also had a sort of poet who would compose songs adapted to popular melodies which the Club would sing. These songs were sometimes humorous, often satirical, but more commonly sad and sung in a minor key. . . . I have heard good music in my day, but I do not think I ever listened to singing that impressed me as that did."[2]

The stage setting for the evening was both perfect and uncommon, Jones believed, observing that "the boom of artillery and the constant hiss of minié balls by day prepared the audience to appreciate the beautiful in the peaceful songs by night. Both the Blue and Gray enjoyed these serenades, and during their continuance a deep hush fell upon the contending forces." Applause from "Our friends the Enemy" was often as loud as that from the Confederates.

The club was not above adding a touch of humor to its repertoire, and Jones remembered one number ending:

> Swear, boys, swear Vicksburg shall ne'er surrender,
> Swear, boys, swear that not one vandal foe
> Shall tread her soil while one arm can defend her,
> Unless her rations get damnation low.[3]

Concern with rations seemed to be a recurring theme of the Club's renditions. Private A. Dalsheimer of the Third Louisiana Regiment, apparently

277

with that theme on his mind, had another composition written to the tune of "Life on the Ocean Wave." The last two stanzas:

> *The bullets may whistle by,*
> *The terrible bombs come down;*
> *But give me full rations, and I*
> *Will stay in my hole in the ground.*

> *Oh! a life on the Vicksburg hills,*
> *A home in the trenches deep,*
> *A dodge from the Yankee shells,*
> *And the old pea-bread won't keep.*

Over and above its glee club, the redan, highly perched to overlook the Jackson Road in both directions, was a fortress to be reckoned with. Ever since the May 22 assault, when McPherson's several thrusts against the stronghold had been thwarted, the redan had been a major target of the Federal offensive. It was close to the center of the Confederate defenses, regarded by the Federals as the "Key Fort" on the Vicksburg line, and, since the first attack, had been considerably strengthened.

Occupying so important a position gave its garrison a sense of proud responsibility. General Louis Hébert, holding that section of the fortifications under General Forney, told the Third Louisiana Regiment that they held "the key to the city, on the most exposed portion of the line." Sergeant Tunnard wrote with justifiable pride, "Perhaps no body of men were actuated by feelings of more determined courage, and a spirit of resistance even unto annihilation."

The Federal troops and commanders held equal respect for the redan, Captain Andrew Hickenlooper, McPherson's chief of engineers, calling it "the most formidable redoubt [redan] on the entire [Confederate] line. . . . Because of its strength, commanding position, and heavy armament, this redoubt became the main objective point of the engineering operations of the Seventeenth Army Corps."[4]

During the truce of May 25, Hickenlooper had inspected the ground around the fort, fixed in his mind its salient points, and studied all possible methods of approach. Before the end of May, he had had his strategy completed.

Some four hundred yards east of the Third Louisiana Redan, the Shirley House was a natural center for Union operations on this section of the line. On Grant's arrival, Mr. and Mrs. James Shirley and their son had been moved first to a cave, then to a place of safety three miles behind the Union camps, and the two-story mansion, known to Federal troops as "the White House," became a rendezvous and observation point.

On the eastern slope, to the side of the house, caves and bombproof shelters honeycombed the hillside, sheltering the troops and men of the Forty-fifth Illinois Infantry of Brigadier General Mortimer D. Leggett's brigade of Logan's division. Whether or not they knew it then, theirs was the mission of taking the redan. The Shirley House itself was unprotected, silhouetted on the rising land to make a perfect target; yet it miraculously survived repeated shelling and was still standing in the late years of the nineteen seventies.

Starting at a point 200 yards southeast of the Shirley House, men of Logan's Third Division began digging their approach to the redan. Working in details, one by day, the other by night, they burrowed in zigzag fashion until they reached a high point 130 yards short of the fort. Here they constructed an earthwork known as Hickenlooper's Battery.[5]

From the beginning of the project, the diggers were protected by a somewhat new form of mobile shield or sap-roller. According to Willie Tunnard it resembled the frame of a flatcar—which it was—piled high with bales of cotton and pushed on wheels ahead of the workers. This movable breastwork, the sergeant wrote, "became a perfect annoyance to the regiment, and various plans were proposed for its destruction. . . . Some of the men actually proposed to make a raid on it, and set it afire, a plan which would have been the height of madness."[6]

It was about this time that Grant complained that the Confederates were using "exploding bullets," a device which he branded "barbarous." The source of his misinformation might have been the "happy invention" by which the Louisianians sought to destroy the four-wheeled monster on their front. The idea was credited to Lieutenant Colonel Samuel D. Russell of the Third Louisiana. Russell discovered that cotton fibers soaked in turpentine and stuffed in the recess at the base of a bullet could be fired by musket to ignite almost any combustible material.

The regiment watched with utmost interest as Russell tested his invention on "the hated object. The initial blast," wrote Sergeant Tunnard, "was followed by the glittering ball as it sped from the breastworks straight to the dark mass of cotton-bales, like the rapid flight of a firefly."

Nothing happened. Keenly disappointed, the troops gave up on Russell's invention. They had retired for the night, when, an hour or so later, one of the watchers on the parapets exclaimed, "I'll be damned if that thing isn't on fire!"

There was a general rush to the breastworks. "Sure enough," wrote Tunnard, "smoke was seen issuing from the dark mass." The fire that had been apparently smoldering for hours was ready to burst into flame—which it shortly did, casting a brilliant light on the Federals who were trying frantically to extinguish the blaze. Confederate riflemen kept up a constant shower of bullets on and around the target, cheering and taunting the firefighters, until the flatcar was "reduced to ashes and a mass of smouldering embers."[7]

"The achievement," Tunnard recorded, "was a source of general satisfaction and rejoicing." Until the Federals built another sap-roller to replace the flatcar, their forward progress had been temporarily halted; all the Confederates had to contend with for the moment were Logan's troops in rifle pits on their front. After a brief respite, however, the Federals put in operation another sap-roller, this one consisting of a wicker casing packed with cotton and far less destructible.

At this point, another example of Yankee ingenuity appeared, not far from the redan. A short distance from the Hickenlooper Battery a curious-looking structure mushroomed. The war in the East had already introduced balloons for high-level observation; almost a year earlier the Confederates had built such a balloon from ladies' silk pantaloons and frocks. But Lieutenant Henry C. Foster of the Twenty-third Indiana Infantry had his own conception of aerial reconnaissance.

Known as "Coonskin" for the Davey Crockett hat he wore, Foster was an unerring shot, according to his commanding officer, Lieutenant Colonel W. P. Davis, "and woe to the Confederate heads that appeared above the parapet." At first, Foster crept out by night and dug himself a burrow with a peephole and slit to fire through in front of the Confederate earthworks in the Jackson Road sector. He took with him enough food and water for several days and passed the time picking off every Confederate head that showed itself.

But being below the walls of the redan put the marksman at a disadvantage. He would prefer shooting down on targets sighted from above. And so, Davis substantiates:

> Taking advantage of the night hours, Coonskin built himself a tower of loose railroad ties. . . . Working several nights, he at length built the tower so high that by climbing toward its top he could actually look over the Confederate parapets. . . . Then taking aim through the chinks of the logs, he would pick off the enemy. The tower was a terror to the Confederates. . . . All they could do was to fire musket-balls at it, which whistled around its corners or buried themselves in its logs.[8]

Shortly, Coonskin introduced new equipment to his lofty crow's nest, turning it into a giant periscope. Large mirrors were strategically placed atop the tower, providing a view of the redan's interior for the benefit of gunners on the ground. The mirrors could be shattered by bullets, of course. But this was one way of getting the Confederates to waste their diminishing ammunition, with no danger to the Federals, and new reflectors could be hauled up to replace those damaged.

With the garrison in the redan, Sergeant Tunnard came to feel that the whole campaign for Vicksburg, the whole war in fact, was capsuled in this struggle for the fort. There was the same ebb and flow of combat—with the antagonists tracking each other's movements with "the ferocity and vigilance of a tiger seeking prey." And along with that, the inevitable camaraderie of men at war, which in listless periods sought to span the forbidding line between blue and gray.

Jared Sanders, with Smith's division, wrote on June 22, of the proximity of the contestants—"so close that they [the Yankees] throw over notes & put them on wild canes & hand them to our boys. . . . They swap knives, canteens, etc., with our men. By agreement we do not fire upon each other unless one party commences to work."[9]

Another soldier with Bowen's division, a Missourian, saw a Missouri regimental battleflag on Blair's trenches. "I'm going out to shake hands with those fellows," he would say. Soon soldiers of both sides were meeting between the lines, to inquire of friends and relatives in the opposing army, to trade "Lincoln coffee" for Confederate tobacco, to exchange good-natured challenges and gibes.

"Keep your head down after daylight, Johnnie," one would warn on parting. "I don't aim to miss."

"You do the same, Yank. I got an Enfield rifle now."

Then, noted Captain Jones, they would return to their respective lines and "shoot at each other's heads with all the eagerness of sportsmen. . . . What a study is human nature, and how seemingly contradictory."[10]

By the third week in June, under the protection of the Hickenlooper Battery, Federal troops and engineers had extended their approach trench—eight feet wide and seven deep—to within twenty yards of the redan. The intention was plain. Since the guns of the battery had only nicked holes in the parapets, which were easily repaired at night, and since the early assaults had proved futile, they planned to blow up the redan.

Under the circumstances the high-rising parapets became, for the Confederates, as much a handicap as a protection. Though equipped now with new Enfields, more accurate than their old rifles, it was hard to depress the barrels sufficiently to fire down on the besiegers. The garrison rolled fused shells and thunder barrels down upon the enemy. Both sides tossed hand grenades freely; sometimes these were caught and thrown back. Once a dead rattlesnake soared through the air and landed inside the breastworks, perhaps as a sort of voodoo warning.

Inside the redan by day and night, the garrison listened curiously to the chip-chip, clink-clink of the Union miners, somewhere underneath their fort. Countermining operations were begun. A vertical shaft was sunk through the floor of the redan, from which the Confederates could intercept the Federal tunnel and destroy it.

General Hébert took other precautions. He could not, perhaps, stop enemy efforts to blow up the fort. But he could prepare for a Federal charge through the breastworks if the mine's explosion opened up a gap. He had breastworks constructed at the rear of the redan, behind which the garrison could make a stand, minimize the effects of the explosion, and repel an attack that might follow.

In an effort to keep the Federals at bay, the Confederates resorted to throwing light shells with short fuses as well as conventional hand grenades. Sergeant Tunnard described the grenade used, as "an iron shell weighing roughly a pound, shaped like a hen's egg, and filled with powder. From one end projected a rudder of feathers, from the other a percussion rod was held extended by a spring. When the shell was hurled at the enemy, the tail feathers kept the nose of the missile forward so that, on striking the target, the rod sprang back and struck a cap to detonate the powder."[11]

On June 22 Captain Hickenlooper reported: "We reached the rebel fort today at 10 o'clock, and cleared away a place to commence mining operations." Thirty-five former coal miners, assigned to eight-hour shifts for day and night duty, began digging a tunnel beneath the redan. The main gallery ran forty-five feet forward, then divided into three branches, one ahead, one to the left, and one to the right. By the time they had penetrated forty feet, Hickenlooper recorded, "Can hear the rebels at work on counter-mines very distinctly."[12]

By June 24 this strange subterranean warfare became a race to determine who would blow up whom, as miners of both sides tunneled like warring termites underneath the firm loess soil, each trying to get below the other. Would the fort go first? Or would the invaders be buried by Confederate explosives planted beneath their deep-dug crypts? Hickenlooper spent an anxious night and awoke on Thursday, June 25, to find that in his absence his men had been frightened by the sound of Confederate countermining and had quit work.

Wrathfully the captain drove them back into the gallery and "had them rush it ahead" to completion by 9:00 A.M. The men then began toting into the tunnel twenty-five pounds of powder at a time, in gunny sacks. Reported Hickenlooper, "Deposited 1,500 pounds in three different branch mines (500 in each), and 700 pounds in center; 2,200 pounds in all. . . . Mines tamped with cross-timbers, sandbags, etc., and already to explode at 1 P.M."[13]

Grant postponed the explosion to 3:00 P.M. If this was indeed to be Gabriel's last trump, the blast that was to bring down the walls of Vicksburg and decide the fate of the Confederacy, it should be heralded by a massive, doomsday bombardment of the city. All artillery on the Union line was to take part in the cannonade.

2:00 P.M. The Forty-fifth Illinois crouched in the approach leading to the redan. Up front were Captain Hickenlooper and the "pioneers," advance squads of engineers, prepared to facilitate passage for the infantry through the exploded Confederate defenses. Farther back other regiments waited in the ravines near the Shirley House. Remembered Captain Hickenlooper, "As far as the eye could reach, to the right and left, could be seen the long winding columns of blue moving to their assigned positions behind the besiegers' works."

2:30 P.M. One mile to the south, Isaac Jackson noted: "The rifle pits were all filled, and all was ready to commence firing as soon as the explosion should take place." Hickenlooper observed that, "Gradually, as the hour of 3 approached, the boom of artillery and incessant rattle of musketry . . . suddenly subsided, and a deathlike and oppressive stillness pervaded the whole command. Every eye was riveted upon that huge redoubt standing high above the adjoining works."

3:30 P.M. After a half-hour delay, the mine was sprung, all four charges going off at once. To Hickenlooper, "It appeared as though the whole fort and connecting outworks commenced an upward movement, gradually breaking into fragments and growing less bulky in appearance, until it looked like an immense fountain of finely pulverized earth, mingled with flashes of fire and clouds of smoke, through which could occasionally be caught glimpses of some dark objects,—men, gun-carriages, shelters, etc."[14]

Sylvanus Cadwallader recorded: "The burst was terrific. For a few seconds . . . the air was filled with dirt, dust, stockades, gabions, timbers, one or two gun carriages, and an immense surging white cloud of smoke which fairly rose to the heavens, and gradually widened out and dissipated."[15]

Two factors diminished the blast's effect for the Confederates. The vertical mine shaft in the center of the fort carried the force of the explosion upward rather than outward, limiting its range of damage, and, knowing what was coming, the garrison had already withdrawn to earthworks erected at the rear of the redan. When the debris settled, what was left between them and the enemy was a yawning crater some forty or fifty feet in diameter and twelve feet deep.

Toward this breach raced the Forty-fifth Illinois Infantry regiment, while, observed Hickenlooper, "Firing along the entire [Union] line instantly opened with great fury, and amidst the din and roar of 150 cannon and the rattle of 50,000 muskets, the charging column moved forward to the assault." The charge was slowed by the mass of debris left by the explosion, and, from behind their new line, the Confederate riflemen turned the crater into a death trap for the first wave of advancing Union soldiers.[16]

In their prepared defenses at the rear of the fort, the Third Louisiana Regiment was reinforced by the Sixth Missouri Infantry led by Colonel Eugene Erwin, a grandson of Henry Clay. Erwin was something of a white-knight figure to his men, and he appeared at this moment of crisis at his bravest. A survivor of many wounds and many battles, he had risen from a sick bed earlier that morning to join his regiment in the redan. Now, mounting the parapet in the face of enemy fire, he drew and waved his sword as a signal to attack. Two minié balls killed him instantly.

Erwin's death so shocked and disheartened the Sixth Missouri that no sortie was made. Wilbur Crummer, pushing through the crater with the Forty-fifth Illinois Regiment, recorded that the Confederates

met us with a terrible volley of musketry, but on the boys went, up and over the embankment with a cheer, the enemy falling back a few paces to an inner or second line of breastworks where are placed cannon loaded with grape and canister, and these cannon belched forth their death-dealing missiles. . . . The line wavers, staggers, then falls back into the crater. The enemy charges on us, but we repel them at the west bank, and a hand-to-hand conflict rages for hours.[17]

McPherson's troops tried to consolidate their hold upon the crater by bringing up logs with peepholes through them, behind which they could fire. Confederate bullets, in turn, sliced flying splinters from the logs, which did more damage than bullets could. Yet a detail of two Federal companies held the crater for thirty minutes. According to Crummer, "their rapid firing causing the rifles to become hot and foul, and the men weary and worn," at which point they would be replaced by a fresh detail. From their emergency breastworks, noted Hickenlooper, the defenders tossed short-fused shells at the invaders, which, "rolling down into the crater crowded with soldiers of the assaulting column, caused the most fearful destruction of life ever witnessed under like circumstances. The groans of the dying and shrieks of the wounded became fearful. . . . "

Sergeant Tunnard briefly chronicled the action of his Louisianians and the Missouri troops, which had fought shoulder to shoulder in the past and "loved each other as brothers. . . . They rushed into the desperate melee unfalteringly, and after a short struggle succeeded in repulsing the enemy with terrible loss." With the embattled Forty-fifth Illinois Regiment, which had borne the brunt of the Union fighting, Wilbur Crummer thought the engagement "a terrible sacrifice," while General Logan, seeing his wounded carried from the crater, exclaimed sorrowfully, "My God! They are killing my best men in that hole!"[18]

As the sun dropped toward the horizon, Tunnard observed that it shrouded its face in a bluish haze, "as if ashamed to shine bright and clear upon such a scene of butchery and bloodshed." Alexander Abrams, a distant observer of the engagement, mistakenly estimated that 400 Federal troops had been killed or wounded in the crater, while Pemberton reported 94 Confederate casualties. The furious action would be recompensed by very little gained on either side. At the end of the savage twenty-four-hour fight, Union troops held tenaciously to a parapet thrown up across the crater, and the Confederates clung to their battered traverse. In between was a meaningless no-man's-land of bodies, blood, and rubble.

In Vicksburg, that hot and blazing Thursday, June 25, had begun like many other mornings. Rowland Chambers found the mortar fire from the river merely a nuisance he was getting used to. But when in midafternoon artillery and rifle fire roared like thunder from the east, followed by the blast of the exploding mine, civilian terror was tempered by resurging hope. Such furious action could mean only one thing: Johnston had crossed the Big Black River and was attacking Grant's forces from the rear.

So it had been predicted by Bob Lowder when he had assured the people that Johnston would arrive in three to five days. Even among the military, Jared Sanders noted, of the great explosion and rifle fire: "All of opinion that Johnston is coming in. May it be so!" The five prophetic days had passed. The liberator had arrived.[19]

Later the truth was learned. The fact that what was probably Grant's last assault on the Confederate defenses—the battle in the crater—had been gallantly repulsed could not override the bitter disappointment. Johnston's Army of Deliverance had not come. It had all been sound and fury, signifying nothing.

That evening, when the tensions of the day had ended, the Lords' cave became, again, a haven of relief, as weary officers came in for relaxation. "One young lieutenant," wrote Lida Lord, "had a beautiful voice, and gave us 'Widow Malone' in fine style. . . . Another, his bosom friend, was an artist, and carved our profiles in bas-relief on the cave walls. . . . So we passed the time trying to be gay, though every face was pale from the recent shock, and every heart heavy with grave anxieties."[20]

Mary Loughborough could not be gay, though she tried to maintain a front. "I am told by my friends, who call, that I am looking worn and pale," she wrote, "and frequently asked if I am not weary of this cave life. I parry the question as well as possible, for I do not like to admit it . . . yet, I *am* tired and weary—ah! So weary!"[21]

All Vicksburg was weary, and though like Mary many were reluctant to admit it, all were fearful of that breaking point beyond which they could not endure. Dora Miller found herself on the ragged edge. Every night she had "lain down expecting death, and every morning rose to the same prospect." Yet she had not broken. But June 25 was "A horrible day—the most horrible yet to me!" And something snapped.

A shell, one of many that had pierced the house in recent days, plunged through two floors into their basement almost shearing off her husband's leg. The cellar was not a refuge but a trap. Before she could fully collect herself, she learned that a neighbor had her thigh bone crushed by fragments of another shell, while her own black servant had had her arm sheared off.

"You must get me out of this horrible place," she shouted to her husband. "I cannot stay; I know I shall be crippled."

Though she would later regret that loss of control, and the look of alarm on her husband's face, it had its effect. Yes, Anderson Miller promised her, he would get her out of the city somehow. For himself, an ablebodied male, it would be impossible to leave. But for a woman, native of the foreign island of Saint Croix, it might be possible. He would see what he could do.[22]

To Rowland Chambers, "The prospects look gloomy." He had been losing sleep for several nights, sitting up with a shotgun to protect his peach orchard and vegetable garden from famished marauders. In the delicate balance between soldiers and civilians in a war-torn city, there was a sad, inevitable conflict between them, in the battle for survival.

The *Daily Citizen* reluctantly reported the case of William ("Big Bill") Porterfield—married to one of Jefferson Davis's nieces and owner of the Porterfield mansion—who had been forced with his shotgun to wound two of three soldiers pillaging his property and kill the third. Neither the *Citizen* nor the authorities condemned Porterfield for this action, though to publisher Swords it emphasized the need for greater discipline among the garrison's officers and greater tolerance among the citizens.[23]

For the Vicksburg garrison, it was the worst of times—the waiting, the weariness, the hunger, not to mention the inaction, for the daily shelling from Porter's fleet was more ritual than action. In fact, the Confederate signal tower on the Devil's Backbone, a hill on the north edge of the city, had long since cracked the admiral's semaphore code and knew beforehand what to expect.

More disheartening was the uncertainty evident among their leaders. They had heard too often that Johnston was coming. Where was Johnston? Pemberton had promised them relief. But there was no relief. In an address to the troops, the general had told his men that they could count upon him never to yield the city and to disregard rumors that he intended "to sell Vicksburg."

When the last pound of beef, bacon and flour, the last grain of corn, the last cow and hog and horse and dog shall have been consumed, and the last man shall have perished in the trenches, then, and only then, will I sell Vicksburg.[24]

Perhaps they could count on his resolve; but they were still anemic, hungry, thirsty. Recorded Colonel Ashbel Smith of the Second Texas Infantry, "The cisterns in the neighborhood being exhausted or forbidden, the men were soon reduced to the sipe [siphoned ?] water got from shallow wells dug in the hollows. This was barely sufficient for our scanty cooking and drinking. Our rations were reduced to little more than sufficient to sustain life. . . . All gradually emaciated and became weak."

It was largely rumor and the gloating imaginations of the Northern press that reported the city surviving on dogs, cats, rats, and mice. Dora Miller, however, noticed that dogs and cats had virtually disappeared from the streets of Vicksburg; she did not know where they had gone. Editor Swords, in the *Citizen*'s social notes, commented on a dinner for eight, shared by friends and pronounced "delicious," that had featured "rabbit" stew. Swords noted pointedly that one of the city's veteran cats had simultaneously disappeared and declared the felines of Vicksburg an endangered species.

No meat, no fresh fruit or vegetables, and a diet of pea bread were nothing strange to Mary Loughborough. She improvised as best she could, but she and her two-year-old daughter were both weak from lack of nourishment. When a kindly soldier brought to their cave a little jay bird to amuse the child, the girl's interest quickly languished and she turned away.

"Miss Mary," said the housemaid, Cynthia, "she's hungry; let me make her some soup from the bird."

It seemed heartless to eat a family pet, but the jay had not yet established itself in that inviolable role, and Mary reluctantly consented. Soon the child was seated before a cup of soup and a dish of delectable white meat which she consumed with innocent relish.[25]

The anguish felt by a mother for her starving young was, perhaps, worse than the pangs of hunger to the child. Annie Harris remembered that, before fleeing Vicksburg, her mother had prepared to spank her for a childish misdemeanor and had seized her by the arm. "As she felt its thinness," wrote Annie, "she burst into tears, and cried out, 'Oh, I cannot, my poor little half-starved child; it is not naughtiness, it is hunger.' "[26]

In the last days of June, 5,900 officers and enlisted men were in hospitals, and many troops who stayed at their posts were ill and suffering from intermittent fever. Malaria and dysentery were commonplace. Cases of highly contagious erysipelas often led to gangrene, for doctors were virtually out of drugs and medicines with which to treat their patients. An epidemic of measles broke out in the city, attacking especially the young, and the recommended antidote was straight corn whiskey. Annie Harris found a dosage of this nostrum "frightful in strength and effect."

Not only food and medicines, but ammunition as well, was running dangerously low. One regiment that might have been considered average could count "only 54 rounds to a man, all told." And in the city, Mary Loughborough witnessed a tragic consequence of this scarcity, as she and her daughter watched two Confederate soldiers dismantling a Parrott shell to salvage the powder. She remembered one of the soldiers well. His name was Henry, and it was he who had given her daughter the pet bird, since unconscionably eaten.

Without warning, the Parrott shell exploded, and the blast was followed by agonized cries. Mary was paralyzed by the scene before her. "Oh, poor Henry! —holding out his mangled arms—the hands torn and hanging from the bleeding, ghastly wrists—a fearful wound in his head—and blood pouring from his wounds." The other soldier was nowhere to be seen; he was found later, mangled and dead, at the bottom of a ravine.[27]

The subterranean war went on. To make it tit for tat, early the next morning the Confederates exploded two of their own mines near the head of Ewing's approach outside the Stockade Redan. The blasts knocked down trench bastions and filled in Federal countermines.

Despite the fact that the explosion at the Third Louisiana Redan had accomplished nothing, Hickenlooper's men began at once on another tunnel to plant another mine beneath the fort. It was the triumph of hope over experience. But Grant was aware that, with Johnston approaching his rear, time was growing short.

On Wednesday, July 1, at 1:00 P.M., the second mine was sprung. "The result," reported division commander Forney, "was the entire demolition of the redan, leaving only an immense chasm where it stood. The greater portion of the earth was thrown toward the enemy, the line of least resistance being in that direction. Our interior line was much uninjured. Nine men who were countermining were necessarily lost, and a large number of those manning the works were killed and wounded." The crater this time was twenty feet deep, and it was estimated that a ton of powder had been used.[28]

Inside the redan, those men working in the central shaft were killed instantly by the blast. One black miner was blown like a cannon ball through the air to drop behind the Union lines, miraculously only bruised. Asked later how far he thought he had traveled, he replied, "Dunno, massa, but t'ink about tree miles." General Logan enlisted the black in his crew of camp custodians.

The explosion was anticipated. The aftermath was a surprise. Confederate troops standing guard at their defense line behind the crater, General Hébert wrote, were "instantly ready to meet the foe and once more teach him that he could not take our works." But the Federal soldiers, as ordered, remained passive in their trenches. "No attempt to charge was made at this time," wrote Grant, "the experience of the 25th admonishing us." His plan was to continue to mine the Confederate works—but he would not risk another assault until the time was ripe.

Meanwhile the last days of June faded out in heat and haze. The lines were close, and drawing ever closer, and conversation between the troops was generally taunting but congenial.

"When are you coming into town, Yank?" was a customary Confederate gibe.

"As soon as you fellows start showing better manners," had been the usual reply. But now, Grant remembered, his men had a more positive answer: "We propose to celebrate the Fourth of July there."

Among themselves, the Union troops discussed at length the time when they might enter Vicksburg. Isaac Jackson thought they would take the place "soon, by storm, if we prepare for it." Osborn Oldroyd was more specific. He pointed out that the army had all the drums and flags and bands they needed for a celebration; hence July 4 would be an appropriate date to raise Old Glory over Vicksburg. He canvassed his regiment on the matter, and all agreed to share a glass of beer in town on Independence Day.[29]

Editor Swords of the *Daily Citizen* seized upon this debate as he did on any other bit of rumor. With all his sources of news dried up, his columns admittedly had become "a rehash of speculation." One of his better efforts in this direction was an account of Robert E. Lee's invasion of the North, now reaching its climax at Gettysburg, but in Swords's account having only just crossed the Potomac.

The Army of Northern Virginia, Swords told his readers, had scattered the Yankees everywhere they met them, "throwing dust on the heels of the panic stricken Federals," and no resistance was anticipated. "Today Maryland is ours, tomorrow Pennsylvania, and the next day Ohio. . . . "

Turning attention to the boasted timetable of the Union troops at Vicksburg, the July 2 *Citizen*—surprinted on wallpaper patterned with green, pink, and yellow flowers—carried the paragraph:

ON DIT: That the great Ulysses—the Yankee Generalissimo, surnamed Grant —has expressed his intention of dining in Vicksburg on Saturday next, and celebrating the 4th of July by a grand dinner and so forth. When asked if he would invite Jo. Johnston to join he said, "No! for fear there will be a row at the table." Ulysses must get into the city before he dines in it. The way to cook a rabbit is "First catch the rabbit," etc.[30]

Grant himself was making no prophecies, abiding by no calendar. He had Vicksburg in his hand for now, surrounded by his troops on three sides, with Porter's gunboats holding the river, and Sherman protecting the rear of the Federal siege line. The next move was not Grant's. Or even Sherman's. It was up to Johnston.

From his headquarters camp near Canton, fifty miles northeast of Vicksburg near the left bank of the Big Black River, General Johnston was explaining to himself and Jefferson Davis the cause of his delay in coming to Pemberton's rescue—principally want of transportation and supplies. Reinforcements arriving by rail, some from as far away as Georgia, had brought only themselves. The general needed wagons, gun carriages, caissons, mules and horses, and provisions, which in the ravaged country around Jackson were difficult to find.

From the first week of June, he had the equivalent of four infantry divisions and one cavalry division, including that of Loring's which had joined him after Champion Hill, a force of 32,000 infantry, artillery, and cavalry. On June 28 he was able to write, "The necessary supplies and field transportation having been procured, the equipment of the artillery completed, and a serviceable floating-bridge finished . . . the army was ordered to march next morning to the Big Black River." Actually, Johnston's army started marching toward Vicksburg on July 1 at a slow pace. By the following day the general had concentrated three of his infantry divisions east of the Big Black River. The fourth, under Major General John C. Breckinridge, was at Bolton. All were within thirty miles of Vicksburg and almost face to face with a portion of Sherman's defense line stretching from the Yazoo to the Big Black railroad bridge.

At this point, Johnston's narrative needs no elaboration. In the light of subsequent events, it tells it all:

This expedition was not undertaken in the wild spirit that dictated the dispatches from the War Department of the 16th and 21st of June. I did not indulge in "the sentiment" that it was better for me to waste the lives and blood of brave soldiers, "than through prudence even," to spare them; and therefore intended to make such close and careful examination of the enemy's lines as might enable me to estimate the probability of our being able to break them, and rescuing the army invested in Vicksburg. There was no hope of saving the place by raising the siege.[31]

So, for the next three days, he would reconnoiter Sherman's lines, particularly north of the Southern Railroad, gather up food and wagons that would be needed for the Vicksburg troops, and decide on a route for their escape and a place of rendezvous with his army. Unsuccessful in finding an opening, Johnston decided on July 5 to scout for feasible crossings of the Big Black River below the bridge.

He did not, meanwhile, expect any further word from Pemberton; there was not enough time between now and the moment of deliverance. And Pemberton, in turn, was uncertain of receiving further word from Johnston. But when the Vicksburg general returned to his quarters the last day in June, he found an unexpected message waiting for him—one that was like the writing on the wall.

❦ 22 ❦

The Glorious Fourth

I T had been slipped under the door of the general's office, during Pemberton's temporary absence—an anonymous letter headed simply AN APPEAL FOR HELP. The first few paragraphs commended the commander for his patriotic leadership and praised the army for "its patient endurance" during the weary weeks of siege—and then continued:

> Everybody admits that we have all covered ourselves in glory, but alas! alas! general, a crisis has arrived . . .
> Our rations have been cut down to one biscuit and a small bit of bacon per day, not enough scarcely to keep soul and body together, . . . there is complaining and general dissatisfaction throughout our lines. . . .
> Men don't want to starve, and don't intend to, but they call upon you for justice, . . . you must adopt some means to relieve us very soon. The emergency of the case demands prompt and decided action on your part.
> If you can't feed us, you had better surrender us, horrible as the idea is, than suffer this noble army to disgrace themselves by desertion. I tell you plainly, men are not going to lie here and perish, if they do love their country dearly. Self preservation is the first law of nature, and hunger will compel a man to do almost anything.
> You had better heed a warning voice, . . . This army is now ripe for mutiny, unless it can be fed.[1]

At the bottom was inscribed: MANY SOLDIERS. But what soldiers? It could be one alienated trooper, or a disgruntled few, or even a plant by an enemy agent seeking to undermine the general's confidence. But Pemberton had long since recognized that he could not keep on forever. He had told Johnston that he could hold the city till July 10. Beyond that date, he was afraid to look.

There was a lot of granite in Pemberton's character, and he read the same endurance into his officers and troops. In his official report of these critical days, he refused to recognize hunger or lack of provisions as major factors in his situation, writing of his army in the first week of July:

> It must be remembered that for forty-seven days and nights these heroic men had been exposed to burning suns, drenching rains, damp fogs, and heavy dews, and

290

that during all this period they never had by day or night the slightest relief. . . . Confined to the narrow limits of a trench, with their limbs cramped and swollen, without exercise, constantly exposed to a murderous storm of shot and shell, while the enemy's unerring sharpshooters stood ready to pick off everyone visible above the parapets, is it strange that the men grew weak and attenuated?[2]

Yet, he insisted, they had "cheerfully encountered danger," borne their hardships with scarcely a murmur, and driven back every assault that the well-fed, well-equipped Federals had launched against their breastworks. That they would continue to do so, he had no doubt. But it was his own compassion and wish to spare them further sacrifice that led him to seek ways to save his army if he could. He drafted a letter to his four division commanders, Forney, Stevenson, Smith, and Bowen, saying essentially the same to each:

GENERAL: Unless the siege of Vicksburg is raised or supplies are thrown in, it will become necessary very shortly to evacuate the place. I see no prospect of the former, and there are many great, if not insuperable, obstacles in the way of the latter. You are, therefore, requested to inform me with as little delay as possible, as to the condition of your troops and their ability to make the marches and undergo the fatigues necessary to accomplish a successful evacuation. . . .[3]

What means he would use to evacuate the city, he did not make clear. The most likely route would be south by the Warrenton Road, as he had suggested earlier to Johnston, thence to team up with Johnston at Hankinson's Ferry, or even join General Gardner at Port Hudson.

On the following day, July 2, the four divisional leaders submitted their replies to his proposal. General Forney, whose troops had been in the center of things throughout the siege, wrote that he concurred "in the unanimous opinion of the brigade commanders, that the physical condition and health of our men are not sufficiently good to enable them to accomplish successfully the evacuation. The spirit of the men is still, however, unshaken, and I am satisfied that they will cheerfully continue to bear the fatigue and privations of the siege."[4]

Other responses were sadly similar. Some of the brigades had been reduced by illness and debilitation to half their normal strength. Hardly a single brigadier general reported his men as capable of undergoing a long fatiguing march, possibly encountering enemy forces, although General Stevenson believed that, in his division, "most of the men, rather than be captured, would exert themselves to the utmost to accomplish it."

That night, after a conference with his commanders, Pemberton drafted the most difficult communication of his life, a letter to Grant which read in part:

GENERAL: I have the honor to propose to you an armistice for several hours, with a view to arranging terms for the capitulation of Vicksburg. To this end, if agreeable to you, I will appoint three commissioners to meet a like number, to be named by yourself, at such place and hour today as you may find convenient.

I make this proposition to save the further effusion of blood, which must

otherwise be shed to a frightful extent, feeling myself fully able to maintain my
position for a yet indefinite period.[5]

He had dated the letter July 3 and would give it to Bowen, hero of Port
Gibson, to deliver under a flag of truce. Bowen had known Grant in the old
days, and later as neighbors in Missouri, and would best know how to talk with
him. Lieutenant Colonel Louis M. Montgomery, Pemberton's aide-de-camp,
would accompany Bowen at nine o'clock the following morning.

Still stubbornly printing his *Daily Citizen* on flowered wallpaper, J. M.
Swords sought as always to buoy Vicksburg's flagging spirits. Things were
looking up, not down. Union General Nathaniel Banks, the editor noted on
July 2, was doing no better against Port Hudson than Grant was doing with
his siege of Vicksburg. "ENEMY TWENTY-FIVE TIMES REPULSED," headlined
the *Citizen*'s report, which stated, "The Federals are despondent, believing
they cannot take Port Hudson by assault."

General Johnston's forces, it was said, had taken possession of the Big Black
River, "driving the Yankees away from it." Kirby Smith's troops were harass-
ing Grant's supply line on the west bank of the Mississippi, and, in the East
—"GLORIOUS INTELLIGENCE!" Robert E. Lee had driven across Maryland into Pennsylvania, and Washington and Baltimore were in a state of
panic.

As for Vicksburg's situation, Swords reminded his readers that "Gen. Pemberton . . . is reported to have stated that he would not surrender our city so
long as there were a mule or dog left on which the men could subsist." And
the editor could attest to the prevalence of mule meat in the city; he had
personally found it "very palatable."

As to the annoying presence of Grant's Yankees, take heart! "Fever, dysentery, and disgust are their companions. . . . The boys are deserting daily,
cussing Grant and abolitionists generally." And in another column Swords
observed that, from the current lassitude of the besieging Federals, "We are
led to the belief that they are sick of the undertaking."[6]

Dora and Anderson Miller found no comfort in these reports, whether they
were true or not. All they wanted was out of this insufferable situation.

Miller finally got a pass to leave the city and secured a boat by which to cross
the Mississippi. But the boat, wrote Dora, "was a miserable, leaky one," and
when it began to founder they started rowing back toward the shore. At that
point a Confederate river battery opened fire on the couple and Dora was
afraid that they would both be killed. They reached shore safely, however, and
the artillery officer apologized; he had not known they had a pass.

So it was back to the cellar again, wrote Dora, "shells flying as thick as ever.
Provisions so nearly gone . . . that a few more days will bring us to starvation
indeed. Martha says rats are hanging dressed in the market for sale with mule
meat,—there is nothing else. . . . We have tried to leave this Tophet and failed,
and if the siege continues I must summon that higher kind of courage—moral
bravery—to subdue my fears of possible mutilation."[7]

Throughout Vicksburg was a sense of watching, waiting, and a blend of
apprehension and anticipation. The feeling that some sort of climax was impending seemed contagious. Rowland Chambers wrote the final entry in the

diary he had begun in June of 1862, when Farragut had threatened Vicksburg: "It is evident that great events will be developed in a very few days."

Courier James H. Pepper also made a final entry in the journal he had started back in May. He had written the day before, "No Johnston yet, and if not soon *we* will have no use for him." Now, on the evening of July 2, he noted: "Quite a stir today. Something to be done soon . . . taken prisoner or relieved next. (God grant the latter.)"

Dr. Joseph Dill Alison, too, closed his journal with the observation, "All the men I have seen today are very much depressed, and look for surrender soon. I am still hopeful and try to keep their spirits up." Vicksburgian Edward S. Gregory observed: "The faith that something would and *must* be done to save the city was desperately clung to till the last."

Sergeant Willie Tunnard's antennae caught the whispers of unbelievable surrender passing through the troops. It was like a dark cloud, he wrote, enveloping them in gloom. And as it grew darker, "the men actually raved at the idea of surrendering, after their long, gallant, and heroic defense. Their spirits were unconquerable."[8]

The suspense was heightened on July 3 when, wrote Margaret Lord, "Early in the morning came the startling news that Generals Pemberton and Bowen with other officers were to have an interview with General Grant. . . . What could it mean? A sickening dread and anxiety filled our hearts."[9] The news seemed confirmed when two mounted officers, one bearing a flag of truce, were seen to leave the Confederate breastworks and ride toward the Union lines.

Their appearance was as bewildering to the Federal troops as to most of the Confederates. Wrote Captain W. H. Claiborne, who had issued a cease-fire order to his troops: "A thousand conjectures and rumors afloat as to the meaning of the flag. Some say it is to send out some prisoners captured a day or two since; others, to point the locality of our hospitals so they will not be fired on; while they again say it is to ask permission to remove the women and children to a place of safety." But, added Claiborne smugly: "*I* know what it means, tho' we have as yet no official information on the subject and the army will know very shortly."[10]

Outside his headquarters tent Grant watched the approaching figures with the flag of truce, but made no move to meet them. He could guess the gist of the message that they carried. And so, he believed, could the rest of the army. He later noted:

> It was a glorious sight to officers and soldiers on the line where those white flags were visible, and the news soon spread to all parts of the command. The troops felt that their long and weary marches, hard fighting, ceaseless watching by night and day in a hot climate, exposure to all sorts of weather, to disease, and, worst of all, to the gibes of many Northern papers that came to them, saying all their suffering was in vain, Vicksburg would never be taken, were at last at an end, and the Union sure to be saved.[11]

General A. J. Smith met the emissaries, and Smith received Pemberton's written proposal. Bowen had expressed to Smith the hope to meet and talk with his old friend, the Federal commander, personally. Grant sent back word that they would renew their friendship after Vicksburg had surrendered, not before. Then he read Pemberton's letter to his staff, without soliciting their comments. He was still "Unconditional Surrender" Grant, and he needed no advice in framing his reply.

He rejected Pemberton's suggestion that commissioners be chosen from both sides to discuss terms. There were no terms to discuss. He told the Vicksburg commander: "The useless profusion of blood you propose stopping by this course can be ended at any time you may choose, by the unconditional surrender of the city and garrison. Men who have shown so much endurance and courage as those now in Vicksburg will always challenge the respect of an adversary, and I can assure you will be treated with all the respect due to prisoners of war."[12]

With this written note, he sent to Bowen a verbal message, saying that if Pemberton so desired, Grant would meet him in front of McPherson's corps at three o'clock that afternoon.

Precisely at that hour Grant, accompanied by corps commanders Ord and McPherson and division commanders Logan and A. J. Smith—Sherman being some twelve miles east, watching out for Johnston—waited near a stunted oak between the lines. Pemberton arrived with Bowen and Montgomery, seemingly in a belligerent and peevish mood. Eavesdropping nearby, Charles Dana observed that the Confederate commander "was much excited and impatient in his answers to Grant." The interview was off to a bad start.

Yet Dana analyzed Pemberton's feelings with compassion, writing,

> Penned up and finally compelled to surrender a vital post and a great army to his conqueror, an almost irremediable disaster to his cause, Pemberton not only suffered the usual pangs of defeat, but he was doubly humiliated by the knowledge that he would be suspected and accused of treachery by his adopted brethren, and that the results would be used by the enemies of Davis, whose favorite he was, to undermine the Confederate administration.[13]

With the two leaders appearing to get nowhere in their dialogue—Pemberton remarking at one point that further talk was useless, and Grant agreeing—their respective subordinates, Bowen and Montgomery, Smith and McPherson, were given the task of carrying on negotiations and arriving at acceptable terms. Grant and Pemberton meanwhile sat beneath the oak tree, the Union general chomping on his unlit cigar, Pemberton chewing on a blade of grass, and neither speaking. The oak tree, Grant recorded later, was afterwards chopped up for souvenirs, producing more chips of memorable wood than did the True Cross.

Bowen's subsequent proposal that "the Confederate army should be allowed to march out with the honors of war, carrying their small arms and field artillery," was summarily rejected by Grant. The conference disbanded, with Grant declaring that he would send his final terms to Pemberton that evening, and the Confederate general promising an immediate reply. In the interval, all hostilities would cease.

Hostilities, from all appearances, had already ceased. Surveying the scene from the fortifications, Confederate Colonel Robert S. Bevier remembered:

Now the two armies stood up and gazed at each other with wondering eyes. Winding around the crests of hills—in ditches and trenches hitherto undreamed of by us—one long line after another started into view, looking like huge blue snakes coiling around the ill-fated city. They were amazed at the paucity of our numbers; we were astonished at the vastness of theirs.

With the parallels of both sides pushed, in many places, within twenty feet of one another, Bevier observed:

Conversation was easy, and while the leaders were in consultation, the men engaged in the truly national occupation of "swapping" whatever our poor boys could muster to stake a "dicker" on for coffee, sugar and whisky. None supposed the result of the official interview would be the striking of our gallant flag, and when that *was* known, the curses of our men were both loud and deep.[14]

That night Grant called for a meeting of all his corps and division commanders, which he characterized as his nearest approach to a council of war. The terms he proposed submitting to Pemberton were a departure from his policy of unconditional surrender. The Confederate garrison would not be treated as prisoners of war, but would all receive paroles, on their honor not to take up arms against the Union until properly exchanged. Officers would be allowed to keep their side arms and their private property. Mounted officers would retain one horse apiece.

The offer of parole was generous, but not without advantages to Grant. To guard and ship so many prisoners to distant parts of the Union would tie up much of his army's strength and means of transportation, just when he needed both to hurl new blows against the Confederacy.

Moreover, he later wrote, the Confederates had fought so well that "I did not want to humiliate them. I believed that consideration for their feelings would make them less dangerous foes during the continuance of hostilities and better citizens after the war was over." He also secretly believed that the average soldier in the Vicksburg garrison was so weary of the fighting that, even though paroled, he would not be eager to take up arms again.[15]

The collective terms as sent to Pemberton provided that, following Pemberton's acceptance, Grant would march into the city at eight o'clock the following morning, with one division, and begin parole procedures. The Confederates would meanwhile post white flags along their breastworks, both to indicate acceptance of the terms and to prevent any renewal of firing between the troops.

Receiving this letter around ten that evening, Pemberton summoned his generals into conference. The consensus was that these were probably the best terms they could get—better, perhaps, than had been hoped for. Two brigade commanders still advocated holding on, or cutting their way out. Presenting his own opinion, South Carolinian Stephen D. Lee stated emphatically: "I do not think it is time to surrender this garrison and post yet. Nor do I think it practicable to cut our way out. . . . I still have hopes of Johnston relieving the garrison."[16]

Accepting the majority decision, Pemberton himself had one reservation, held "in justice to the honor and spirit of my troops, manifested in the defense of Vicksburg." The men had vowed that no Union soldier would set foot in

Vicksburg while they manned the parapets. Therefore, Grant was not to march into the city, as proposed. Instead, the Confederate garrison would march out in military formation, at 10:00 A.M., carrying their rifles and regimental flags, and stack their arms outside the lines. With the city evacuated, Grant could then march in and take possession.

It was perhaps a minor point, but one with major symbolic significance, and Grant, humanely aware of this, wrote back his acceptance of these conditions, with the understanding that Confederate troops would then return behind the defense perimeter and remain there until paroled. Both had yielded a little in the negotiations; yet Pemberton, in reality, had lost everything—even his honor in the eyes of some.

Had he any choice? Colonel Allen Thomas of the Twenty-eighth Louisiana, who was present at that last war conference in Vicksburg, summarized the Confederate predicament. The garrison had been reduced by illness and starvation to scarcely 11,000 effective troops. They were hopelessly lacking in rations and small-arms ammunition. There were not enough horses to haul the artillery.

The troops had not the physical strength to cut their way out. They had no assurance that Johnston was coming—or would ever come—to their assistance. Their capture was only a matter of time, and in the interval more lives would be sacrificed to no avail. And Thomas paid tribute to the one man who would lose the most from these compelling circumstances:

> The capitulation was, therefore, universally assented to; and I am sure there was not an officer present—and there were not a few who were heroes of many hard-fought fields—but was convinced that General Pemberton had done all that the most exalted patriotism, or the most punctilious soldierly honor, could have demanded.[17]

Isaac Jackson, like most of Grant's troops, had been aware of the negotiations going on. All, including the Confederates on the breastworks, had seen the white flags of the emissaries, and the conference of officers between the lines. "The Rebs & us had quite a holiday on the third, no firing the whole day . . . parties met between the forts and had quite a social time indeed."[18] Though they fraternized freely, the word "surrender" remained unspoken. Instead, according to James Wilson, the troops exchanged good-natured gibes. From the Confederates a common question: "Yank, why don't you all make a general assault and end this thing?" Or: "When are you going to attack again and close up this siege?"

And a common answer: "Don't be impatient, Johnny, we are in no hurry. We are just guarding prisoners and it would be inhuman to fire on them unless they undertake to break out." There were repeated Union promises to celebrate the Fourth of July with their Southern brethren—inside the city.[19]

In Vicksburg, "No one seemed to know," wrote Mary Loughborough, "why a truce had been made; but all believed that a treaty of surrender was pending. Nothing was talked about among the officers but the all engrossing theme. Many wished to cut their way out and make the risk their own; but I secretly hoped that no such bloody hazard would be attempted."[20]

The McRaes, whose abandoned house was occupied by Colonel Allen

Thomas and a few staff officers, were in a position to know more than Mrs. Loughborough as to what was going on. "On the evening of the 3d of July," wrote Lucy McRae, "all was quiet; people could be seen walking around, concluding that the silence meant dreadful things on the morrow."

> We were sitting outside the cave, twilight approaching, when father came in sight. Mother thought father had decided to die with his family the next day, for everybody thought that Grant would make the effort of his life to take the city on the 4th. Father came to mother, looking sad, with tears in his eyes, and said, "You can all come home for a night's rest. General Pemberton has surrendered, and General Grant will enter the city in the morning."[21]

All knew before they slept that night, in homes or caves or trenches, that the unconquerable city had surrendered.

In the hot and hazy hours of the early morning, in a silence so intense that it was almost audible, Sergeant Charles Wilcox recorded in his diary:

> Saturday, July 4th—This day in American history is only second to the one of which today is the eighty-seventh anniversary. The fate of the American Republic has positively been decided this day. . . . The heart bereaved by the loss of a husband, brother or son in the battle for Vicksburg, will forget its sorrow. All will sing "Hallelujah!" "The heroic city has fallen!" "Vicksburg is ours!"[22]

With General Smith's division, in almost the center of the Union siege line, Isaac Jackson noted:

> About 10 o'clock, from where we were, we could see the Stars & Stripes floating on a Rebel fort on our left. Then on the next, a white flag appeared. We now knew that the forts were ours. And as the white emblem appeared on fort after fort, from left to right, the cheering went up from crowds opposite the different forts. This was the most Glorious Fourth I ever spent.[23]

To Sergeant William Tunnard, the Glorious Fourth was a day of mortification. Members of the Third Louisiana Infantry expressed themselves in "a fearful outburst of anger." To surrender on this, of all days, was the ultimate humiliation. Many smashed their rifles against the trunks of trees and scattered their ammunition over the ground. Rather than yield their battle flags, they tore them in pieces and passed around the shreds for souvenirs.[24]

In general, however, the gray- and butternut-clad troops comported themselves with military rectitude. Mounted on horseback, John Clifford Pemberton, tall, immaculate, erect, rode past in review of his troops. Then, promptly at 10:00 A.M., wrote Colonel Thomas Waul of the Texas Legion, "The command marched out of the intrenchments with their colors flying and band playing." Outside the lines they stood in formation, saluted their colors, and stacked their arms.

All down the eight-mile front, regiment after regiment followed suit in perfect discipline. However emaciated and fatigued, the men held their heads erect, ranks steady, footsteps firm. They carried their colors high, although William Chambers noticed one soldier with his regimental flag wrapped around his waist as if only death would part him from it. Brigade Commander F. A. Shoup thought he read in the sad faces of the men the message, "This is pretty bad, but we can stand it."[25]

For their part, the Federal soldiers watched them pass with undisguised respect and sympathy. Many were tempted to salute; this being barred, they showed their emotions in other ways. Samuel Lockett recalled that "a hearty cheer was given by one Federal division 'for the gallant defenders of Vicksburg!' " For the most part, however, there was little cheering, no triumphant exaltation. Only an almost reverential silence that seemed to toll like muted bells above a fallen foe.

It was only when, without flags or rifles or marching bands, they returned behind the lines that the Confederates gave way to their emotions. A war correspondent had written from the battlefields of Vicksburg, "the dying never weep." But now, in this dying city, "some of us wept," confessed William Chambers, "for we realized that this was the end of all our sacrifices. . . . Thus perished the glory so dearly won—thus had fallen the Confederate Saragossa."

Wrote Chambers elsewhere in his diary, "I realized more forcibly than I had ever done before, the strategic importance of the position we held, and the magnitude of its loss to the Confederacy. . . . oh, how burned the haggard cheek with shame and indignation to realize that on *that* day of all others Vicksburg should be surrendered! Why could not the deed have been consummated yesterday or tomorrow."[26]

Lucy McRae remembered of that morning of the Fourth:

> . . . how sad was the spectacle that met our gaze: arms stacked in the center of the streets, men with tearful eyes and downcast faces walking here and there; men sitting in groups feeling that they would gladly have given their life-blood on the battlefield rather than hand over the guns and sabers so dear to them!

The instruments of the band of a Tennessee regiment were piled on the corner in front of the McRae house, and the drummerboy gave his drum to Lucy's brother rather than have the Federals take it from him. Another soldier gave the McRaes his horse, with the initials "C. S." branded on its flanks, and Lucy's brothers hid it in the yard. Both the drum and the horse disappeared after the Union soldiers came.[27]

Mary Loughborough remembered her husband coming to the cave that morning and telling her: "It's all over! The white flag floats from our forts! Vicksburg has surrendered!" Then the captain hurried off, presumably to join his regiment. Mary went to the door of the cave, where she happened to see an old gray-headed soldier pass.

He stopped, touched his hat, and said: "It's a sad day this, madam; I little thought we'd come to it, when we first stopped in the intrenchments. I hope you'll yet be happy, madam, after all the trouble you've seen." To which Mary responded, "Amen."[28]

All was strangely quiet outside the cave where Dora Richards Miller had been guest for the night. She started back to her home and ran into editor Swords of the *Citizen,* who told her "the last shell has been thrown into Vicksburg; it is surrender." Back in her house, she found a group of wan

Confederate soldiers hopefully waiting for scraps of food, something that she had grown accustomed to.

"Good morning, madam," one said to her; "we won't bother you much longer." He thanked her warmly for the morsels from her kitchen which, he alleged, had helped to keep some of them alive.

"Is it true about the surrender?" Dora asked.

"Yes . . . and the men in Vicksburg will never forgive Pemberton. An old granny! A child would have known better than to shut men up in this cursed trap to starve to death like useless vermin."

Dora observed the fury that burned in the soldier's eyes as he said to her: "Haven't I seen my friends carted out three or four in a box, that died of starvation! Nothing else, madam! Starved to death because we had a fool for a general."

But like Dora's dissembling husband, Anderson Miller, Pemberton was a native Yankee, and perhaps for that reason she came to his defense. Wasn't the soldier being rather hard on him? she asked. Wasn't it Pemberton's duty to sit tight and wait for Johnston?

"Some people may excuse him, ma'am, but we'll curse him to our dying day."[29]

Though Margaret, Willie, and Lida Lord were able to leave their cave for good and return home, Mrs. Lord found little consolation on that "saddest of days." For, "All the weary way home, I wept incessantly, meeting first one group of soldiers and then another, many of them with tears streaming down their faces." She found the rectory "a scene of desolation you can hardly imagine," some rooms destroyed, all damaged, not a pane of glass remaining in the windows. But this, she wrote, was of comparatively little matter, for

> Our poor soldiers came in a continuous stream past the house, so pale, so emaciated, and so grief stricken, panting with the heat and Oh! saddest of all, without their colors and arms. . . . We all congregated on the piazzas with buckets of water to quench their thirst and their "God bless you, ladies," and "nothing but starvation whipped us" could be heard on all hands.[30]

Along with the hordes of the disconsolate, the soldiers of defeat, another spectral band emerged, as if rising from the grave. One by one, then in pairs, then by scores and hundreds, the cave dwellers came back into the air. Pale, gaunt women and children, old men stooped over by confinement, blinked their eyes at the unaccustomed daylight and looked about them, in stunned disbelief, at the cratered hillsides and the ruined buildings.

Many did not realize they had been so close to the trenches and the fighting. They filled the streets leading to the center of the town, like an army of refugees, bent beneath bundles of bedding, pots and pans, and other accouterments of meager living. In long columns they trudged back to their homes—fearful of what they might find when they arrived.

Shortly before noon Dora and Anderson Miller saw a Union flag rise over the cupola of the court house and wave slowly in the breeze. Miller drew a long sigh of relief. "Now I feel once more at home in mine own country," he declared.

Soon Logan's division, selected to lead the occupying forces, marched into the city, banners streaming, bands playing "Yankee Doodle," bayonets and sabers shining bright, and the horses of the officers prancing. Few civilians watched their coming. "You may be sure," wrote Margaret Lord, "that none of us raised our eyes to see the flag of the enemy. . . . Every house was closed and every house filled with weeping inmates and mourning hearts."

Dora Miller, however, watched the entrance of the Union army with relief and admiration:

> What a contrast to the suffering creatures we had seen so long were these stalwart, well-fed men, so splendidly set-up and accoutered. Sleek horses, polished arms, bright plumes,—this was the pride and panoply of war. Civilization, discipline, and order seemed to enter with the measured tramp of these marching columns. . . .[31]

Witnessing "this embodiment of modern power," Dora felt a "fervent gratitude" that her Vicksburg ordeal was over and she herself remained unscathed among the widows and the wounded.

Grant—who would later write, "the fate of the Confederacy was sealed at Vicksburg"—rode toward the city with James Wilson and his staff and stopped as a matter of courtesy at the Rock House, where Pemberton and some of his officers were sitting on the porch. Wrote Wilson, "They were received with the coldest formality. No one even offered Grant a seat, and when he asked for a glass of water a member of the Confederate staff merely told him where he could find it. The situation was trying in the extreme. . . . "

Three Confederate officers, however, including Samuel Lockett, were "polite and courteous," Wilson remembered, "in recognition of which their haversacks and canteens were well filled with provisions and whiskey when they bade us goodbye."[32]

All eyes now turned to the Mississippi River, as Grant rode to the city wharf, to greet and congratulate Admiral Porter. The fleet, as it passed in review, presented a spectacle that even loyal citizens admired. Wrote Lucy McRae: "The inspiring grandeur of gunboat after gunboat, transport after transport, with flags flying to the breeze, broadside after broadside belching forth in honor of a victory dearly won, bands playing, made a picture that can never fade from memory."[33]

Once the formalities were over, the men of both armies began to mix freely in a newfound camaraderie, with little distinction between the victors and the vanquished. William Chambers noted that he heard not a single Yankee boast of having "taken Vicksburg." Rather, he heard many praise the Confederates for their "wonderful defense." When her husband returned after the surrender ceremonies, he told Mary Loughborough that "the Federal troops had acted splendidly," far different from what he had expected. Not a jeer or taunt came from any of the troops in blue, rather a good deal of empathy as bygones became bygones.

Union soldiers shared their supplies with hungry Confederates. "I myself," wrote Grant, "saw our men taking bread from their haversacks and giving it to the enemy they had so recently been engaged in *starving* out. It was accepted with avidity and thanks."[34] And on every street corner, the blue and gray troops exchanged mementoes and experiences of the campaign. A Union rifleman recognized Samuel Lockett as the man he had seen riding up and down the Confederate lines on tours of inspection.

"See here, Mister," he shouted, "you on the little white horse! Danged if you ain't the hardest feller to hit I ever saw; I've shot at you more'n a hundred times."[35]

Though Grant had refused Pemberton's demand to guarantee the safety of civilians, private homes and property were generally respected. There was little looting, as at Jackson. But when the Federal troops were told that speculators had been hoarding flour, wines, and spirits to be sold at exorbitant prices, Willie Tunnard was pleased to notice:

> A retributive justice speedily descended upon the speculators, as the Federals broke open their stores, completely plundering them. The Southerners looked on this work of destruction with something akin to satisfaction, and felt as if a portion of their wrongs were avenged.
>
> Wines for which the sick had pined in vain, were brought to light; luxuries of various kinds were found in profusion. The Federals brought them into the streets, and throwing them down, would shout, "here, rebs, help yourselves, you are naked and starving and need them." What a strange spectacle of war between those who were recently deadly foes.[36]

Isaac Jackson almost missed the excitement in the city. His regiment was on standby orders, to be ready to join Sherman's forces in pursuit of Johnston. "But," wrote Isaac, "I was bound to see the place we had been trying to get to for 6 months, so I put out about noon and 'went to town.' " He found the city "a desolate looking place," and the Confederate soldiers a sad-looking lot:

> They were nearly starved. I was talking with one who had been eating mule meat for four days & but one biscuit a day for over a week. This is a fact. It looked hard to see the poor fellow pitch into our "hard tack" which our boys gave them, we had plenty, and they carried them off by armloads. Poor fellows, they needed them.[37]

Jackson talked with some little girls who had lived in a cave throughout the siege, on mule meat, peas, and corn. They pleaded with him for a bit of cheese or candy, which he did not have but promised to bring when he returned— knowing sadly that he could not keep that promise. Grant had already sent instructions to Sherman to "go for Joe Johnston," destroy his army or drive him from the state, and Sherman had ordered his troops "to give one big huzza and sling the knapsacks for new fields."[38]

It was not all over—not, in any event, the campaign for the Mississippi Valley. Johnston would have to be eliminated as a threat in Mississippi, and most of the troops which had manned the siege line would join Sherman's forces in pushing the Confederate general back toward Jackson. Port Hudson, though invested by Banks's army, was still holding out, although General Gardner had heard of the July Fourth victory salutes from Porter's river fleet, and knew then that the game was up. It was only a matter of time—five days, as it turned out—before his depleted and starving garrison would be forced into surrender.

But for Grant the immediate task was done. It had not been too costly a victory for what was gained. He estimated his losses in men, from the time he began marching down the west side of the Mississippi to the fall of Vicksburg, to be a bit over 10,000 killed, wounded, and missing, about half this number lost at Vicksburg. Confederate casualties during the same period had been thousands less, but far greater in ratio to the size of Pemberton's army.

In addition, the surrender of Vicksburg yielded 172 Confederate cannon, 60,000 stands of arms—many rifles superior to those in the Union army—and quantities of artillery ammunition. This, along with 29,500 prisoners, the largest army ever captured in the active phase of the war, the largest so far in American history.[39]

But statistics told only a part of the story. With the fall of Vicksburg and the subsequent surrender of Port Hudson, the entire Mississippi River was in Federal hands, never to be relinquished. As Lincoln remarked, "The Father of Waters again goes unvexed to the sea." The Southern states west of the river were now isolated; men and supplies from that region would no longer be on call from Richmond. The Confederacy was split in two, a mortal wound from which the South could not recover.

A thousand miles away at Gettysburg, General Robert E. Lee expressed the Confederacy's feelings on that fateful day—when the white flags waved at Vicksburg and Lee's all-out assault on Cemetery Ridge had failed. "This has been a sad, sad day for us," said the Virginia general to cavalry officer John Imboden. "Too bad! *Too bad!* OH! TOO BAD!"[40]

Yet essentially Lee had been only checked in Pennsylvania; the tide in the East may have turned, but his army would survive to fight again. At Vicksburg, the heart of half a nation had stopped beating. "Yesterday," wrote General Josiah Gorgas, chief of ordnance for the Confederacy, "we rode on the pinnacle of success—today absolute ruin seems to be our portion. The Confederacy totters to its destruction."[41]

J. M. Swords would publish no more editions of the *Daily Citizen*. With the occupation of Vicksburg by Grant's army, he had fled the city for parts unknown. In his printing shop, Federal troops found the type still standing from the issue of July 2, with its gibe at Grant's intention to dine in Vicksburg on July 4: "The way to cook a rabbit is first catch the rabbit." Union soldiers therewith ran off another printing of the same edition, with one important paragraph added at the bottom, headlined NOTE:

July 4th, 1863

Two days bring about great changes. The banner of the Union floats over Vicksburg. Gen. Grant has "caught the rabbit"; he has dined in Vicksburg, and he did bring his dinner with him. The "Citizen" lives to see it. For the last time it appears on "Wall-paper." No more will it eulogize the luxury of mule-meat and fricassed [sic] kitten—urge Southern warriors to such diet never more. This is the last wall-paper edition, and is, excepting this note, from the types as we found them. It will be valuable hereafter as a curiosity.[42]

❧ 23 ❧

In the Wake of the Storm

I T was all over—except for Joe Johnston's army east of the city, and Port Hudson holding on precariously 240 miles downriver.

With Vicksburg's collapse, there was no hope left for Franklin Gardner's garrison, already pounded and starved to near submission after more than forty days of siege. On July 9 Gardner surrendered Port Hudson to Nathaniel Banks, and the Union troops walked into the citadel they had been trying to subdue by force since late May.[1]

It took Sherman's troops less than a week to drive Joe Johnston back into the Mississippi capital, which, after a brief stay, the Confederates evacuated on July 16. Then Sherman pulled back from Jackson to his former position on the Big Black River, there to encamp for a two-month respite after the arduous campaign. Grant remained for the summer in Vicksburg, headquartering in the William Lum house beyond the southern edge of town, to superintend the city's military and civilian needs.

Though they might be geographically separated in the months ahead, Grant and Sherman were more than ever a team, and one that would, in large degree, decide the outcome of the war. They had learned much about military strategy, much about each other, in the Vicksburg campaign, and now, wrote Sherman, "We were as brothers—I the older man in years, he the higher in rank. We both believed in our heart of hearts that the success of the Union cause was not only necessary to the then generation of Americans, but to all future generations."[2]

That fall Grant sent Sherman's divisions north in support of Rosecrans and, himself, took over command of Union troops around Chattanooga. Appointed general in chief of all Federal forces, he relinquished command of the Army of the Tennessee to Sherman. In May 1864 the teammates began their joint, deadly thrusts at the dismembered Confederacy, Grant setting his sights for Lee in Virginia, Sherman marching through Georgia to Atlanta and the sea.

In Georgia, Joseph Johnston once again faced his former rival, Sherman, and did his best to outwit the Union general with his skillful Fabian tactics. But, in the background, smoldered his feud with Jefferson Davis. At a critical point before Atlanta, Davis replaced him with John Bell Hood. By then one of the best-loved generals in the Southern army, Johnston's removal was a crushing disappointment to the troops. When Hood was defeated around Atlanta and later for good and all at Nashville, the once magnificent Army of Tennessee (not to be confused with the Union Army of *the* Tennessee) chanted in retreat:

> *And now I'm going southward*
> *For my heart is full of woe*
> *I'm going back to Georgia,*
> *To find my "Uncle Joe." ³*

Johnston, however, regainèd command of the Army of Tennessee and fought Sherman to the bitter end in North Carolina. Two and a half weeks after Appomattox, the two met face to face at Hillsboro, in an atmosphere of "extreme cordiality" and mutual admiration. Sherman proposed, and Johnston accepted, the same terms of surrender that Grant offered General Lee. Kirby Smith fell in line in May and yielded the Trans-Mississippi region to the Union.

In Johnston's later-published *Narrative of Military Operations* and in Pemberton's "Official Report" of the siege of Vicksburg, both leaders sought to place the blame for Vicksburg on the faulty vision of the other. Objectively, the Pennsylvania general emerges as the more ill-used of the two, and as one of the tragic figures of the Civil War. Ill-starred by his Yankee birth, constantly under undeserved suspicion, he did his best with what he had. Davis never doubted his loyalty, and Marmaduke Shannon, in August, published a moving tribute to Vicksburg's late defender.

After being "paroled" by Grant in Vicksburg and instructed to report to his superior, Pemberton finally caught up with Johnston seated on a knoll outside his Mississippi camp. Of that meeting with the Virginia general who had seemingly deserted him, Pemberton's grandson wrote:

> Unheralded, and of a sudden coming up the hill toward him, Johnston observed "a tall, handsome, dignified figure." He sprang up to greet the officer now recognized, extended his hand, saying in the meantime, "Well, Jack old boy, I am certainly glad to see you."
>
> The proffered hand, unclasped, was slowly lowered as Johnston's staff saw Pemberton salute his superior officer punctiliously, pause for the barest second and reply, "General Johnston, according to the terms of parole prescribed by General Grant, I was directed to report to you, sir!"
>
> Both stood motionless, and in silence. Then Pemberton saluted once more and turned away. It was the last meeting for these two.⁴

The South needed a scapegoat for the fall of Vicksburg, and a court of inquiry was proposed to investigate his role in the affair. Due to the exigencies of war, the court never assembled. Pemberton, however, resigned his commission as lieutenant general, later to accept a lesser rank as lieutenant colonel of artillery in the defense of Richmond. Meanwhile he had had a chance to visit his wife and children, after four months of separation, in their refugee home in Gainesville, Alabama.

With tired steps the general approached the unfamiliar house, to see his thirteen-year-old daughter Patty playing in the yard. He stretched out his arms to her, but she backed away with no sign of recognition, only a questioning expression in her eyes. Who was this old man with the thin face and the snow-white hair? Surely not her father. Her father's hair was black; and besides, he was a much younger man.[5]

Union General John A. McClernand would never forget the injustice he felt had been dealt him at Vicksburg by Grant and President Lincoln. Early in 1864 he finally regained command of the Thirteenth Corps, then scattered in Louisiana and Texas. Shortly after his entry into the Red River Campaign, he became sick and returned to Illinois to recover. Still plagued by health problems he resigned his commission on November 30, 1864. In subsequent years McClernand was active in politics in Illinois and continued to write bitter critiques of his one-time commander, General Grant.

Of James Birdseye McPherson, commander of the Seventeenth Corps at Vicksburg, Sherman had written, "If he lives, he'll outdistance Grant and myself . . . the best hope for a great soldier." McPherson would not have a chance to prove or disprove that prediction. During the Battle of Atlanta in the summer of 1864, he was reconnoitering the Union lines, when "The sound of musketry was heard, and McPherson's horse came back, bleeding, wounded, and riderless." McPherson's body was later found with a bullet through the chest.[6]

Admiral Farragut, once Port Hudson fell and the Mississippi was secure, returned to the Gulf and directed his efforts toward taking Mobile Bay, in conjunction with Union infantry—thus slicing off another piece of the Confederacy. It was at Mobile Bay, approaching the two defending forts, that Farragut gave his famous order, "Damn the torpedoes, full speed ahead!" Fitting his action to the words, he turned a near disaster into victory. He was named vice admiral in 1864 and admiral in 1866.

David Dixon Porter, having received the thanks of the Congress for "opening the Mississippi river," cooperated with Nathaniel Banks in the Red River expeditions of early 1864. Thereafter, as he was made head of the North Atlantic Blockading Squadron, Porter's fleet assisted the army in capturing Fort Fisher in North Carolina. After the war, he became superintendent of the United States Naval Academy at Annapolis and later "adviser" to the secretary of the navy, under President Grant.

The services of the former music master Benjamin Grierson and his cavalry were, after Port Hudson surrendered, in immediate demand from both General Banks and Grant. Grant summoned the brigadier general to Vicksburg and made him chief of cavalry of the Sixteenth Army Corps.

But the man who hated horses suffered malicious retribution. Boarding a steamer to conduct his men to Tennessee, Grierson was kicked in the knee by a horse and suffered his most serious wound of the war. Returning on crutches to Jacksonville, Illinois, to recuperate, he was given a musical ovation by his former concert band and was lauded by speakers as a cavalry leader who had "far more in him than *bugle blowing.*"[7]

James Wilson's career after Vicksburg was little short of meteoric. Essentially an engineer till then, he found his future in the burgeoning glory of the Union cavalry. Following Grant to Chattanooga and then Virginia, he was assigned at Grant's request to Philip Sheridan's command in 1864.

"I believe he will add fifty percent to the effectiveness of your cavalry," Grant later wrote to Sherman. Wilson fulfilled that promise. Given command of mounted forces in the West, he twice routed the hard-riding troopers of Nathan Bedford Forrest, in what his biographer termed "the longest and greatest cavalry movement in the Civil War."[8]

John Rawlins, too, would rise in rank and responsibility in accordance with the rise of Grant. But, during that summer in Vicksburg, there was an interruption. He met the bewitching Mary Hurlburt of Danbury, Connecticut, who was serving as governess to Annie Harris. "The courteous Rawlins," according to Annie, "courted her so assiduously and ardently, that she changed the hated enemy into a beloved husband when peace was proclaimed."

Rawlins, doomed by consumption, was never far from Grant's side in the final years. Grant was instrumental in securing his promotion to brigadier general, and in 1865 he became chief of staff of the regular army. When Grant was elected President in 1868, Rawlins served as his secretary of war before his untimely death in 1869.[9]

Charles Anderson Dana followed General Grant to Chattanooga, the Wilderness, the siege of Petersburg, and Appomattox. His admiration and friendship for the general increased, and he helped achieve for Grant the latter's appointment to lieutenant general. After a two-year stint as assistant secretary of war under Stanton, Dana in 1868 became proprietor of the New York *Sun* which effectively supported Grant's election to the Presidency.[10]

Like Dana, Sylvanus Cadwallader stayed close to Grant through his subsequent battles and campaigns. He was beside the general near Appomattox, when Lee's first surrender note arrived and Grant's expression was as revealing as "last year's bird nest."[11] Switching his allegiance from the Chicago *Times* to the New York *Herald,* Cadwallader's reports of the last days of the Confederacy and the subsequent era of reconstruction are among the best accounts of that turbulent period.

Of the men in the ranks, inside and outside Vicksburg, few would go on to such glory, squalor, bloodshed, and excitement as they had known that spring and summer. Many Confederates, as Grant had surmised in allowing the parole, took off for their homes to avoid exchange and further service in the Southern armies. Soon the crops would be ripening, and there was work to be done on the farms and plantations. Besides, they had had enough of the war. Vicksburg and Mississippi were now in the Union; what many had fought for was already lost.

On July 11, one week after the surrender, the paroled Confederate army marched out of Vicksburg with Pemberton riding in the lead. They were headed for parole camps in Alabama and Mississippi, but most were furloughed for a short period before these camps were reached. Some slipped away and deserted; others diverged from the column and gorged themselves on the bountiful produce of the countryside. One succumbed to this gluttony and was buried by the roadside, with a warning marker at the grave site, "Died from eating too much green corn."

Sergeant William Tunnard eventually found himself exchanged along with others of the Vicksburg garrison, for a like number of Federal prisoners. A year after the surrender of Vicksburg, he was back in the ranks of the Third

Louisiana Infantry. Encamped first near Alexandria, later Shreveport, Louisiana, Tunnard never saw serious action again. After the war, he made use of his literary flair to become, at different times, editor of the Shreveport *Times* and the Shreveport *Journal.* [12]

Like the sergeant, William Chambers also found himself exchanged. In December he was at Dalton, Georgia, with Johnston's Army of Tennessee, battling Sherman's march from Chattanooga to Atlanta. Wounded near Atlanta, Chambers returned to Mississippi, where he later married, resumed his teaching, and became a poet and writer of considerable note—still asking himself in his diary, of the struggle for Vicksburg, "What was it all about?"[13]

Jared Young Sanders, after the surrender, sought to return to the family plantation in St. Mary's Parish but found it in enemy-occupied territory. As soon as exchanged, he rejoined the Twenty-sixth Louisiana Infantry to fight in Georgia in the campaign for Atlanta, which ended with Hood's defeat in Tennessee. Disheartened and at loose ends, Sanders tried unsuccessfully to organize a company of cavalry, then again rejoined his regiment in Alexandria, Louisiana, writing at the time, "Oh, war, war, how I hate Ye!"[14]

Sanders's commander, Colonel Winchester Hall, was still convalescing from his leg wound and unable to leave Vicksburg. Hall's friend of prewar days, Union General William Orme, called on the family and found the colonel, his wife, and four children in "destitute circumstances."

Orme offered to help but was politely turned down. "They are a proud people," he wrote to his wife, equating the Halls with Southerners in general, "and do not like to appear asking for anything."[15] Returning to civilian life, Hall served as a judge in Louisiana and in the state legislature, before moving to New York to resume his legal practice.

Sergeant Charles Wilcox of the Thirty-third Illinois Infantry, who had hoped for promotion after his company's success at Vicksburg, achieved his goal in a signal way. That September he resigned from the regiment to accept the captaincy of Company B, Ninety-second United States Colored Infantry. He remained with the Negro troops till the end of the war, when he took over a home colony for blacks on Braxton Bragg's plantation in Louisiana, under the auspices of the Freedmen's Bureau.[16]

Hugh Moss, after the surrender, turned his sights homeward and, with fourteen other Confederate parolees, walked "step after step with sore limbs and blistering feet" to the lower reaches of the Big Black River. They passed Yankee pickets who waved them on congenially, were entertained at Southern plantations as heroes even in defeat, and via the Mississippi reached southwestern Louisiana.

Moss found his native village of Lake Charles aswarm with extravagantly dressed, top-hatted blacks "strutting about as proud as peacocks," and wondered, "What will befall the Nation!" If exchanged, would he fight for the South again? A clue appears in the last entry in his diary, dated July 29, and reading "there may be many things connected with a man's life that will prevent him from leaving home for bloody scenes, and war is a very serious affair when we take it from a moral point of view."[17]

Among the troops of Grant's triumphant army, there was a general itch to be transferred east, where the action was, and continue the victorious momentum they had gained in Mississippi. The capture of Vicksburg had been a heady tonic, and their devotion to Grant and Sherman coursed like adrenalin in their veins. Neither general could be characterized as lovable nor was either on easygoing terms with the men they commanded, but both were winners, and one stayed with winners.

Isaac Jackson of the Eighty-third Ohio Infantry accompanied Sherman's forces in routing Johnston from the Mississippi capital, but reported nothing more strenuous than "hot marching." He returned to Vicksburg to remain with the Federal occupation forces through the summer, thence, with his regiment, to New Orleans. For a year he skirmished in the bayou country of Louisiana, keeping careful track in his diary of what and how much he ate and the condition of his stomach (his weight had increased by thirty pounds since he joined the army). The last action he saw was in land operations against the forts east of Mobile in March and April, 1865.[18]

Osborn Oldroyd of the Twentieth Ohio became, after the war, a bookseller in Springfield, Illinois, where he witnessed the arrival of the funeral train bearing the body of the assassinated President in May of 1865. Possibly moved by this, he went to Washington, to become custodian of William Petersen's boarding house, across the street from Ford's New Theater, where Lincoln died.

Vicksburg would always be the high point in his life, and Oldroyd began collating his experiences for a book to be later published. It closed with an appropriate poem of unacknowledged authorship. Perhaps it was his own, composed at the time of the surrender:

> The armies of the Union
> Round Vicksburg long had lain;
> For forty-seven days and nights
> Besieging it in vain. . . .
>
> The siege is done, the struggle past.
> On this eventful day
> Glad triumph crowns us, as, at last,
> Our thanks to God we pay.[19]

Candlelight and quiet, and the "peace which passeth understanding." One was safe again. The guns were silenced. For most, the heartache was yet to come, when they fully realized the extent of all that they had lost. As of now, wrote Dora Miller:

It is evening. All is still. Silence and night are once more united. I can sit at the table in the parlor and write. Two candles are lighted. I would like a dozen. We have had wheat supper and wheat bread once more.

Her husband, Anderson Miller, rocked in a chair beside her, saying, "It seems to me I can hear the silence, and feel it, too. It wraps me like a soft garment; how else can I express this peace?"[20]

But the euphoria was a passing reaction, in contrast to the noise and horror of six long weeks of siege. It was a time for taking stock . . .

After the surrender, many whom war had brought to Vicksburg from other parts of the Confederacy sought to leave the stricken city. Natives who had already fled, before the siege made flight impossible, sought means of returning, while those who had burrowed underground until the storm blew over returned to their houses to make repairs and rebuild their shattered lives.

Some had lost everything—their homes, their money, their family treasures, and their slaves, the latter an asset on which their former mode of living had depended. One elderly widow found her life savings paid out in wages to the faithful black who had served her without pay for thirty years. There was nothing left, as one returning native wrote, "but to endure."

Through the efforts of her officer-husband, Mary Loughborough obtained a pass to leave the city. A week after the capitulation, she and her daughter crossed the river, and "Vicksburg, with her terraced hills—with her pleasant homes and sad memories, passed from my view in the gathering twilight."[21] Settling in Little Rock, Arkansas, and left a widow by the death of her husband, Mrs. Loughborough founded what became the highly successful *Southern Ladies Journal,* later publishing her acclaimed account of *My Cave Life in Vicksburg.*

For Emma Balfour, the surrender of Vicksburg meant that her house was safe for living again, while Mahala Roach shifted from cave life to her home on Mulberry and Depot streets overlooking the unfamiliar masts and funnels of the Mississippi riverboats that were back in service once again. Mahala began sorting out the pages of the diary she had started when the siege began, but "The task will be a sad one for me, for I will have to turn back my glances to a happy life, now alas! passed away forever."[22]

For Lucy McRae, as well, returning home meant simply moving from their cave back to the red-brick family house on Monroe Street, where workmen cleared away the broken glass and fallen plaster and repaired the damaged walls. Lucy was there to greet her homecoming brother, Allen McRae, who had been serving with Lee in Virginia. He was the last man, wrote Lucy, to stand guard at Jefferson Davis's tent, and when discharged was given a horse and a twenty dollar gold piece by the President. "My brother rode from Virginia to Vicksburg on that horse, carrying the gold piece in the bottom of his boot."[23]

Dora Miller, after the surrender, found herself "thoroughly pulled to pieces in Vicksburg circles; there is no more salvation for me." Her husband arranged to get passes for both of them to New Orleans, where Anderson died two years later. Dora got along by teaching school and, under the influence of author George Washington Cable, supplemented her income by writing of her experiences in the war for *The Century Magazine.*

Rowland Chambers, the itinerant dentist, found life in Vicksburg more and more intolerable under Union rule. He destroyed his orchard, as the only means of preventing marauding soldiers from making off with his fruit, and blasted away with a shotgun at any who tried to steal his truck garden. Despite the harassments, which he tended to exaggerate, Chambers stayed on in Vicksburg as a practicing dentist for the three more years remaining to him, dying at his son-in-law's house in 1866.[24]

John Bobb, whose Greek Revival manor with its boxwood and magnolia gardens was the pride of Vicksburg, suffered more tragically from Federal harassment. Finding some Union soldiers pillaging his gardens, he harshly ordered them off the property. In the altercation that followed, Bobb was shot dead. It was an atrocity which brought swift retribution. On Grant's insistence, the culprits were court-martialed and a number hanged.[25]

The week after July 4, Margaret Lord called on Grant, to obtain permission to leave the city. She found the general "a kindly gentleman . . . anxious to aid the people all he could." And he expressed admiration for the women of Vicksburg, who, he said, "cannot be conquered." He gave the Lords passports and passage on a steamer carrying sick and wounded Confederates to New Orleans and Mobile.

Leaving everything they owned behind them in the rectory, which was later vandalized by maverick Union soldiers, they boarded the Mississippi steamboat, on the deck of which young Willie Lord saw his family as "refugees adrift upon the hopeless current of a losing cause."[26] Dr. Lord accompanied the family to Mobile and thence to South Carolina, where they remained until the Episcopal minister was able to return to Vicksburg to take over the pulpit of the newly built Holy Trinity Church.

With the siege of the city still clear in her mind, Annie Laurie Harris wrote, "My enthusiasm and love of country grows stronger, as the old scenes spring into life, the ruined homes, poverty, distress and death." Annie didn't think she ever wanted to see the City of a Hundred Hills again. But from afar she noted, "Our grandmother's home [the William Lum house] was taken and used for General Grant's headquarters." But Grant did not evict the family, as Annie gratefully acknowledged. "The upper half was retained by my relatives, and the lower was used by the General, his family and officers . . . the General treated all with kindness and consideration, insisting that officers should do the same."[27]

In the Washington Street house young Fred Grant found a playmate of his own age in the Lums' young pigtailed daughter. Their friendship ripened to the point where Fred permitted the girl to ride his pony around the grounds. But the two were forcibly parted when Grant was ordered east, and the homestead the general had vowed to protect was razed, to make way for a military facility named, in honor of Grant's chief of staff, Fort Rawlins. A similar fate befell the famed Castle of Castle Hill, which was leveled to make room for a Federal fort designed to repel any future Confederate attempts to retake Vicksburg.

Lavinia Shannon warned her refugee daughter that "Vicksburg is not the place it once was, neither is home." But Alice Shannon had "had enough of the Yankees at Raymond." She returned to rejoin her parents in Vicksburg, where "every time I raise my eyes I see that hateful flag flying from the court house." She declared, "I don't think I shall wear blue any more, I hate the very sight of it."[28]

Marmaduke Shannon's *Whig* would never get on its feet again, and the publisher turned to different fields, becoming first postwar sheriff of Vicksburg in 1865.

J. M. Swords of the *Citizen,* apparently more resigned and pliable than Shannon, adjusted to the new conditions. He revived his newspaper under the name of the Vicksburg *Herald,* filling its columns with casualty lists of Vicksburg sons who were fighting in Georgia and Virginia or eastern Tennessee.

For Ida Barlow, still at her grandfather's house outside the nearly abandoned Union lines, the aftermath of war continued after the surrender. She was gathering bluebells in the yard when she heard a moan and discovered a wounded Confederate soldier lying in the garden. He was one of the vanguard of parolees that were stumbling out of Vicksburg toward their homes in Mississippi. For the rest of her life the scent of bluebells would remind her that:

> For days and weeks we had to endure the pitiable sight of our men struggling homeward—there were no trails in running order—and with bare feet, gaunt, and partly naked on they came in a steady stream; but the poor starved creatures were still afraid and would only stop for a drink until out of the Yankee lines, and many was the poor fellow who fell by the wayside.

Leaving the grandfather's house several weeks later, the Barlows returned to their home in Vicksburg, where, wrote Ida, "One by one our own dear ones returned to us—one with an arm gone, another with a leg gone."[29]

Matilda Champion, on whose plantation the critical battle for Vicksburg had been fought, returned in July to find much of her house destroyed and the negro workers gone. Her husband was still serving with the Mississippi cavalry, but Matilda had enough with which to carry on till Sid came back. But, "Oh God, when will this war end and let severed families be united." Sidney would return to the plantation after Appomattox, and Champion Hill would remain with the family for generations in the future.[30]

With the Mississippi in Federal hands, it took a long time for news to travel west of the river to Lamar County, Texas. Not till the end of July, did Kate Stone learn that "Vicksburg is taken without a doubt. . . . How have the mighty fallen!" Shortly after that, came news of her brother Coley's death in Mississippi, the second brother she had given to the Cause. Dreaming ever of the plantation in Louisiana, Kate and her family returned to Brokenburn in the fall of 1865 when she wrote on November 16:

> At home again but so many, many changes in two years. It does not seem the same place. The bare echoing rooms, the neglect and defacement of all—though the place is in better repair than most—and the stately oaks and the green grass make it look pleasant and cheerful, though gardens, orchards, and fences are mostly swept away.

The words "never, never, nevermore," echoed in Kate's heart "like a funeral knell at every thought of the happy past." Yet, "We must bear our losses as best we can. Nothing is left but to endure."[31]

"The town, situated on a high bluff with the sunlight on its hills and roofs and fortifications, was a fine sight," wrote Boston journalist John Townsend Trowbridge, aboard a packet approaching Vicksburg at Christmastime in 1865. Trowbridge had set out shortly after war's end to visit the principal cities of "The Desolate South," for a book of that title he had been assigned to write.

He reached Vicksburg before it had fully recovered from the wounds of war. The caves and "gopher holes" were being covered up, to prevent their being used as garbage dumps; the streets were being repaired, the craters filled; the brick and wood houses had been repaired. The desolation of the South was not immediately apparent in the City of a Hundred Hills. It was there, but neatly covered over with a brave veneer.[32]

Natives of Vicksburg no longer dreamed the impossible dream. For them the storm was over, and the war had moved away, leaving heartbreak and disillusion in its wake. The Confederacy had drifted past the far horizon, no more substantial than a cloud of smoke. They were in the Union, like it or not, and the city would be under Federal rule until peace came.

The immediate problem was one of survival, relying on the enemy's commissary for provisions, and trying to rebuild their homes and adjust to new and unfamiliar patterns of existence. No more, the gracious, hedonistic life.

One thing, however, remained constant. King Cotton still governed the economy. The lure of enormous profits to be made from cotton and from cotton-growing real estate drew a horde of newcomers to the city—land speculators, builders, profiteers, traders, and promoters, Wrote one chronicler of this period: "Like vultures descending on a carcass, they swarmed into Vicksburg, eager to pick the bones. If a man was lucky, and able, and not too scrupulous, fortunes waited for the taking."[33]

The river, which had brought war and death to Vicksburg, now became its leading benefactor. In mid-July the side-wheeler *Imperial,* its tall twin funnels saluting the city with columns of black smoke, stopped at the wharf on its way from Saint Louis to New Orleans, and the Mississippi was back in business as the artery of western commerce. Five years later Vicksburg citizens would crowd the levee and hilltops to watch the *Robert E. Lee* pass well ahead of the *Natchez* in their famous race over the same route.

Vicksburg again became an important river port, being forced to use wharf-boats (one of them the retired *Natchez*) as surrogate warehouses to accommodate the flow of cotton. In the single decade from 1860 to 1870, its population tripled to 12,443, surpassing that of Natchez, Jackson, and Columbus, and making the city the largest in the state.

Sylvanus Cadwallader, returning to Vicksburg in late July 1863, found the citizens ambivalent in attitude and actions toward the Federal army of occupation. He complained that they took what they could get, at the same time, "cherishing the utmost bitterness and malignancy towards us. . . . " What Cadwallader expected from a people beneath the heel of a conqueror, he did not say but charged: "Here no duplicity is too low; no cunning or treachery too base, to practice towards us." As illustration:

> The people as a whole are the most ungrateful on the face of the earth. They should either act honorably, or refuse to receive their daily bread from our hands. Probably more than ten thousand rations are daily issued to rebel citizens on the score of humanity, to prevent starvation, and probably there are not ten of these but would glory in betraying us . . .[34]

Grant, however, was far more sympathetic to the people's plight. He sent orders to Sherman, and himself followed the directive, that the Union troops should conduct themselves "in an orderly manner, abstaining from taking anything not absolutely necessary for their subsistence. . . . They should try to create as favorable impression as possible upon the people."[35]

The commanding general directed that medicines be made available to the ill and wounded in the city. Food, provisions, and forage were ordered drawn from army supplies and distributed to the natives in both Vicksburg and the countryside, for "I thought it only fair that we should return to these people some of the articles we had taken while marching through the country."

But Grant would not be in charge for long. He had urged Halleck to send him against Mobile, while his troops were still imbued with the spirit of victory, but Halleck, he observed, found it "very much easier to refuse a favor than to grant one." So the general trekked to New Orleans to discuss his next move with Banks. During the trip he was thrown from his horse and painfully injured. He was still bedded down when ordered by Halleck to send substantial reinforcements to the aid of Rosecrans at Chattanooga. Sherman was placed in charge of these troops.

With Grant's departure in mid-October to assume command of all Federal forces at Chattanooga, supervision of business and commerce in Vicksburg fell to agents of the Treasury Department, who tried to keep control by licensing all who did business in the city. It was an open invitation to defiance, evasion, and deceit. Political adventurers among the horde of new arrivals infiltrated the city government, with only self-betterment in mind, until one treasury agent wrote despairingly that even "corruption was corrupted."

No amount of shenanigans, however, could stop the surge of progress and prosperity. The old-time businesses started up again; new firms and industries arrived. By the end of August, most of the stores were open and doing a thriving business, and citizens who had been without the simplest of luxuries for many months discovered "you can buy anything you want." Like the other planters, Amanda Stone raised a healthy crop of cotton at Brokenburn, though it cost her $25,000 to do so, most of the money going to wages for labor that had once been free. William Crutcher got his hands on 2,500 bales of cotton, on which he hoped to clear $15,000 to $20,000 from eager buyers.

The big consumer market for cotton, tobacco, and other Mississippi Valley products was, of course, the occupying army. Few Southerners in and around Vicksburg had the money to make substantial purchases, and there was no virulent stigma attached to trading with the conqueror. As William Crutcher noted, "It was every man for himself." If one could milk the Union government of whatever it was prepared to pay, so much the better for the cause of individual enterprise and Vicksburg's reconstruction. Only the Richmond authorities deplored this trade, which they regarded as treason and collaboration with the enemy.

On top of these shifting sands was the problem of the emancipated slaves. The blacks who had worked the plantations often remained, as paid hands, with their former masters. The house slaves in the city were a different problem. Often arrogant, frightened, and without direction, they paraded the streets of Vicksburg in shiny clothes that were the uniform of freedom, hoping to find utopia around each corner and being forever disillusioned. The establishment of the Freedmen's Bureau promised hope and guidance, but Vicksburg was not up to facing a problem that in time would be a national disgrace. It had too many problems of its own, not the least of which was acceptance of its new position.

By the time the first anniversary of the surrender rolled around, on July 4, 1864, J. M. Swords of the *Citizen* was disposed to write, "No city in the Union has so good a reason to celebrate the Fourth of July as Vicksburg, and we trust it will be an occasion of a cordial greeting among the citizens and soldiers of a common country." With war still on, it was a sweeping reversal of position for the editor who, a year before, was writing that the South had divested itself of the Union for all time to come.

But it was a symptomatic recognition of reality. The following year, 1865, editors J. W. Kinsley and E. B. Kinsley of the newly established Vicksburg *Journal* revived the days of siege in hyperbolic prose ("the angel of death spread his wings to the blast") and noted that "all these things have passed away. Peace with her many blessings once more hovers o'er her land and good and true hearts are trying to heal the wounds inflicted in the past." The editors concluded:

We have accepted the issue of the war in good faith; and while it would be hypocritical for us to say we have not mourned over the downfall of our hopes, we are prepared to do all that can be required of us.[36]

They did all that and more, without, somehow, compromising the integrity and individual courage of the city that refused to die.

"We used to plow past the lofty hill city of Vicksburg, downstream; but we cannot do that now. A cutoff has made a country town of it. . . . There is . . . a big island in front of Vicksburg now. You come down the river the other side of the island, then turn and come up to the town."[37]

So wrote Samuel Clemens, or Mark Twain, in the 1880s—for the Mississippi of its own volition had accomplished what Grant's troops had failed to do, cutting a new channel through the De Soto Peninsula and leaving Vicksburg high and dry. It did not matter greatly; the railroads were beginning to absorb the river traffic, and the golden age of the paddlewheel steamers was on the wane.

The city still kept in contact with the river by means of a diversion canal extended to the Yazoo River, and Mark Twain was able to observe that "Vicksburg is a town of substantial business streets and pleasant residences; it commands the commerce of the Yazoo and Sunflower Rivers; is pushing railways in several directions, through rich agricultural regions, and has a promising future of prosperity and importance."

That was in 1883. Vicksburg today is one of the pleasantest of Mississippi cities, and one that seems drifting backward into time. The gaslights, of course, are gone; the up-and-down streets are no longer paved with stones and bricks; and while two paddle-wheel steamers, their calliopes playing, bring visitors to the landing, these craft are only entertaining souvenirs. Still, the past broods over the town like the touch of a gentle ghost, and time seems to move more slowly, perhaps to compensate for the marathon years of 1862 and 1863.

A number of the city's antebellum homes and buildings are preserved. The court house with its four-face clock on the cupola still dominates the skyline, housing the local historical society's archives and museum. One can see or visit the home that Annie Harris preferred to the safety of a cave; the Klein house, "Cedar Grove"; the house where Pemberton stayed on Crawford Street; the red-brick Planters Hall, where Lucy McRae and her family lived; the Shirley

House, from which the Federals charged into the crater of the Third Louisiana Redan—and many more, not greatly changed since the days of swords and roses.

Above all, there is the magnificent Vicksburg National Military Park: 1,800 acres embracing the city on the north and east. Well tended as it is, the restored earthworks and trenches are softened by green rolling turf, and the 132 cannons stand mutely like children's innocent toys. There is none of the raw, bleeding earth that once told of a mighty battle fought here, nothing that speaks of pain and death. . . .

Except the towering monuments of marble and granite. The state of Massachusetts started it off by emplacing a fifteen-ton boulder topped by a bronze military figure. Oxen hauled the granite base from the city to a site near the position of Grant's headquarters. Other state memorials followed, erected at appropriate sites by nearly all of the twenty-eight states of North and South represented here. Hundreds of monuments and tablets call attention to regiments, forts, batteries, trenches, and significant combat areas. Scores of bronze busts and bronze portraits identify field commanders.

Some 118 acres are encompassed in the Vicksburg National Military Cemetry, which provides a final resting place for more Union soldiers than any other burial ground. Under a rolling canopy of green, 17,000 Federal veterans are interred. Of this number, three-fourths comprise the nameless dead. All that is known about them, all that really need be known about them, is that they died for the greatest of all causes, something they believed in.

Lest we forget . . .

Notes

(Unless specifically indicated here, publication data and sources for the following books, publications, and manuscripts are provided in the bibliography.)

Chapter 1. THE IMPERIAL RIVER

1. Scott in a letter to W. H. Seward, March 3, 1861. His exact wording: "Say to the seceded States, 'Wayward sisters, depart in peace.' " A profile of the aging general in these twilight years is presented in Margaret Leech, *Reveille in Washington,* pp. 1–4, and a capsule biography, pp. 451–52.
2. Bruce Catton, *The Coming Fury,* pp. 438–41. For McClellan's counterproposals to the Anaconda Plan, see p. 438.
3. Lincoln's riverboat days are presented in Carl Sandburg, *Abraham Lincoln, The Prairie Years* (New York: Harcourt, Brace, 1926), I: 78, 83–87.
4. *Harper's Magazine,* February 1900, p. 413.
5. Hodding Carter, *The Lower Mississippi,* p. 222.
6. *Confederate Military History,* XII: 2: 17.
7. Lloyd Lewis, *Sherman: Fighting Prophet,* pp. 72, 131, 161.
8. Frederick J. Turner, *The Frontier in American History,* p. 187. The words are those of General James Wilkinson, ranking officer of the United States Army at the beginning of the century.
9. The story of James Eads and his gunboats is told by the captain himself in *Battles and Leaders* (hereafter cited as *B & L*), I: 338–46, including comments on Admiral Foote's participation. For a biography of the inventor and naval architect, see Louis How, *James B. Eads* (Boston: Houghton, Mifflin, 1900).
10. *B & L,* I: 338 (n.). The writer here is naval historian, Charles B. Boynton.
11. H. A. Gosnell, *Guns on Western Waters,* pp. 15–18.
12. C. B. Long with Barbara, *The Civil War Day by Day, an Almanac,* p. 89.
13. *B & L,* II: 13.
14. Sylvanus Cadwallader, *Three Years with Grant,* p. 53. What particular reason Cadwallader had for detesting Porter, he does not reveal. But he devotes a good many high-powered paragraphs to the subject.
15. *B & L,* II: 24.
16. Ibid., pp. 24–25.
17. Ibid., pp. 27–28. See also Christopher Martin, *Damn the Torpedoes!,* pp. 160–61.
18. George Cable, "New Orleans Before the Capture," *B & L,* II: 14–17. Born in New

Orleans in 1844, Cable would have been seventeen at the time (though he writes of being younger), and would shortly enlist and serve for two years in the fourth Mississippi Cavalry. After the war, of course, he became a distinguished American author of books about the South, oriented on Louisiana.

19. Ibid., p. 15.
20. John Fiske, *The Mississippi Valley and the Civil War,* pp. 117–20. For Fiske's appraisal of the military importance of New Orleans, see pp. 111–12.
21. Dora Richards, "War Diary of a Union Woman in the South," pp. 931, 934. Dora Richards, later to become Mrs. Anderson Miller, presumably never met or knew of George Cable during her stay in New Orleans. But it was Cable who, after the war, encouraged her to publish the diary she had kept of her experiences in New Orleans and during the siege of Vicksburg. The work was published anonymously, edited by George W. Cable, in two issues of *The Century Magazine,* and Dora referred neither to herself nor her husband-to-be by name.
22. Shelby Foote, *The Civil War,* I: 361.
23. Annie Laurie Harris's manuscript, headed "A Recollection of Thirty Years Ago," consists presently of twenty-one (now typescript) pages, following no precise chronological order and giving no dates. Her comments appear in this book where they logically seem to apply. This quotation, p. 5.
24. The immortal "Dixie" may well have been born in Vicksburg. Or at least the Hill City can split that honor with New Orleans. Director Gordon Cotton of the Old Court House Museum points out that publisher Werlein was a native of Vicksburg and conducted his music operations from offices in that city as well as in New Orleans.
25. Kate Stone, *Brokenburn,* p. 13.
26. Edward Pollard, *The Lost Cause,* p. 324.

Chapter 2. CITY OF A HUNDRED HILLS

1. *A General Directory for the City of Vicksburg,* H. C. Clarke, publisher, 1860 (hereafter cited as *City Directory*). On file in the Old Court House Museum, the directory gives names and addresses, and sometimes professions or businesses, of nearly 700 residents. No blacks are included in the list, which covers only residents within the corporate boundaries as defined in 1825, thus excluding a vast number of farmers and planters surrounding the city on both sides of the river.
2. Vicksburg *Evening Post,* July 1, 1963, 1: 2. This special Centennial Edition of the *Post* devotes the first of five sections to the founding and growth of Vicksburg, including biographies of Newet Vick (sometimes spelled Newitt or Newit) and other members of the family, and a list of the initial settlers.
3. Ibid., p. 14.
4. Ibid. See also B. A. Botkin, *Treasury of Mississippi River Folklore,* pp. 222–25, for a full account of the war against the Vicksburg gamblers.
5. Vicksburg *Evening Post,* July 1, 1963, 5:8. "Railroads Play Big Role in Area's Growth."
6. Compiled from listings in *City Directory.*
7. Annie Harris, "A Recollection of Thirty Years Ago," p. 2.
8. Miscellaneous papers, item undated, Old Court House Museum.
9. Vicksburg *Evening Post,* July 1, 1963, 2:18.
10. Kate Stone, *Brokenburn,* pp. 3–12.
11. Ibid., p. 35.
12. *City Directory,* prefatory "Sketch of the City of Vicksburg."
13. Vicksburg *Evening Post,* July 1, 1963, Pt 2., p. 8.
14. Ibid., p. 19.

15. Diary of Mahala P. H. Roach, pp. 367–69. Mahala Roach's diary is close to being a novel of life in Vicksburg during the war years, and through its pages pass virtually every well-known figure in the city, with the reactions thereto of the writer's own volatile temperament. It never got beyond the manuscript stage, which is a pity; it would have made a good book.

16. Biographical data on Rowland Chambers, along with his rather slipshod diary, are in the Louisiana State University Archives. At fifty-six, too old for military service, Chambers began his diary in Saint Louis in May of 1849, and subsequent entries are dated from Panama City, Natchez, Satartia (Miss.), Vicksburg, Madison (La.), and back to Vicksburg in early 1862. Since his spelling and grammar are atrocious, quotations used hereafter have been arbitrarily corrected for the sake of clarity.

17. Mary F. Lacey, *Intellectual Activities of Vicksburg Prior to 1860.*

18. *City Directory,* prefatory "Sketch . . . "

19. *Confederate Military History,* XII:2:6. The words are those of Governor McWillie, in an address to the Mississippi legislature, November, 1859.

20. Harris, "Recollection," p. 10.

21. Vicksburg *Daily Whig,* October 10, 1860.

22. Vicksburg *Weekly Whig,* November 14, 1860.

23. Vicksburg *Daily Citizen,* December 22, 1860.

24. Dora Richards, "War Diary of a Woman in the South," p. 931.

25. Vicksburg *Weekly Whig,* January 23, 1861.

26. City Council Minute Book, Old Court House Museum, Vicksburg, 1860–69, p. 57.

27. *Confederate Military History,* XII: 2: 10–11.

28. John Monroe Gibson papers, Old Court House Museum, item undated.

29. Stone, *Brokenburn,* pp. 18, 24, 31.

30. Harris, "Recollection," p. 10.

31. *Confederate Military History,* XII:2, p. 17.

32. C. B. Long, *The Civil War Day by Day, an Almanac,* p. 35.

Chapter 3. THREAT FROM THE SOUTH

1. David Dixon Porter, "Opening of the Lower Mississippi," *B & L,* II: 29–30.

2. Ibid., pp. 31–32.

3. Charles L. Dufour, *Ten Flags in the Wind,* p. 167.

4. Porter, "Opening," pp. 34–37.

5. Christopher Martin, *Damn the Torpedoes!,* p. 195.

6. William Meredith, "Farragut's Capture of New Orleans," *B & L,* II: 71.

7. Porter, "Opening," pp. 39–40.

8. Ibid., pp. 42–47. For other accounts of Farragut's running of the forts, see John Fiske, *The Mississippi Valley and the Civil War,* pp. 123–28; Martin, *Torpedoes,* pp. 183–94; and John R. Bartlett, "The *Brooklyn* at the Passage of the Forts," *B & L,* II: 56–69.

9. Porter, "Opening," p. 45.

10. Dufour, *Ten Flags,* p. 165. Also, *Confederate Military History,* X:1:35–36.

11. George Cable, "New Orleans Before the Capture," *B & L,* II:20.

12. Ibid.

13. Porter, "Opening," pp. 50–53.

14. Dufour, *Ten Flags,* p. 168.

15. Albert Kautz, "Incidents on the Occupation of New Orleans," *B & L,* II:91–92.

16. Diary of Mahala P. H. Roach, p. 102.

17. Annie Harris, "A Recollection of Thirty Years Ago," p. 12.

18. Roach, pp. 103–104.
19. Hugh Moss, *The Diary of A. Hugh Moss,* p. 18. Moss arrived at Vicksburg on May 5 with the Eighth Louisiana Artillery Battalion, under Major F. N. Ogden, which became part of the river batteries defending the city.
20. Roach, p. 108. At this time Mahala described herself as "all adrift," and she contemplated leaving the city for her mother's plantation, which she shortly did, though returning from time to time to look after her home in Vicksburg.
21. Charles Allen, "Plantation Book," p. 71.
22. Vicksburg *Daily Whig,* May 5, 1862.
23. Samuel H. Lockett, "The Defense of Vicksburg," *B & L,* III:482.
24. *War of the Rebellion: Official Records, Union and Confederate Armies* (hereafter cited as O.R.) Ser. 1, Vol. XV, p. 7.
25. Vicksburg *Daily Whig,* May 15, 1862.
26. *Official Records, Union and Confederate Navies,* 1:XVIII:491–493. The naval records show that, when Phillips Lee reached Vicksburg, he had with him not only his five-ship flotilla, but also two transports loaded with infantry. An additional transport arrived on May 19.
27. Ibid.
28. Ibid.
29. Ibid.
30. *O.R.,* 1:XV:7.

Chapter 4. MENACE FROM THE NORTH

1. Paul Wood, *Illinois at War, 1861–1865,* p. 6.
2. Bruce Catton, *Grant Moves South,* pp. 46–47.
3. John A. Foote, "Notes on the Life of Admiral Foote," *B & L,* I:347.
4. Ulysses S. Grant, *Personal Memoirs,* I:230–31, 255–56. Facsimile edition.
5. Ibid., pp. 245–46.
6. Quoted in Lloyd N. Lewis, *Sherman: Fighting Prophet,* p. 260.
7. Grant, *Memoirs,* I:270–80.
8. James Eads, "Recollections of Foote and the Gun-boats," *B & L,* I:343–44.
9. Ibid., pp. 339–42.
10. Jesse Taylor, "The Defense of Fort Henry," *B & L,* I:369.
11. Ibid., p. 730.
12. Grant, *Memoirs,* I:315.
13. Henry Walke, "The Western Flotilla at Fort Donelson," *B & L,* I: 433–34.
14. Robert S. Henry, *First with the Most Forrest* (Indianapolis: Bobbs-Merrill, 1944), pp. 58–59.
15. Halleck to McClellan, March 3, 1862. *O.R.,* VII:679–80.
16. The friction between Grant and Halleck, and President Lincoln's concern and intervention, are discussed in Catton, *Grant,* pp. 200–7.
17. Walke, "Western Flotilla," pp. 339–40.
18. Ibid., pp. 442–43.
19. Ibid., pp. 444–45.
20. Alfred W. Ellet, "Ellet and His Steam-rams at Memphis," *B & L,* I:453.
21. Ibid.
22. Walke, "Western Flotilla," pp. 447–49.
23. Ibid.
24. Kate Stone, *Brokenburn,* pp. 100–1. The citizens of Vicksburg and its environs, as indicated by their diaries, appeared to remain calm during the peril to Memphis. Mahala Roach did not mention that city in her diary; she was more concerned with her daughter's birthday, which fell on the day the Union fleet at-

tacked; while Kate Stone noted, "All are busy plaiting hats." It is likely that none of them knew what was going on upriver. The Memphis *Bulletin,* on which both Shannon and Swords relied for news from the north, had suspended publication, and thereafter would be under Federal control. The Vicksburg *Daily Whig* would not report the fall of Memphis until July 11.

25. Dora Richards, "War Diary of a Woman in the South," pp. 936–39.
26. Annie Harris, "A Recollection of Thirty Years Ago," p. 12.
27. Ellet, p. 454.
28. Ibid., p. 456.
29. Ibid. For other accounts of the battle for Memphis, see John Fiske, *The Mississippi Valley and the Civil War,* pp. 236–37; Willard Webb, *Crucial Moments of the Civil War,* pp. 134–36; H. A. Gosnell, *Guns on the Western Waters,* pp. 92–100.
30. Ellet, p. 459. Ellet's reference here to "ironclad" enemy vessels is misleading. Only the prows of Confederate rams were metal-armored.

Chapter 5. FIRM AS THE ETERNAL HILLS

1. Kate Stone, *Brokenburn,* p. 107.
2. Jared Sanders, "Diary in Gray," April 27, 1862. Jared Sanders, of St. Mary's Parish, Louisiana, entered the Confederate service in March of 1862 at age twenty-three. The diary he kept thereafter was incomplete and fragmentary and was later filled out, for the Louisiana Genealogical Register, with letters to his family, written during the campaign for Vicksburg.
3. Granville L. Alspaugh, Civil War Letters, to Mrs. A. E. Alspaugh, May 11, 1862. Private Alspaugh's letters are dated from late March 1862 to April 25, 1863. All were written to his mother or sister, on any kind of paper available, and, though his punctuation and grammar were haphazard, he wrote with feeling and a curious sixteen-year-old eloquence.
4. Dr. William Wilberforce Lord, alone among the members of his family, kept no surviving record of his Vicksburg war years.
5. Rowland Chambers, Diary, May 27 and 28, 1862. Chamber's timing is incorrect. The shelling on May 27 began at 5:30 P.M., not 3:00, as he recorded.
6. Mahala Roach, Diary, entries written at Woodfield, May 28 and 29, 1862.
7. Ibid.
8. William W. Lord, Jr., "A Child at the Siege of Vicksburg," p. 44.
9. Peter F. Walker, *Vicksburg, A People at War,* p. 94.
10. *Confederate Military History,* XII: 2: 70.
11. Isaac N. Brown, "The Confederate Gun-boat Arkansas," B & L, III: 572.
12. Ibid.
13. Shelby Foote, *The Civil War,* I: 547–48. Farragut was laying it on pretty thick here, probably for Butler's edification. In Civil War times it would have been impossible to move 20,000 men an hour by rail.
14. Foote, *The Civil War,* I:547.
15. Ibid.
16. John C. Curtis to his father, June 28, 1862. Letter in the possession of Milton W. Bond of Fairfield, Connecticut.
17. Vicksburg *Daily Whig,* June 5, 1862.
18. Vicksburg *Daily Citizen,* June 20, 1862.
19. Samuel H. Lockett, "The Defense of Vicksburg," *B & L,* Vol. III, p. 483.
20. Granville Alspaugh to Mrs. A. E. Alspaugh, "Civil War Letters," June 14, 1862.
21. Stone, p. 122.
22. *Diary of A. Hugh Moss,* p. 4; *Diary of Rowland Chambers,* June 27, 1862.
23. Lockett, p. 483.

24. *Confederate Military History,* XII:2:73.
25. Vicksburg *Daily Whig,* July 1, 1862.
26. Ibid.
27. *O.R.,* 1:XV:14.
28. Soley, "Naval Operations in the Vicksburg Campaign," *B & L,* III:554.
29. Stone, pp. 126–27.
30. Curtis, letter, June 28, 1862.
31. *Confederate Military History,* XII:2:74.
32. Earl S. Miers, *Web of Victory,* pp. 32–33.
33. Richard B. Irwin, "Military Operations in Louisiana in 1862," *B & L,* III:583.
34. Vicksburg *Daily Whig,* July 11, 1862.
35. Ibid.
36. Foote, *The Civil War,* p. 549. Also Bearss, *Rebel Victory at Vicksburg,* pp. 192–93.

Chapter 6. "THE *ARKANSAS* IS COMING!"

1. Isaac N. Brown, "The Confederate Gun-boat *Arkansas,*" B & L, III: 572. Familiar to most students of the Civil War, the *Arkansas* story is deservedly one of the great legends of American history.
2. Brown, p. 572.
3. Ibid. Also, H. A. Gosnell, *Guns on the Western Waters,* p. 104.
4. Gosnell, p. 106.
5. Ibid., pp. 108–109.
6. Brown, p. 575.
7. Ibid.
8. Gosnell, p. 110.
9. Vicksburg *Evening Post,* July 1, 1961, 3:3. The *Post* writer might have paraphrased Churchill's words: seldom have so many owed so much to just a single ship.
10. Brown, p. 576.
11. Gosnell, p. 122.
12. Ibid., p. 124.
13. Ibid., p. 125.
14. Diary of Mahala Roach, July 15, 1862.
15. Brown, p. 577.
16. Gosnell, p. 130.
17. Brown, p. 578.
18. Shelby Foote, *The Civil War,* I:556.
19. *Confederate Military History,* XII:2:79.
20. Rowland Chambers, Diary, July 20, 1862.
21. Diary of Mahala Roach, July 19, 31, 1862.
22. Dora Richards, "War Diary of a Union Woman in the South," pp. 942–43.
23. Annie Harris, "A Recollection of Thirty Years Ago," p. 14.
24. Kate Stone, *Brokenburn,* p. 109.
25. Sanders, "Diary in Gray," letter to his mother, Mrs. William G. Sanders, August 8, 1862.
26. Ibid.
27. Brown, p. 578.
28. Gosnell, p. 133.
29. Brown, p. 579.

Chapter 7. A GALAXY OF GENERALS

1. Ulysses S. Grant, *Personal Memoirs,* I:395. There were multiple reasons for Grant's anxiety. With the departure of Henry Halleck to Washington, unified command in the West ceased to exist until revived some two years later. At this time, the summer of 1862, Grant was taking command of the army he had led earlier in the year without any clear orders or formulated plan.

2. William T. Sherman, *Memoirs,* I:255–56.

3. Grant, *Memoirs,* I:392–94.

4. Joseph E. Johnston, "Jefferson Davis and the Mississippi Campaign," B & L, III:472.

5. Mary B. Chesnut, *Diary from Dixie,* p. 117. Mary was in a gloomy mood. She had written two days earlier, "New Orleans is gone, and with it the Confederacy! Are we not cut in two?" She considered this setback "fatal," adding: "The Mississippi River ruins us if it is lost."

6. John C. Pemberton, *Defender of Vicksburg,* Appendices, pp. 289–90.

7. Diary of Mahala Roach, November 10, 1862.

8. Diary of Jared Sanders, August 8, 1862; Alspaugh to his mother, November 17, 1862.

9. A summary of press reactions to Pemberton's assumption of command in Vicksburg, from the Pemberton collection of manuscripts, newspaper clippings, etc., at the Library of the University of North Carolina, appears in his grandson's *Defender of Vicksburg,* pp. 43–48.

10. Pemberton, p. 14.

11. T. Harry Williams, *Lincoln and His Generals,* pp. 190–94. Williams finds this whole affair hard to explain; as others might. Among his conclusions, "the autumn of 1862 was simply a period when Lincoln's powers of human evaluation were not as sharp as usual. It was his bad time, his time to pick poor generals."

12. David Dixon Porter, *Incidents and Anecdotes,* p. 122.

13. Ibid., pp. 122–23.

14. Ulysses S. Grant, "The Vicksburg Campaign," *B & L,* III:493.

15. *O.R.,* XVII:2:260–61.

16. Grant, *Memoirs,* I:426–27.

17. *O.R.,* XVII:1:469.

18. Johnston, "Jefferson Davis," p. 473.

19. Hudson Strode, *Jefferson Davis,* p. 342.

20. William Chambers, *My Journal,* pp. 253–54.

21. Johnston, "Jefferson Davis," p. 474.

22. Grant, *Memoirs,* I:430–31.

23. Isaac Brown, "Confederate Torpedoes in the Yazoo," B & L, III:580.

24. James R. Soley, "Naval Operations in the Vicksburg Campaign," B & L, III: 559.

25. Sherman, I:285.

26. Bruce Catton, *Grant Moves South,* p. 538.

27. Lloyd Lewis, *Sherman: Fighting Prophet,* p. 258.

28. Springfield (Ill.) *Journal,* December 29, 1862. Other details of the general's wedding festivities provided by Mrs. Jaqueline Wright of Springfield.

29. Sherman, I:287–88.

Chapter 8. ASSAULT ON THE BLUFFS

1. Van Dorn's raid on Holly Springs is recounted in *Confederate Military History,* XII:2:98–99; and John Fiske, *The Mississippi Valley and the Civil War,* pp. 198–99. Both accounts include Forrest's synchronized cavalry thrust on Grant's supply bases in Tennessee.
2. Ulysses S. Grant, *Personal Memoirs,* I:432–33.
3. Sylvanus Cadwallader, *Three Years with Grant,* pp. 38–40.
4. Ibid., p. 40. Reference to "Yocknapatafa" may refer to Yocknapatalla River. No town of that name appears to have existed.
5. Grant, *Memoirs,* I: 435.
6. Diary of Rowland Chambers, December 26, 1862.
7. Vicksburg *Daily Whig,* December 30, 1862. Pemberton's proclamation dated December 27.
8. William Chambers, *My Journal,* October 17, 1862, pp. 252–53.
9. Diary of Mahala Roach, December 1, 20, 1862.
10. Vicksburg *Daily Whig,* December 30, 31, 1862.
11. Ibid.
12. Kate Stone, *Brokenburn,* pp. 165–66.
13. Roach, December 30, 31, 1862.
14. William T. Sherman, *Memoirs,* I:287–88.
15. Ibid., p. 289.
16. Jared Sanders, "Diary in Gray," Vol. XVII, No. 1, p. 16.
17. David Dixon Porter, *Naval History of the Civil War,* pp. 289–94.
18. Sanders, p. 18.
19. Ibid.
20. Sherman, I:291.
21. George T. Morgan, "The Assault on Chickasaw Bluffs," p. 467.
22. Ibid.
23. Sanders, p. 19.
24. Sherman, I:292.
25. Ibid., p. 295.
26. Morgan, p. 463.
27. Sherman, I:292.
28. David D. Porter, *Incidents and Anecdotes of the Civil War,* p. 129.
29. Shelby Foote, *The Civil War,* II:77.
30. Liddell Hart, *Sherman: Soldier, Realist, American* (New York: Dodd, 1929), p. 165.
31. Porter, *Incidents,* p. 130.
32. Hart, pp. 165, 171.
33. Sherman, I:296.
34. Foote, *Civil War,* II:134–35.
35. Sherman, I:298.
36. Ibid., pp. 299–300.
37. Isaac Jackson, *Some of the Boys,* p. 50.
38. Sherman, I:301.
39. Grant, *Memoirs,* I:440.
40. Ibid., p. 441.
41. Ibid., p. 442.

Chapter 9. OF TIME AND THE RIVER

1. Vicksburg *Daily Whig,* January 8, 1863.
2. Ibid., including quotation from *The New Mercury.*
3. New York *Times,* January 19, 1863.
4. Ulysses S. Grant, *Personal Memoirs,* I:443.
5. *Harper's Weekly,* Vol. VII, January 24, 1863, p. 50.
6. Shelby Foote, *The Civil War,* II:56.
7. Halleck to Grant, January 21, 1863, *O.R.,* XXIV:1:9.
8. Grant, *Memoirs,* I:446.
9. Foote, *Civil War,* II:145.
10. Vicksburg *Daily Whig,* January 6, 1863.
11. Sylvanus Cadwallader, *Three Years with Grant,* pp. 46–47.
12. Sherman, *Memoirs,* Vol. I, p. 305.
13. Isaac Jackson, *Some of the Boys,* pp. 58–59.
14. Cadwallader, p. 54.
15. Foote, *Civil War,* II:146–47.
16. Cadwallader, p. 49. The canal entrance lay three miles below Young's Point.
17. Foote, *Civil War,* II:79.
18. Vicksburg *Daily Whig,* January 22, 1863.
19. Ibid., January 10, 1863.
20. Jackson *Mississippian,* December 30, 1862.
21. Reprinted in the Vicksburg *Daily Whig,* January 6, 1863.
22. John C. Pemberton, *Defender of Vicksburg,* pp. 69–70
23. Vicksburg *Daily Whig,* December 30, 1862.
24. William Chambers, *My Journal,* pp. 256–57.
25. Willie H. Tunnard, *A Southern Record,* pp. 217–18.
26. Jared Sanders, "Diary in Gray," Vol. XVII, No. 1, p. 19. Letter to "Dear Friend," dated January 4, 1863.
27. Vicksburg *Daily Whig,* January 10, 1863.
28. Dora Richards, "A Woman's Diary of the Siege of Vicksburg," p. 767.
29. Hudson Strode, *Jefferson Davis,* II:363–64.
30. Diary of Mahala H. P. Roach, December 31, 1862.
31. Kate Stone, *Brokenburn,* pp. 168–69.
32. *O.R.,* XXIV:3:7. The projected route involved canals connecting the Mississippi, above and below Vicksburg, with Lake Providence, Baxter Bayou, Bayou Macon, the Tensas River, Black River, and Red River.
33. Ibid.
34. Grant, *Memoirs,* I:448.
35. Ibid.
36. Norman Shavin, *The Atlanta Century* (Atlanta, I/D Publishers, 1965). Reprint of newspaper records for February 15, 1863.
37. Vicksburg *Daily Whig,* January 27, 1863.

Chapter 10. THE QUEEN AND THE DUMMY

1. Sylvanus Cadwallader, *Three Years with Grant,* p. 53.
2. Shelby Foote, *The Civil War,* II:199–200.
3. Earl S. Miers, *The Webb of Victory,* p. 89.
4. Cadwallader, p. 55. Why Cadwallader did not accompany his fellow correspondents on Ellet's eventful mission with *Queen of the West* is hard to say, unless he felt it was his duty to the paper to stay close to Grant. Though the Chicago

reporter complained that Grant was too easily put upon by those around him, he wangled a personal stateroom for himself aboard the *Magnolia,* in quarters normally reserved for naval officers.

5. David Dixon Porter, *Naval History of the Civil War,* pp. 296–97.
6. Miers, p. 91.
7. Ibid., p. 92.
8. Chicago *Tribune,* February 15, 1863.
9. Ibid. See also, H. A. Gosnell, *Guns on Western Waters,* p. 187. Gosnell gives a full account of the adventures of the *Queen,* pp. 179–92, based largely on Bodman's dispatches to his New York paper.
10. Gosnell, p. 188.
11. Ibid.
12. Ibid., p. 190.
13. Miers, p. 104.
14. Ibid.
15. Ibid., p. 105.
16. Ibid.
17. Bruce Catton, *Never Call Retreat,* pp. 78–79.
18. Vicksburg *Daily Whig,* February 7, 1863.
19. David Dixon Porter, *Incidents and Anecdotes,* pp. 134–35. Porter describes in some detail the building of his dummy craft.
20. Ibid. See also Gosnell, pp. 199–200.
21. Vicksburg *Daily Whig,* March 18, 1866, a reprint of the story of the "Turreted Monster," which first appeared under that title in the Richmond *Examiner.*
22. Ibid.
23. Ibid.
24. Kate Stone, *Brokenburn,* p. 174.
25. Dora Richards, "A Woman's Diary of the Siege of Vicksburg," 767–68.
26. Vicksburg *Evening Post,* July 1, 1963, Pt. 3, 7.
27. Granville Alspaugh, Letters, to his mother, March 15, 1863.
28. Diary of Rowland Chambers, March 5, 1863.
29. Reprinted in Norman Shavin, *The Atlanta Century,* March 8, 1863.
30. Ibid., February 22, 1863.
31. Isaac Jackson, *One of the Boys,* p. 73.
32. Shavin, *Atlanta Century,* March 8, 1863.
33. John Fiske, *The Mississippi Valley and the Civil War,* p. 225.
34. Ulysses S. Grant, *Personal Memoirs,* I: 449.

Chapter 11. BATTLING THE BAYOUS

1. James H. Wilson, *Under the Old Flag,* pp. 150–52. Lieutenant Colonel James Harrison Wilson had joined Grant's forces in November, as the general's chief topographical engineer. He had not been cut out for the job; his inclinations were toward the cavalry. But he did his homework well. Recognizing that Grant was neither a good organizer nor greatly concerned with technical details, "I got together a force of civil and military assistants and photographers for gathering information, surveying, sketching, and mapping the country." (p. 139) When Grant assigned him the task of finding a water route to the rear of Vicksburg, he was well equipped to do so. In fact, like John Rawlins, who befriended Wilson on his arrival from the East, the major became one of the more influential men behind the scenes in Grant's campaign for Vicksburg.
2. John Fiske, *The Mississippi Valley and the Civil War,* p. 216.

3. Earl S. Miers, *The Web of Victory,* p. 110.
4. David Dixon Porter, *Incidents and Anecdotes,* p. 140. In preceding pages, Porter discusses the planning and early stages of the expedition.
5. Wilson, pp. 151–52.
6. Ibid.
7. Miers, p. 111.
8. John C. Pemberton, *Pemberton: Defender of Vicksburg,* p. 77.
9. Miers, pp. 112–14.
10. Pemberton, p. 77. See also Samuel Lockett, "The Defense of Vicksburg," p. 485.
11. Miers, p. 112.
12. Ibid., p. 113.
13. Ibid., p. 115.
14. Vicksburg *Daily Whig,* March 18, 1863.
15. Ibid.
16. Ibid., March 10, 1863.
17. Peter F. Walker, *Vicksburg, a People at War,* p. 148. De Bow (real name: De Bienville Randolph Kleim) was editor of the influential journal, *De Bow's Review,* and, during the war, acted unofficially as an investigative agent for the Mississippi legislature.
18. Porter, *Incidents,* p. 144.
19. Ibid., p. 137.
20. William T. Sherman, *Memoirs,* I:306.
21. Porter, *Incidents,* p. 145. In the following pages, Porter gives a comprehensive account of the Steele's Bayou expedition.
22. Ibid., p. 149. The words, of course, are those that Porter imagines being sent; there was no telegram.
23. Ibid., pp. 146–47.
24. Ibid., p. 149. For the disruption of life among the planters in the Delta, as a result of this amphibious invasion, see Frank E. Smith, *The Yazoo River,* pp. 130–35.
25. Porter, *Incidents,* p. 150.
26. Ibid., pp. 151–52.
27. Ibid., pp. 153–55.
28. Ibid., p. 159.
29. Ibid., p. 160.
30. William Chambers, *My Journal,* pp. 259–60.
31. Porter, *Incidents,* p. 161.
32. Sherman, I:308–10.
33. Ibid.
34. Ibid., p. 312.
35. Porter, *Incidents,* pp. 169, 171.
36. *Harper's Magazine,* April 1863, p. 455.

Chapter 12. LAST DESPERATE GAMBLE

1. William C. Everhart, *Vicksburg,* p. 2. Telegram, Halleck to Grant, dated March 20, 1863.
2. Bruce Catton, *Grant Moves South,* pp. 394–95. The acrimonious correspondent was Murat Halstead of the *Gazette* who, according to fellow newspaperman Sylvanus Cadwallader, "had joined in the hue and cry against Grant from the outset." The vicious gibes quoted here were part of a letter Halstead wrote to Secretary Salmon P. Chase, dated February 19, 1863, copies of which found their way to certain newspapers (reprinted in the Chicago *Tribune,* for one), and more

significantly to the President in Washington. Grant couldn't have had a more antagonistic press, as he admits in his *Personal Memoirs,* I:458–59. Examples of the verbal pummeling he took appear in Sylvanus Cadwallader, *Three Years with Grant,* pp. 113–15, Earl S. Miers, *The Web of Victory,* and Lloyd Lewis, *Sherman: Fighting Prophet,* pp. 262–63.

3. John Fiske, *The Mississippi Valley and the Civil War,* p. 225.
4. Van Wyck Brooks, *The Flowering of New England* (New York: Dutton, 1940), pp. 243–45.
5. Charles A. Dana, *Recollections of the Civil War,* pp. 30–34.
6. Ibid. Despite Dana's initial subterfuge, Grant freely discussed his military plans with him, which the latter, in turn, presented in his *Recollections.*
7. Catton, *Grant Moves South,* p. 408.
8. *O.R.,* 1:XXIV:3:168. In Union reports, Snyder's Bluff was often mistakenly referred to as Haynes Bluff. Haynes Bluff was three miles north of Snyder's.
9. Lloyd Lewis, *Sherman: Fighting Prophet,* pp. 270–71.
10. Isaac Jackson, *Some of the Boys,* p. 82.
11. Dana, pp. 33–34.
12. Mary A. Loughborough, *My Cave Life in Vicksburg,* p. 12.
13. Ibid., pp. 13–14.
14. Dana, pp. 36–37.
15. Diary of A. Hugh Moss, p. 21.
16. James H. Wilson, *Under the Old Flag,* pp. 163–64.
17. Loughborough, p. 23.
18. William Chambers, *My Journal,* pp. 262–63.
19. Dora Richards, "A Woman's Diary of the Siege of Vicksburg," p. 768.
20. William T. Sherman, *Memoirs,* I:317–18.
21. Kate Stone, *Brokenburn,* pp. 182–83.
22. Ibid., pp. 188–91.
23. Franc B. Wilkie, *Pen and Pencil,* pp. 307–10.
24. Richards, p. 768.
25. John C. Pemberton, *Pemberton: Defender of Vicksburg,* p. 97.
26. Ibid., p. 90.
27. Ulysses S. Grant, *Personal Memoirs,* I:468–70.
28. Dana, p. 38.
29. Jacob W. Wilkin, "Personal Reminiscences of General U. S. Grant," p. 134.
30. Charles E. Wilcox, "With Grant at Vicksburg." The diary of Charles Wilcox, which covers the period of April 30, 1860, to August 30, 1863, was edited by Edgar L. Erickson for the *Journal of the Illinois State Historical Society,* January 1938, selecting those entries applying to the campaign for Vicksburg. For his description of the army's movement from Vicksburg to New Carthage, see pp. 456–66.
31. Lewis, p. 272.
32. Grant, *Memoirs,* I:459.
33. *O.R.,* 1:XXIV:3:50.
34. Pemberton, p. 94.

Chapter 13. RAID OF THE HELLIONS

1. D. Alexander Brown, *Grierson's Raid,* pp. 23–25. Grierson's unpublished autobiography remains in manuscript form at the Illinois State Historical Library in Springfield, along with his letters and personal papers.
2. Henry Steele Commager, *The Blue and the Gray,* II:656. Under the title of

"Colonel Grierson Discovers that the Confederacy is a Hollow Shell," the editor presents Grierson's account of the raid through Mississippi, quoting directly from the commander's reports in *O.R.,* 1:XXIV:1.

3. Brown, *Grierson,* pp. 5–6. By far the most available and readable account of this extraordinary raid, Dee Brown's volume follows, with minute and colorful detail, the day-by-day progress of each regiment in the battalion. There is hardly need to look further for particulars of Grierson's exploit, which was the first true success of Union cavalry in the Civil War.
4. Richard Surby, *Grierson's Raids,* p. 21.
5. Brown, *Grierson,* pp. 5–6.
6. Ibid., p. 4.
7. Commager, p. 657.
8. Stephen Forbes, "Grierson's Cavalry Raid," p. 102.
9. Brown, *Grierson,* pp. 74–75.
10. Surby, pp. 33–34.
11. Ibid., pp. 36–38.
12. Brown, *Grierson,* pp. 107–12.
13. John C. Pemberton, *Pemberton: Defender of Vicksburg,* p. 293.
14. Ibid., p. 103.
15. Ibid., pp. 103–04.
16. Ibid., pp. 112–13.
17. Brown, *Grierson,* p. 114.
18. Dora Richards, "A Woman's Diary of the Siege of Vicksburg," p. 767.
19. Kate Stone, *Brokenburn,* p. 191.
20. Vicksburg *Daily Whig,* April 29, 1863.
21. Ibid., April 30, 1863.
22. Ibid.
23. Ibid., May 2, 1863.
24. Isaac Jackson, *One of the Boys,* p. 85.
25. Grenville M. Dodge, *The Battle of Atlanta and Other Campaigns,* pp. 119–25. In these pages, Dodge includes Streight's own, detailed account of the raid through northern Alabama. Also, Samuel Carter III, *The Last Cavaliers,* pp. 133–47.
26. Brown, *Grierson,* p. 147.
27. Ibid., pp. 148–49.
28. Surby, pp. 75–76.
29. Brown, *Grierson,* p. 162.
30. Commager, p. 660.
31. Brown, *Grierson,* pp. 186–87.
32. Ibid., p. 191.
33. Ibid., p. 201.
34. Commager, p. 661.
35. Brown, *Grierson,* p. 206.
36. Ibid., p. 236.
37. Ibid., p. 210.
38. Ibid., p. 215.
39. *O.R.,* 1:XXIV:1:33–34.
40. Brown, *Grierson,* p. 223.
41. Commager, p. 662.

Chapter 14. "THE ROAD TO VICKSBURG IS OPEN"

1. Charles E. Wilcox, "With Grant at Vicksburg," p. 467.
2. Bruce Catton, *Grant Moves South,* pp. 424–25.
3. Charles A. Dana, *Recollections of the Civil War,* p. 43.
4. Lloyd Lewis, *Sherman: Fighting Prophet,* p. 272.
5. *O.R.,* 1:XXIV:3:800.
6. William T. Sherman, *Memoirs,* I:319.
7. Ulysses S. Grant, *Personal Memoirs,* Vol I:480–81.
8. William Chambers, *My Journal,* pp. 263–64. Chambers's comment on the beauty of Port Gibson reflects Grant's own opinion that "Port Gibson is too beautiful to burn." Apart from minor battle scars, the city was not damaged.
9. Dana, pp. 44–45.
10. Frederick Dent Grant, "Reminiscences," Vicksburg *Evening Post,* July 1, 1963.
11. Ulysses S. Grant, *Personal Memoirs,* I:491–92. Despite Grant's quoted statement, he continued to rely on supplies from Grand Gulf for many days to come.
12. Catton, *Grant,* p. 436.
13. John C. Pemberton, *Pemberton: Defender of Vicksburg,* p. 296, Appendices.
14. Ibid., p. 122.
15. Ibid., pp. 111, 124.
16. Isaac Jackson, *One of the Boys,* p. 90.
17. Dana, pp. 49–50.
18. Osborn H. Oldroyd, *A Soldier's Story of the Siege of Vicksburg,* pp. 11–12.
19. William Chambers, *My Journal,* pp. 266–67.
20. Shelby Foote, *The Civil War,* II:358.
21. Oldroyd, p. 9.
22. Sylvanus Cadwallader, *Three Years with Grant,* p. 67.
23. Oldroyd, pp. 16–17.
24. Peter F. Walker, *Vicksburg, A People at War,* p. 159.
25. Cadwallader, pp. 70–72.
26. Grant, *Memoirs,* I:499.
27. Joseph E. Johnston, *Narrative of Military Operations,* pp. 172–73.
28. Ibid., p. 506, Appendix.
29. Oldroyd, p. 21.
30. Cadwallader, pp. 73–74. Also, Fred Grant's "Reminiscences," Vicksburg *Evening Post,* July 1, 1963.
31. Grant, *Memoirs,* I:507.
32. *Civil War Times,* February 1977, p. 7.
33. James A. Fremantle, *The Fremantle Diary,* p. 87.
34. Samual H. Lockett, "The Defense of Vicksburg," p. 487.
35. Mary A. Loughborough, *My Cave Life in Vicksburg,* pp. 28, 34.

Chapter 15. HILL OF DEATH

As Grant's army starts its march toward Vicksburg and the fighting with Pemberton's Confederates begins in earnest, this and subsequent chapters lean more heavily for source material on *O.R.,* 1:XXIV:2. In this series are ninety-seven reports of leading commanders and their subordinates, covering generally the period between May 19 and July 4, 1863. Seventy of these entries are the records of Union officers. The balance of twenty-seven sections contains the reports of Confederate units and their commanders. In some instances these reports refer back to action occurring before May 19.

1. Ulysses S. Grant, *Personal Memoirs,* I:507–08.

2. Ibid., pp. 508–09.
3. Charles A. Dana, *Recollections of the Civil War*, p. 52.
4. Sylvanus Cadwallader, *Three Years with Grant*, p. 77.
5. John C. Pemberton, *Pemberton: Defender of Vicksburg*, p. 54.
6. Ibid., pp. 146–48.
7. Joseph E. Johnston, *Narrative of Military Operations*, p. 527, Appendix.
8. Earl S. Miers, *The Web of Victory*, p. 181.
9. Ibid., pp. 182–84.
10. S.H.M. Byers, "Some Recollections of Grant," pp. 346–56.
11. *O.R.*, 1:XXIV:2:88.
12. Pemberton, pp. 156–65. Along with his account of the battle in these pages, Pemberton discusses, with understandable bitterness, the disappearance of Loring and his division, which the commander believed had caused the Confederate disaster. Certainly it was a vital factor, and even Secretary of War James A. Seddon confessed, a few months later, that Loring's conduct was "incomprehensible to me."
13. Vicksburg *Herald*, July 26, 1870.
14. Wilbur F. Crummer, *With Grant . . . at Vicksburg*, pp. 104–06.
15. Charles A. Dana, *Recollections of the Civil War*, pp. 54–55.
16. Cadwallader, p. 80.
17. Grant, *Personal Memoirs*, I:519–20.
18. William T. Sherman, *Memoirs*, I:323. The "affectionate niece" referred to here was most likely Joseph's granddaughter, Lise.
19. William Chambers, *My Journal*, p. 269.
20. Frederick Dent Grant, "With Grant in Vicksburg," Webb, *Crucial Moments*, pp. 153–55.
21. Ulysses S. Grant, *Personal Memoirs*, I:524–26.
22. Samuel H. Lockett, "The Defense of Vicksburg," p. 488.
23. Diary of Emma Balfour, May 17, 1863.
24. Mary A. Loughborough, *My Cave Life in Vicksburg*, pp. 40–41.
25. Dora Richards, "A Woman's Diary of the Siege of Vicksburg," p. 771.
26. Loughborough, pp. 44–45.
27. Balfour, May 17, 1863.
28. Diary of Joseph D. Alison, May 17, 1863.
29. Diary of Rowland Chambers, May 17, 1863.
30. Richards, May 17, 1863.
31. Loughborough, p. 46.
32. *Harper's Pictorial History of the Great Rebellion*, pp. 466–67.
33. Jared Y. Sanders, "Civil War Letters and Diary," May 18, 1863.
34. Alison, May 18, 1863. Alison is anticipating the worst. As Albert Scheller points out, Vicksburg was not totally invested until a week later, May 25.
35. Sherman, I:324.
36. Osborn H. Oldroyd, *A Soldier's Story of the Siege of Vicksburg*, pp. 26–27.
37. Grant, *Memoirs*, I:528. "I do not claim to quote Sherman's language," the general noted, "but the substance only."

Chapter 16. CORDON OF STEEL

1. *O.R.*, 1:XXIV:2:329–30. See also, Samuel H. Lockett, "The Defense of Vicksburg," p. 488. How Grant perceived the city's defenses, and formed his own siege line accordingly, is described in his *Personal Memoirs*, I:532–41.
2. Lucy McRae, "A Girl's Experience," p. 12.
3. John C. Pemberton, *Pemberton: Defender of Vicksburg*, pp. 176–77. Pemberton's

several communications with Johnston at this critical period are in *O.R.*, XXIV:1:273.

4. Ibid., p. 178.
5. Ibid., p. 179.
6. Bruce Catton, *Grant Moves South,* p. 450.
7. Osborn H. Oldroyd, *A Soldier's Story of the Siege of Vicksburg,* p. 27.
8. Charles E. Wilcox, "With Grant at Vicksburg," pp. 476–77. Wilcox, like Dr. Alison earlier, is exaggerating. Vicksburg was not completely invested until May 25.
9. Shelby Foote, *The Civil War,* II:381–82.
10. J. H. Jones, "The Rank and File at Vicksburg," pp. 19–20. Captain (later colonel) J. H. Jones served with the Thirty-eighth Mississippi Infantry, forming a part of Hébert's brigade in Forney's division.
11. Ibid.
12. Earl S. Miers, *The Web of Victory,* p. 204.
13. Ibid.
14. Lloyd Lewis, *Sherman: Fighting Prophet,* pp. 280–81.
15. Sylvanus Cadwallader, *Three Years with Grant,* pp. 87–88.
16. Diary of Emma Balfour, May 20, 1863.
17. Mary A. Loughborough, *My Cave Life in Vicksburg,* pp. 50–51.
18. Ibid., p. 54.
19. A. A. Hoehling, *Vicksburg,* pp. 27–28.
20. Pemberton, p. 183.
21. Diary of Margaret Lord, p. 3.
22. Lida Lord, "A Woman's Experience During the Siege of Vicksburg," p. 923.
23. Hoehling, pp. 29–30.
24. William W. Lord, Jr., "A Child at the Siege of Vicksburg," pp. 44, 46.
25. McRae, p. 12.
26. Vicksburg *Evening Post,* July 1, 1963, 3:13.
27. Ibid.
28. James A. L. Fremantle, *The Fremantle Diary,* pp. 93–99.
29. Ibid., p. 95.
30. Pemberton, p. 184.
31. Ulysses Grant, *Personal Memoirs,* I:530–31.
32. Ibid., p. 530.
33. J. H. Jones, p. 20.
34. Willie H. Tunnard, *A Southern Record,* pp. 237–38.
35. Oldroyd, p. 30.
36. Diary of Joseph D. Alison, May 21, 1863.

Chapter 17. RIVETS OF BRAVE HEARTS

1. E. B. Long with Barbara Long, *The Civil War Day by Day, an Almanac,* May 22, 1863. At this time also, Davis suggested that Robert E. Lee might send a division or corps from his Army of Northern Virginia to Pemberton in Vicksburg. Which raises one of those tantalizing "What if?" questions of the Civil War. It is a question suggested by Joseph E. Johnston in his *Narrative of Military Operations,* pp. 225–26. Bewailing the transfer of troops from Braxton Bragg instead of from Lee, as too little and too late, Johnston insists that Longstreet's corps *could* have been detached from the Virginia army. He notes: "The military condition in Virginia seems to have been such in the spring of 1863, that the corps was not required in General Lee's army, for in all that time it was detached . . . in some service far less important, certainly, than that which might have been given it at

Vicksburg." Perhaps Lee's invasion of Pennsylvania might therefore have been delayed or canceled; Gettysburg might never have been fought. But a fresh, veteran army corps under Johnston, attacking Grant's rear, might well have saved Vicksburg, the Mississippi Valley, and even the Confederacy. Northern sentiment could not have survived another major military defeat, without a public outcry for negotiations with the South.

2. J. H. Jones, "The Rank and File at Vicksburg," p. 20.
3. Osborn H. Oldroyd, *A Soldier's Story,* pp. 31–32.
4. Sylvanus Cadwallader, *Three Years with Grant,* pp. 89–90.
5. William T. Sherman, *Memoirs,* I:326.
6. J. H. Jones, p. 21.
7. Earl S. Miers, *The Web of Victory,* pp. 209–10.
8. Charles E. Wilcox, "With Grant at Vicksburg," pp. 479–80.
9. Cadwallader, p. 90.
10. Miers, p. 211.
11. Sherman, I:327.
12. Miers, p. 213.
13. Cadwallader, p. 91.
14. Sherman, I:327.
15. William Chambers, *My Journal,* p. 272.
16. Cadwallader, p. 92.
17. Bruce Catton, *Grant Moves South,* p. 453.
18. Ulysses S. Grant, *Personal Memoirs,* I:531.
19. Diary of Emma Balfour, May 23, 1863.
20. Diary of Margaret Lord, p. 3. Lida Lord, "A Woman's Experience . . .," p. 924.
21. Mary A. Loughborough, *My Cave Life in Vicksburg,* pp. 56–58.
22. Dora Richards, "A Woman's Diary of the Siege of Vicksburg," p. 771.
23. Diary of Rowland Chambers, May 22, 23, 1863.
24. Willie H. Tunnard, *A Southern Record,* p. 239.
25. Balfour, May 23, 1863.
26. Catton, *Grant,* p. 453.
27. Grant, *Memoirs,* I:532.
28. John C. Pemberton, *Pemberton: Defender of Vicksburg,* p. 195.
29. Tunnard, p. 240.
30. Oldroyd, pp. 36–37; Isaac Jackson, *One of the Boys,* p. 97.
31. Samuel H. Lockett, "The Defense of Vicksburg," p. 490.
32. Tunnard, p. 241.
33. Jared Y. Sanders, "Civil War Letters and Diary," May 25, 1863.
34. Diary of A. Hugh Moss, p. 30.
35. Tunnard, pp. 241–42.
36. William Chambers, *My Journal,* p. 274.
37. Pemberton, p. 199.

Chapter 18. THE NOOSE DRAWS TIGHTER

1. Ulysses S. Grant, *Personal Memoirs,* I:535. Grant is writing of the first week in June 1863, the third week of the siege; and he here describes the strengthening of his position, the troops turning-to as engineers, the use of sap-rollers, etc.
2. William C. Everhart, *Vicksburg,* p. 40.
3. Wilbur F. Crummer, *With Grant . . . at Vicksburg,* p. 118.
4. Grant, *Memoirs,* I:537.
5. Bruce Catton, *Grant Moves South,* p. 460.
6. Hudson Strode, *Jefferson Davis,* II:409–10. There had been previous vandalism

at the Davis plantations, during the period when Butler's troops from New Orleans were following Farragut up the Mississippi in May and June of 1862, but none could date the crimes or identify the culprits.

7. William Chambers, *My Journal*, p. 274. Chambers's closing, underscored comment is surely an overstatement. The Confederates were cautioned against wasting ammunition; they were not forbidden to fire.
8. Diary of Emma Balfour, May 30, 1863.
9. A. A. Hoehling, *Vicksburg*, p. 92.
10. Mark Twain, *Life on the Mississippi*, p. 216. Twain does not identify the couple from whose narrative he quotes.
11. Balfour, May 30, 1863.
12. Dora Richards, "A Woman's Diary of the Siege of Vicksburg," p. 772.
13. Ibid., June 7.
14. Ida Barlow, Manuscript recollections of the siege of Vicksburg, p. 1. Ida Trotter Barlow's six-page manuscript, with no dates given, is in the Mississippi State Archives. Ida lived with her father and stepmother, and two smaller children, less than a mile northeast of the Vicksburg fortifications. Her oldest brother, Captain James A. Barlow, had been killed fighting under General Lee in Virginia just a year before—no doubt contributing to their militant antagonism toward the enemy around them.
15. Ibid., pp. 2–3.
16. P. M. Angle and Earl S. Miers, *The Tragic Years 1860–1865*, p. 616.
17. Catton, *Grant*, p. 419.
18. Ibid., p. 463. Also Earl S. Miers, *The Web of Victory*, p. 244.
19. Sylvanus Cadwallader, *Three Years with Grant*, p. 103.
20. Ibid., p. 104.
21. Ibid., pp. 106–107.
22. Ibid., p. 109.
23. John C. Pemberton, *Pemberton: Defender of Vicksburg*, p. 202.
24. *American Heritage Songbook* (New York: American Heritage Publishing Co., 1969), p. 133.
25. M. M. Quaife (ed.), *Absalom Grimes, Confederate Mail Runner* (New Haven: Yale University Press, 1926), pp. 122–28. Albert Scheller, who so kindly reviewed this manuscript, states that "there are so many errors and inconsistencies in Grimes's account" that it does not warrant serious consideration. But I have kept it for what it is worth.
26. Pemberton, p. 194. The ratio of ammunition to musket-caps was roughly two to one.
27. Shelby Foote, *The Civil War*, II:406.
28. Pemberton, pp. 203–04.
29. Charles A. Dana, *Recollections of the Civil War*, pp. 86–87.
30. Grant, *Memoirs*, I:545.
31. Charles E. Wilcox, "With Grant at Vicksburg," p. 490.

Chapter 19. THE MOUNTING FURY

1. Osborn H. Oldroyd, *A Soldier's Story*, pp. 51–52.
2. Bruce Catton, *Grant Moves South*, p. 466. Grant's letter to Pride is in the archives of the Missouri Historical Society.
3. Richard B. Harwell, ed., *The Confederate Reader*, p. 196.
4. Diary of Joseph D. Alison, June 10, 1863.
5. Mary A. Loughborough, *My Cave Life in Vicksburg*, p. 72. Since its publication in 1864, Mary Loughborough's small book has become a treasury of life in

Vicksburg under siege. "Caves were the fashion—the rage—over besieged Vicksburg," Mary wrote, observing that her own underground refuge was five city blocks up from the Mississippi levee.

6. Lida Lord, "A Woman's Experience . . . " pp. 924–25.
7. Vicksburg *Evening Post,* July 1, 1963, Pt. 3, p. 6.
8. Lucy McRae, "A Girl's Experience," p. 13.
9. A. A. Hoehling, *Vicksburg,* p. 29.
10. Lida Lord, p. 925.
11. W. W. Lord, Jr., "A Child . . . at Vicksburg," p. 47.
12. Wilbur Crummer, *With Grant . . . at Vicksburg,* pp. 149–50; Earl S. Miers, *Web of Victory,* p. 256.
13. P. M. Angle and E. S. Miers, *The Tragic Years, 1860–1865,* pp. 625–26.
14. O. R., 1:XXIV:2:409.
15. Angle and Miers, p. 615.
16. James H. Wilson, *Under the Old Flag,* pp. 184–86.
17. Ibid.
18. Quoted in Lloyd Lewis, *Sherman: Fighting Prophet,* p. 58.
19. Ibid., pp. 205–06.
20. O.R., XXIV:1:278.
21. Joseph E. Johnston, *Narrative of Military Operations,* p. 199.
22. Vicksburg *Daily Citizen,* June 16, 1863.
23. Dora Richards, "A Woman's Diary of the Siege of Vicksburg," p. 772.
24. Vicksburg *Daily Citizen,* June 13, 1863.
25. Annie Harris, "A Recollection of Thirty Years Ago," p. 12.
26. Willie H. Tunnard, *A Southern Record,* p. 242. Tunnard's and Anderson's sentiments were echoed by observant soldiers in the Union lines—among them Osborn Oldroyd who wrote of the women within the beleaguered city, "Their sacrifices and privations are worthy of a better cause, and were they but on our side how we would worship them."
27. Hoehling, pp. 110–13.
28. *Civil War Times Illustrated,* August 1978, p. 41.
29. Loughborough, pp. 81–82.
30. Richard B. Irwin, "The Capture of Port Hudson," B & L, Vol. III, p. 595.
31. Barlow, MS, pp. 3–4.
32. Hoehling, p. 167.
33. Lida Lord, p. 925.
34. Jackson *Mississippian,* June 17, 1863. Just the day before, the newspaper had reported: "Officers who have lately left the garrison at Vicksburg concur in representing the troops in the very best of spirits. The idea of surrendering never enters the head of any of them, from General Pemberton to the lowest private."

Chapter 20. "HO! FOR JOHNSTON!"

1. Willie Tunnard, *A Southern Record,* p. 250. The rumor of Johnston's strength and intentions was, of course, largely incorrect.
2. Diary of James H. Pepper, pp. 12, 15. James Pepper began his diary on the siege of Vicksburg on June 4, 1863, with some flashback entries of his recollections during May. The manuscript, in the Mississippi Department of Archives and History, is headed: "Personal Knowledge while a Courier for Brigadier Gen. Moore of Fornie's [sic] Division." The original consisted of penciled notes on rough tablet paper, not always dated. All references here are from the twenty-two-page typed copy of this original. The page numbers noted are those of the original diary, as indicated in the typed transcript.

3. *Diary* of A. Hugh Moss, p. 39.
4. Charles A. Dana, *Recollections of the Civil War,* p. 84.
5. Vicksburg *Daily Citizen,* June 18, 1863.
6. William A. Drennan, Diary, Vol. II, pp. 20–21.
7. Joseph E. Johnston, *Narrative of Military Operations,* p. 200.
8. Ibid.
9. Ibid., p. 201.
10. A. A. Hoehling, *Vicksburg,* p. 192.
11. *O.R.,* 1:XXIV:2:293.
12. John C. Pemberton, *Pemberton: Defender of Vicksburg,* p. 214.
13. Osborn H. Oldroyd, *A Soldier's Story,* p. 59.
14. Tunnard, p. 255.
15. Dora Richards, "A Woman's Diary of the Siege of Vicksburg," p. 773.
16. Lucy McRae, "A Girl's Experience," p. 13.
17. Carl Sandburg, *Abraham Lincoln: The War Years,* II:349.
18. Mary A. Loughborough, *My Cave Life in Vicksburg,* p. 74.
19. Lida Lord, "A Woman's Experience . . . ," p. 924.
20. Vicksburg *Daily Citizen,* June 20, 1863.
21. William Drennan, Civil War Papers, Vol. II, p. 18.
22. Lida Lord, p. 925.
23. Pemberton, pp. 210–11.
24. Ibid., p. 213.
25. Tunnard, p. 264.
26. Ulysses S. Grant, "The Vicksburg Campaign," pp. 528–29.
27. McRae, p. 13.
28. Tunnard, p. 263. Though Lida Lord, among others, denied that the people of Vicksburg were reduced to eating rats, the tales persisted, embellished to include cats, dogs, mice, and virtually everything that moved or crawled within the city. But substantiation is hard to come by; only mule meat was admittedly consumed in generous quantities.
29. Hoehling, p. 250.
30. Thomas N. Waul Papers, Duke University, *Rebellion Record,* Vol. VII, p. 57.
31. Ida Barlow, MS, p. 4.
32. Lida Lord, p. 926.
33. Pemberton, p. 215.
34. Ibid.
35. Ibid., p. 216.
36. Grant, "Vicksburg Campaign," p. 526.
37. Dana, p. 85.
38. Lloyd Lewis, *Sherman: Fighting Prophet,* p. 290.
39. Isaac Jackson, *Some of the Boys,* p. 109.
40. James H. Wilson, *Under the Old Flag,* p. 224.

Chapter 21. BLOW, GABRIEL, BLOW

1. Willie Tunnard, *A Southern Record,* p. 245. Being with the Third Louisiana Infantry, Tunnard, of course, was himself with the garrison manning the Redan throughout most of the siege. The Third Louisiana Regiment was withdrawn after the second explosion of a mine. Missouri troops took over, to remain for as long as the siege continued.
2. J. H. Jones, "The Rank and File at Vicksburg," p. 26.
3. Ibid., p. 27.
4. Andrew Hickenlooper, "The Vicksburg Mine," p. 539.

5. Ibid., p. 540, with diagram showing construction of the Federal approaches from the Shirley House to the redan.
6. Tunnard, pp. 246–47.
7. Ibid. The day-by-day efforts of Federal troops and engineers to approach the Confederate fort, by trenches and tunnels, is detailed in O.R., 1:XXIV:2:199–203.
8. *B & L,* Vol. III, p. 541, editors' footnote. Actually, Foster was assisted in building his tower by members of his regiment.
9. Jared Sanders, Diary, June 22, 1863.
10. J. H. Jones, p. 23.
11. Tunnard, p. 259.
12. *O.R.,* 1:XXIV:2:202.
13. Ibid.
14. Hickenlooper, p. 542.
15. Sylvanus Cadwallader, *Three Years with Grant,* p. 121.
16. Hickenlooper, p. 542. Source material used for describing the affair of the crater: *O.R.,* 1:XXIV:2. Notable among these reports, on the Confederate side, are those of General Hébert, pp. 372, 375–76; and General Forney, pp. 365, 369. Notable among Union reports is that of Logan's Chief Engineer S. R. Tresilian, pp. 207–08.
17. Quoted in Earl S. Miers, *Web of Victory,* pp. 281–82.
18. Ibid., p. 283.
19. Sanders, June 25, 1863.
20. Lida Lord, "A Woman's Experience . . . ," p. 926.
21. Mary A. Loughborough, *My Cave Life in Vicksburg,* p. 114.
22. Dora Richards, "A Woman's Diary of the Siege of Vicksburg," p. 773.
23. Vicksburg *Daily Citizen,* June 23, 1863.
24. Carl Sandburg, *Abraham Lincoln: The War Years,* II:111.
25. Loughborough, pp. 136–37.
26. Annie Harris, "A Recollection of Thirty Years Ago," p. 14.
27. Loughborough, p. 129.
28. *O.R.,* 1:XXIV:2:368.
29. Osborn H. Oldroyd, *A Soldier's Story,* pp. 68–69.
30. Vicksburg *Daily Citizen,* July 2, 1863.
31. Joseph E. Johnston, *Narrative of Military Operations,* pp. 202–03.

Chapter 22. THE GLORIOUS FOURTH

1. *Official Records of the Union and Confederate Navies,* 1:XXV:118.
2. John C. Pemberton, *Pemberton: Defender of Vicksburg,* pp. 223–24.
3. Ibid., pp. 221–22.
4. *O.R.,* 1:XXIV:2:368. Among the replies submitted by the various commanders, there was only one dissenting voice. Wrote Brigadier General W. S. Baldwin, "I object to a surrender of the troops, and am in favor of holding the position, or attempting to hold it, as long as possible" (p. 405).
5. Pemberton, p. 225. At the meeting held at Pemberton's headquarters to consider Grant's written terms of surrender, Brigadier General Stephen D. Lee joined Baldwin in opposing surrender.
6. Vicksburg *Daily Citizen,* June 30 and July 2, 1863.
7. Dora Richards, "A Woman's Diary of the Siege of Vicksburg," p. 774.
8. Willie Tunnard, *A Southern Record,* p. 264.
9. Margaret Lord, Journal, p. 7.
10. A. A. Hoehling, *Vicksburg,* p. 265.
11. Ulysses S. Grant, *Personal Memoirs,* I:557.

12. Ibid., pp. 557–58.
13. Charles A. Dana, *Recollections of the Civil War,* p. 96.
14. R. S. Bevier, "Confederate Reminiscences," in appendix of Oldroyd, *A Soldier's Story,* p. 179.
15. Grant, *Memoirs,* I:561.
16. *O.R.,* 1:XXIV:2:352.
17. Quoted in Pemberton, pp. 232–33.
18. Isaac Jackson, *One of the Boys,* pp. 111–12.
19. James H. Wilson, *Under the Old Flag,* p. 22.
20. Mary A. Loughborough, *My Cave Life,* p. 139.
21. Lucy McRae, "A Girl's Experience," p. 13.
22. Charles E. Wilcox, "With Grant at Vicksburg," p. 495.
23. Jackson, p. 112.
24. Tunnard, p. 271.
25. *O.R.,* 1:XXIV:2:410.
26. William Chambers, *My Journal,* p. 281.
27. McRae, p. 13.
28. Loughborough, pp. 139–40.
29. Richards, p. 774.
30. Margaret Lord, p. 9.
31. Richards, p. 775.
32. Wilson, p. 223. The Rock House, to which Pemberton presumably had moved from Crawford Street, was on the Jackson Road a half mile west of the defense line.
33. McRae, p. 13.
34. Ulysses S. Grant, "The Vicksburg Campaign," p. 534.
35. Samuel H. Lockett, "The Defense of Vicksburg," p. 492.
36. Tunnard, p. 272.
37. Jackson, p. 112.
38. Lloyd Lewis, *Sherman: Fighting Prophet,* p. 292.
39. Both Grant and Sherman in their *Memoirs* give statistics on casualties and captures in the siege of Vicksburg, on pages 572 and 333 respectively.
40. Bruce Catton, *Never Call Retreat,* p. 192.
41. William C. Everhart, *Vicksburg,* p. 53.
42. Vicksburg *Daily Citizen.* The date of July 2, 1863, still remained on the masthead.

Chapter 23. IN THE WAKE OF THE STORM

1. Richard B. Irwin, "The Capture of Port Hudson," *B & L,* Vol. III, pp. 586–98.
2. William T. Sherman, "The Grand Strategy . . . ," *B & L,* Vol. IV, p. 250.
3. Samuel Carter III, *Siege of Atlanta,* p. 384. The fate of the Army of Tennessee, perhaps the most magnificent military force ever fielded in America, is beautifully told in Thomas L. Connelly's *Autumn of Glory* (Baton Rouge: Louisiana State University Press, 1971). In the epilogue, Connelly relates Johnston's resumption of command, and his last stand against Sherman in the Carolinas.
4. John C. Pemberton, *Pemberton: Defender of Vicksburg,* p. 241.
5. Ibid., p. 249.
6. William T. Sherman, *Memoirs,* II:27.
7. D. Alexander Brown, *Grierson's Raid,* p. 239.
8. *Dictionary of American Biography* (New York: Scribners, 1930).
9. Records of the Scott Fanton Museum in Danbury, Connecticut, show that Rawlins made his family home in that city, even while absent in Washington, and his wife and two children are buried there.

10. *Encyclopedia Brittanica,* 1949, VII:11.
11. Sylvanus Cadwallader, *Three Years with Grant,* introduction, pp. x–xi.
12. A. A. Hoehling, *Vicksburg,* p. 295.
13. Diary of Rowland Chambers, May 16, 1863, written at camp near Meridian, Mississippi.
14. Jared Y. Sanders, "Civil War Letters and Diary," January 2, 1865.
15. William Ward Orme, letter to his wife dated July 7, 1863. *Civil War Letters,* pp. 293–94.
16. Edgar L. Erickson, *Journal of the Illinois State Historical Society,* Vol. XXX, No. 4, January 1938, pp. 502–03.
17. Diary of A. Hugh Moss, July 12 through 29, 1863, pp. 48–56.
18. Isaac Jackson, *Some of the Boys,* July 26, 1863, through April 13, 1865, pp. 114–249.
19. Osborn H. Oldroyd, *A Soldier's Story,* pp. 74–75.
20. Dora Richards, "A Woman's Diary of the Siege of Vicksburg," p. 774.
21. Mary A. Loughborough, *My Cave Life in Vicksburg,* pp. 145–46.
22. Roach-Eggleston Papers, Southern Historical Collection, University of North Carolina.
23. Lucy McRae, "A Girl's Experience," p. 13.
24. Biographical data on Rowland Chambers from the Archives of the Louisiana State University Library.
25. Vicksburg *Evening Post,* July 1, 1963, 5:4, 23.
26. Diary of Margaret Lord, p. 12; W. W. Lord, Jr., "A Child at the Siege of Vicksburg," p. 53.
27. Annie Harris, "A Recollection of Thirty Years Ago," pp. 22–24.
28. Peter F. Walker, *Vicksburg, A People at War,* pp. 220–21.
29. Ida Barlow, MS, p. 6.
30. A. A. Hoehling, *Vicksburg,* p. 292.
31. Kate Stone, *Brokenburn,* p. 364.
32. John T. Trowbridge, *The Desolate South* (New York: Duell, Sloane & Pearce, 1956), p. 190.
33. Walker, pp. 215–16.
34. Sylvanus Cadwallader, *Three Years With Grant,* p. 127.
35. Ulysses S. Grant, *Personal Memoirs,* I:577.
36. Reprinted in Vicksburg *Evening Post,* July 1, 1963, 5:2.
37. Mark Twain, *Life on the Mississippi,* p. 214.

Bibliography and Sources

Abbot, Willis J., *Blue Jackets of 1861*. New York: Dodd, Mead, 1886.

Abrams, Alexander S., *A Full and Detailed History of the Siege of Vicksburg*. Atlanta: Intelligencer Press, 1863.

Alison, Joseph D., Diary. Southern Historical Collection, University of North Carolina, Chapel Hill.

Allen, Charles B., "Plantation Book." Manuscript, and typescript, Mississippi Department of Archives and History, Jackson.

Alspaugh, Granville L., "Civil War Letters." *Louisiana Historical Quarterly,* Vol. 29, No. 4, October 1946, pp. 1229–1240.

American Heritage, *Picture History of the Civil War,* text by Bruce Catton. New York: Doubleday, 1960.

Anderson, Ephraim McD., *Memoirs.* St. Louis: Times Printing Co., 1868.

Angle, P. M., and Miers, E. S., *The Tragic Years, 1860–1865,* 2 vols. New York: Simon & Schuster, 1960.

Annals of the War Written by Leading Participants North and South. Philadelphia: Weekly Times, 1879.

Balfour, Emma, Diary. Typed manuscript, Mississippi Department of Archives and History, Jackson.

Barlow, Ida (Trotter). Manuscript recollections of the siege of Vicksburg, Mississippi Department of Archives and History, Jackson.

Bearss, Edwin C., "Battle of Chickasaw Bayou." Vicksburg *Sunday Post,* November 13, 1960, and January 29, 1961.

———. *Decision in Mississippi.* Jackson: Mississippi Commission on the War Between the States, 1962.

———. *Hardluck Ironclad: The Sinking and the Salvage of the Cairo.* Baton Rouge: Louisiana State University Press, 1966.

Bettersworth, John K., *Confederate Mississippi.* Baton Rouge: Louisiana State University Press, 1943.

Bevier, Robert S., *History of the First and Second Missouri Confederate Brigades 1861–1865.* St. Louis: Bryand, Brand & Co., 1879.

Botkin, B. A., *Mississippi River Folklore.* New York: Crown, 1978.

Brown, D. Alexander, *Grierson's Raid.* Urbana: University of Illinois Press, 1954.

Brown, Isaac N., *Arkansas. Battles and Leaders,* Vol. III, pp. 572–80.

Byers, S. H. M., "Some Recollections of Grant," *Annals of the War,* pp. 342–56.

Cadwallader, Sylvanus, *Three Years with Grant.* New York: Knopf, 1955.

Carter, Hodding, *The Lower Mississippi.* New York: Farrar and Rinehart, 1942.

Carter, Samuel III, *The Siege of Atlanta.* New York: St. Martin's Press, 1973.

———, *The Last Cavaliers.* New York: St. Martin's Press, 1979.

Catton, Bruce, *Grant Moves South.* Boston: Little Brown & Co., 1960.

———. *Never Call Retreat.* New York: Doubleday & Co., 1965.

———. *This Hallowed Ground.* New York: Doubleday & Co., 1956.

Chambers, Rowland, Diary. Typescript from original, Library Archives, Louisiana State University, Baton Rouge.

Chambers, William P., *My Journal.* Jackson: Publications of the Mississippi Historical Society, Vol. V, 1925.

Chesnut, Mary B., *Diary from Dixie.* New York: D. Appleton, 1905.

Civil War Times, "Struggle for Vicksburg." Gettysburg: Historical Times, Inc., 1967.

Commager, Henry Steele, ed., *The Blue and the Gray,* 2 vols. Indianapolis: Bobbs-Merrill, 1950.

Coulter, E. Merton, "Commercial Intercourse with the Confederacy in the Mississippi Valley, 1861–1865." *The Mississippi Valley Historical Review,* Vol. V, No. 4, March 1919.

Crozier, Emmet, *Yankee Reporter, 1861–65.* New York: Oxford University Press, 1956.

Crummer, Wilbur F., *With Grant at Fort Donelson, Shiloh and Vicksburg.* Oak Park (Ill.): privately printed, 1915.

Cunningham, Edward, *The Port Hudson Campaign, 1862–1863.* Baton Rouge: Louisiana State University Press, 1963.

Curtis, John C., Civil War Letters. Property of Milton Bond, Fairfield, Connecticut.

Dana, Charles A., *Recollections of the Civil War.* New York: D. Appleton, 1898.

Dictionary of American Biography. 20 vols. New York: Scribner, 1948.

Dodge, Grenville M., *The Battle of Atlanta and Other Campaigns.* Council Bluffs (Iowa): Monarch Printing Co., 1911.

Drennan, William A., Civil War Papers. Mississippi Department of Archives and History, Jackson.

Dufour, Charles L., *Ten Flags in the Wind.* New York: Harper & Row, 1967.

Eads, James B., "Recollections of Foote and the Gun-boats." *Battles and Leaders,* Vol. I, pp. 338–46.

Eaton, Clement, *Jefferson Davis.* New York: Macmillan, 1977.

Ellet, Alfred W., "Ellet and his Steam-rams at Memphis." *Battles and Leaders,* Vol. I, pp. 453–59.

Evans, Clement A., ed, *Confederate Military History.* Vols. X and XII. Atlanta: Confederate Publishing Co., 1899.

Everhart, William C., *Vicksburg.* Washington, D.C.: National Park Service Handbook Series No. 21, 1954.

Fiske, John, *The Mississippi Valley and the Civil War.* Boston: Houghton Mifflin, 1900.

Foote, John A., "Notes on the Life of Admiral Foote." *Battles and Leaders,* Vol. I, p. 347.

Foote, Shelby, *The Civil War,* 3 vols. New York: Random House, 1954–1978.

Forbes, Stephen A., "Grierson's Cavalry Raid," Illinois State Historical Society, *Transactions,* 1907.

Fremantle, James A. L., *The Fremantle Diary.* London: André Deutsch, 1956.

General Directory for the City of Vicksburg. Vicksburg: H. C. Clarke, 1860.

Gift, George W., "The Story of the *Arkansas.*" *Southern Historical Society Papers,* Vol. XII, Nos. 1–5, January–May, 1884.

Gosnell, H. A., *Guns on the Western Waters.* Baton Rouge: Louisiana State University Press, 1949.

Grant, Frederick Dent, "Reminiscences." Vicksburg *Evening Post,* July 1, 1963, Pt. 3, pp. 12, 19.

———. "With Grant at Vicksburg." *The Outlook,* July 2, 1898. Reprinted: Willard Webb, *Crucial Moments of the Civil War.*

Grant, Ulysses S., *Personal Memoirs.* 2 vols. New York: Charles L. Webster, 1885. Facsimile edition, New York, Bonanza Books.

———. "The Vicksburg Campaign." *Battles and Leaders,* Vol. III, pp. 493–539.

Gregory, Edward S., "Vicksburg during the Siege." *Annals of the War,* pp. 112–33.

Grimes, Absalom, *Confederate Mail Runner.* New Haven: Yale University Press, 1926.

Guyton, Pearl V., *Campaign and Siege of Vicksburg.* Natchez: privately printed, 1944.

Hall, Winchester, *The Story of the 26th Louisiana Infantry.* No place or publisher, 1890.

Harper's Illistrated History of the Great Rebellion. New York: Fairfax Press, 1866.

Harris, Annie Laurie (Broidrick), "A Recollection of Thirty Years Ago." Manuscript, Southern Historical Collection, University of North Carolina Library, Chapel Hill.

Harwell, Richard B., ed., *The Confederate Reader.* New York: Longman's, Green, 1957.

Henry, Robert S., *The Story of the Confederacy.* Indianapolis: Bobbs-Merrill, 1931.

Hickenlooper, Andrew, "The Vicksburg Mine." *Battles and Leaders,* Vol. III, pp. 539–42.

Hoehling, A. A., *Vicksburg.* Englewood Cliffs: Prentice-Hall, 1969.

Hoge, A. H., *The Boys in Blue.* New York: E. B. Trent, 1867.

Irwin, Richard B, "Military Operations in Louisiana in 1862." *Battles and Leaders,* Vol. III, pp. 582–84.

Jackson, Isaac, *Some of the Boys.* Carbondale (Ill.): Southern Illinois University Press, 1960.

Johnson, R.U., and Buel, C.C., eds, *Battles and Leaders of the Civil War.* 4 vols. New York: Century Co., 1884.

Johnston, Joseph E., "Jefferson Davis and the Mississippi Campaign." *Battles and Leaders,* Vol. III, pp. 472–82.

———. *Narrative of Military Operations.* New York: D. Appleton, 1874.

Jones, Archer, *Confederate Strategy from Shiloh to Vicksburg.* Baton Rouge: Louisiana State University Press, 1961.

Jones, J. H., "The Rank and File at Vicksburg." *Publications of the Mississippi Historical Society,* Vol. VII, pp. 17–31.

Jones, Jenkin L., *An Artilleryman's Diary.* Madison: Wisconsin Historical Commission, 1914.

Jones, Joseph, "The Siege and Defense of Vicksburg, 1862–1863." Manuscript, Library Archives, Louisiana State University, Baton Rouge.

Kane, Harnett T., *Deep Delta Country.* New York: Duell, Sloan & Pearce, 1944.

Lacey, Mary F., *Intellectual Activities of Vicksburg Prior to 1860.* Thesis submitted for the degree of Master of Arts, Duke University, 1937.

Leech, Margaret, *Reveille in Washington.* New York: Harper, 1941.

Lewis, Lloyd, *Sherman: Fighting Prophet.* New York: Harcourt, Brace, 1932.

Lockett, Samuel H., "The Defense of Vicksburg." *Battles and Leaders,* Vol. III, pp. 482–92.

Long, E. B., with Barbara Long, *The Civil War Day by Day, An Almanac.* New York: Doubleday, 1971.

Lord, Lida (Reed), "A Woman's Experience During the Siege of Vicksburg." *Century Magazine,* Vol. LXI, April 1901, pp. 922–28.

Lord, Margaret (Mrs. William W.), record kept during the siege of Vicksburg. Manuscript. Library of Congress, Washington, D.C.

Lord, William W., Jr., "A Child at the Siege of Vicksburg." *Harper's Monthly Magazine,* Vol. CXVIII, December 1908, pp. 44–53.

Loughborough, Mary A., *My Cave Life in Vicksburg.* New York: D. Appleton, 1864.

Macartney, Clarence E., *Grant and His Generals.* New York: McBride, 1953.

McRae, Lucy (Bell), "A Girl's Experience in the Siege of Vicksburg." *Harper's Weekly,* LVI, June 8, 1912. pp. 12–13.

Martin, Christopher, *Damn the Torpedoes!* New York: Abelard-Schuman, 1970.

Maurey, Dabney, H., "Van Dorn, the Hero of Mississippi." *Annals of the War,* pp. 460–66.

Meredith, William T., "Farragut's Capture of New Orleans," *Battles and Leaders*, Vol. II, pp. 70–73.

Miers, Earl S., *The Web of Victory.* New York: Knopf, 1955.

Miller, A., *The Mississippi.* New York: Crown, 1975.

Miller, Francis T., ed., *Photographic History of the Civil War,* Vol. VI. New York: Review of Reviews Co., 1911.

Milligan, John D., *Gunboats Down the Mississippi.* Annapolis: U.S. Naval Institute, 1965.

Morgan, George W., "The Assault on Chickasaw Bluffs." *Battles and Leaders,* Vol. III, pp. 462–70.

Moss, A. H., *The Diary of A. Hugh Moss.* Copy in Library of Congress, dated 1948, no name or place of publisher.

Nevins, Allan, *The War for the Union,* Vols. V, VI, VII. New York: Scribner, 1960.

Official Records of the Union and Confederate Navies in the War of the Rebellion. 30 vols. Washington, D.C.: Government Printing Office, 1896.

Oldroyd, Osborn H., *A Soldier's Story of the Siege of Vicksburg.* Springfield (Ill.): Published by the author, 1885.

Orme, William Ward, *Civil War Letters.* Journal of the Illinois State Historical Society, Vol. XXIII, No. 2, July 1930.

Pemberton, John C., *Pemberton: Defender of Vicksburg.* Chapel Hill: University of North Carolina Press, 1942.

Pepper, James H., Diary kept during the siege of Vicksburg. Typed manuscript, Mississippi Department of Archives and History, Jackson.

Pollard, Edward, *The Lost Cause.* New York: E. B. Trent & Co., 1867.

Porter, David Dixon, *Incidents and Anecdotes of the Civil War.* New York: D. Appleton, 1886.

———. *Naval History of the Civil War.* New York: Sherman Publishing Co., 1886.

Pratt, Fletcher, *Civil War on Western Waters.* New York: Henry Holt, 1956.

Randell, J. G., *The Civil War and Reconstruction.* Lexington (Mass.): D. C. Heath & Co., 1937.

Richards, Dora (Miller), "War Diary of a Union Woman in the South," *Century Magazine,* XXXVIII, October, 1889, pp. 931–46.

———, "A Woman's Diary of the Siege of Vicksburg," *Century Magazine,* XXX, September, 1885, pp. 767–75.

Roach, Mahala P. H., *Diary.* Roach-Eggleston Family Papers, Southern Historical Collection, University of North Carolina, Chapel Hill.

Russell, William H., *My Diary, North and South.* London: Bradley & Evans, 1863.

Sandburg, Carl, *Abraham Lincoln, The War Years.* 4 vols. New York: Harcourt, Brace & World, 1939.

Sanders, Jared Y., "Diary in Gray, Civil War Letters and Diary," edited by Mary Elizabeth Sanders. Louisiana Genealogical Register, Vol. XVI, 1969, and Vol. XVII, 1970.

Shavin, Norman, *The Atlanta Century.* Atlanta: I/D Publishers, 1965.

Sherman, William T., *Memoirs.* 2 vols. New York: D. Appleton, 1875.

Silver, James W., ed., *Mississippi in the Confederacy.* Baton Rouge: Louisiana State University Press, 1961.

Smith, Frank E., *The Yazoo River.* New York: Rinehart, 1954.

Soley, James R., "Naval Operations in the Vicksburg Campaign." *Battles and Leaders,* Vol. III, pp. 551–70.

Stern, P. Van Doren, *Soldier Life in the Union and Confederate Armies.* New York: Crown, 1961.

Stone, Kate, *Brokenburn.* Baton Rouge: Louisiana State University Press, 1955.

Streight, Abel D., "Report on the Raid through Alabama," in Grenville M. Dodge, *Battle of Atlanta and Other Campaigns.* Council Bluffs (Iowa): Monarch Printing Co., 1911.

Strode, Hudson, *Jefferson Davis.* 2 vols. New York: Harcourt, Brace & World, 1955, 1959.

Surby, Richard W., *Grierson's Raids.* Chicago, privately printed, 1865.

Tunnard, Willie H., *A Southern Record.* Baton Rouge: Printed for the author, 1866.

Turner, Frederick J., *The Frontier in American History.* New York: Holt, Rinehart and Winston, 1962.

Twain, Mark, *Life on the Mississippi.* Boston: Osgood & Co., 1883.

———. "The Private History of a Campaign that Failed." *Century Magazine,* Vol. XXI, No. 2, December 1885.

Vandiver, Frank E., *Their Tattered Flags.* New York: Harper & Row, 1970.

Vicksburg *Daily Citizen.* Selected issues from January 1861 to July 2, 1863.

Vicksburg *Daily Whig.* Selected issues from November 1859 to May 5, 1863.

Vicksburg *Evening Post,* Centennial Edition, July 1, 1963.

Vicksburg *Herald,* "Our Women at War," Supplement, April 16, 1908.

Vilas, William F., *The Vicksburg Campaign.* Madison: Wisconsin Historical Commission, 1908.

Walke, Henry, "The Gunboats at Belmont and Fort Henry." *Battles and Leaders,* Vol. I, pp. 358–67.

Walker, Peter F., *Vicksburg, A People at War.* Chapel Hill: University of North Carolina Press, 1960.

War of the Rebellion, Official Records of the Union and Confederate Armies. 70 vols. Washington, D.C.: Government Printing Office, 1880–1901.

Wayman, Norbury L., *Life on the River.* New York: Crown, 1971.

Webb, Willard, *Crucial Moments of the Civil War.* New York: Crown, 1961.

Wells, Seth, *The Siege of Vicksburg from the Diary of Seth Wells.* Detroit: Wm. H. Rowe, 1915.

Wheeler, Richard, *The Siege of Vicksburg.* New York: Thomas Y. Crowell, 1978.

———. *Voices of the War.* New York: Thomas Y. Crowell, 1976.

Wilcox, Charles E., "With Grant at Vicksburg," Edgar L. Erickson, ed., *Journal of the Illinois State Historical Society,* Vol. XXX, No. 4, January 1938.

Wiley, Bell I., *The Life of Billy Yank.* Indianapolis: Bobbs-Merrill, 1951, 1952.

———. *The Life of Johnny Reb.* New York: Doubleday, 1971.

Wilkie, Franc B., *Pen and Powder.* Boston: Ticknor & Co., 1888.

Wilkin, Jacob W., "Personal Reminiscences of General U. S. Grant." *Transactions of the Illinois State Historical Society for 1907,* pp. 131–40.

Williams, T. Harry, *Lincoln and His Generals.* New York: Knopf, 1952.

Wilson, James H., *Under the Old Flag,* Vol. I. New York: D. Appleton, 1912.

Winters, John D., *The Civil War in Louisiana.* Baton Rouge: Louisiana State University Press, 1963.

Wood, Paul, *Illinois at War, 1861–1865.* Springfield: Illinois Office of Education, no date.

Index

345